MODERN RETAILING MANAGEMENT
Basic concepts and practices

MODERN RETAILING MANAGEMENT
Basic concepts and practices

DELBERT J. DUNCAN, Ph.D.
Professor of Marketing, Emeritus
Schools of Business Administration
University of California, Berkeley

CHARLES F. PHILLIPS, Ph.D., LL.D., L.H.D., Litt.D.
President Emeritus
Bates College

STANLEY C. HOLLANDER, Ph.D.
Professor of Marketing
Graduate School of Business Administration
Michigan State University

Eighth Edition 1972
RICHARD D. IRWIN, INC.
Homewood, Illinois 60430
IRWIN-DORSEY LIMITED Georgetown, Ontario

Earlier editions of this book were published under the title *Retailing: Principles and Methods.*

Eighth Edition

First Printing, January, 1972

Library of Congress Catalog Card No. 72–168298

Printed in the United States of America

To

MARY H. DUNCAN
FRANK G. PHILLIPS
SELMA D. J. HOLLANDER

PREFACE

It was noted in the previous edition of this volume entitled *Retailing: Principles and Methods,* that "Retailing continues in a state of ferment, accentuated by the technical developments of recent years as well as by changes in the environment within which retail stores must operate. New management methods are being devised and new tools are being utilized as executives become increasingly aware of their opportunities and responsibilities under the highly dynamic conditions of today." These statements apply with equal, if not greater, force today as changes continue at an increasingly rapid pace.

Many aspects of the business recession of the early 1970s, including continuing inflation, curtailed buying by consumers, and uncertainty in fashion in the apparel field, among others, caused grave concern among retailers. Nevertheless, that recession also induced needed managerial actions. To mention but a few: It forced a critical reappraisal of both short- and long-range plans; it resulted in more stringent buying policies and a reevaluation of suppliers; it compelled a close scrutiny of the various merchandise classifications' and departments' contributions to profit; it focused attention on the critical increase in stock shortages and stimulated vigorous attempts to control this drain on operating revenues; and it led to a serious reappraisal of managerial and other personnel. In brief, in all progressive organizations the recession resulted in a tough, thorough reevaluation of policies, practices, and people—a course of action probably long overdue.

The environment in which retailers must operate also continues to change in many other ways. Changes in consumer location, age-distribution, tastes and shopping patterns affect retail planning; new legislation modifies retail decision making; retail technology is developing with increasing use of electronic data processing and other automation equipment; and the competitive strengths of various types of retailers have altered considerably in recent years. We have attempted to outline these many elements of change in this Eighth Edition of our textbook, retitled *Modern Retailing Management: Concepts and Practices.* And we have particularly tried to emphasize the new techniques and managerial measures required for successful retail operation in this new environment.

Among the major changes in the present edition, in addition to the extensive updating of all the material, are the following:

1. The title has been changed to *Modern Retailing Management: Concepts and Practices* from *Retailing: Principles and Methods.* This reflects an emphasis on management responsibilities under current conditions and highlights the newer concepts and practices which have been adopted to serve American consumers.

2. The individual chapters have been revised and rewritten to provide a "tighter" coverage of the same material in fewer pages without any sacrifice of important subject matter.

3. Several changes have been made in chapter titles, and in content and organization of the material included. Two examples may be cited. Chapter 3 has been retitled "Careers and Opportunities in Retailing" to reflect the career growth possibilities for students with diverse educational backgrounds and from diverse educational institutions. The final chapter has been enlarged to include discussions of management by objectives and the social responsibilities of retail management.

4. The chapter on retail insurance has been eliminated because of its complex nature and the fact that detailed treatment of this subject is beyond the scope of the introductory course in retailing.

5. To improve continuity and content flow for the reader from chapter to chapter, the annotated supplementary readings, previously given at the end of each chapter, have been consolidated in a separate section immediately preceding the index. This arrangement permits easy reference for students interested in broadening their knowledge in all major areas of retailing management.

6. Despite the rapidity of change in the areas of automation and electronic data processing, and the possibility that devices and methods now employed may be rendered obsolete in a few months or years, an attempt

has been made to describe and illustrate some of those in current use as this is written. Nowhere, perhaps, is the responsibility of the teacher "to keep current" more evident than in the application of electronics to retailing operations.

We have carefully reviewed the relevancy of the entire contents of this edition and previous ones to improve the book's effectiveness as a teaching/learning instrument and to meet current shifts in the organization and emphasis of retailing courses in our colleges and universities. In addition, opinions of students, our associates and other teachers, and businessmen —too numerous to name here—have been sought and have helped shape the final product. We are deeply grateful for this assistance.

Dr. Charles F. Phillips did not actively participate in this revision and should not be held responsible for any of its shortcomings. However, his many contributions to the previous editions have helped build this one.

December, 1971

DELBERT J. DUNCAN
STANLEY C. HOLLANDER

CONTENTS

PART VIII. Coordination and management

INDEXES

PART I

Retailing in transition

chapter chapter chapter 1 chapter

RETAILING TODAY: ITS STRUCTURE AND ENVIRONMENT

Retailing—the activities involved in selling consumers' goods to ultimate consumers—has undergone vast changes during the last three decades. Tremendous changes in the broad environment within which retailers of all kinds must operate—including social, economic, technological, and competitive aspects—have forced adjustments in policies, methods, and in managerial strategy that justify the term "fantastic." And the end is not yet in sight!

The retailer must appreciate the nature and implications of these changes, since current developments may make retailing tomorrow significantly different from retailing today. The development of such an appreciation is the goal of this chapter. To this end, we shall, first, note certain basic facts about the present status of retailing in the United States. Second, we will consider some of the current major environmental changes affecting retailing operations. Finally, we will examine retailing's responses to these changes.

Relatively few statistics will be included in this chapter. The reader seeking statistical support for the trends cited can find it by referring to the subject index at the end of this volume.[1] The index can also be

[1] Additional background material may be obtained from the chapters dealing with retailing institutions in a basic marketing text. Cf. C. F. Phillips and D. J. Duncan, *Market-*

used to locate definitions of any terms with which the reader may not be familiar.

THE NATURE OF RETAILING IN THE UNITED STATES

A study in contrasts There are slightly less than 1,800,000 retail establishments in the United States.[2] Some of these retail units are very small, with daily sales of as little as $20; others have sales of $100,000 or more each business day. Some carry small assortments of very limited lines of goods—for example, the tobacco shop and the small newsstand. In contrast, department stores carry broad assortments of many kinds of goods. Some stores extend a large number of services along with the goods they sell—credit, delivery, sale on approval, adjustments, personal shopping service are a few. Others offer their goods for sale in establishments where the service is so limited that the customer has to serve herself. Certain stores are well managed and operated; others show obvious signs of poor management. Some stores are organized as proprietorships, others as partnerships and cooperatives; still others are corporations. Alongside of the independently owned and operated store, we find the store controlled by an organization with a thousand or more units. Truly, a study of retail structure in this country is a study in contrasts.

Yet if we look beneath some of the contrasting features of the 1,763,000 retail establishments in the United States, we find that the operators of these stores have more in common than is apparent at first glance. As already indicated, practically all of them are engaged in the final stage of the marketing of consumers' goods: They obtain goods from various sources of supply and resell to ultimate consumers. More specifically, retailers exist to serve their customers and prospective customers through providing wanted goods and services at the proper times, places, and prices. Performance of these tasks involves certain basic activities or functions. Generally speaking, these are the same as the marketing functions and are classified in the same manner. For example, buying and selling are known as functions involving transfer of title; transporting, storage, and plant maintenance are functions involving physical supply; and financing, risk taking, market information, and personnel management are termed "facilitating functions."[3]

Retailing methods The retail functions are performed by organizations

---

ing: Principles and Methods, 6th ed. (Homewood, Ill.: Richard D. Irwin, Inc., 1968), chaps. 6–11.

[2] Cf. Table 1–1, p. 5.

[3] For detailed discussions of the marketing functions, see any of the "standard" textbooks on marketing.

that reach customers in one or more of four ways: through stores, the mail, house-to-house salesmen, and automatic vending machines. Of these ways —commonly termed "methods of retailing"—stores are most important, accounting for about 97 percent of all retail sales. Mail-order retailing and house-to-house selling are each responsible for nearly 1 percent. Although 1967 *Census of Business* data show sales through vending machines of $2 billion or about 0.6 percent of all retail sales, these figures considerably understate the importance of this method of retailing. Many vending machines are located in stores and their sales are reported in the figures for these establishments. Actually, vending machines probably dispensed about $4.5 billion worth of merchandise in that year. Since then their sales have increased about 10 percent per year.[4]

□ Our retailing structure

Number and sales of retail stores Table 1–1 shows the number of retailers, total retail sales, and average sales per store for selected years beginning in 1929.

Changes in the price level have caused some of the increase in dollar sales volume shown in this table. The actual physical volume of goods sold

TABLE 1–1

Retailers and sales, selected years, 1929–1969

Year	Number of establishments (000 omitted)	Total sales (000,000 omitted)	Average sales per store
1929	1,476	$ 48,330	$ 33,000
1933	1,526	25,037	16,000
1939	1,770	42,042	24,000
1948	1,770	130,521	74,000
1958	1,788	199,646	112,000
1963	1,708	244,202	143,000
1967	1,763	310,214	176,000
1969	n.a.	351,633	n.a.

Source: The 1929–1967 data are from the *Census of Business*. The sales estimates for 1968–1969 are from the *Survey of Current Business*, December 1970, p. 5–11. Data for different years are not completely comparable. Figures prior to 1963 do not include sales made in Alaska and Hawaii. Military post exchange and commissary sales, which amounted to approximately $1.8 billion in 1963 and $2.8 billion in 1967, are not included in any of the above figures. Some industrial, institutional and club cafeteria, restaurant and canteen sales are also excluded.

[4] "Census of the Industry: Total Vended Dollar Volume," *Vend*, May 1, 1971, p. 36–4.

at retail has not fluctuated as much as the dollar figures might suggest. Nevertheless, adjusting those figures for differences in the price level indicates that physical volume probably quadrupled between 1929 and 1969.

Although total dollar sales have increased from a low of $25 billion in 1933 to a high of over $350 billion in 1969, the total number of retail stores has remained surprisingly steady since 1939.[5] Consequently, the average sales per store have risen rapidly from a low of $16,000 in 1933 to $176,000 in 1967 and have likely increased further since that time.

Sales by type of outlet Table 1–2 shows the 1967 sales of different types of retail outlets. The relative importance of food retailers is evident from the fact that they accounted for 22.7 percent of total retail sales. This figure increases to 30.3 percent if eating and drinking places are also included. The automotive group transacted 17.9 percent of all sales and department stores accounted for 10.4 percent.

Independent and chain stores Both in numbers and in total sales volume, the small single-unit store is still the predominant retail institution in the United States. Eighty-seven percent of our retail establishments are operated by firms that have only one store in the same general kind of business. These stores account for 60 percent of all retail sales. Firms operating more than one store in the same general kind of business control about 13 percent of all stores and do 40 percent of all retail sales.[6]

The importance of these multiunit and chain-store organizations varies greatly by kind of business. In contrast to their 40 percent of total retail sales, in 1967 they did about 83 percent of all business in variety stores, 62 percent in shoe stores, 58 percent in food stores, 39 percent in drugstores and 28 percent in furniture stores.[7]

Retail firms operating more than one unit accounted for about 30 percent of all retail trade in 1929, when the first census of retail distribution was compiled; by 1967 their share had grown to about 40 percent. But almost all of this growth in the multiunits' share has occurred during the last 15 years. The greatest growth in market share has taken place among firms with four or more stores. Although variations in census classifications make precise comparisons difficult, chains and department-store ownership groups with four or more stores seem to have accounted for about 24 percent of all retail business in 1929; 27–28 percent in 1933; 25 percent in 1935;

[5] A sample survey, conducted by Audits & Surveys, Inc. of New York, indicates a decline in total retail establishments to slightly less than 1,700,000 in 1970. (Company press release, 1970.)

[6] *1967 Census of Business, Retail Trade—Single Units and Multiunits* (Advance Report), BC67(A)-RS-2 (Washington, D.C.: U.S. Department of Commerce, 1970), p. 2.

[7] *Ibid.*, pp. 2–16.

TABLE 1–2

Retail sales by type of outlet 1948, 1954, 1958, 1963, 1967 (in billions of dollars)

Type of outlet	1948	1954	1958	1963	1967	% change 1963 to 1967
Food	$ 29.2	$ 39.8	$ 49.3	$ 57.1	$ 70.3	23.1
Automotive group	20.1	29.9	31.9	45.4	55.6	22.6
Filling stations	6.5	10.7	14.2	17.8	22.7	27.9
Eating and drinking places	10.6	13.1	15.3	18.4	23.8	32.7
Apparel and accessory stores	9.7	11.1	12.6	14.0	16.7	18.7
Department stores	9.4	10.6	13.4	20.5	32.3	57.5
Lumber and building materials group	11.1	13.1	14.3	14.6	17.2	17.8
Furniture and appliance stores	6.6	9.0	10.1	10.9	14.5	33.1
Variety stores (limited prices)	2.5	3.1	3.6	4.5	5.4	19.1
General and general merchandise stores	3.9	4.2	4.9	4.9	5.8	17.4
Drug and proprietary stores	4.0	5.3	6.8	8.5	10.9	28.8
Miscellaneous retail stores	15.2 (with Non-store)	15.6	18.5	21.3	27.3	28.0
Non-store (mail order, automatic vending, and direct selling)		4.5	5.4	6.2	7.6	29.9
Totals	$128.8	$170.0	$200.4	$244.2	$310.2	27.0

Source: Same as Table 1–1, except that the figures have been adjusted to the more recent census definitions for each type of outlet.

23–24 percent in 1939, 1948, and 1954; 27 percent in 1958; and 34 percent in 1967.[8]

The current importance of various-sized chains is indicated in Table 1–3, which shows each size group's 1967 sales volume.

TABLE 1–3

1967 sales of retail multiunit organizations

	Sales (in millions)	Percent of total U.S. retail sales
Total U.S. retail sales	$310,214	100.0
All multiunits	123,505	39.8
2 establishment multiunits	12,185	3.9
3 establishment multiunits	5,912	1.9
4 and 5 establishment multiunits	6,114	2.0
6 to 10 establishment multiunits	8,488	2.7
11 to 25 establishment multiunits	11,245	3.6
26 to 50 establishment multiunits	8,794	2.8
51 to 100 establishment multiunits	13,036	4.2
101 or more establishment multiunits	57,731	18.6

Source: *1967 Census of Business, Retail Trade, Single Units and Multiunits* (Advance Report), BC67-RS-2 (Washington, D.C.: U.S. Department of Commerce, 1970), p. 2.

Small and large stores The small size of the typical retail establishment often astonishes the person unfamiliar with retailing. Using annual sales as the measure of size and relying upon 1967 data, 25.2 percent of all stores had sales of less than $20,000 in that year; and they transacted only 1.4 percent of all retail business.[9] These stores, together with those in the $20,000–$49,999 class, which accounted for 23.3 percent of all stores and 4.2 percent of all sales, may be considered as small stores. Hence, stores with sales under $50,000 account for 48.5 percent of all stores and 5.6 percent of sales. At the other extreme, 6.3 percent of the stores each had sales of $500,000 or over; and these stores together did almost three-fifths (57.2 percent) of all retail business.

When another measure of size is used—the number of employees—the

---

[8] *Ibid.;* also Fifteenth Census of the U.S. [1929], *Census of Distribution,* Vol. 1, p. 28; *Census of American Business 1933, Retail Distribution,* Vol. 1, p. 27; *Census of Business 1935, Retail Distribution,* Vol. 1, p. 1–44; *Census of Business 1939,* Vol. 1, Part 1, p. 10d, Table 3A; *Census of Business 1948,* Vol. 1, Part 1, Table 3D; *1954 Census of Business,* Vol. 1, p. 19; *U.S. Census of Business 1958,* Vol. 1, *Retail Trade—Summary Statistics,* p. 4–2.

[9] *1967 Census of Business, Retail Trade, Sales Size* (Advance Report), BC67(A)-RS-1 (Washington, D.C.: U.S. Department of Commerce, 1970), p. 2.

TABLE 1–4

Relative distribution of retail establishments in operation November 15, 1967, by number of paid employees

Number of employees	Percentage of establishments
0–5	78.2
6–9	9.2
10–19	7.4
20–49	3.9
50–99	0.9
100 or more	0.4
Total	100.0

Source: *1967 Census of Business, Retail Trade—Employment Size*, BC67-RS-3 (Washington, D.C.: U.S. Government Printing Office, 1970), p. 3–1. Figures are for establishments operated during the entire year.

small size of our typical retail store becomes even more apparent. Table 1–4 reveals that 78.2 percent of the retail establishments employed 5 persons or less and that 94.8 percent of them had 19 or fewer employees. Despite the fact that sales of retail stores of all sizes have increased substantially in recent years, our retail structure is still composed of a very large number of small stores, a fairly large number of medium-sized establishments, and a very small number of gigantic stores.

Some large retail organizations The figures in Table 1–5 show the importance of some of our largest retail organizations; that is, for 1969 it shows the approximate average number of employees, the sales volume, and the earnings of the twenty-five largest firms measured by sales. Most of these companies operate primarily supermarkets, department stores, variety stores, or discount houses; but drug, hardware, automatic vending, and men's clothing chains are also represented on the list.

■ THE CHANGING ENVIRONMENT OF RETAILING

With the foregoing brief background on the structure of retailing, let us turn to the tremendous changes taking place in the environment[10] within which retailers must operate. In reality, this environment consists of several

[10] Although some readers will have covered similar material to that in this section in the basic marketing course, numerous others will not have done so. In any event, both groups should benefit from a review of the environmental factors currently affecting retailing.

TABLE 1–5

Employees, sales, and earnings of the 25 largest retailers, 1969

Rank	Company	Number of employees[1]	In thousands: Sales	In thousands: Net income after taxes	Net income as percent of sales
1	Sears, Roebuck (Chicago)	355,000	$8,862,971	$440,954	5.0
2	Great Atlantic & Pacific Tea (New York)[2]	135,000	5,700,000	52,000	0.9
3	Safeway Stores (Oakland)	91,400	4,099,647	54,593	1.3
4	J. C. Penney (New York)	105,000	3,756,092	110,927	3.0
5	Kroger (Cincinnati)	80,500	3,477,164	38,730	1.1
6	Marcor (Chicago)[3]	127,100	2,715,150	66,950	2.5
7	F. W. Woolworth (New York)	92,200	2,272,570	70,658	3.1
8	S. S. Kresge (Detroit)	76,500	2,185,298	54,089	2.5
9	Federated Department Stores (Cincinnati)	77,500	1,998,863	85,942	4.3
10	Food Fair Stores (Philadelphia)	30,000	1,555,431	12,062	0.8
11	Acme Markets (Philadelphia)	31,700	1,471,080	10,745	0.7
12	Jewel Companies (Melrose Park, Ill.)	19,800	1,464,318	21,416	1.5
13	Lucky Stores (San Leandro, Calif.)	23,000	1,259,198	21,336	1.7
14	Gamble-Skogmo (Minneapolis)	26,300	1,257,580	13,206	1.1
15	Winn-Dixie Stores (Jacksonville)	14,800	1,249,996	26,506	2.1
16	W. T. Grant (New York)	63,000	1,214,666	41,809	3.4
17	Allied Stores (New York)	50,000	1,201,796	22,163	1.8
18	National Tea (Chicago)	31,000	1,192,628	7,194	0.6
19	May Department Stores (St. Louis)	54,000	1,134,237	28,919	2.5
20	Grand Union (East Paterson, N.J.)	24,300	1,113,338	15,196	1.4
21	City Products (Des Plaines, Ill.)	28,400	1,096,958	24,275	2.2
22	Spartans Industries (New York)	35,000	957,658	23,962[4]	2.5
23	Dayton Hudson (Minneapolis)	27,000	888,357	23,673	2.7
24	R. H. Macy (New York)	38,000	878,480	24,366	2.8
25	Allied Supermarkets (Detroit)	15,000	877,894	1,722	0.2

[1] Yearend or average annual employment
[2] *Fortune* estimate
[3] Formerly Montgomery Ward and Container Corp.
[4] Influenced by special, nonrecurring charge or credit

Source: "The 50 Largest Retailing Companies," *Fortune*, Vol. 82, No. 5, May 1970, pp. 208–209. Reprinted from the Fortune Directory by special permission; © 1970 Time Inc.

significant forces or elements such as social, economic, technological, and competitive, each of which for practical purposes may be considered an environment by itself. The retailer should be familiar with these forces because they have a vital impact on his policies, practices, and ultimate success.

□ Major social forces

Multitudes of social forces have influenced the conduct of retail enterprises over the years and these forces have been particularly strong since World War II. Only a few of them may be mentioned here, but those discussed indicate the broad spectrum of developments with which retailers must cope in our growing, dynamic economy.

Population growth In the 60-year period between 1910 and 1970, the population of the continental United States grew from 92 to 204 million. The total population, including Alaska and Hawaii, now exceeds 205 million. Over 50 million of this population growth has come in the last two decades, an increase of over one-third since 1950. Projections for the next two decades indicate still further growth—over 227 million in 1980 and over 250 million by 1990.[11] The rate of increase has been slowing down in recent years, however, and these projections may have to be revised downward if present trends continue.

The rate of household and family formation is of special interest to the retailer, since these groups are the significant buying units for many products and services. The number of households in the United States has been increasing at an annual rate of about 1,400,000 units in recent years. Although this rate may also slow down in the future, we may have as many as 68 to 70 million households by 1975.[12]

Population growth in certain age groups The teenage and young adult segments of our population have increased very substantially during recent years. Almost one-fifth of the 1969 population was between 10 and 20 years of age. Another fifth was in the 20 to 34 year age bracket, a period in the life cycle that is usually marked by low rates of saving and high rates of consumption expenditure. However, the number of individuals under age 10 actually declined between 1960 and 1969.[13] Consequently, in forthcoming years, the percentage of the population that is in the 10–30 year old age groups will decline. Nevertheless, young people will undoubtedly

---

[11] U.S. Bureau of the Census, *Current Population Reports,* Series P-25, No. 448, August 6, 1970, page 1 (Projection Series D).

[12] U.S. Bureau of the Census, *Current Population Reports,* Series P-25, No. 387, February 20, 1968; 394, June 6, 1968, and *Statistical Abstract, 1970,* pp. 35, 36.

[13] *Current Population Reports,* Series P-25, No. 441, March 19, 1970, pp. 12, 16; and *Statistical Abstract, 1970,* Table No. 8, p. 10.

continue to exert strong influences on popular tastes and fashions.[14]

The "over 65" segment of our population continues to grow rapidly and will probably gain about 50 percent between 1960 and 1985. By the latter year, there may well be over 25 million of these "oldsters."[15]

Population mobility Retailing is also affected by the degree to which people move from place to place. The mobility of the American population is a long-standing phenomenon. Since colonial days our people have shifted from the East to the new agricultural lands of the West, from rural and farm areas to the urban centers, and from the major cities to the suburbs. Mobility is still a national characteristic. In one fairly typical year alone—March 1969 to March 1970—almost 19 percent of our population moved from one address to another. More than a third of the movers, comprising almost 7 percent of the total population, relocated in a different county.[16] Since many of these people are inclined to remain loyal to the firms they patronized at their former location, statewide, regional, and national chains have an advantage in retaining mobile consumers.[17]

The number of Americans living on farms has been greatly reduced during the last 40 years. During the 1960 decade alone, our farm population decreased at an average rate of one-half million persons per year.[18] Many smaller cities and communities continue to be important retail centers in spite of the population movement toward the metropolitan areas. One study found a far greater retail sales increase between 1958 and 1967 in Ohio cities with 25,000 to 50,000 population than in the state's metropolitan areas (the large cities and their contiguous suburbs).[19]

---

[14] The importance of the "under-25" market is discussed in Sheldon Zalaznick, "The Youthquake in Pop Culture," *Fortune,* Vol. 79, No. 1 (January 1969), pp. 84–87 ff.; and in Melvin Helitzer and Carl Heyel, *The Youth Market* (New York: Media Books, 1970). For some other views, including comments on possible overemphasis of the "youth influence," cf. Ira J. Bravin, "Is Youth Losing Its Grip?" *Stores,* Vol. 52, No. 4 (April 1970), pp. 4–8; "Why 'Youth' Needs a New Definition," *Business Week,* December 12, 1970, pp. 34–35; and Lee Templeton, "The Youth Thing Has Been Oversold and Overbought," *Retail Overview,* Vol. 3, No. 3 (Fall 1970), pp. 24–29.

[15] *Current Population Reports,* Series P-25, No. 448, August 6, 1970, p. 11.

[16] *Current Population Reports,* Series P-20 *(Population Characteristics)* No. 210, January 15, 1971, p. 1.

[17] James E. Bell, *Selection of New Suppliers by the Mobile Family* (East Lansing, Michigan: Bureau of Business and Economic Research, Michigan State University, 1969), p. 64.

[18] *Current Population Reports,* Series P-27, No. 41, June 18, 1970, p. 1. Very preliminary analysis of the 1970 Census suggests that the farm population is now becoming stable in size. Cf. "U.S.A.–1970," *Newsweek,* December 28, 1970, p. 11.

[19] Peter S. Carusone, "A Shift in the Point of Patronage," *MSU Business Topics,* Vol. 18, No. 4 (Autumn 1970), pp. 61–69. Also cf. Eli P. Cox and Leo G. Erickson, *Retail Decentralization* (East Lansing, Michigan: Bureau of Business and Economic Research, Michigan State University, 1967) which reports higher *per capita* retail sales growth rates for nonmetropolitan areas than for metropolitan districts.

Suburban living The movement of people into metropolitan areas, and particularly into the suburbs, has brought about important changes in their modes of living, in their buying behavior, and in their future expectations as members of our society.

Our great middle class has, as one informed observer has expressed it, "suddenly experienced a widening horizon of the economic good life: [these people want] a better house, . . . better education for their children, improved health and medical care, opportunity to develop all kinds of personal interests and hobbies, vacations, travel, sports, a second car, and all the expensive household conveniences of the modern age."[20] These desires for casual living, for more and better quality merchandise, and in general for a better standard of living, have generated demands which have exceeded current income in many instances. One result has been a tremendous surge in "buying on time." Today the amount of consumer credit outstanding is at the highest level in our history.[21] Although this "widening horizon" is not confined to residents of our suburbs, it is probably most pronounced in those areas.

Leisure Our environment may also include increased leisure time, with marked opportunities for recreational activities such as boating, bowling, swimming, travel, concert attendance, and self-education. Consumers with more leisure time would certainly want more recreational and cultural equipment; they also might want more retail activities that combine shopping and entertainment, for example, exhibits and festivals at shopping centers. The average industrial workweek has been declining in recent years, which suggests that leisure may indeed increase. However, some experts believe that this will be more than offset by foreseeable increases in the number of people who "moonlight," or hold two jobs; in the percentage of working wives; in time spent traveling to and from work; and in the demand for services that provide little opportunity for use of time-saving machinery.[22]

Other social forces One extremely unfortunate social change, concerned with the degree of adherence to ethical and moral standards, is reflected in an increased rate of shoplifting, pilferage, and store-employee theft. No one knows exactly how much these crimes cost, but many merchants are now experiencing loss rates of 2 to 5 percent of sales and even more. These rates sometimes equal or exceed the store's profits and

---

[20] M. P. McNair, in an address entitled "Change and Challenges in the Department Store Industry," New York City, October 5, 1964.

[21] For details, cf. p. 17, and Chapter 22.

[22] Cf. Gilbert Burck, "There'll Be Less Leisure than You Think," *Fortune*, Vol. 81, No. 3 (March 1970), pp. 87–89; also cf. Sebastian De Grazia, *Of Time, Work, and Leisure* (New York: The Twentieth Century Fund, 1962).

inevitably affect the prices that merchants must charge to stay in business.[23]

Examples of other changes in the social environment of retailing include the following: (1) Better-educated and better-informed buyers, notably reflected in the so-called "culture explosion," with the consequent accelerated demand for better-quality merchandise and a higher standard of living; (2) a sharpened "fashion consciousness" among all segments of our population, but especially among teenagers and the under-25-year-old group—and, although to a lesser degree, among adult men, evident not only in wearing apparel but also in cosmetics; (3) changes in the composition of our working population, reflected in a higher proportion of better-educated and skilled men and in the number of married women employed; (4) the continued expansion of services of various kinds; (5) the growth of our suburbs which has contributed to the deterioration of the downtown areas of the larger cities; and (6) the possible rebirth of some downtown areas as a result of urban renewal and other programs.

□ Government regulation

Federal, state and local laws and regulations affect retailing, just as they influence all other types of businesses. Many of these laws concern specific aspects of retail management, such as personnel relations or buying practices, and we will discuss those laws in the chapters devoted to those topics. At this point, we should note two types of regulation that are growing in importance: (1) federal restrictions on mergers and acquisitions, which affects the growth of chains, and (2) consumeristic legislation which affects all types of retailing.

Restrictions on mergers and acquisitions Part of the recent growth among large retail organizations has resulted from *internal* expansion, *i.e.* the opening of additional stores and enlargement of existing ones, and part has been achieved through mergers and acquisitions. Recently, however, the Federal Trade Commission and the Department of Justice have moved to restrict external growth through mergers and purchases of other stores by the very large organizations.

Only a few of the Commission's restrictive actions can be cited here. It has announced that food-chain mergers and acquisitions that result in over $500 million food store sales per annum will "warrant attention and consideration," [which suggests that they probably will be prohibited]; also

---

[23] "Shoplifting: The Pinch That Hurts," *Business Week,* June 27, 1970, pp. 72–73; Samuel Feinberg, "Internal Shortages Major Factor in Lower Profits," *Women's Wear Daily,* May 13, 1970, p. 22; and "Spartans to Share List of U.S. Shoplifters," *New York Times,* June 12, 1970, p. 53. Also cf. the discussion in Chapter 13, pp. 328–30.

that food chain mergers and amalgamations resulting in combined food store sales between $100 and $500 million will "warrant investigation."[24] Several specific orders of the Commission as well as consent agreements, issued in 1965 and 1966, limited or restricted merger activity on the part of such grocery chains as the Grand Union Co., the National Tea Company and the Winn-Dixie Stores. About the same time, the Commission obtained agreements from Federated Department Stores, Broadway-Hale Stores, Inc., and May Department Stores, Inc., to refrain for specified periods of time from any department-store mergers or acquisitions that did not have the Commission's specific prior approval. Still other Commission orders have restrained merger activity among discount stores, shoe stores, and other kinds of retail organizations.[25]

Of even greater significance than Federal Trade Commission action, however, was a decision of the United States Supreme Court in 1966, *un*-merging Von's Grocery Company and Shopping Bag Food Stores, both of Los Angeles. The merger had taken place in 1960 and the combined sales of the two firms constituted 7.5 percent of the area's retail grocery sales. Breaking new ground, the Court in effect ruled that "mergers of substantial, healthy competitors must be blocked in a market that is still highly competitive but tending toward an oligopoly—where a few giants operate."[26]

To date, at least, the government has tried mainly to restrict mergers and acquisitions that involve large groups of similar stores—for example, two food chains. Amalgamations that unite different types of stores such as supermarkets and discount houses, however, have gone relatively unchallenged, resulting in important implications for the diversification policies of large retail organizations as we will note later in this chapter.

Consumerism The "consumerism" or consumer protection movement of the 1960s has inspired a number of laws and regulations that have significant implications for retailers as well as other marketers. The laws and codes already enacted, discussed in detail at the appropriate points in the chapters that follow, affect retail advertising and promotion practices, credit operations, warranty and service arrangements, and pricing. Some far-sighted merchants and other businessmen have responded to this movement by changing and expanding the ways in which they communicate with their customers, by collecting new types of information about consumer needs, and by providing new types of information and services for their customers.

---

[24] Statement of the U.S. Federal Trade Commission, "Commission Enforcement Policy with Regard to Mergers in the Food Distribution Industry," January 17, 1967 (*Commerce Clearing House Trade Regulation Reporter*, paragraph 4520).

[25] Cf. Irving Scher, *Manual of Federal Trade Regulations Affecting Retailers*, New ed. (New York: National Retail Merchants Association, 1969), pp. 76–81.

[26] *United States* v. *Von's Grocery* Co., 384 U.S. 270 (1966).

The National Association of Food Chains, for example, has sponsored a series of "shopper dialogues" with customers throughout the country.[27]

The consumeristic movement appears likely to grow in the near future and probably will induce additional government intervention in the marketing process. The basic problems in framing consumer legislation are providing safeguards that the consumer really needs and will use and protecting the ethical merchant from unethical competition without either inhibiting vigorous competition and innovation or burdening the distribution system (and thus the consumer who pays the bills) with excessively costly and cumbersome procedures.

□ Major economic forces

Personal income Personal income, providing spending capacity for consumers and strongly affecting total retail sales, rose steadily in the United States during the years from 1940 to 1970. The period from 1958 to 1970 alone, saw total individual incomes increase from $360 billion to $800 billion. Not all of this income, however, could be translated into purchases of increased *amounts* of goods and services since some of the gain in personal income was consumed by rising prices and higher taxes. But *total* real personal disposable income (after taxes and adjusted for price changes) did grow by almost 65 percent from 1958 to 1970.[28] *Per capita* personal income also increased. After again adjusting for price and tax increases, each member of our increased population had on the average about 40 percent more purchasing power in 1970 than in 1958.[29]

Income distribution The general prosperity of the post–World War II period in the United States is reflected in the substantial improvement in income distribution during the late 1940s, 1950s, and 1960s. Families with annual incomes of $5,000 and over increased from 19 percent of the total in 1947 to 80 percent in 1969. In the latter year almost 45 percent of all American families had incomes of $10,000 or over. Of course, much of this change in dollar income was absorbed by price increases. But the real income of the average American family, after adjusting for price changes, still increased by about 88 percent from 1947 to 1969.[30]

---

[27] Cf. "Sponsoring Your Own Shopper Dialogues," *Chain Store Age,* March 1968, p. 35. Also see "Business Responds to Consumerism," *Business Week,* September 6, 1969, pp. 94–108, for a discussion of the movement and of vendors' responses. A number of significant articles concerning the consumer movement are assembled in David A. Aaker and George S. Day, eds., *Consumerism* (New York: The Free Press, 1971).

[28] *Survey of Current Business,* Vol. 51, No. 1, January 1971, p. 11; *Statistical Abstract of the United States 1960* (Washington, D.C.: U.S. Government Printing Office, 1960), p. 309.

[29] *Ibid.*

[30] U.S. Bureau of the Census, *Current Population Reports,* Series P–60, No. 75, De-

Consumer credit The great growth in credit buying is another significant aspect of the economic environment for retailing. Consumer credit outstanding at the end of the year, aside from residential mortgages and cash loans, grew from approximately $4 billion in 1945 to approximately $84 billion in 1969. The 1969 consumer debt included the following: automobile installment credit, $37 billion; other installment credit, $28 billion; retail charge accounts, $8 billion; service credit, $7 billion; and home repair and modernization loans, $4 billion. In addition, consumers had about $39 billion outstanding in personal cash loans, much of which was also used to acquire goods and services.[31] The University of Michigan Survey Research Center reports that slightly more than half of all American families owed some installment debt at the beginning of 1969.[32]

It is clear that we are in a credit economy, one providing great opportunities and challenges to the retailer. But obligations are equally great. There is a vital, growing need for more careful appraisal of credit risks, closer scrutiny of the regularity of payments, and prompt follow-up on past-due accounts. The personal bankruptcy rate has increased quite sharply during the last decade and more.

□ Technological advances

Large retailers are increasingly using electronic computers, new data-processing systems, and other technological devices and methods to improve their operating techniques and procedures. Some medium-sized merchants are also beginning to participate in the "computer revolution." These merchants either use time-sharing computer systems or send part of their daily and weekly records to outside data-processing bureaus for summarization and analysis.

The major retail organizations have used their electronic data-processing systems mainly for employee payroll records, customer credit accounts, inventory control, and accounts payable. But most authorities agree that such usage only scratches the surface of what EDP systems can and will do in retail stores of the future.[33]

Automated merchandise control systems that maintain balanced stocks

---

cember 14, 1970, p. 1. More precisely, median family income, calculated in constant 1969 dollars, increased from about $5,000 in 1947 to $9,400 in 1969. Preliminary reports indicate that the median family income in 1970, after adjustment for price changes, was approximately the same as in 1969; *ibid.*, No. 78, May 20, 1971, p. 1.

[31] *Federal Reserve Bulletin*, January 1971, p. A54, figures rounded to nearest billion.

[32] George Katona et al., *1969 Survey of Consumer Finances* (Ann Arbor, Michigan: University of Michigan, 1970), p. 21.

[33] *E.g.*, David L. Fleisher, "Merchandising and the Computer: A Performance Gap," *Retail Overview*, Vol. 3, No. 2 (Summer 1970), pp. 33–42.

and "spot" fast and slow selling items, thus helping to predict future sales, are coming into use. And the computer has great, relatively untapped, potentialities for use in retail research. Opportunities exist, for instance, in studying which customers buy what merchandise and how they respond to different prices and promotional tactics, also in helping schedule the use of part-time salespeople, and in forecasting.[34]

Many other technological changes are also affecting retailing. Automation, for example, has had considerable impact in food retailing—a field where chain stores and voluntary and cooperative groups predominate. It is evident in automatic merchandising, in office procedures, and in various physical handling activities of store, warehouse, and distribution center operations.[35]

□ The changing competitive environment

Our earlier discussion of retailing structure has shown that the competitive environment of retailing is characterized by many types and sizes of stores, located in all kinds of areas, offering various assortments of merchandise, and providing a wide range of services to their customers. A brief examination of some of the competitive forces and developments now taking place will demonstrate how retailers are responding to their changing environment; that retailing is an ever-changing field; that constant vigilance on the part of the retailer is necessary to strengthen or even maintain his competitive position; and that continuous innovation is a prime requisite of success under the turbulent conditions of today. This exploration takes place in the next section of this chapter.

■ RETAILING'S RESPONSE TO ENVIRONMENTAL CHANGES

The environmental changes we have just described have supported the growth of new types of retail institutions and practices and have encouraged changes and developments among the older types. We will discuss some of the more significant of these retailing innovations on the pages that follow. We will give particular attention to the growth of branch stores, discount houses, and "convenience" stores; to the use of leasing and franchising ar-

---

[34] Electronic data-processing equipment and its current and potential retail applications are discussed at several points in the chapters that follow. Cf., especially Chapters 5, 13, 22, and 25.

[35] Cf. Chapter 15.

rangements; to diversification tendencies among large retailers; and to the use of private brands.

But first we might note the important role that market considerations have played in evoking these changes. For instance, the growing suburban pattern of living provided markets for the planned shopping center with its department store branches and also contributed much to the meteoric expansion of the general merchandise discount house, with its mass displays, extended opening hours, and check-out type of operation. Many of these suburban consumers wanted the reasonably priced goods and the informal, self-service, drive-in family-shopping conditions that the discount stores offered. But many consumers, in the suburbs and elsewhere, also wanted to be able to obtain selected food items from a nearby outlet with minimum shopping effort and were willing to pay a reasonable premium for the service of a "convenience" food store. Similarly, rising incomes, increases in the number of working wives, and other factors led to an increase in the market for "take out" foods and tasty, inexpensive meals. This market provided opportunities for many new "fast food" stores and restaurants.

Many of the organizations that entered the discount store field, however, had to turn to department leasing arrangements; and many of the entrants into the fast food, convenience store and other service markets had to use franchising (both old retailing practices which took on new importance) in order to be able to grow as rapidly as they desired. Expanding markets, both in the United States and abroad, also encouraged growth and mergers among the established large retail firms, but governmental restrictions as well as market factors channeled some of this expansion into diversification and internationalization.

Not all firms have been as alert to market opportunities as the ones we have been discussing. Some were reluctant to depart from traditional operating patterns until their competitors' actions forced them to change. To mention but one illustration, the lethargy and inertia of many department stores during the 1950s helped permit more aggressive entrepreneurs, such as the discounters, to enter the field and compete actively for consumer patronage.

□ Branch stores

As we have noted, the rapid growth of our suburbs following World War II, their increasing importance as high consumption markets, the deterioration of downtown areas, the widespread use of private cars, and the growth of planned suburban shopping centers finally convinced most department store managements that they had to take their stores to the places where their customers were now living and wanted to do their shopping.

Yet some of the oldest and best-known stores in all sections of the country failed to recognize the need for suburban branches. Established in their downtown "ivory towers," they considered themselves impregnable to the great social and economic changes swirling around them. Several paid the ultimate price—failure—for their oversight.

Fortunately these stores were in the minority and today branch stores are "a way of life" among successful department stores throughout the country.[36] By 1969, approximately 62 percent of all department store sales volume emanated from the branches, which thus had become more important as a group than the downtown or parent stores. As one might expect, the branch percentage of total volume tended to be highest for the larger firms in the larger cities.[37]

□ The discount house

This institution in its "primitive" form has existed for more than four decades, but its emergence as a going, highly competitive retailer has come since 1950. Its nature and significance, in response to the changes taking place in our economy, can best be understood by examining its characteristics.

Characteristics What this text refers to as a discount house has all or most of these features:

1. A broad merchandise assortment, including both "hard" and "soft" goods and frequently food as well.
2. Price lines aimed at low- and middle-income families.
3. Emphasis on rapid turnover of merchandise. Through relatively low prices and a rigid limitation of merchandise to the fast-moving items, the typical discount house turns its inventory about six times a year. However, a few firms manage to achieve from 12 to 15 stock turns annually.
4. Price as the main sales appeal. To this end, every effort is exerted to reduce operating cost.
5. Buildings, equipment and fixtures are relatively inexpensive, although the newer discount houses tend to have somewhat more costly buildings and furnishings.
6. In many cases, low rent locations, often as a separate, "free standing" store with its own parking lot. Some of the newer discount houses, however, are located in planned shopping centers.
7. An emphasis on self-service operation with a minimum of salespeople

[36] Also cf. the discussions of these stores in Chapter 4, "Store Location," and Chapter 7, "Structure of the Retail Firm."

[37] Jay Scher, *Financial and Operating Results of Department and Specialty Stores, 1969* (New York: National Retail Merchants Association, 1970), pp. vi.

where self-service is not applicable. Whereas payroll in a department store may equal 18 percent of sales, in the discount house this cost may be between 10 and 15 percent.

8. Limited customer services such as credit and delivery, or the offering of these services at a special charge to the customer.
9. Less use of merchandise and accounting controls than in the typical chain or department store.
10. Low profit as a percentage of sales (1 to 2 percent is quite common). However, the return on investment is very satisfactory (10 to 20 percent is not unusual).
11. Long hours, frequently from 10:00 A.M. to 10:00 P.M. and often including Sunday.
12. Large stores, with 50,000 to 100,000 square feet on one floor being common, and 200,000 square feet or more not being exceptional.
13. Large parking area.
14. A carnival atmosphere based on extensive sales promotional activities, including advertising, in-store display and promotions, and major special events.
15. Often associated with, or containing, a supermarket.

Approximately 11 percent of all new supermarkets opened in 1969 were built as parts of discount houses and another 11 percent were located adjacent to discount houses.[38]

Importance of full-line discount houses *The Discount Merchandiser* magazine estimates that at the beginning of 1971 there were more than 5,000 retail institutions with the characteristics outlined in the previous section. Of these, about 800 were opened during 1969 and 1970. Total sales in 1970 were about $24.4 billion, up from about $2 billion in 1960 and $22.2 billion in 1969.[39]

Other low-margin retailers There are many other retailers with some of the features of the full-line discount house, and some of these frequently add the word "discount" to their name. The food supermarket which has added a limited number of nonfood lines sometimes tries to capitalize on the current popularity of the discount house. Other food supermarkets have adopted the designation "discount food stores" for some of their units after (1) giving up trading stamps, (2) limiting their stocks to the more rapidly moving items, (3) eliminating their carry-out service, and (4) reducing their markups. Some women's apparel retailers have placed their dresses on pipe racks, adopted self-service selling, and entered into an aggressive promo-

[38] *Facts about New Super Markets Opened in 1969* (Chicago: Super Market Institute, 1970), p. 17.

[39] "The True Look of the Discount Industry," *The Discount Merchandiser*, June 1971, p. TL–4.

tional program under the designation of "discount house," instead of the more accurate term "apparel supermarket." Appliance retailers and operators of hardware stores have likewise switched to the new name. Some of the older bargain-type stores, which operate without a basic inventory, depending heavily on out-of-season, closed-out, and discontinued items, are termed discount houses by some retail students. In this text all of these retailers are excluded from the discount house classification.

Future of the discount house It is evident that the discount house has assumed a role of importance among our retailing institutions. In this process it has had a strong impact on other retailers mainly in two directions. First, in a relatively few years, discount houses have achieved annual sales of more than $22 billion that otherwise might have gone to other retail institutions. Second, they have forced many of the more conventional retailers to adopt some of the discounters' policies and methods to guard against the loss of additional sales volume. For example, some department stores such as Macy's in New York and Abraham & Straus of Brooklyn have reduced prices to meet all competition. Others have attempted to "trade-up" their merchandise and service to attract a different clientele. Still others have turned to self-service basement stores, longer store hours with more night openings, and more extensive promotions.

Among the variety and junior department store chains, which have probably been hurt by the discount house more seriously than any other retailer, Woolworth and Kresge have developed their own discount house chains—the former with 164 Woolco Department Stores, the latter with 411 K-Marts as of June 1971. Both have numerous additional units underway, and scheduled for the future. W. T. Grant is also opening large retail units as well as converting some of its smaller units to a junior-type discount operation. Aldens, a division of Gamble-Skogmo, Inc., which operates mainly on a mail-order basis, has a number of discount houses under the name of Shoppers World and more are in the planning stage. Walgreen Company, a drug chain, is expanding a discount house chain through purchases and opening of new units. Melville Shoe Corporation, operator of Thom McAn shoe stores, is leasing shoe departments in discount stores. Women's apparel chains, such as Diana Stores, a part of the Daylin Corporation, and Franklin Stores, are buying discount stores, opening their own, and operating leased departments.

Conventional department store organizations are also opening discount subsidiaries. Federated Department Stores has established its Gold Circle and Gold Triangle units; Dayton-Hudson Corporation operates the Target discount houses; and The May Company is opening Venture stores. The discount store business has also attracted many highly successful supermarket organizations. The J. M. Fields stores are owned by Food Fair, Turn-Style Family Centers by Jewel Companies, Inc., and Bradlees by Stop and Shop.

It would seem that the appeal of the discount house to potential customers should have declined in the affluent society that existed in the 1950's and 1960's. But this was not the case! Despite some failures—characteristic of all retailing—well-managed discount firms have manifested an awareness of the changing status of their customers and potential customers by "trading up" their stores, their merchandise, their services, and their public relations. As a result their growth has continued and, if such alertness is demonstrated in the years ahead, the future of this retailing institution is assured.

□ Small, convenience-type stores

These establishments, often called "bantam stores," are another recent development. They offer a limited selection of brand-name merchandise but usually compensate for this by convenient locations and typically long hours —frequently 7 A.M. to 11 P.M.—on a seven-day a week basis. Sunday is their busiest day. These "vest-pocket" supermarkets cater to workers whose odd hours prevent their shopping regularly elsewhere and to customers who desire fast service. They operate with a minimum of personnel and are usually slightly higher on prices than their larger namesakes. Although the average sale may be between 50¢ and $1, their careful inventory control and low labor costs often enable them to earn more per dollar of sales than the conventional supermarkets.

Many of these convenience stores are operated in large chains. For example, at the beginning of 1969, Southland Corporation operated about 3,000 7-Eleven Stores in 30 states; Consolidated Foods Corp.'s Lawson Milk division had about 680 convenience stores in Ohio, Pennsylvania, and Michigan; Fairmont Food Corporation maintained 350 UtoteM stores in the southern and western parts of the country; and General Host Corporation had 380 Li'l General stores in 7 states.[40] All of these chains, and many others, have since added many additional convenience outlets. That stores of this type are fulfilling a genuine need is shown by the fact that their number increased from an estimated 5,000 in 1964 to 9,600 in 1968. Estimated sales in the latter year were $1.6 billion.[41]

□ Leased departments

Leasing arrangements A "leased department" is a sales department that is operated by a firm (or individual) other than the one that owns the store

---

[40] *Moody's Financial Manual, 1970.*

[41] "Convenience Stores Show Continued Growth," *Progressive Grocer,* May 1969, pp. 86–87; also cf. "Bantams Keep Flowering in Houston," *Supermarketing,* May 1970, pp. 53–54.

in which the department is located. Usually no indication is given that the department is operated by an outsider, and the customer usually cannot tell whether she is shopping in a store-owned or in a leased department.[42]

Leasing arrangements vary widely, but the lessor (the store) usually provides the necessary space, fixtures, heat and light, and bookkeeping services, plus credit and delivery services similar to those offered in the store's wholly owned departments. The lessee assumes responsibility for merchandise handled and for management of the department. The lessee pays the store a flat monthly rental charge or a percentage of its sales or some combination of the two charges.

Some leased department operators have very large organizations. To illustrate, Consolidated Millinery Company maintains leased departments in large stores throughout the country; both the Glemby Corporation and Seligman & Latz run leased beauty salons in some 500–600 department stores in the United States and abroad; and Unishops, Inc., operates men's and boyswear departments in discount stores in 33 states.

Wide use of leasing For many years some department stores have leased out such merchandise and service departments as millinery, beauty parlors, jewelry, furs, shoes, soda fountains, and restaurants. Leased departments produced about 5.6 percent of all department store sales in 1969.[43] Supermarkets have also long used leased departments to expand their offerings in such areas as drugs, liquors, flowers, and other nonfood items. Even some meat and produce departments have been leased to outside operators.

But, in recent years, leasing has been especially important to the discount store firms. Many of them leased their "difficult" departments to outside specialists and thus were able to expand much more rapidly than would have been the case if they had had to use their own funds and staffs to operate those departments.[44] Even such large chains as Woolco (F. W. Woolworth Company) and K-Mart (S. S. Kresge Company) rely upon leasing for some of their departments.

Advantages and problems The basic advantage to the store, of course, is that it does not have to provide its own capital and staff to operate the department. Consequently, it can expand much more rapidly and can also readily experiment with new departments at minimum risk. It also benefits from the lessee's specialized management and (in the case of large lessees)

---

[42] Occasional exceptions to this rule may include travel agency branches in department stores (if the name of the national agency is an important sales tool), and in-store podiatry, optometrist, and optician's departments (when state law requires such identification).

[43] Jay Scher, *op. cit.* p. ii.

[44] Cf. W. R. Davidson, A. F. Doody, and J. R. Lowry, "Leased Departments as a Major Force in the Growth of Discount Store Retailing," *Journal of Marketing*, Vol. 34, No. 1 (January 1970), pp. 39–46.

buying power. The leasing organization, in turn, gains by being able to concentrate upon its specialized merchandise lines. It uses the store's fixtures and services. And it benefits from the customer traffic generated by the other departments and the store's overall promotion.

Nevertheless, the store and the lessee may eventually disagree over basic policies and procedures. Leasing increases the store's coordination problems, and a single poorly operated leased department can harm the entire store's image. Pricing flexibility is reduced, since the store cannot cut prices in the leased department to attract customers for the other departments. And the lease places a ceiling on the income that can be obtained from the department.[45]

The future of leasing Merchants disagree about the relative importance of the advantages and disadvantages cited above. But many of the advantages become less significant as the store organization (the landlord) becomes more firmly entrenched, acquires more capital, and develops its own staff of capable executives. As the lessor (landlord) firm grows it often decides to operate many of the departments previously leased. Consequently, some observors predict that there will be much less leasing, especially among major discount chains, in the future. At least one expert, however, believes that leasing will continue to be used to some degree for departments with complicated inventory problems, such as shoes; that require considerable technical knowledge, such as watch repairs and cameras and photo supplies; and those with service and operating problems, such as restaurants and snack bars. He also believes that the leasing organizations will survive by working with the smaller chains and by diversifying into store ownership themselves.[46]

□ Franchising

The term "franchising" covers a variety of arrangements under which one firm (the franchisor) licenses a number of retail or service outlets (the franchisees) to operate in accordance with a pattern it has developed. The franchisor may provide the merchandise that the franchisee sells, or he may simply license the use of his name, trademark, and operating style. The franchisor's compensation may come from an initial fee charged each franchisee, from royalties imposed on the franchisees' sales, from sales of mer-

[45] The lessee also experiences some disadvantages. The department develops good will for the store rather than for the lessee. The rental charge may be quite high in some cases. And, after developing a good business, the lessee may lose his lease since the landlord store may decide to operate the department or rent to someone else.

[46] Cf. Robert Drew-Bear, *Mass Merchandising: Revolution & Evolution* (New York: Fairchild Publications, Inc., 1970), pp. 272–75.

chandise, supples and/or services to the franchisees, or from some combination of these charges.

As was also true of leased departments, franchising is really an old and well-established practice despite the present emphasis given the arrangement. Automobile dealerships (under which the independent dealer is licensed to sell only one make of car, displays the manufacturer's name, and operates at least partially under instructions from the manufacturer) are examples of franchising, as are most gasoline service stations and soft-drink bottling plants. A great many other franchise systems have emerged during the last 15 years in such fields as motels (Holiday Inns), automobile rentals (Hertz and Avis), "fast-food" restaurants and snack bars (MacDonald's, Kentucky Fried Chicken, International House of Pancakes), pet shops (Doktor's Pet Centers), dress shops (House of Nine, Bride's Showcase), and automobile equipment and repair (Midas Muffler).

The variety of franchise arrangements prohibits any precise statement of the total number of firms involved or their dollar sales. One commentator, however, cites an estimate of 1,200 franchisor companies, 400,000–600,000 franchised outlets, and annual sales of about $90 billion. (The latter figures undoubtedly include automobile and gasoline sales.)[47] Friction sometimes develops between the franchisor and his franchisees. Many franchise systems have been over optimistically promoted and have failed to yield the promised support and profits to the franchisees. But the better and more successful franchise systems have proven very rewarding to most of their participants.

□ Diversification

Many of the largest retail firms have been expanding into highly diversified lines of business. *Chain Store Age,* for example, notes that more than half of the 50 largest supermarket corporations now also own some nongrocery subsidiaries such as chains of gasoline service stations, quick-service restaurants, discount stores, drugstores, and nonretailing businesses.[48] The Dayton-Hudson Corporation, which was basically a department store firm,

---

[47] Charles G. Burck, "Franchising's Troubled Dream World," *Fortune,* Vol. 81, No. 3 (March 1970), pp. 116–21. Many articles have been written about franchising. The Winter 1968–69 issue of the *Journal of Retailing* was devoted exclusively to this topic; for other sources cf. "A Business of Your Own . . . The Growth of Franchising," *U.S. News & World Report,* December 8, 1969, pp. 56–59; "Franchising: Too Much, Too Soon," *Business Week,* June 27, 1970, pp. 54–59; "Franchising's Busy Helpers," *Business Week,* February 21, 1970, pp. 132–33; and D. N. Thompson (ed.), *Contractual Marketing Systems* (Lexington, Mass.: D. C. Heath and Co., 1971).

[48] "Now Retailing Conglomerates?" *Chain Store Age* (supermarket executives edition), August 1969, p. E 33.

now owns the Target and Lechmere discount chains, the B. Dalton bookshop chain, a number of independent specialty jewelry stores, and the Team Central high-fidelity stores franchising operation. The Thrift Drug Company is a J. C. Penney subsidiary. Sears, Roebuck's insurance subsidiary is well known and the company is now experimenting with other financial services. At least one-quarter to one-third of our largest retail firms now operate two or more different types of stores and/or engage in some business outside of retailing.[49]

Several forces are responsible for the movement toward diversification. The more vigorous firms perceived growth opportunities in new fields during the long post–World War II period of prosperity. Diversification is also seen as a safety measure, since profit opportunities in new lines might offset poor competitive conditions or changing customer tastes that could reduce profits in the firm's basic business. And government limitations on mergers within the same line of business, already noted, have stimulated mergers and acquisitions that cut across traditional retail lines.

□ Internationalization

A number of American retail firms have also expanded abroad. Many have Canadian subsidiaries, and some have ventured even farther afield. Sears has numerous branches in Mexico, Central and South America, and has also opened stores in Spain; Woolworth has had a partly owned British subsidiary for many years, has important German and Mexican divisions as well as newly opened stores in Spain. The Jewel Company is a partner in a major Belgian retailing firm, G. B. Enterprises; and the J. C. Penney Co. now owns Sarma, another important Belgian chain. Wickes Hardware has established a branch in the Netherlands; Safeway operates supermarkets in Great Britain, West Germany, and Australia; and S. S. Kresge Co. is a partner in a chain of Australian K-Marts. Some direct-selling companies, such as Avon, Tupperware, and Singer have literally worldwide operations.

Relatively fewer foreign retailers are active in the United States, but there are some. George Weston, Ltd., a Canadian firm with substantial holdings in Western Europe, owns the Loblaw and National Tea grocery chains in this country. The Orbach department and specialty stores in the New York and Los Angeles areas are part of C. & A. Brenninkmeyer, a very large Dutch firm. A considerable number of European designers and stylists have franchised outlets in the U.S., and some foreign dealers in fine jewelry, art objects, and other luxury products also have American branches. The in-

[49] For company-by-company details, cf. *Fairchild's Financial Manual of Retail Stores* (New York: Fairchild Publications). Published annually.

creasing ease of communication and the growing similarity of middle-income consumer purchasing habits around the world may well encourage more such internationalization in the future.[50]

□ National versus private brands

For many years retailers with adequate resources and sufficient prestige to consider the problem have had to decide what sort of balance should be maintained in their merchandise offerings and sales promotional efforts between national brands and private brands.[51] The degree of emphasis given each type of brand has varied from company to company and even from time to time within a firm; but, in general, many retailers favor national brands because of the substantial advertising expenditures and aggressive merchandising tactics of their manufacturers.

Nevertheless, most large food retailers probably obtain between 5 and 15 percent of their sales (aside from fresh meat and produce) from private brand merchandise. *Chain Store Age* estimates that private brands account for about 10 percent of all grocery sales.[52] By far the greater share of branded merchandise in Sears and Wards is sold under the stores' private labels, and private branding is also widely used in apparel, variety, and other chains. Even though most stores usually sell their private brand merchandise for less than comparable national brand items and thus receive a competitive advantage, they also usually enjoy a greater gross margin (the difference between the store's cost and selling price) on the private lines. And well-accepted private brands help build customer loyalty to the store, since the same brand cannot be obtained from competitive outlets. The battle of the brands is far from over.

□ Other forms of response

In addition to the responses already mentioned, retailers have adopted numerous other measures to meet their changing environment. The number is so great, in fact, that only a sampling of them can be mentioned here and even these must be presented in summary form. Many of these developments, however, are discussed in some detail in later chapters.

---

[50] Cf. the Special International Issue, *Journal of Retailing,* Spring 1968; and S. C. Hollander, *Multinational Retailing* (East Lansing, Michigan: Institute for International Business and Economic Development Studies, Michigan State University, 1970), for a further discussion of this topic.

[51] As the terms are used here a "national brand" is a manufacturer's brand whereas a "private brand" is a middleman's or reseller's brand. Cf. the discussion in Chapter 19.

[52] "Behind the Private Label Boom," *Chain Store Age* (supermarket executives edition), August 1968, p. 56.

1. Stores are being relocated in suburban areas and outlying shopping centers because of the deterioration of many downtown sections and the movement of population to the suburbs.[53] Scientific methods are being employed in the choice of these relocation sites to insure attraction of sufficient patronage to realize a profit.
2. Recent emphasis seems to be on the establishment of larger outlying stores with more departments featuring wider selections of merchandise.
3. Modernization of existing stores has continued at a high rate with many improvements in materials, fixtures, and equipment.[54]
4. Changes are being made in the organizational structure of department stores and other multiunit retailers to strengthen controls over merchandise stocks and operating activities.[55]
5. Shifts in store hours are being made to accommodate the needs of customers; several night openings plus Sundays—particularly for food stores—are becoming increasingly common.[56]
6. In the area of sales promotion techniques, the use of both trading stamps and such games as "Bonus Bingo" and "Win-a-check" continues, although they have lost some popularity among supermarkets and other stores because of unfavorable customer reaction and the move toward "discounting."[57]
7. Growing recognition is being given to imported merchandise in regular merchandise inventories and for special sales events. In some areas, "import stores" have been established to meet the demand.
8. More store space is being given to "leisure-time" merchandise offerings and to art objects, antiques, and similar items demanded by a growing culture-conscious population.
9. The tendency for retailers to broaden and extend the lines carried within each store—"scrambled merchandising"—continues, with the result that competition in the retail field is intensified. No longer does the small-appliance dealer compete only with similar specialty stores. He is also in keen competition with the discount house, supermarket, drugstore, variety retailer, department store—and frequently the gasoline service station and auto-supply outlet as well.
10. A constant alertness is being manifested by retailers in changing their "mix" of merchandise and operating policies and methods. Some seek a more profitable mix through store modernization programs, self-

[53] Cf. Chapter 4.
[54] Cf. Chapter 5.
[55] Cf. Chapter 7.
[56] Cf. discussion of "Retail Working Conditions" in Chapter 9.
[57] Cf. Chapter 19.

service operation, and the promotion of private brands; others place their emphasis on widespread promotional activities for bargain-price merchandise; and still others prefer to maintain "regular" prices with greater attention to improved personal salesmanship. Change in the retailing mix is still another factor intensifying competition among retailers.

11. In response to technological developments, retailers are increasingly using data-capturing and data-processing equipment for such activities as merchandise planning and control, pricing, checking credits, accounting for receivables and payables, improving turnover, payroll, and sales audit and analysis.[58]

REVIEW AND DISCUSSION QUESTIONS

1 What factors, in your judgment, are responsible for the continuing growth of giant retailers? Explain.

2 As the proprietor of a small, independent store what measures would you adopt to meet the growing competition of the large retailers?

3 Why is it so important for all retailers to keep informed regarding changes in the environment in which they must operate?

4 Summarize significant developments in the following environmental areas during recent years: (a) social; (*b*) economic; and (c) political.

5 Prepare a paper of some 1,500 words on one of the following subjects: (a) "The Teenagers—What Retail Stores Should Do about Them"; (*b*) "The Oldsters (65 and over)—Retailers' Opportunities for Service and Profit"; (c) "Implications for the Retailer under Current Economic Conditions."

6 How do you explain the continued growth of the "discount house" in the United States?

7 Name and explain briefly five significant recent changes in the competitive environment of retailing.

8 Prepare a list of the franchised stores in your community or in the neighborhood of your school. How do these stores differ from their nonfranchised competitors in the same area? Do these differences help explain the recent growth of franchising? Discuss.

9 Argue both sides of the question—"Resolved: The traditional depart- partment store's future is very uncertain in retail trade."

10 Evaluate the pros and cons of private branding by retail stores as compared with the handling of nationally advertised brands exclusively.

---

[58] Cf. the discussion of "The Retailer and Electronic Equipment," in Chapter 5.

PART II

Retailing opportunities and careers

chapter 2

BASIC REQUIREMENTS FOR SUCCESSFUL STORE MANAGEMENT

Successful operation of a retail business, in the rapidly changing market conditions and in the social, political, economic, and competitive environment discussed in the previous chapter, is a very challenging task. Some of the main requirements for performance of that task can be classified into five broad groups: (1) the personal qualifications of the proprietor or of top management; (2) an adequate financial structure; (3) necessary physical facilities; (4) effective policies and procedures; and (5) competent, loyal, and productive personnel in both sales and sales-supporting activities. Effective combination and correlation of these factors will result in satisfied customers and in profit for the retailer.

PERSONAL REQUIREMENTS OF MANAGEMENT

Most young people who enter retailing eventually hope to become store owners or department, division, store, or area managers. We should therefore examine this goal, the executive function, at this early stage in our study of retailing. What is the retail executive's role? What personal qualifications are necessary for success as a retail executive? What is the retail executive's social contribution?

□ The executive's functions

The key executives (or the management) are the most significant single ingredient in the success of a retail business. As one writer points out, they must perform three basic functions: (1) *Giving direction* to the firm (establishing goals, framing policies, developing operating programs, initiating action and coordinating activities to achieve the goals); (2) *representing the company to the public* ("the most underrated of management's multiple responsibilities"); and (3) *evaluating results,* that is, examining the company's performance, analyzing the causes of deviations from the goals, and determining what must be done to improve operations.[1] The retail executives who perform these functions successfully are usually hard-working, self-disciplined men and women who are willing to accept significant responsibilities and to give unstintingly of themselves to serve their organizations. In the informal world of retailing, these executives are likely to be highly active and energetic people who maintain close relationships with their associates and with their firm's day-to-day operations.

Thus the retail manager may be viewed as a teacher or a coach. He molds his associates into an effective team by teaching them how to work together and by training them for greater responsibilities. He must build morale within his organization and provide the drive and leadership necessary for accomplishment of the organization's goals. He should also keep himself informed about developments in his own firm, in the entire retail field, and in the overall environment in which the store operates. Otherwise, he will fail to adjust his operations to shifting conditions. He plays a significant role in long-range planning and policy formation and institutes procedures to be sure the plans and policies are put into effect. In addition, he and/or his high-level associates represent his company in the community, at public functions and in community betterment activities designed to fulfill the social responsibilities of all businesses today. The breadth and time-consuming aspects of his many tasks are obvious.

□ The retail executive's personal qualities

Satisfactory performance at the management level in retailing requires the same personal characteristics, in general, as are needed for good management in most lines of business.[2] Certain characteristics, however, should

[1] W. N. Mitchell, *The Business Executive in a Changing World* (New York: American Management Association, 1965), pp. 48, 58, 60, 75.

[2] Some social psychologists might disagree with this statement and claim that retail executives have greater sensitivity to short-term changes in business activity, greater aesthetic awareness, and somewhat less analytical ability than executives in other organizations.

be emphasized. These include: a market orientation, knowledge, experience, drive, friendliness, leadership, judgment, decisiveness, vision, effective expression, and character. The need for overall administrative ability overlaps all of these characteristics.

Market orientation The retail executive must be sensitive to market demands and market opportunities. He must understand consumer buying motives and habits and he must become skilled in developing satisfactory relations with his customers.

1. The consumer is king The retailer's business and profits depend upon satisfying his customers, thus ensuring their continuous patronage. He must offer them the goods and services they want, when, how, and where they want them, and at the prices they are willing to pay. An experienced grocery merchant once expressed the same thought in these words: A retailer must so please his customers that they will "never go to another store. They might like it better there, and never come back."[3]

This requirement is illustrated by one author's explanation of the success of the J. C. Penney Company: Its executives "never lost sight of the elementary fact that without customers they could not remain in business. They looked upon their customers as their *real* board of directors. They realized that the success of their stores and the security of their own jobs were decisions completely within the keeping of the public."[4] Or, as an eminent merchant once put it:

> You'll get along fine so long as you never forget it's the *people* in our business who make it a business. Management, merchandisers, buyers, salespeople, but most of all, customers are *people*, not sales figures.[5]

2. The marketing concept In recent years retailers and marketers in general who accept and practice this "consumer is king" philosophy are said to be using the marketing concept. Specifically, they accept "customer needs and wants . . . (as) . . . the starting point for all their efforts."[6] Consequently, they plan their merchandise assortments, the services they render, their physical facilities, and their personnel policies so as to meet these needs and wants. Everyone in the firm takes his "marching orders from the market."[7]

---

[3] "The Agile Man Who Built Third Avenue," *Fortune*, Vol. 71, No. 5 (May 1965), p. 146.

[4] Norman Beasley, *Main Street Merchant: The Story of the J. C. Penney Company* (New York: Whittlesey House, McGraw-Hill Book Co., Inc., 1948), p. 80.

[5] James McCreery, quoted by Margaret Dana, "Listen to What Your Customers Tell You," in *Readings in Modern Retailing* (New York: National Retail Merchants Association, 1969), p. 75.

[6] E. H. Fram, "Application of the Marketing Concept to Retailing," *Journal of Retailing*, Vol. 41, No. 2 (Summer 1965), p. 19.

[7] Wroe Alderson and P. E. Green, *Planning and Problem Solving in Marketing* (Homewood, Ill.: Richard D. Irwin, Inc., 1964), p. 5.

Knowledge The retail executive needs to know a great deal about (1) human relations, including the effective leadership and direction of employees as well as for developing satisfactory customer relations, (2) retail operating methods and procedures, and (3) merchandise and sources of supply. As noted previously, the successful retailer of today must also understand the nature and structure of retailing and the current developments and trends in its environment.

Experience Large retail organizations now assign their young executives much more responsibility and authority at an earlier age than they did in the past. The major variety chains, for example, are now promoting their executive trainees to the position of store manager in about half the time required for promotion ten years ago.[8] But some years of meaningful experience in performing or dealing with the major retail activities is a necessary qualification for top management.[9] The young man or woman who wants to "reach the top" in a large retail organization should try to obtain experience in successfully handling increasingly difficult assignments in several major phases of store operations. And the individual who wants to run a store of his own would be well advised to gain considerable knowledge of retailing problems and techniques as an employee before venturing on his own.[10]

The successful retailer must learn the relationships involved in all of the following functions and activities, and he will benefit greatly from experience in as many of them as possible:

1. Effective buying.
2. Judicious pricing.
3. Sound merchandising control methods.
4. Creative advertising and sales promotion.
5. Constructive salesmanship.
6. An adequate store system.
7. Enlightened personnel administration.
8. Customer-attracting customer services.
9. Effective expense control.

---

[8] "Who'll Run the Stores of the 70's," *Chain Store Age* (Variety Stores Executives Edition), November 1970, p. 40.

[9] The young lady who was appointed president of a 30-store shoe chain at age 26 is very definitely an exception to the general rule. Cf. "Jane Evans: The Whiz Kid Who Fills I. Miller's Shoes," *Chicago Tribune*, December 6, 1970, sec. 5, p. 8; also cf. Mary Quant, *Quant by Quant* (New York: G. P. Putnam Sons, 1966) for the autobiography of a very successful unconventional young merchant and clothing designer.

[10] Yet some franchising organizations which train their franchisees in their own highly structured operating methods prefer to deal with people who have had no previous retailing experience.

But experience must be something more than mere "time on the job." Anyone who wants to develop mature judgment and an ability to make wise decisions has to analyze his activities, determine the causes for his successes and failures, and avoid repeating his mistakes. He must learn to appraise situations systematically and deliberately, to recognize the value of assembling all relevant and pertinent data (in so far as time permits), to evaluate alternative courses of action, and to think objectively and logically.

Drive Old fashioned ambition and hard work are usually prerequisites for success in retailing. The way to a top management post, as one merchant has expressed it, is to "forget the glamour, accept the responsibilities, and work like the devil." Drive—not the kind typified by the man who works hard for a few days and then loses his enthusiasm, but the type which perseveres year after year—is a key ingredient for the progressive retailer. In this respect, retailing differs little from most other worthwhile and challenging businesses and professions that demand constant effort and devotion. But the successful retail executive must expect to deal with a wide variety of obligations in a vigorous and zestful manner.

During his working hours, the executive must think constantly about a wide range of problems, meet a steady demand for new ideas, and face everlasting competition both from inside and from outside his company. He must attend numerous conferences and meetings, travel to distant places when necessary, and take an active part in the life of the community. This latter obligation includes participation in Community Chest campaigns, church work, youth movements, leadership of clubs, and speaking engagements. Someone has said that "success consists not only of doing extraordinary things but of doing ordinary things extraordinarily well." The dynamic retail executive gets keen satisfaction from doing the best possible job in every assigned task. Moreover, he is one who builds a reputation for doing the job right the *first* time.

Friendliness The retail executive should sincerely try to get along well with people: his employees, his superiors, and his business associates. Winning the friendship and respect of his staff is not an easy task. A good supervisor leads rather than drives his employees, but he loses their respect if he fails to enforce company rules and regulations. Any necessary criticisms should be constructive, based upon careful study of the circumstances, and expressed to the employee in private. Unjust criticism, or even justified criticism made under improper conditions, can do considerable harm to the individual criticized as well as to the executive.

The typical retail executive does a great deal of his work in association with other people. The major problems of the firm are frequently solved in executive conferences. Moreover, the various executives have to consult with each other very frequently to coordinate and harmonize the various aspects of their integrated operations. Most large retail organizations need a very considerable number of middle management executives, who stand between top management and the employees and who have to think in terms of both groups' needs and interests. The individual who does not like to work with people will be at a very great disadvantage in a business as humanized as retailing. His talents probably could be better used elsewhere.

Leadership A good manager inspires the confidence of others in his ability as a leader. He communicates assurance to his staff and arouses their confidence in and their enthusiasm for the firm's goals, policies, and procedures. He uses his authority to guide his organization and he motivates his associates to ever-higher levels of performance. He demands constant improvement, but he shows his people how to achieve it and encourages them to strive for excellence. The retail executive does not automatically receive his authority and leadership capacity from the title on his door. They must be earned through the confidence, respect, and support of the people with whom he works. He gains authority when he demonstrates his ability to assume it.

Judgment The successful executive must be able to judge the probable outcome of his own decisions. Also, he must gauge the effect of outside events on his own business. The ability to reason, to draw valid conclusions from facts, to withstand some pressures and give way to others, and to sift good advice from bad—all these call for judgment on his part. Frequently he is called upon to exercise judgment on merchandise; in such cases his aesthetic taste, his sense of style, and his appreciation of merchandise may be important in reaching valid decisions. Of course, his judgment will not be infallible, but his wise decisions must outweigh his faulty ones.

Decisiveness Retail management involves a never-ending series of decisions: decisions about merchandise, prices, promotional programs, space allocations, personnel, customer relations, business policy, *etc.* Many of these decisions are subject to pressing time deadlines. Often at least some of the facts that the executive would like to know are unavailable, despite all the data that modern information and control systems provide. Yet procrastination and failure to reach a decision is often tantamount to making a very bad decision. For example, the merchandising executive who delays too long in selecting his Christmas or his Mother's Day stocks will undoubtedly have a very poor assortment of goods for a peak selling season. The capable manager learns to make sound and timely decisions, and to translate thought into action.

An executive must be willing to make unpopular decisions if his best judgment tells him to do so. And he must constantly keep in mind the overall well-being of the company. The man who says, "We'll take care of our own department; let the others solve their own problems," takes far too narrow a view. Top retail positions should be filled by individuals who continuously strive to fulfill the purposes and aims of the entire organization.

Vision As we have already noted, retailing is a highly dynamic, changing industry. Tomorrow's customers are likely to live in different places, shop in different fashion, and want different merchandise than today's shoppers. Competition constantly presents new challenges. The retail executive must be able to look beyond his company's immediate problems and goals and to plan for the future. He should be able to anticipate and to lead change. And all of his current problem-solving decisions should be designed to strengthen the firm's future growth, reputation, and organization. In order to do this, he must develop a vivid picture of what he believes should be his company's ultimate goals.

The manager's vision of the future must go far beyond the confines of his business and embrace the entire environment in which his firm operates. Thus, in addition to achieving effective internal operations, he must do his best to help maintain a free and viable economy in a healthy social system.

Effective expression Having a vision of desirable changes is only half the battle: The retail executive must also be able to "sell" the vision to his associates, his customers, and the public. Consequently, effective communication—the ability to use the English language convincingly and persuasively, both orally and in writing—is important to his success.

Character A good retail executive is both reliable and courageous. He never forgets his obligations to his firm's customers, employees, stockholders, and sources of supply. He knows that his reputation for keeping promises is his business livelihood, that his character is reflected in the actions of his company, in the quality of the product it handles, and the services it renders. He is aware that honesty in dealing with his customers and employees is not just the *best* policy but that it is the *only* policy upon which continued patronage and employee loyalty can be founded.

Administrative ability Another approach to many of the characteristics already discussed is to say that the executive must have a high degree of administrative ability. One authority believes that successful administration rests upon three basic and related skills—technical, human, and conceptual—which he defines as follows:

> *Technical skill* [which] implies an understanding of, and proficiency in, a specific kind of activity, particularly one involving methods, processes, procedures or techniques. . . . It involves specialized knowledge, analytical ability within that specialty, and facility in the use of the tools and techniques of a specific discipline.
>
> *Human skill* is . . . the executive's ability to work effectively as a group member and to build cooperative effort within the team he leads. As *technical skill* is primarily concerned with working with "things" (processes or physical objects) so *human skill* is primarily concerned with working with people.

Conceptual skill . . . involves the ability to see the enterprise as a whole; it includes recognizing how the various functions of the organization depend on one another, and how changes in any one part affect all the others; and it extends to visualizing the relationship of the individual business to the industry, the community, and the political, social and economic forces of the nation as a whole. Recognizing these relationships, and perceiving the significant elements in any situation, the administrator should then be able to act in a way which advances the overall welfare of the organization.[11]

In the retail field the executive who possesses such skills and utilizes them with discretion and judgment is likely to be a *good* administrator. Exercising the leadership which such skills imply and remaining in close touch with the major activities of his business should give satisfactory results both in the short and the long run.

Thus the successful retail executive is a composite of many qualities. Adequate knowledge, practical experience, and certain personal attributes are all essential. The knowledge necessary for advancement in retailing comes from a variety of sources—formal academic training, careful observation, reading and study on one's own initiative, and experience. But, there is no substitute for experience in the learning process. The actual doing of jobs, the performance of specialized tasks, personal observation of customer buying habits, and intimate contact with day-to-day problems as they arise are an important part of the retail executive's training.

□ The retail executive's social contribution

The retailer's most basic social contribution[12] comes from the successful and efficient operation of his business. A prospering, continuing business in any field provides a livelihood for many people, both directly for its own employees and indirectly for the employees of its many suppliers. But the well-conducted retail business also performs other functions in our complex market economy. We are so accustomed to visiting stores that we can easily forget their vital role as supply points for the necessities and amenities of life. The successful retail business, at the very heart of the marketing system, is in close touch with both consumers and suppliers. It can act as coordinator between the manufacturer's product development, merchandising and promotional activities, and the requirements and aspirations of the consumer market. Convenient, reliable, and attractive retail establish-

[11] R. L. Katz, *Executive Skills* (Hanover, N.H.: Amos Tuck School of Business Administration, 1954), pp. 4–6.

[12] Also cf. the discussion of social responsibilities of retailers in Chapter 26.

ments facilitate consumer purchasing, help stimulate economic expansion, and play a significant part in raising our standard of living.

Many merchants go beyond this basic task in personal and corporate service to society. The International Executive Service Corps, a private non-profit organization that provides consultants to assist struggling businesses in the developing countries, finds that some of its most successful and helpful volunteers are retired chain store and supermarket executives.[13] Other retailers render their contributions closer to home. A British writer notes that American and Canadian stores have "a genuine sense of civic responsibility towards the community they serve. They tend to be leaders rather than followers in charity drives, patriotic occasions, even municipal politics."[14]

Senior store officials often play prominent roles in municipal development and rehabilitation efforts. Some stores have developed active programs for training and promoting disadvantaged workers. Department stores frequently sponsor youth groups, sometimes in cooperation with magazines and suppliers, that engage in a wide variety of civic, charitable, and educational activities. One firm that works with stores in developing these groups comments:

> Today, youth is intensely interested in people and their problems—in community service and action
>
> Today, the progressive retail store is actively involved in the welfare of its community
>
> Community service is the meeting place—For retailing, which wants to attract more creative and dedicated young men and women . . . For youth, seeking a challenging opportunity for community participation.[15]

■ FINANCIAL STRUCTURE

The second basic requirement of successful retail management is adequate capital. Regardless of one's personal qualifications and interest in the field, profitable operation of a retail store is impossible without sufficient funds. The need for funds permeates all phases of the business from the exploratory and planning stages up to the final payments for merchandise and employee services.

---

[13] For discussions of the International Executive Service Corps, cf. Robert Sheehan, "Those 'Retired' Management Missionaries," *Fortune*, Vol. 76, No. 3 (September 1, 1967, p. 106); and "This Isn't Minneapolis, Mr. Moran," *Sales Management*, Vol. 98, No. 10 (May 15, 1967, p. 66).

[14] Ann Roush, *Selling to North American Stores* (London: Routledge & Kegan Paul, for the British Export Council, 1969), p. 15.

[15] Quoted from the summary of the 1968–1969 Bonne Bell Community Service Citations.

The capital needed should be very carefully estimated before establishing a new store or buying an established one. Many would-be retailers have seriously underestimated their initial expenses and overestimated their early sales and profits. Consequently, these estimates should be checked and rechecked before the business is started (or purchased). The sources from which those funds will come should then be determined.[16] The retailer must also be prepared for unexpected demands for funds not included in his estimates. After he has gone through the difficult opening period and first few months of operations, he should be able to formulate reasonably accurate merchandise, expense and overall financial budgets.[17] But he certainly should leave considerable "room for error", *i.e.*, a reasonable safety margin in his initial plans.

■ BUILDINGS AND PHYSICAL FACILITIES

Adequate physical facilities, the third broad group of factors underlying the successful operation of a retail store, include a satisfactory building—properly located and arranged—suitable fixtures and equipment, and other devices and mechanisms necessary to provide customers with needed merchandise and services in a pleasant environment. Recent years have witnessed important advances and improvements in site selection, store arrangement, merchandise handling and storage, and the use of electronic equipment—to mention but a few of the major areas. These matters are discussed in considerable detail in Chapters 4, 5, and 6.

■ EFFECTIVE RETAILING POLICIES

Effective, well-maintained policies for operation of the business constitute the fourth major requirement for profitable store management. Business policies are the written or implied rules of conduct under which the firm operates. A policy establishes a definite and uniform course of action which all members of the organization must follow under substantially similar and recurrent circumstances.

In small businesses, these "rules of conduct" are often simply the ideas the proprietor keeps in mind as to the way he wants to operate his store. He

[16] These points are developed more fully later in "Financing Methods," pp. 60–62.

[17] The merchandise budget is discussed in Chapter 13 and the expense and financial budgets in Chapter 24.

adopts policies when he decides to sell on account rather than for cash only and when he decides to pay his salespeople bonuses in addition to their regular salary. Larger retailers, however, usually put their policies in writing because they must be communicated to many people, frequently at several locations.[18] All policies should be clear and definite, workable, stable and consistent as long as circumstances are similar, and adjusted promptly when fundamental conditions change. Policies that meet these requirements can be very useful management tools for the retail store proprietor or executive.

☐ Need for effective policies

We have already noted that the retail stores of today operate under trying conditions. Competition steadily intensifies, many stores are broadening their "product mix," discount houses are growing rapidly, and traditional retailers are revising their services. Population shifts, particularly the growth of suburban areas, complicate the problems of downtown stores. High taxes make it difficult to generate internal funds for expansion purposes; and high construction, modernization, and interest costs tend to deter necessary or desirable changes in physical facilities. The potential growth of retail unions and the increase in government regulations place restrictions on some of the retailer's former freedoms. Shorter working hours, higher wage rates, and night and Sunday openings have raised "break-even" points and made profitable operation more difficult.

These changing and trying conditions necessitate carefully established policies. Otherwise the retailer may be swept along with the tide—merely trying one opportunistic adjustment after another without thinking through the long-run implications of those adjustments. Stated positively, the retailer who goes through the mental process of determining policies has a set of standards to guide his and his associates' actions; he does not drift off the main road because of the superficial attractiveness of some bypath.

At the same time, changing conditions may well call for policy adjustments. In fact, as has already been emphasized, a policy is valid only so long as the circumstances which brought it into existence remain substantially the same. But the retailer who has carefully established his policies for a certain set of conditions, will usually be the one who is willing to make adjustments in them *after investigation* indicates changes are necessary.

Well-established policies reduce the number of decisions that key executives have to make. Comparable cases can be settled on a routine basis ac-

---

[18] The advantages that even the small merchant gains from putting policies in writing are discussed in: "Save Time, Avoid Confusion: Write a Policy Manual," *Hardware Retailer*, February 1969, pp. 173, 179.

cording to predetermined and well-understood rules. Thus, the time of major executives is conserved by allowing others in the organization to make decisions based on the company's policies. Sound policies that insure consistent and equitable treatment of similar situations will reduce the danger of improperly treating one customer, employee, or supplier more favorably than another.

□ Steps in policy formulation

Careful study of the problems to be solved is the first step in policy formation. Accurate and complete information should be secured, rather than relying upon hunches and guesswork. The business's objectives, the anticipated operating conditions, the possible alternative policies, and their potential results should be carefully analyzed. Then the policies may be properly formulated.

Considerations influencing choice of policies While the proprietor's, management's, or the board of directors' judgment is the final determinant in each policy decision, the business policies of any firm will depend upon what is desired and what is possible. What is desired, of course, is not always possible. Like most businessmen, the retailer must constantly make compromises to meet the situations that confront him and especially to meet the restrictions placed upon his choice of alternatives. These include, among other factors, legal restrictions, public opinion, cost considerations, activities of competitors, vested interests of individuals in his own organization, his personal preferences, the services his customers expect, and the limits of the resources at his command.

Responsibility for policy formulation Responsibility for establishing retail policies varies with the size and type of store and with the form of business organization. Most small firms and some rather large ones are individual proprietorships or partnerships. The proprietor or the partners, sometimes along with other family members, frame the rules for conducting these businesses. The board of directors should play a major role in policy formation for the incorporated small store. Unfortunately, however, the boards of small corporations often have only a purely nominal existence to satisfy legal technicalities and do not participate in policy formation.

The boards of directors of larger retail firms, such as corporate department stores and chains, are usually responsible for major policies, but they normally give the president or possibly a management committee authority to approve other policies. In so far as possible, though, the people who will be expected to carry out a policy should play some part in its development, regardless of where the final authority lies and regardless of who drafts the actual policy statement. Their experience and insights will not only help in framing the policy but they will become committed to its successful implementation.

Many retailers become so busy with daily routine affairs that they fail to devote enough time to policy formation. Despite the constant stream of daily matters demanding his attention, every retailer should reserve sufficient time and energy for consideration of policy questions. The proprietor or chief executive should never forget that formulating suitable policies (in cooperation with his board of directors, if one exists) is one of his major tasks.

□ Areas of policy decisions

The retailer must make policy decisions concerning numerous aspects of the business, including, for example, kind and quality of merchandise to be carried, forms of customer service to be rendered, types of sales promotion to be used, and personnel administration problems. Policies concerning each of these and other matters are discussed in subsequent chapters and need not be treated at this point. In passing, however, let us consider briefly two other areas in which policies should be established—participation in community activities and membership in trade associations.

Participation in community activities Many retailers—small and large—belong to service clubs such as the Kiwanis, Lions, or Rotary. Membership is considered a mark of distinction because of the interest such organizations take in community affairs and because of the exchange of ideas on business problems. Other retailers are members of chambers of commerce, local school boards, Community Fund committees, hospital boards, and parent-teacher associations. Still others serve as Boy Scout leaders, aldermen, city officials, and church officers. In deciding how active a part he will play in the life of the community, the retailer will be governed by his desire to serve, the time involved, and his judgment of the long-run effect such participation will have on his sales and profits.

Membership in trade associations Sooner or later the retailer is confronted with the question of whether he should join an association of stores in his field. His decision will be based largely upon the services the association can render him, the cost involved, and the time he will have to devote to it. Recent years have witnessed a continued growth in the membership of such associations because of the increase in services provided to members. Today there exist strong associations—local, state, and national—in almost every field of retail enterprise; and their membership lists include most of the successful retailers in the country.[19]

---

[19] For a comprehensive list of retail and non-retail trade associations, see the *Encyclopedia of Associations*, 6th ed. (Detroit: Gale Research Corp. 1970).

☐ Policy enforcement and review

Policies and procedures Once policies have been established, operating procedures must be developed to carry them out. These procedures should be as simple and clear-cut as possible so as to be easily understood and applied by the people who will be using them. Otherwise, the time spent developing procedures is wasted and the business cannot function according to plan.

A simple illustration will clarify the relationship between policies and procedures. When the owner of a supermarket decides he will offer delivery service to his customers, he is adopting a policy. In choosing a method of handling the goods sold so that they will be delivered to customers as promptly and as economically as possible, he is establishing operating procedures.

Policy enforcement No policy, however well conceived, can be of value to a retail store unless it is adhered to closely and consistently throughout the organization. Continual follow-up and enforcement are necessary to assure such adherence, especially in regard to the rank and file of employees.

Many store employees tend to disregard rules and regulations, not because of disagreement with those rules but because of unwillingness to spend the time and effort to become familiar with them. Others are particularly averse to making changes, to being forced to learn "something new." Consequently the employees must be educated in the purposes of the new rules as well as in the advantages of conformance to them. Employees will accept the situation more readily and adjust themselves to it more quickly, if they can be shown the new procedure is simpler in operation, that it saves time, that it achieves the firm's objectives substantially better than the old method, or it results in greater customer satisfaction.

Unfortunately many retail executives become lax about insuring compliance with the company's policies. They become so engrossed in major decisions relating to immediate profits that they neglect the essential continuous reemphasis of established policies and procedures. Their own negligence contributes significantly to the carelessness of their employees.

Coordination Top management must also make certain that the policies and activities of the various sections of the business are coordinated and contribute to the overall objective of providing needed goods and services and thus keeping the business profitable. Departmental and divisional personnel sometimes think of a store as a number of separate parts, each of which operates in its own interest. As a result, insufficient attention is given to the necessity of integrating these parts effectively.

Adjusting policies to changing conditions The dynamic nature of retailing necessitates continuous policy development and adjustment. Policies, like retail prices, are constantly on trial. Top management must constantly examine its policies in the light of experience and make whatever adjustments are necessary when conditions change to a significant degree.

Policy changes and adjustments call for some caution. Occasionally a policy will be discarded as an apparent failure after a short period of trial when actually the program of implementation rather than the basic policy itself was the cause of failure. Further investigation would have revealed the true problem. All of which suggests again that the successful operation of a retail store depends to an important degree upon how closely the proprietor or chief executive officer remains in contact with the essential activities of his business. Systematic and thorough follow-up of policies and procedures substantially influences profits.

■ COMPETENCY AND LOYALTY OF RETAIL PERSONNEL

The importance of the human factor in retailing, the fifth basic requirement of success in this field, has already been stressed in previous pages. It should be emphasized further, however, that profitable store operation is impossible unless an adequate sales and sales-supporting staff is carefully selected, effectively trained, adequately compensated, and properly supervised. Competency in the particular activities in which they are engaged, loyalty to top management and their immediate supervisors through close adherence to established policies and practices, and performance of duties and responsibilities efficiently and at reasonable cost are major obligations of every employee. Likewise, it is the obligation of the proprietor or of top management to be so objective, logical, and progressive in policies and practices that employees respond with loyalty and respect. Chapters 8 and 9 are devoted to personnel management in the retail store.

■ REVIEW AND DISCUSSION QUESTIONS

1 How is the "Revolution in Retailing" related to retail management requirements? Be specific.

2 Explain the "marketing concept," and its applicability to retailing. How widely is it employed in the retail field?

3 What do you consider the essential personal qualifications of an effective retail executive? Defend your answer.

4 Discuss: "Retail Management is More Art than Science."

5 Define "retailing policy" in your own words and point out the characteristics of a *good* policy.

6 Explain why effective policies are essential to success in retailing and illustrate three areas in which they are required.

7 Based on your observation in retail stores or your recent reading, give examples of policy changes by specific retail firms. Explain, where possible, the circumstances which brought about the changes.

8 As a retailer, precisely how would you keep acquainted with current developments and improvements in merchandising methods?

9 Assume that your first job following graduation is in a retail store and that the controller asks you to suggest ways through which better adherence to established rules and regulations can be obtained. Prepare a brief report covering this assignment.

10 Discuss: "Adjusting Retail Policies to Changing Conditions."

chapter 3

OPPORTUNITIES AND CAREERS IN RETAILING

Retailing offers many opportunities for stimulating and rewarding careers. It employs almost as many people as the combined fields of construction, transportation, communications, public utilities, real estate, insurance, banking, and finance. Moreover, retail stores are diverse enough and positions in stores are sufficiently varied to provide opportunities for almost every kind of ability, training, ambition, need, and desire. Top management has become increasingly aware of the advantages of community college and university training for success in this field.

■ SCOPE OF THE CHAPTER

Many retail employees are unskilled and poorly trained. Often employed on a part-time basis, they hold little or no authority and executive responsibility, but yet seem reasonably satisfied with their work. Our discussion here, however, concentrates on the opportunities for students who wish to advance to responsible positions in retailing, with commensurate salaries, where their abilities will be fully used. Of course, advancement involves accepting the responsibilities along with the rewards. Many people want to avoid the obligations inherent in higher positions. Some, for example, will refuse promotions that involve supervising other people's work. The opportunities in retailing—or elsewhere—for such people are definitely limited.

Students will find career opportunities in small, medium-sized, and large retail establishments located in various-sized communities. We cannot safely generalize, however, as to the size of store or community that provides the greatest possibilities. The opportunities in any particular retail venture depend upon the store itself—regardless of size, the suitability of its merchandise and service to its market, the progressiveness and alertness of its management, general business and competitive conditions, the managerial candidate's own qualifications, and to some extent, the "breaks" that he receives or creates for himself.

For convenience, this chapter is divided into five parts: (1) General employment aspects of retailing; (2) prospects in small and medium-sized stores; (3) prospects in department and specialty stores; (4) prospects in chain stores; and (5) "pro's" and "con's" of retailing careers.

■ GENERAL EMPLOYMENT ASPECTS OF RETAILING

Career-minded students should note the following major aspects of retail employment:

□ A decentralized industry

Retailing offers opportunities, as an employee or proprietor, in every city, town, and village in the country. Talented and ambitious individuals can receive highly useful experience near their homes in one of the almost 1,800,000 stores scattered throughout the country. Many large retailers believe that store experience, as well as training, are prerequisites for promotion. Students seeking employment and careers in the large firms can often obtain valuable early experience in their home town stores.

□ Many kinds of stores

The *1967 Census of Business* shows 82 separate classifications of stores, such as automobile dealers, drugstores, hardware stores, and millinery shops, as well as many types of "non-store" retailers. The stores within a classification also often differ greatly in character and personnel requirements, since some may feature style, others service, and still others low prices. The different types of experience, knowledge, abilities, tastes, and desires that these various stores require furnish opportunities for people with very different interests and talents.

☐ Large number employed

Retail stores in the United States employed about 11.3 million persons in 1970, or slightly more than twice the 1945 figure and about 1.5 million more than in 1965.[1] The U.S. Department of Labor forecasts that increased consumer expenditures, continued suburbanization, and longer store hours will raise future retail employment. Mechanization and self-service will supplant some lower level jobs, resulting in a moderate net increase throughout the 1970's.[2]

☐ Stable employment for full-time employees

Employment is more stable in retailing than in many other industries. Some retail businesses, such as food stores, experience little seasonal fluctuation in sales. Seasonal variations are significant in other retail fields but are not as great as the production fluctuations in many manufacturing industries. The increasing use of part-time employees in retailing permits adjustment to fluctuating conditions without altering the size of the regular staff.

☐ Shifting employment opportunities

Retailing is a stable industry, but not static. Total retail volume and employment fluctuate with, and are dependent upon, national income. Some groups of retail stores are increasing in importance, while others are decreasing. Table 3–1 shows some shifts in retail employment between 1963 and 1967. The first eight types of business listed, with substantially increased employment, are examples of "growing industries" that may provide more opportunities for young men and women than the declining or static fields listed in the second part of the table. Employment and career possibilities also appear in newer retailing developments, such as: the growth of "bantam, convenience-type" food stores, the expansion of stores that rent rather than sell merchandise, the increased development of franchising, and the emergence of various new style boutiques.

---

[1] U.S. Department of Labor, *Employment and Earnings*, Vol. 17, No. 12 (December 1970), pp. 55–58.

[2] U.S. Department of Labor, Bureau of Labor Statistics, *Occupational Outlook Handbook* (1970–71 edition, Washington, D.S.: U.S. Government Printing Office), pp. 775–76.

TABLE 3–1

Changes in employment by type of retail store, 1963 and 1967

Employment increased substantially in the following types of retail businesses from 1963 to 1967:

Type of business	Number of employees 1963	Number of employees 1967
Department stores	970,802	1,174,351
Motor vehicle dealers	656,440	734,820
Grocery stores	1,080,905	1,241,767
Shoe stores	91,728	108,367
Home furnishings stores	56,068	70,521
Garden supply stores	10,281	13,806
Florists	42,803	57,277

While it remained nearly constant or actually declined in these types:

Type of Business	Number of employees 1963	Number of employees 1967
Lumber and other building materials	188,152	188,715
Hardware stores	85,471	82,035
Candy, nut, and confectionery stores	21,808	21,341
Women's accessory and specialty shops	48,410	38,050
Fuel and ice dealers	102,273	101,227
Hobby, toy, and game shops	11,607	10,882

Source: *Census of Business 1967, Retail Trade: United States Summary BC67-RA1* (Washington, D.C.: U.S. Government Printing Office, 1970), pp. 1–6 to 1–9.

□ Variety of occupations

Mention retail employment and most people think of selling or cashiering. Yet only a fraction of the employees in many large organizations meet the customer on the sales floor. Jewel supermarkets, for example, employs 3.12 people behind the scenes for every cashier the customer sees.[3] One department store lists 800 different job classifications.[4] Many retail stores need buyers, fashion experts, accountants, advertising men and women, traffic and delivery experts, research directors, and personnel specialists as well as salespeople.

[3] Donald S. Perkins, "The Low-Income Consumer—A Human Problem and a Selling Problem," Executive Lecture Series, University of Notre Dame, March 2, 1970.

[4] Richard J. Braun, "The Retailing Specialist," in *Marketing, Business and Office Specialists,* ed. Garland D. Wiggs (Chicago: J. G. Ferguson Publishing Co., 1970), p. 215.

☐ Numerous women employees

Retailing has traditionally been a field offering employment to a large number of women. Almost 50 percent of all retail employees in 1968 were women,[5] and the current figure may be higher. The percentage of women employees varies widely with the kind of business, being low in tire and automotive supply stores, for example, and high in millinery shops.

The promotional opportunities for women are also good. Women compete with men on a much more equal basis in retailing than in most industries. Department stores in fact often prefer to have women, rather than men, as buyers and managers in many of the important ready-to-wear departments. In many high-fashion specialty shops all buyers may be women, except possibly the shoe, fur, and, occasionally, the coat buyer. Women fill about half of the supervisory and executive positions in department stores, including often one-third to one-half of the buying posts. Promotion above the rank of buyer has been more restricted, but women have often been publicity and fashion directors and are beginning to assume more senior management functions. For example, the downtown San Francisco store manager and the two merchandising vice presidents of Macy's California division are women, and Macy's New York recently promoted five women to vice presidential status.[6]

Apparel chains have appointed an increasing number of women as store managers, and variety, supermarket, and general merchandise chains are beginning to do the same thing. The McCrory-McLellan-Green chain assigned many of its stores to women managers in 1969, and the J. C. Penney Company appointed its first female store manager in 1970.[7]

☐ Training essential for key positions

Training, through academic background, trade or business school education, in-store development programs, and/or experience, is essential for many key retailing positions. Large retail firms recruit promotable young

[5] *Occupational Outlook Handbook, op. cit.,* p. 57. This figure includes part-time workers.

[6] Samuel Feinberg, "From Where I Sit," *Women's Wear Daily,* November 27, 1970, p. 11.

[7] "Who'll Run the Stores of the '70s?" *Chain Store Age* (Variety Stores Executives Edition) November 1970, p. 42; "Mary Boulette," *Penney News,* October 1970 (special issue on "Women in the Penney Company"), p. 10. Also cf. "Carole Bitter Breaks Barriers . . . ," *Supermarket News,* September 21, 1970, p. 12 (Stop & Shop's first woman reserve supermarket manager), and "For Women, a Difficult Climb to the Top," *Business Week,* August 2, 1969, pp. 42–46 (including a brief sketch of Mrs. Edith Grimm, vice president, Carson Pirie Scott & Co., a major Chicago department store).

men and women at community colleges, universities, and graduate schools, and in some cases have sponsored employee and prospective employee enrollment in community and senior colleges.[8] They also often implement their "promotion from within" policies by establishing development programs for the academically-trained and other promotable individuals in their organizations. These programs vary in extent, format, and effectiveness, but usually involve rotating work experience in various sectors of the firm. They may also include lectures and discussions with corporate officials and selected outsiders, attendance at evening courses and short seminars, correspondence study and other activities.[9]

□ Retailing salaries

Salespeople and nonselling employees Table 3–2 shows average hourly wages, working hours and weekly wages for full-time and part-time *nonsupervisory* workers in selected retail trades. These figures do not include any executive, professional, or managerial personnel. Salaries for beginning salespeople in small communities tend to be close to the statutory minimum

TABLE 3–2

Average hourly earnings, weekly hours and weekly earnings of nonsupervisory employees in selected retail trades, September 1970

Type of store	Average hourly wage	Average weekly hours	Average weekly earnings
Retail trade (except eating and drinking establishments)	$2.48	33.9	$ 84.07
General merchandise stores	2.44	32.1	78.32
Department stores	2.61	31.8	83.00
Grocery, meat and vegetable stores	2.81	33.3	93.57
Apparel and accessories stores	2.30	31.9	73.37
Shoe stores	2.43	31.5	76.55
Men's and boys' apparel stores	2.64	33.8	89.23
Motor vehicle dealers	3.29	40.3	132.59
Furniture and home furnishings stores	2.98	37.0	110.26

Source: U.S. Department of Labor, *Employment and Earnings*, Vol. 7, No. 12 (December 1970), p. 84.

[8] Cf. the three year cooperative program conducted by Wickes Home Supply Stores and Building Supply Centers and Delta (Community) College, "Manpower: The Key to Expansion," *Building Supply News*, April 1968, pp. 70–72.

[9] Department and chain store training programs are discussed more fully at pp. 63-71 in this chapter, and Chapter 8.

of $64 for 40 hours.[10] Beginning salaries for routine saleswork in stores in larger cities are somewhat higher—one recent union contract provides a $2.50 an hour minimum. But capable, experienced specialty salespeople in shoes, clothing, and "big ticket" appliance departments may earn $150 to $300 per week.

Trainees' initial salaries Retail executive trainees also tend to receive relatively low starting salaries, although some firms have improved their compensation substantially in recent years. For example, an analysis of over 8,000 job offers received by male bachelor's degree candidates at 133 colleges in 1969–70 shows that "merchandising and related firms" (wholesaling, retailing, advertising, etc.) offered about 15 percent less than the all-industry average. Merchandising offers to master's degree candidates, however, were at about the average for all industries.[11] Similarly, the salaries offered to women as merchandising or sales promotion trainees were only slightly under the average for all nontechnical business positions.[12] Clearly, retail organizations should do more to meet the inducements of other industries. Beginning salaries must be raised and qualified trainees must be advanced even more rapidly than in the past.[13]

Top executive salaries The chief executives of the large firms earn very substantial incomes. Sears, Roebuck & Co. paid its chairman $375,000 and its president $275,000 in 1970; the four senior executives in Federated Department Stores received compensation ranging from $200,000 to $265,000; Kresge's two top executives received $170,000 and $275,000; the chairman of F. W. Woolworth, slightly over $300,000; and the chief executive of Kroger Co. earned about $192,000.[14]

Obviously, only a few persons entering retailing will reach these levels. But as indicated later in this chapter, middle-management executives in retailing are also usually very well paid. Unfortunately, relatively low executive trainee salaries and the prospect of some Saturday, Sunday, and evening work (often heaviest during the first few years of employment) drive many able young men and women away from retailing careers. Yet those who have the necessary personalities and abilities and who can "stick out" the first hard years will eventually obtain very large financial rewards.

---

[10] Effective February 1, 1971 for stores with sales between $250,000 and $1,000,000 per year; effective earlier for larger stores.

[11] "Men's Salary Survey," *Study of 1969–70 Beginning Offers by Business and Industry* (Bethlehem, Pa.: The College Placement Council, 1970). Detailed breakdowns within the so-called "merchandising" group are not available, but retail firms probably provided most of the offers included in the average figure.

[12] "Women's Salary Survey," *ibid.*

[13] Cf. J. L. Goldstucker, "Competent Retail Trainees—Where Are They?" *Journal of Marketing*, Vol. 27, No. 2, April 1963, pp. 38–41.

[14] *Business Week*, June 19, 1971, pp. 68, 76.

Nonfinancial rewards Although dollar compensation is an important part of executive motivation, it is not the whole story. The successful retail executive can expect many nonmonetary satisfactions in addition to his monetary earnings. There is the personal sense of achievement and the recognition of his accomplishments within the company and in the community. He can derive satisfaction from service to the community, in providing job opportunities for many people, in assuming leadership roles in community betterment programs, and in his significant contribution to today's high standard of living. And he can enjoy the constant stimulation and intellectual challenge of experimenting with new ways of operating his store or department, of constantly meeting new competitive thrusts, and of working with people in an active, vigorous, ever-changing environment.

□ Working conditions in retailing

The following discussion is in general terms since working conditions vary greatly among different types of work in a given retail firm, among firms in the same field, among fields, and among sections of the country.

Hours Retail working hours have been sharply reduced in recent years. The proprietor, his family members, and the few employees of a small store may work 48, 54, or more hours per week, but larger retail organizations generally observe a 40-hour week, with some overtime at peak periods. The five day workweek has also become common in spite of the increase in Sunday openings. In fact, work schedules in retailing are frequently far more regular than in such fields as airline transportation, newspaper and television communications, medicine, or law. And those who are willing to undertake hard work during their first years in retailing will find this time and effort amply compensated for later on.

Surroundings The retail employee's surroundings vary greatly with the kind of work, the particular store, and the community. Although office and nonselling areas are being increasingly modernized, many retailers have concentrated upon decorating and improving the selling departments where customers see the results. Consequently nonselling employees and middle-level store executives often work in relatively unattractive surroundings. While overly elaborate offices are not appropriate to the informality of most retail organizations, top executives, senior headquarters staff, and more and more middle managers work in attractive offices and are provided competent secretarial assistance.

Retailers are also recognizing the need for improving the mental and social conditions of work. Libraries, house organs, concerts, athletic contests, recreation rooms and similar amenities contribute to the rank-and-file employees' *esprit de corps* and contentment. Many retail workers find the social contacts and opportunities to talk with customers and fellow employees even more pleasurable and stimulating.

Vacations Vacations in retailing are comparable to those in most other businesses. The larger retailers offer regular employees at least a week with pay, usually increased to two, three, or even five with added years of service. Vacation periods have normally been confined to the relatively slow summer months, but winter vacation options are becoming more popular. Executives have great flexibility in scheduling vacations.

Job security Retailing is a stable business and consequently provides substantial job security for most types of regular workers. Technological unemployment has not been a problem, as in some industries, and should not be significant in the reasonably foreseeable future. In spite of further developments in warehouse mechanization, computerized accounting and record-keeping, and self-service, retailing is likely to continue to require large numbers of employees and executives. The employees of the larger firms especially are benefiting from increased personal security through expanded corporate group insurance, health insurance, and pension programs in addition to governmental provisions for medicare, old-age, and unemployment benefits.[15]

Unions[16] Although labor unions have less influence in retailing than in some other industries, they have become more important in recent years.

Future prospects In spite of night and Sunday openings, overall retail working conditions will undoubtedly continue to improve in the coming years. Working hours, however, are not likely to decline for either the small store owner who must compete on the basis of customer service and convenience or for the ambitious junior executive who is seeking to get ahead. Promotion and success in any business usually require long hours, often for additional study as well as directly on the job, and hard work along with the assumption of increased responsibilities.

■ PROSPECTS IN SMALL AND MEDIUM-SIZED STORES

Some students plan careers in small and medium-sized stores because of opportunities to participate in, and ultimately manage, a family or friend's business. Others are attracted by the possibility of buying or establishing their own stores, although, of course, this alternative involves the capital and experience requirements noted in the previous chapter and amplified

---

[15] These benefits are discussed in Chapter 9, "Retail Personnel Management—Continued."

[16] Cf. the discussion of retail labor unions in Chapter 9, pp. 227–30.

below. However, many students must postpone store ownership, and in some cases even entry into the family business, until they have gained experience and training through a job in someone else's store.

□ Limited opportunities as an employee

The student or graduate who seeks experience in a small or medium-sized store should hold his long-run career objectives clearly in mind. He should recognize that employees who are not members of the owner's family seldom have an advantageous opportunity to acquire the business in which they are working. Consequently, he should concentrate on training possibilities rather than on immediate compensation or future promises. He should avoid the many small establishments whose methods are too outmoded to be of any real training value. Stated positively, he should seek employment in a progressive independent store where he can get experience in all aspects of retailing, including knowledge of merchandise and suppliers, operating methods, sales promotion, relations with customers, and store records and controls. He should read relevant trade magazines, textbooks, and government and commercial reports and carefully study other retailers' practices and policies to supplement his store work.

□ Store ownership

Students who have thought only about "big business" overlook the possible rewards of ultimately owning their own stores.

Many possibilities Few fields still offer as many opportunities as retailing does for independent business ownership. There are approximately 1½ million single-unit independent retail establishments in this country. The prospective storeowner can always find some available for purchase, perhaps because of the retirement or death of the owner. Some will be advertised in newspaper and trade publication classified sections, and people in the trade, such as manufacturers and wholesalers and their salesmen, will often know of others that may be available.

Manufacturers, wholesalers, store designers and builders, and equipment houses are usually eager for outlets and sales. They will often provide considerable assistance, through advice and credit extension, in finding a store to buy or in establishing a new one. Many franchising companies, including automobile manufacturers and gasoline refiners, act as "management consultants" for their new (and old) dealers. Some voluntary chain wholesalers, especially grocery firms, will find a location, erect a building, and stock it for the new owner. Even the growth of large organizations, such as chain discount houses, provides some opportunities for smaller leased department operators. Those who wish to own stores can indeed find many opportunities to do so.

Moreover, even though chains and other large organizations are handling an increasing portion of total retail sales, as we noted in Chapter 1, opportunities for *profitable* independent store ownership remain and will persist. Two analysts who see growing strength in small retailing emphasize: (1) The small retailer's ability to gain some large-scale advantages through franchise and voluntary chain arrangements; (2) the limitations of large, corporate retail organizations, including burdensome union contracts and difficulties in providing middle-management incentives; and (3) the increasing diversity of consumer markets which creates new opportunities for highly flexible, specialized small operators.[17]

Of course, the small retailer who hopes to be successful must expect to work very hard. If he operates entirely independently, he must often be an innovator, or at least differentiate himself from competitors, and offer products, services, convenience, or an "atmosphere" that is unavailable in larger establishments. And, if he participates in a voluntary chain or franchise system, he must be willing to sacrifice some independence, for both his own and the entire system's benefit.

Profitability and failure The returns from independent store ownership vary considerably, but can be quite attractive. One study, for example, found that the proprietors of small flower shops with sales of about $125,000 per year received average incomes of approximately $17,500. Proprietors of stores in the $25,000 to $60,000 class, however, only averaged about $9,000 per year.[18]

Concerning franchises, a consultant notes that earnings will be affected by the size of the individual establishment; by the skills, effort and capital the franchisee provides; whether the franchisee joins the system early or late in its development; and, of course, by the quality and fairness of the franchise arrangement. But he concludes that "although few franchisees can attain the fantastic profits sometimes promised . . . many of them do quite well financially."[19]

Various expense studies which show retail profits of only 1 to 4 percent

---

[17] A. F. Doody and W. R. Davidson, "Growing Strength in Small Retailing," *Harvard Business Review*, Vol. 42, No. 4 (July–August 1964), pp. 62–69.

[18] Paul R. Krone, *Starting and Managing a Retail Flower Shop*, Small Business Administration Starting and Managing Series (Washington, D.C.: U.S. Government Printing Office, 1970), p. 4.

[19] Louis M. Bernstein, "Does Franchising Create a Secure Outlet for the Small Aspiring Entrepreneur?" *Journal of Retailing*, Vol. 44, No. 4 (Winter 1968–69), p. 33. For a more adverse view of franchising, cf. Robert M. Dias and Stanley I. Gurnick, *Franchising: The Investor's Complete Handbook* (New York: Hastings House, 1969).

of sales often encourage the belief that retailing is unprofitable. But these apparently small ratios often equal a return of 10 to 20 percent or more on *net worth* and, in small stores, are *in addition* to the proprietor's salary or drawing account for services rendered to the business.

But along with these profit possibilities, independent store ownership also involves risks, including the danger of failure. There are no universally accepted figures, and the failure rate varies from field to field and from year to year, depending upon general economic conditions. But often 10 to 20 percent of the new store owners fail within the first year, and perhaps 30 to 40 percent within the first five years of operation. While this rate may seem high, it certainly is no higher than for those who begin their own wholesaling or manufacturing businesses. Moreover, the most important reasons for retail failures include lack of capital and incompetence resulting from inexperience and absence of managerial ability.[20] The student who secures proper financial backing, acquires adequate experience, and develops his managerial abilities before opening his store may well succeed in his retailing venture.

Financing methods The size of the establishment and the types of merchandise handled help determine the capital requirements for an independent store. Typical initial requirements for a pet shop are $15,000, $22,000, and $30,000, depending on the size of the business.[21] A small camera shop in rented premises might require about $10,000 in addition to the merchandise inventory.[22] In contrast, the average modern supermarket involves an investment of almost $500,000, including the building.[23] However, the various sources discussed in later paragraphs will often supply financial support for some of these capital outlays.

1. Determining requirements The purchaser of an *established business* can estimate his financial needs fairly easily: He uses the purchase price plus rough estimates for the costs of layout changes, inventory adjustments, additional working capital requirements, living expenses, and contingencies until store revenue becomes available.

The retailer who wants to establish a *new business* should take several steps. He should try to get information from friendly, comparable retailers in other communities concerning investments in fixtures and equipment, merchandise inventory, accounts receivable (if credit sales are contem-

---

[20] "Business Failures," *Dun's*, September 1970, p. 101. Also cf. "Who's Failing," *Retailing Today*, December, 1970, p. 3.

[21] Joe Ross and Stan Gores, *Starting and Managing a Pet Shop* (Washington, D.C.: U.S. Government Printing Office, 1970), p. 17.

[22] Morrie Bragin, *Starting and Managing a Small Retail Camera Store* (Washington, D.C.: U.S. Government Printing Office, 1969), pp. 17–18.

[23] *Facts about New Supermarkets Opened in 1970* (Chicago: The Super Market Institute, 1971), pp. 4, 12.

plated), and other working capital items. Possible equipment cost increases, an allowance for unforeseen contingencies, and the cost of living and operating expenses until the store opens and develops reasonable sales volume must be added to these figures.

The resultant sums should be compared with all data available from relevant trade associations, business publications, university research bureaus, and the Small Business Administration. Then all of this information should be checked against the prospective retailer's own estimates for each major item. For example, he can check fixture and equipment costs by obtaining bids from two or three equipment firms. Reputable franchisors also will indicate capital requirements for their franchisees, but unfortunately unscrupulous firms often understate this figure.

Finally, all estimates and purchase or franchise contracts should be checked very carefully by a knowledgeable accountant and attorney. We cannot overemphasize the importance of these careful reviews in avoiding future disappointment and hardship.

2. Securing financial backing The new owner's own capital is usually the most important single source of funds for the venture. As a general rule, subject to many exceptions, he should provide at least 50 percent of the total opening investment. It may be difficult to secure additional funds from other sources without a personal investment of this size. Moreover, excessive dependence upon borrowed capital will raise interest costs to a dangerous level.

Several sources are available for the remaining 50 percent. The wholesalers or manufacturers from whom he buys will usually supply at least part of the inventory on 30-, 60-, or 90-day credit. The fixtures and equipment may be purchased on an installment basis. A short-term loan may be available from a commercial bank if the prospective retailer can show that it will be repaid within the bank's time limits.

Friends may provide loans, or in the case of a corporation, purchase stock. In the latter case, the retailer must be careful to retain control of his business. Perhaps the seller will accept a well-secured note from the buyer for part of the purchase price if a going business is being acquired. The federal government's Small Business Administration provides loans to some retailers who are unable to obtain funds elsewhere.

Special financial assistance is available in a few retail fields. Wholesalers and other voluntary chain sponsors (variety, food, hardware, and drug stores) are sometimes willing to accept a note from the buyer for a substantial part of the store equipment and merchandise investment. Automobile manufacturers often give their new dealers substantial aid, a typical arrangement being that the dealer provide at least one quarter of the total investment. Many franchising companies either extend some financial assistance or help arrange loans. The major gasoline companies often help equip and stock their service stations, so that the dealer may only have to arrange working capital, which may be as little as $10,000.

Buying an established business or starting a new one The choice between buying an on-going business and starting a new store depends on many factors. These include: the availability of a business for purchase, the price the seller will accept, whether a good location is available for a new store, whether the community can support an additional establishment, and which of the two propositions is easier to finance.

The prospective purchaser should try to determine why the present owner wants to sell the business. Does the store have a poor location? Is it suffering from new competition? Are the present customers moving away?

An entirely new business has some strong advantages. Its stock can be completely "clean" and fresh. New fixtures, equipment, and layout provide an attractive shopping atmosphere and may reduce operating expenses. There are no payments for good will, and the new proprietor isn't burdened with any "ill will" the former owner might have created.

But an on-going business frequently offers compensating advantages. The new owner doesn't have to spend a lengthy period of time acquiring fixtures and equipment, assembling inventory, engaging personnel, and establishing recordkeeping systems. Some steady customers will "stay with" the store. The purchase of a going business does not increase the total number of stores in the area, which would divide the existing trade among more retailers.

Thus the question of "whether to buy an established store or start a new one" often comes down to the price the seller will accept for his business. If it is low enough, even a poorly equipped and stocked store may be a good purchase. The appraised value of the store's assets is, however, only the starting point for establishing the sale price. Payment of a premium over "book value" may be both necessary and profitable for a store with an attractive location and a well-developed clientele; in other cases, the reverse is true. In any event, the final price is usually subject to considerable bargaining. The buyer will do well to have the store's assets appraised carefully and its profit possibilities estimated before bargaining, so as to have a sound basis for judgment.

Legal form of organization The general advantages and disadvantages of the proprietorship, partnership, and corporate forms of organization are discussed in many business law, accounting, corporation finance, and business management texts,[24] and need not be analyzed here. Most small retail

---

[24] For example, Pearce C. Kelley, Kenneth Lawyer, and Clifford M. Baumback, *How to Organize and Operate a Small Business*, 4th ed. (Englewood Cliffs, N.J.: Prentice-Hall, Inc., 1968), pp. 192–201.

businesses in this country are operated as individual proprietorships because of (1) the resultant tax savings, and (2) the relatively greater complications and legal problems of incorporation. However, the corporate form's limited liability, and the fact that it is not automatically terminated by the proprietor's death, make it more attractive for the retailer who is investing a substantial part of his savings or borrowing heavily to begin a new venture. The new retailer who begins with a proprietorship or partnership may find it advisable to convert to a corporation as soon as his business has shown some growth.

■ PROSPECTS IN DEPARTMENT AND SPECIALTY STORES

We have already noted that department store employment increased by more than 20 percent between 1963 and 1967 alone.[25] The more alert and progressive department and large specialty store firms have been actively improving their merchandise efforts during the past two or three decades and have been opening numerous branch and suburban stores. This growth greatly increased the need for qualified managerial personnel. Many of the leading firms have instituted or expanded strong programs for recruiting and developing executive trainees. For example, R. H. Macy & Co., which created one of the first retail programs in 1919, sought only about 25 to 40 potential executives in 1945; by the late 1960s it was hiring 200 young men and women a year for the executive training squad.[26]

Again, as in other fields, the executive promotional opportunities vary considerably from company to company. Promotion will be slow in stores that have "gone to seed," or that have a full staff of seasoned, stable executives and no real growth prospects, or where management prefers to fill most executive positions from outside. In contrast, progress may be very rapid in fast-growing or expanding firms that have policies of promotion from within. Vacancies through resignation, retirement, or otherwise also create many chances for promotion. Everything considered, students can find many attractive career opportunities in department and specialty stores.

More information about salaries appears in the subsequent discussions of opportunities in various department store divisions, but junior retailing executives usually earn from $6,500 to $9,500 yearly. Many buyers receive between $10,000 and $35,000 annually, and major division heads range from $20,000 to $75,000.

---

[25] P. 52, above.

[26] Samuel Feinberg, "50 Years of Macy's Executive Training," *Women's Wear Daily*, July 2, 1969, pp. 1, 12.

□ Junior executive training programs

The growth of executive training programs is a highly favorable feature of the department store field. Employment in the better programs is often highly competitive, and is based on interviews with store executives, evaluation of the prospective trainee's academic, extracurricular, and employment record, and perhaps personality tests. But the people selected for participation receive an opportunity to learn practically all aspects of the business in a relatively short period. R. H. Macy & Co. describes its Executive Training Squad as ". . . a post-graduate program in business, but a post-graduate program in which you learn by doing as well as studying . . . and get paid at the same time." Federated Department Stores says that the essence of its program ". . . is to produce entrepreneurs . . . young men and women who, early in their careers, are eager and able to run a small business [such as a merchandise department] as if it were their own."[27] The executive trainee can also be very sure that top management will watch and be quite aware of his or her progress (or lack of progress).

□ Merchandising division opportunities

Department stores and large specialty stores are usually organized into several main divisions, such as merchandising (buying and selling), operations, publicity, accounting or control, and personnel.[28] About sixty percent of the executive jobs are in merchandising.

Promotion from a selling position in a department store is usually fairly slow for anyone who has not been specifically hired as a potential executive. The normal promotional path, if advancement comes, is from salesperson to head of stock, then assistant buyer (often now called assistant department manager), buyer (department manager), and finally merchandise manager. The latter two are very responsible positions. Figure 3–1 shows a typical promotional path for merchandising executives in a large department store, in this case Dayton's—Minneapolis-St. Paul.

The head of stock usually supervises the merchandise in one of the department's sections, keeping it clean and orderly, notifying the buyer of needed items, and instructing and helping new salespeople. He may also assist in departmental administrative work, such as helping prepare advertising copy (in the smaller stores); planning departmental and window dis-

[27] Company brochures.

[28] Figure 7–3, p. 161, shows the relationships of these divisions in a typical department store.

FIGURE 3–1 Promotional paths for merchandising executives, Dayton's—Minneapolis-St. Paul

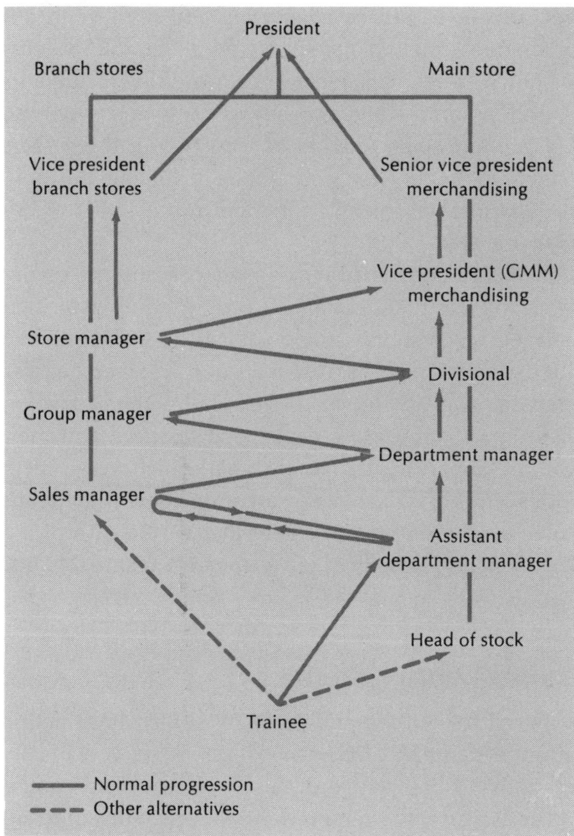

Source: Company brochure.

plays; and handling some of the merchandise records and inventory clerical work. The head of stock is sometimes authorized to prepare reorders for basic items, subject to the buyer's approval. He normally earns $10, $20 or $30 a week more than salespeople in the department. Executive trainees also often spend a period performing similar duties.

The assistant buyer or assistant department manager's activities may vary from head of stock's work-up to some of the buyer's functions, depending upon the particular buyer, the assistant's experience, the size of the department, and whether or not the buyer is in town. Salaries, depending upon store, individual, and department, range from $100 to $200 per week.

Traditionally, the buyer has been in complete charge of his department just as if it were his own small store. He selects and purchases merchandise; supervises stock and recordkeeping; plans advertising and displays in cooperation with appropriate departments; and supervises actual sales to customers. The growth of branch stores has created new positions for departmental sales managers, and in some stores the buyers no longer supervise sales. A mature, capable young trainee requires at least two or three years experience, usually longer, to qualify for and obtain a buying position. Earnings depend upon departmental sales volume and profit, but run between $10,000 and $35,000 a year.

A small store may have only one merchandise manager, and the owner or proprietor may assume the position. In larger stores, a number of divisional merchandise managers, each supervising possibly 5 to 20 buyers, are responsible to the senior or general merchandise manager. The merchandise manager generally supervises and advises his buyers, helps them develop merchandise plans and programs, and exercises general financial and merchandising control over his departments. His income, which varies with volume and often includes a bonus or profit-sharing arrangement, depends upon ability to get results to an even greater extent than in the case of the buyers. But merchandise managers usually receive from $15,000 to $45,000 or even more.

□ Publicity division opportunities

Advertising positions call for writing and planning ability, imagination and originality, and an understanding of human nature. Some actual sales experience, to provide first-hand knowledge of customer reactions to merchandise and sales appeals, is also often required. Applicants with some advertising experience may begin as copywriters, or as window trimmers and display people, and will earn from $100 to $200 per week.

The successful advertising employee may advance to publicity director or manager at $8,000 to $25,000 per year or more. There are very close ties between advertising and merchandising, and some organizations will also promote good copy writers to buying positions, especially in fashion departments.

□ Service or operating division opportunities

The operating division's responsibilities involve merchandise receiving, warehousing, marking and delivery; building and equipment maintenance; store security; supply procurement; and a wide variety of customer services that may include store restaurants and workrooms for custom-made merchandise. Executives in this division may supervise highly advanced systems research, procurement or traffic specialists; skilled craftsmen such as plumbers, carpenters and electricians; or large numbers of relatively unskilled workers. The operating division, however, ordinarily offers lower salaries and fewer promotional opportunities than the merchandising division. Even the store superintendent or operating manager, who must be a man of considerable ability and experience, usually earns between $15,000 and $40,000, which is less than what the successful merchandise manager will receive. The promotional path for operating executices at Dayton's is shown in Figure 3–2.

FIGURE 3–2 **Promotional path for operating executives, Dayton's—Minneapolis-St. Paul**

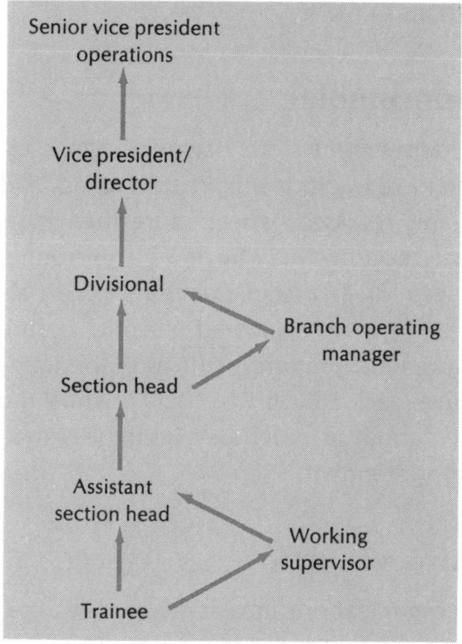

Source: Company brochure.

☐ Accounting and control opportunities

The controller heads the accounting and control division, and is responsible for administering the store's finances, collections, credits, and accounting records. Numerous federal and state recordkeeping requirements and new developments in systems and electronic data processing have substantially increased the opportunities in this division. The more important opportunities require a thorough knowledge of accounting or systems, accuracy and precision in handling figures, and the ability to analyze and interpret those figures in the light of broad store policy. An accounting or control executive needs an orderly mind that can create systems for recording voluminous data and that can summarize those data for easy interpretation by other executives.

Beginning bookkeepers, credit clerks, correspondents, and other trained clericals may start at $85 to $100 per week. Accounting majors will receive perhaps $125 to $175; and head cashiers, head bookkeepers, paymasters and other such supervisors between $8,000 and $15,000 annually. Credit managers, office managers, and the manager of the statistical office have higher salaries, although compensation usually is not as high as in merchandising. The controller may receive as much as $50,000 in the largest firms, considerably less in smaller organizations.

□ Personnel division opportunities

The increasing opportunities in department store personnel work include training activities, where women have traditionally predominated, and various forms of personnel analysis and research, where more men have been employed. A potential personnel executive may begin as a personnel clerk, as assistant employment manager, or as a staff training worker, although some experience on the selling floor is considered essential before good work can be done in those departments. Junior executives in the training, employment, and personnel offices earn $5,000 to $10,000, while the chief personnel executive may receive about as much or slightly less than the controller and operating store superintendent.

■ PROSPECTS IN CHAIN STORES

The great growth of many chain organizations in recent years has created numerous opportunities for career-minded men and women. The need for promotable people is illustrated by a statement in the J. C. Penney Company's 1967 report: "A conservative estimate indicates that about 5,000 of our associates will either achieve managerial positions or move up to higher management positions during the next five years." Along with store executives, Penney noted that it would require "buyers, merchandising managers, architects, computer programmers, fashion consultants, financial analysts, attorneys, distribution experts, accountants, advertising copywriters, catalog merchandisers, credit managers, and people with many other skills."[29]

[29] *Annual Report,* 1967, p. 4.

The major variety, junior department store, department store and mail-order chains recruit executive trainees from various academic institutions in their sales territories. Some of the important food and drug chains, such as The Kroger Co., Jewel Companies, Inc., Walgreen Co., and The Stop and Shop Companies, Inc., also have active recruiting programs. But most food and specialty chains do little campus recruiting. Consequently, the man or woman who wants a career with those firms must usually take the initiative in approaching the chain's personnel officer. Yet many of these companies offer fine employment opportunities, in part simply because only a limited number of trained people may be competing for the top executive posts. Naturally the opportunities vary from company to company and are greatest in those firms that are engaged in soundly-financed, well-considered, vigorous expansion programs.

☐ Store management and supervisory opportunities

The store operating division usually provides the largest number of managerial positions in a chain store organization.[30] Store management trainees start at about $6,000 to $8,000 per year, depending upon the firm and the trainee's academic preparation. The number of steps in the training program and their duration depend upon several factors in addition to company policy and the trainee's ability. These factors include: (1) The size of the stores used for training (promotion to assistant manager will require more experience and there will be more intermediate levels in large stores than in small ones); (2) the variety of functions performed in the stores (for example, the prospective manager has more to learn and consequently will need more time in those firms where the stores handle part or all of their own credit activities); and (3) the merchandise lines involved (fashion merchandise may require more experience than staple products).

Variety store training programs Figure 3–3 diagrams the principal steps in managerial training in the S. S. Kresge Co., operators of Jupiter and Kresge variety stores and K-Mart discount houses. Promotional patterns are somewhat similar in other major variety chains, such as W. T. Grant, Woolworth, McCrory-McLellan-Green, and G. C. Murphy Co. These programs often start with a relatively short period of general orientation and experience in some phases of sales and/or sales-supporting work. The trainees are usually placed in several different stores during the program, to obtain guidance from different managers and to experience a variety of personnel,

---

[30] The organizational structures of three representative chains are shown in Figures 7–5, 7–6, and 7–7, pp. 174–76 below.

FIGURE 3–3 **Executive development chart, S. S. Kresge Co., 1970**

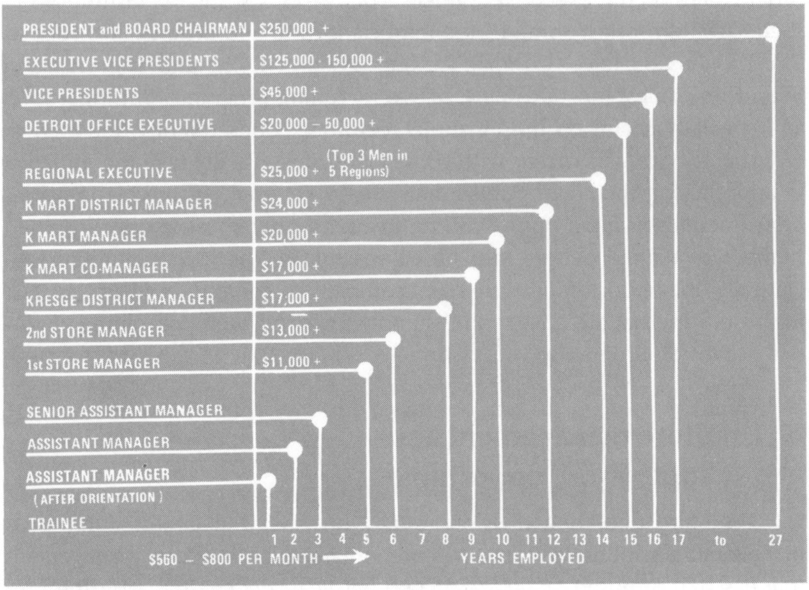

Position	Salary
PRESIDENT and BOARD CHAIRMAN	$250,000 +
EXECUTIVE VICE PRESIDENTS	$125,000 - 150,000 +
VICE PRESIDENTS	$45,000 +
DETROIT OFFICE EXECUTIVE	$20,000 – 50,000 +
REGIONAL EXECUTIVE	$25,000 + (Top 3 Men in 5 Regions)
K MART DISTRICT MANAGER	$24,000 +
K MART MANAGER	$20,000 +
K MART CO-MANAGER	$17,000 +
KRESGE DISTRICT MANAGER	$17,000 +
2nd STORE MANAGER	$13,000 +
1st STORE MANAGER	$11,000 +
SENIOR ASSISTANT MANAGER	
ASSISTANT MANAGER	
ASSISTANT MANAGER (AFTER ORIENTATION)	
TRAINEE	

1 2 3 4 5 6 7 8 9 10 11 12 13 14 15 16 17 to 27

$560 – $800 PER MONTH → YEARS EMPLOYED

Source: S. S. Kresge Co.

operating, and market conditions. Some merchandising and supervisory responsibilities are normally assigned to the trainee during the first several months or year of employment, and these responsibilities are then steadily increased. Two or three years training leads to the level immediately below store manager, with the title "assistant manager," "senior assistant manager," "comanager" or "merchandise manager" in different companies. Three to six years training leads to appointment as a store manager, usually with assignment to a small store. The current tendency, however, is to shorten the training period, especially for individuals with some retailing or administrative experience.[31] The store manager's compensation includes incentive payments that may be based upon store sales, expense control, or profits. Earnings range from a $10,000–$11,000 minimum in very small stores to $70,000 and higher in large establishments.

Discount, supermarket, and general merchandise chains Discount chains differ considerably in their training and promotional paths for store management. Variety store chains and other old, well-established organizations operate many of today's modern large discount stores. These firms have included the new discount units within their training program, as il-

[31] "Who'll Run the Stores of the '70's?" *op. cit.*, pp. 40–43.

lustrated in Figure 3–3. Some experience in managing one or more conventional smaller stores is often required before promotion to the managership of a large discount store. An exception to this rule arises when the discount stores are a major departure from the company's traditional line of business. Supermarket chains that enter the general merchandise discount store business often have to hire some managers from outside in order to acquire people with knowledge of textiles and nonfoods retailing.

The firms that started more or less directly as discount store chains during the 1950s and 1960s (including many of the pioneers in the business) often promote junior executives much more rapidly, have much less formalized training programs, and engage many managers and assistant managers from outside. They also tend to offer less job security than the older chains.[32]

Recent help-wanted advertisements for discount store managers have offered earnings ranging from $15,000 to $25,000.[33]

Supermarket chains have shortened the training period and now appoint many 25 to 30 year old individuals as store managers.[34] The average food store manager (stores of all sizes combined) earns about $9,000 to $10,000, but managers of large stores may make two or even, in some cases, three times as much.[35] Chain drug store managers (of whom only about two-thirds are registered pharmacists) mainly earn between $12,000 and $17,000.[36] As already noted, store managerships tend to take longer to acquire in the department store and general merchandise field, where the establishments are very large and conduct complex operations. The financial rewards, however, are very good and there are many intermediate positions at satisfactory compensation levels.

☐ Supervisory and area management positions

Some chains employ functional supervisors who are responsible for overseeing a particular activity in a group of stores. Some variety chains, for example, have district or regional fountain and lunch-counter supervisors who coordinate lunch counter operations in their areas, inspect the physical

---

[32] Cf. Robert Drew-Bear, *Mass Merchandising: Revolution and Evolution* (New York: Fairchild Publications, Inc., 1970), pp. 412–13.

[33] *Discount Store News*, December 14, 1970.

[34] "Young Men in a Hurry," *Chain Store Age* (Supermarket Executives Edition) October, 1968, p. 27.

[35] Cf. "Food Store Manager," in *The Encyclopedia of Careers and Vocational Guidance*, ed.-in-chief, William E. Hopke (Garden City, N.Y.: Doubleday & Co., Inc., 1967), pp. 126–29. Figures quoted above adjusted for post-1967 changes.

[36] *Management of Managerial Resources* (Washington, D.C.: National Association of Chain Drug Stores, 1967) p. 26; figures adjusted.

facilities to insure proper maintenance, and help train new food-service department managers for the stores. Many supermarket chains have traveling meat and produce supervisors who advise the store managers on the special problems of handling their particular types of merchandise. Compensation in this position varies greatly with the amount of responsibility, the requirements for technical knowledge and managerial judgment, and the total sales volume involved.

The district manager is directly responsible for several stores. He performs general supervisory tasks, acts as a link between the store managers and headquarters, sees that the stores conform to company policy and practices, and usually pays close attention to the management development program in his district. He recommends trainees for transfer and promotion. Satisfactory experience as a store manager is a prerequisite for this position, although the managers of the largest and most profitable stores may earn almost as much as, or even more than, their district managers.

The large chains divide their district managers into regional groups, each reporting to a regional or area manager. Regional management positions carry great responsibility, and hence the opportunity of a large financial reward. Regional managers will earn at least $25,000 per year, and profit sharing may increase their compensation substantially.

Most chains have traditionally used successful store managers to fill the majority of their headquarter and top executive positions. Technical specialists, such as architects and attorneys, were once the only exception to this rule, and most chains still prefer store experience as a background for headquarter's responsibility. But an increasing number of very large organizations that need a variety of talents, including Sears, Roebuck Co., J. C. Penney Co., Inc.; and Montgomery Ward & Co., Inc., are now recruiting trainees for direct assignment to central buying, advertising, traffic, and systems analysis staffs at headquarters.

■ "PROS" AND "CONS" OF RETAILING CAREERS

In spite of the career opportunities that retailing offers, many students have a negative view of the field.[37] In some cases this view rests upon a careful self-appraisal which indicates that the individual's talents and interests fit some other business or profession more satisfactorily. In other cases, the negative impression may result from some unexciting employment as a routine part-time retail worker while in school, or from partial or erroneous information about retailing careers.

---

[37] "Retailers Have Difficulties Recruiting College Students," *Women's Wear Daily*, June 2, 1969, p. 14.

Some of the merits and limitations of careers in this broad and varied field are summarized below. In the final analysis, only the student himself can decide whether or not retailing should be his field of endeavor. But his decision should be based upon a careful evalution of all relevant facts, his own preferences and experiences, and the knowledge that the rewards for high-quality work and accomplishment in retailing—as in other trades and professions—go far beyond monetary income.

Disadvantages of retailing careers The following are some of the negative aspects of retailing as a career field:

1. Beginning salaries are frequently lower in retailing and have increased less in the past two decades than in other areas of employment. Fortunately, progressive retailers have recognized this fact and raised starting salaries.
2. The working hours are sometimes longer than in other fields, and may include some Saturday, Sunday or evening hours.
3. Initial work activities, including selling duties, in stores that have poorly organized training programs may discourage the trainee.
4. Some retailing positions, but not all, involve more competitive pressure, physical strain, and nervous tension than would be experienced in a number of other occupations.
5. Chain store personnel are sometimes required to relocate rather frequently, which is disagreeable to the person who wants "to get his roots established" in a community as soon as possible.
6. Some students dislike the impersonal atmosphere of some large and medium-sized retail stores, where the major executives are not known and seldom seen by the employees.
7. Some people assert that retailing lacks social prestige as compared with banking and finance, for example; that it does not offer a sufficient "intellectual challenge" for those with "creative talents"; and that it gives but a limited opportunity to serve others.

Advantages of retailing careers The disadvantages cited above do not apply to all retailing positions, however, and in many cases may be offset by some of the following advantages:

1. There is a wide range of opportunities in all parts of the country for men and women of various talents and interests.
2. The size and growth of retailing to meet our rapidly expanding needs provides an increasing number of executive positions for qualified personnel.
3. Men and women of demonstrated ability can advance to positions of responsibility with commensurate salaries more rapidly than in most other fields of employment.

4. The knowledge and experience that one gains may be easily transferred from one business to another, including the establishment of one's own store.
5. The many personal contacts, and in some positions opportunities for extensive travel, are stimulating and enjoyable and broaden perspectives.
6. Reasonable security results from the relatively great stability of retail sales volume from year to year. Inefficiency, however, is just as unacceptable in retailing as in any other field.
7. Interested and qualified personnel in retailing find considerable personal satisfaction through the significant contributions they make to the welfare of the community in which they are located.

REVIEW AND DISCUSSION QUESTIONS

1 Prepare a five minute talk outlining and evaluating the major factors students consider as they seek a career.

2 Talk with owners and managers of various retail stores in your community and summarize their opinions regarding the opportunities which retailing affords. What do they consider to be the chief limitations?

3 What are some of the more recent developments in retailing which encourage (discourage) students to seek careers in this field?

4 What are the opportunities for women in retailing? How do they compare with other fields?

5 Prepare a brief essay on the subject "Probable Changes in Working Conditions in Retail Stores during the Next Decade."

6 Assuming that you expect to own and operate your own small independent store in the future and desire to obtain the best experience possible to prepare you for this task, would you prefer to obtain that experience in a small store, a department store, or a chain store? Why?

7 How would you proceed, and what factors would you take into account, in determining whether or not you would open a retail store of your own?

8 Assume that you have an interview with a recruiter for a department store concerning possible employment with the firm upon your graduation. Explain briefly (*a*) how you would prepare for such an interview and (*b*) the questions you would want answered before accepting a position if one were offered.

9 Outline the "promotional ladder" of a general merchandise chain.

10 Prepare a paper of about 2,000 words on the subject: "A Constructive Program for Attracting Qualified Executive Trainees into Retailing."

PART III

The retail store

chapter 4

STORE LOCATION

The location of a retail store determines to a large degree the sales made and the profits realized, thus playing a vital part in the store's success. Some retailers, such as those selling variety store merchandise and women's apparel, consider location so important that they prefer to pay a larger-than-usual rental to obtain desirable sites, even if this means other expenses must be restricted. Good locations frequently offset deficiencies in management, but poor locations seriously handicap even the most skillful merchandisers.

■ LOCATION: A CONTINUING PROBLEM

Most discussions of retailing emphasize the choice of a location for a *new* store, but the problem is even broader. Because of population shifts, the movement (in or out) of other retailers, the improvement or deterioration of buildings, and the establishment of shopping centers, suburban and roadside stores, and discount houses, good locations of one period may gradually become poorer (or better) ones.[1] Consequently, locations should be evaluated at frequent intervals to determine if they are meeting current

[1] Cf., for example, "The Changing Face of Fifth [Avenue, New York City]," *Women's Wear Daily*, June 11, 1969, pp. 1, 8, and "Fifth Avenue Suits Korvette's to a T," *ibid.*, January 26, 1970, pp. 1, 44.

expectations and are likely to meet future goals. As one expert in store location has written: "In our dynamic urban economy the life-span of most retail facilities is comparatively short. Even successful chain stores are faced with the problem of store mortality due to obsolescence and other factors. . . . Typically a store has a life cycle of three successive stages: ascent, peak, and decline. The ascent and decline stages may be very steep or gradual, and the peak stage may be of long or short duration."[2] Retailers, therefore, are always faced with a location problem.

□ Location and the landlord

A location suitable to the successful conduct of business is important to the owner of the land and building occupied by the store as well as to the retail merchant. The value of a lease is dependent upon the ability of a tenant to realize a profit under it, and only through careful selection of tenants can a reasonable and regular return upon property investment be assured. Moreover, it is axiomatic that property values are maximized only when a site is used so as to extract the greatest economic utility from it. The best locations tend to be held by the better store managers because these managers are able to obtain greater productiveness from such locations than are less capable competitors.

□ General neglect of the location problem

Despite its significance, many retailers still decide upon a location without proper analysis. Frequently, shopping center developers, chain stores, and voluntary chain organizations are singled out as among those who plan locations on a scientific basis. To a degree, of course, this is true, since some developers and large-scale retailers conduct careful studies of locations before final decisions are made. For example, one organization will not approve a site for a proposed shopping center until it is subjected to a searching analysis, covering such factors as current population in the trading area, population trends, current and potential per capita income of the area, competing centers or retailers, shopping loyalty of potential customers, road patterns, and expected sales by major classes of merchandise. Frequently, outside consultants on locations are used to conduct the study. Similar investigations are conducted by Sears, Roebuck and Co., J. C. Penney Company, W. T. Grant Company and other leading chains before they authorize a contract for a new store.

---

[2] William Applebaum "Store Performance in Relation to Location and Other Characteristics," *Chain Store Age* (Executives Edition), November 1965, p. E14.

In contrast to the foregoing procedures, however, is the practice of a local drug chain which relies largely on the judgment of one of its chief executives who usually appraises a site "just by taking a ride around a particular area, talking to some of the people living there, and getting a general feel of the site's expansion possibilities."

Thousands of small stores are opened each year in particular sites largely because locations are available, with little or no effort to analyze them. This situation exists because many retailers fail to appreciate the significance of location. Moreover, most prospective retailers have the confident expectation of doing better in a particular location than their predecessors and hence consider it unnecessary to study the past history of a site. They also consider research to be too costly. Still others are eager to start "tending the store" and do not want to take the time needed for a worthwhile site-selection investigation.

Even some retailers who recognize the importance of location research and are willing to spend money and time on it consider it too complex a problem for them to approach entirely on a scientific basis. They point out that research techniques in this area have made little progress in recent years, a statement with which the location experts are forced to agree.[3] Furthermore, while these retailers may gather and analyze statistical data on a site, they believe that the validity of the decision rests with the man making the final judgment—and that his judgment cannot be replaced with a computer.[4] To quote the real estate vice president of a leading variety-discount house chain: "People with experience in looking at sites are better 'computers' than any computer can be—because we cannot yet feed accurate information, reduced to definite numbers, into a location-evaluating machine."

The foregoing factors *explain* why the location problem is often neglected by some retailers; but they do not *justify* this neglect. Even the criticism that research cannot "produce all the answers" is beside the point, since no one claims that it does. In brief, location plays such an important part in determining sales and profits that the retailer should assemble and evaluate carefully all available information in choosing a location for his store. And these tasks become more difficult as choice locations become scarce for individual stores and shopping centers alike. One prolific writer

---

[3] Cf., however, Elliot Zweibach, "Research for Sites Pays off at Ralphs," *Supermarket News*, December 22, 1969, p. 18. This 62-store food chain triple-checks prospective sites to minimize errors, using the research department of its parent company (Federated Department Stores) and its own real estate division and store operations department.

[4] Yet, states one location expert, "Computers can handle vast amounts of information and interrelate it faster, cheaper and with greater refinement than we now do with conventional cartographic methods." William Applebaum quoted in Jan Calkins, "Computers to Map Store Sites," *Supermarket News*, March 31, 1969, p. 1.

forecasts many innovations in location-study, predicting "that between 1975 and 1980 there will be . . . a strong trend toward the following startling concepts in store location . . . : underground, high above the ground, and adjacent to water."[5]

■ BASIC FACTORS IN LOCATION

Factors governing the choice of a location for a retail store may be divided logically into two groups: (1) Those that influence the choice of a city or trading area in which to locate and (2) those that determine the particular site within the chosen city or trading area.[6] These groups of factors are closely related. For example, the availability of desirable sites in a certain city or shopping center obviously affects the decision to locate or not to locate in that area. Yet, for purposes of analysis, the distinction between the two groups is helpful.

Although this discussion is in terms of a *new* store, the factors involved are equally applicable—as already indicated—to the appraisal of an established store. Moreover, the number of factors mentioned must not cause one to forget the basic determinants in any location, that is, the sales and profit potentials which can reasonably be expected assuming suitable store facilities and customer services are provided.

□ Selecting a city or trading area

At the outset of our discussion it should be noted that the small retailer is at a serious competitive disadvantage when it comes to choosing a city in which to locate. In contrast to the chain store and the shopping center developer, he has neither the financial resources nor the manpower to conduct a systematic review of cities, suburban areas, or even shopping centers. His decision is often based on considerations of health, climate, or nearness of relatives and friends. It is evident, however, that his chances of success will be greater if he assembles and evaluates all pertinent information. In this process he should take advantage of the aid offered by the manufacturers and wholesalers from whom he makes or expects to make

---

[5] These innovations are discussed in E. B. Weiss, "Retailing Branches Skyward, Seaward and Downward," *Advertising Age*, April 28, 1969, pp. 70, 73. Underground stores and facilities have existed, of course, for some years. An underground shopping plaza in Montreal, Quebec, located at Place de Vielle Marie and Place Bonaventure, has been highly successful.

[6] Many of the factors included in this analysis are also applicable (1) to the location of shopping centers and (2) to the selection of sites within such centers. Also cf. the discussion of shopping center on pp. 95–98, below.

purchases, his banker, the Chamber of Commerce in the area considered, and any studies available from shopping center developers.[7]

Type and character of industries The number, type, and character of the industries within the confines of a city and its surrounding trading area influence (1) the amount and the stability of potential customer income and (2) the kind of goods customers will want. The alert retailer will attempt to locate, as far as possible, within an area where income is regular, assured, and substantial in amount. Generally speaking, income is more stable and assured in cities with diversified industries than in areas where one single industry dominates the picture. In the former situation, not all the firms will be affected by seasonal factors or by fluctuations in general business conditions in the same manner or at the same time. Only in a comparatively few instances, such as major depressions, will income for the area as a whole be sharply reduced and severe declines in sales experienced.

One factor in the stability of income from local industries is the labor-management relationship. Investigation of this factor is important, since the existence of a poor relationship may mean constant labor strife and periodic strikes. The effects of such strikes on retail sales may be significant: for the cash store, they may result in violent fluctuations in volume; for the credit store, they may encourage an overextension of credit.

The retailer will also be interested in the growth of local industries. Obviously, an area in which industry is progressive and expansion is likely has advantages over an area in which maximum development has already been attained. Towns and cities from which industries are moving have serious limitations as retail locations.

Population of the trading area The population of the city and the surrounding trading area determines the number of potential customers of the retail store. But knowledge of those currently living in the area is not sufficient; equally important is information on the rate of growth (or decline).[8]

Even the casual reader is aware of the growth of our population, despite the recent decline in the birthrate from 25.3 in 1957 to 1.4 in 1968[9]—the

---

[7] For a list of factors influencing the choice of a trading area, cf. William Applebaum, "Guidelines for a Store-Location Strategy Study," *Journal of Marketing*, Vol. 30, No. 4 (October 1966), pp. 42–45. Also cf. Earl Dash, "Target: Central Florida," *Women's Wear Daily*, April 14, 1971, pp. 4–5.

[8] *Current Population Reports, Population Estimates*, published frequently but irregularly by the Bureau of the Census of the U.S. Department of Commerce, contains a variety of information concerning population such as growth, shifts, and age groupings by regions and states. Special censuses covering numerous cities and areas are also available from the Bureau. Also cf., E. B. Weiss, "Surprise for 1980s: The Big City Population Explosion Will Fizzle," *Advertising Age*, May 4, 1970, pp. 65–66.

[9] The birthrate increased somewhat in 1969 and 1970, rising to 18.2 in 1970. U.S. Public Health Service, *Monthly Vital Statistics Report*, Vol. 19, No. 12, March 4, 1971, p. 1.

lowest in our history—and of the fact that this expansion is unevenly distributed among regions, states, cities, and their environs. Between 1960 and 1970 the urban dwellers increased from 70 to 73.5 percent of our total population.[10] During this same period the Western states led other regions with a 38.9 percent population gain. Among states 1970 data reveal that the highest rates of population increase occurred in Nevada (71.3 percent), Florida (37.1 percent), Arizona (36.1 percent), Alaska (33.6 percent), and Colorado (25.8 percent). Three states lost population: West Virginia, North Dakota, and South Dakota.

As regards cities, the pattern of growth varies widely among them. Some cities, of course, remain almost stationary as regards population; but this fact alone does not mean, necessarily, that they are undesirable as areas in which to locate stores. In such cases, however, the need is apparent for a careful investigation of the reasons for lack of growth and the impact of this factor on the retailers of the area.

Attention should also be given to seasonal shifts in population. Many trading areas gain people during the summer and lose them during the winter months. Thus communities in such states as Maine, Vermont, Michigan, and Colorado have a large influx of summer residents who substantially increase the potential customers for several months each year. In contrast, Florida, California, and Arizona experience population gains during the winter months.

Progressiveness of the city Closely related to the type and character of industries, to population trend, and to factors discussed in the following paragraphs is the progressiveness of an area. Is it one in which there is an active Chamber of Commerce or industrial development group attempting to attract new industries? Is there an urban renewal program? Is the local school system adequate, so that people are encouraged to move into the area? Is an effort made to attract conventions that bring to the area another group of customers? Are local service clubs active in community betterment? Is there a local area-sponsored recreation program, indicating a community interest in promoting better citizenship? Do the local merchants work together in the sponsorship of periodic events—dollar days, festivals, and fairs—to expand the trading area? Do the streets allow for a free flow of traffic? What about the availability of off-street parking areas? Is there adequate public transportation? All of these factors and others must be given careful consideration in forecasting the city's future.

Buying habits of potential customers The selection of an area in which to locate is also influenced by the buying habits or practices of the populace,

---

[10] *1970 Census of Population, Advance Report,* PC (VI)-1 (Washington, D.C.: U.S. Department of Commerce, February 1971), p. 4.

such as the extent to which potential customers do their buying at the most convenient and accessible locations; their preference to concentrate their purchases in shopping centers; the importance they attach to large assortments of merchandise offering a wider range of choice; their willingness to drive 25, 50, or more miles to do their shopping because they can combine the shopping expedition with a pleasure trip; the kinds of stores they prefer to patronize for particular types of merchandise and the extent to which they divide their purchases among such stores; the services, such as credit and delivery, which they customarily require and expect; and the influence of age distribution on their purchases. Consideration should be given also to the differences in buying practices among various nationalities and races residing in the trading district. The more familiar the prospective store owner is with the customary buying habits, preferences, and prejudices of the people in the area, the greater the assurance that his location will meet with their approval.

Purchasing power of the population Total retail sales in an area are closely correlated with the purchasing ability of the nearby population.[11] The number of people employed, the total payrolls of the industries located in the district and the average wage, the regularity and frequency of payment of wages and salaries, social security payments to the elderly,[12] and the amount of and trend in bank deposits are among the significant factors indicative of the purchasing power of the area under consideration.[13] As a matter of fact, skilled retailers can frequently use these factors as the basis of a reasonably accurate estimate of the sales that a proposed store can achieve.

Dispersion of wealth The dispersion of wealth is another factor influencing sales and profit opportunities. A retailer who proposes to open a store dealing in fancy groceries, high-priced dresses, or custom-made men's clothes should not seek an area populated largely by persons with low incomes. In this connection, it is important to note that the rise in earnings during the 1950s and 1960s, widely distributed among the population,

---

[11] The correlation between population changes and retail sales in 1958 and 1967 for each state and the country as a whole are given in R. C. Sizemore, "Census Reveals Retail Potential," *Women's Wear Daily*, September 15, 1970, pp. 1, 18. For a study in much greater depth, cf. Ben-chieh Liu, "Relationships among Population, Income and Retail Sales in SMSA's 1952–66," *Quarterly Review of Economics and Business*, Vol. 10, No. 1 (Spring 1970), pp. 25–40.

[12] In 1970 and 1971 increases in Social Security payments added billions of dollars to personal income. And with inflationary pressures persisting, further increases were reasonably certain in the years ahead.

[13] Some retailers develop their own special ways of judging the purchasing power of an area. To illustrate: Sears, Roebuck and Co. uses its mail-order sales. Experience has demonstrated that an area producing $1 million in mail-order business can support a Sears store. *Time*, January 21, 1966, p. 69B.

brought about considerable "trading up," with people buying better-quality merchandise and patronizing higher-class stores.

Some specific evidence of the relationship between (1) family income, and (2) the sales and profits of the retailer is given in Table 4–1. This table classifies the sales and profits achieved by each unit of a chain according to the annual income of the families which it served. Note that the units in areas having the highest annual incomes had over three times the sales and nearly twice the profits of the units in the lowest annual income areas.

TABLE 4–1

Sales and profits of stores in a chain classified by annual income of families served

Annual income of families served	Index of store	
	Sales	Profits
Under $3,000	100	100
$3,000–$4,999	160	112
$5,000–$7,999	240	125
$8,000 and over	320	188

Source: William Applebaum, "Store Performance in Relation to Location and other Characteristics," *op. cit.*, p. E15.

In an effort to determine the dispersion of income in a trading area, the prospective store owner finds the following information of value: the types or kinds of homes, the proportion of home owners, the educational level of the community, the number of telephones, the number and makes of automobiles, per capita retail sales, and the number of credit accounts. Reports of the 1970 population census also contain considerable data which enable the retailer to judge the extent of his potential market and to arrive more accurately at anticipated or planned sales figures against which actual results may be checked.

Nature and strength of competition The number, type, floor space, and location of competing retail stores, viewed in the light of the economic need of the community for a store of the type being considered, also influence the choice of a city or of a shopping center in which to locate. Competing stores must be analyzed carefully to determine the services they offer, the extent to which they are alert to the present and prospective demands of consumers, and their merchandising methods in general.

In this process the retailer should recognize the trend toward "scrambled merchandising." Today much of the competition for an electric appliance store may come from auto supply stores, department stores, or hardware stores, while drugstores are feeling the effects of the nonfood lines of supermarkets. And the women's wear shop is in competition with many items sold by the variety store, the mail-order house, and the discount store. In other words, the study of competitors must be made on a realistic basis and not just on the basis of the name given to a particular kind of retail establishment.

State and local legislation The nature of existing legislation related to the number and types of taxes that must be paid—including the trend in tax rates—and the various licenses which must be obtained in the city often influence the decision on location. Variations in sales tax rates among nearby cities and across state lines are particularly troublesome elements. Fair-trade laws and unfair-trade-practice acts must also be taken into account. And local or state regulations concerning hours of business are significant in view of the increasing night and Sunday openings for many stores.

Other factors influencing choice of a city Several other factors influence the choice of a city or trading area in which to locate a store. At times practically all retailers find it necessary to secure bank loans to finance expansion plans, seasonal inventories, or larger-than-usual credit accounts. Hence, the existence in the community of bankers who have some understanding of the retailer's financial problems is much to be desired. Likewise, the attractiveness of a community is increased if suitable advertising media are available; if police and fire protection are satisfactory; if trade-union regulations are not so restrictive that profitable operation is difficult; if adequate merchandise resources are conveniently located; and if the area is served satisfactorily by the highways and public transportation facilities leading into it.

☐ Selecting a specific site

The selection of a particular location within the chosen city or trading area is determined by the following major considerations.

Estimated volume of business Early in the appraisal of a possible store site the retailer should estimate the potential annual sales that can be obtained, because volume is vital in determining whether a store in the location will be profitable.

For independent stores, this estimate is often based on estimates of sales of nearby competitors. In addition, wholesalers and manufacturers' salesmen well acquainted with the area can provide well-informed guesses. Sometimes the independent may have an estimate prepared for him based on family incomes in the area. This approach is not always reliable, however, because many cities attract a large amount of trade from outside the immediate area. That is, they serve as trading centers for the surrounding area or they attract many tourists or business visitors.

Among chain stores, the sales estimate is sometimes based on the per capita annual sales of company stores of comparable size located in cities of about the same population, type of industries, and number of persons employed; in other cases, annual sales per counter-foot in company stores approximately equal in size are relied upon. These inside-the-company forecasts are commonly supplemented by estimates of sales of competitors in the city. Such "educated guesses" are obtained by measurements of the counter-feet space in directly competing stores, by customer counts in such stores at various times of the day, and by ascertaining the number of salespeople in these stores at specific hours and on certain days. Finally, outside experts may be used in forecasting sales for a specific location.

One successful supermarket chain, Lucky Stores, Inc., projects a proposed store's volume as follows: "The number of residents for each trading segment [area] is multiplied by $7 (the average per capita weekly food expenditure) minus projected competition volume plus spill-over volume from other segments."[14] To illustrate: If a trading area has 600 residents, a $4,200 weekly volume can be generated. If a competitor is in the area, 50 to 60 percent of the total volume might be captured depending on the competitor's strength, with perhaps as much as 20 percent of sales coming from outside the trading area.

1. *Long-run considerations* In estimating the volume of business for a particular site, long-run considerations are essential. The past history and the probable future of the district should be studied and any shifts or movements in the business sections should be weighed carefully to ascertain their probable effects on the traffic stream. No business site stands still in value. The main shopping block in a city today may be several blocks removed from the one of three decades ago. And an undeveloped and outlying piece of land today may be a flourishing shopping center five years from now.

2. *Accuracy of sales estimates* Some idea of management's ability to forecast sales in a specific store is given by the supermarket data of Table 4–2. Using the Supermarket Institute definition of sales within plus or minus 10 percent of the estimate as being "on target," the forecast was accurate, for example, in 34 percent of the cases in 1970. However, 30 percent of the stores opened that year produced sales substantially above the estimate and 36 percent fell appreciably below. These data make it clear that far better techniques of sales forecasting for the individual store are needed.

---

[14] Tim Simmons, "Air Photos Help Lucky Pick Sites," *Supermarket News*, May 12, 1969, p. 58.

TABLE 4–2

Actual sales versus estimated sales

Year	Percentage of supermarkets		
	With sales more than 10 percent above preopening estimate	With sales as estimated	With sales more than 10 percent below preopening estimate
1966	30	45	25
1967	40	38	22
1968	29	43	28
1969	34	37	29
1970	30	34	36

Source: *Facts about New Super Markets Opened in 1970.* (Chicago: Super Market Institute, 1971), p. 7.

Customer buying habits in relation to types of goods sold We have noted that customer buying habits influence the choice of a city or town. They are equally important in the selection of a site. A store handling staple groceries, for example, ordinarily will be located (1) close to the homes of the customers it hopes to serve or (2) in shopping centers or areas where parking facilities are available and which can easily be patronized when the customer is also after other merchandise. A department store, on the other hand, should be situated within an area where other stores of the same type are located since such stores thrive best in groups. This fact is being increasingly recognized by shopping center developers through their efforts to bring two, three, or more department stores into a single center. When customers are attracted on bases other than convenience and opportunity for shopping, the store proprietor has a greater degree of freedom in choosing a location. Accessibility remains important, however, with the result that stores handling goods of this type are commonly located in the chief shopping districts, either on the main thoroughfare or on a better-class side street, or in shopping centers.

Good roads, increased use of automobiles, urban decentralization, shopping centers, and discount houses, are all bringing changes or reflecting shifts in buying habits. Consequently, revisions in plans and in methods by executives responsible for locations have been necessary.[15]

Customer traffic: the traffic count The amount, kind, and distribution of potential customer traffic by hours of the day and days of the week significantly affect location. There is an old "rule of thumb" which says: "The

[15] Cf. "Decentralization of Retailing," pp. 92–93, below.

heavier the pedestrian traffic, the greater the volume of business, other things being equal." But other things are never equal and, during recent years, retailers have given increased attention to qualitative analyses of such traffic as opposed to the previous emphasis upon quantity alone.[16]

The fundamental purpose of traffic analysis, of course, is to estimate the proportion of pedestrians who constitute potential customers and who would probably be attracted into a store of the type proposed. The usual method employed to analyze traffic is the traffic count. Prior to making the actual count, however, it is necessary (1) to determine who shall be counted —such as all pedestrians, those of one sex, or just those within certain ages; and (2) to decide the days of the week and the length of the times when counts are to be made. Streams of pedestrian traffic are now being analyzed to ascertain reasons for passing a particular site at a given time. In other words, attention is given to the state of mind of the individuals in the traffic stream, to their purchasing power, and to other factors of a similar nature. Customer counts are also frequently made in the stores of chief competitors.

In passing, it should be noted that the significance of a flow of potential customers past a store varies widely from one retailer to another. To illustrate: A high traffic count may be essential for a cash-and-carry variety store which depends mainly upon small purchases from a large number of customers. In contrast, the retailer of fancy groceries who appeals largely to the "carriage trade" through a telephone sale-credit-delivery type of service will be less interested in a high-traffic-count location.

Location in relation to competitors and other stores The proximity of his store to his chief competitors and to other types of retail establishments requires close study by the prospective retailer. For some types of stores, location in the central shopping district or in a large shopping center is almost essential to success; for others, successful operations may be conducted outside such areas. A retailer of automobiles, for example, may find it highly desirable to locate near his competitors on "automobile row." A women's wear store may also seek a site near other similar shops or near a department store to make it more possible to sell to customers who desire to shop from one store to another. Other retailers, perhaps those selling drugs and groceries, may seek neighborhood locations which are removed from direct competitors.

For many retailers the reputation and merchandising methods of the other stores in the immediate area are important considerations. An exclusive dress-shop operator will not seek to locate beside a "cut-rate" drugstore or near a retailer of low-priced women's wear. A children's shop will

---

[16] The limitations of traffic pattern studies "that are apparently not widely recognized" are discussed in D. T. Kollat and R. D. Blackwell, "Recognizing the Limitations of Customer Traffic Pattern Studies," *New York Retailer*, December 1968, pp. 3–7.

not rent a building contiguous to a liquor store. Some areas have obtained reputations as locations for "good" merchants, and this fact is significant to the retailer who seeks to acquire a comparable designation.

Accessibility Despite its obvious significance, accessibility is often neglected by retailers eager to find a site and "get in business." Especially are employees' needs given inadequate attention. Among the numerous factors relating to accessibility which warrant detailed investigation are the following:

1. Public transportation facilities to the proposed store, such as streetcars, buses, and subways.
2. Distance of the proposed store from residences of potential customers and employees.[17]
3. Amount of traffic congestion prevailing in the district and the variations in this congestion during hours of the day and days of the week.
4. Parking facilities available within convenient walking distance of the proposed store and the charges therefor.
5. Side of the street upon which the site is located (in many towns and cities, one side is more popular than the other).
6. Width of the street, so that potential customers are not discouraged from visiting the store because of being jostled or by a slow flow of street traffic. Streets with marked inclines and dead ends are also less desirable.
7. The part of the block in which the site is located, i.e., whether it is a corner location or an "inside" location and, in the case of a large store, whether entrances may be made available on two, three, or four streets.

It should be emphasized that some retailers may successfully overcome part of the inaccessibility of a particular location by means of a low-price appeal. This possibility is well illustrated by stores which make use of basement or second-floor locations. Similarly, other retailers attempting to "build up" locations frequently sell at low prices for a time.

Return on capital investment Of major concern is the retailer's return on his capital investment in a specific site. This involves such considerations as the equipment and fixtures he plans to use, the size and turnover of his merchandise inventory, and the rent to be paid, or the cost of the site and building.[18] Although he may be willing to accept a small return in the

---

[17] One study indicates that about three-fourths of those shopping at a specific shopping center live within a 15-minute drive of the center. Cf. J. A. Brunner and J. L. Mason, "The Influence of Driving Time on Shopping Center Preference." *Journal of Marketing,* Vol. 32, No. 2 (April 1968), p. 61.

[18] One authority points out, however, that return-on-investment techniques "are neither necessary nor practical for a large retail chain in assessing the potential of a proposed new store." He proposes that a set of standard investment norms be estab-

short run, over a longer period he needs to obtain a reasonable return on his overall investment.

Site characteristics detrimental to retail outlets Site characteristics which decrease the retailer's ability to attract customers include the following: (1) smoke, dust, disagreeable odors, and noise; (2) proximity to garages, hospitals, taverns, and similar places; (3) poor sidewalks; and (4) old and worn-out neighboring structures.

Availability of the site Other considerations may be favorable, but the desired site may not be available under terms and conditions satisfactory to the retailer. Although the type and construction of the building may be suitable either with or without remodeling, it may be impossible to work out a favorable leasing arrangement covering the period desired, the amount of rental, privilege of renewal, and similar matters. If mutually satisfactory leasing arrangements for a given structure cannot be completed, one alternative is to investigate the possibilities of obtaining land and constructing a building. In such an instance, zoning regulations, land cost, building-construction costs, and taxes must be carefully weighed.

Some other factors affecting choice of site In the case of the chain organization, or the parent store considering the establishment of a branch, certain operating factors should be carefully considered in selecting a specific site. The distance of the proposed unit from headquarters, the parent store, or from a warehouse, to permit effective supervision and servicing; the incremental advertising expense required; and the availability of qualified personnel at the firm's existing pay rates are of major concern.

■ FROM CITY TO METROPOLIS TO MEGALOPOLIS

Earlier we noted that in the decade of the sixties the number of people living in our urban areas increased from 70 to 73.5 percent of the total population.[19] This trend has accelerated more recently so that the percentage of our people now classified by the census as urban dwellers is at an all-time high.

□ Growth in suburbia

It is very important for the retailer to interpret correctly the growth of our urban areas. Particularly it should be emphasized that in recent decades

---

lished "against which . . . the expectations of a projected outlet [can be] conveniently judged." Cf. H. L. Green, "Investment Norms in Chain Store Expansion," *Harvard Business Review,* Vol. 46, No. 4 (July-August 1968), p. 143.

[19] Cf. p. 82, above.

the relative gain in urban population has taken place largely in the *suburban* areas. Actually, and subject to notable exceptions, the central areas of our larger cities are now growing very slowly or not at all. To be specific, between 1960 and 1969 the population in older central cities gained but 2 percent, whereas their suburban rings jumped 30 percent. Moreover, a smaller proportion of our metropolitan population resided within central cities in 1969 (45 percent) than in 1960 (51 percent).[20]

The relative shift of population to the suburbs may be partially explained by a desire for improved living conditions and for a more open type of housing with larger lots, trees, flowers, and grass. The shorter workweek, longer vacation periods, new Monday holidays to provide three consecutive "weekend" days, and more paid holidays—estimated to give the average American 125 days a year away from his job—encourage people to live some distance from their work. Many persons have sought to escape from the high taxes prevalent in large cities. In addition, private housing developments as well as the related activities of the federal government have made possible the ownership of property at lower interest rates and with relatively larger mortgages than were heretofore considered practicable.[21]

Regardless of the reasons for the population shift, in the outlying areas a way of life has gradually developed that is quite different from that of the typical city dweller. With a higher per capita income, the suburbanite is more apt to own a home and to buy more furniture, appliances, garden tools, records and books, and sportswear than his city contemporary. He also engages in a different variety of leisure-time activities.

□ The metropolitan area

As a result of the foregoing trends, the last 25 to 35 years have witnessed the emergence of a new metropolis or metropolitan area as a social and economic unit. Defined by the census as a "county or group of contiguous counties . . . which contains at least one city of 50,000 inhabitants or more or 'twin cities' with a combined population of at least 50,000," in practice it consists of a declining or slowly growing central city and an exploding suburban area. The 1967 Census of Business lists some 230 such areas with 71.4 percent of all retail sales.[22] Of these areas 66 had 500,000 or more people in 1970. And a leading student of these "large conglomerations"

[20] U.S. Bureau of the Census, *Current Population Reports,* Series P-23, No. 33 (September 1970), p. 2.

[21] The tight-money situation that prevailed in 1969–70, however, sharply curtailed home building and raised mortgage rates to an all-time high.

[22] *1967 Census of Business, Retail Trade: United States Summary,* BC RA1, p. 1–98. Also cf. D. W. Twedt, "Toward a Simple System of Standard Geographic Unit," *Journal of Marketing,* Vol. 32, No. 3 (July 1968), pp. 71–73.

refers to them as "the most efficient producing-consuming units that mankind has ever devised."[23]

□ Trend toward megalopolis

Today the conglomeration is becoming even larger! As metropolitan areas expand, some of them begin to overlap to produce what we refer to as a "megalopolis": Witness the coming-together of the Boston, New York, Philadelphia, Baltimore, and Washington metropolitan areas so that they—in effect—form a single stretch of urban and suburban areas.[24] Similar megalopolises are gradually taking shape in other parts of the country, especially along the California coast, along Puget Sound in the Northwest, and in the lower Lake Michigan area. And there is abundant evidence that "the big retailers are zeroing in on the megalopolis and metropolitan areas."[25]

□ Decentralization of retailing

Close observers of retailing trends in recent decades are well aware that the growth of Suburbia has been accompanied by a relatively large gain in the retail sales of such areas. Although retail sales in many of the older downtown central shopping districts of our metropolitan areas have declined, the total retail sales of these same areas have advanced.[26] It is quite clear that retailing has been decentralizing. Why?

Some reasons for decentralization It is axiomatic that the retailer must follow his customers. Consequently, we may say that:

1. The pronounced shift of population to the suburbs is clearly the first reason for the rapid development of retail facilities in the outlying areas. But there are other factors as well.
2. Changes in shopping habits of women during the last 20 years and more. The desire to compare merchandise and prices in more than one store is no longer so great, with the result that one-stop shopping has become increasingly common. Women are continually broadening their interests outside their homes; consequently, they have less time for shopping.

---

[23] P. M. Hauser, "Is the Market Moving away from You?" *A View to 1970* (Chicago: Super Market Institute, 1965), p. 11.

[24] By far the best treatment of megalopolis is found in Jean Gottman, *Megalopolis* (New York: Twentieth Century Fund, 1961).

[25] Cf. Isadore Barmash, "Chain Stores Focus on Megalopolis Vigor," *New York Times*, April 27, 1969, p. F15.

[26] On the trend toward retail trade decentralization in ten *nonmetropolitan* Ohio cities in the period 1958 to 1967 cf. P. S. Carusone, "A Shift in the Point of Patronage," *MSU Business Topics*, Autumn 1970, pp. 61–69.

Moreover, the rapid and widespread dissemination of fashion information through motion pictures, radio, television, newspapers, and magazines probably has brought about an increased willingness and desire on the part of women to rely on their own judgment in selecting styles. As a result, they patronize to an increasing extent the women's specialty stores located near their homes, visit nearby shopping centers, or make their selections from advertisements of stores in the central shopping district and place their orders by telephone or mail.

3. The increased use of the automobile. This factor is closely related to, or even a part of, the changes that have taken place in buying habits. Use of their cars for shopping has a wide appeal among women, especially in the better-class suburbs; and it is likely that this appeal will continue to grow. Incidentally, it is this greater use of the automobile which has made possible a substantial growth of roadside retailing. Today such retailing goes far beyond gasoline stations and farmers' stands; it includes men's and women's clothing, furniture, and other shopping goods.
4. The rapid rise in the cost of public transportation facilities used to reach the downtown areas and the traffic congestion which exists there. For example, residents of East Bay sections in the San Francisco metropolitan area must pay a minimum of $1.00 round-trip bus fare to the downtown area, plus as much as 50 cents for additional transportation by bus or streetcar to reach the major downtown stores.
5. The lack of economical and convenient parking lots in the central shopping districts. Even though the customer willingly confronts the traffic congestion in downtown areas, she is faced with the problem of finding a conveniently accessible parking space at a reasonable cost.
6. The excellent retail facilities which have been developed in the suburbs. Since many of our best retail buildings—containing the most modern equipment and fixtures and stocked with both broad and deep assortments of merchandise—are now found in the newer shopping centers and as free-standing units scattered about metropolitan areas, the customer no longer finds the "pull" of downtown what it was 20 years ago.

■ RETAIL STRUCTURE OF THE METROPOLITAN AREA

Turning now to the anatomy of our 230 metropolitan areas, it should be noted that, although significant differences exist among them, a structure analysis applicable in a general way to all of them is possible. Each area seems to contain an older central shopping district, one or more older secondary shopping districts as well as the newer shopping centers, several scattered but large free-standing stores, some neighborhood business streets, and many scattered areas with single units or clusters of small stores.[27]

□ The older central shopping district

The central shopping district is the heart of the retail structure of the city which, in turn, is an integral part of each metropolitan area. All means of intracity communication converge on this district. Here are concentrated many of the area's leading shopping and specialty-goods stores—department stores, departmentized specialty stores, and limited-line independent and chain stores engaged in selling such merchandise as apparel, furniture, shoes, and jewelry. They are much larger in both floor space and sales than the average store in the city, and draw a far greater part of their total business from nonresidents than do the other city retailers. In addition, there are a number of convenience-goods retailers—drugstores, cigar stores, and food stores. Although the area covered by this district is small, it draws customers from the entire metropolitan area, and its total sales form a substantial but declining part of the total sales of the whole metropolitan area.

□ The older secondary shopping districts

The older secondary shopping districts came into existence mainly as the city increased in population and spread over a broader area. Gradually it became more convenient for some of the people to buy at least part of their requirements outside the older central shopping district. Consequently, the stores located on a neighborhood business street expanded to supply more of the wants of the people living in the vicinity. Several centers which have developed in this manner may be found in practically every large city, each well located on the main traffic arteries leading from residential districts to the older central shopping district. In addition, some of these secondary shopping districts developed within the smaller towns which have gradually been absorbed by the metropolitan area. Regardless of their origin, the kinds of goods sold here are generally similar to those sold in the main shopping district; but the stores are smaller, selection is more limited, people are not attracted from such wide areas, and the sale of convenience goods predominates.

---

[27] Cf. J. B. Schneider, "Retail Competition Patterns in a Metropolitan Area," *Journal of Retailing,* Vol. 45, No. 4 (Winter 1969–70), pp. 67–74. Supermarket's place in this picture is discussed by Bryan Thompson, "Intraurban Retail Structure: The Supermarket Structure," *ibid.,* Vol. 45, No. 3 (Fall 1969), pp. 69–80.

□ The newer shopping centers

Nature and growth One major response to (and also a factor encouraging) the decentralization of shopping areas is the rapid growth of outlying shopping centers on a planned or controlled basis. They have even been viewed as the nucleus around which new cities will spring or included as the anchor in establishing new towns.[28] Usually the entire center is an integrated development, under single ownership, with coordinated and complete shopping facilities, and with adequate parking space. The stores in the center are leased to various retailers. Frequently, all of the stores in the center engage in joint advertising and adopt a unified public relations program. Such joint activities are usually required by or are actually carried out by the central organization which owns the center.

A few of these newer shopping centers were established earlier but the overwhelming majority have been built since the end of World War II. From 1,000 centers at the end of 1955, the number advanced spectacularly to 4,500 at the close of 1960, and to an estimated 12,500 by December 1, 1970. By 1985 an additional 12,000 were expected to be in operation.[29] They probably account for 30 percent or more of *all* retail sales.

Shopping center developers Based on sponsorship, there are two main types of shopping centers. The most numerous are those centers which have been built by real estate organizations, that is, firms which expect to make a profit on their investment by leasing the units of the center to others. Many centers, however, have been developed by large retailers who sometimes dictate the kinds of stores to be located in the center.[30] In some cases, a large chain has organized what is, in effect, a subsidiary corporation to develop centers. Examples are Food Fair Properties, Inc., sponsored by Food Fair Stores, Gamble Development Co. organized by Gamble-Skogmo, Inc., and Sears' Homart Development Co. In other instances the developer is a large department store which operates the department store in the center and leases the remaining buildings to others. Centers developed by May Department Stores (through its subsidiary, May Realty & Investment Com-

---

[28] In 1970, for example, it was announced that Sears, Roebuck and Co., Marshall Field & Co., and the Urban Investment & Development Co. were planning to establish a new Century Town of 15,000 to 18,000 people some 30 miles north of Chicago's Loop. Sears and Field's would have major stores in the center surrounded by other facilities and services required in a community of this size. For details, cf. "Sears, Field's Plan a Town," *Women's Wear Daily*, July 30, 1970, pp. 1, 28.

[29] Information supplied by *Chain Store Age*. For more details cf. its "Executives Edition," February 1971, p. 25.

[30] Cf. John Osbon, "Sears Defends Its Role in Shopping Center Mix," *Women's Wear Daily*, May 15, 1968, p. 24. Also cf. his "Sears Finds Developing Malls Less Profitable," *ibid.*, April 9, 1971, p. 15; and "Ward Maps Center Growth," *ibid.*, April 15, 1970, pp. 1, 68.

pany) and the Broadway Department Store in southern California, and Allied Stores Corporation in Seattle through its affiliate, Bon Marche, are examples of this type. The Southdale Shopping Center, near Minneapolis, Minnesota, developed by Dayton's, provides still another illustration.

Trends and problems The dynamic nature of retailing is no better demonstrated than in the case of shopping center development. Continuous improvements are being made to attract customers, to make it more convenient for them to park and shop, and to provide merchandise and services comparable to those "downtown" or in the older central shopping districts. Some of the other major current trends and problems of this development are as follows:

1. Currently there is a strong trend toward the fully-enclosed-mall-air-conditioned type of shopping center. Although the first of this type dates just from 1956 (Southdale near Minneapolis), it has accounted for the large majority of regional centers built in recent years. Moreover, many existing centers are including these features in their modernization and expansion programs.
2. In contrast to the early large centers which included just one major department store, today's large centers attempt to attract at least two full-line department stores and a few centers with three or four stores of this type are in existence. And giant complexes are increasing in number.[31]
3. Along with the development of new centers, successful established centers are also expanding. These expansion programs are giving many retailers an opportunity to enlarge their stores. During lease negotiations, some retailers now seek a clause which guarantees them an area for later expansion if it proves desirable.
4. In locations with limited acreage or very high land costs, multilevel centers are being built. Likewise, a limited number of centers are providing vertical parking facilities.
5. There is growing recognition of the fact that more careful planning and research is necessary, both for the center developer and the lessees of the space occupied. Far too many centers have been built without a sufficient number of "lead in" roads; or they have generated more traffic than the nearby road system can handle, with the result that customers have difficulty entering or leaving the center. Additional marketing research data are also needed regarding customer preferences, wants, buying motives, and buying habits.

---

[31] One such complex—the largest in the west—is the Northridge Fashion Center in the San Fernando Valley of California. The center, consisting of some 140 stores anchored by four major tenants, will occupy 72 acres, cost $200 million, and is expected to generate sales of $155 million a year. Parking for 6,700 cars will be provided.

6. Improved methods and devices for projecting sales volume in new shopping centers are required. A variety chain found that its methods of forecasting volume for new stores in established central shopping districts and smaller communities were inaccurate for shopping center units.
7. As more centers are built in a single metropolitan area so that the small retailer has a choice of centers, he needs outside aid in reaching a decision.
8. Discount houses are evidencing a growing interest in shopping center locations. The attitude of existing tenants is mixed. Some believe that these low-margin operators draw traffic to the center and represent a favorable development. Others either fear the competition afforded by the discount firms or believe that their presence cheapens the center and object to their entry.
9. As real estate taxes rise, the insertion of tax escalation clauses in shopping center leases is gaining despite opposition by many center tenants. Landlords and tenants are joining together in an effort to fight the proposed increases which they believe are excessive.
10. A few planned shopping centers have found locations in downtown business districts as a part of the urban renewal activities.
11. Shopping centers catering primarily to farmers are being established. One such development, under the direction of National Farm Stores of Minneapolis, is planned as a nationwide chain and is "designed to provide all the needs of farmers on one 40-acre tract, plus facilities for the marketing of livestock."[32]
12. Determining uniform and profitable hours of operation, including Sunday openings, constitutes a problem for operators of shopping centers. It is made more difficult because of disagreement among tenants on the number of nights (and which nights) they wish to remain open. The trend seems to be toward as many as three to five nights per week plus Sunday.
13. Merchants' associations are being discussed more frequently, with emphasis on whether membership should be a condition of the lease. Although it is recognized that the success of such an association depends on the cooperation and participation of the tenants, the consensus among them is that active leadership by the developer of the center is the basic factor in success.
14. Seeking to overcome the tight money situation prevailing in 1969–70, numerous innovations have been made to improve shopping center operations. Among these are the use of "outside" general merchandise

---

[32] "Shopping and Selling Centers for Farmers Set," *New York Times,* February 23, 1969, p. F17.

managers, each serving a number of centers as a consultant, and the building of "showcase" stores of "innovational units" by large retail chains such as E. J. Korvette and Sears, Roebuck and Co. which will set the pattern and techniques of stores yet to come.[33]

Future Despite a long-persisting worry that the country will become "over-stored," there seems no question but that the development of shopping centers will continue. But this growth does not insure the success of each center. As has been indicated in previous paragraphs, great care is necessary in choosing locations, studying competition, designing buildings, providing adequate parking space, selecting tenants, preparing leases, and arranging proper promotion. A major failing of many shopping centers being built today is lack of careful economic appraisal prior to their development.

Some criticism has also been directed toward the roles large stores play in shopping center developments. It is sometimes alleged that department and chain stores too often assume the "self-appointed position of Prime Minister," without giving adequate consideration to the needs and preferences of smaller, independent tenants. Certainly there needs to be closer cooperation among tenants in shopping centers in considering each other's problems. Such cooperation is needed, also, among developers and tenants to insure the "partnership" relationship essential for mutual success. Despite these problems and others, the continued growth of the shopping center seems assured.

In concluding our discussion of shopping centers, let us note the comments of the vice president-real estate of Carson Pirie Scott of Chicago, Illinois.

> Sophisticated management will meet the challenge of the 70's, but the rate of technological change will be much more accelerated. . . . Chances are [that] new technology will come faster than we can possibly absorb it. Instant communication and rapid advances in transportation technology will permit radically changed future relationships between customer residence location and the retail store. With greatly increased mobility, the opportunities for land use and development will be unsurpassed. Certainly cheap atomic power will change mechanical facilities and the structures for them. Our present-day store buildings could become obsolete before their useful life has ended. Because business may be remotely controlled, store premises as we know them today may cease to exist or may be remodeled for other uses.[34]

---

[33] Cf. Isadore Barmash, "Retail Innovations Aid Shopping Centers," *New York Times,* April 4, 1970, p. 39. Also cf. Samuel Feinberg, 'Should Shopping Centers Have General Merchandise Manager?' in "From Where I Sit," *Women's Wear Daily,* January 30, 1970, p. 40.

[34] Harold Spurway, "Changing Trends in Shopping Center Development and Management," in a paper delivered before the World Congress of Retailers, Dublin, Ireland, June 2, 1970.

☐ Large free-standing stores

Another development of some significance is the large free-standing store. Normally located in the suburban parts of the metropolitan areas, this store is usually: (1) a discount store, (2) a department store, or (3) a departmentized specialty store. If it is one of the latter two types, it is typically a unit of a chain or a branch of a downtown store.

The free-standing discount house Discount houses are not always welcomed into the newer shopping centers. As a result, some discount retailers have turned to the free-standing store as an alternative to the center or have established centers of their own.[35] States the real estate vice president of S. S. Kresge Company, "[For our K-Marts] we favor free-standing units . . ."[36] Back of this policy is the belief of many discount retailers that the free-standing store gives them a lower rental, complete freedom of choice on merchandise lines (in centers, merchandise restrictions are typically included in leases), better parking facilities (usually around a great part of the store building), and a greater flow of traffic for the types and quality of merchandise they offer for sale. By "ringing a city" with units (for example, E. J. Korvette, Inc., has used the "cluster" approach around New York, St. Louis, Chicago, and Baltimore), a substantial promotional program is possible at a relatively low cost per store.

The department store and the departmentized specialty store During the late 1920s and the 1930s, as Sears, Roebuck and Co. began to develop its chain of department stores, the firm's management correctly interpreted the trend to the suburbs and began to open free-standing units in such areas. At the same time, a few downtown department and departmentized specialty stores started to serve these areas through branches, that is, stores usually smaller than (and dominated by) the parent stores.

It was not until after World War II, however, that the number of these stores, both chain and branch, became important. In the greater Los Angeles area, for instance, the six department and departmentized specialty stores located in that city have opened more than 40 branches, some of which are located as far away as Palm Springs—90 miles from the Los Angeles central shopping district. And the trend is nationwide, with branches now operated by such well-known organizations as Marshall Field & Company and Carson Pirie Scott & Co. of Chicago; William Filene's Sons Company of Boston; R. H. Macy & Company and Lord & Taylor of New York City; Woodward & Lothrop of Washington, D.C.; Bullock's, Inc., of Los Angeles; and the Em-

[35] Cf., however, "Discount Shopping Center Is Planned in Matawan, N.J.," *Women's Wear Daily*, February 18, 1970, p. 13.

[36] "Nailing down Locations is the Key to Kresge's Expansion," *Chain Store Age*, (Executives Edition), December 1965, p. E15. In contrast, practically all of the Woolco units of the F. W. Woolworth Company are in shopping centers.

porium in San Francisco. Moreover, the branches continue to gain in size, although the majority of them still make no pretense of carrying as complete a stock as does the parent store.

Benefits and problems of branch stores Through branches, downtown stores follow their customers to the suburbs. Branches attract business because of the downtown store's prestige and also acquaint people with the firm, so that even the parent store acquires new customers. The nonmerchandising departments of the parent store are able to perform additional work, such as accounting and advertising, without a significant increase in total overhead cost. The net result is that the branch store has added substantially to the total profit of the organization.

Branch stores, however, are not without their problems. Sometimes they cut substantially into the sales of the parent store; some are in such poor locations that they result in losses rather than yielding additional profits. Effective management is still another problem. Some organizations attempt to solve this problem by assigning the merchandising function, for example, to the parent store with the branch responsible mainly for selling; others allow the branch to select merchandise from parent-store stocks; still others authorize the branch to buy directly in wholesale markets; but, increasingly, chain-store principles of organization are being adopted.[37] None of these solutions, however, has eliminated all the friction and overlapping of responsibility between branch and parent stores.

□ Neighborhood business streets

Far more numerous than the foregoing types of locations in the metropolitan area are neighborhood business streets, made up mainly of convenience-goods stores located very close together. Here are the grocery stores, superettes, meat markets, small bakery shops, fruit and vegetable stores, small variety stores, and drugstores, as well as smaller shopping- and specialty-goods stores. In the majority of cases these streets follow the main arteries of traffic throughout both the city and its satellite towns and villages. The stores are relatively small and attract business from the immediately surrounding area.

In recent years a development somewhat comparable to the controlled shopping center has taken place in neighborhood business streets. Instead of developing gradually as in the past, in some areas a large building—sometimes known as a "shopping plaza"—has been constructed and its various sections rented out to several retailers. Ample parking space is usually provided.

[37] Cf. the discussion of organizational practices for branch stores in Chapter 7, pp. 166–67.

In spite of competition from stores in other parts of the metropolitan area, those located on the neighborhood business streets (as well as those situated in small clusters and scattered, discussed below) have demonstrated a remarkable vitality. It is not difficult to rationalize this endurance. People in general are creatures of habit and tend to follow lines of least resistance. They are not always value conscious nor do they take time to seek the "best buys." Frequently they fail to anticipate their needs and as a result make their purchases at the most convenient store when their wants are immediate or urgent.

□ Small clusters and scattered stores

The clusters or scattered individual small stores of the metropolitan area are distinguished from the neighborhood business streets largely by the number of stores. Typically, the stores are complementary; that is, a cluster may be made up of a grocery store, a drugstore, and one or two other noncompetitive stores. Recently, such clusters are being located in a centrally owned plaza or retail development. Sometimes, however, there may be only a single small grocery store or drugstore in the area dealing mainly in convenience-type goods. They attract most of their customers from the adjacent area.

□ Probable future of the central shopping district

The decentralization of shopping areas has proceeded so rapidly that it gives rise to the question: Does it eventually mean the end of the central shopping district? Both retailers and customers agree that today's downtown presents great problems for them: Customer access difficulties, limited parking, high land cost, substantial property taxes, high building cost, soaring rentals, declining sales volume, difficulties in moving merchandise into the store and in delivering it to the customer, split ownership of land and buildings, and old retail structures. The late Frank Lloyd Wright even proclaimed that the downtown shopping center will disappear.

The authors believe, however, that the center shopping district, while declining in importance, will probably remain a significant contributor to retail sales volume. Many of our cities are still gaining population within their old boundaries. Urban renewal programs, downtown high-rise residential buildings, and relatively low-cost government-subsidized housing are inducing many middle-income families to return to the cities and others to remain.

In the larger cities the great congregation of stores in the downtown area offers a breadth of merchandise assortment not matched by the largest of the planned shopping centers. The desire to "make a day" of a shopping trip still brings many from the outlying areas to the central shopping area while the thousands who work in that area or who come to the city as out-of-town visitors find it convenient to buy there.

Moreover, in many cities the downtown merchants in cooperation with transit authorities and city-federal governments are making efforts to increase the attractiveness of downtown shopping. Express highways leading directly to the heart of the city are being built. Public transportation systems are being modernized and unified to give better schedules. More parking facilities are becoming available, some through additional parking lots, some by underground developments, and still others by creating ramps or mechanical devices to provide above-the-ground parking. A combination of fringe parking lots plus public transportation (in some instances, without charge or at a nominal cost) to the central shopping area is being used in some cities. Downtown merchants are modernizing their stores, establishing shopping malls,[38] adopting night and Sunday hours, and joining together on promotional programs similar to those of the shopping center. Presently, there is considerable optimism among many merchants about the future of downtown.[39]

■ REVIEW AND DISCUSSION QUESTIONS

1 "Location problems are not confined to *new* stores; they are also faced by established stores." Explain why this statement is true, and illustrate your point of view by reference to the situation in your local community.

2 Explain briefly the main reasons for neglect of the location problem by retail stores. Be sure to include the factors responsible for the limited amount of money spent on location research even by large-scale retailers.

3 Summarize, in sufficient detail to make your meaning clear, six of the basic factors influencing the choice of *a city* or *trading area* in which to locate a store.

---

[38] Cf. M. A. Puglisi, "The Urban Mall," *New York Retailer,* December 1969, pp. 13–22; "Macy 34th St. Mall Boasts Some 23 Shops," *Women's Wear Daily,* September 15, 1970, p. 42; "Fifth Avenue Turns into a Mall," *Business Week,* July 18, 1970, p. 22; and E. B. Weiss, "Expect 1,000 Pedestrian Shopping Malls by 1980," *Advertising Age,* September 21, 1970, pp. 50, 52.

[39] Cf., for instance, "Downtown Stores Buoy Federated," *Women's Wear Daily,* June 4, 1969, pp. 1, 36, which reports that the company's downtown stores continue to become more profitable although not growing as fast as the branches. Also cf. "Downtown USA Now Boomtown USA," *ibid.,* pp. 1, 26.

4 Follow the same instructions as those in question (3) concerning the selection of a specific site within the chosen city or trading area.

5 Visit a leading retailer in your city and determine from him the considerations which dictated the choice of his particular location. Contrast these considerations with those given in the text relative to the choice of the city and the site.

6 Define "suburbia," "metropolis," and "megalopolis." From the point of view of retail location, discuss current population trends in relation to each of these terms.

7 Discuss the major factors responsible for the decentralization of retail trade.

8 Describe concisely the major elements in the retail structure of the metropolitan area.

9 Explain five current trends in shopping center development, supporting each one with specific evidence.

10 As a researcher for the retail trade board of a city of 500,000 people you have been asked to make recommendations for revitalizing the downtown area and prevent further loss of sales to suburban stores. What steps would you follow to fulfill this assignment? Why?

chapter 5

THE STORE BUILDING, FIXTURES, AND EQUIPMENT

After a suitable location has been chosen, a building must be pre-pared for occupancy. This preparation involves the following: (1) Constructing a new building or making the necessary structural changes in an existing one to provide the space and facilities required; (2) providing adequate lighting equipment, properly colored walls and ceilings, and suitable floor coverings; (3) procuring the fixtures and equipment essential to the conduct of the business; and (4) arranging and locating the merchandise, fixtures, and equipment in such a manner that customers may be served promptly and satisfactorily at the lowest cost.

■ THE STORE BUILDING AS A SELLING INSTRUMENT

A well-designed store is one embodying features that attract customers and facilitates their movement inside the store, provides a pleasant environment in which they may shop, makes possible economical operations and maintenance, and has adequate space for selling and sales-supporting activities currently and in the foreseeable future. Well-designed stores are as essential to profitable operation as good assortments of merchandise at reasonable prices. Contemporary architects realize that "form follows function" and that store buildings must be effective selling instruments. Experience demonstrates that effective store planning may result in sales 10 to 100 percent higher than in the poorly planned unit. Consequently, interest in better design permeates the whole field of retailing.[1] Through the cooperation of store executives, building architects, lighting and ventilating engineers, and specialists in store equipment and layout, marked progress has resulted.[2]

□ Land, building, and equipment expenditures

Building and land costs are high and continuing to increase. For instance, land, building, and equipment for a large supermarket may cost $500,000 or more, a modern full-line drugstore $200,000 to $300,000, a large discount house may require an investment of $2–3 million, and a free-standing full-line department store may range between $5 and $15 million.[3] As a result retailers are becoming increasingly cost conscious in their store building programs with some delaying construction[4] and many large firms assigning to their architects and engineers the task of achieving equally efficient and impressive facilities at lower costs.

Some organizations have attempted to achieve their economy goal by reducing the construction period through more careful integration of all phases of the job, including use of the Program Evaluation and Review Technique—commonly known as PERT. Others have found that a newer, and less costly, material may be substituted and that less expensive fixtures may be installed. Perhaps a prefabricated structure or section of a building may be used.[5] Corporate and voluntary chains often develop a prototype or pat-

---

[1] Cf., as illustrations, Pat Terry and Susan Grant, "Design Research's New Glass House," *Home Furnishings Daily*, December 12, 1969, pp. 4–5; Ron Williams and Joe Valliant, "Retailing: New Art Form," *ibid.*, February 13, 1969, p. 7; Suzy Farbman, "Display," *Women's Wear Daily*, January 6, 1970, p. 89—describing some of our country's "best recent developments in store design"; and Pat Terry, "Display," *ibid.*, February 17, 1970, p. 38—illustrating a jewelry store.

[2] How newly designed branch stores are revitalizing W & J Sloane operations in Northern California is explained in Betty Kilich, "Sloane's New Face," *Home Furnishings Daily*, February 24, 1970, p. 5.

[3] These figures are based on retailers' statements to the authors. On the average building costs per square foot in supermarkets, cf. *Facts about New Super Markets Opened in 1969* (Chicago: Super Market Institute, 1970), p. 12.

[4] The *Progressive Grocer* reports that construction of grocery (food) stores declined from 4,850 in 1969 to 4,130 in 1970. Cf. issue of April 1971, p. 104.

[5] In 1970 it was reported that "mass-produced stores of modular construction may be innovated by Montgomery Ward in both large metropolitan areas and smaller communities." Cf. John Osbon, "Prefabricated Ward Stores Seen Coming," *Women's Wear*

tern store which reflects such savings and can be approximately duplicated many times.

□ Common features of the newer-store buildings

No store building can be described as the "typical" one of today, but common features of the newer buildings may be noted. Reinforced concrete and concrete and cinderblock tile, as well as brick and highly finished tile, are being widely used, often forming a plain, functional, and windowless building—although display windows are typically constructed on the ground-floor level. Roofs are often flat, pitch and gravel being used for the surface. For floors, terrazzo and vinyl tile are common in basements, the heavy traffic-bearing first floor, and washrooms; asphalt or vinyl tiles are generally used on the other selling floors, although carpeting placed over concrete is appearing in more and more departments; and concrete in the receiving areas. Glass block is sometimes used for at least part of the outside walls to admit natural light. Entrances and exits, as well as interior aisles, are planned for maximum movement of customers. Overall, however, the tight money situation prevailing in 1969 and 1970, rising costs, and the development of new building materials and techniques—plus management's concern over security—forced a careful review of building plans and brought numerous changes in construction patterns.[6]

■ THE STORE FRONT AND EXTERIOR

Since "the front often sells the store," it should give the impression of a going concern and reflect neither stagnation nor decline. Moreover, it should typify the spirit of the organization and the nature of the activity within. By suggesting stability and permanence the front and exterior create confidence and good will. The massive stone columns in front of Marshall Field & Company in Chicago and Selfridge's in London give this impression. Since identification is another function of the store front and exterior, symbols and distinctive store fronts—as well as large signs—have long been used. Furthermore, a minimum maintenance cost and protection of the store's windows and interior from sun damage require attention.

Daily, March 2, 1970, p. 1; and "Ward's Stores Go 'Modular'," *Business Week*, November 28, 1970, p. 21.

[6] Cf., for example, "Planners Confront the Cost Crisis," *Chain Store Age* (Executives Edition), March 1971, pp. E24–E29 ff.; and "Tight Money Speeds Up Changes," *ibid.*, May 1970, pp. E26–E27.

Finally, an accelerated development of some significance is the disappearance of traditional parts of the retail store façade such as glass windows and entrance ways. To illustrate: White Front Stores' new 130,000 square-feet store in San Carlos, California "is largely glassless, boasts a split face, brick-concrete paneling integrated with poured-in veneer panels," while Bamberger's (a subsidiary of R. H. Macy & Company) new unit in East Brunswick, New Jersey will have a glassless exterior. Among the reasons for these design changes are the desire to improve security in case of civil disorders, to obtain better control of the interior environment at a lower cost, and to benefit from new merchandising techniques that have diminished the value of store windows.[7]

Figures 5–1, 5–2, 5–3, 5–4, and 5–5 provide examples of the exterior appearance of modern and rather unique store buildings.[8]

FIGURE 5–1 A modern store of Weinstock's, Fresno, California

Courtesy: Weinstock's

☐ Customer entrances

Entrances should be wide and inviting,[9] with doorsills preferably at the street level. To avoid congestion and concentration of customer traffic, two entrances are advisable for stores with a frontage of 75 feet or more. Entrances on two streets are preferable for corner locations. Doors should

[7] Cf. "Chains Cut Use of Store Front Glass," *Chain Store Age* (Executives Edition), October 1970, pp. E32–E33.

[8] Additional illustrations of shopping centers and stores in them are given in "Shopping Centers," *Architectural Record,* March 1970, pp. 119–32.

[9] The main entrance of F. R. Lazarus and Co., Columbus, Ohio, department store, is over 33 feet wide. Open winter and summer, merchandise displays are brought close to customers. When the store is closed, folding doors protect the entrance.

FIGURE 5–2 **A fashion specialty store in San Diego, California** Note lack of windows and unusual roof treatment.

Courtesy: Joseph Magnin & Co.

FIGURE 5–3 **The new three-story Liberty House store in San Jose, California with spacious parking area**

Courtesy: Amfac Merchandising Corp.

permit easy access;[10] in fact, some retailers have replaced them with "curtains of air" (warm or cold, depending on the weather), thus eliminating them as a deterrent to entrance by the customer. Whether or not revolving doors are used depends on the size of the store, willingness of the retailer to meet the cost, and the climate.

[10] Cf., however, "Rivalry Sharpens Doorless Designs," *Chain Store Age* (Executives Edition), March 1971, pp. E60–E61.

FIGURE 5–4 **The R. H. Macy & Company, Inc.'s department store, Queens Boulevard, Queens, New York** Opened in 1965 with over 330,000 square feet of area, this unusual structure parks 1,500 cars on its roof and ramps.

Courtesy: R. H. Macy & Co., Inc.

□ Show windows

The use of windows to display merchandise offered for sale has been an almost universal practice, with supermarkets and some discount houses the most notable exceptions. Recent years, however, have witnessed a decline in their use by other stores, particularly chain organizations, department and specialty stores, for reasons already mentioned. Yet as the "eyes" of the store, they continue in use by most stores as a desirable feature of the store exterior from the sales point of view because the impressions customers receive from the window displays largely determine whether or not they will enter the store.[11] Consequently, even some of the so-called "windowless" stores have windows at the ground level to "show their wares."

The size and type of windows used in a particular establishment are determined by the kind of store and the goods displayed. To illustrate: Many department stores, with items varying in size from furniture suites to notions, have large and deep windows to accommodate many different types of merchandise; variety stores frequently use large, shallow windows with

[11] As an example, in a recent promotional effort Young-Quinlan of Minneapolis used six main display windows to "catch the eye" in an ingenious manner. Dominating each window was a back-drop of an eye with the soft-look in eye makeup. Shown with each "eye do" was the appropriate color and style handbag, gloves, jewelry, neckwear, hosiery and other accessories.

FIGURE 5–5 **A multi-story specialty store facing Union Square in San Francisco**

Courtesy: I. Magnin & Co.

no backgrounds above eye level, thus affording an unobstructed view of the store's interior; and some jewelry stores favor the so-called "invisible" window, which consists of a curved sheet of glass so formed as to cast reflections downward and away from the observer's eye, thus giving the effect of an open window.

Backgrounds Among stores using show windows, three general types of window backgrounds are found: (*a*) The open background, which permits the passer-by to see into the store, as in grocery stores, candy stores, and florists' shops; (*b*) the semiclosed background, with a partition extending to a height below the line of vision, sometimes found in drugstores and hardware stores; and (*c*) the closed background, which shuts off the window completely, as in department stores and in specialty stores handling men's and women's wearing apparel. Retailers using closed or semiclosed backgrounds claim that they focus attention upon displays, provide attractive settings for the merchandise shown, and permit more effective illumination.

Visual fronts Still found in some stores is the open or visual store front, which has no formal window; instead, the customer looks through glass directly to the store's interior displays. This front enables the customer to grasp more quickly the scope of merchandise offered for sale. It also adds selling space, reduces the time required to trim windows, permits greater use of natural light, and creates a more open and attractive shopping "atmosphere."

■ THE STORE INTERIOR

Regardless of the reasons why the customer enters the store, her impression of the interior must be favorable. Such an impression may be created by, for example, an open area inside the entrance, aisles wide enough to readily accommodate customer traffic, good light, ceilings of the proper height, and colorful displays. Also helpful in this connection are floor, wall, and ceiling finishes, store equipment and fixtures—including lighting, elevators and escalators, and air conditioning, and the proper harmonizing of these factors.

□ Floors, walls, and ceilings

The retailer may choose from among more than 50 floor finishes made of such materials as wood, marble, tile, linoleum, rubber, and cork. Different types, of course, are required for different purposes; the finish in the receiving or marking room, for example, would be unlike that required on the second floor of a department store. Likewise, exclusive specialty shops,

FIGURE 5–6 **Interior section of a high-fashion specialty store**

Courtesy: *Joseph Magnin & Co.*

where wall-to-wall carpeting is growing in popularity, require a floor different from that of a neighborhood grocery store. Figure 5–6 shows one section of the Joseph Magnin & Co. fashion specialty store in La Habra, California.[12] In general, however, the trend is toward the newer types of vinyl and other resilient tiles as replacements for the older masonry and wood floors because of their durability and attractiveness.

Wall and ceiling finishes are dictated by considerations of attractiveness, economy, and preference of store executives. While many economy-type stores rely heavily on paint spread directly on cinder or concrete blocks for much of their wall area, even these establishments usually finish off some areas with wood panels, reclaimed brick, or some of the plastic laminates. In other stores, plastered walls finished with paint or decorative wallpaper are common. The newer vinyl fabrics, while involving a larger original cost, are preferred by many retailers because they can supply texture and color effects not possible with paint, and the increased cost is largely offset by longer life and reduced maintenance costs. The use of "super graphics," or very large-scale photographs and geometric designs for wall decoration and departmental location indicators, as shown in Figure 5–7, is a very modern and colorful development.

The color of the store's interior makes the store more attractive and aids in the sale of specific merchandise. Color combinations are also employed to emphasize the individuality and character of a store and to reduce lighting costs.

☐ Store fixtures and equipment

The appearance of the store's interior and its effectiveness as a retail facility are determined in large measure by the fixtures and equipment used. The terms "store fixtures" and "store equipment" are often used interchangeably by students of retailing: Some retailers speak of the lights they install as "light fixtures" while others refer to their "lighting equipment." Despite such loose usage, however, the term "fixtures" is properly reserved for those durable goods which the retailer uses directly in the sale, display, storage, and protection of merchandise, such as display cabinets and cases, shelves, counters, and tables; whereas the term "equipment" refers to such other durable goods as elevators, escalators, air-conditioning units, sales registers, and delivery trucks, which are used throughout the store to facilitate both selling and nonselling activities.

[12] Note especially, in addition to the carpeted floor, the grid ceiling with movable lighting fixtures, the inset hanging rods with overhead lighting, and the platform stage used for display with dressing rooms, store rooms, and a wrapping desk below.

FIGURE 5–7 **Super graphic design in the J. L. Hudson Company store, Fox Park Mall, Toledo, Ohio, opened July 1971**

Selecting fixtures and equipment In choosing fixtures and equipment, certain factors, in addition to cost, are decisive. First is the clientele or class of trade to which the store intends to cater; second, those chosen should not divert customers' attention from the merchandise; third, they should be adjusted to the type of merchandise handled, including such closely related factors as size, value, need for protection from theft and deterioration or spoilage, and the methods employed to display and sell it;[13] fourth, the type of service rendered in connection with the merchandise, *i.e.*, whether

[13] Cf. "New S. Klein Fixtures Put All Stock on Selling Floor," *Home Furnishings Daily*, March 13, 1970, pp. 1, 11.

the store is a self-service or full-service one; fifth, the original cost and maintenance expense; and sixth, the types and kinds of items available for use in the particular kind of store under consideration.

□ Lighting the modern store

Effective lighting is essential for the conduct of both selling and non-selling activities. While cost of equipment and economy in operation are basic considerations, the retailer is also interested in how his lighting—among other things—improves the store's interior and if it adds to the customer's shopping pleasure, steps up sales personnel productivity, makes self-selection easier, increases merchandise turnover, decreases shoplifting, ties in with the kind of merchandise he sells, and adds to the effectiveness of his displays. In other words, he thinks of lighting as a sales tool.[14] (See Figure 5–6.)

Typical of the questions the retailer should answer as he attempts to solve his lighting problems are the following:

1. Does the lighting arrangement make it easy for customers to find and identify the store during evening hours through effective use of electric signs, luminous façades, and well-lighted parking lots?
2. Does the lighting plan cause the customer to look where it is desired that she look?
3. Are the lighting conditions most effective for buying decisions through providing for the best rendition of color on all types of merchandise?
4. Does the lighting add emphasis to merchandise and yield maximum results from display space?
5. Is lighting used properly to identify departments and direct customers?
6. Is the lighting used at check-out counters and sales registers of the kind that permits easy reading of prices and the writing of sales slips, yet avoiding glare reflections from surfaces on merchandise and sales registers?
7. Does the lighting plan speed stocking and order filling in the storage areas of the store, thus improving production?
8. Is the lighting arrangement one that minimizes the maintenance of cleaning light fixtures, replacing lamps, and similar work?

---

[14] Cf. "Incandescents Put Goods in New Light [Filene's of Boston]," *Chain Store Age* (Executives Edition), October 1969, pp. 26 ff. Mercury vapor lamps, which emit a softer, more attractive glow than fluorescents, are also being used, especially in supermarkets and discount houses. Cf. "Giant Food Boosts Light, Cuts Power with M.V.s," *ibid.,* January 1971, p. E41.

9. Does the complete lighting program provide an atmosphere where the customer can shop pleasantly and cause her to return to the store to make additional purchases?

The technical nature of lighting makes it advisable for the retailer to consult a qualified lighting engineer to solve his problems in this area.

◻ Equipment for handling vertical customer traffic

Handling vertical customer traffic, especially during peak periods, is a problem for retailers who operate on more than one level. Stationary stairways are adequate for many stores with just a basement or perhaps only one floor above the street level, but other stores find they must install elevators and escalators or moving stairways. R. H. Macy & Company, New York City, to cite an extreme example, found 70 escalators and 29 passenger elevators were necessary to provide vertical transportation for its 150,000 daily customers.

The marked improvement in elevator types has increased their usefulness because large numbers of customers can be handled more rapidly and more comfortably than formerly. Automatic stopping, microleveling, and power-operated doors have all contributed to greater speed.

Escalators were long considered as unsightly, impractical equipment but today they are a "must" in the larger stores. Improved design, "streamlined" effects, and inlaid lighting have contributed to this growth. Moreover, their advantages over elevators are increasingly being recognized including the following: elimination of waiting for elevators and reduction of congestion and crowding—thus saving the customer's time and energy; provision of fast and comfortable transportation between floors while affording a good view of adjacent merchandise offerings; and finally, in large stores which need to provide for considerable vertical transportation, they occupy far less space than elevators, require no operators, and provide continuity of motion with low power cost.

Among smaller stores the elevator is usually more advantageous than the escalator. If a single elevator is adequate, it will require but one-third as much space as an escalator and installation cost is lower. An observer of the heavy loads carried by escalators during the peak Christmas business in the larger stores, however, wonders how they operated without escalators for so many years. But even in these stores some elevators are needed, especially to provide rapid movement for customers wishing to move vertically several floors at one time, for those who are aged or infirm, and for those who prefer to ride in them.

☐ Growth of air conditioning in retail stores

Currently, practically all major department and departmentalized specialty stores as well as chain stores are air conditioned, at least in part. In fact, most of the new stores being built today are air conditioned, regardless of their type or location. And in shopping centers even the malls are being treated in this manner by means of automated controls to provide the desired "climate."[15]

The main advantage of air conditioning is its attractiveness to the customer. It encourages shopping on warm days and it increases impulse sales to people drawn into stores just "to cool off." It also improves employee morale, resulting in better performance as well as contributing to a cleaner store and merchandise. Finally, if a retailer's chief competitors adopt air conditioning, he may well be forced to do so to maintain his competitive position.

Some limitations Despite its growing popularity and advantages, air conditioning has not been universally adopted. In fact, only a low percentage of the smaller independent stores use it in marked contrast to the larger stores where air conditioning is common. Its limited use in small stores is due to the facts that initial, operating, and maintenance costs of various types of equipment are relatively high[16] and some sales or storage space is lost. Even the fact that a competitor has installed such equipment should not cause undue alarm, unless that competitor also practices effective retailing methods. Air conditioning a store will not overcome unsound merchandising practices.

☐ Other kinds of equipment

For selling activities Exclusive of service equipment,[17] various other kinds of equipment are required to facilitate the handling of sales transactions. The types and amounts of these kinds of equipment used in particular stores and departments will depend upon existing needs and conditions. In grocery stores, for example, weighing machines or scales are essential in

---

[15] Cf. Herbert Argintar, "Automated Control of a Store's Internal Climate," *Stores*, October 1969, pp. 41–42.

[16] The formation of a nationwide network of independent service companies, working with 800 manufacturers' engineers to provide maintenance on air conditioning and climate control service—Sure Air Ltd.—is outlined in "Preventative Maintenance Service Spans Country for Chain Stores," *Air Conditioning, Heating & Refrigeration News*, February 9, 1970, pp. 20–21.

[17] Service equipment, such as sales registers, is discussed in Chapter 25, "Control of Sales Transactions."

selling bulk goods, fruits, and vegetables. In department stores, certain departments—candy, for instance—also require scales. For stores that sell yard goods or piece goods and therefore need linear measurements, there are machines available that measure such merchandise accurately.

For sales-supporting activities A wide variety of equipment is required to carry out sales-supporting functions. This equipment, which has contributed to improved performance and to reduced costs, may be classified as follows: (*a*) Mechanical equipment used in receiving, marking, checking, and delivery rooms, including small floor trucks, mobile marking tables, price-ticket machines, marking machines, time-stamp machines, belt conveyor systems, and wastepaper baling machines; (*b*) labor-saving devices used in the general offices for handling correspondence and other clerical work such as typewriters and machines used for calculating, duplicating, bookkeeping, addressing, and stamping; (*c*) store communication devices, such as call systems—bells, lights, or electronic—for store executives, private telephone systems, and dictagraphs; and (*d*) miscellaneous equipment, including time clocks, signature-recording machines for timekeeping purposes, and sewing and textile-repair machines in workrooms. Relatively few stores, of course, use all of these types of equipment; but retail executives should be aware of the fact that such equipment is available when, as, and if it may be used advantageously.

Electronic equipment The use of electronic data-processing systems and the equipment required for their effective functioning, is growing rapidly. Frequently referred to as EDP, these systems provide a means of gathering, storing, and processing data to provide the retailer with the information he requires.[18] Already so complicated that no one man knows a large computer's wiring diagram in full detail, many new electronic machines with even greater complexity continue to be developed. In fact, it may prove true that the machines now being used are Neanderthal models compared to what is coming in the relatively near future.

1. *Current uses of EDP in retailing* In the hands of an able operator, usually referred to as the programmer, EDP equipment can provide timely information on such matters as (1) sales by classifications, departments, or stores and even by individual items broken down by price lines, sizes, colors, or other factors, (2) inventories, (3) expenses, (4) purchases, (5) accounts payable, (6) accounts receivable, (7) gross margin, and (8) returned goods.[19] Clerical work can be minimized, and speed and accuracy maxi-

[18] One source estimates that retailers will increase their expenditures for EDP some 60 percent by 1976 or from $500 million to $800 million, with inventory control the prime target. Cf. "Retail EDP Costs to Hit $800 million," *Chain Store Age* (Executives Edition), February 1971, p. E17.

[19] In later chapters, including our discussions of merchandise management, credit, and sales registers, some of these uses of EDP are developed at greater length.

mized, by using EDP to prepare payrolls, to reorder certain items automatically, to supply open-to-buy reports, and to prepare checks for merchandise and other purchases. Eventually, some retailers expect that—by "feeding" into the machines certain basic data—the desirability of a store location may be analyzed, the most efficient truck routing determined, and a judgment on the advisability of adding a new product may be secured.

2. Limitations and probable future of EDP in retailing EDP systems are very costly with the prices of computers varying widely according to the capabilities they provide. Although some of the new mini-computers—"easy to use as a typewriter"—sell below $25,000, other small and medium-sized installations are in the $25,000 to $150,000 range and the larger ones are priced at $200,000 to $5 million. Perhaps 90 percent of such equipment is rented. To cite some specific examples of the leading producer in the field: One of IBM's smallest computers, the System/3 Model 6, configured with a typical amount of input-output equipment, rents at $1,015 per month and the purchase price is $48,250. Comparable figures for a medium-sized computer, the System/370 Model 145, are $14,950 and $705,775.

Considerable expense is involved in the year or two of study leading to the selection of the equipment and in the comparable "breaking-in" or testing period after the equipment has been installed. Consequently, the purchase or full-time lease of EDP systems is open just to the large retail organizations. Yet the medium-size retailer can still secure some of the advantages of these systems by renting their use for a few hours at a time. Both equipment manufacturers and independent firms now offer a rental service, including the aid of programmers and other skilled personnel, throughout the country.

In view of the cost involved, there is a wide range of opinion, even among large retailers, as to how rapidly they should adopt electronic equipment. Certainly the retailer should precede his purchase or "time sharing" of such equipment with a careful study of his needs, exercise great care in retraining his people to think in terms of the new machines, and not expect his new equipment to serve as a panacea for all his problems. He should keep firmly in mind the facts "that these new devices are only tools" to aid his judgments and that some "data refinements of the precision which these devices make possible may not be needed at all by many astute executives in making many business decisions."[20] As a matter of fact, some very successful retailers operate with a minimum of reports. One large English retailer, for example, abolished many of his reports, thereby eliminating 8,000 out of 28,000 jobs, reduced his prices, and added to his sales and

[20] W. N. Mitchell, *The Business Executive in a Changing World* (New York: American Management Association, 1965), p. 77.

profits.[21] Some discount houses also operate with a minimum of records. How to balance the gains from added information against the cost of obtaining it is not one of the retailer's easy decisions. Present indications, however, are that in the foreseeable future retailers will seek more aid from the newer electronic equipment.

Leasing fixtures and equipment Previous reference to the fact that retailers often lease electronic equipment is illustrative of a trend toward the leasing of fixtures and equipment in general. Faced with a growing need for capital in the "tight money" situation prevailing as this is written, plus other factors, many retailers have found it advisable to practice leasing to ease their problems. To illustrate, some large retailers lease a complete fleet of trucks, many of their store fixtures, and their headquarters' bookkeeping and billing equipment.[22]

■ STORE MODERNIZATION

Store modernization may be defined as bringing and keeping up to date the physical appearance, the fixtures, and the equipment of a store to increase its attractiveness to customers and to aid in obtaining continuous patronage. Moreover, it is designed to minimize operating costs and improve profit possibilities by such means as increasing the flow of traffic through the store, stepping up employee productivity in both selling and nonselling activities, and cutting maintenance expenses. As a continuing responsibility of the retailer, modernization involves the utilization of improved construction materials and techniques as well as the most modern equipment and fixtures suited to his requirements.

□ Modernization expenditures

During comparatively recent years, the United States has experienced its greatest retailing modernization program in history. Progressive retailers of all types, regardless of their location, are well aware of the necessity of keeping their stores up to date. They know modernization is essential for satisfactory service to customers and for the maintenance of one's competitive position. And they spend large sums in the process: For 1971 alone, despite the business situation and rising costs of labor and materials, chain organizations in various fields and their landlords budgeted $485 million to

---

[21] "The English Unorthodoxy of Marks & Spencer," *Dun's Review and Modern Industry,* October 1966, p. 128.

[22] On this subject, cf. "Growing Lure of Leasing," *Business Management,* January 1970, pp. 40–41 ff., and D. P. Vall, "Lease versus Loan as Comparable Investments," *Stores,* January 1969, pp. 20–21.

remodel 9,461 stores, an average of some $51,413 per job. Comparable figures for 1970 were $556 million to remodel 13,100 stores, an average of over $42,000.[23] In fact, in 1971 they modernized more old stores than they opened as new units (9,185). During the same year, department stores were expected to spend $38 million to refurbish existing units and half of the hardware stores with annual sales over $100,000 planned expenditures averaging $4,000 on improvements.[24] In a recent year, Marshall Field & Company had a total capital expenditure of $4.9 million, of which $3.2 million was for modernization; and, in 1969, the J. C. Penney Company, Inc., spent $13.7 million to modernize and renovate older stores with its landlords contributing an additional $71.5 million.[25] The average annual modernization expenditure of the Emporium-Capwell Company of San Francisco is $6 million.

The continuing nature and significance of store modernization is also well illustrated by the supermarket field. During 1969, the number of remodelings exceeded the number of new units opened. The total number of supermarkets only increased by about 4.5 percent, but about 7 percent of the existing markets were remodeled. Major remodelings were also planned for 7 percent of the stores in 1971.[26] That such major remodeling programs are expensive is suggested by a study among independent supermarkets: The average modernization job cost $42,660 in 1969 but declined to $41,420 in 1970.[27]

□ Modernization programs

As retailers have modernized their stores, some of them, for financial reasons, have limited their expenditures to new store fronts, or, perhaps, to improved interiors. Changes of this nature often result in a substantial sales increase. More extensive programs such as constructing new façades or rearranging departments to utilize newly designed fixtures also have produced excellent results. Large stores have centered major attention upon elevators, escalators, air conditioning, improved illumination, and additional selling and nonselling space; and small retailers have emphasized better illumination, more attractive windows, and—to a substantially lesser degree —air conditioning.

---

[23] "$3.7 Billion for New, Remodeled Stores," *Chain Store Age* (Executives Edition), January 1971, p. E19.

[24] "What Competitors Are Spending," *Hardware Retailer*, April 1970, p. 47.

[25] *Annual Report 1969*, p. 25.

[26] *The Super Market Industry Speaks 1971* (Chicago: Super Market Institute, 1971), pp. 9–11.

[27] "New Store Construction and Store Remodeling," *Progressive Grocer*, April 1971, p. 106.

Large retailers can retain experts in layout, lighting, and other aspects of modernization, sometimes establishing their own store-planning departments.[28] Smaller ones often find these services too expensive. The latter rely to a considerable extent on the assistance provided by their trade associations. For example, the National Retail Hardware Association not only advises its members to "Consult Your Association First on All Store Modernizations," but it also encourages modernization by the preparation and dissemination of printed material.

Other small stores—and some larger ones—are aided by wholesalers and by manufacturers of fixtures, equipment, glass, and paint.

■ FUTURE BUILDING AND MODERNIZATION PROSPECTS

The growth of our population, urban renewal programs, and the surge in shopping centers and large free-standing stores, among other factors, suggest that the present new-store building boom will continue, but temporarily at a reduced rate. In turn, the competition offered by these new units will further stimulate the trend toward store modernization. Despite high break-even points, narrowing profit margins, current high interest rates, and the sharp increase in modernization costs, today's merchants are convinced that improved buildings and better equipment are essential to their preservation at a satisfactory level of profit. Furthermore, remodeling and renovation are encouraged by the development of new materials, equipment, and devices which tend to make those in use obsolete.

In view of the foregoing, it is not surprising that by 1970 chain store annual expenditures on new construction and modernization had exceeded $3.9 billion, up from $3.6 billion in 1968, and that further rises were anticipated. Most small retailers will probably continue to operate as they have in the past, rationalizing their actions on the ground that they cannot afford to make extensive structural and equipment changes. The more progressive stores, however, both large and small, will modernize to increase their attractiveness to customers and their efficiency as selling instruments.

■ REVIEW AND DISCUSSION QUESTIONS

1 Account for the growing emphasis on well-designed and attractive retail store buildings despite increasing construction costs.

---

[28] One such department, in Allied Stores Corp., is explained and illustrated in "Diverse Stores Tied Together," *Chain Store Age* (Executives Edition), August 1970, pp. E9–E12.

2 Explain some of the common features of the newer store buildings and the main factors responsible for their adoption.

3 Discuss the reasons for the trend toward disappearance of traditional parts of the retail store façade (principal face or front) such as glass windows and entrance ways.

4 Explain briefly what you consider to be the essential elements in providing an attractive, desirable store interior to induce regular customer patronage.

5 (*a*) Differentiate between the terms "store fixtures" and "store equipment." Give examples of each.
(*b*) Summarize the decisive considerations in the choice of fixtures and equipment by the retailer.

6 Visit a lighting engineer or an executive of a modernized store in your community—or a nearby one—and determine the most recent developments in lighting equipment and methods. What is his opinion regarding the potential of mercury vapor lights in retail stores?

7 Based on the brief treatment in this chapter, what are the major current uses of EDP (Electronic Data Processing) in the field of retailing. Be specific!

8 Evaluate the growing practice of equipment leasing among retailers.

9 Speculate on future building and modernization developments in two types or kinds of retail stores of your own choosing. State your reasons in each case.

10 Some observers contend that many of our metropolitan areas are becoming "overstored," *i.e.*, there are more stores than needed to meet customers' needs. How may such a situation be determined?

chapter 6

ARRANGING THE STORE'S INTERIOR—LAYOUT

In the previous chapter, some of the factors involved in preparing the store building for use were developed. In the present one, we devote attention to its interior arrangement or layout. Specifically, we concern ourselves with arranging and locating the merchandise, fixtures, and equipment so as to provide the desired standard of customer service at the lowest cost to the retailer.

DEFINITION OF AND FACTORS INFLUENCING LAYOUT

The layout of a retail store refers to the arrangement of equipment and fixtures, merchandise, selling and sales-supporting departments, displays, aisles, and check-out stands where needed in proper relationship to each other and in accordance with a *definite plan*. According to this concept, stores that have "just grown" on a haphazard basis are not actually "laid out" despite the fact that, broadly speaking, they are arranged in a particular manner.

☐ Factors influencing layout

The layout of any retail store is affected by such factors as (1) the size and shape of the space to be occupied, including the number of floors; (2) the location of the unloading dock or area, elevators, escalators, and other permanent installations; (3) the kinds and amounts of merchandise to be handled; (4) the type of operation to be employed, such as self-service; (5) the characteristics and buying habits of the clientele to be served; (6) the nature and quantity of the fixtures and equipment to be installed; and (7) the personal preferences of the retailer.

In considering the foregoing factors, the retailer will seek a layout designed: (1) To make the store as attractive, inviting, and convenient as possible to the customer; and (2) to provide the most effective and efficient utilization of the space. He will especially emphasize the sales promotion aspect of layout, including maximum exposure of goods to sale. Perhaps the only important exception to this rule is afforded by certain exclusive specialty shops where the layout is deliberately planned to hide merchandise from the customer's view. In one store, for example, the only ready-to-wear shown is that displayed on a few mannequins; the merchandise is brought by sales personnel to customers who sit at small tables. Such personal service is possible in only few retail stores; most retailers find it too expensive.

☐ Increasing emphasis on layout

The trend toward larger stores, the desire to gain more sales space at the expense of nonselling areas,[1] the development of stores on shopping center malls, the "shop within a shop" concept,[2] new kinds of fixtures and equipment, and the tremendous growth of simplified selling, self-selection, and self-service have outmoded old store arrangement patterns and resulted in more attention to and far-reaching changes in the layouts of stores of all types. Currently, layouts are being designed to permit easy access to merchandise by customers; to facilitate selection through grouping of related items, which permits comparison of brands and prices; to allow for

---

[1] The president of Goldblatt Bros., Inc., a 39-store regional operation centering in Chicago, reports that an increase of 20 to 30 percent in selling areas in an increasing number of its stores has significantly improved both sales per square foot and margins. Cf. John Osbon, "Goldblatt's Departments Plan to Steal Scenes," *Women's Wear Daily*, May 27, 1969, p. 52. Also cf. "Showcase Stairway [at Roos-Atkins] Adds to Sales Area," *Chain Store Age* (Executives Edition), September 1970, p. E70.

[2] Cf. "Shop-within-a-Shop," *Women's Wear Daily*, January 13, 1970, p. 36; and the description of Saks Fifth Avenue's "Street of Shops" on the fifth floor of its New York City store in "Design Environment," *ibid.*, January 12, 1970, p. 44.

future expansion of the store; and to provide sufficient checkout stands and trained cashiers to insure fast customer service. Moreover, retailing literature has continued to stress the importance of layout while retail trade journals, trade association literature and meetings, the obvious success of other stores which have changed their layouts, and the efforts of equipment and fixture manufacturers—all these, and others, have made both large and small retailers more conscious of the need to study layout problems.[3]

■ LAYOUT PROCEDURE

To accomplish the main purposes of layout we have mentioned, a logical procedure is essential. Appropriate steps include a survey of space requirements; a review of the characteristics of satisfactory layouts; visits to other stores; the securing of recommendations from equipment and fixture manufacturers, merchandise resources, store engineers, and architects; and the tentative location of selling and sales-supporting departments on paper for review. In addition, the layout should remain sufficiently flexible to allow for adaptations to the changing needs of both the customers and the retailer.

In going through these steps, it is usually desirable that the retailer be guided by a competent store architect and, in some instances, by an engineer. The large retailer may have well-qualified architects and engineers on his staff, although on many occasions even these need to be supplemented by outside experts who can bring in a "fresh" point of view. The small retailer usually hesitates to engage an architect because of the added cost, but a competent architect can often recommend cost savings which more than offset his fee.

□ Survey space requirements

Sales forecast This step requires an estimate of sales, both immediately and in the future.[4] Once the immediate sales forecast is at hand, the minimum square footage of the store can be determined by dividing into it what experience has indicated is a reasonable projection of sales per square foot[5]

---

[3] Note, however, the following statement regarding food stores: "Although store design and layouts change, equipment developments advance, and methods of merchandising are altered, the important reasons for store selection by shoppers—everyday low prices, convenience of location, quality and freshness of meats, variety and selection of merchandise, and friendly personnel—have remained reasonably constant over the years." "Super Markets of the 70's," *Progressive Grocer,* July 1969, p. 58.

[4] Cf. "Estimated Volume of Business," pp. 85–86, above.

[5] Allied Stores Corporation has set $70 to $80 sales per square foot guidelines for future store expansion goals as compared with the former $50 to $60 sales level. The advance was made "to meet higher building and fixturing costs and soaring interest

based on the merchant's previous experience (if any), cost trends, trade association data, and studies reported in trade papers. If a substantial future sales increase seems likely, provision should be made to enlarge the area at a later date—perhaps by a new wing to the building or by adding a floor or floors. To make such a step practicable, the Macy store illustrated in Figure 5–4 (page 109) was constructed strongly enough to carry one additional floor.

In estimating his space requirements the retailer should avoid one error which is all too common—the idea that a high figure for sales per square foot can be attained merely by constructing a large store without worrying too much about its layout. As a matter of fact, large stores frequently waste space simply because they have so much of it.

Checklist of Space Needs A valuable guide in analyzing space requirements is a detailed checklist of the merchandise, functions, and facilities for which space must be provided within the store. This list, naturally, will reflect store policy and procedure. Moreover, the kinds and amounts of merchandise stocked and the services rendered will depend on the type of store. But, in general, each retailer should ask if, to illustrate, he has provided space for the following:

1. Merchandise departments, including the necessary space for storing, displaying and selling goods in appropriate fixtures and on shelves.
2. Sales-supporting departments of all types—receiving and marking goods, reserve stock storage space, deliveries, returns and adjustments, storage of supplies, and similar activities.
3. Comforts and conveniences for customers and employees.
4. Office space, including areas for purchase of merchandise.
5. Workroom space.
6. Heating, lighting, air conditioning, and ventilating equipment and fixtures.
7. Stairways, elevators, and escalators.
8. Aisles wide enough to permit free flow of customer traffic.
9. Window space of the form or type desired, if any.
10. Suitable areas for EDP equipment and other demands of the new technology.

In reviewing this checklist, the prospective store proprietor will find that the experiences of other retailers are very helpful. For example, the prospective supermarket retailer can benefit from the information available

rates." Cf. Harry Berlfein, "Allied Hikes Sales Goals," *Women's Wear Daily*, June 18, 1969, p. 1.

from the Super Market Institute; the department store from that furnished by the National Retail Merchants Association; and the hardware store from that supplied by the National Retail Hardware Association.

□ Review characteristics of good layouts

The desirable characteristics of a good layout from the point of view of both the customer and the retailer should be reviewed carefully.

Customer point of view The logical basis for sound layout decisions should be consumer satisfaction. In other words, the needs and expectations of his potential customers, more than any other factor, should dictate the retailer's arrangement of his store's interior.

Generally speaking, customers want an attractive place in which to shop, convenient access to merchandise throughout the store, aisles wide enough to prevent crowding during normal business days, freedom from obstructions that prevent a general view of the floor, related merchandise together, similar locations of merchandise in the stores in which they concentrate their purchases, infrequent changes in the location of departments, privacy for the fitting of garments, and daylight rather than artificial light to judge the color of certain merchandise. In addition, stores catering primarily to women but wishing to attract men to certain departments may need layouts that permit men to enter these departments without going through other areas of the store.

Developing a layout to meet customer wishes is not always easy, a point which is illustrated by the problems encountered by department stores in bringing together related merchandise. At first thought it may seem easy to set up a bath shop (with "everything for the bathroom," from towels and bath mats to marbletopped lavatories) and a ski shop (including men's and women's ski clothing as well as ski equipment). But such arrangements immediately raise such questions as: Who buys the men's clothing for the ski shop—the shop personnel or the buyer in the men's clothing department? Can a seller in the ski shop be trained to sell both men's and women's clothing as well as ski equipment? Will garments on sale in the ski shop be duplicated in the women's apparel departments?

In practice, there is no single answer to any of these questions. For instance, some stores let the ski-shop personnel do all their buying while other retailers spread the buying function among regular department buyers. But each store must find its own answers since this practice of classification merchandising and selling by category continues to increase.

Retailer point of view Although customers' preferences are vital in laying out a store, other considerations are also important. Because of the increase in night and Sunday openings, shorter working hours, and the higher rates of pay received by employees in recent years, layouts which will increase employee productivity are required. Consequently, store plans are sought which will reduce both the time required to complete sales transactions and the amount of walking necessary by customers and salespeople.

To encourage self-selection and impulse buying, layouts designed to facilitate the movement of traffic throughout the store are increasing in number.[6] Many recently modernized stores have adopted the so-called "wandering aisle," which replaces the more or less straight aisles with a series of circular, octagonal, or oval counters around which traffic moves so that more merchandise is brought into the customer's view. Still others have moved in the opposite direction, to a mall-type or wide central aisle which encourages the flow of traffic in a predetermined pattern. Under such an arrangement, each department in the store fronts on this main aisle, with two advantages: (*a*) The department is easily located by the customer; and (*b*) the department can use this front as a promotional spot.

The relation of layout to profit is suggested by the efforts of many retailers to place high-margin merchandise where it gets maximum customer exposure. One self-service retailer found that since the first two aisles near the entrance carried the most traffic, his better margin-yielding departments were moved to these areas with a resulting gain in profits. Other retailers have discovered that the amount of merchandise of a particular kind displayed on a shelf, as well as the location of the shelf in the store, is important from a sales point of view and have rearranged their stocks to take advantage of this fact.

Figures 6–1, 6–2, and 6–3 illustrate layouts in various stores intended to meet the needs of both customers and the retailer. To make certain that the characteristics of good layouts are carefully considered for each new store, many retailers have developed checklists.

Sources of information on layouts A study of available literature on store arrangement is invaluable to the retail merchant. Such action familiarizes him with the opinions of authorities on the subject concerning the desirable characteristics of good layouts and also with current developments in this field. Such sources as the United States Department of Commerce (including the Small Business Administration), trade associations and trade

---

[6] Mr. E. B. Weiss forecasts that traffic flow will eventually be facilitated by the installation of moving aisles. Cf. his "What Will Retailing Be Like in 1975?" *Advertising Age*, March 7, 1966, pp. 119–20 ff.

FIGURE 6–1 **A shoe department in a high-fashion store**

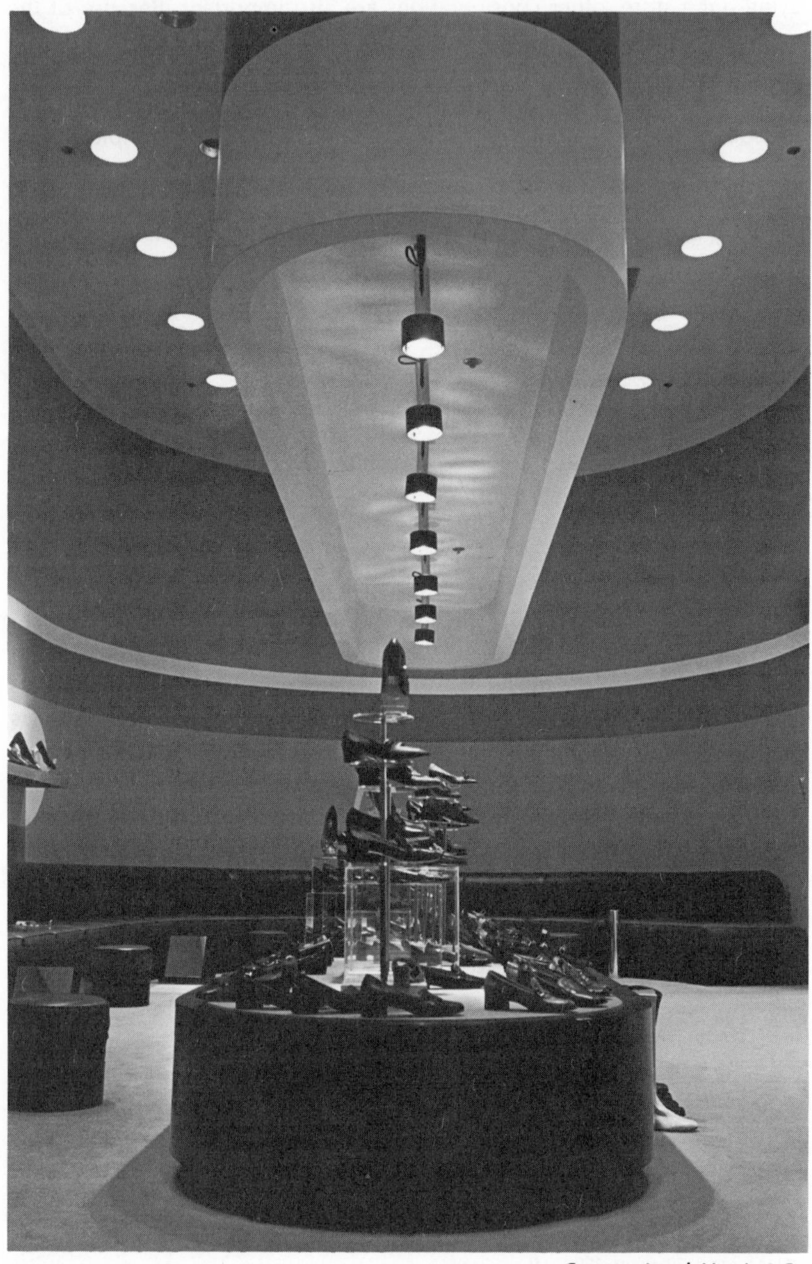

Courtesy: Joseph Magnin & Co.

FIGURE 6–2 **A men's clothing department adjacent to shoe and hat departments in a branch store**

Courtesy: The Emporium-Capwell Company

magazines in the retail field, equipment manufacturers, and periodicals such as *Architectural Record* provide numerous services useful in solving layout problems.

☐ Visit new stores of same type

Although most written material on store arrangement includes diagrams and illustrations to facilitate understanding, many retailers find it advisable to visit new and recently remodeled stores similar to their own and to observe the layouts and the flow of traffic. They are then in a better position to judge the wisdom of arranging their stores along similar lines.

FIGURE 6–3 **F. W. Woolworth store in Bethesda, Maryland** Maximum exposure of merchandise, ready accessibility, and height of fixtures permitting salespeople to view large areas and thus reduce pilferage are emphasized.

Courtesy: The Merchandiser/Magazine of Mass Retailing

□ Secure recommendations from outside sources

Recommendations of manufacturers from whom equipment, fixtures, materials, and merchandise have been or may be purchased are valuable guides in deciding upon the arrangement of the store's interior. These firms are well qualified to make suggestions based upon their experience in solving such problems and upon their researches in this field. Some of them, voluntary chain wholesalers and equipment manufacturers, for instance, have developed prototype layouts for stores of different sizes, which are available to the retailer. And a few have constructed small-scale model fixtures and equipment to enable the retailer to visualize exactly how his store will look. Because of their interest in selling store equipment, or in promoting the sale of the manufacturers' products, no charge is ordinarily made for these services.

☐ Locate selling and sales-supporting departments

In locating each particular selling and sales-supporting department the major considerations are as follows: (1) Providing the best possible service to customers based on their known buying habits; (2) establishing the most effective coordination of selling and sales-supporting activities; and (3) maximizing the selling area in relation to other functions. Their basic objective, of course, is to increase sales and minimize expenses.

Locating particular departments is commonly done through the preparation of diagrams or blueprints, because of the convenience afforded in visualizing relationships of departments and the ease with which plans may possibly be changed. It should be noted, however, that regardless of the care exercised in drafting the proposed layout, unless it is based on a well thought-out selling policy founded upon one's own experience or that of others, it may be doomed to failure. It is helpful, also, both in planning the layout and in judging its effectiveness, for the retailer to obtain the ideas and opinions of associates in whose judgment he has confidence.

A specific example How selling and sales-supporting departments in a department store may be placed in close proximity to each other is well illustrated in Figure 6–4. Designed to provide the maximum in economy and efficiency, the main feature of this arrangement is a "magic core" occupying 36,000 of the store's 297,000 square feet of floor space. Despite its size, customers are almost unaware of the core because it is partially hidden by display counters. Yet all the facilities for handling merchandise and customer traffic are present. Each of the three main shopping floors has two levels in the "magic core" and the upper one (the mezzanine) is connected with the floor on which the goods will be sold. Goods are carried by elevators to the mezzanine where they are checked and marked. Then they are sent to the appropriate stockroom on the same floor or delivered by chute to the level below.

Variations in space value within a store Wide variations in the value of space exist in different parts of the store with respect both to sections of a single floor and to floors, when more than one floor is occupied, a fact well known to management. Particularly in large stores, the equitable as-

FIGURE 6–4 **An illustration of the "magic core" of Famous-Barr's Southtown store in St. Louis, Missouri** A truck ramp leads to the basement platform (1), where goods are unloaded and later stored on various levels of the operating core (2), then fed to the various sales floors (3).

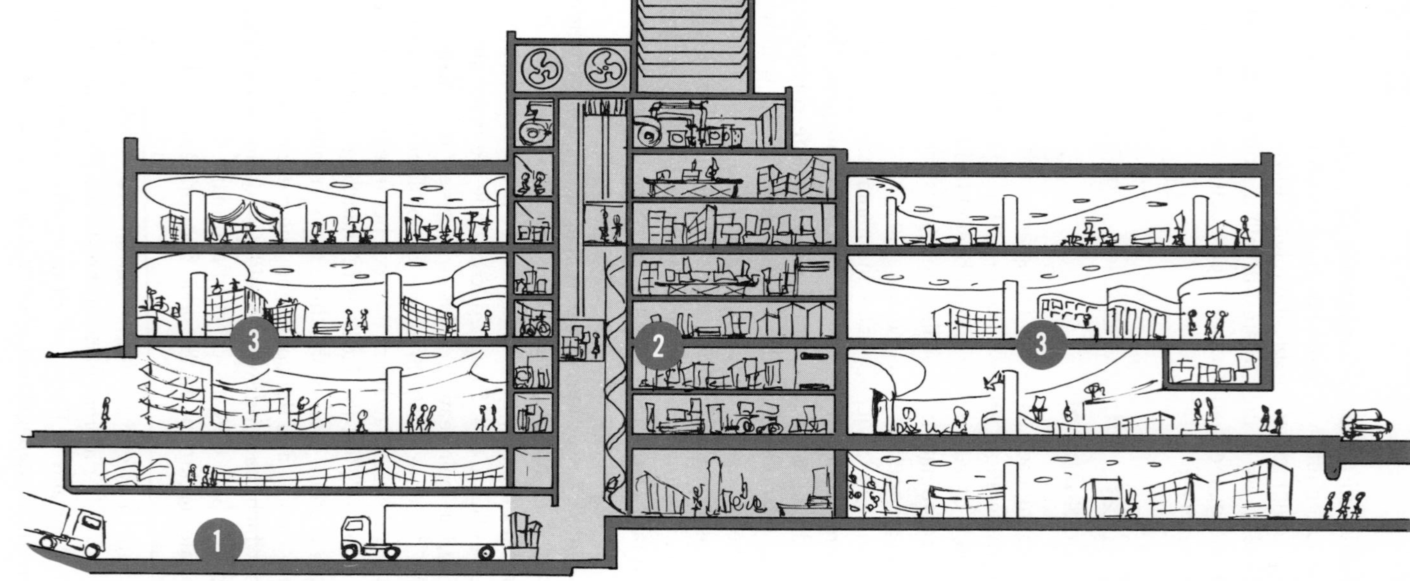

Courtesy: *Famous-Barr and* Business Week

signment of values to specific areas or sections is a continuing problem.[7] These values are based upon the management's estimate of the sales and profit possibilities of each area and thus are chiefly arbitrary in nature. Generally speaking, space charges decrease from the front to the rear of a one-story building and as one moves away from the traffic lanes. In multiple-story structures, the charges assigned to each floor decrease as the height of the floor increases; that is, space on the second floor is less valuable than space on the first, and so on.

□ Layout flexibility

Once the layout of the store has been decided, the problem is by no means permanently solved. As noted, even the original layout should give the retailer the maximum degree of flexibility to make future changes. Adjustments may also be necessary because of shifting seasonal demands, changes in buying habits and in tastes of customers, and new policies and practices of competitors. Or, it may be advisable to expand the areas where merchandise is growing in popularity and to shrink that devoted to items losing in customer acceptance. Furthermore, analysis of developments may dictate the conversion of certain departments or areas to self-service.[8] "Change is the order of the day" in retailing, and store layout is not exempted from this rule.

■ STORE LAYOUTS ILLUSTRATED

A suggested layout for a hardware store, reflecting consideration of the steps discussed, and intended primarily to stimulate the thinking of the retailer in arranging his store and afford the necesssary security against pilferage, is shown in Figure 6–5. The layout in Figure 6–6 shows the first three floors and basement of the five-floor F. W. Woolworth & Co. store in Boston, the company's largest. Figure 6–7 shows an effective layout used in a one-floor unit of Montgomery Ward & Company. Especially noteworthy is this layout's broad aisles which funnel store traffic in a pre-determined pattern for maximum merchandise exposure. Finally, Figure 6–8 provides a detailed plan of a supermarket revealing location of selling and nonselling departments and other facilities.

A comparison of the layouts in Figures 6–5 to 6–8 with those of other retailers will suggest that there is no ideal layout which will meet the needs of all stores handling the same kinds of merchandise. Local circumstances and individual preferences markedly influence the particular arrangement

---

[7] The allocation of rental charges to specific departments is discussed in Chapter 24.

[8] Cf. the discussion of self-service on pp. 143–47, below.

FIGURE 6–5 Layout of an "average" hardware store showing suggested control areas and devices

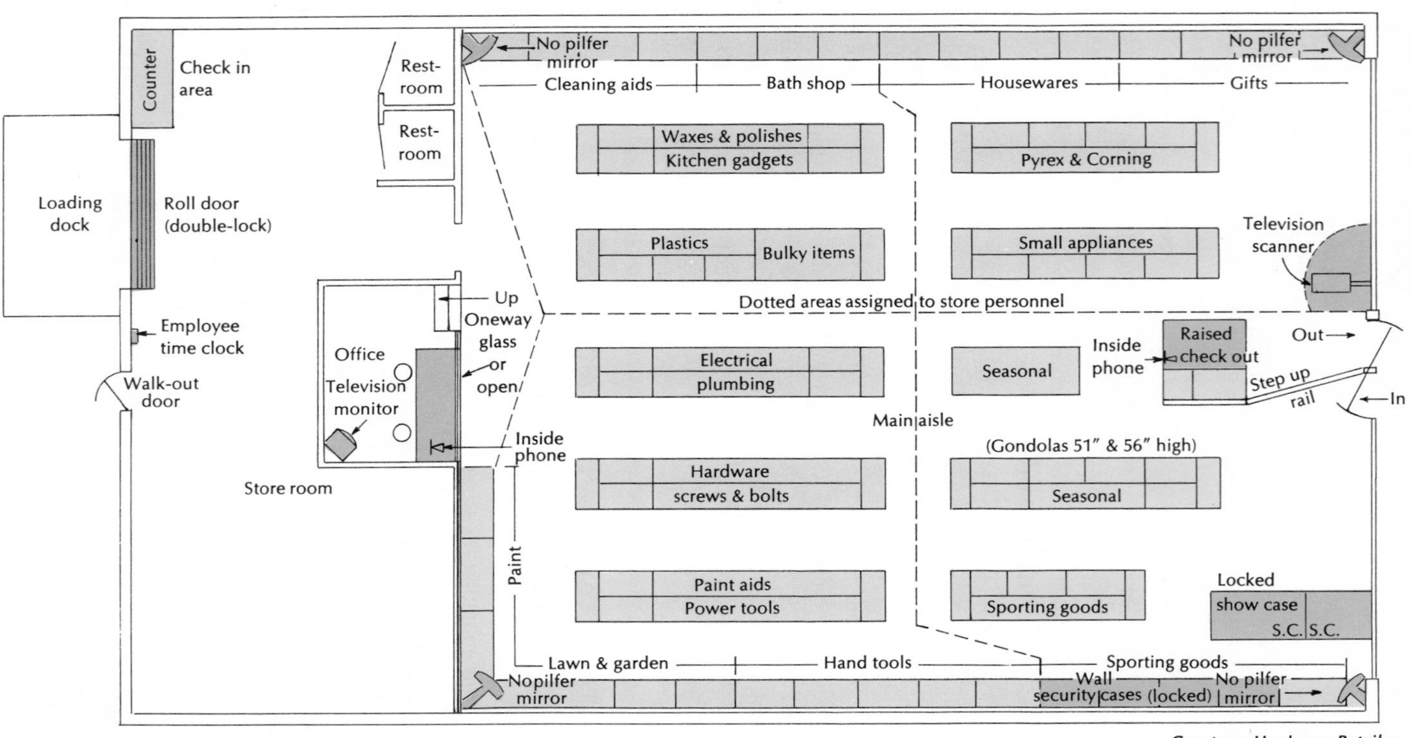

Courtesy: Hardware Retailer

FIGURE 6–6 **Layouts of three floors and basement of F. W. Woolworth Co.'s Boston store, largest in the chain with 133,400 square feet of space** The selling floors are topped by a four level 1,000 car-capacity parking garage.

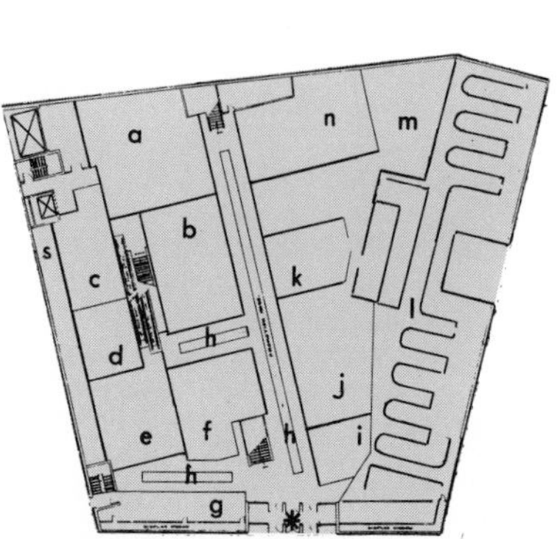

First floor. a- toiletries; b- cosmetics; c- handbags; d- hair goods; e- style accessories; f- jewelry; g- hosiery; h- promotional mdse.; i- novelties; j- candy; k- delicatessen; l- restaurant; m- stationery; n- gift shop; s- stockroom areas; *store entrance.

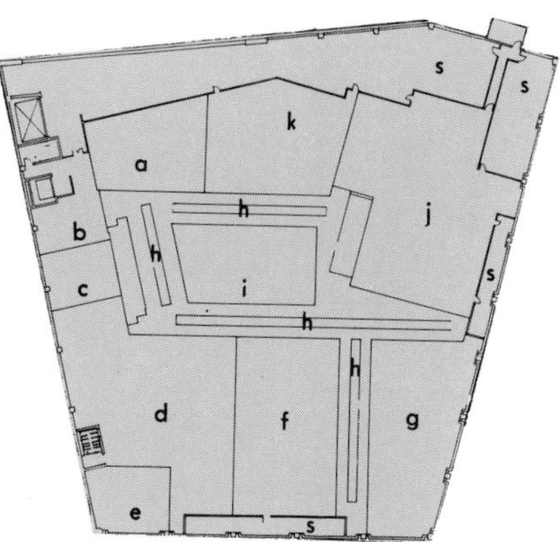

Second floor. a- music shop; b- plants; c- pet shop; d- toys, books, and games; e- hobby shop; f- fabric and sewing shop; g- bedding-bath-curtains; h- promotional merchandise; i- kitchen wares; j- home decor lines; k- household lines; and s- stock areas.

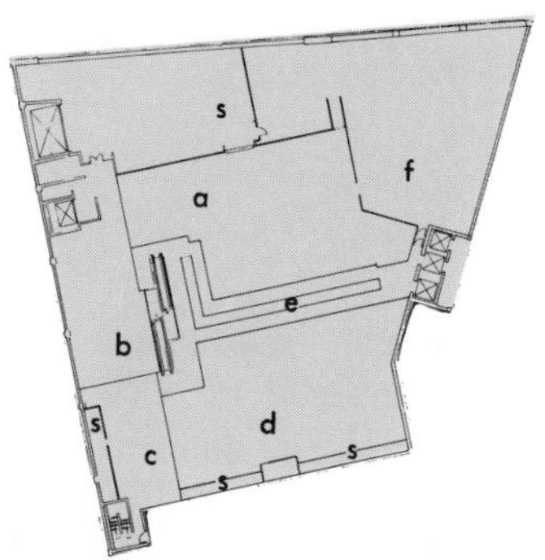

Third floor plan. a- sporting goods; b- tools and paints; c- men's and boys' shoes; d- men's and boys; e- promotion mdse.; f- offices and employees quarters; s- stockroom areas. (Main stock area located in sub-basement, not shown).

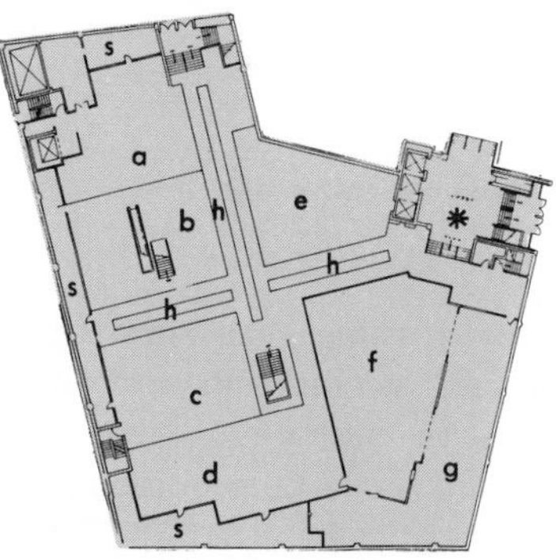

Basement. a- shoe dept.; b- ladies dept.; c- sportswear; d- infant's and toddler shop; e- intimate shop; f- restaurant; g- utilities; h- promotional merchandise; s- stockroom areas; *subway-level store entrance.

Courtesy: The Merchandiser/Magazine of Mass Retailing

FIGURE 6–7 A one-level Montgomery Ward & Company store located on a shopping center mall

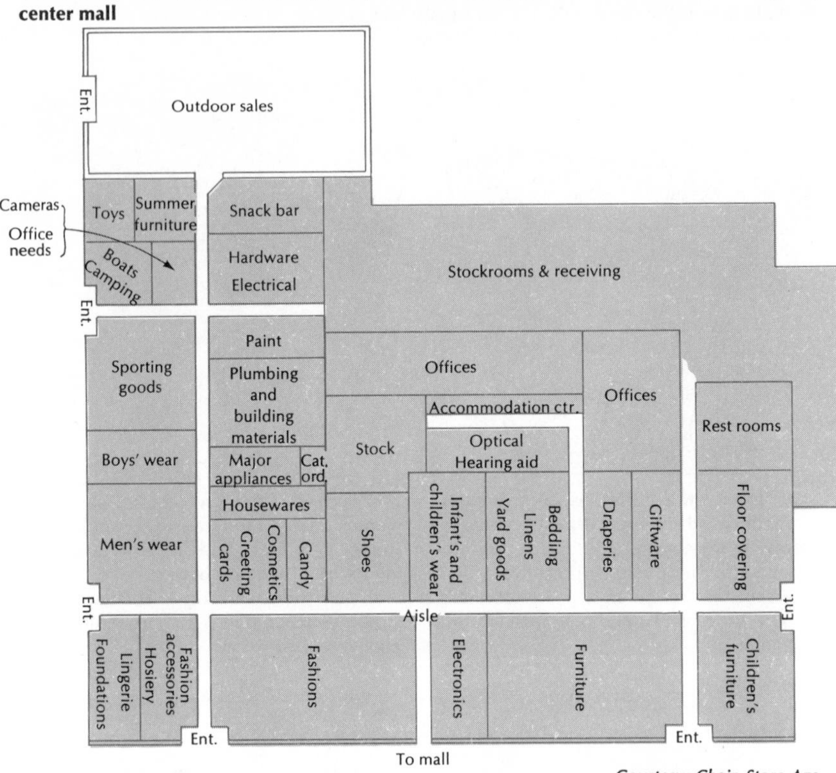

Courtesy: Chain Store Age

adopted. Some chain-store organizations, however, have adopted some standard layouts with a resulting economy in the cost of opening new stores. To illustrate, Colonial Stores have developed five different sizes of standardized layouts for food stores in the process of which all the steps we have mentioned were taken. Final decisions were made by a store-planning committee. These standardized arrangements are changed periodically to incorporate improvements and suggestions from store personnel.

■ DISPLAY: A MAJOR FACTOR IN LAYOUT

As already mentioned, layout may be considered a form of sales promotion. An effective layout facilitates sales from the point of view of both the customer and the store proprietor and display considerations are insep-

FIGURE 6–8 Detailed layout plan of a supermarket showing location of selling and nonselling facilities

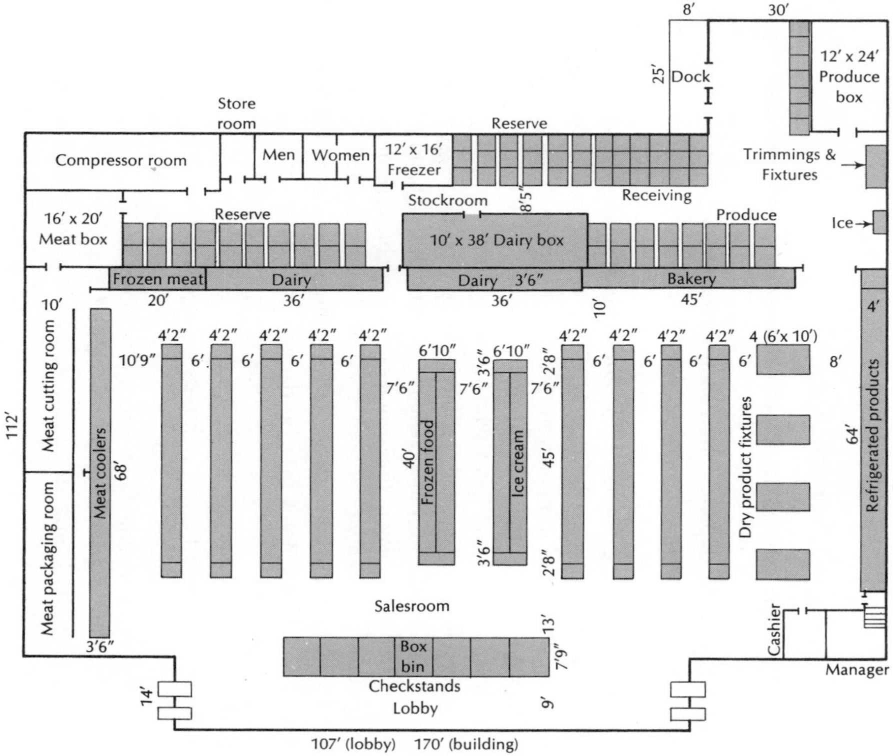

Facilities	This Layout		Type III Stand's	
Ground area		21,288 sq.ft		18/21,000 sq.ft.
Salesroom		14,200		
Total display		1,347 (L.f.)		
Product		144		
Dry	80		72/85	
Refrigerated	64		60/72	
Meat		68		56/72
Dry grocery		810		630/725
Bakery		45		30/45
Dairy		72		72
Freezer		208		165/200
Meat	20			
Ice cream	47			
Frozen foods	141			
Checkstands		6		4/8
Refrigerated storage		1,180 sq.ft.		
Freezer box	192			200
Dry box	380			408
Produce box	288			288
Meat box	320			320
Pallets		70		72
Grocery	56		58	
Produce	14		14	

Courtesy: Safeway Stores, Inc.

arable from layout. Display[9] means simply that goods are exposed to customers to facilitate observation, examination, and selection—and the way a store displays its merchandise has much to do with its sales volume. A study of over 300 shoppers in New York City department and specialty stores a few years ago revealed that about one-third of them entered these stores without any intention to buy. Attractive merchandise displays, however, induced over half of this group to make purchases.

Since most types of retail stores carry large assortments of merchandise, management is faced with problems concerning the amount of display and the kind of display to give certain items. These problems are not easy ones to solve, since, at some point, the variety of merchandise becomes confusing to the customer. In addition, retailers must decide on the best time and the length of time to display merchandise. As is true in other areas of responsibility, however, certain general rules are available for guidance.

□ Types of interior display

The primary purpose of interior display is to enhance sales and profit possibilities within the store; but the type of display for any specific item or group of items depends upon such characteristics as perishability, bulk, value, risk of breakage, packaging, danger to customers, attractiveness, seasonableness, and fashion. The significance of these factors can be demonstrated with a few examples from various kinds of merchandise, as follows: While cured meats can be openly displayed without special equipment, fresh meats demand refrigeration; passenger-car tires, which are bulky, may be displayed with little thought of the danger of theft, but pilferage is a consideration for small items which can be slipped into a pocket or handbag; valuable jewelry usually requires closed display cases; mechanical toys may be damaged if they are available for everyone to handle; packaging encourages open display in that it makes the merchandise more attractive and reduces the possibility of deterioration. Special precautions should be taken for items which create hazards: Poisons should be out of the reach of customers and heavy items may be dangerous if hung on display over store aisles. Unattractive items, such as bulk vinegar in a food store, may not even be placed on display. As for seasonableness and fashion, it is evident that the time factor and fashion rightness are decisive factors.

Display variations by type of store Wide differences exist among retail stores in planning their interior displays and in the frequency with which they are used to promote the sale of specific merchandise. Discount houses, food, and drug stores, for example, make extensive use of "merchandise islands" in their layouts—that is, tables, counters, cases, or a small

[9] Also cf. the discussion of "Interior Displays" in Chapter 18.

group of any or all of these—upon which merchandise is displayed and which are surrounded by adequate aisle space. Many of the display materials (racks, stands, signs) placed on these aisle tables are provided by merchandise resources. Shelves and racks are also used extensively to display wares with less-frequent use of closed display fixtures, such as cabinets or cases. The latter are commonly employed by department store and specialty shops. Jewelry stores, camera stores, and others handling expensive merchandise enclose their displays to provide the necessary protection.

Food stores place considerable emphasis upon displays as "silent salesmen"; upon the merits of "talking signs" which give convincing reasons for purchase; upon "mass displays" for the purpose of impressing the customer with the quantity of items sold at a particular price;[10] upon "dining-room" displays for delicatessen and dairy products; and upon the arrangement of merchandise items in a manner designed to induce customers to pick them up, as opposed to balanced symmetrical arrangements designed chiefly for decorative purposes.

Other types of retail stores are guided in their display problems by such considerations as the following: (1) The type of product, its value, size, and appeal to the buyer; (2) the purpose of the display, *i.e.*, the actual sale of the article or the creation of prestige or "atmosphere"; (3) suitable location; (4) attractiveness; (5) timeliness as related to seasonableness; and (6) desired frequency of change.[11] Originality and distinctiveness should continually be sought by most stores in order that they may be set apart from their competitors.

□ Exterior displays

Although some retailers have long made use of out-of-door displays—for example, food stores and the department stores of Sears, Roebuck and Co.—today there is also a strong trend for many other kinds of retailers to employ exterior displays. Branch department stores, many discount houses, the so-called home and garden stores, and supermarkets typically have their own parking areas which serve as locations for displays of lawn and garden supplies and tools; plants, shrubbery, grass, seeds, and weed killers; automobile tires and tubes; Christmas trees and other seasonal items. In general, such displays are rather crude, boxes of the merchandise being placed on the parking area surface or on plain tables. Frequently the display is unpro-

---

[10] Rearrangement of the display area of five produce departments resulted in a substantial increase in the percentage of produce sales to total store sales in one food store. Cf. D. L. Anderson and P. F. Shaffer, "Display Location and Customer Service in Retail Produce Departments," (Washington, D.C.: U.S. Department of Agriculture, Marketing Research Report No. 501, 1966), p. 1.

[11] These considerations and others are developed and illustrated in E. M. Mauger, *Modern Display Techniques* (New York: Fairchild Publications, Inc., 1965).

tected from the weather, although canopies—either canvas or permanent—are also being used. Figure 6–7 shows the location of the "outdoor sales" area of a Montgomery Ward & Company store.

Outside display offers such advantages as (1) inexpensive selling space, (2) opportunity to show additional merchandise in natural settings, (3) a place for bulky and untidy goods, (4) visibility to a greater number of potential customers, and (5) customer convenience, since much of this merchandise is not suited to shopping cart usage.

□ Aisle tables

We have noted that many retailers use "merchandise islands" in promoting the sale of certain articles. When tables are located in the main aisles of the store and used as islands, as is often done in department and specialty stores, they are referred to as "aisle tables."

Aisle tables may be used to display either regular or special merchandise. In a service store, they usually have a salesperson regularly assigned to each and a cash register is placed on or near the table. When tables are arranged in units of four in the form of squares and when merchandise is offered at reduced prices or at featured prices as a regular practice, they are known as "bargain squares." Some stores prefer the "Y" arrangement.

Whether or not a store uses aisle tables will depend largely upon the type or types of merchandise handled, upon the clientele to which the store caters, and upon the desire of the store management to avoid congestion in customer traffic, particularly during busy periods such as the holiday season.

■ SELF-SELECTION AND SELF-SERVICE

A major problem associated with store arrangement concerns the retailer's decision regarding the extent to which he will allow access to merchandise by customers and permit them to serve themselves, with aid being provided by sales help if needed. This decision obviously influences the entire layout of his store as well as the kind and amount of store equipment he purchases.

□ Definition of terms

When a store is operated on a *self-selection* basis, merchandise is so displayed and arranged that the customer can make her selection without the aid of a salesperson. Typically, open display shelves and tables are used, frequently supplemented by racks, stands, and islands. Once the selection is made, the merchandise is usually handed to a nearby salesperson, who takes the further steps necessary to complete the sale. This type of operation has long been characteristic of variety stores such as those operated by F. W. Woolworth and S. H. Kress although they have turned increasingly to self-service in recent years.

Under *self-service* operation the customer not only makes her selection, but brings the goods to a check-out stand where she makes payment and her purchases are wrapped or "sacked." Credit, delivery, and other special customer services commonly found in service stores ordinarily are not offered by the self-service store, since a low operating cost is one of its major goals. Although, technically speaking, the term "self-service store" should refer to one with all of its sales on this basis, many stores described by this name handle a substantial amount of business on a service basis. To illustrate: Many self-service discount stores provide salesperson service for jewelry, cameras and supplies, major appliances, and for bakery products, meats, and fruits and vegetables in their supermarket areas.

For some years it has become customary, especially among department and specialty store retailers, to speak of *simplified selling.* Within the scope of this term they include both self-selection and self-service—and much more, such as better fixtures, improved layouts, more effective packaging, displays which lead to increased sales, and techniques and devices to speed up sales transactions. So broad is this usage that, for present purposes, we shall limit our discussion to self-selection and self-service as defined above; however, we should recognize that where self-selection and self-service techniques are used, many of the other aspects of simplified selling are also involved.[12]

□ Historical development

Contrary to much current opinion, neither self-selection nor self-service operations are particularly new, especially the former. As mentioned, self-selection has long been used in variety stores. Moreover, for years the trend in stores of many types has been toward open displays which encourage self-selection. Yet self-selection has been widely adopted since World War II and today it is practiced in varying degrees by stores of practically all types.

In food stores The self-service plan of operation was employed by a few grocery stores in southern California at least as early as 1912. Immediately after World War I, the Piggly-Wiggly grocery stores began to expand on this basis. Moreover, there were some early successes in the ready-to-wear and drug fields; the S. Klein store in New York City and the Pay-Less Drug Stores on the Pacific Coast are good illustrations.

[12] Cf. the discussion of "Requirements for Self-Selection and Self-Service," below.

Despite this earlier development, as late as 1927 only two of the major food chains in the Los Angeles market—the area in which self-service first developed to any significant degree—used the self-service method. Consequently, we may conclude that it was during the depression of the early thirties, which also saw the development of the supermarket, that self-service became popular in the food field. As retailers sought ways to reduce their costs, they were naturally attracted by any method which would lower their payments for wages—the greatest single item in the cost of operating a store. The trend was further encouraged by the manpower shortage of World War II and by the "profit squeeze" of the 1960s. Today 79 percent of some 7,380 supermarkets surveyed by the Super Market Institute were found to be fully self-service in all four major departments—grocery, meat, produce and dairy—an increase of 10 percent since 1964.[13]

In other stores Following the success of self-service in food stores, and recognizing that "service" provided by the salespeople in many stores leaves much to be desired, self-service has been adopted by many kinds of stores handling a wide variety of merchandise and operating independently or as chains. Among those now offering self-service in some or all of their departments are department stores, discount houses, and stores selling drugs, variety merchandise, shoes, stationery, and home furnishings. To take a few specific illustrations: During 1969 Walgreen's, continuing its expansion and diversification program, added 53 new stores, most of which were self-service. Among these, its Globe Division ("Shopping Cities") consists of 16 full-line self-service department stores.[14] And in February 1971 the J. C. Penney Co. opened its fourth store designed for self-service shopping. Both general merchandise with ten check-out stands and a supermarket section with eight check-out locations were featured. In the stores operated by R. H. Macy & Company the basements have been almost completely converted to self-service and self-selection operations. Moreover, while retaining personal selling for major home appliances and higher-priced fashion merchandise, the trend is still in the direction of additional stores and departments on the self-service principle.

□ Requirements for self-selection and self-service

Experience with self-selection and self-service reveals that among the factors essential to success are the following:

---

[13] *The Super Market Industry Speaks 1970* (Chicago: The Super Market Institute, 1970), p. 22.

[14] *Walgreen's Annual Report 1969*, p. 7.

1. Sound merchandising decisions made in advance regarding the following: (a) the basic stocks to be carried with particular reference to styles, types, price lines, sizes, and colors; (b) the amount of space that will be required for each style, size, and price line; and (c) the extent to which feature items will be used and the importance that will be given to them.
2. Good fixturing. The merchandise to be stocked will govern the types of fixtures to be used. Sometimes good fixtures prove unsatisfactory because of improper use.
3. A layout which allows for, and encourages, the flow of customer traffic.
4. Adequate check-out facilities.[15]
5. Well-filled stocks and appropriate signs. Unbalanced stocks, poorly designed signs, and incorrect prices irritate customers and lose sales.
6. Attractive packages. Because competition for the customer's attention is strong under self-selection and self-service arrangements, attractive packages are essential.
7. Cooperation of personnel. When a shift to a self-service plan is contemplated, resentment within the department or store will be minimized if the personnel involved are kept fully informed.
8. Training of personnel in new duties. Particular emphasis should be placed on the need for proper coverage of the floor to provide satisfactory service to customers and to prevent pilferage, currently at an all-time high.

In general, arrangement of a store for self-selection or self-service operation is motivated by the same considerations which determine the layout of any store—that is, attractiveness and convenience from the customer point of view, exposure of merchandise for sale, and satisfactory sales volume and economical operation from the point of view of the retailer. But attainment of these goals is no easy matter and, whether a new store is being opened or the conversion of a service store into one providing less service is being weighed, the favorable and unfavorable elements of the self-selection and self-service plans should be studied carefully. So far as self-service is concerned, these elements, many of which are also applicable to self-selection, are summarized in the next two sections.

Merits of self-service operation The chief merits of self-service operation are as follows.

1. Generally speaking, stores arranged on the self-service plan have wider aisles with fewer obstructions, thus encouraging circulation of customers and minimizing congestion in customer traffic.

[15] The need to improve check-out operations is emphasized in "Checkouts Call for a Revolution," *Women's Wear Daily*, January 19, 1970, pp. 1, 13.

2. Many customers prefer self-service because it enables them to leisurely examine merchandise, make selections based upon their own judgment, and overcome their dependency on salespeople who may lack the courtesy and helpfulness expected.
3. Fewer salespeople and other personnel are required, thus reducing selling expenses and personnel problems.
4. Economies in operation make it possible to sell at lower prices than others and to appeal to customers on this basis.
5. Self-service arrangements permit larger and better displays of merchandise which, in turn, contribute to greater sales.
6. Customers of self-service stores purchase more at one time, both in amount and in variety, than patrons of other stores. This occurs because customers shop in a more leisurely manner and examine more merchandise and because self-service encourages impulse purchasing.

Limitations of self-service operation The publicity given to successful stores and departments using the self-service plan frequently has resulted in failure to consider the shortcomings of this type of operation, such as the following:

1. Since self-service arrangement requires more floor space for a given sales volume than the counter-service plan, the physical makeup of the store —its size, shape, and location—may not be adaptable to self-service.
2. Many customers prefer to be served by salespeople and dislike having to locate specific merchandise and bring it to the check-out counter.
3. The large sales volume of some stores creates congestion at check-out points, especially during rush periods. The result is both inconvenience for the customer and more errors by the check-out operators.[16]
4. Since self-service arrangement and operation are most successful in stores catering to middle- and low-income groups and offering well-known brands of packaged merchandise, retailers appealing to upper-income groups and selling unadvertised goods which are not customarily packaged find it difficult to operate profitably on the self-service plan.
5. Shoplifting and common thievery are easier and more prevalent in self-service stores, and consequently losses are greater. Presently, this is a problem of some magnitude.
6. Certain types of high-priced products such as mechanical durable goods, drug prescriptions, women's hats, and many other items, require the ad-

---

[16] One study some years ago disclosed that errors were made on 11.3 percent of all the items "rung up" by the check-out operators of food stores, the final result being an undercharge equal to .7 percent of sales. Cf. E. M. Harwell, *Checkout Management* (New York: Chain Store Age Publishing Co., 1963), p. 7.

vice and service of salespeople. Nevertheless, the experience of discount houses reveals that many customers like to serve themselves even when buying such items as shoes, dresses, and millinery.

7. An impersonal atmosphere is common in the large self-service store and the shopper may fail to develop any emotional attachment or loyalty toward it.

□ Future prospects

The recent tremendous increase in self-selection and self-service seems likely to continue in the foreseeable future. Moreover, further improvements in techniques will undoubtedly be developed. To illustrate, one of the present serious problems of self-service operations is that the shopper must bring purchases to the check-out point. In this process, pilferage takes place, merchandise is damaged, customer time is involved and fatigue results. Yet many stores are taking these risks to reduce the substantial payroll costs that service by salespeople involve. Even prestige stores are adopting it.[17] One authority, however, is convinced that mechanization will eventually make it unnecessary for the shopper to bring purchases to a check-out point.[18]

All conversions to self-selection and self-service, however, are not—and will not be—successful. Despite the care with which they are planned, conditions in every case may not be suited to such methods of operation. A case in point is the experience of Famous-Barr Company in St. Louis. A few years ago check-out merchandising operations were instituted on an experimental basis in the basements of three stores. Discontinued two months later, management reported the check-out failed because of (1) the high fashion level of much of the merchandise, (2) the large share of "big ticket" items sold, and (3) inability to handle efficiently the large number of transactions on peak days.

The future of self-selection and self-service will depend mainly upon (1) the continued willingness of customers to serve themselves in return for the savings they realize on their purchases; (2) improvements in fixtures, displays, and package design that will enable customers to locate and examine desired items more easily; and (3) the conviction of retail store management that these methods afford excellent opportunities to increase sales, reduce expenses, and alleviate some of their problems in the existing profit squeeze.

---

[17] Cf. "Prestige Store Goes Self-Service," *Chain Store Age* (Executives Edition), September 1968, p. 50.

[18] Cf. E. B. Weiss, "Robot Retailing Inches Along," *Advertising Age*, April 5, 1965, pp. 131–32.

REVIEW AND DISCUSSION QUESTIONS

1 Explain concisely the major factors which influence the layout of a specific store.

2 Assume that you are planning to construct a new store. Precisely, how would you proceed to determine your space requirements for layout purposes?

3 What do you consider to be the major problems regarding layout facing departments stores today? Compare these problems with another type of retailer of your own choosing and preferably in your own community.

4 Visit a branch store in or near your local community and compare its layout with the main or parent store of the company which owns it. Give special attention to location of specific departments, size of space devoted to particular merchandise, width of aisles, and use of displays.

5 Discuss the relationship of store display to layout.

6 Explain carefully how the type of display employed by a store depends upon each of the following: value of the item, bulk of the item, perishability, staple or impulse character of the item, hazards, packaging, and profitability.

7 Compare and contrast the interior displays typical of self-service food stores with those of department or specialty stores.

8 Distinguish among self-selection, self-service, and simplified selling. Explain the factors responsible for the growth of these methods in recent years.

9 Discuss briefly the basic requirements of a successful self-service operation. Appraise a local self-service store in the light of these requirements.

10 Visit two types of retail stores (*i.e.*, supermarket, department store, furniture store) in your local area and review their layouts. Suggest what changes you believe would be desirable to improve customer convenience and probably lead to increased patronage and higher profits. State your reasons.

PART IV

Retail organization

chapter 7

STRUCTURE OF THE RETAIL FIRM

Every business has to have a structure or organization to perform its work. The structure or organization of a retail firm will vary with such factors as size, kinds of merchandise sold, services rendered, and preferences and desires of the executives. But the organization plan for any retail business—a three-man company with little division of labor or a giant enterprise with thousands of specialists—must be designed to meet the company's individual needs and requirements. Moreover, an organization plan that was satisfactory at one point in a firm's history may be unsuitable at a later date; the structure must be flexible enough to meet changes in fundamental conditions.

This chapter, therefore, (1) discusses the meaning of "organization," (2) examines the various structures that retailers have developed to meet their specific needs, and (3) notes some major trends in retail organization.

THE MEANING OF "ORGANIZATION"

Organization has been defined in various ways.[1] One expert describes organization as ". . . the framework within which work takes place; its

[1] Our discussion here is concerned with organization for *operation,* or *administra-*

major function is to facilitate work."[2] Another analyst considers organization as a process that includes: "(1) breaking down the work necessary to achieve the objective into individual jobs and (2) providing means of coordinating the efforts of the jobholders."[3] Still other authorities include personnel selection as a part of organization.

Probably the most useful approach for our purposes is to define "organization" in terms of its component parts. Using this approach, we may say that organization involves four aspects, as follows:

1. Arranging the activities that the retailer has decided to perform in convenient groups for assignment to specific individuals.[4]
2. Providing for the selection of the personnel to whom the activities will be assigned.
3. Assigning responsibility for each group of activities and determining the authority that is to go with the responsibility.
4. Providing for control of and harmonious adjustment among the individuals to whom responsibilities are assigned.

This chapter discusses three of these four aspects of organizational structure, while personnel selection is among the topics considered in the next chapter.

□ Organization charts

The preparation of a written or printed organization chart is an important step in planning or revising the firm's structure, since drawing the plan on paper exposes inconsistencies, forces clear thinking, and encourages logical arrangement. The organization chart shows the relationship of functions within the firm and helps everyone visualize the company as a whole. Montgomery Ward & Co.'s organization manual aptly describes the value of carefully prepared organization charts:

A company's success and progress are in great measure related to the efficient utilization of the efforts of its management representatives. To achieve success we must adhere to a plan which clearly establishes areas of responsibility and lines of author-

---

tive purposes. For detailed discussion of the concept of *legal form of organization* (in other words, use of single proprietorship, partnership, and corporate forms of ownership) consult any standard business organization or business finance textbook.

[2] Douglas C. Basil, *Managerial Skills for Executive Action* (New York: American Management Association, Inc., 1970), p. 53.

[3] Ernest Dale, *Management: Theory and Practice*, 2d ed. (New York: McGraw-Hill Book Co., Inc., 1969), p. 178.

[4] The *selection* of the particular activities which a specific retailer will undertake —for example, credit extension, comparison shopping, and delivery service—is a matter of *policy*, not of organization.

ity within the company's structure. To provide complete understanding and consistent interpretation, it is necessary that this organization plan, by which the company operates, be set forth in writing.

[Our] charts and accompanying [job] descriptions mirror the plan for guiding and controlling the activities of the business. . . .

It is essential that you be completely knowledgeable about your authority and responsibility. It is also important that you know the functions, responsibility and authority vested in other management positions. . . .

You are expected to become familiar with this manual. In so doing, you will be better able to view your individual activities in relation to all Company activities. You will be better able to visualize how your specific actions affect other segments of the business and the attainment of Company objectives, and how your own areas of responsibility are affected by the actions of other managers.[5]

Although organization charts are highly useful for all types of retailers, and particularly so for the larger ones, some of their limitations must also be recognized. An organization chart should not be mistaken for an organization. A firm may have a fine-appearing chart and still fail to function effectively. A business organization is a group of human beings; attention must be paid to their individual personalities as well as to the formal relationships shown on the chart. Members of different departments must constantly work together and cooperate in handling joint problems and activities without referring every question to their individual superiors as shown on the chart. And, as indicated below, organization charts must be revised frequently in fast-moving, everchanging businesses such as retailing.

□ Need for flexibility in organization

The organizational task is never completed. Different structural patterns may be required as the firm adds or drops activities, as the number of branch stores changes, or as the relative importance of different merchandise lines change. The firm's management may discover a better way of grouping present activities, or become convinced that the business will function better if the lines of authority are shifted. The idea of a "plural" chief executive was unknown a few years ago, yet a number of firms now divide the chief executive's functions among two or three individuals who operate as a "team."[6]

But the fact that the organization plan probably will have to be changed in the future never eliminates the need for careful preparation of the current

[5] Montgomery Ward Organization Manual (June 1970), courtesy: Montgomery Ward & Co., Inc.

[6] Samuel Feinberg, "Top Management Teams Grow for Future Needs," *Women's Wear Daily*, November 4, 1969, p. 17; and "Macy's Top Management Gets Major Realignment," *New York Times*, January 14, 1971, pp. 53, 57.

structure. Good organization defines the relationships of the various departments, specifies each unit's authority and function, determines responsibility for the various objectives of the firm, encourages specialization of effort and the development of skill in particular tasks, facilitates planning, reduces waste effort, and increases productivity.[7]

SMALL STORE ORGANIZATION

The structural requirements and organizational problems of small stores differ greatly from the organizational characteristics of the large retail businesses.

The term "small store" covers a variety of establishments that ranges from the one-man newsstand, the gasoline service station with several attendants, and the neighborhood grocery store to more complex businesses that employ a fairly large number of people. We will use the term to indicate stores that are too small to be divided into separate departments.[8]

The small retailer usually carries on fewer activities than his large competitor: He may provide fewer services; often carries a narrower variety of merchandise; may have a more limited advertising program or none at all; and probably uses less elaborate planning techniques. Consequently he can have a much simpler organizational structure.

Moreover, there will be much less specialization of labor in the small store. In the one-man store, all aspects of organization center around the question: How can the store owner best plan *the use of his own time?* And even where there are several employees, each will be expected to perform a wider range of duties than is customary in the large establishment. In contrast, the large retailer must assign specific responsibilities to many different persons, determine each one's authority, and provide for harmonious adjustment of all the different parts of the business.

Figure 7–1 illustrates the restricted activities and limited specialization typically found in small stores.[9] It shows the organization of a store employing four persons in addition to the proprietor. Although the organizational plan shown in Figure 7–1 is very simple in structure, it provides all three aspects of organization discussed in this chapter: It groups the firm's activities for assignment; it assigns authority to employees and fixes responsibility for carrying out activities; and it provides—in the person of the proprietor

[7] Wilbur B. England, *The Purchasing System* (Homewood, Ill.: Richard D. Irwin, Inc., 1967), pp. 133–34.

[8] The small department store (a large establishment in comparison to the stores mentioned above) is discussed below, on pp. 159–60, along with other types of departmentalized stores.

[9] Comparison of Figures 7–2 and 7–3 will demonstrate the way activities tend to increase with store size.

FIGURE 7–1 **Organization of a small store**

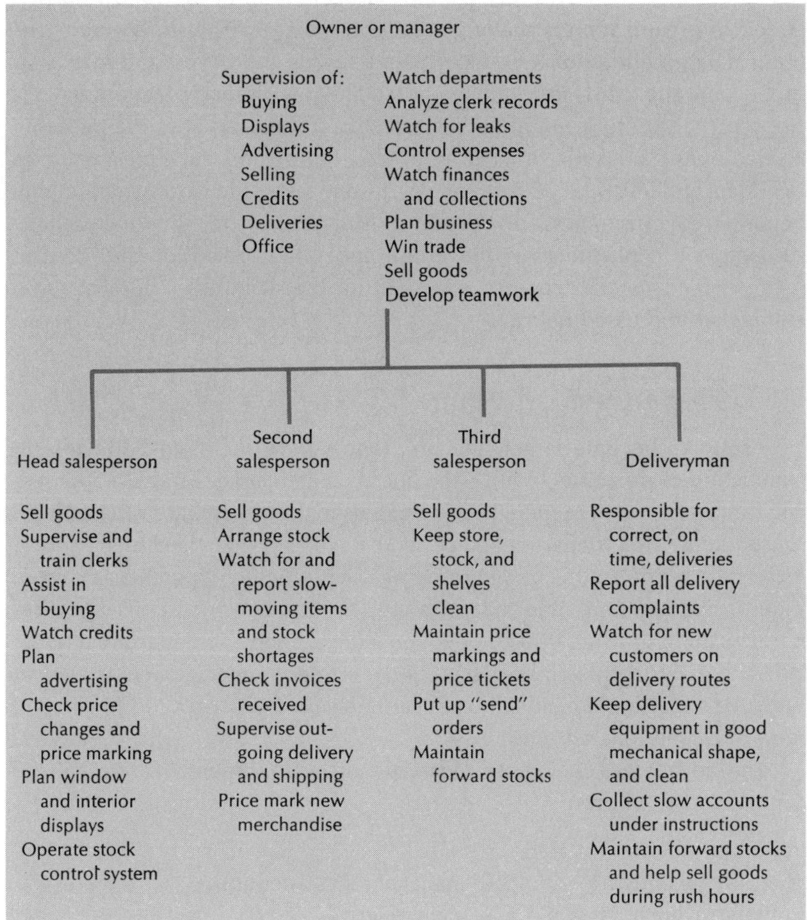

himself—a means of control and of making any necessary adjustments among the store's personnel.

■ ORGANIZATION IN THE LARGER FIRM

In larger firms, such as department stores and chain stores, the problem of organization relates primarily to the variety of merchandise handled, the numerous functions performed, the specialization of personnel, and the need for coordination and control of all the activities required to accomplish the firm's objectives. We should particularly note the following two aspects of organization in the large retail business: (1) The store's merchandise is divided into groups or departments so that the buyers and sales staff can become specialists in handling particular types of goods. Departmentalization can be useful even in fairly small stores;[10] it is an absolute necessity in large ones. (2) As the firms grow in size, the owners and top executives spend less and less time performing day-to-day tasks, such as buying, selling, preparing advertisements, or designing displays. Instead, they increasingly concentrate on planning for the future and on coordination and control of the executives and workers who perform the daily tasks. Both of these features are discussed below.

□ Departmentalization

As stores become larger, the proprietors have increasing difficulty in maintaining close contact with each line of merchandise, and become less able to locate (and eliminate) the weak spots in their merchandising activity. Consequently they departmentalize, that is, they divide their merchandise into a number of groups or departments, each of which operates as a more or less separate unit. Information about the store's operations becomes more meaningful when broken down on a department-by-department basis; and each department can be placed under a middle-management executive (buyer or department head) who concentrates on that merchandise line and perhaps closely related ones.

The advantages of logical and systematic departmentalization can be summarized as follows:

Profitable lines are revealed.
Unprofitable lines are brought to management's attention.
Profitable average margin can be maintained.
Margins can be easily adjusted on each kind of merchandise.
Necessary markup can be computed for each line.
Inventory is more easily controlled.
Stockturn is increased.
Responsibility is more easily assigned among personnel.
Salespeople can be assigned by departments and specialize on selling a line of merchandise.
Specific assignment of responsibility to salespeople gives them a greater incentive to work and to take a greater interest in the business.

---

[10] "Why Departmentalization Is a Prime Industry Need during the '70's," *Hardware Retailer,* October 1969, pp. 82–84.

"Leaks" and losses are more easily located and checked.
Customers can more easily find what they are seeking.
Management is simplified.
Any part of the business can be checked at any time.
Better control is possible over each part of the business.
Larger profits are obtained.

Steps in departmentalizing The following steps are usually followed in departmentalizing the store:

1. The merchandise is divided into well-defined and related groups.
2. A decision is made as to the number of departments and the groups of merchandise assigned to each department. The number depends upon the size of the store and the variety of goods handled, but each department usually handles a complete line or two or more related smaller lines. Creating too many departments is a mistake that should be carefully avoided.
3. Each department is assigned a definite location within the store. The customers' buying habits, the types and kinds of merchandise involved, and the size and shape of the available space influence the selection of locations.[11]
4. Henceforth, many of the store's records are kept on a department-by-department basis and the business results of each department are analyzed separately:
   (a) Each department is charged with its direct expenses, such as the wages of its own sales staff. Indirect expenses, such as rent, light, heat, and power, are often allocated to the various departments on some reasonable and equitable basis.[12]
   (*b*) The gross margin—the difference between merchandise cost and net sales—that each department obtains is recorded. Different margins will be realized on various items in a department, but the department head will try to sell a satisfactory amount of high-margin merchandise in order to increase his (operation's) profit or minimize any loss.
   (c) Purchases, returns to vendors, sales, price reductions and customer returns are recorded on a departmental basis.

Regrouping merchandise lines Although departmentalization is helpful to almost all stores and necessary in the larger ones, it also creates problems. The customer who needs a set of items for a particular purpose may

[11] Cf. the discussion of "Regrouping Merchandise Lines," below.

[12] Methods of allocating expenses to departments are discussed in Chapter 24, "Expense Control: A Requisite of Profitable Operation."

be forced to trudge through many different departments to get everything he or she wants. To illustrate: A ski enthusiast may want to buy a pair of skis (normally sold in sporting goods), stretch ski pants (men's or women's sportswear), ski hose (hosiery), and an overnight case (luggage). Many stores are now bringing all of these items and other related products together in ski shops, so as to provide better service and make shopping easier for the customer. Similarly, large stores have developed cruise shops, sports shops, gun shops, bath shops, junior miss shops and many other types of specialized sections to match customer interests.

But this regrouping in terms of customer interests creates its own problems and disadvantages. First, different customers buy similar items for different purposes. Some customers may buy small electrical appliances for use as wedding or anniversary presents and would be best served if the appliances were in the gift shop, where they could be compared with alternative gifts such as pottery or tableware. Other customers, who are purchasing the appliances for their own use, expect to find them in the appliance department. Similarly, the overnight case, mentioned in the illustration above, might be sold to someone going on a ski trip, to a college student going back to school, or to a traveling salesman for business use. Yet the store will have excess inventory if it tries to maintain complete assortments of suitcases in the ski shop, in the college shop, in the cruise shop, and in the luggage department.

Another problem is an organizational one. Will the ski-shop personnel purchase the skis, stretch pants, ski hose, and overnight case, or will the regular sporting goods, men's wear, hosiery, and luggage buyers (each of whom is a specialist in his line) handle the buying? Stores are experimenting with both plans; no one has yet found a perfectly satisfactory system.

□ General management

In the large retail organization, as we have already noted, the top executives devote their time and efforts to performing general management's major function, that of providing leadership and direction for the firm, while their subordinates oversee the day-to-day operations of the business. The prime obligations of general management are: (1) To formulate and announce basic policies; (2) to direct, correlate and coordinate the activities of the various divisions, so that the business operates effectively and profitably; (3) to make decisions (subject to approval by the board of directors) concerning the firm's future growth and expansion; and (4) to represent the business in major civic, social, and public activities. The proprietor or head of a small store can spend only a part of his time on these functions, but the chief executives and general management of a large enterprise can give these responsibilities their full attention.[13]

DEPARTMENT STORES

Although there are many similarities in the organizational problems and structures of the two major types of large retail businesses, (1) department and departmentalized specialty stores and (2) chain stores, there are also some differences between them. Consequently, in the paragraphs that follow, we will first study department store organization and then turn to the special characteristics of chain stores. We should note, however, that in recent years the growth of suburban branches[14] and other factors have caused many department store firms to adopt some of the features of chain store organization.

The larger department store businesses, which produce by far the major share of total department store sales volume, have all the elements of large-scale retailing: wide range of activities, departmentalization, many staff functions, intensive specialization of labor, and all operating duties located below the general management level. In contrast, the small department store has at least one similarity to other small establishments: The general manager often takes direct charge of either merchandising or operating activities.

The small department store

Small department stores often use a two-function plan that separates such operating activities as store maintenance, adjustments, and deliveries, from the merchandising tasks of buying and selling. Figure 7–2 shows this organizational structure.[15] This plan also provides for two staff officers, a combination treasurer-controller and a personnel director, who report directly to the general manager or proprietor. These two officers have store-wide duties; placing them in staff positions permits them to carry out their activities without interfering with the line executives' day-to-day operating functions.

The organization plan shown in Figure 7–2 is well suited to the small

[13] Cf. the further discussion of the coordinating functions of general management in Chapter 26, "Coordination and Retailing Management."

[14] Cf. the discussion of branch store organization, pp. 166–67, below.

[15] The specific responsibilities of the merchandising-sales promotion director and the store operations director are discussed at greater length in connection with the description of large store organization, pp. 162–65 below.

FIGURE 7–2 **Two-function organization chart for a small department store**

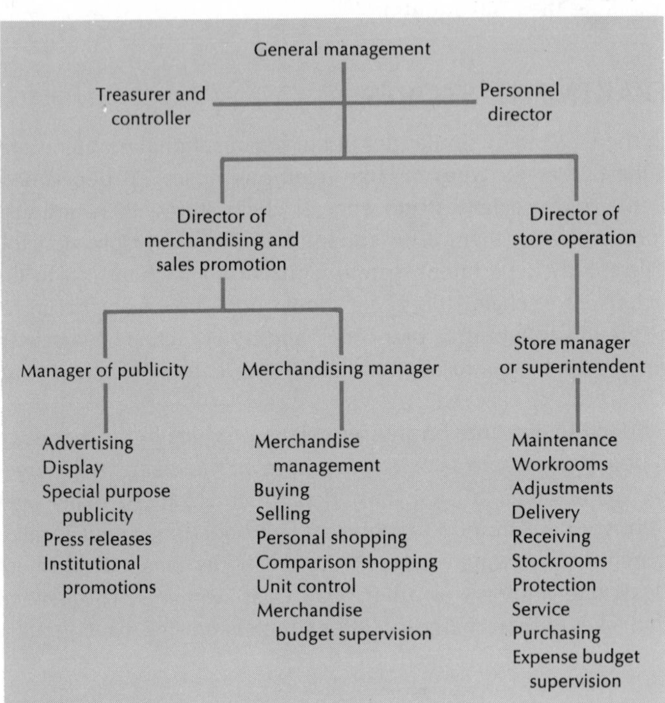

department store. It is simple and uncomplicated, yet it establishes a desirable degree of specialization. It permits the personnel director to function on a store-wide basis; it centralizes responsibility for control activities in the treasurer-controller; and it unifies buying and selling activities. The specialized publicity manager reports directly to the director of merchandising and sales promotion, so that publicity work is closely integrated with the whole merchandising process.

□ Four function or Mazur Plan

Many medium-sized and large department stores use a four-function plan, illustrated in Figure 7–3, that divides the store's activities into the following groups: (1) Merchandising, (2) publicity, (3) store management or operations, and (4) accounting and control. This widely accepted organizational structure is often called the Mazur Plan in honor of its proponent,

FIGURE 7–3 The four-function organization chart of a department store

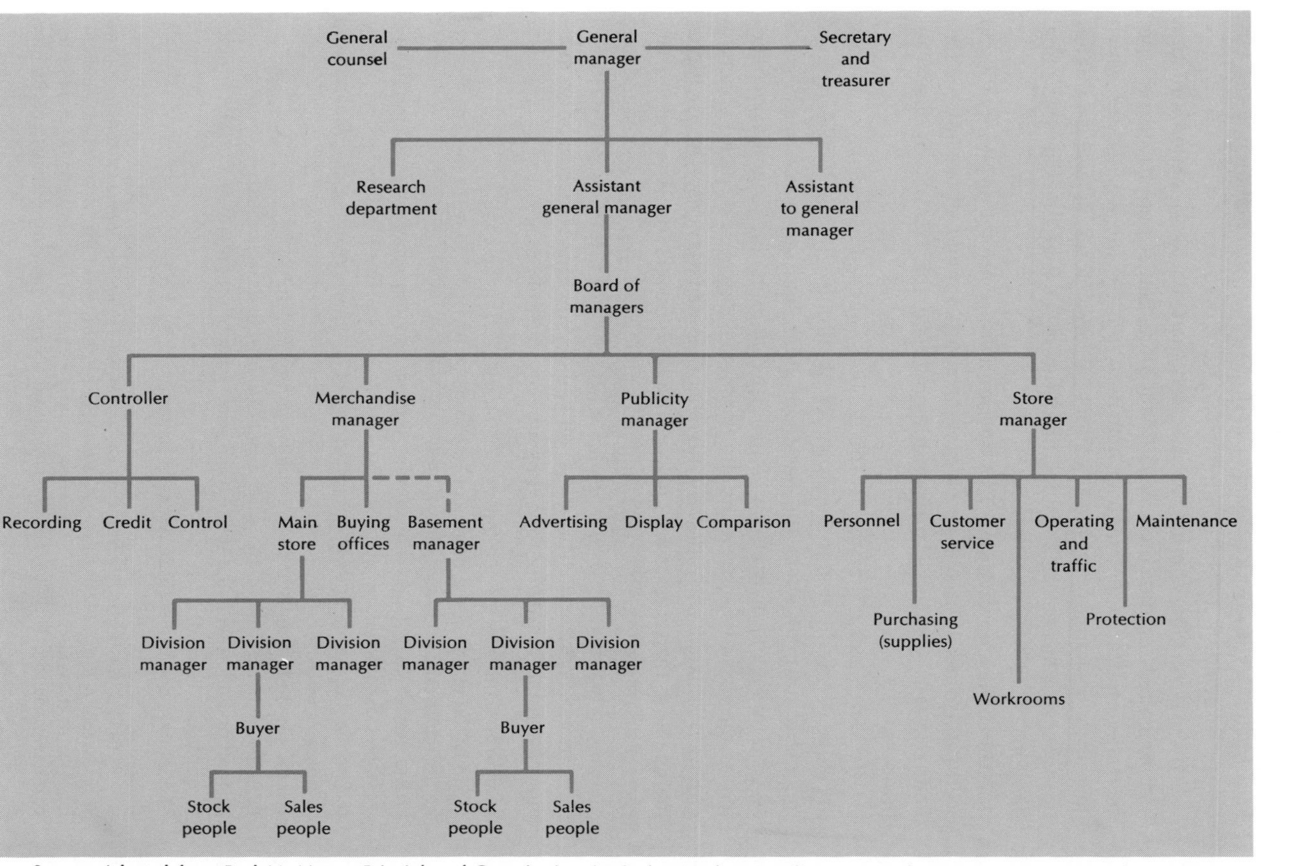

Source: Adapted from Paul M. Mazur, *Principles of Organization Applied to Modern Retailing* (New York: Harper & Bros., 1927), frontispiece.

Paul Mazur, an investment banker and chairman of a National Retail Dry Goods Association special committee on store organization.[16]

The Mazur Plan is more complicated than the two-function structure recommended for the small department store, but it permits greater specialization and a wider range of activities. It has some weaknesses which have lead to changes and modifications in some stores, as discussed later; but first we will analyze the specific duties of each of the four traditional divisions.

Merchandising division This division is responsible for all buying and selling activities. It usually receives the greatest amount of executive attention, since its functions are considered to be the "heart" of the retail business.

1. Merchandise managers The general merchandise manager, who is in charge of this division, supervises merchandising activities in all locations, including the main store, the basement store, and buying offices.[17] He is assisted by several divisional merchandise managers, their number depending on the size of the store and the number of departments, who supervise groups of related and adjacent merchandise departments. The divisional merchandise managers work closely with their buyers (or department managers), coordinating the departments, guiding the buyers' merchandising plans, and helping the buyers evaluate present and future merchandise and sales trends. More specifically, the general and divisional merchandise managers have the following functions and responsibilities:

a) Interpret and execute the merchandising policies of the company.
b) Unify the efforts of all buyers or department managers so as to present a single "image" to the buying public.
c) Aid buyers to get and use current information regarding business trends and market conditions.
d) Provide the buyer with an objective point of view regarding his department's operation.
e) Establish and administer a merchandise control system.
f) Assist each department in planning and carrying out its individual buying plans.
g) In cooperation with the publicity or sales promotion division, plan sales promotions.
h) Supervise departmental activities of buyers.

---

[16] Cf. P. M. Mazur, *Principles of Organization Applied to Modern Retailing* (New York: Harper & Bros., 1927). Also cf. the excellent discussion of the Mazur Plan and modifications of it by R. C. Bond, "Department Store Organization," in National Retail Merchants Association, *The Buyer's Manual,* 4th ed. (New York: The Association, 1965), p. 11–22.

[17] The basement store typically operates as a separate unit with its own merchandise manager and buying staff. Some stores refer to the basement store as the "Budget Floor," while others designate it as the "Downtairs Store" or "The Store of Lower Prices." Increasingly basements are being used for self-selection, check-out operations.

i) Assist buyers in locating and developing new resources.
j) Plan and supervise comparison shopping (unless assigned to the publicity division).[18]

2. *Buyers or department managers* Under the Mazur Plan, the buyers have major responsibility for buying and selling activities within their departments and consequently are very important individuals in the merchandising operation. Their buying duties generally include preparing preliminary merchandise plans or budgets under the guidance of the divisional merchandise manager; making contacts with manufacturers, wholesalers, and other sources of merchandise; studying fashion trends and price movements; obtaining proper qualities and grades of merchandise in styles suited to the customers' tastes; securing deliveries of merchandise at the proper times; and making purchases at prices which permit resale at a desired markup.

The buyer's responsibilities for selling activities include: Planning the number of salespeople needed for his department; determining their qualifications; and, in cooperation with the personnel department, maintaining the proper size selling force at all times. He gives the salespeople information about the merchandise he has purchased and about fashion trends in general. He supervises the department closely; cooperates in the preparation of merchandise displays; and does everything possible to insure customer satisfaction and the profitability of department operations.

But the buyer does not have sole responsibility for sales efforts, even under the four-functional plan. Problems often arise because the selling function is actually divided among three major divisions: The merchandising division, as indicated; the publicity division, with its advertsing and display efforts; and the store management division, which is responsible for recruiting and maintaining a satisfactory sales force. The growth of branch stores, which often extends the department's sales efforts to a number of remote locations, also makes it difficult for the buyer to be an effective sales manager. Consequently, as discussed later in this chapter, many stores are now changing or reducing the buyer's responsibilities for sales activities.

Publicity division The publicity, or sales promotion and advertising, division is responsible for all selling efforts not classified as personal selling. Specifically, its responsibilities include:

1. All forms of advertising.
2. Window displays.
3. Interior displays, usually excluding counter displays.
4. The planning and executing of sales-promotion events, in cooperation with the merchandising division.

[18] This list is based on that developed by E. J. Brown in his chapter on "The Merchandising Division" in *The Buyer's Manual, op. cit.*, pp. 29–30.

5. Special forms of sales promotion, such as fashion shows and educational exhibits.
6. Advertising research.
7. Public relations.
8. Comparison shopping (unless assigned to the merchandising division).

The publicity or advertising manager, who heads this division, works with the personnel department to recruit, train, and maintain an adequate advertising and display staff. He supervises the methods used in special forms of sales promotion and tries to devise special events that are more interesting and effective than his competitors'. And he reviews his plans and programs with top management to make certain that all forms of publicity conform to store policy. Top management decisions govern, for example, the size of his budget and the extent to which he will use purely institutional advertising. And, moreover, he must work very closely with the merchandising division. Because such close cooperation is necessary, many stores make the publicity division virtually subordinate to the key merchandising executive.

Store management or operating division This division, headed by the store manager or store superintendent, covers a greater variety of activities than any other. In fact, it is usually responsible for all activities not directly associated with buying, selling, accounting or financial control. Its duties have actually increased over the years as it absorbed functions the other divisions refused to assume.

The store manager is usually responsible for the following functions:

A. Store maintenance.
   1. Construction.
   2. Repairs and renovations.
   3. Maintenance of mechanical equipment.
   4. Ventilation, including air conditioning.
   5. Heat, light, and power.
   6. Janitor service.
B. Customer service.
   1. Adjustment bureaus.
   2. Service superintendents.
   3. Floor service supervisors.
   4. Personal service bureaus.
C. Operating activities.
   1. Receiving, checking, and marking.
   2. Stock rooms.
   3. Warehouses.
   4. Shipping rooms.

5. Deliveries.
6. Returned goods.

D. Purchasing of store supplies, equipment, and other property.
1. Supplies needed for store use.
2. Fixtures and equipment of all kinds.
3. Fuel.

E. Store and merchandise protection.
1. Special service operators.
2. Night watchmen.
3. Service shopping.
4. Outside protection agencies.
5. Insurance (in cooperation with control division or treasurer).

F. Personnel.[19]
1. Employment.[20]
2. Training.
3. Compensation.
4. Health and welfare.
5. Employment stabilization.

G. Workrooms.
1. Cost departments, such as restaurants, soda fountains, beauty shops, and drapery workrooms.
2. Manufacturing departments, such as candy and ice-cream making, and bakeries.
3. Expense workrooms, such as laundries and employee cafeterias.

Control division The controller, or occasionally, the treasurer, heads this division. His chief tasks are to protect the company's assets and to obtain adequate working capital to meet the needs of the business. He contributes a "show-me" attitude, taking very little for granted until the results reflect accomplishment. His detailed responsibilities usually include:

1. Devising and maintaining adequate accounting records.
2. Planning, taking, and calculating the physical inventory.
3. Credits and collections.
4. Merchandise budgeting and control (in cooperation with the merchandising division).
5. Expense budgeting and control.

---

[19] There has been a definite trend in recent years toward removing the director of personnel from under the jurisdiction of the store manager and making the personnel officer a major executive reporting directly to the general manager. Cf. p. 170, below.

[20] With the employment function growing rapidly in size and complexity some students believe it may be advisable to give it a place of its own in the organization structure.

6. Development of procedures to provide the desired control.
7. Preparing reports for general management.
8. Insurance (often the responsibility of the treasurer).
9. Safekeeping of all records prepared by or furnished to him.
10. Familiarity and compliance with governmental rules and regulations, city, state, and federal.
11. Preparing reports for governmental and other agencies.

Increased responsibilities The controller's responsibilities and prestige have increased greatly in recent years. His duties have widened and he has added many specialized assistants as a result of the growth of credit transactions, the increased use of electronic data-processing and scientific control methods, and the increasing complexity of federal and local tax and other regulations. The expansion of his functions and personnel is illustrated by the fact that in many stores the credit department alone now employs as many people as the entire control division did a few years ago.

□ Changes in department store organization

Since World War II particularly, many department stores have modified the Mazur Plan or adopted other organizational structures to meet changing conditions. Three of the major changes have been: (1) Adjustments made necessary by the growth of branch stores, (2) separation of buying and selling activities, and (3) changes in the number of divisions.[21]

Branch organization The development of branch stores, which now account for more than half of all department store sales, presented difficult organizational problems for their parent companies. No single best method of coordinating parent and branch operations has yet emerged, but three general patterns are quite clear.

1. "Brood hen and chick" organization Under this plan, the parent store organization operates the branch: The parent publicity director advertises for the branch; the controller and store superintendent perform their functions for both parent and branch store; and parent store buyers or department managers are responsible for all buying. The employees in the branch have a line responsibility to the branch manager, but the branch department sales supervisors and maintenance supervisor, for example, must work closely with parent store buyers and store superintendent. The "brood hen and chick" plan is usually followed for the first few branches, especially if they are considerably smaller than the parent store.

---

[21] A fourth change, the expansion of staff services, is discussed separately later in this chapter, pp. 178–80.

2. *"Separate store" plan* As the number of branches increases or as the branches grow in size, however, the obvious limitation of the "brood hen and chick" structure is soon reached: The parent store, especially its buyers, cannot continue indenfinitely to absorb the additional work load. At this point, a few firms—especially those with large branch units—have decided to treat each branch as a separate store with its own management and buying staffs organized on the same basis as the parent unit. This plan provides maximum flexibility and adjustment to local conditions, but it involves multiplication of management and buying salaries, travel costs, and other expenses. The separate store arrangement also reduces the stores' combined buying power and interferes with efforts to build a consistent "store image" for the parent and branches. Bullock's of Los Angeles, long the best-known advocate of this plan, is now changing to more closely coordinated operations.[22]

3. *"Equal store" structure* Many other firms with numerous branches have moved in the opposite direction, and centralized major management functions, *including buying,* at a single headquarters. Selling responsibilities are separated from buying[23] and the downtown store and the various branches all become sales units with equal organizational status. As we shall see, the "equal store" structure (illustrated in Figure 7–4) follows long-established chain store organizational principles. Although department stores are still experimenting with various branch store structures and modifications, the "equal store" plan will probably become dominant as the number of branches increase. This central control arrangement seems the most likely to give department store organizations the economies and efficiencies of chain store systems.

Separation of buying and selling responsibilities As we have noted, department stores that use the Mazur Plan or other traditional structures give the buyer or department manager responsibility for both buying and selling activities. The major arguments for combining these functions are:

1. Separation of buying and selling will result in lack of responsibility for department profits.
2. The person who buys the merchandise should be responsible for selling it.
3. The buyer needs direct consumer contact so that he can interpret correctly the consumer's wants.

---

[22] Cf. Eleanore Carruth, "Federated Department Stores: Growing Pains at Forty," *Fortune*, Vol. 79, No. 7 (June 1969), p. 145. Bullock's is now a Federated subsidiary. In contrast, Titche-Goettinger, a Dallas store with five branches is now installing the unit system in its fashion departments. "Titche Moving Buyers out to Branches to 'Involve' " *Women's Wear Daily*, January 15, 1970, p. 35.

[23] Cf. the discussion of separation of buying and selling immediately below.

FIGURE 7–4 An organization model for department or specialty stores with four or more selling units

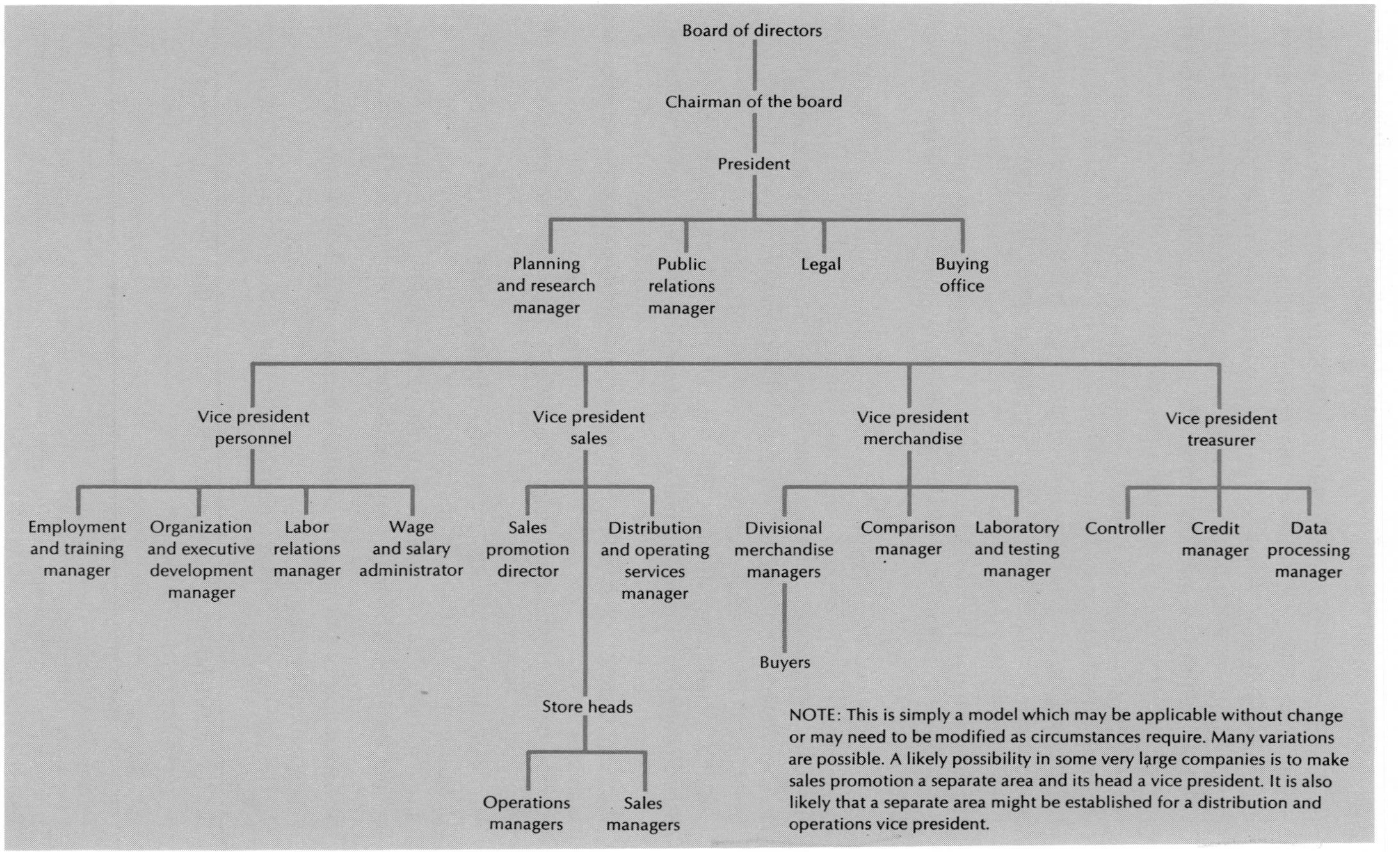

Source: Milton Woll, "Store Organization: How to Build in the Capacity for Change," *Stores*, October 1961, p. 20.

4. Only the person who buys the merchandise can convey the necessary information and enthusiasm to the salespeople.
5. Separation is too expensive, since it makes dual staffs (sales managers *and* buyers) necessary.

Reasons for separation Despite these arguments, there is a definite trend today towards separating buying and selling responsibilities in department stores. The growth of branch stores has been the most basic force supporting this trend, since the buyer cannot supervise sales activities in a number of locations and still perform his buying duties properly. But the following arguments for separation are relevant regardless of the number or existence of branches:

1. Buying and selling are different jobs which require different types of ability, personality, and training.
2. Combining buying and selling has resulted in buying becoming predominant and overshadowing selling.
3. Suitable emphasis on selling can be obtained only by setting up a sales organization which is divorced from buying.
4. Separation of buying and selling works well in chain stores, even those handling fashion merchandise.
5. Modern merchandise control systems can now provide proper coordination even if different persons are responsible for buying and selling.
6. The regrouping of merchandise into such combinations as cruise shops, sport shops, gun shops, and ski shops suggests that the best combinations of goods for buying purposes are not necessarily the most strategic combinations for sales purposes.[24]
7. Separation of buying and selling makes it easier to shift salespeople among departments according to need.
8. To obtain efficiency in buying, frequently one man should buy for several departments; if he does, he has little time to handle the selling function.

Organization for separation Various organizational plans have been used to separate buying and selling activities. In one plan, with complete separation, both a merchandise director who heads all buying and a sales director who heads all personal selling and publicity report directly to general management. Other retailers have left the merchandise manager responsible for both buying and selling, and made the separation at lower levels. Under this arrangement, one of the merchandise manager's subordinates supervises all buying and another supervises all sales work. The key executives' personal preferences, the personalities involved, the partic-

[24] Cf. the discussion of "Regrouping Merchandise Lines," pp. 157–58, above.

ular needs of the firm, management's willingness to experiment, and the size of the business tend to influence the decisions on how (and whether) to divide sales and buying responsibilities.

Changes in the number of divisions Many stores have raised the personnel function to major divisional status, with the director of personnel reporting directly to top management. This change, which makes personnel a fifth division in stores that otherwise use the Mazur plan, is due to the increasing complexity of personnel activities and problems—the result of new labor legislation, growth of labor unions, shortened working hours in spite of expanded store hours, rising wages, development of new training techniques, and the need to improve the employees' productivity.

The separation of buying and selling, discussed above, often also adds another divison to the traditional pattern. Some stores, however, have reduced the number of divisions; others have simplified their organization (at least at the upper levels of the charts) by concentrating responsibility in just three or even two divisions. Publicity and sales promotion are frequently made subordinate to merchandising in the three-divisional organization. All activities are concentrated in merchandising and store operations in the two-divisional firm.

□ Ownership groups

Some of our leading department stores, once independently-owned and operated, have been merged into ownership groups such as Federated Department Stores, Inc., Allied Stores Corporation, Cities Stores Company, and Mercantile Stores Company, Inc. These groups differ from chains of more or less uniform stores, such as Sears' and Montgomery Wards' department stores, discussed later in this chapter. Actually, they are department stores which have usually been in existence for a long time and which were gradually brought together under common ownership. The stores retain their original name, in most instances, and few customers are aware of the group ownership.[25]

While management responsibilities in some ownership groups have been centralized much as is true of chain-store operation, in most of them —Federated Department Stores, Inc., for example—the stores have retained many of the management functions they had when they were individual units. Each store typically has its own merchandising, publicity, operations,

[25] For example, Federated Department Stores' 16 major divisions include The Boston Store (Milwaukee), Bloomingdale's (New York), Abraham & Straus (Brooklyn, N.Y.), Bullocks-Magnin Co. (California), and Shillito's (Cincinnati). Allied Stores Company includes Bon Marche (Washington, Oregon & Utah), Jordan Marsh (Boston & Miami), Joske's (Houston) and Donaldson's (Minneapolis-St. Paul) as well as other divisions in other cities. McAlpin's (Cincinnati), Jones (Kansas City), Gayfer's (Alabama & Florida) and Lion (Toledo, Ohio), are part of the Mercantile Stores Co.

and control divisions. The group's central management establishes basic policies and provides certain services for the benefit of its units—such as financing, research, central market-buying facilities, exchange of operating statistics. In addition, it helps each store set overall goals, thereby stimulating local management to improve its operating results. It also has a small staff of experts to aid each store in the solution of problems. However, the central managements of these groups currently seem to be increasing their influence over basic decisions, although the individual units still have considerable autonomy.

■ CHAIN STORE ORGANIZATION STRUCTURE

Chain store companies vary in organization because of differences in types of merchandise handled, in services performed, in size of individual retail units, and in territory covered. Company policy, past experience and the executives' preferences and personalities also influence organization structure.

□ Some common characteristics

Most chain store companies have the following characteristics:

1. Major responsibilities are centralized in the headquarters or home office, regardless of the chain's geographic spread. Decentralized responsibility for sales is the chief exception to this rule.
2. The organization is divided into more main divisions than is typical of department stores. These often include real estate and maintenance, merchandising (buying), sales promotion, store operations, personnel, control, and, perhaps traffic, transportation and warehousing, and others.
3. Trained and capable executives are employed to direct these divisions.
4. Recognition of the personnel division's importance, and appointment of the personnel director or manager as a major executive. As noted, many department stores are now following the same policy.
5. Careful supervision and follow-up of store activities.
6. An elaborate system of reports to keep headquarters informed on operations and to enable the executives to maintain effective control over all activities for which they are responsible.

□ An apparel chain

Many of the above characteristics may be found, for example, in the organizational structure of a 100-store apparel chain. This company's stores are divided into 10 districts, with a manager for each store, and a field manager or supervisor for each district.

There is a well-defined division of responsibilities between store managers and field managers. The store manager's main function is the sale of merchandise, with its selection and purchase largely centralized at the chain's headquarters. The store manager actually makes some sales himself, hires and trains a sales staff which varies from 4 to 20 persons, arranges store displays, and reports daily sales to headquarters. The field manager is the connecting link between headquarters and the store. He hires store managers, takes physical inventories, checks displays, and gives the buyers at headquarters the store managers' requests for merchandise to meet local demand.

At headquarters, a merchandise manager, aided by five buyers and eight divisional distribution managers, supervises buying and merchandise control. Each buyer purchases a specific type of merchandise, such as dresses or hosiery. The divisional distribution managers then control the shipment of this merchandise to the stores, with each manager responsible for 10 to 20 stores. Purchases and shipments are based upon the information contained in the stores' daily sales reports (including ticket stubs for all items sold), and the buyers' and distribution managers' knowledge of styles, prices, and consumer buying trends.

□ A variety store chain

A national variety store chain has a relatively similar structure. A brief description of its chief executives and their responsibilities will indicate the similarites and differences in function between chain store officials and the department store executives discussed earlier in this chapter. The president of this particular firm is charged with the overall administration and coordination of the company's operations. In making his policy decisions, he pays close attention to analytical studies conducted by the research manager and to legal advice obtained from the general counsel. The treasurer is responsible for handling company funds, arrangements for financing, and the purchase and management of insurance.

Six operating officials also report directly to the president. The controller's responsibilities are similar to those of his department store counterpart,[26] except (1) there are no credit and collection problems since this firm sells for cash, (2) the treasurer handles insurance probems, and (3) supervision of the physical inventory count is a function of the retail operations department. The advertising director prepares the basic advertising budget,

[26] Cf. pp. 165–66, above.

subject to top management approval, and then plans and initiates sales and promotional campaigns within the budgetary limits.

The merchandise manager is concerned with the buying of merchandise and supplies and with related activities. He establishes retail prices and prepares merchandise bulletins for store managers. In this particular firm, he also is in charge of company-operated warehouses and supervises shipments; although in some large chains, these duties fall to other executives.

The actual operation of this chain's retail units falls to the director of retail operations, although the director of real estate and maintenance is responsible for obtaining the stores, planning layouts, installing fixtures, and maintenance. All district managers report to the retail organizations director, and each store manager to the district manager of his district. Finally, the personnel director performs duties comparable to those already outlined on page 165 for the department store.

☐ Some other chains

Figure 7–5, which shows the basic organization structure of Colonial Stores, Inc., a 425-store regional food chain, and Figure 7–6, which shows part of Montgomery Ward & Co.'s organizational plan, illustrate other facets of chain store organization. Both show the separation of selling (store and mail-order) activities from buying and merchandising; both show the existence of a large number of staff and advisory functions; and both show more divisions reporting to the president than is customary in department store organization. Figure 7–6 is especially interesting in showing how Montgomery Ward has faced the problem of integrating chain store and mail order activities.

The individual store managers in these, and other chains, are supervised by district or area managers (various titles are used in different firms) who have been successful store managers themselves. The district manager's main task is to help each store manager operate his store more effectively. Regional officials or vice presidents then coordinate the work of the various district managers. Figure 7–7, based on part of The Kroger Co.'s organization plan, shows how district product specialists work in a staff capacity to advise and assist both store managers and the respective product department heads within the stores.

☐ Decentralization of chain store organization

Many years ago, most chains exercised such tight control over their stores that one could almost say: "When a store manager sneezed, the presi-

FIGURE 7–5 Organization chart of Colonial Stores, Inc., a food processing firm and regional food chain with approximately 425 stores

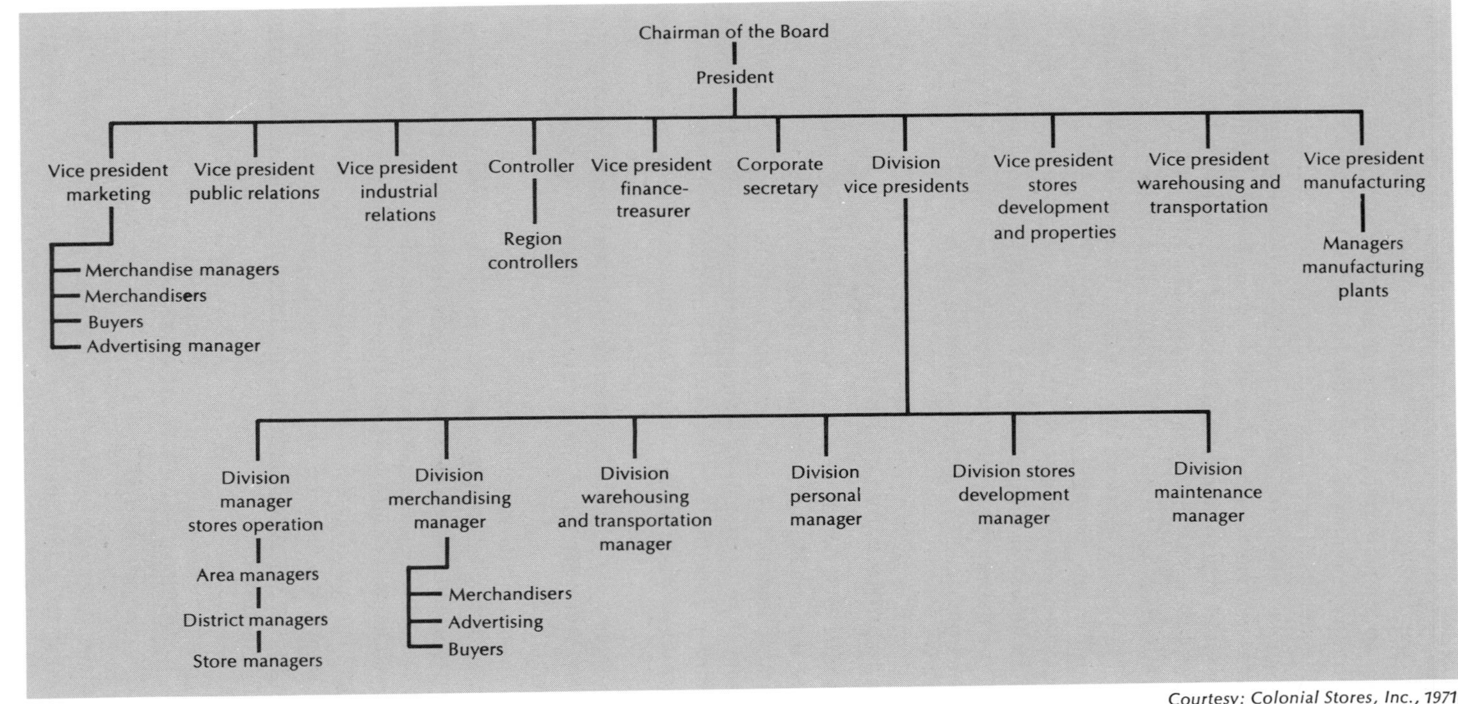

Courtesy: Colonial Stores, Inc., 1971

FIGURE 7–6 **Organization chart, Montgomery Ward & Co., Inc., a subsidiary of Marcor, Inc.** Eastern Region and Merchandising Division shown in greater detail than other regions and divisions.

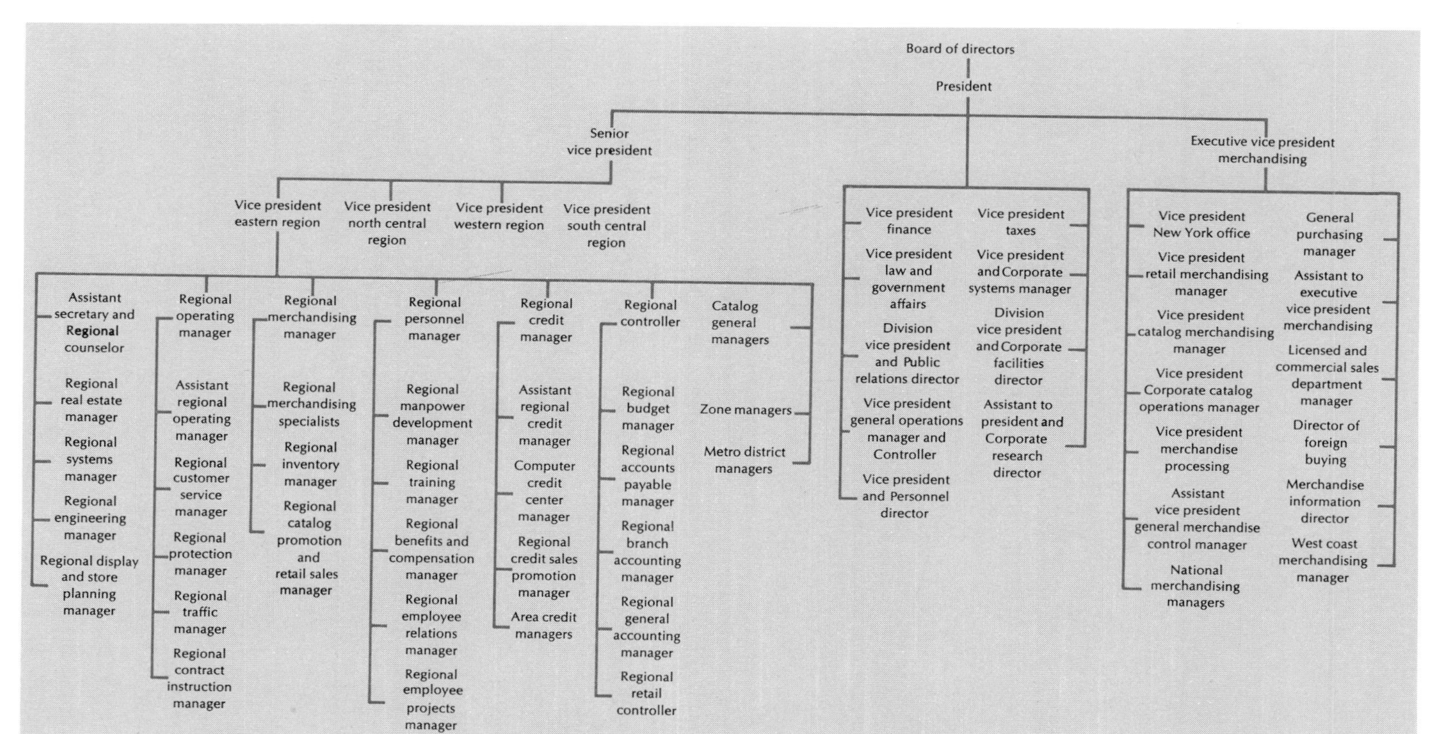

Source: Montgomery Ward & Co., Inc., *Organizational Manual*, 1970, adapted.

FIGURE 7–7 **Line and staff relationships of product supervisors and managers in Kroger Food Stores, a division of The Kroger Co.**

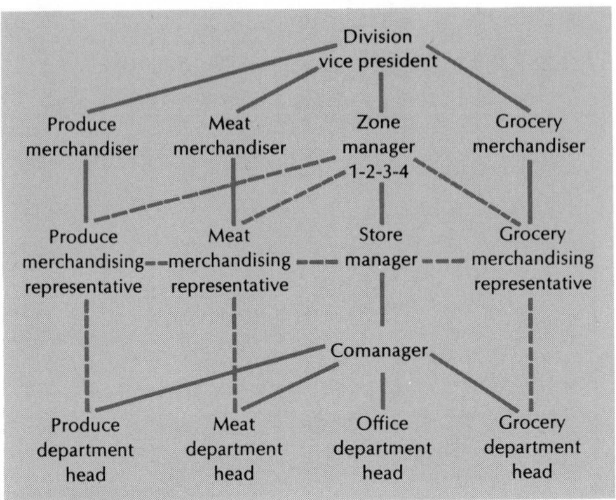

Source: The Kroger Co.

dent—seated in his office hundreds of miles away—said 'Gesundheit.' " Some chains still maintain very close control; the increased information flowing to headquarters through the new data-processing systems has actually increased centralization in a few firms. Nevertheless, the current trend in chain store organization is towards decentralization of buying, selling, and sales promotion activities. In some cases, divisional headquarters perform or control these functions for groups of stores. Other chains, especially those with large stores, have delegated more authority to the zone, district, or store managers.

Some illustrations of decentralization Company after company illustrates this tendency toward decentralization. Sears, Roebuck & Co. has divided its stores into five regions supervised by regional vice presidents. Each of these executives has a considerable degree of autonomy within his region, and as a director of the company, also plays an important role in overall policy determination. Although much of Sears' buying is still centralized, store managers have freedom to select many of their merchandise items from lists prepared at headquarters.[27] Montgomery Ward & Co. has revised its operating methods so that:

> . . . where almost every merchandising decision of the entire chain was once made on Chicago Avenue [national headquarters] Ward now manages 115 retail

[27] Cf. "Why Sears Stays the No. 1 Retailer," *Business Week,* January 20, 1968, pp. 65–73.

stores in nineteen major urban areas through metropolitan district management staffs whose say-so extends to merchandising, distribution, advertising, warehousing, inventory and expense controls.[28]

Even the supermarket chains, once perhaps the most highly centralized of all retail groups, are now becoming much more decentralized. A & P, for example, recently gave its 33 divisional headquarters a considerable part of the buying and operating authority that was formerly concentrated in the New York headquarters.[29] Firms such as Kroger and Jewel have transferred many important decisions to regional and zone managers, and have also given the store managers increased authority. A knowledgeable analyst says that Safeway's "decentralization of retail pricing and merchandising decisions . . . to conform more closely with local competitive supply and demand conditions" is probably fairly typical of the chain supermarket industry.[30]

Centralization trends Despite the developments mentioned, not all retail firms are decentralizing. We have already noted a tendency toward some reduction of decentralization among department store ownership groups. The trend toward the "equal store" structure and away from the "separate store" plan for department store branches constitutes a centralization of buying along with decentralization of sales responsibility. We also noted, in Chapter 1, that many discount chains were acquiring and operating departments that they once leased to outsiders. The leading discount chains have substantially reduced the proportion of their total sales handled through outside leases.[31] Some large franchising organizations are now buying back some of their franchised outlets and operating them as parts of wholly owned chains.[32]

Many voluntary and cooperative chain groups are also showing signs of centralizing in several ways: (1) The central headquarters or wholesaler-sponsors are purchasing and operating some of the formerly independent member stores; (2) many of these chains are placing greater emphasis on

---

[28] "Marcor: How's It Managing," *Dun's Review*, August 1969, p. 73. Headquarters buyers, however, still retain considerable control over merchandise selection, inventory assortments, and retail prices. Cf. "The Strategy That Saved Montgomery Ward," *Fortune*, Vol. 81 No. 5, May 1970, p. 170.

[29] "A & P Finally Waking Up?" *Chain Storge Age* (Supermarket Executives Edition), June 1969, pp. 23–27; "The A & P Study—Part II—How New Thinking and New People Are Making an Old Company Young," *Progressive Grocer*, March 1970, pp. 46–59; and "Part IV—Expanding Role for the Store Manager," *ibid.*, June 1970, pp. 54–63.

[30] Daniel I. Padberg, *Economics of Food Retailing* (Ithaca, N.Y.: Cornell University Food Distribution Program, 1968), p. 173.

[31] Cf. Robert Drew-Bear, *Mass Merchandising: Revolution & Evolution* (New York: Fairchild Publications, Inc., 1970), pp. 272–76; and "S. S. Kresge Steams Ahead," *Women's Wear Daily*, January 7, 1971, p. 13.

[32] Alfred R. Oxenfeldt and Anthony O. Kelly, "Will Successful Franchise Systems Ultimately Become Wholly Owned Chains?" *Journal of Retailing*, Vol. 44, No. 4 (Winter 1968–69), pp. 69–83.

centrally-purchased private brands; and (3) the affiliated members are relying upon the central headquarters' services (store planning, financing, accounting, and supervision) to a greater degree than ever before.[33]

Balancing centralization and decentralization The problem of balancing centralization and decentralization is to retain the advantages and economies of group purchasing and sales effort while encouraging the appropriate store and district officials to use their initiative in adjusting to local conditions. Even the chains that are decentralizing retain many functions at central or regional headquarters, where they can be performed on a group basis. An experienced chain store merchant says:

> "The name of the game in chain-store operation is central direction, taking full advantage of the combined power of the chain, including the immense power of good store managers. . . .
>
> The central core of chain-store effectiveness is centralization. Centralization of decision-making in marketing brings grave responsibility but great rewards."[34]

No chain ever finds the absolutely perfect point of balance between centralization and decentralization, if such a point even exists. Constant experimentation and adjustment, however, will keep the chain from becoming either excessively loose and uncoordinated or overly rigid and inflexible.

■ ENLARGED STAFF AND MANAGEMENT INFORMATION SERVICES

The larger and more progressive department and chain store firms have established many staff units within their organizations to gather, analyze, and summarize information and to furnish advice for top management and other executives responsible for decisions.

□ Management information and advice

Research units Although research findings can never replace executive judgment, top executives in retailing, as in other fields, are increasingly using research studies as an aid in making well-informed decisions.[35] The research department or unit within the large firm is responsible for conduct-

---

[33] Cf. Daniel Padberg, *op. cit.*, pp. 40–41.

[34] Robert F. Chisholm, *The Darlings: The Mystique of the Supermarket* (New York: Chain Store Age Books, 1970), pp. 14, 105.

[35] Cf. the discussion of research as a coordinating function in Chapter 26, "Coordination and Retail Management.

ing some of the necessary studies and for analyzing and supervising the flow of information purchased from outside organizations. The research department, which serves in a staff capacity, commonly reports directly to the general management because its investigations cover all divisions of the business as well as outside conditions.

Long range planning Although only a few large retailers have long-range planning and development staffs, their number is steadily increasing. This planning unit is normally headed by a very competent vice president for (or director of) planning and development who works with a few skilled assistants. His task is to help the president or chief executive answer two critically important questions:

1. What should be this firm's position 5 (10, 20) years from now?
2. What policies and actions must we adopt to reach that position?

Policy and planning committees In some companies, the board of directors and top management may also turn to a policy committee for advice and suggestions on major decisions. The policy committee usually consists of the firm's key executives plus perhaps an outside consultant and one or two board members. These committees are not new to retailing, but they have assumed greater importance in recent years. Their growing significance indicates the emphasis that many firms now place upon consideration of all relevant points of view when making fundamental decisions.

In some cases, if the board of directors wants to play a very active role in long-range planning, it may set up a committee for this purpose. This committee will usually consist of selected board members and the chief executive, supplemented perhaps by one or two other executives and an outside consultant. In such instances, the director of long-range planning may report to this committee, either directly or indirectly through the chief executive. The chief executive and the board of directors as a group remain responsible for their major decisions. The policy committee, the research director, the planning director, or even the planning committee cannot assume those responsibilities. But their information, insights, analyses, and opinions can be of substantial assistance to top management.

□ Other staff services

Various other staff services have grown in usefulness and in personnel in the large retail organizations. Additional firms are adopting merchandise testing, which results in better buying on the store's part, more satisfied customers, and reduced merchandise returns.[36] Public relations and con-

[36] Cf. "Consumerism Is Here to Stay, Stores Do Something about It," *Editor and Publisher,* February 28, 1970, pp. 16, 40.

sumer relations staffs are assuming increasing importance. Comparison shopping plays a growing role as retailers find themselves faced with an ever more-competitive market.[37] Some retailers have established industrial engineering and systems staffs to apply work simplification methods to repetitive activities such as merchandise handling and information processing. Fashion coordinators have been appointed to make certain that the store is in touch with current style trends and to coordinate quality and fashion position in the various departments.

Place on the organization chart Retailers disagree as to where these various staff services should be located in the organization structure. In some instances, a number are grouped together and placed under a staff vice president. Or, the activities may be distributed among various qualified personnel throughout the organization. For example, the heads of merchandise testing and comparison shopping might report to the general merchandise manager, the fashion coordinator to the advertising and sales-promotion manager or to the general merchandise manager, with the research and public relations directors responsible to the general manager. As is true with so many aspects of organization, existing personnel and management preferences play leading roles in determining exactly where these staff services will report within each company.

■ SUMMARY OF ORGANIZATIONAL CHANGES AND TRENDS

The trends and tendencies discussed in this chapter do not exhaust the list of organizational developments in retailing. Other significant organizational arrangements that apply to specific retail activities are analyzed in the chapters devoted to those activities. Buying committees, for example, are discussed in Chapter 10. But a recapitulation of some of the overall trends noted in this chapter may be helpful:

1. Merchants are experimenting with various groupings of merchandise lines and various bases for departmentalization.
2. Many department stores are changing their organizational structure to accommodate an increasing number of branches. No single best answer has yet developed, but stores with a large number of branches are tending to use the "equal store" ("chain store") approach.
3. Department stores are increasingly separating buying and selling responsibilities.

---

[37] Cf. p. 244, below.

4. Many department stores have departed from or modified the traditional Mazur four-functional organization structure.
5. Many chain store firms have decentralized important functions and decision-making power to regional, district, and store levels.
6. Despite the growth in decentralization among chain organizations, centralization tendencies continue among many firms, including department stores, ownership groups, voluntary chains, and franchising organizations.
7. Personnel directors and controllers have assumed increased responsibility and importance in both department and chain store firms.
8. Staff and informational services have also grown greatly in importance and use among the large retailers.

Clearly, retail organization is in a state of flux.

■ REVIEW AND DISCUSSION QUESTIONS

1 Compare and contrast the organization needs of each of the following: (*a*) a small food store and a large food chain; (*b*) a general store and a department store; (*c*) a mail-order company and a chain selling similar goods.

2 "An important aspect of retail store structure is departmentalizing." What is meant by "departmentalizing" and what steps would be involved in departmentalizing a women's clothing store?

3 Discuss the causes for the current regrouping of merchandise lines and the organizational problems that result from such regrouping.

4 Explain the traditional or orthodox organization of a department store in sufficient detail to make clear the major duties and responsibilities of each division. What are the major weaknesses of this organization plan?

5 What are the principal organizational patterns for branch-downtown store relationships? What are the strengths and weaknesses of each such pattern?

6 Summarize the arguments for and against separating buying and selling.

7 "Chain-store companies vary in organization because of differences in types of merchandise handled, in services performed, in size of individual store, and in territory covered." Explain how each of these factors has an influence on the organization structure.

8 Compare and contrast the general characteristics of chain-store organization with the four-function department-store organization.

9 How do you account for the trend among chain stores toward decentralization as some other multiunit retailers are moving toward centralization? Give examples of these trends.

10 What is meant by the term "staff services"? Why are they being expanded in retail stores? Give examples of their expansion.

chapter 8

RETAIL PERSONNEL MANAGEMENT

The importance of personnel—the human factor—in the success of a retail enterprise was emphasized in the previous chapter. Many factors, as discussed below, have increased the variety and complexity of personnel problems in all types of retail businesses today.

SCOPE AND AIMS OF PERSONNEL MANAGEMENT

Personnel management is concerned with the organization's employees. The major retail personnel activities include: selecting, training, and compensating employees; maintaining adequate performance levels; conducting service activities for employees; and hearing and trying to adjust employees' complaints. The successful performance of these activities requires understanding and application of the basic principles of human relations.

The immediate objective of personnel activities is the development of a staff that will perform the other retail functions satisfactorily from both the retailer's and the customer's point of view. The personnel department must cooperate closely with the executives and other store divisions, since its basic task is to help the other departments operate more effectively. The ultimate aim is to help maximize the store's profits; thus, in the final analysis, personnel management is a dollar and cents matter.

INCREASING EMPHASIS ON PERSONNEL MANAGEMENT

The primary significance of personnel management lies in the fact that retailing is a "humanized" business involving frequent contact between the firm's customers and its employees. In fact, it is often said that the impression the customer receives from employees does "as much as, if not more than, anything else to build and maintain the store's image."[1] Despite the importance of the employee, only in recent decades has personnel management been widely recognized as an important activity of the retailer. In 1882 a general store owner-operator handled many of his personnel problems by simply posting the following:

Rules for Clerks

1. This store must be opened at Sunrise. No mistake. Open 6 o'clock A.M. Summer and Winter. Close about 8:30 or 9 P.M. the year round.
2. Store must be swept—dusted—doors and windows opened—lamps filled, trimmed and chimneys cleaned—counters, base shelves and show cases dusted—pens made—a pail of water also the coal must be brought in before breakfast, if there is time to do it and attend to all the customers who call.
3. The store is not to be opened on the Sabbath day unless absolutely necessary and then only for a few minutes.
4. Should the store be opened on Sunday the clerks must go in alone and get tobacco for customers in need.
5. The clerk who is in the habit of smoking Spanish cigars—being shaved at the barbers—going to dancing parties and other places of amusement and being out late at night—will assuredly give his employer reason to be ever suspicious of his integrity and honesty.
6. Clerks are allowed to smoke in the store provided they do not wait on women with a "stogie" in the mouth.
7. Each clerk must pay not less than $5.00 per year to the Church and must attend Sunday School regularly.
8. Men clerks are given one evening a week off for courting and two if they go to prayer meeting.
9. After the 14 hours in the store the leisure hours should be spent mostly in reading.[2]

---

[1] J. E. Stafford and T. V. Greer, "Consumer Preference for Types of Salesmen: A Study of Independence–Dependence Characteristics," *Journal of Retailing,* Vol. 41, No. 2 (Summer 1965), p. 27.

[2] Carson Pirie Scott & Co., *"We" and Our Business* (Chicago, 1927), p. 20.

■ EXTERNAL FACTORS RESPONSIBLE FOR GROWING EMPHASIS ON PERSONNEL MANAGEMENT

The intensified personnel-consciousness of businessmen in general during the last half-century may be attributed to such factors as the following: The development of new management concepts with increased emphasis on human relations; the changing social and political climate; the growth of labor unions; employee demands for extensive "fringe" benefits; shortages of qualified workers during much of the post–World War II period; and the growth of federal and state legislation. Major labor laws include those dealing with wages and hours, social security, unemployment insurance, and mandatory collective bargaining, as well as legislation banning job discrimination based on "race, color, religion, sex, national origin or age."[3] These factors have affected retailers as well as other businessmen, but the retailers have also gradually recognized a number of other, more specifically retailing-related reasons for the growing emphasis upon personnel management. These factors require further analysis.

□ Causal factors within retailing

Good people bring good results Progressive retailers realize that the success of the store depends as much upon skillful handling of personnel activities as upon the store's merchandise or its fixtures and equipment. Competing stores often have similar merchandise, equipment, and sales promotion, so that personnel becomes the distinguishing feature. There is an old saying in big league baseball: "If you want to be a good manager, get good ball players." This also applies to the general manager of a retail store: "If you want to run a successful store, get (and keep) good people."

Customer goodwill and repeat business Customer goodwill rests upon personal contact with the proprietor in the very small store. But the customer gains her impressions of larger stores through her experiences with all types of employees—salespeople, telephone operators, elevator operators, credit interviewers, deliverymen, and complaint adjustors. She will feel favorably towards the store if these people are courteous, alert, friendly, and helpful; but even extensive advertising cannot overcome the ill-will that results when the employees lack these qualities. Dissatisfaction with

[3] Title VII, Civil Rights Act of 1964, as amended (42 U.S.C. 2000 e) and Age Discrimination in Employment Act, 1967 (Public Law 90–202, 81 *Stat.* 602); Also cf. Richard Wightman, "Now Age Joins Hiring Taboos," *Women's Wear Daily*, May 17, 1968, pp. 1, 6.

employees and their attitudes probably drives far more people away from stores than does discontent with the merchandise.

Pressure An obvious fact is that customer-employee contacts in retailing are not evenly spaced throughout the week and the year. Instead, they are often concentrated in hectic periods when both the customer and the employee may feel a sense of pressure. Consequently, personnel must seek to develop a working force that can remain calm and cheerful under trying conditions. The J. C. Penney Company's employee magazine describes the requirements half-humorously but accurately:

The Joy of Survival

You're surrounded by an army of customers. It's the second night you've worked this week and your feet are killing you. You probably won't be getting home 'til at least 10 and then you have to stay up and wrap a few more gifts and address a few more cards . . . and, oh, are you tired .

Sound familiar? It should, because that's the way we all feel at one time or another during the Christmas holidays. Yet there's no other time during the year when our customers need us more . . .

"I'm looking for something for my aunt. She's very old . . ." "Does this come in purple? Then can you order it for me?" "He's six years old, but I haven't seen him since he was a baby. He was very big then. What size might he take?"

And there's no time when we have more customers.

It's exciting and it's fun, but it *is* exhausting. And just to add to our survival problems we find ourselves combining our busiest working season with our busiest social season.

It seems that 90 per cent of the year's parties are squeezed into these few short holiday weeks and somehow we also have to find the time and energy to shop for gifts, decorate the house, write cards and maybe even sleep a little . . .

Little wonder that the last joy of Christmas comes when it's over—when you know you've made it and can finally rest.

No matter how much you love the season, no matter how keenly you anticipate its coming, when it's all over there's a unique joy in knowing you've survived another Christmas—and the next one is a whole year away.

Merry Christmas and a Happy and Healthy New Year![4]

Human relations in retailing Thoughtful retailers have been worrying about the constant deterioration in the quality of selling service, about lowered employee morale,[5] and about the number of able young people who fail to consider retailing as a career because of (what they consider to be) unsatisfactory working relationships. These merchants are seeking to solve such problems through improvement of human relations within their firms. They approach their personnel situations from the point of view of the peo-

[4] *Penney News* November–December 1970, p. 14.

[5] Similar problems arise in other fields, Cf. "Rising Worry about the Will to Work," *Time*, October 17, 1969, p. 96.

ple involved, and ask why some supervisors and personnel specialists achieve so much better results than others. Why is employee morale and productivity so much higher in some departments or stores than in others with identical working conditions and compensation?

Part of the answer seems to be some human relations principles that can be applied to all relationships with people.

1. We do not like to be dominated by others.
2. We are more likely to agree with those we like personally.
3. All of us like to feel important, to be recognized as individuals, and to do work that is significant.
4. We want to be in the "know."
5. Emotions, as well as objective analysis, are important in our reactions to situations.
6. We accept change slowly.
7. In our job, we want good working conditions, a fair wage, a chance to get ahead, and to feel secure.

A recent study reports that salespeople are most productive when their jobs permit relatively full expression of their individual potentials; that is, when the work situations coincide with the predispositions and aims that the employees bring to the job.[6] Of course, the retailer must exercise common sense and balance. He must not be so "soft" that his employees begin to feel sorry for themselves and neglect their tasks. Yet he must not be so "tough" that employees lose all initiative because of their fear of him.

Many inexperienced employees Young people, without previous business training, often take rank-and-file retail positions as their first jobs. Many leave after a period of time, to get married or to seek employment elsewhere, and must be replaced by other new workers. An increasing number of inexperienced older workers, especially married women, are also entering retail employment. All of these people often need special training and supervision.

High rate of employee turnover High employee turnover rates in retailing result from many factors: business seasonality; poor supervision; poor training leading to resignations or discharges; many young and inexperienced employees; high percentage of women employed; belief that better jobs are available elsewhere; employee dissatisfaction with immediate superiors or general management; and employee restlessness, low morale, poor health, or dislike of a particular community. Turnover rates vary widely among stores of different sizes and types, but may rise to 50 percent or

[6] Grady D. Bruce and Charles M. Bonjean, "Self-Actualization among Retail Sales Personnel," *Journal of Retailing,* Vol. 45, No. 2 (Summer 1969), pp. 73–84.

more,[7] thereby adding substantially to the store's hiring, training, and unemployment compensation insurance costs.

Close management attention is usually essential whenever the turnover rate is above 25 to 35 percent. The following steps, discussed in later paragraphs, often help reduce excessive employee turnover.

1. More careful selection.
2. Better training.
3. Using a compensation plan which the employees consider fair and which results in an annual income at least equal to that which can be secured in similar work elsewhere.
4. A well-conceived promotion policy.
5. Adequate employee service activities.
6. Hearing and seeking satisfactory adjustments to employees' complaints and grievances.
7. Introducing a pension system.
8. Recognizing the importance of morale in effective performance, even to the point of employing outside agencies to conduct "morale surveys" as a step toward better human relations within the store.

Cost of executive training and replacement The labor turnover problem also extends to the management level. A variety chain executive, for example, reports that over a 10-year period 70 percent of his firm's management trainees withdrew or were let out before finishing the third year of employment. This executive estimates the cost of training a manager at $8,000 or more. Department and specialty stores, supermarkets, and discount house chains have experienced similar executive turnover difficulties. This is a major problem since many retailers, department stores for example, require about one executive for every ten employees.

Large number of part-time employees Wide fluctuations in retail sales, both from hour to hour and seasonally, and night and Sunday openings that extend store hours far beyond any individual's working hours, have led to widespread use of part-time personnel. Fifty-six percent of the supermarket personnel covered in one large 1970 survey were part-time workers.[8] Skillful part-time employees are increasingly difficult to find and consequently retailers are hiring inexperienced people who require much more extensive training. Moreover, training and other employee communications are more difficult when workers are on a variety of different full-time and part-time schedules.

---

[7] A 50 percent turnover means that the number of workers leaving the store's employment during the course of the year equalled 50 percent of the average number of people simultaneously on the payroll during the year.

[8] *The Super Market Industry Speaks 1970* (Chicago: Super Market Institute, 1970), p. 5.

Expansion of many retail firms Some retailers' personnel problems come, in part, from rapid expansion. For example, between 1967 and 1969, Sears, Roebuck & Co.'s payroll grew by 40,000 employees, from 315,000 to 355,000; the J. C. Penney Company from 87,000 to 105,000; Gamble-Skogmo, Inc., from 22,700 to 26,300; and Lucky Stores, Inc., from 10,400 to 23,000.[9] And many smaller retailers are also modernizing and enlarging their establishments. Some of the smaller food chains, for example, are growing even more rapidly than the larger firms.

High wage-to-sales ratio Wages commonly represent more than one-half of the retailer's total expense, another reason for emphasis on personnel work. No retailer faced with normal competitive conditions and low profit ratios can ignore such a large part of his total operating expense.

Various kinds of ability needed Employees perform many different kinds of jobs, especially in the larger stores. Different selling and sales-supporting positions require different qualifications. The retailer needs people with various types of skill and intelligence—check-out girls, stock room boys, store managers, basement salespeople, fur department saleswomen, heating engineers, watch repairmen, garage mechanics, testing laboratory technicians, registered nurses, dieticians, accountants, pharmacists, economists, and top management people.

Employees' requirements The retailer must either satisfy his employees' many legitimate wants in varying degree or pay the penalty of bad personnel relationships. His employees want good working conditions, satisfactory wages and hours; employment security; recognition for good work and suggestions; paid vacations; purchasing discounts; treatment as individuals rather than as cogs in a machine; a feeling of importance; a chance to work to their full capacities and to use their maximum abilities and aptitudes; and, in many cases, opportunity for advancement. Although the employee demands can be costly, failure to meet them may be even more expensive, especially if a strike should result. Personnel management must try to reconcile the employees' desires with the employer's resources.

This reconciliation is difficult, however, since many aspects of retailing work against high wages, short hours, and employment security at the submanagerial levels. The individual retailer who faces keen competition from other merchants cannot raise prices in order to pay higher wages. Many of the rank-and-file jobs do not demand unusual physical abilities or high levels of education, experience or formalized training and thus are unlikely to command high salaries. Steadily increasing store hours already require

[9] "The Fifty Largest Retailing Companies," *Fortune*, Vol. 81 (May 1970), pp. 208–9; and "The Fifty Largest Merchandising Companies," *ibid.*, Vol. 77 (June 15, 1968), pp. 212–13.

much part-time and double shift employment and thus tend to block any reduction in normal working hours. Seasonal fluctuations in retail sales preclude employment security for all workers. Even in the relative stable drugstore business, December sales are normally double January's. Many retailers also experience sales peaks before Easter and during back-to-school days. Sales volume also varies among different days of the week and hours of the day. The job stability of "regular" employees has been greatly improved in recent years through increasing use of "part-time" and "extra" workers, but this has transferred the insecurity to these latter employees.

DEFINITE PERSONNEL POLICIES ESSENTIAL

Personnel policies should be clear and definite—which, where practicable, means they should be in writing; carefully formulated; consistently administered; stable, yet flexible enough to meet changing conditions; cover all major aspects of employee-management relationships; and widely publicized among employees. Definite, well-publicized policies are especially important in large-scale retailing where minor executives make many decisions that affect store personnel. Unless these officers know and follow the firm's policies, employee ill-will is inevitable.

Definite personnel policies should cover, among other areas:

1. The personnel division's authority and responsibilities, and its relationships with other divisions and departments.
2. Personnel recruitment and sources of supply.
3. Selecting personnel—number and types of interviews, use of tests, and similar devices.
4. Training methods and content of training—for new and existing personnel.
5. Compensation and compensation methods.
6. Working conditions—hours of work, number of days per week, and vacations.
7. Induction of new employees.
8. Promotions, transfers, and terminations.
9. Personnel reviews and ratings.
10. Employee discounts on purchases.
11. Employee cafeterias and lunchrooms.
12. Personnel complaints and methods of handling them.
13. Unions and labor organizations.

■ CONDUCTING PERSONNEL ACTIVITIES

The proprietor or manager of a small store usually conducts all of his own personnel activities. He normally knows the store's few employees well and has close working relationships with them. Consequently he has to spend relatively little time on formal personnel work. Hiring, training, and other personnel activities require more attention in the medium-sized establishment with 15 or 20 employees. A "sponsor" may be appointed to handle some of the training work.[10] Chain store district offices may absorb some personnel responsibilities for the units, particularly the smaller stores in their areas, but the store managers will still handle most personnel tasks.

Personnel work assumes more significant proportions and requires more elaborate programs in the larger retail organization. The mere number of employees creates a hiring and training problem in the large chain store, department store, or discount house. Lack of direct association between the executives who formulate general policies and the employees can generate misunderstandings and ill will which must be minimized. Consequently, personnel departments or divisions are needed, both to perform personnel tasks and, even more importantly, to help the operating supervisors understand and fulfill the firm's personnel policies.

Actually all the store's executives and employees, whether in the personnel department or not, are involved in personnel work. Many will have specific responsibilities for training new people, and executives on the promotion ladder are often expected to develop their own successors. But every individual's actions contribute to the development of good, or poor, human relations within the store. The chain organization superintendent who ridicules or undermines his firm's manager-training plan weakens the entire personnel program. The department manager who fails to understand human relations and tries to dominate his subordinates invariably increases labor turnover and complicates the personnel department's employee-selection program. In contrast, the executive who leads his associates to successful performance of their tasks bolsters the firm's personnel objectives.

■ EMPLOYMENT PROCEDURE

Recruitment of capable retail employees involves at least four important steps: (1) Making careful job analyses and preparing adequate job

[10] Cf. pp. 199–200, below.

specifications or descriptions; (2) developing satisfactory sources of supply; (3) using application forms, interviews, tests, and physical examinations to select employees; and (4) introducing the new employees to the store and to their jobs. Large-scale retailers frequently also have to maintain a contingent force and a file of prospective employees.

□ Job analyses and job specifications

A job analysis is a complete study of the job to determine: (*a*) the exact work to be done, (*b*) the expected quantity and quality of work, (*c*) the best-working methods, and (*d*) the desired characteristics of the employee. Information is obtained about the physical effort, experience, mental keenness, leadership qualities, dependability, accuracy, and other personal characteristics that the job requires; the working conditions—work environment and safety hazards—involved; hours normally worked; and the job's evaluation.[11]

The job analysis should be the basis for a "job specification" or "job description," which outlines the qualifications needed to fill the job satisfactorily.[12] This specification is useful in finding persons to fill jobs, in setting up placement tests, and in transferring present employees to more suitable jobs. It helps the training department and supervisors to decide what kind of training is desirable for employees performing various jobs. It facilitates interstore comparisons since it gives common titles to similar jobs in other stores. In securing the data, the management obtains a better understanding of working conditions and what is required of each employee; and such information is the first step toward improvement. In addition, the job specification facilitates the delegation process since it shows employees exactly what is expected of them, especially if management uses the information to set up employee guides or work charts.

□ Sources of personnel

The retailer is ready to look for people with the desired qualifications once he has obtained a more or less precise idea of the type of person needed. Some people who are good candidates for at least some of the open positions may have already applied to the store for jobs, either in person or by correspondence. Many stores keep availability files and hire qualified

[11] For a discussion of job evaluation, cf. pp. 217–18, below.

[12] For an extended discussion of job analysis and description, cf. J. A. Patton, C. L. Littlefield and S. A. Self, *Job Evaluation*, 3d ed. (Homewood, Ill.: Richard D. Irwin, Inc., 1964), Part II.

employees in order of application. Employees and customers often recommend other desirable candidates.

However, most retailers have to seek out people if they want the best available. Many different sources may be used to help locate good prospects. High schools, business schools, community colleges, and university employment and placement units are often good sources. When people are needed, the retailer may also use government and private employment agencies; and window signs and display pieces, as well as classified or regular space newspaper advertising. If an executive position is open, the store's own personnel should be reviewed carefully, inquiries may be made among vendors and others familiar with the organization, and specialized employment agencies may be used.

Some retailers use well-developed recruiting programs to attract graduating students. A few, especially chains and department stores, have gone beyond this and established summer or part-time employment programs for college and high school students. These merchants hope that the participants will ultimately want permanent careers with their stores and also will encourage their classmates to become interested in retailing. A drug chain, in addition to offers of loans and part-time jobs to pharmacy school students, also attempts to attract high school students through weekend work. Some retail trade associations—the National Retail Merchants Association, for example—have also undertaken programs to encourage more college students to enter the retail field.

☐ Selecting personnel

The next step is to acquire knowledge of the various candidates' qualifications so as to select the ones who best meet the store's requirements. Information may be obtained through: (1) Application forms, (2) references, (3) preliminary interviews, (4) tests, (5) physical examinations, and (6) final interviews. Although the order may vary from firm to firm, most large retailers use all six sources of information about the applicant. In contrast, the proprietor of the small store usually limits himself to interviews and references.

Application forms and references Some retailers use a very simple one-page preliminary application form. The form, which calls for a brief description of the applicant's experience, education, type or job sought, and expected salary, provides a quick screening without imposing a lengthy form upon either the candidate or the personnel department.

Retailers' regular application forms—while not so lengthy as they once were—contain many questions. These questions concern the applicant's personal and family background, present living conditions, health, schools attended, academic record, previous employment, reasons for leaving previous employers, and reasons for desiring the job under consideration. The applicant may be asked to submit a transcript of his high school or college record, and asked to supply the names of several persons as references.[13]

Preliminary interviews After receiving the information described, and possibly immediately eliminating some candidates, the personnel manager —or the small store proprietor—is ready for relatively brief preliminary interviews with the prospective employees. The interviewer seeks information about basic interests and fields of proficiency, and tries to get an impression of the applicant's voice, appearance, use of English, poise, self-confidence, and attitude toward work. He tries to study the applicant by letting him do most of the talking.

Tests Retail personnel men hold widely differing opinions about the value of the four main types of employment tests—intelligence, aptitude, skill, and personality. Some retailers, especially department store firms, require every applicant to take an intelligence or mental ability test. Some of these firms believe that there is an appropriate intelligence quotient range for every job: People with IQ's below the desired range will not be able to handle the job while those with higher IQ's will get bored and quit. However, probably fewer than 15 percent of all large-scale retailers, including perhaps only 25 to 30 percent of the department stores, use intelligence tests.

Aptitude tests differ from intelligence tests in attempting to measure accomplishment potential rather than merely capacity for learning, and probably have somewhat wider use among retailers. For example, the New York State Employment Service has developed a sales aptitude test battery which the Service claims helps predict probable performance in sales jobs. Some retailers claim considerable success with aptitude tests and they are being used by a growing number of firms.[14] Yet others have been disap-

---

[13] For differences of opinion about the value of some of the information usually requested on application blanks, cf. Charles N. Weaver, "An Empirical Study to Aid in the Selection of Retail Salesclerks," *Journal of Retailing*, Vol. 45, No. 3 (Fall 1969), pp. 22–26, which reports sales performance significantly correlated with age, education, and marital status; Robert F. Hartley, "The Weighted Application Blank Can Improve Retail Employee Selection," *ibid.*, Vol. 46, No. 1 (Spring 1970), pp. 32–40, which recommends a technique for giving exact weights to various items on the blank; and James C. Cotham III, "Using Personal History in Retail Salesman Selection," *ibid.*, Vol. 45, No. 2 (Summer 1969), pp. 31–38, which reports little correlation between personal history data and the sales records of different retail major appliance salesmen.

[14] Among 348 supermarket organizations, 46 percent used "aptitude and other tests" in 1970 as compared with 22 percent in 1955. Cf. *The Super Market Industry Speaks, 1970*, *op. cit.*, p. 28.

pointed in the results and the great majority of merchants still have little faith in aptitude testing.

Many retailers use skill, job, or trade tests that measure very specific abilities in evaluating prospective employees for certain nonselling jobs. For example, a prospective stenographer may be tested on speed and accuracy in taking dictation and in typing. A deliveryman may be given a test on local geography. Prospective salesclerks are sometimes tested for arithmetic skill and ability to prepare an accurate salescheck, but very few retailers have found any satisfactory way to test for selling skills.

Personality tests assume that certain personality traits (friendliness, flexibility, sociability, stability) are essential to success and that measurement of these traits will help predict an individual's success or failure. Retailers and other businessmen are showing increased interest in these personality tests, but no reliable estimate of their retail use is currently available. Some observors believe that none of the tests developed to date accurately measures significant personality characteristics; others think that some firms give excessive weight to such tests in making personnel decisions.[15] Many merchants have found these tests helpful. Sears, Roebuck and Co. recently reported considerable success with the use of an elaborate management game as a combination personality and executive aptitude test to help screen managerial trainees.[16]

In summary, tests have been used to an increasing extent in recent years, as psychologists have improved their measuring techniques and as retailers have recognized the value of tests in avoiding serious selection mistakes. Some retailers also use outside testing agencies to help select executives and to assist in upgrading present employees. But, most retail personnel people still believe that the tests described above are primarily useful as supplementary tools in personnel decision making and that they should never be the sole criterion for any decision. That is, they should only be used in conjunction with interview, reference, and personal history information.

Physical examinations Many small and medium-sized stores do not require physical examinations, and even some large retail organizations put them on a voluntary basis. This is probably unwise. Retail work is often quite demanding and may be too difficult for people in poor physical condition. Recognition of this fact is leading to greater use of mandatory physical examinations. The examinations may also help to reduce costly accidents and injuries. The growth of employee pension and health insurance plans also argues for more pre-employment physicals.

---

[15] Cf. Samuel Feinberg, "How Valid Are Psychological Tests, Job Resumes," *Women's Wear Daily*, September 20, 1968, p. 11.

[16] "How to Spot Executives Early," *Fortune*, Vol. 78, No. 7 (July 1968), pp. 106–11.

Final interviews The applicant is usually given a final interview after the test and examination results become available. At this time, an effort is made to give him additional information about the job and to judge what he knows and thinks about its conditions and circumstances. The department manager or the applicant's "boss," perhaps assisted by a key interviewer from the personnel department, often conducts the final interview in large stores. Chain-store firms typically have an experienced interviewer conduct the final interview, commonly at central or branch headquarters.

In view of the reliance placed upon interviews, we may well ask: How satisfactory are they as a means of selecting employees? This question is difficult to answer. Because of lack of care in interviewing, disagreement as to qualities desired, and divergence of opinion concerning the outward indications of those qualities, various interviewers frequently give a single individual widely different ratings. All of these difficulties cannot be completely overcome, but some may be minimized through use of carefully drawn specifications and experienced, trained interviewers. The interview is a useful selection tool under such conditions. In the future, the interviewers' conclusions may become even more valid when they are checked against computerized comparisons of job requirements and applicant characteristics.

□ Introducing the employee to the store and to his job

Broadly speaking, the selection process has not been completed until the new employee has been introduced to his job and to his associates. All too frequently this step is neglected. In many stores no effort is made to acquaint the new employee with the firm's history, organization, and policies. Even his introduction to his immediate associates is perfunctory, and little effort is made to make him "feel at home." Yet this indoctrination task is essential, if the new employee is to enter upon his work feeling that he really "belongs."

What can the retailer do to introduce the employee to the store and to the job with more satisfactory results? In the small store, the proprietor should inform the employee about the store and its promotion opportunities. He should also take the time to introduce the new worker to the other employees, and to explain the nature and extent of his duties, hours, and other working conditions.

Employee induction is a joint responsibility of the employment and training departments in the well-run large retail organization. The training department takes over after the applicant is employed, and uses store tours, classes, conferences, and handbooks to instruct him in store organization, policy, and in his specific duties. A sponsor, the department head or the store manager, or a member of the personnel division then introduces him to his immediate colleagues.

□ The contingent force and prospect file

Because most medium-sized and large retail organizations need persons upon short notice, they usually keep a so-called "contingent force" upon the payroll. The contingent force members are not assigned to any particular department. Some stores use their most experienced salespeople, who can serve successfully in new and unfamiliar departments, for this purpose. Other organizations build their contingent force from part-time workers or from inexperienced new employees who give promise of being satisfactory workers after some service in the store.

A store's contingent force can only take care of sudden emergencies, such as special sales and sickness among employees. Where turnover of help is imminent, it is desirable to maintain a "prospect file," or list of people who have been passed upon by the employment office. By keeping it up-to-date and by steadily adding new names to it, the employment office seeks to fill all personnel requisitions soon after they are received.

■ TRAINING EMPLOYEES

A second major responsibility of personnel management is employee training, an activity that clearly demonstrates the axiom: "Personnel work is a dollar and cents matter." Adequate training results in more effective job performance and greater productivity; it insures conformance with established rules and regulations, thus reducing errors and increasing customer satisfaction; it lowers short-run and long-run selling costs, thus enhancing profits; it increases the employees' earnings through better job performance; it reduces employee turnover, improves morale and strengthens loyalty; and it simplifies management's supervisory tasks. Consequently, retailers of all sizes and types have been trying to improve their training programs in recent years to help protect their stores against the widespread general decline in the quality of service.[17]

---

[17] One commentator says: "The deficiency at the retail sales level has been—and is—notoriously bad." Earl Lifshey, "If You Ask Me," *Home Furnishings Daily*, November 4, 1968, p. 39.

□ Centralized and decentralized training

Organized training may be either centralized, that is, conducted by a central department, or decentralized to the actual job supervisors. The proprietors and managers normally do most of the training work right on the job in the small and medium-sized stores. Training is also being increasingly decentralized in the larger stores, since management often feels that the department heads and operating executives have more knowledge of job requirements than people in the training department and thus can more readily obtain the trainee's respect. Also, training is a constant responsibility and is more economically handled by supervisors who are in constant contact with the workers.

When training is largely decentralized, the central training department may concentrate on three major functions: (1) providing a certain amount of introductory schooling for new rank-and-file employees; (2) organizing some special courses, seminars, and other special activities; and (3), of most importance, helping the department heads and supervisors develop their training programs and abilities or, in other words, "training the trainers." Moreover, the central training staff often prepares films, other visual aids, and other materials to be used in the various units of a chain store system or in the departments of a large store. Some chains also try to assign as many new employees as possible, particularly managerial trainees, to specially designated training units where the managers are especially adept in personnel development and training.[18]

□ Determining the extent of the training program

Executive attitudes, personnel turnover rates, the store's service objectives, and the size of the store often determine the extent of a store's training program. A minimum of formal training will be used if the store does not aim at a high service standard, if its personnel turnover is low, and if the executives do not believe strongly in training programs. A comprehensive training plan is likely to be maintained under opposite conditions.

The store size also affects the training program. In the small store, whatever training may be provided is usually limited to the salespeople, some of whom may be inexperienced, whereas others have had various amounts of

---

[18] Two chain-type programs in which the central trainers come to the stores are described in: "Training: Wetterau's 251 Regional Schools," *Chain Store Age* (Supermarket Executives Edition), July 1968, pp. 47–48; and "Trailers for Training," *ibid.*, August 1968, p. 24.

previous training. Since the small store specializes in a limited line of merchandise, a comparable training program can be used for practically all new employees, with some adjustments because of previous experience.

The training program becomes more complicated as the size of the store increases. A considerably greater number of employees must be trained for a wide variety of selling and sales-supporting jobs involving many different types of goods. The training of part-time employees also becomes more complicated. Furthermore, some of the present staff, who are candidates for promotion, must be trained for advancement. Finally, extensive employee training programs are most likely to receive strong support from key executives in large and growing firms. Consequently, such firms often spend many thousands of dollars per year on their training programs.

□ The training program

In view of the factors mentioned in the previous section, it is logical to begin our discussion of the content of the training program with the kinds of employees to be trained.[19] Broadly speaking, these may be classified as follows: (1) New, inexperienced employees; (2) new, experienced employees; (3) current regular employees; and (4) "extras," that is, individuals employed for short intervals such as the pre-Christmas period.

Training new, inexperienced employees We will distinguish between sales and sales-supporting employees although there are some basic similarities in training both groups.

1. Salespeople New salespeople in large retail establishments often receive fifteen to twenty hours of very specific instruction, sometimes concentrated in a few days and sometimes spread over the first week or two, in organized selling classes. The salesperson-to-be is given a picture of the store's organization—made more vivid, perhaps, by a trip through the store. She is taught how to prepare sales slips, use sales registers, and keep stock. Store policies are explained concerning returned goods, credit, adjustments, absences from work, dress regulations, employee discounts, and safety regulations. Methods of greeting customers, showing merchandise, and closing sales are also usually discussed.

The proprietor or manager of the small store usually supplies this instruction right on the selling floor, as we have already noted. Some medium-sized and larger stores also provide much of this training through the "sponsor" system—an experienced salesperson who also acts as a training department representative in the selling department—since they believe

[19] Academic recruitment and training programs have already been covered in Chapter 3, "Opportunities and Careers in Retailing," so they are excluded from the present discussion.

this approach is more effective than the use of formal classes. Sponsors are also often used as a supplement to sales classes for such functions as introducing the new employee to the other workers, teaching selling techniques, helping correct individual difficulties, perhaps periodically rating each new worker, and especially building morale through regular follow-up.

Some retailers, particularly the larger organizations, have developed extensive sets of slides, movies, posters, other visual aids, and written materials to supplement the information that is provided by their sponsor systems, classroom lectures, workshop groups and role playing demonstrations. These supplementary materials may demonstrate right and wrong tactics to use with different customers, illustrate suggestion selling, remind the staff of basic matters such as courtesy to customers and care in preparing sales slips, explain store policies, and to instill pride of service in the salespeople. The written material is being increasingly reorganized for programmed instruction, that is, systematically presented so that the student can absorb it by himself either from a book or a teaching machine.

Several retail trade associations have also prepared helpful manuals on selling for use by their members[20] and some manufacturers provide details concerning the merchandise they sell. In recent years, many stores and groups of stores have employed specialized outside agencies to help develop training programs for inexperienced salespeople. The smaller store can gain access to training materials and skills it could not afford to develop on its own through joint or part-time use of the outside agency and even large stores find these organizations helpful. The outside training must be supplemented, however, by some internal instruction on the systems used in the employee's own store.

Many local school systems offer distributive training programs that are supported in part through federal grants. These courses usually include basic and career development retail job training for students who often assume part-time positions in local stores.[21] Some school systems also provide in-service refresher and advancement distributive education courses for experienced employees and storeowners. The Vocational Education Acts of 1963

---

[20] "New Advanced Course in Hardware Retailing Ready," *Hardware Retailer,* February 1969, p. 117, describes a course prepared by the National Retail Hardware Association; and "Retail Training: Teaching the Old Salesman about the New Consumer," *Training in Business and Industry,* October 1969, pp. 33–38, outlines some of the steps in the development of the National Retail Furniture Association's selling course.

[21] "For Hire: 104,000 Careerists," *Chain Store Age* (Supermarket Executives Edition), May 1968, pp. 64–65 describes the advantages of using distributive education students in these positions. Cf. U.S. Department of Health, Education, and Welfare, *Distributive Education in the High School* (Washington, D.C.: U.S. Government Printing Office, 1969); and John A. Beaumont, "How Distributive Education Helps Small Business," *Small Marketers Aids No. 14* (Washington, D.C.: U.S. Small Business Administration, 1961, reprinted 1968).

and 1968 provide additional support for curriculums for youths with socio-economic or other handicaps. Many retail firms have established special programs, in some cases with government cooperation, to train disadvantaged and minority group potential employees for sales and other positions. Such programs are underway in department store, discount, variety, supermarket, and drug chains.[22] However, many of the programs have encountered more difficulties and have been less extensive and effective than was envisaged at the outset.[23]

Despite all the training efforts discussed above, some experts feel that retail management fails "to appreciate the real contribution that creative sales effort can have on the final sale."[24] One observer states that retailing lags far behind manufacturing "in sophisticated training."[25] These opinions may be harsh, but they emphasize the need for constant attention to the sales training programs for new (and experienced) salespeople. Such programs are the best possible means for improving sales effort and the prestige of selling positions.

2. *Sales-supporting employees* The same two general techniques, employed in training salespeople—class sessions for a short period and the sponsor system—are also used when sales-supporting employees, such as deliverymen, elevator operators, and cashiers, are trained. Movies, demonstrations, group discussions, individual conferences, store manuals and programmed instruction are also used. Much of the instruction is decentralized and delegated to operating supervisors and employee sponsors even if the program is planned by, or in cooperation with, the central training department.

But, unfortunately, many stores, including a large portion of those that do train salespeople, fail to give their sales-supporting personnel any formal training. Still others limit the programs for nonselling employees to a brief introductory period. Relatively few stores take the trouble to give the new receiving clerk or marker an understanding of his place in the retail organization. This attitude has undoubtedly hurt performance standards and made the nonselling employees more receptive to unionization. If these workers are to feel that they are an essential part of the organization, their training should go beyond the question: How is my job performed?

---

[22] "Chains Enlisted in Ghetto Jobless Drive," *Chain Store Age* (Supermarket Executives Edition) May 1968, pp. 88–100; and "Opportunities at Bullock's Grow under Yolanda Chambers," *Women's Wear Daily*, April 29, 1968, p. 22.

[23] Cf. "Jobs Plan Ailing," *Women's Wear Daily*, June 20, 1968, pp. 1, 14.

[24] James C. Cotham, "The Case for Personal Selling," *Business Horizons*, Vol. 11, No. 2 (April 1968), pp. 75–81.

[25] E. B. Weiss, "Let Me Put It This Way," *Stores*, March 1970, p. 47; also cf. Bird McCord, "The Training Department as an Aid to Management Planning," *Journal of Retailing*, Vol. 44, No. 3 (Fall 1968), p. 68.

Training new, experienced employees New employees with previous retail experience do not need as elaborate introductory training as inexperienced employees. In the small store, such employees are usually put quite completely on their own after a minimum of instruction concerning the exact duties of the job and peculiarities of the store's system. In the large retail organization, however, some formal training in store organization, policies, and methods is necessary. A few class meetings or a brief period under sponsorship usually accomplishes this task satisfactorily.

Training regular employees Although retail training programs still emphasize the new employees, increasing attention is being given to workers who have been on the staff for some time. Progressive retailers recognize that training should be a continuous process for all employees. Few new employees fully absorb all of the material that is set forth in the few class hours of initial training. New questions, not covered during the introductory training, arise out of actual work experience. Even veteran cashiers, salespeople, stockroom personnel, and other staff can become overconfident, careless, or forgetful of the basic rules of courtesy and need follow-up programs. New fashion and merchandise developments must be outlined for the employees. Formal training for promotion may prod some who are slightly lethargic into seeking advancement and will help satisfy and retain the ambitious employee who expects his firm to assist him in moving ahead. Some stores make this training a more or less implicit precondition for promotion, while other merchants believe that the best results can be obtained by putting the formal programs on a more voluntary basis.

1. Follow-up or job training Follow-up training often consists of private conferences to discuss ways the individual employee can improve his performance. Classes are also used for large numbers of employees. Department store buyers often hold weekly meetings to give employees information about fashion trends and new merchandise. Suppliers' representatives may participate in some of these meetings to supply additional product data, and other store executives and training staff may be brought in to discuss salesmanship, the use of sales quotas, or the ways the salespeople can help reduce expenses. Chain store and branch store managers and department heads hold similar meetings, often with the help of a constant flow of pamphlets, films, bulletins, selling tips, and other training aids from central headquarters.

Some firms carry out job training by switching employees from one branch of the business to another, thus providing a complete view of the firm's operations. Still another technique is sending small groups of salespeople out from time to time to observe competing or affiliated stores. This technique stimulates interest and encourages employees to notice things that will improve their performance. Such observation trips are followed by group conferences in which experiences are exchanged.

2. *Promotional training* The majority of successful retailers agree that a policy of promotion from the ranks is highly desirable. Most of them would echo the statement of Mr. Irving Edison, president of Edison Brothers Stores, Inc., a national shoe chain:

> For over 40 years, we have followed an inviolate policy of elevating our shoe salesman to the higher posts in our company. Our 508 stores are managed by 508 of our former salespeople. Our 30 regional managers are our former salespeople. Every buyer in our home office and most of our officers are former salespeople of our company. We believe that, if we do not have qualified, trained personnel in our company for the bigger positions that become available, the fault is ours.[26]

Promotion from within builds employee goodwill, improves morale, attracts forward-looking individuals, provides officers who are well trained in the store's policies and practices, and is a relatively inexpensive method of securing executives.

A house organ can supplement the training program. News of employee promotions may stimulate other persons to greater efforts. Data on new lines of merchandise, on the use of good salesmanship, on outstanding or unusual services rendered to customers, and on certain of the store's policies may also be covered in the store paper.

For maximum effectiveness, a policy of promotion from within the firm should be accompanied by an adequate training program for promotable personnel. This may involve company-planned conferences and courses in various aspects of the business, work-study arrangements with universities, evening courses in colleges, correspondence courses, job rotation, and the use of sponsors.

Unfortunately, most of the advanced training (and much of the other training as well) given by stores to nonexecutive employees is largely technical in nature and designed to explain how certain jobs are performed. This type of training is important, of course, but if the store is really eager to stir the interest of its workers in jobs in the retail field, the training needs to be broader. It should give the employee a picture of the significance of retailing in our economy, of major trends in the retail field, and of the importance of the individual to the success of the store. Moreover, it is quite likely that most retailers have been too slow to advance those who have taken advantage of promotional training opportunities. A decrease in this time lag could be a significant factor in educating retail personnel as to the dollar and cents advantage of such training.

3. *Training supervisors* No retail training program can be really effective without the full support and cooperation of the supervisory force. Consequently, some large retailers have adopted various measures to involve the

[26] Quoted by Samuel Feinberg in "From Where I Sit" *Women's Wear Daily*, May 28, 1965, p. 7.

supervisors in the training process, to improve their training abilities, and to make them aware of training's significance. Some provide the supervisors with special self-study programs which make use of textbooks, correspondence courses, phonograph records, and (in a few instances) teaching machines. Still other retailers have rather formalized training courses, which may include lectures, films, and business games, that emphasize leadership qualities and stress the wise application of company policies and procedures. Supervisors are taught that their job is to maintain good human relationships through proper indoctrination and on-the-job training of employees, through frequent personnel reviews, and through appropriate salary, promotional, transfer and release recommendations. Chain store supervisors may receive all or part of this training through meetings at regional or main office headquarters. The personnel division, of course, plays a key role in carrying out all of these activities within the framework of the firm's general policies.

4. Advanced management programs Some progressive retail firms offer an elaborate assortment of management advancement programs. For example, Stop & Shop, a New England-based supermarket and discount chain, has used approximately 20 different management development programs. These include trade association-sponsored seminars, an 11-session course in effective communications, a 50 percent tuition grant for job-related evening college courses, assistant buyers' seminars conducted in its discount division, a 15 session management improvement course for Boston area middle-level executives taught by M.I.T. faculty, a one-week intensive human-relations training session for senior executives, and a six to eight month Accelerated Management Development Program for potential store managers. The latter program includes on-the-job training in stores, headquarters sessions, and an intensive four-day leadership conference held at a Cape Cod resort.[27] The McCrory-McLellan-Green variety chain conducts a rigorous three-week course for district manager candidates; offers seminars for experienced district managers; prepares its own training films; and encourages its executives to take outside courses in mathematics and other subjects.[28]

Carson Pirie Scott & Co., a Chicago department store, forms a group of selected executives who study and discuss corporate-wide problems in addition to performing their specific functions within the firm. The group participates in meetings concerned with all phases of the company's opera-

[27] "Stop and Shop: Today a Retailing Complex," *Chain Store Age*, (Supermarket Executives Edition) December 1968, pp. 35–40. Also cf. "Jewel Lets Young Men Make Mistakes," *Business Week*, January 17, 1970, pp. 90–92.

[28] "How Do You Train A District Manager—or a Buyer—or a V.P.?" *Chain Store Age* (General Merchandise Managers' Edition), July 1969, pp. 34–37.

tions, and two representatives attend each Board of Directors' meeting to report on specific projects. The company also uses middle-management seminars and discussion programs in which the executives analyze both classical books and contemporary psychological studies for their insights into human relations. Several R. H. Macy Company divisions use a "Work Simplification Program," that has the executives consider and plan ways of improving operations. These projects produce beneficial changes in store methods, but the company considers the executives' discussions and training in problem-solving as the most valuable contributions of the program.[29] Other alert firms are using a wide variety of similar techniques to encourage and nurture executive growth.

Training extras The short period that most extras are on the payroll seldom makes intensive training worthwhile, yet these employees may account for one-third or more of a store's sales. Moreover, as we have already noted, the current shortage of "extras" forces retailers to hire less satisfactory employees, so that the training task is more difficult than at an earlier period.

The larger stores usually give the "extras" a one- (sometimes two-) day "cram" session covering, in abbreviated fashion, the material given to new inexperienced employees. Then a sponsor takes over. Some retailers, both large and small, rely practically entirely on the sponsor system, perhaps supplemented by printed material. One variety chain gives each extra employee a short manual which covers such matters as store policies and regulations, care of stock, and the manner of approaching customers. In a few cases, retailers in a city have cooperated in arranging initial general training of holiday employees through a local business school or college.

Regardless of the training given extras before they begin work, the retailer must depend in large measure upon the aid and advice they receive from his regular employees. Through its house organ "Field Glass," Marshall Field & Company appeals to its employees for this necessary cooperation as follows:

Let's Welcome Them

Christmas hiring has started. Between now and the end of November we will nearly double our number of employees. These new people come in to aid us during the greatest rush of the year—it is only through their efforts added to our own that we will be able to give our large number of holiday customers the traditional courtesy and service that spell FIELD'S.

Let's welcome them—remembering our own first days in the store, let's help them. We know the store. We know its systems, its locations, its habits and its people. And all these are strange to our new members. We can do much to help

[29] Eugene Kalina, "A Re-Appraisal of Effective Executive Training," and Alfred Nieman, "Work Simplification Program," in *Recruiting and Developing Store Executives* (New York: National Retail Merchants Association, 1967), pp. 46–53, 55–64.

them overcome their strangeness, and to make their work here the pleasant experience we all want it to be. Let's increase our constant effort to do this during the next few weeks—let's resolve that each new member will learn of Field's courtesy and service from personal experience—will learn that these qualities are genuine and are extended to customers because they are practiced "at home."

□ Appraising the training program

The precise value of employee training is very difficult to measure.[30] But some checking techniques will give management a rough indication of what the training is accomplishing. Larger retailers often send professional shoppers into their stores to act as customers and then report on their experiences with specific sales personnel. These shopping-service reports, however, are expensive and are likely to be influenced by chance factors (an employee may be approached when specially tired or bothered) and by such human elements as the shopper's own training and background. Records of employee average sale and the number of errors and complaints reported have some value as indicators when used with appropriate caution. Periodic examinations sometimes afford a fairly satisfactory check.[31] Personnel reviews at regular intervals are also used for this purpose.

In the final analysis, however, the effectiveness of the training program is measured by the general morale of the store's employees, the opportunities for advancement and the extent of promotion from within, the quality of supervision, the number of customer complaints, the rate of employee turnover, and—most important of all—the quality of customer service and its reflection in profits.

■ REVIEW AND DISCUSSION QUESTIONS

1 "It is old-fashioned to think of personnel management as a dollar-and-cents matter; instead it must be thought of as a means of keeping people happy on their jobs." Discuss.

2 Explain the main factors responsible for the increased emphasis on personnel management in retail stores in recent years.

3 Select three of the seven "human relations principles" listed on page

[30] Cf. Ann Karlsson, "Does Retail Training Pay?" *Training in Business and Industry*, February 1969, p. 25; April 1969, pp. 33–34, 58.

[31] These tests need not be written. The "test sale" is becoming a popular means of checking on the effectiveness of sales training programs. The employee who has finished her initial training is required to demonstrate the sale of specific merchandise with another salesperson or an employee of the training department as the customer.

187 and comment on some of your personal experiences which seem to support or invalidate these "principles."

4 "It must be recognized that, in a sense, personnel work is performed by every employee and executive of a store, regardless of whether he is or is not in the personnel department." Give three illustrations of this statement.

5 Discuss the important steps involved in recruiting an adequate force of retail employees.

6 What are the most common sources from which a store may draw employees? Which sources seem the most satisfactory for (a) the small drugstore, (*b*) the large chain drug company, (c) the discount house, and (*d*) the department store? Would your answer be affected by the type of jobs available? Give your reasons.

7 Discuss the value and the use of each of the following factors in the selection of employees: the application blank, the preliminary interview, aptitude tests, the physical examination, and the final interview.

8 What is meant by the term "induction of employees"? Indicate the significance of the induction program from both employer and employee points of view.

9 Compare and contrast the training program of a small retailer in your home town with that of a competing large-scale retailer handling the same general types of merchandise. To what extent does the large-scale retailer use centralized training? What are the organization chart positions and duties of his personnel and training directors?

10 What kind of follow-up training would you recommend (*a*) in a small specialty shop, (*b*) in a large clothing store for men, and (c) in a department store? Explain.

chapter 9

RETAIL PERSONNEL MANAGEMENT (continued)

A third very important personnel responsibility involves working out compensation plans for selling and sales-supporting personnel, including such managerial personnel as buyers or department managers, store managers, and key executives. Dissatisfaction with compensation plans is a common source of complaint.

■ COMPENSATING RETAIL PERSONNEL

It is very difficult to devise any method of payment which is satisfactory to personnel performing a wide variety of tasks that require different skills and abilities. Some of the difficulties may be made clear if we establish the requisites of an ideal plan and then see how closely the plans in use conform to this goal.

□ Goals of a compensation plan

An ideal compensation plan, designed to meet the requirements of both the store and the employee as far as this is practicable, should:

1. Keep wage costs under control. The store's payroll costs, expressed as a percentage of sales, should be compared frequently with labor costs in fairly similar stores. Simple comparison of the store's present rate with its past experience is not adequate, since past wage costs may have also been excessive.
2. Minimize discontent among employees and help to reduce labor turnover. It should not only *be* fair but should be *considered* fair by employees.
3. Be easily understood by employees and easily administered by management.
4. Provide an incentive for better work, rewarding improved performance and penalizing inefficiency.
5. Guarantee a minimum income and regular periodic payments, so as to give the employee a sense of security.

□ Compensating salespeople

The four main compensation plans for salespeople are:

1. Straight salary.
2. Salary plus commission on *all* net sales.
3. Quota bonus, also known as salary-quota bonus.
4. Straight commission (usually with drawing account).

Some stores use combinations of these plans to meet particular requirements and practically all retailers employ various salary supplements to stimulate their salespeople.

Straight salary The employee is paid a definite amount each payday—for example, $80 each Friday. It is the most common method of compensating salespeople, being almost universally used in small stores and in chain stores selling convenience goods.

The straight salary plan has many advantages. It is especially suitable for the small store where the employee performs so many different jobs that it is difficult and perhaps unfair to pay him on any other basis. Adequate salaries can minimize employee discontent and hold those individuals who might be attracted to other firms. This plan is easily understood, and the fixed regular payment meets the objections of many who dislike the insecurity of a fluctuating income.

These advantages are so significant that straight salary, accompanied by a well-conceived personnel-rating program[1] to provide incentive, is probably the best single method of compensating retail salespeople. But, when

[1] Cf. pp. 219–20, below.

used without personnel-rating, it fails to offer an immediate incentive to greater effort. Straight salary also lacks any degree of automatic flexibility so that the wage-cost ratio may get out of control. This disadvantage is especially serious if sales decline significantly, since the retailer may hesitate to reduce salary rates because of union contracts, fear of employee discontent, or hope for a reversal of the sales trend. Consequently the payroll ratio may increase sharply.

Salary plus commission on all net sales This plan, which is even more common in the very large stores than straight salary, usually calls for a salary which is somewhat less than would be paid in the absence of a commission but adds a relatively low commission rate on *all* net sales. Currently, the commission rate ranges from ½ to 1 percent. Thus a person with a $75 weekly salary and weekly net sales of $500 would receive a total of $77.50 (on a ½ of 1 percent commission) or $80 (with a 1 percent rate).

Adding a small commission to the salary helps answer some of the objections to the straight salary method. Some immediate incentive to greater effort is provided; and the wage ratio becomes somewhat more flexible since commission payments will fluctuate with sales. At the same time, the main advantages of the straight salary plan are retained by keeping the basic salary large relative to the weekly pay.

Quota bonus Increasingly, some large and small retailers selling shopping and specialty goods use a basic salary plus a commission on all net sales in excess of a certain quota. This plan involves four steps:

1. Determining the weekly (or monthly) quota. Typically, past sales are the basis of this decision, with adjustment for changed conditions and for seasonal fluctuations. If records suggest that $900 weekly sales is about average, this figure may be used as the quota. To be of greatest value, the quota should remain within the reach of practically all the salespeople. Yet, it cannot be too low or everyone will reach it without much effort.
2. Establishing the basic salary. This salary is usually determined on the basis of the past wage-cost ratio adjusted in the light of competitive practices. If this ratio has averaged about 7 percent, the basic salary might be established at 7 percent of the quota; that is, $63 on a $900 quota.
3. Setting the commission rate for sales in excess of the quota. In practice this commission is usually set considerably below the store's average wage cost. If 7 percent is the average wage cost, the commission may be set at 3 or 4 percent. In some cases the bonus is a specific dollar amount, rather than a percentage of sales in excess of the quota.
4. Deciding whether each period involves a "fresh start" (non-cumulative plans) or whether salespeople who fail to make their quota in one period

have to fill the deficiency before becoming eligible for a bonus in the next period (cumulative plans). Most plans today are noncumulative.

How does this plan compare with our "ideal" requirements? (1) The wage-cost ratio remains relatively inflexible, since the basic salary makes up the bulk of the total wage payment. (2) The plan may minimize discontent by giving each salesperson a chance to earn as much as any other salesperson. (3) Any change in quotas, however, may be interpreted as an attempt to reduce wage payments and hence, may lead to dissatisfaction. (4) The computation of payments adds some clerical work. (5) Assuming the quotas are not set too high, the commission on excess sales provides an incentive for greater effort. (6) Yet it is difficult to adjust the quota to periods of falling and rising sales. (7) The employee will find it rather complicated; and incentive is lost, if the commission payment is held off for a considerable period. (8) The basic salary does provide a steady income.

Straight commission Under the straight commission plan of wage payment, salespeople receive a specified commission on all goods they sell. This commission varies from 3 to 8 percent of sales, depending on the type of merchandise and its profitableness, the store, and the season of the year. This method of payment is most common in stores and departments selling items of high unit value, such as furniture and rugs, women's apparel, and shoes.[2]

In actual practice, the straight commission is often supplemented with a drawing account. That is, payments are made to salespeople at regular intervals, and these are charged against commissons earned each month when reconciliations are made.

The straight commission provides the most flexibility in wages and the greatest control over wage costs. It is easily understood by employees, and the payments can be computed without difficulty. Since income varies directly with sales and payment follows closely upon the expenditure of effort, an incentive is offered. When supplemented with a drawing account, a regular income is assured.

Paradoxical though it may seem, the incentive provided by the straight commission plan has proved to be one of its weaknesses, especially for stores that desire to build a reputation for service to all customers. Salespeople paid on commission may try to avoid persons who seem merely to be "looking" or who are interested in low-priced merchandise. Stores some-

[2] Some commission salesmen and saleswomen earn rather substantial incomes. Top retail furniture salesmen in New York and Los Angeles are reported to make about $300 per week, some shoe and clothing salespeople about $150 to $200, and leading appliance salesmen $250 to $400. Samuel Feinberg, "New Pact Could Be Best Ever Macy's Investment," *Women's Wear Daily,* February 11, 1970, pp. 1, 18; "Labor's Los Angeles Move Hits Snags," *Home Furnishings Daily,* March 18, 1970, p. 7.

times minimize this disadvantage by the use of a call system, which usually provides for a man to welcome each customer and assign a salesperson to take care of her wishes. In this way, salespeople get an equal chance to make sales and cannot "pick" their customers. However, there is still the objection that the salesperson, trying to increase his income, may exert pressure on the customer to buy. Some customers object to such tactics. Another difficulty is that new salespeople, without a "following" or experience, often find it difficult to make a sufficient number of sales to obtain what they feel is an adequate income.

Salary supplements for salespeople Some retailers also provide their salespeople with opportunities for earning extra compensation which may add from 10 to 15 percent to their regular salary. Sometimes this is done through profit sharing. The percentage of retail workers and executives participating in profit-sharing plans has grown significantly in recent years, and is higher than in any other major industry group.[3] About 25 percent of the supermarket chains share profits with *all* employees.[4] Montgomery Ward & Company adopted a general profit-sharing plan covering sales and sales-supporting personnel as well as store managers, superintendents, and major executives in 1963. The J. C. Penney Company and Sears, Roebuck and Co., however, have long had such plans and both firms cite them as a significant factor in their success.[5] In contrast, other retailers—Woodward and Lothrop, a Washington, D.C., department store company, for instance—have abandoned profit sharing, believing the relatively small payments going to sales personnel and the lack of clear-cut evidence of relationship between effort and reward minimize the impact of this form of salary supplement.

Prize money (P.M.'s) or extra commissions, another kind of salary supplement, may be paid for selling certain kinds of merchandise, such as private brands. Dollar awards are used to encourage courteous treatment of customers. Some retailers hold sales contests in which salespeople can win valuable prizes, such as major appliances, wardrobes, and winter trips to Florida.

Many department and specialty stores allow employee discounts on all purchases made in the store—and, of late, retailers are liberalizing this arrangement. Whereas, formerly, some weeks or months of service were quite typically required, today the discount privilege is granted almost im-

---

[3] Gunnar Engen, "A New Direction and Growth in Profit Sharing," *Monthly Labor Review*, July 1967, pp. 6–7.

[4] An additional 27 percent have profit sharing limited to certain managerial personnel. Seventy percent of the companies pay an annual bonus (21 percent to all full-timers). *The Supermarket Industry Speaks, 1970* (Chicago: The Super Market Institute, 1970) p. 27.

[5] Cf. "The Booming Benefits of Profit Sharing," *The Reader's Digest*, August 1969, pp. 111–14.

mediately. Moreover, many retailers have increased their discounts; the former 10 to 15 percent figures have been replaced by 15, or, in even more cases, 20 percent. With employee discount purchases amounting to over 4 percent of department store sales and 2 percent of specialty store sales, retailers consider the discount as a way to promote the store's merchandise to employees as well as an important aid in retaining personnel.[6] In contrast, just 6 percent of the food chains grant employee discounts and even in these firms the discounts are held within the 5 to 10 percent range. With their relatively low mark-ups and the possibility that the discount privilege might be abused (employees purchasing for friends and relatives), these chains tend to minimize this form of salary supplement.

Still other salary supplements are the cash award given for usable suggestions and the special bonus, based on length of service or other factors, often given at Christmas time. Finally, various pension programs have been developed to provide compensation after the salesperson's retirement.[7]

☐ Compensating sales-supporting employees

Straight salary is the most popular way of compensating these employees. Widespread use of the salary plan results in part from the difficulties involved in setting quotas or in finding a satisfactory basis for a commission. Yet a standard unit of output can be set for some nonselling jobs and commissions paid on the number of units produced. Department store and chain store industrial engineering and "work study" bureaus have developed new methods and devices to measure productivity in an increasing number of sales-supporting jobs. Thus, the number of units marked may serve as a basis of commission to people who mark goods; the number of packages put up as a basis for paying packers; and the number of pages or lines typed, for stenographers. But even in these instances, it is hard to get a standard unit of output. For the typist the number of lines typed depends somewhat upon the material, and this is a variable factor. Not all goods are marked in the same way, and various-sized packages have different time requirements for packing.

Incentive plans for nonselling employees are limited almost entirely to the large retail firms. However, in retail stores of all sizes, sales-supporting

[6] Richard Rosenthal, "Employee Discount Buying Rings up 4% of Store Sales," *Women's Wear Daily,* December 1, 1965, p. 8. For further details on this study by the National Retail Merchants Association, cf. *Retail Employee Discounts* (New York: The Association, 1965). Recent union agreements with the Gimbel and Bloomingdale department stores in New York provide for a 25 percent discount on some merchandise categories. "Store Union, Gimbels OK New Pay Pact," *Women's Wear Daily,* June 11, 1969, p. 2.

[7] Cf. p. 226, below.

employees are usually eligible for most of the salary supplements given to selling employees, especially discounts on purchases, profit sharing, cash awards, and special bonuses.

□ Compensating managerial personnel

Most compensation plans at the managerial level include an immediate incentive to greater efforts.[8]

Department store and specialty store buyers Practically all department and specialty stores pay their buyers some form of bonus, in addition to salary; and the specific arrangement is usually set forth in a definite written contract.

Six common methods are employed for determining the bonus, as follows:

1. Bonus based on sales—either stated as a percentage of the total sales of the department (such as 1 percent) or as a stated percentage of the increase in sales over a quota. A stated minimum gross margin is also often required.
2. Bonus based on increased sales plus increased gross margin or net profit. For example, a store may agree to pay "1 percent of sales increase over previous year plus 5 percent of additional net profits after income taxes."
3. Bonus based on total store operations. Such an arrangement is designed to induce buyers to "merchandise" with a storewide approach to problems. The amount the buyer receives is dependent on a management review of the department's operation during the year.
4. Bonus based on departmental net profit, either before or after federal taxes. The bonus may vary from 1 to 10 percent and it may not apply until after a stated dollar amount of net profit has been reached, e.g., $10,000.
5. Bonus based on a department's contribution. "Contribution" is usually defined as the dollar gross margin of the department minus specified controllable expenses. The bonus is calculated as a percentage of the department's contribution and commonly ranges from 1 to 3 percent.
6. Bonus based on departmental gross margin, such as 3 percent or more of the gross margin realized.

Chain store managers Variety, discount, and junior department store chains often pay a salary and then give the manager from 10 to 15 percent of the profits made by his store. Other firms use a drawing account and give

[8] Also cf. the discussion of top management compensation in Chapter 3.

the manager from 10 to 20 percent of the profits minus what he has already received from a drawing account. Such compensation plans give the manager a direct incentive to make his store produce profits. Even when a salary is paid, it is kept relatively low, so that a large part of the manager's income results from his store's profit.

Food and drug chains, on the other hand, usually base their incentive payments on sales, a common plan being a salary plus from 1 to 2 percent of sales. Although this arrangement encourages the manager to seek volume irrespective of profits, the chains feel that other controls will insure profitability. In some cases the store manager is paid a substantial straight commission on sales and is expected to pay his employees out of his commission. Such a plan has the major advantage of keeping wage costs under definite control.

Chain organizations in several other fields—auto supplies, for example—also use bonuses based on the store's contribution to company profits. Frequently, the bonus is paid only on the contribution above an established goal for the store; and it may be divided between manager and assistant manager on a 3 to 1 or some other fixed basis.

The chain store manager compensation plan should be suited to the company's needs. Specifically, it should help top management attract and hold desirable personnel by providing incentive for above-average efforts and satisfactory operating results, furnishing extra rewards for outstanding accomplishment, and comparing favorably with the compensation plans of leading competitors.

Major executives Previous mention has been made of the search for executive talent.[9] An attractive compensation plan is only one major factor in attracting and retaining properly qualified retail executives. Studies indicate that the fundamental satisfactions desired by those who operate their own stores or who serve in executive positions for others are as follows:

1. Financial rewards commensurate with the responsibilities of the position.
2. Freedom of action within the individual's sphere of responsibility with commensurate authority.
3. Adequate title and prestige of position.
4. Stability of position, with adequate provision for retirement.
5. Satisfactory working quarters and conditions. Many executives report that they want comfortable offices with adequate light and ventilation and good furnishings. One company president who had recently moved into a new office was heard to say: "I'd gladly take $5,000 a year off my present salary if it were necessary to justify my present office facilities."

[9] Cf. pp. 63–72 and 193, above.

6. Association with an organization that is "moving ahead," so that one may take pride in being a part of it.
7. A position that offers an opportunity of public service.

Despite the fact that financial reward is by no means the only consideration important to retail executives, a fact which is currently not given sufficient attention in the retail field, dollar compensation *is* significant.

The majority of small store proprietors pay themselves a regular weekly or biweekly salary. This salary may be adjusted from year to year according to the proprietor's judgment as to the expected profits. Moreover, it may be supplemented from time to time or at the end of each year by extra withdrawals of funds if the profit position is satisfactory.

While the executives of some large retail organizations are paid by salary only, the incentive aspect is so important that most of them receive a salary plus some form of bonus or profit-sharing arrangement, all or part of which may be deferred until after retirement when the recipient will be (presumably) in a lower tax bracket. Option plans which permit the executive to benefit (by paying a capital gains tax rather than an income tax) from advances in the price of the firm's stock are also common.[10] Still other typical elements in the executive compensation package are insurance payments and pension plans.

In some instances the firm's bonus or profit-sharing arrangement is not formalized, the amount paid being determined each year by the president or the board of directors. But most firms set aside a fixed percentage of net profits as a bonus or profit-sharing fund, to be divided among key executives in ratio to their salaries or according to some other predetermined formula. One careful study of 14 major chains suggests that such profit sharing is effective. The seven chains with profit-sharing plans were substantially more successful than the seven lacking such plans.[11]

The long-run nature of the executive compensation plan should not,

[10] An executive or other employee in a rapidly growing corporation may receive very substantial benefits from profit sharing paid in the form of corporate stock. For a description of a company pilot in charge of corporate aviation for a hardware and building supply store chain, who accumulated over $1 million through profit sharing bonuses, cf. John Corcoran, "Don't Tell Max Freeman [Chief Pilot, Lowe's Companies, Inc.] 'Corporate Aviation Is a Nice Way to Earn a Living, but You'll Never Make a Million,' " *Professional Pilot,* May 1971, pp. 62–64.

[11] J. J. Jehring and B. L. Metzger, *The Stockholder and Employee Profit Sharing* (Evanston, Ill.: Profit Sharing Research Foundation, 1960). A followup study shows that the performance of the profit sharing retail chains improved even more, relative to the nonprofit sharers, during the years 1958 through 1969. B. L. Metzger and J. A. Colletti, *Does Profit Sharing Pay?* (Evanston, Ill.: Profit Sharing Research Foundation, 1971), p. viii. Research and other lines of business also shows superior results for companies with profit sharing plans. Cf. R. L. Wood, "Determination of the Profit Sharing Formula," in D. X. Murray, ed., *Successful Profit Sharing Plans—Theory and Practice* (Chicago: Council of Profit Sharing Industries, 1968), p. 19.

however, force the company to retain incompetent officials. The plan should include equitable separation arrangements and, in some cases, early retirement at a reduced pension.

Finally, the executive compensation plan should be reviewed frequently. In part, such a review is necessary because constantly changing taxation and inheritance laws alter the tax status of different executive remuneration techniques. But the plan also needs periodic review from the point of view of individual executives. An executive's needs change with the various stages of his career cycle. In his thirties and early forties his main requirement may be for cash; from forty-five until his mid-fifties, he may be able to forego some immediate cash in favor of stock options or a long-range incentive bonus plan; and as he approaches retirement, a deferral arrangement may be attractive.

□ Job evaluation and the compensation plan

Job evaluation is simply a carefully worked out program for appraising the value of jobs and obtaining an equitable relationship among them—a program founded upon common sense and good judgment. Job evaluation has been carried on in a more or less formal way in industrial plants for many years but only recently has it received the close attention it deserves from retail personnel executives.

Objectives of job evaluation The five major objectives of job evaluation are as follows:

1. To implement a company policy of equal pay for equal work, thereby building employee good will.
2. To pay all employees in proportion to their responsibilities and to the difficulty of their work.
3. To recognize monetary differentials for different quality and quantity of work, thus giving employees an incentive for improved performance.
4. To provide a basis for explaining to employees why a job is valued as it is.
5. To establish pay rates in keeping with those for similar work in the community.

Job evaluation methods A great variety of methods are employed to evaluate jobs in retail stores. The plan adopted by any specific firm should, of course, be tailored to its own conditions, reflect the considered judgment of the firm's executives, and be based on adequate study of all pertinent factors. One progressive store, for example, evaluates all jobs on the basis of four major groups of factors, with weights within each group assigned as follows:

1. *Skill requirement factors,* including education, 10 percent; job knowledge, 15 percent; customer contact, 10 percent; personal contact (other than customer contact), 10 percent; special aptitudes, 7 percent.
2. *Responsibility requirement factors,* including supervision, 12 percent; and responsibility, 15 percent.
3. *Effort requirement factors,* including mental effort, 9 percent; and physical effort, 6 percent.
4. *Working conditions factor,* 6 percent.

A job evaluation committee composed of the store superintendent, the personnel director, the industrial engineer, the controller, the merchandise manager, and the president of the store uses these factors as its yardstick. Summaries of evaluations are prepared for each division and distributed to the divisional manager concerned. Inequities are promptly corrected, after which the personnel manager prepares a total store summary and forwards it to top management.

Steps should be taken to gain employee acceptance before any job evaluation program is instituted. Unless employees understand the reasons for its adoption and how it will affect their work, the program will not produce its maximum results. Management should avoid such errors as lack of simplicity, failure to apply common sense, and general impatience for results. Job evaluation is a painstaking process, and its value will depend upon the care with which it is planned and carried out.

Significant by-products of job evaluation In addition to the many direct advantages produced by properly conducted job evaluations, such as more equitable wage rates, better wage progression, and improved employee morale, important by-products also result. These include increased emphasis upon job study and improved personnel performance, stimulation of employees by presenting a clearer picture of promotional opportunities, a reduction in labor turnover, fair and frequent reviews of individual performance, suggestions for presenting management's point of view in collective bargaining on wages, and the information needed by management to explain wage rates satisfactorily to employees.

A survey of 98 department stores some years ago found 47 percent used some kind of job evaluation.[12] While this figure is far too high for retailing as a whole, the gains from job evaluation are so significant that the practice will undoubtedly receive increasing attention from retail store executives in the future. Experience has proven it a necessary and useful tool in determining and maintaining a satisfactory compensation program.

---

[12] I. L. Sands, "Personnel Practices in Department Stores," *New York Retailer,* June 1957, p. 20. Comparable data for more recent years are not available.

■ OBTAINING SATISFACTORY PERSONNEL PERFORMANCE

As already emphasized, personnel management's responsibility does not end with the hiring and initial training of employees. Some of the most important personnel functions involve maintaining and improving the present staff's performance level. To a degree, achieving this goal depends upon the spirit which management injects into the firm's personnel—the birthday corsage to saleswomen, the breakfast for the contest winner, and the picture of the "best manager of the week" in the weekly house organ.

More than enthusiasm, however, is needed to stimulate employees to a higher-level performance of their responsibilities: There must be personnel activities leading to a suitable compensation plan, preferably based on sound job evaluation; continuous evaluation of personnel; promotion, transfer, demotion, and discharge of some workers; adequate working conditions; appropriate employee service activities; and successful handling of employees' complaints. Compensation plans and job evaluation have already been covered; the other activities will be discussed in the remaining sections of this chapter.

□ Evaluating personnel

Personnel evaluation seeks to give the retailer a carefully formed opinion as to the value of each employee to the firm. Such evaluation is important as the basis for salary adjustments, promotions, transfers, and terminations and also as a method of encouraging employees to do better work. It aids in detecting employees who are "slipping," before they have fallen to such a low performance level that termination of employment is necessary. The evaluation process brings the management into closer touch with the employee, which leads to greater mutual understanding.

Careful evaluation of personnel is difficult because the value of an employee depends, in part, on so many factors which cannot be measured objectively. Not only is the employee's production important; his ability, loyalty, honesty, and attitude toward the store and his work are also significant. Many of these latter elements are matters of opinion, and various individuals may differ in rating the same employee. In spite of such difficulties, worthwhile results can be obtained if the retailer will maintain adequate up-to-date records, set up objective standards wherever possible, get opinions from a number of sources, and carry out the process on a regular schedule.

In the small store Many small store proprietors fail to use definite, objective standards in personnel evaluation; hence personal likes and dislikes excessively influence their opinions. Greater objectivity may be obtained, however, through recognition of the importance of evaluation and the establishment of certain criteria to use as a yardstick. A salesperson, for example, might be judged on the basis of sales, both in dollars and in number of transactions, customer complaints, errors in filling orders and recording sales, the number of times late or absent from work, and the ratio of dollar value of goods returned to sales. If the store has several employees, the proprietor may periodically ask each one to rate the other employees on a number of personal qualities—loyalty, honesty, courtesy, and attitude toward work. The proprietor may occasionally get customer reaction to certain employees by interviewing a number of patrons. Fairly similar techniques may be used to evaluate any sales-supporting employees.

In the large store A committee, frequently consisting of the personnel director and two or three other executives, supervises the systematic evaluation of personnel or the "personnel review" in most large retail firms. This committee originates forms for recording the performance of each employee (see Figure 9–1) and his ratings. Although each individual may be rated as often as once a month or as infrequently as once a year, about every six months is usual. To minimize personal prejudice, each employee is usually rated by two to four associates. The factors appraised usually include some or all of the following: personality, attendance, sales, industry, initiative, cooperation, knowledge of the job, loyalty to the firm, accuracy, appearance, treatment of customers, health, and willingness and ability to assume responsibility.

Another type of personnel evaluation for salespeople is the "shopping report" prepared by an outside organization. This report covers important points regarding salesmanship, the appearance of the salesperson and the department, and the extent of compliance with the store system.[13]

The committee reviews the individual performance records and ratings and employees are divided into several groups as follows: (1) Those who deserve promotion; (2) those who should stay where they are; (3) those who should be shifted to some other department in the organization in the hope that they will do better there; (4) those who should be discharged if they do not improve before the next periodic review; and (5) those who have previously been warned that they must improve, have failed to improve, and so should be discharged.

---

[13] Cf. the discussion of service shopping at p. 206 above.

FIGURE 9–1 **Job performance form**

TO: ____________ DATE: 2-15-

Guppy, Joseph — Name of Person to be Rated
Asst. Mgr. — Position
971-6 — Department
House Number

Please check the appropriate squares below to indicate the above-named person's present job performance. Give detailed comments below, on all ratings checked Deficient or Poor. For example, if you have checked Quantity of Work as deficient, you might comment that the cause is lack of interest; or lack of stamina; a personality clash with a fellow worker; lack of knowledge of his job; or lack of planning.

	POOR	DEFIC	AVER	GOOD	EXCEL
QUANTITY OF WORK				✓	
QUALITY OF WORK					✓
LEADERSHIP (Includes training and supervision of subordinates)				✓	
INITIATIVE (Can he see things to be done?)					✓
AMOUNT OF SUPERVISION REQUIRED					✓
ATTITUDE TOWARD OTHERS (Is he pleasant, courteous, tactful, cooperative, self-confident and aggressive?)					✓
ORGANIZING ABILITY (Can he analyze a problem or a bad situation and effect a solution smoothly and easily?)					✓
OVER-ALL RATING					✓

comments; Mr. Guppy has become a valuable assistant in the department. Is learning shoe know-how rapidly. Sees his job and does it thoroughly.

PROMOTIONAL POSSIBILITIES: Is this person promotable immediately? Yes What more responsible position do you think he could fill ably? Asst.-larger shoe dept. What more responsible position does he have as a goal, if any? Mgr.-shoes If not immediately promotable, when do you think he will be? 6 months

M Manager — Signature of Department Manager
Joe Guppy — Signature of Person Rated
D. Smith — Signature of Divisional Manager

After discussing this rating with the Employe, please return as soon as possible to the Personnel Office

Courtesy: The Emporium, San Francisco

☐ Relocating personnel

The relocation of employees is common in retail stores, just as it is in practically every career field. Some relocations will be *promotions;* others will *transfer* the person to a job in another store or department or to a position within the same department with about the same responsibility and pay; still others will involve *demotion* because of unsatisfactory performance.

Promotions Promotion from within an organization serves both management and employees. Management gains the qualified manpower to fill responsible executive positions. The able employee obtains an opportunity to exercise his ability and the satisfaction of being part of an organization in which ability is recognized and rewarded. There are few better ways of building employee goodwill, of offering an incentive for improved performance, and of holding valuable employees than assuring them that they have a "job with a future."

Transfers Frequently transferring a worker to another job will benefit both employer and employee. Some transfers are made to find an assignment for which the employee is better suited by training, ability, and temperament. Others result from the employer's desire to stimulate the employee's interest in the business by "getting him out of a rut" or by reducing the monotony associated with the steady performance of a certain task. Sometimes the transfer is designed to broaden the employee's background and to prepare him for advancement: This use of the transfer is important especially in chain and department stores.

Demotions As a general rule, no demotion should take place until the retailer is convinced that successful transfer is impossible. Demoting employees requires great skill and understanding. All too often, the demoted employee takes his new job with a feeling that he has been "railroaded" and not treated fairly by the firm. Unless his goodwill can be retained (or soon regained), it is best to sever his connection. Satisfactory demotions can sometimes be carried out—for instance, during periods when the firm has to contract its operations, or when the employee realizes that age or physical defects preclude continuing his present assignment. But the retailer should recognize the difficulties faced when he contemplates demoting an employee.

□ Terminations

Employers today regard terminations with increasing disfavor. This attitude is partly the result of the growth of unions, with the employer hesitating to discharge a worker for fear he may be accused of antiunion activities. But other factors have also played a part. Many retailers have intensified their efforts to maintain continuous employment so as to reduce their payments under unemployment compensation provisions of federal and state social security laws. In addition, merchants realize that an excessive number of terminations may cause other employees to worry about their jobs and, as a result, lower morale. Moreover, a termination means that the firm has lost its investment in the employee's training. Since this investment may be considerable, termination should ordinarily be considered only after serious attempts at relocation have been made and the employee has been given adequate warning.

In spite of a growing dislike for terminations, management should not hesitate to face the employee with its decision when a termination is required. Certainly the employee has a right to at least an interview with the proprietor of the small store or with someone from the personnel department in the large organization and, in most cases, to receive the reasons leading to the termination. The store will reap benefits if it can retain some of the discharged employee's goodwill, so that he will not go into the community and spread unfavorable comments. Although not even the most carefully conducted termination procedure can always avoid this unfortunate result, much success can be achieved by a well-handled final interview.

□ Retail working conditions

The personnel department has the duty of reviewing and suggesting improvements in working conditions.[14] This requires detailed studies of such matters as lighting, heating, ventilation, rest periods, working hours, safety, and vacations from the employee's viewpoint. Perhaps certain employees can be given somewhat reduced hours and still accomplish as much or more than when working longer hours. Rest periods may increase efficiency. An employees' cafeteria may provide good food at reasonable prices, and still pay its own way or at least cover its direct costs.

Employee hours The hours that retail stores are open for business have increased greatly in recent decades with the increasing trend towards night and Sunday openings.[15] But the individual retail employee's working hours have been progressively shortened in recent years. The 40-hour workweek is fairly standard for retail workers in metropolitan areas, and the workweek is only slightly longer in rural area stores. Staggered hours or a double shift of employees is used when stores are open six or seven days a week. Some stores pay substantial premiums for Sunday work.[16]

Safety provisions Retailers are now more "safety conscious" than ever before. Safety provisions and preventive measures receive constant attention

[14] Also Cf. the discussion of this subject on pp. 56–57, above.

[15] Cf. the discussion of store hours in Chapter 21, "Customer Services."

[16] Cf. "Premium Pay Lure Drawing Sunday Help," *Women's Wear Daily,* November 3, 1969, p. 23.

and have reduced accidents. The increasing number of government regulations concerning working conditions has also imposed additional safety requirements.

□ Employee service activities

Retailers are increasingly providing employee benefits in addition to the unemployment insurance, workmen's compensation, and old-age pensions (social security) established by law. The largest retailers spend very substantial sums every year for employee vacations, group life insurance, purchase discounts, illness allowances and medical care, profit sharing, pension funds, and other benefits. The survey of 98 department stores cited previously disclosed that 73 percent sponsor athletic and recreational activities; 62 percent aid employees to locate living quarters; 62 percent offer a fully equipped medical department; 77 percent provide group insurance; and 43 percent offer savings and loan programs.[17] Still other retailers engage in educational activities, and offer counseling services on a wide variety of subjects, including preparations for retirement.

Sometimes the service work immediately pays for itself, as when a retailer offers health services which increase productivity. It is quite impossible to say whether the costs of other services, such as pension systems, are offset by greater effort. But the fact remains that the retailer's service activities are important in attracting and keeping employees, and competition is forcing more and more employers to undertake them.

Medical and health services Large retail establishments furnish medical and health services on a formalized, continuous basis, with one or more full-time doctors and a staff of nurses. The smaller firm may use a doctor only part time, often having regular hours during which he is at the store to serve employees. A visiting nurse may be retained to aid employees confined to their homes. Some organizations have set up dental clinics. Vacations, which are steadily being liberalized, are still another way to improve the health of employees.[18]

Increasingly retail organizations have encouraged and aided their employees to take medical and hospitalization insurance, often through organizations like "Blue Shield" and "Blue Cross." Under these plans, both the store and the employee pay part of the cost, with the latter's contribution being deducted from his pay. The present emphasis on medical care is also demonstrated by the frequency with which union negotiators seek greater

[17] Sands, *op. cit.*, pp. 20–21. More recent comparable data are not available, but these percentages have probably increased sharply.

[18] Cf. p. 57, above.

medical and dental benefits.[19] And, of course, both employer and employee pay a compulsory payroll tax in support of the medicare hospitalization and medical programs.

Recreational and educational activities One effective method of building goodwill is through store-sponsored recreational activities such as orchestras, glee clubs, dramatics, athletic events, all-store picnics, costume parties, dances, and other social events. Some stores provide rented or store-owned facilities for the groups they sponsor: An auditorium where the glee club and dramatic group may entertain, an athletic field, a hall for social gatherings. Management, however, should go slowly in "pushing" recreational activities, and all signs of paternalism must be avoided. Probably the retailer's best approach is to sponsor only those activities in which the employees take some initiative. A common method of ascertaining employee interest is to establish one or more recreation clubs which are partly supported by employees' dues.

Educational activities of retailers, other than those directly connected with the training program, are not widespread but are steadily becoming more common. Some of the larger firms have long maintained libraries, and increasingly they are offering financial assistance, through scholarships and work-study arrangements, to encourage employees to continue their education in business schools, colleges, and universities.

Employee financial benefit plans Retailers extend other kinds of financial aid to their employees through group insurance, mutual-aid associations, old-age pensions, and savings and loan programs.

1. *Group insurance* Low-cost group life insurance plans, under which both employer and employee make a contribution, are restricted chiefly to large stores and chain organizations. Employee contributions are deducted from pay checks. There are no age restrictions and no physical examination is required. But the insurance lapses if the employee leaves the company (although some plans permit conversion of some or all of his group insurance to another kind of policy); and, since it is term insurance, it has no cash value.

2. *Mutual-aid associations* These voluntary associations provide sickness, accident, and death benefits for employees not covered by workmen's compensation and insurance plans. They also render extensive assistance in times of financial stress. They are usually incorporated, to have a legal

[19] A recent R. H. Macy Co. union contract, which provides a minimum wage of $2.50 per hour, also includes insurance against major (catastrophic) medical costs, increased allowances for doctors' home and office visits, paid vacation increasing to four weeks after 20 years' service and five weeks after 25 years, and a paid holiday on the worker's birthday. "Macy's Sends 65¢ Pay Hike to Employees," *Women's Wear Daily,* February 5, 1970, pp. 1, 22.

existence separate from that of the store. Contributions come from both employees and employer; and the employees usually control the association, although employees and management may cooperate in its operation. In some cases the employer underwrites the establishment of the association and then leaves it up to employee contributions to carry on from that point.

3. *Old-Age Pensions* The federal Social Security pension plan applies to retail, as well as other, employees. Both the employer and the employee contribute 4.6 percent (5.0 after 1973) on wages up to $7,800 per year. Upon retiring at ages 62 to 65, the worker receives a pension ranging between $51.20 and $434.40 per month, depending upon age and date of retirement, average earnings subject to social security, and number of dependents. The plan also provides disability income benefits and partial benefits for widows and other surviving dependents. In addition, an increasing number of firms have their own retirement plans to supplement these payments.

4. *Savings and loan plans* Some large retailers have established savings plans. The employee usually makes periodic cash deposits, which are then supplemented through a contribution from the employer. For example, employees of one large retailer may deposit 3 percent of their annual pay in the savings plan and the company—depending upon its annual earnings—will contribute an amount equal to 25 to 50 percent of each employee's deposit. In a recent year, this firm contributed over $1.7 million to this savings plan. Many retailers, both large and small, encourage the purchase of government savings bonds through deduction of agreed amounts from the employee's regular pay check. Others offer emergency loan services through which a worker may secure funds to be repaid by wage deductions. Management may encourage the establishment of a credit union to handle such loans.

□ Handling employee complaints

Employee complaints cover a wide range of subjects—hours, wages, promotions, working conditions, "fringe" benefits, and tactics of other salespeople. Many retailers go to great lengths to minimize or eliminate such complaints. Practically all of the work of the personnel division, as well as the employee-service activities discussed in the previous section, are helpful in reducing complaints. Many retailers use a so-called "exit interview" to ascertain the causes of dissatisfaction when an employee resigns and to permit remedial action. Figure 9–2 shows the exit interview checklist used in one retail firm. Still other companies encourage their employees to elect representatives to meet with management and discuss problems of mutual interest. Employer-employee committees are established to consider

FIGURE 9–2 **Exit interview checklist**

Date
Name Department
Date Employed Last Day Worked Salary or Rate ______
Why is employee leaving? ______
What, if anything, was especially disliked about work? ______
Were working conditions satisfactory? (light, heat, atmosphere, etc.) ______
Was equipment for your job satisfactory? ______
Were your rest periods—eating periods satisfactory? ______
Was salary satisfactory? (increase?) ______
Do you have any unfinished financial business with the company? (Credit Union, etc.) ______
Was treatment received from this office satisfactory? ______
How was the treatment from the other employees? ______
Do you think a person has opportunity for advancement in this firm? ______
Does employee have any suggestions for improvement on anything within organization? ______
Does employee think management is interested in employee? ______
Was ample training given on job? ______
Would employee be interested in working again for the company? ______
Other comments: ______________________________

__________________ __________________
Signature of Interviewer Signature of Employee

especially difficult problems, such as improving working conditions and the more advantageous planning of vacations.

Nevertheless, complaints continue to develop and provision should be made to handle them promptly and effectively. The proprietor of the small store usually handles them directly and informally; but the large operation needs a definite procedure for dealing with them. Such a procedure has been made imperative by the growth of retail trade unions, since the union demands that there be some responsible executive with whom it can negotiate and from whom it can expect action when agreements have been reached. The personnel director, or a special assistant well versed in personnel relations, is usually given the duty of dealing with complaints.

☐ Labor organizations in the retail field

Growth of retail labor unions Unions in the retail field are not a new development. Several unions composed solely of store employees existed as early as 1882.[20] Their main aim of seeking shorter hours earned them the

[20] P. H. Nystrom, *Economics of Retailing* (New York: Ronald Press Co., 1930), Vol. 2, p. 281.

name of "Early Closing Societies." Although these early unions had some successes and experienced some growth, the limited development of trade unions that has taken place in the retail field has occurred mainly since the early 1930s.

Although local retail operations are specifically exempted from the 1935 National Labor Relations Act, interstate retail firms are subject to the Act's prohibitions against interference with unions, discrimination against union members, and refusal to bargain with unions. In other words, if a majority of the employees of an interstate retail organization form a union and send representatives to talk over certain grievances, the management must negotiate concerning the complaints.[21] Whereas at an earlier time the store could decide whether to set up an agency to handle employees' complaints, today the machinery must exist in any retail establishment with organized employees. A few states have passed laws that place intrastate employees in the same position as employees of interstate retailers.

Unionization has spread slowly in the retail field despite both the favorable legal situation mentioned and union success in obtaining the closed shop and checkoff in some department and chain stores. Probably somewhat less than 10 percent of all retail employees are unionized, although unions have made strong inroads in some cities and among some sales-supporting employee groups, such as truck drivers, warehousemen, elevator operators, and maintenance staffs. However, membership in the major retail unions has grown substantially in recent years. The Retail Clerks International Association (AFL-CIO) had over 550,000 members at the end of 1969; the Retail, Wholesale & Department Store Union (AFL-CIO), 175,000; the National Council of Distributive Workers of America (independent), 40,000; and the Amalgamated Meat Cutters and Butcher Workmen of North America (AFL-CIO) had about 200,000 members employed in wholesale and retail food firms.[22] These unions are currently trying to attract more discount house, supermarket, department store and specialty store employee members, and have conducted some long and costly strikes in the process.

Union aims In general, retail unions have sought such goals as union recognition, the closed shop, shorter hours, higher wages, extra pay for overtime, paid vacations, health and welfare programs, grievance proce-

---

[21] Actually, the union may represent the firm's employees in a given geographic area, such as greater Los Angeles, and not necessarily throughout the country. Moreover, it may represent just certain types of employees, such as restaurant workers, sales personnel, or clerical employees. Cf. "Unions Will Sell Harder in Stores," *Business Week,* February 6, 1965, p. 46.

[22] U.S. Department of Labor, *Directory of National and International Labor Unions in the United States, 1969* (Washington, D.C.: U.S. Government Printing Office, 1970).

dures, seniority rights, and job security.[23] In some cases, the unions have achieved formal contracts that provide substantial gains, especially in regard to hours, wages, paid vacations, and overtime pay. The efforts to achieve job security are illustrated by the provisions in some of the contracts in the supermarket industry, one of the more unionized segments of retailing. Agreements with the Amalgamated Meat Cutters in some cities forbid the retail sale of prepackaged meats.[24] The National Retail Labor Relations Board has upheld a supermarket union contract which specified that suppliers' deliverymen could not place merchandise on store shelves (a common practice in distributing bakery products and certain other types of merchandise) since, under the contract, this work was to be reserved for store employees.[25] To forestall union activities, retailers in some cities have formed their own voluntary agreements to establish improved wages, hours, and other benefits.

Wage and hours laws The retail unions have supported both state and federal wage and hour laws as one step toward higher wages. A few states have had such laws for some time but it was not until 1961 that the federal Fair Labor Standards (Wage and Hour) Law was amended to cover a substantial number of retail workers. A 1966 amendment broadened the law to cover practically all retail establishments with sales of $250,000 per year or more. The minimum wage has been raised several times and is now $1.60 per hour.[26] Workers, except executive, professional, and certain higher-paid commission sales employees, must be paid at 1½ times their regular rate for all work in excess of 40 hours per week.

Certain implications of the minimum wage and hour laws for the retailers covered are quite clear. One is that retailers are compelled to maintain the differential between those whose wages are advanced by the minimum and other workers already exceeding it. Another is that the rising minimum has accelerated the move toward self-service and automation and caused many retailers to place greater emphasis on productivity.

---

[23] For a general discussion of union objectives, including a $4 hourly wage, "portable" or transferable pensions, and a 35 hour week, cf. "Clerks Want More of the Good Life," *Chain Store Age* (Supermarket Executives Edition), February 1969, pp. 30–31.

[24] *Cf.* Herbert R. Northrup, *Restrictive Labor Practices in the Supermarket Industry* (Philadelphia: University of Pennsylvania Press, 1967). Sausages and other prepared meats are, of course, normally exempted from this restriction.

[25] *Retail Store Employees Local Union No. 876, R.C.I.A.* et al. v. *Independent Biscuit Company* et al. (70 LRRM 1213, February 12, 1969, reversal denied, CA-6, 1970, 73 LRRM 2582). The impact of such rules on retail management decision making is discussed in R. D. Michman, "Union Impact on Retail Management," *Business Horizons,* Vol. 10, No. 1 (Spring 1967) pp. 79–84.

[26] U.S. Department of Labor, *Handy Reference Guide to the Fair Labor Standards Act (Federal Wage-Hour Law)* (Washington, D.C.; U.S. Government Printing Office, 1970), p. 2.

Management response to unions Although management's first reaction to the spread of unionism was to look for some method of "smashing the union," increasing numbers of enlightened retailers, like alert businessmen in all fields, soon decided to try to improve conditions and minimize grievances. The leading retailers in some cities have agreed to "codes of ethics" calling for better working conditions, shorter hours, and higher wages. A number of firms have actively encouraged a degree of employee participation in management. Other companies are distributing "jobholders' annual reports" and employee policy books, and making other efforts to acquaint employees with their labor policies, what management is already doing for its workers, and what it hopes to do in the future. In the past, all too often, major difficulties in personnel relations have been caused by management weaknesses. Fortunately, alert executives recognize this fact and are taking measures to correct the situation.

The facts that retailing is a field of relatively small establishments with close relationships between proprietor and employees, that many retail employees hope to establish their own stores at a later time, and that many employees are on a part-time basis while many others look upon retailing as a temporary means of making a living, are deterrents to labor organizations. Yet it seems likely that retail unions will demonstrate greater strength and continue to grow.

Many retailers see only "bad" results from union growth, especially loss of control over personnel. In contrast, a few argue that the end result may be employees who are more appreciative of the problems of management, more willing to cooperate in making suggestions for improving operations, and—because of a greater feeling of security—are more enthusiastic about their jobs. In large measure, securing these benefits depends upon a progressive personnel program, which is believed in and adhered to by the management and made absolutely clear to all employees.

Regardless of a specific retailer's attitude toward retail unions, he cannot afford to overlook his legal and moral responsibilities to his employees. Familiarity and full compliance with city, state, and federal labor regulations are essential. In addition, his personnel policies must anticipate and prepare for future developments. Above all, he must provide an environment in which employees can work pleasantly and effectively.

■ REVIEW AND DISCUSSION QUESTIONS

1 Are there any characteristics of retailing which make it difficult to devise a satisfactory compensation plan for retail personnel? Explain.

2 As the proprietor of a retail store, under what conditions or circum-

stances would you adopt each of the main methods of compensating salespeople?

3 Analyze the pros and cons for paying salespeople a straight commission in (a) a drugstore, (*b*) a new car agency, (*c*) a men's clothing store.

4 Evaluate the employee discount policies of three specific retailers in your area.

5 Explain the major current compensation plans for sales-supporting employees.

6 What do you think are the most satisfactory ways for compensating (a) department-store buyers, (*b*) chain discount-house managers, (*c*) chain women's ready-to-wear shop managers, (*d*) general managers of the branches of a mail-order house, and (e) major executives in large retail firms? Explain.

7 Discuss the meaning, objectives, and methods of job evaluation.

8 What are the main current trends in retail working conditions? Discuss the impact of these trends on the activities of the personnel department.

9 What, in your judgment, are the probable future developments in retailers' employee-service activities? Give reasons for your answer.

10 How do you account for the relatively slow growth of retail trade unions in this country and what do you think of their future growth possibilities?

PART V

Merchandise management: Buying, handling, control, and pricing

chapter chapter 10 chapter chapter

BUYING THE RIGHT MERCHANDISE: BASIC CONSIDERATIONS

There is an old saying among retailers that "goods well bought are half sold." One might go further and add that goods not well bought cannot be profitably sold.[1] Since our most successful retailers place much emphasis on the buying function, this subject warrants examination in some detail.

As we embark upon the study of buying, however, the reader should bear in mind that this function is an integral part of merchandise control. In fact, one fundamental purpose of merchandise control is to provide information that helps buyers determine what and how much to purchase. Yet the merchandise itself cannot be really controlled until it has been bought; hence it is advisable to discuss the basic considerations involved in buying the right merchandise prior to analyzing the more formal aspects of merchandise control or management.

■ THE BUYING FUNCTION

In general conversation the term "buying" simply connotes the act of purchase. As used by the retailer, however, the term includes far more

[1] The closing of a well-known store on Fifth Avenue, New York, has been partially attributed to improper buying. Cf. Samuel Feinberg, "Best Couldn't Keep up with Trends in Buying," *Women's Wear Daily*, October 6, 1970, pp. 1, 18.

than the act of purchase. Specifically, it involves six steps: (1) Formulating effective buying policies; (2) determining customer wants; (3) selecting sources of supply; (4) determining suitability of the merchandise offered for sale; (5) negotiating terms of sale; and (6) transferring title. In this and the following chapter each of these steps will be considered.

The work of persons known in various retail organizations as "buyers," may consist of less or more than the activities mentioned. In a large shoe chain the buyer may have nothing to do with the formulation of buying policies, the general manager assuming these activities. In contrast, in the smaller retail store the proprietor generally does the buying in addition to serving in such other capacities as salesman, advertising director, and general manager. And, in the large department store, the buyer may be in charge of both selling and buying in his department. Our interest lies in how the buying function is performed, irrespective of the title carried by the individual or individuals engaged in performing that function.[2]

FORMULATING EFFECTIVE BUYING POLICIES

The first step in buying is the establishment of clear-cut policies[3] covering all aspects of the purchasing function. Its importance may be illustrated in connection with selecting sources of supply. Decisions must be made on such questions as to whether to buy from jobbers or wholesalers rather than directly from manufacturers, the degree to which buying will be concentrated with a few resources, and whether joint purchasing with other retailers will be undertaken.

Wide differences exist among stores as to the importance of the foregoing considerations. In all of them, however, two basic elements are decisive in buying-policy formation. First, buying policies should be "in tune" with the general objectives of the organization, reflecting a harmonious relationship with the types and assortments of merchandise handled,[4] including the emphasis placed on fashion leadership; the clientele to be served; the funds available in the merchandise budget; the knowledge, experience, and preferences of the buyer; the nature and extent of competition; general business conditions, including seasonal and cyclical variations; and the

[2] The "personal qualifications needed for success" in performing the buying function are set forth in J. W. Wingate and J. S. Friedlander, *The Management of Retail Buying* (Englewood Cliffs, N.J.: Prentice-Hall, Inc., 1963), pp. 13–19.

[3] The reader will find it helpful to review the discussion of policies in Chapter 2, pp. 42–47, above.

[4] On the importance of merchandise selection in attracting customers cf. P. R. Stephenson, "Identifying Determinants of Retail Patronage," *Journal of Marketing*, Vol. 33, No. 3 (July 1969), pp. 57–61.

general needs of the community as a whole. The increasing fashion and quality consciousness of consumers is particularly noteworthy in all types of merchandise.[5] And one provocative observer predicts that by 1980 "fashion, style, design and creative innovation will dominate practically all merchandise lines and will become thoroughly integrated."[6]

The second basic consideration in establishing buying policies is that they should serve the needs of the store's customers.[7] Actually, all successful purchasing begins with a clear-cut idea on the buyer's part of *what* is wanted, or at least what the buyer thinks will be wanted when it is called to the attention of potential customers. The buyer's personal likes and dislikes are unimportant; he is the "purchasing agent" of the customers.[8] He should know customers' preferences as to price class of goods, quality, materials, styles, colors, and the like—a task made more difficult as customers achieve higher standards of living and become more discriminating ("fussy" is the word often used by retailers) in their purchases. In this connection, the shifts in consumer spending and buying habits growing out of the factors already outlined in Chapter 1 should be given careful consideration. Take, for instance, the situation prevailing in 1970. Caught in an "inflationary squeeze," many customers were shifting to lower-priced merchandise than formerly, particularly in apparel. One men's clothing manufacturer faced with declining sales reduced his retail base from $95 to a $75 minimum with the result that "his sales quickly picked up and his whole line showed a new impetus."[9] Moreover, numerous retailers, aware of their cus-

---

[5] Cf., for example, June Weir, "Sears—New Fashion Face," *Women's Wear Daily,* July 14, 1969, pp. 8–9; Sidney Rutberg, "Marcor Draws Big Fashion Growth Plan," *ibid.,* January 7, 1970, pp. 1, 42; Samuel Feinberg, "[Neiman-Marcus] Competes on Quality Not on Size of Stocks," *ibid.,* June 13, 1968, p. 16; Bess Winakor, "Goldblatt's Striving for a Fashion Image," *ibid.,* January 2, 1970, p. 13; and Roger Beardwood, "Melville Draws a Bead on the $50 Billion Fashion Market," *Fortune,* Vol. 80, No. 7 (December 1969), pp. 110–14 ff.

[6] E. B. Weiss, "Fashion Creativity Demands Diversity in Manufacturing," *Advertising Age,* June 30, 1969, pp. 72, 74.

[7] States the vice-president of R. H. Macy & Co.: "It is the retailer's job to be the representative for the consumer. It is our job to pick merchandise that is priced right, usable and safe. And it is our responsibility to act upon the consumer's right to be heard." Rona Cutler, "Macy's Puts Itself on Side of Consumer," *Women's Wear Daily,* June 30, 1970, p. 1. Also cf. "What Makes the New Consumer Buy," *Business Week,* April 24, 1971, pp. 52–58.

[8] Despite the increase in "family" buying with night and Sunday openings quite prevalent, many retailers find that the majority of their customers are women. One authority suggests it is "the ever increasing duties of the wife who serves as household purchasing agent." H. O. Whiteside in Reavis Cox, Wroe Alderson, and S. J. Shapiro, *Theory in Marketing,* Second Series, (Homewood, Ill.: Richard D. Irwin, Inc., 1964), p. 270. Among hardware stores, however, men are more important, comprising 61 percent of the customers. Cf. "Who is Your Customer?" *Hardware Retailer,* October 1969, p. 86.

[9] Isadore Barmash, "Manufacturers vs. the Consumers," *New York Times,* July 5, 1970, p. F9.

tomers' desire for inflationary relief, were conducting special promotions featuring merchandise at sharply reduced prices. These actions, specially the former, represented a drastic (temporary?) reversal of the trading-up policy prevalent for many years.

Considerable knowledge of what consumers want, however, does not insure success in buying. Sound decisions on the quantity of the desired merchandise to be purchased are also necessary. In the balance of this chapter, we shall examine the ways in which stores of various sizes and in different fields obtain information concerning *what* particular goods their customers want and the *quantities* of such goods they should buy.

DETERMINING MERCHANDISE CUSTOMERS WANT

Information as to the types, kinds, and prices of goods wanted by a retailer's present and potential customers may be gathered both inside and outside the store. The major sources of such data are as follows: (1) Inside sources—including past sales, returned goods and adjustment data, credit department data, customer inquiries, suggestions of salespeople, and the judgment of buyers; (2) outside sources—comprising the goods sold by other successful stores, vendors' offerings, central market representatives, trade papers, newspapers, and general publications, and customer surveys. Both of these sources require some explanation.

Inside sources of buying information

Past sales Past sales constitute the most valuable inside source of information on customers' wants for both staple merchandise and fashion goods.

1. The basic stock list for staple goods Analysis of past sales of the more staple items permits preparation of a basic stock list for them. Such a list usually consists of (1) the items to be carried in stock, classified as to size and other important factors; (2) the minimum quantities to have on hand at any time[10]—adjusted to seasonal requirements; and (3) the quantity to order when reordering takes place.

The quantity to order at a particular time will depend upon such factors as the quantity discounts allowed by the vendor, the cost of transporting

---

[10] In terms of a formula, the minimum stock is equal to the quantity normally sold during the delivery period plus a safety factor (additional units to meet maximum possible demand); thus, minimum stock equals delivery period quantity plus safety factor.

orders of various sizes, the speed of deterioration of the product, and the unit in which the product is packed.[11]

Some means, of course, should be used to acquaint salespeople when the minimum stock point has been reached; otherwise the buyer will not be notified. While periodic visual inspection of inventory may supply this information, many retailers employ some kind of "automatic reminder." Perhaps a cardboard divider or a tape may be used to separate the minimum stock from other merchandise, or a two-bin system is employed under which one bin holds regular-sale merchandise and the other the minimum inventory. Sometimes a perpetual inventory system—described below—and perhaps employing electronic equipment may be used under certain conditions.

Many manufacturers offer aid to retailers of their products in the development of a basic stock list. For example, the Telechron division of the General Electric Company provides its dealers with a 40-page booklet on *Retail-Tested Selling Ideas and Profit Pointers* which offers basic stock lists for electric clocks as well as ideas on inventory control, displays, promotions, and other aspects of retailing. In most fields, the retailer will find similar aids available to him from manufacturers and trade associations.

a) Perpetual inventory for staple goods—Sometimes the basic stock list is supplemented by a perpetual inventory system to indicate the quantity of stock on hand at any time. A card showing the minimum stock and the reorder quantity may be kept for each item carried. When a purchase is made, the quantity of the item received is entered on the card. Sales are also entered. Thus, a glance at the card will tell the quantity on hand. The person keeping the perpetual inventory control informs the buyer when the stock reaches the minimum or reorder point.

Among large retailers, recent developments in electronic tabulating equipment suggest that eventually more complete inventory data may be available more promptly than ever before.[12] Safeway Stores, Inc., Food Fair Stores, F. W. Woolworth, S. S. Kresge, J. C. Penney and many other chains are already using electronic data processing, in part, to control inventories and furnish sales information to buyers.[13]

Most stores find that a perpetual inventory control system, regardless of whether it is based on clerical work or on electronic devices, is too complicated and expensive for their needs. Drug and grocery stores, including some chains, find it satisfactory to have the buyer take his basic stock list and

---

[11] For details, cf. "Determining Quantity to Purchase," pp. 247–50, below.

[12] Cf. the previous discussion of EDP on pp. 118–20, above.

[13] In 1970 Montgomery Ward & Company opened a large computerized store with 120,000 square feet of selling space in Rockford, Illinois. More than half of the stock is merchandised by computers which, among other functions, will prepare seasonal merchandise plans, write purchase orders and reorders, noting color, fashion and size trends.

spend a few hours each week canvassing the shelves in his store or his department to find out what items are down to or near the minimum requirements. It seems likely, however, that as electronic computers become more widely used by retailers of lower-priced stable goods, they will be of greater aid in controlling warehouse stocks rather than merchandise already in stores.

b) Revision of basic stock necessary—In any case, the basic stock list should be revised constantly. Not only do some kinds of goods gain in popularity as others lose, shifts take place among competing products, and seasonal changes in demand occur. To illustrate: Sales of men's plain wool hose increase in the fall and winter and decrease in the spring. Food stores sell huge quantities of nuts during the Christmas holidays and the coming of Easter, June graduation, and September's "back-to-school" days spell huge fluctuations in the sales of many staples.

To supplement their basic stock lists many buyers employ a seasonal buying calendar. Such a calendar sets forth all special events, shows the dates on which the buyer should begin his planning, when increased orders should be placed, and when goods should be delivered and ready for display.

In summary, careful analysis of past sales permits a basic stock list to be devised for staple merchandise. Kept up to date and supplemented with a buying calendar and—under certain circumstances—with a perpetual inventory control system, the basic stock list provides a method that makes the actual determination of wants for many staples quite automatic.

Analysis of past sales also reveals helpful information about customer brand preferences, data that have increased in importance with the growth of self-service and self-selection. Based on such information, the buyer can concentrate more on the "best sellers," and obtain better service and prices from suppliers.

2. The model stock for fashion goods A basic stock list based entirely on an analysis of past sales is of little value to the buyer of fashion goods. What sold well last year may not sell well this year. Consequently, the retailer—taking into consideration both past sales and sales expected for the forthcoming period—tries to build up a picture of (a) the total dollar value of the stock and (*b*) a detailed classification of the stock to be carried as to such factors as sizes, types, and price lines. The result is known as a model stock. With reference to planned sales, it contains the merchandise designed to achieve these sales most effectively. Thus, although a model stock is forward looking—that is, it is always built to meet expected or forthcoming sales—it is evident that an analysis of past sales is essential to its existence. It may suggest, for instance, which colors and styles of high fashion ready-to-wear are gaining or losing in popularity as well as help decide on the dollar value of the goods to be carried as well as their general characteristics, that is, the model stock.

a) Dollar value of the stock—The dollar value of the model stock may be determined by past sales and past stocks supplemented by an estimate of the business outlook. Past sales are first broken down on a daily, weekly, or monthly basis. If for example, last year's sales for the month were $20,000 and the present outlook for business is good, sales for the period this year may be adjusted upward by 10 percent to $22,000. If a monthly turnover can be expected, the average stock at retail (the model stock) should be $22,000.[14]

b) Characteristics of goods carried—Past sales can also yield information as to the type of merchandise to be carried, sizes, price lines, and trends in materials and sales. Regarding type, consider a men's shoe store. Past sales indicate that, irrespective of fashion changes, for comparable months the store sells fairly consistent percentages of dress, street, and sport shoes. Variations from month to month can be indicated on a buying calendar.

For most fashion goods the assortment as to size is also fairly constant. For example, irrespective of the year's fashion, a women's dress shop finds its percentage of sales of dresses of various sizes as follows: Size 12, 12 percent; size 14, 22 percent; size 16, 30 percent; size 18, 26 percent; and size 20, 10 percent. It should be recognized however, that the model stock assortment as to size and type should not be necessarily the same as the actual sales distribution. Although 10 percent of all sales are in size 20 dresses, to provide an adequate assortment, this size may account for 15 percent of the model stock.

Past sales also furnish information as to the prices at which a store should offer merchandise. Past trends, by indicating whether the best or the cheapest goods are moving, can show a buyer the merchandise items which appeal most to his customers as well as the price lines that are most popular.[15] Once the price lines are adopted, analysis of past sales will reveal the percentage of total sales in each price line. Finally, and as already suggested, past sales provide information on customer preferences for materials, colors, and particular styles. By keeping a running check on these factors, the buyer is better prepared in placing reorders.

c) Perpetual inventory for fashion goods—Perpetual inventories of fashion goods may be maintained just as they are for staple goods, *i.e.*, through unit-control systems of various types. The system used in the dress shops of Diana Stores Corporation is illustrative. Model stocks are devised

---

[14] This figure would be adjusted upward or downward if the buyer wished to add to or reduce the size of his department's end-of-month inventory.

[15] Price lining is discussed in some detail in Chapter 16.

each month as seasons, fashions, and sales change. Each garment sent to a store is listed at headquarters. When it is sold, headquarters is informed by returning part of the ticket formerly attached to it. By a counting process carried out by electronic computers, buyers at headquarters know exactly what a store has on hand by unit prices, styles, sizes, and colors, and how fast various items are moving.

So important is inventory control for fashion goods that some retailers —such as Diana Stores Corporation, referred to above—have installed electronic computers, in part, for stock control and buying purposes.[16] The Federated Department Stores, Woodward & Lothrop, and Sears, Roebuck and Co. have invested heavily in electronics programs designed to put up-to-date figures in the hands of buyers.[17] Both the National Cash Register Company and International Business Machines have introduced unit stock control and automatic reorder systems which use the sales register tape to "feed" data into the computer. Stores too small to have their own computers can have their tapes processed at nearby computer centers. Despite this "sharing" of computer time, however, the cost of the necessary equipment is so great that, at least for the immediate future, sales register types and electronic computers will probably be used mainly by large retailers—and even many of these will continue to use clerical personnel to get much of the data they need for buying purposes.

d) Summary—For fashion goods, several factors permit a model stock to be built. Past sales yield data concerning the types of merchandise, sizes, and price lines customers prefer, and reveal trends regarding materials and colors. And, when adjusted according to the future outlook, *past* sales and stocks provide a basis for estimating *future* sales and stocks. Yet the model stock in fashion goods is far from a *fait accompli* because unforeseen developments often require changes. Moreover, many stores make special purchases of goods outside of their regular assortments for special promotions, to help the sale of outmoded merchandise, and for prestige. These purchases must be fitted into the model stock plan.

Finally, it should not be forgotten that a model stock plan is as applicable to small stores as to the largest retail organization, a fact often overlooked by both students of retailing and small retailers.

Returned goods and adjustment data Returned goods and customer complaints supply considerable information as to what customers want. Some merchandise may be of inferior material or poor workmanship and

[16] Cf. the previous discussion of EDP on pp. 118–20, above.

[17] Cf. "Computer and Buyer," *Stores,* March 1969, pp. 41–42; "Small Stores Can Up Profit by Computerizing Inventory," *ibid.*, May 1968, pp. 29–30; Irving Geller, "Master Machines of Retailing," *Dun's Review,* October 1969, pp. 107–9 ff.; and "Key Retailers See EDP a Solid Bet in 5 Years," *Merchandising Week,* September 22, 1969, p. 24.

give unsatisfactory service.[18] Women's dresses may fade, and the collars of men's shirts may fray. Knowledge of such facts is obviously of importance to buyers.

In small stores complaints about merchandise and service usually are handled by the owner-buyer. In the large store, however, complaints are registered with the adjustment department and some method must be devised for passing on pertinent information to the buyer. One method is to use the "adjustment-department notice," which contains a brief description of the complaint and of the merchandise against which the complaint was registered.

Credit department data Retailers extending credit find two chief kinds of information available in the credit department useful to their buyers. One is the customers' records of purchases and the kinds and prices of merchandise they return. The second is supplied by the credit application which furnishes a variety of data such as nationality, occupation, age, marriage status, sex, and income.

Credit application analysis is relatively simple for stores that require a large amount of information from their customers. When using credit data, however, the buyer should recognize that the store's credit customers may not form a typical sample of all its customers, and that this inside-the-store information should be supplemented with customer data gathered outside the store.

Customer Inquiries A record of goods desired by customers but not in stock furnishes a helpful guide to the buyer since it reveals customer wants. Although some salespeople in small stores rely on their memory in reporting such requests to the buyer-owner, most stores find it desirable to keep a pad near the sales register on which customer inquiries can be written down. Such a record is nearly indispensable to sound purchasing. Among large retailers more care is necessary in recording customer-inquiries. Here a formal want-slip system is desirable and forms should be provided for entering requests for merchandise not carried in stock. Such slips usually go to the merchandising office for analysis, with a summary sent to the buyer who decides if the items should be purchased.[19]

Suggestions of salespeople Since salespeople are customers in their own right, with wants that frequently are similar to those of other patrons, they can afford the buyer a valuable sample of customer opinion. Urging salespeople to bring in suggestions for purchases and seeking their opinions on the merchandise offered in the market help the buyer in his purchasing.

[18] "Shoddy Merchandise Popping up Everywhere," *Women's Wear Daily*, February 11, 1970, pp. 1, 26.

[19] Cf. Wingate and Friedlander, *op. cit.*, pp. 129–33, for the essentials of a good want-slip system and the chief objections to want slips.

□ Outside sources of buying information

Offerings of other successful stores Turning to outside sources of information as listed on page 238 (we shall return later to the judgment of buyers on page 246), it is evident that no buyer can afford to overlook the goods offered by other successful stores in deciding what he should buy. This source of information is particularly helpful to smaller retailers who cannot afford other costly ways of finding out what customers want. Through such methods as visits to other local stores and those in other cities, study of their advertisements, and the hiring of outside "shoppers" to report on their offerings, employing one's own Comparison Department—if the store is large enough to maintain one—considerable useful buying information may be obtained. Many large stores have comparison departments whose responsibility, among others, is to "shop" competitive stores in the trading area to determine merchandise offerings, prices, and customer response. Frequently goods are purchased for later detailed comparison with the store's own goods. Reports are prepared and submitted to the buyer for his guidance in building proper assortments and establishing prices.

Despite the advantages of knowing what is being stocked and promoted by other successful stores, some retailers owe their success to the fact that they operate unique stores—stores which offer "unusual merchandise." To use the words of one highly successful, small-town retailer: " 'Tain't the money that puts your business up. It's having something that no one else has as good as."[20] In carrying out this philosophy, a small shop selling women's apparel builds its clientele on having "different" dresses or a men's clothing retailer tries to be ahead of his large-scale competitors in having the latest fashions. In fact, one of the advantages of the smaller store is its buying flexibility which gives it an opportunity to "be different" from its larger competitor.

Vendor's offerings All stores, particularly small ones, rely to some degree on the offerings of vendors[21] to learn what goods are "in demand." Perhaps buyers rely too much on vendors who are trying to sell what they are producing rather than first studying customer demand to find out what is wanted. Yet there is a definite trend for vendors to engage in more customer research. As they do, their offerings will reflect customers' needs to a greater degree and thus become a more dependable guide to the buyer. Some vendors use bulletins to inform their customers what is selling.

[20] L. L. Bean, quoted in *Time*, December 7, 1962, p. 89.

[21] "Vendor" is simply another designation for merchandise supplier or merchandise resource. The term includes manufacturers, wholesalers, rack jobbers, etc.—anyone who sells to the store.

This practice is followed especially by sellers of fashion merchandise. Others use salesmen for this purpose and still others have developed inventory control systems—some based on electronic computers—for their retail outlets to provide improved stock control, semiautomatic reordering and similar buying information. Vendors using the franchise system of servicing retailers through a voluntary chain arrangement place special emphasis on supplying "what is selling" data to their outlets.

Central market representatives Many retailers retain central market representatives,[22] often referred to as MR's, to furnish store buyers with information about new and popular items in the market. These representatives study vendors' offerings, watch fashion trends, and check promotions in large city stores. Their conclusions are transmitted to buyers by means of bulletins or verbally when the buyers visit the central markets.

Trade papers, newspapers, and general publications Retailers of all sizes depend on trade and fashion magazines and newspapers for much information as to what customers want. Retailers of women's wear find it worthwhile to study such publications as *Mademoiselle, Seventeen, Charm, Harper's Bazaar,* and *Vogue,* in which the latest fashions are pictured and discussed. *Women's Wear Daily* is another standard source of information in this field. For retailers of men's wearing apparel, *Esquire, Daily News Record,* and *Men's Wear* offer considerable data on fashion trends. Many other fields are also supplied with tradepapers, as illustrated by *Chain Store Age* with its various editions, *Discount Store News, Progressive Grocer, National Jeweler, Hardware Retailer* and *Footwear News.*

Customer surveys Broadly, any activity designed to gather information directly from customers concerning their wants may be classified as a customer survey. Although these surveys are not used extensively by retailers because of the time and cost involved, when employed any one or more of the following methods and devices are used to obtain the desired data: questionnaires either mailed or completed through personal interviews; style counts for fashion goods; and consumer advisory groups. Since surveys may provide the store not only with data as to the goods customers want, but also with information as to the surroundings and services they want with the goods, it is essential that they be conducted and interpreted with great care; otherwise, the results may suggest courses of action not warranted by the facts.

Stores or departments handling fashion goods find the style count of value as a source of customer information. The count is made by placing observers at certain points with instructions to record what people are wearing. The observation points should be selected with care, so that information

[22] Cf. the discussion of market representatives, pp. 264–67, below.

will be obtained on all income classes including the groups that act as local fashion leaders.

When consumer advisory groups or juries are used, the store attempts to organize a single small group which is representative of its customers.[23] The group may be broken down into subgroups, each representing one segment of the store's customers. Thus, one subgroup may be made up of high school or college students, another of newlyweds, and another of middle-income buyers. Such groups or panels may be used not only to pass on merchandise offered by vendors but also to appraise goods already in the store, together with the store's operating policies.

Some agencies conduct customer surveys for retailers or on their own initiative obtain data of value in buying. Many newspapers, such as the *Milwaukee Journal*, the *Cleveland Press*, the *Chicago Tribune*, and the *New York Times*, finance research designed to provide information on consumer buying habits. The A. C. Nielsen Company, through its consumer and dealer panels, supplies valuable information, and the studies of R. L. Polk and Company serve the same purpose. Some resident buying organizations, especially those located in New York City, also undertake investigations of various types for their members.

Judgment of buyers Even after a buyer has made full use of all or a number of the foregoing sources of information, he still has to exercise judgment in his buying decisions. That is, the data he gathers needs to be interpreted. The successful buyer may be distinguished from the unsuccessful one by his "sense" in correctly interpreting the facts.

One leading firm has about 550 buyers at its headquarters' offices in New York City "supervised by 8 merchandise managers, 29 buying department heads, and 22 catalog merchandisers. . . . [They] buy from . . . more than 10,000 vendors."[24] Since the company—J. C. Penney—is shifting its merchandising emphasis from basic, popular-priced goods to a moderate-price "mix" and greater fashion appeal, its buying problems are probably more difficult than formerly. In addition to New York, Penney also has buying offices in Los Angeles, Dallas, and Miami, each concentrating its purchases to specific lines of merchandise.

---

[23] Wingate and Friedlander distinguish among five varieties of consumer panels: (1) The customer advisory group—which makes suggestions concerning store policies, services, and merchandise assortments; (2) the consumer jury that expresses opinion on advertising and sketches of styles; (3) the consumer experience group that reports on performance of products in use; (4) the home inventory group that reports the goods they have on hand; and (5) the continuous-purchase-record group which records and make monthly reports on their family purchasing. *Op. cit.*, p. 102.

[24] Samuel Feinberg, "Penney's—Always Amid Transition," *Women's Wear Daily*, July 30, 1970, p. 21.

For new items retailers increasingly are substituting the judgment of a buying committee for that of a single buyer. For example, three out of every four supermarket chains have established three- to eight-man committees which often include some or all of these: the buyer assigned to the particular group of products under consideration; his superior—head buyer or merchandise manager; the publicity manager; and two or three store supervisors. No new product can be added to stock without the approval of the committee.[25] Similar committees now exist in retail organizations dealing in many kinds of merchandise.

■ DETERMINING QUANTITY TO PURCHASE

Having decided *what* merchandise to buy, the buyer now faces the problem of *how much* to purchase at any particular time. His decision here will rest on four main factors: (1) The period for which purchasing shall be done, (2) estimated sales for the period, (3) goods on hand plus goods already on order, and (4) the desired stock at the end of the period.

□ Period for which purchasing is done

It is evident that customer acceptance of merchandise offerings (sales), whether staple or fashion goods, cannot be estimated without considering a particular period of time. For some goods—fresh vegetables, for example—the period may be only one day but for women's winter coats the selling season may extend over several months and purchases planned for each month.

Hand-to-mouth buying Today numerous retailers practice "hand-to-mouth" buying, that is, they purchase in small quantities at frequent intervals, thus shortening the period for which they buy. The increasing emphasis on fashion has contributed to this development since such merchandise is subject to large markdowns unless it is sold before the crest of the fashion cycle has passed. Many retailers have found that a small inventory with a rapid turnover decreases storage and interest charges, results in a steady flow of new merchandise into the store and increased sales, and reduces the risks involved in long-term commitments. Better inventory control and ordering systems—some of them based on electronic data processing; im-

---

[25] E. Dubbs, "Committee Buying on the Rise," *Merchandising Week*, November 4, 1968, p. 27.

provements in communication—the telephone, telegraph, and teletype; and more rapid delivery, resulting from branch and public warehouses near the retailer, the truck, air express, and fast freight, have made it possible to operate successfully on smaller stocks.

The major disadvantages of hand-to-mouth buying are that it results in the loss of higher-bracket noncumulative quantity discounts, may lead to inadequate assortments with a loss of sales and customer goodwill, contributes to less effective displays because of smaller inventories, and increases transportation and handling costs. There are also dangers that in a rising market, higher prices will have to be paid on later orders and the emphasis on smaller orders and speed in delivery will undermine quality standards on merchandise.

Speculative buying Many retailers follow a policy of speculative buying. That is, when rising prices are expected, buyers place large orders hoping to resell at higher prices later and obtain a larger gross margin; when falling prices are anticipated, they pursue a very close hand-to-mouth buying policy. This policy should be followed with caution and full awareness of the risks involved. Occasionally, a larger order than usual should be placed when rising prices are expected. Sometimes such action is necessary to increase the assurance of getting needed goods. But with respect to speculative buying it may be said that if the retailer is quite consistently right in predicting price-level changes, retailing is not the best field for him. He could make a much larger income speculating on some commodity exchange and not have the problems connected with the operation of a store. In other words, a retailer is in business to make a merchandising profit, not a speculative profit. If he wants to speculate, he does not need to bother with operating a store at the same time. To put it very bluntly: Speculation is a profession in itself and does not under any circumstances come under the head of buying.

It is also dangerous to trim inventories too far when the retailer expects a falling price level. In the words of one experienced retailer:

> Though it is considered sound practice to minimize losses by keeping small inventories in times of shrinking values, from a practical angle this is unsound, for the reputation of carrying a fine stock is more important than the expected loss. Over against the few occasions when normal inventories have been decreased to forestall losses can be set the great majority of occasions when insufficient inventories have given rise to a myriad of intangible costs—ill-will, small repeat orders, and the extra expenses entailed in work stoppages, delays and extra efforts. Within a wide margin, inventory depreciation is the lesser of the two evils.[26]

[26] Oswald Knauth, *Managerial Enterprise* (New York: W. W. Norton & Co., Inc., 1948), p. 103.

In brief, although some inventory variation in response to expected price-level changes is desirable, it must not be carried to excess regardless of whether a higher or a lower price level is expected.

Other considerations Three other factors which influence the period for which purchasing is done require only brief mention at this point. They are (1) quantity discounts, (2) supply conditions, and (3) the retailer's financial resources and storage facilities. Obviously, large discounts will encourage purchasing for a longer period. Likewise, if supply conditions are such that delivery is uncertain, the retailer may well "order ahead." Finally, it is clear that retailers with limited financial resources—including both cash and credit—and without adequate storage facilities are restricted as to the length of the period for which they can buy.

□ Estimated sales for the period

Estimated sales for the period under consideration usually are based on past sales, with allowance for changes in the competitive situation and business conditions. Without detailing this process, three points deserve mention. First, the competitive situation is often the determining factor in the sales outlook for a particular store or department. Even though a store had sales of $10,000 for a certain month last year and business conditions are better this year, the sales estimate may be less for the comparable period this year because of the existence of a new competitor.

Second, the buyer should not be misled by the statistics on the business outlook for the country as a whole. Rather, his concern should be the incomes of his potential customers and their buying intentions. In other words, the general economic situation in the area in which his store is located, particularly as it affects the income of his customers and potential customers and reflects their willingness to spend this income, is far more significant to the retailer in planning his sales than is the business outlook for the country as a whole.

Third, the importance of a careful estimate of sales varies both by kinds of goods and from time to time. Thus, for perishable and fashion goods, considerable caution is needed; otherwise, excessive purchases will result in spoilage of goods or in large markdowns. For staple goods, excessive purchases may mean merely larger-than-necessary inventories for a while, with a temporary tie-up of some working capital. In periods of falling prices, however, overestimates of sales may result in inventory losses.

For new merchandise the buyer may feel it quite impossible to estimate sales even for a relatively short period; as a result, he may buy only a few units to test customer reaction. Although this solution may result in his quickly being out of stock, it may be better than taking markdowns if the new goods fail to sell.

□ Stock on hand and on order

The present stock and that for which orders have been placed affect the quantity to be purchased in a given period. Information as to goods on hand may be obtained from observation, current merchandise control records, or physical inventories. In small stores observation is the usual method. Before placing orders with a salesman, the retailer will look over his stock of the particular items involved. Preceding a buying trip he may make a more careful appraisal of his stock, perhaps going to the expense of an inventory of the items in which he is interested. In some lines a perpetual inventory system may be used,[27] thus providing the buyer with an up-to-the-minute picture of stock on hand.

In large stores buyers maintain or have access to merchandise records which reveal currently the quantity of most items on hand, since proper ticketing of goods permits accurate tabulation of goods purchased and sold. It is an easy matter, therefore, to determine the stock on hand at any given time. It is equally convenient to obtain data concerning merchandise on order from the buyer's own records.

□ Desired stock at end of period

The planned or desired stock at the end of the particular period, our final major consideration in determining how much to buy, represents the best judgment of the buyer after pertinent information has been evaluated. An increasing sales trend, a rising fashion cycle, prospective price advances, supply conditions, and the existence of substantial quantity discounts, may well dictate a relatively large end-of-period stock. The reverse of these factors may induce him to reduce his inventory.

□ Trip buying plan

Before going to market, buyers often develop a trip buying plan covering the specific items they wish to purchase and the amount they intend to spend in the light of their "open-to-buy,"[28] merchandise budget, and the other sources of information which have been described. Figure 10–1 shows the form used by one retailer.[29]

---

[27] See the description of the perpetual inventory system used in a chain shoe store, p. 242, above.

[28] For details on the "open-to-buy" cf. pp. 345–48, below.

[29] For a discussion of buying trips, cf. the following chapter, pp. 262–64.

FIGURE 10–1 **Trip buying plan form**

Stk. & Inv. on Hand Today $________

On Order This Month Del.________

Est. Sales Bal. of Month________

Planned Stock E. O. M.________

Open to Buy This Month________

Planned Sales This Month________

Trip Buying Limit______ (MONTH) Delivery $________

Planned Initial Mark-up %________

On Order Next Month Del.________

Plan Purchases Next Month________

Est. Sales Next Month________

Dep't.________

Store________

Date________

ALL ABOVE SPACES ON THIS PLAN MUST BE FILLED OUT BEFORE BEING SIGNED BY BUYER

1	2	3	4	5	6	7	8	9	10	11	12	13
On Hand	On Order	Total	Estimated Sales Till Delivery	Stock Remain-ing	Planned Stock Desired	Open to Buy	Plan to Buy Now	DESCRIPTION OF MERCHANDISE	Cost	Retail	Total Retail	QUANTITY PURCHASED

Delivery Date________ Signed________ Buyer Approved________ Mdse Mgr.

With data available concerning the merchandise his customers want and the quantities he should purchase, the buyer is in a position to choose his sources of supply, also known as merchandise resources. This subject is discussed in the next chapter.

REVIEW AND DISCUSSION QUESTIONS

1 Name and explain briefly the major factors influencing the buying policies of a specific retailer.

2 In view of the importance of customer knowledge in effective buying, how can you explain the relatively small amount of customer research carried on by retailers?

3 Distinguish between a "basic stock list" and a "model stock." Discuss the problems involved in establishing a basic stock list for staple goods and a model stock for fashion goods.

4 Visit some of the larger retail stores in your city or a nearby one and report on the extent to which electronic computers are being used to improve buying. For any firms using computers, determine the degree of satisfaction that exists with their use.

5 Explain how the buyer is aided in determining what goods to purchase by the information gained by analyzing returned goods and adjustments.

6 Assume that you are the owner-buyer of a men's clothing store or women's apparel shop in a city of 25,000 population. Evaluate the methods you would use to determine what merchandise is selling best in competing stores and by comparable stores in other cities.

7 As the buyer of shoes in a large discount house, what kinds or types of information would you require to fulfill your responsibilities satisfactorily? Where would you obtain it?

8 Discuss the main forms of buying assistance given by vendors to their retail customers.

9 Prepare a concise report on the topic: "Buying Committees: A Critical Appraisal of Their Functions under Present Conditions."

10 Explain in some detail the chief factors which determine the quantity of merchandise to be purchased at a given time.

chapter 11

BUYING: SELECTING MERCHANDISE RESOURCES AND SUITABLE MERCHANDISE

The second main step in buying is the choice of satisfactory sources of supply. The difficulty of this problem is evidenced by the fact that an independent supermarket operator has to assemble from 4,000 to 9,000 different items and a drugstore up to 12,000 items. For the large-scale retailer even these figures seem small; a general merchandise store or a large discount house may stock as many as 40,000 different types, styles, sizes, or qualities of merchandise, and the 200,000 items sold by Sears, Roebuck and Co. come from over 18,000 suppliers. In this chapter we describe and evaluate the "merchandise resources"—as they are known in the trade—from which the retailer purchases these goods. Attention is also devoted to selecting merchandise which is suitable to customers' requirements which, of course, influences the choice of suppliers.

GENERAL TYPES OF MERCHANDISE RESOURCES

Retailers use three major sources of supply—middlemen, manufacturers, and farmers or growers. In view of the typical reader's familiarity with them from his basic marketing course, our treatment can be relatively brief. A few retailers, of course, make some purchases from other retailers. Thus the retailer of men's clothing who is "out" of a shirt of a certain size may go to another retailer and secure one, rather than let his regular customer go there. Or again, so-called "discount" retailers find, on occasion, that some manufacturers and wholesalers refuse to sell them merchandise; their response may be to find other retailers to make the purchases for them. In view of the relative unimportance of these practices, however, we shall not discuss them further.

□ Middlemen as merchandise resources

Wholesalers Wholesalers are merchant middlemen who typically buy from manufacturers in relatively large quantities and sell to retailers in substantially smaller quantities. Probably almost half of all manufactured consumers' goods go through the hands of wholesalers. They may handle as much as 90 percent of all goods in the hardware trade and nearly 70 percent of all drugstore merchandise.

1. Service and limited-function wholesalers Most wholesalers are best described as service wholesalers, despite the growth of those performing only limited functions. The service wholesaler's chief responsibility is to serve as the retailers' "buying agent." He anticipates what retailers will want, goes out in the market to obtain these goods, and has them available when the retailers want them.

Service wholesalers not only assemble goods for retailers; they also render other valuable services, including storage of goods, quick delivery, extension of credit, risk reduction through enabling the retailer to operate on smaller stocks, and furnishing market information.

Limited-function wholesalers extend few of the foregoing services to the retailer. Cash-and-carry wholesalers in the grocery and tobacco fields, for example, limit themselves to stocks of fast-moving items, eliminate salesmen, and offer no credit or delivery service, thus reducing the cost of wholesaling. Most retailers, however, still prefer to use wholesalers because of the important services they perform.

The services rendered by "regular" wholesalers are especially valuable to small- and medium-sized retailers who utilize this source of supply more than any other. In contrast, large-scale retailers such as chain stores, who are able to perform many of the wholesaler's functions themselves, find it more economical to take over many of the services the wholesaler performs for smaller retailers. Even large retailers, however, make some use of wholesalers, relying on them to obtain items temporarily out of stock or for which the demand is limited.[1]

2. Rack jobbers Basically, the rack jobber is a wholesaler of nonfood items who arranges with the managements of supermarkets to stock and maintain an assortment of goods in a fixture or rack in a particular space in each store. A specific percentage of markup—usually 25 to 33 percent, depending upon the type of merchandise and competitive conditions—is guaranteed to the supermarket. The rack jobber selects the items and arranges the displays, making changes whenever he considers such action advisable.

The rack jobber is responsible for much of the rapidity with which supermarkets have added nonfoods. Without his specialized service, these retailers would have been quite reluctant to add toys, housewares, children's books, hardware, and many other items to their inventory. But since the rack jobber delivers the merchandise, arranges for its display, prices it, provides point-of-purchase material and special promotions, removes slow-selling items—and at a guaranteed gross profit margin—the retailer's resistance crumbled. Today the rack jobber is the main source of supply for health and beauty aids in 48 percent of the independent and small-chain supermarkets, and for 64 percent of housewares and soft goods.[2]

Despite the widespread use of rack jobbers among supermarkets some chains have taken over their functions. For instance, such companies as Acme Markets, Inc., Mayfair Markets, and Food Fair Stores have taken this step, and the trend is continuing. One large organization, however, the Great Atlantic & Pacific Tea Company, switched back to rack jobbers recently.

Among the large supermarket chains direct buying of health and beauty aids, housewares, and glassware is also common. Apparently the managements of these chains are convinced that they can perform the rack jobber's services more effectively than he can. Of course, this trend is in line with the chain's desire for as complete integration as proves to be economically feasible. But it is likely that so long as rack jobbers provide needed nonfoods, give good service, and price their merchandise on a competitive basis, they will be widely used as a source of merchandise.[3]

---

[1] Some students believe that certain of the large national and regional supermarket chains should rely more on wholesalers than is currently the case. Cf. L. W. Stern, "Self-Sufficiency: A Fixation in Corporate Supermarket Chains?" *Journal of Retailing,* Vol. 42, No. 1 (Spring 1966), pp. 18–25 ff.

[2] "37th Annual Report of the Grocery Industry," *Progressive Grocer,* April 1970, p. 86.

[3] For "success" stories in rack merchandising, cf. "Sav-A-Stop's Expressway to Sales," *Non-Foods Business,* May 1968, pp. 14–19, "Flickinger: Off to a Flying Start," *ibid.,* March

3. Integration of wholesale and retail functions Among regular chains there is often a high degree of integration of retail and wholesale activities. The voluntary chain also integrates these activities.[4] Although in the latter case the wholesale and retail activities are not under common ownership, a contractual arrangement usually exists under which the wholesaler and retailer agree to coordinate their operations. In practice, the line between regular chain and voluntary chain operations is becoming somewhat obscure: In addition to serving retailers under contract, the voluntary chain wholesaler may operate a chain of his own—or have a substantial financial investment in many of the so-called "independent" stores. Or a retailer may own a whole group of stores (*i.e.*, a chain) and yet have them supplied by merchandise from a voluntary wholesaler.[5] Finally, the retailers may actually own the wholesale organization, an arrangement usually referred to as a cooperative chain.

While voluntary and cooperative wholesalers have developed outside the food field, it is in food that they play their greatest role. In 1970 their annual sales in this area were $21 billion, 8 percent over 1968.[6] If we also take into account the integration of wholesale and retail activities through (1) chain store organizations, (2) voluntary and cooperative wholesalers in nonfood fields, and (3) group buying arrangements,[7] the magnitude of this development comes into focus.

Other middlemen Other middlemen—brokers, commission men, manufacturers' agents, selling agents, and auctions—are used as sources of needed merchandise by some retailers.

The *broker's* main service is to bring buyer and seller together. He is used chiefly in buying and selling grocery specialties, dry goods, and fruits and vegetables. He is more useful to large retailers than to small-scale operators, but small retailers of men's and women's wear, household appliances, furniture, jewelry, hardware, and drugs employ his services to some degree.[8] To illustrate the way the broker operates, consider a large food

---

1968, pp. 12–17, and "Thriftway's Thrift Rack: Wholesaler as Rack Merchandiser," *ibid.*, June 1968, pp. 12–17.

[4] For details on this form of organization cf. Chapter 8, "Group Activities of Independent Retailers," in C. F. Phillips and D. J. Duncan, *Marketing Principles and Methods* (6th ed.; Homewood, Ill.: Richard D. Irwin, Inc., 1968) and K. A. Adams, "Achieving Market Organization through Voluntary and Cooperative Groups," *Journal of Retailing*, Vol. 42, No. 2 (Summer 1966), pp. 19–28, 60.

[5] The *Progressive Grocer* reports that, in 1969, 24 percent of grocery wholesalers sold to voluntary chains with such sales comprising 26 percent of their total volume. Comparable figures for cooperative chains were 32 percent and 29 percent. "38th Annual Report of the Grocery Industry," April 1971, p. 92.

[6] *Ibid.*, p. 90.

[7] Cf. pp. 267–68, below.

[8] Cf. the discussion of the merchandise broker on p. 265, below.

chain which wishes to purchase several tons of sugar. Instead of having its own buyer visit several refiners to see what is available and at what prices, the chain will secure the services of a broker. Perhaps he is told the highest price the chain will pay for its sugar. Since he is a specialist in sugar, he knows prices and the supplies available; hence, he can quickly locate a proper source of supply and carry out the buyer's orders. Title passes not through the broker but directly from the seller of the sugar to the food chain. For bringing buyer and seller together, the broker receives a fee or commission.

Commission men constitute a source of supply mainly for large retailers, especially for those buying dry goods, grocery specialties, and fruits and vegetables. They differ from brokers in that they usually handle the merchandise. They operate typically in central markets, receive merchandise that they display and sell, deduct their commission and other charges from the proceeds of the sale, and remit the balance to their principals.

Selling agents are independent businessmen who take over the entire sales function for their clients. They are employed mostly by small manufacturers of piece goods, clothing, and food specialties who are not large enough to have their own sales organizations. In addition to selling for their clients, selling agents often give advice on styling, extend financial aid, and make collections. *Manufacturers' agents* sell goods similar to those sold by selling agents but they have less authority over prices and terms of sale, are restricted to a more limited area, and sell only part of their clients' output.

Auctions are used mainly by retailers of fruits and vegetables. When produce is received at the auction, it is placed on display and sold quickly to the highest bidder, the proceeds going to the shipper after commissions and other charges have been deducted. Because they lack the skill needed to be good buyers and have little time to attend the auction, most smaller retailers buy their fruits and vegetables from wholesalers.

□ The manufacturer as a merchandise resource

Why retailers buy direct Many retailers purchase their merchandise directly from manufacturers, even though they lose some of the services offered by the regular wholesaler. Manufacturers' salesmen are usually better trained and better informed than those of wholesalers and can advise the retailer on advertising, display, and on the stock needed. This advice is very valuable for high-fashion merchandise. Also, direct buying is frequently accompanied by the manufacturer's cooperation in training the retailer's salesmen in how to sell certain merchandise; providing demonstrators; training employees to repair and install merchandise (by way of illustration, oil burners); and providing advertising and display material.[9]

In regard to fashion merchandise, direct buying also frequently enables the retailer to get merchandise into his store more quickly than if a middleman is involved. For high-fashion items, time is an important consideration. Even for manufactured goods which are somewhat perishable—crackers and cookies, for example—speed in getting merchandise from manufacturer to retailer is essential since customers are constantly demanding fresher merchandise.

For the large retailer, direct buying permits the purchase of goods made according to his own specifications. Montgomery Ward & Company has added many new lines of products made to its own specifications and Sears, Roebuck and Co. specifies the design of 95 percent of the goods it sells. Drug and furniture chains, department stores, and discount houses also follow this practice. His nearness to the customer enables the retailer to assess customer wants; and his testing laboratory[10] serves as an ideal place for drawing up product specifications.

In addition to the foregoing benefits, many retailers buy direct because they are able to obtain lower net prices. In other words—partly by eliminating some of the middleman's functions or absorbing them, and partly by having them performed by the manufacturer—the cost of marketing is reduced and prices to the retailer are lowered.

To achieve some of the advantages of direct-buying, many smaller retailers have joined together. In Cleveland, for example, direct buying by a group of hardware retailers resulted in a reported 10 to 20 percent reduction in purchase prices; and the ability to purchase directly was a major reason for the formation of Casual Corner Associates, an association of independently owned sportswear shops.

Why manufacturers sell direct An understanding of the reasons why retailers buy directly from manufacturers is insufficient to explain the prevalence of this practice. The attitude of the manufacturer also needs to be considered. Many manufacturers prefer to sell directly to retailers because they consider it "good business." They appreciate the necessity of speed in getting fashion and perishable merchandise to the retailer while such goods are saleable. Moreover, the growth of retailers who buy in large amounts, perform part of the storage function, and are good credit risks, encourages

---

[9] Manufacturers selling directly to large retailers cannot provide advertising and other promotional assistance unless the same assistance is offered to small retailers who buy through wholesalers. Cf. the discussion of the Robinson-Patman Act in Chapter 12, pp. 286–87.

[10] Cf. pp. 273–74, below.

the manufacturer to sell direct. And relatively small retailers may concentrate their buying with a few manufacturers to make direct sale economical. Many small retailers of men's clothing, for instance, buy the major part of their suits and overcoats from a few sources. They also purchase substantial quantities for each season at one time, thus increasing the size of their orders.

Still other manufacturers sell directly to secure more aggressive selling, as in the grocery field where many wholesalers have developed their own private brands. The availability of public warehouses and manufacturers' branches as distributing points near their customers is also partly the cause and partly the effect of direct selling.

Manufacturer-retailer integration Just as integration has taken place between wholesaler and retailer, the manufacturer and the retailer have also been drawn together. Some retailers, having purchased for some time from certain manufacturers, have taken the initiative and "bought out"—in whole or in part—some of their resources. Currently, Sears, Roebuck and Co. has sizeable ownership of the manufacturers producing about one-third of the merchandise it sells, and the Great Atlantic & Pacific Tea Company owns—among many others—bakeries, candy factories, ice cream plants, cheese factories, and French-fried potato plants; Bond Stores, Inc., manufactures men's suits, coats, and shirts; and the Thom McAn Shoe Company produces its own shoes.

☐ The farmer as a merchandise resource

The grower is not an important source of supply for retailers, except for some foods. Small retailers may buy a large part of their fresh fruits and vegetables directly from local growers. Large chain retailers, however, may send buyers to distant farmers to procure supplies as is true for the Great Atlantic & Pacific Tea Company. "Its produce-buying division is the largest single factor in the market. Three teams of buyers—on the West Coast, in the Mississippi Valley, and on the East Coast—follow the crops northward as they ripen and keep in constant communication with the central office, and with one another, over a national teletype system."[11] Smaller chains cover a less extensive geographic area, but they, also, frequently by-pass central markets and go directly to growers or, to cooperative marketing associations to which the growers belong. Most agricultural consumers' goods, however, are still bought by retailers from middlemen.[12]

---

[11] "Pinching 500,000,000,000 Pennies," *Fortune*, Vol. 67, No. 3 (March 1963), p. 172.
[12] Cf. pp. 256–57, above.

VENDOR INITIATIVE TO FIND BUYERS

The initiative in bringing the retailer and the source of supply together may be taken by the seller or by the retailer himself, acting individually or in cooperation with other retailers. We begin our discussion with the seller taking the initiative. He employs two methods mainly, (1) catalogs and price lists and (2) salesmen.

Catalogs and price lists

To provide information concerning their offerings, both manufacturers and wholesalers issue catalogs. Of considerable importance at one time and still widely used by some vendors, catalogs today are largely used by retailers for the purchase of staple merchandise needed to fill in their stocks. Even for such merchandise, catalogs are used chiefly by retailers in areas where the total business of vendors is not sufficient to justify frequent visits by salesmen. As catalog sales have fallen off, some vendors have substituted shorter price lists with less complete descriptions of the items offered for sale than formerly.

Catalogs are used by some resident buying offices in cities such as New York to assist their client stores in making purchases. One office, for example, issues a notion catalog describing all the items carried by the stores in its affiliated group. Another publishes a housewares catalog in mimeographed form containing the chief offerings of over 1,200 suppliers.[13]

Salesmen

Using salesmen to sell his products is probably the most important activity initiated by the vendor. When goods sell quite rapidly, salesmen may call upon their customers once a week or more often. In the grocery, drug, and hardware fields, some wholesalers' salesmen telephone their retailer customers daily. In other fields—men's clothing, for instance—visits by the salesmen are less frequent. To some degree the interval between salesmen's visits depends on business conditions. The more difficult it is to sell, the greater the likelihood that calls will be made more often to exert more selling "pressure."

Purchasing through salesmen offers the buyer certain advantages. It relieves him from searching for sources of supply, and permits him to obtain the opinions of his salespeople when samples are shown before purchases

[13] Residents buying offices are discussed on pp. 264–67, below.

are made. The salesman also serves as a source of market information and when buying is done on the premises of the buyer, he can more deliberately check the stock on hand. In view of these benefits, and others, the buyer can do a better job of purchasing.

■ RETAILER INITIATIVE TO FIND VENDORS

Increasingly, retailers are seeking sources of supply, rather than depending on vendors coming to them. They prefer to compare the offerings of several vendors, survey "the market," and exchange ideas with various sellers and retailers handling similar merchandise. Moreover, manufacturers of such high-fashion goods as women's dresses are small and concentrated in a limited area, thus making it more economical for the retailer to take the initiative than for the manufacturer to send out salesmen. In performing this task the retailer may visit local, central, and even foreign markets, use a buying office, and engage in group and central buying.

□ Visits to local markets

Visits to local markets, as we have noted, are common among small retailers of fruits and vegetables and may well result in obtaining their produce at lower prices. Large food retailers also send their buyers into local markets to assure themselves of an ample supply at the lowest possible price. They usually deal with the local middlemen who offer the output of several farmers. Retailers may also take the initiative in dealing with cash-and-carry wholesalers in the local market and occasionally call on certain local manufacturers.

□ Visits to central markets

Facilities available Buying in central markets is practiced mainly by medium-size and large-scale retailers and, to some degree, by all retailers of fashion goods. Most retailers consider New York City the dominant central market for many types of merchandise, particularly women's wear, since about two-thirds of all the dresses manufactured in this country are made there. But, other cities are gaining as central markets, and, for certain goods they overshadow New York. For department store merchandise, San Francisco and Los Angeles have become so important that even buyers from eastern stores visit these cities. For furniture, Chicago; Grand Rapids, Michigan; High Point, North Carolina; and Jamestown, New York, are important markets, in addition to New York City. For many retailers, St. Louis, Dallas, and New Orleans are important central markets.

Central market buyers typically visit the display quarters of individual vendors as well as joint display centers. In most cities vendors of competing goods are located close together and suppliers' offerings can be easily compared. Permanent displays in one large building are also frequently maintained by competing vendors. Chicago's American Furniture Mart houses the permanent displays of many sellers of furniture and related products and its gigantic Merchandise Mart is used for display and selling purposes by vendors in practically all fields. Atlanta's Merchandise Mart likewise has displays covering many lines of merchandise, while the Apparel Mart in Dallas concentrates on all kinds of apparel.

Where central permanent displays are not used, competing vendors often sponsor temporary joint showings of their goods. Thus, New York City has its house-furnishings show and its toy fair; Chicago, its home-furnishings exhibit, its millinery-fashion display, its semiannual furniture markets, and its national shoe fair; and San Francisco, its home furnishings show.

Benefits and methods of central market buying Although the excitement of the large "showings" may not be conducive to careful buying, much can be said from the buyer's point of view in favor of the joint showing. In some instances catalog illustrations may be misleading, so that it is wise to examine samples of the goods before they are purchased. The show meets this need. It also allows the buyer to view all offerings in a minimum of time, to make direct comparisons, and to exchange ideas with other buyers.

Buying in central markets is carried on mainly (1) through store buyers who make periodic trips to market, (2) through store buyers assisted by resident buying offices, and (3) through central market representatives. When the store buyer goes to market and buys without assistance from a resident buying office, he has full authority. Although he still retains this authority when making use of the resident buying office, the latter helps determine what shall be purchased. Where central market representatives are used, the local buyer loses to them much of his authority.

Central market buying trips The frequency of buying visits to central markets is determined by such factors as: (1) Whether or not the buyer's store has a resident buying office; (2) the type of merchandise involved, *i.e.*, staple or fashion goods; (3) the size of the store; (4) business and supply conditions; and (5) the location of the retailer in relation to the central market.

The brevity of the usual market trip makes intensive preparation essential to insure the most productive use of the buyer's time. Once in the market, the buyer must scout it carefully, decide on the number of vendors he will patronize, and maintain a resource file containing information regarding past experience, if any, with each vendor.

1. "Scouting" the market Visits to central markets, especially to purchase fashion goods, enable the buyer to obtain merchandise knowledge before he actually starts to make purchases. Without the assistance of a resident buying office, he usually utilizes his first visit to each vendor as a "sight-seeing" trip to note what is available. But much depends, of course, upon supply and demand conditions. When goods are in short supply, delays in making purchases may result in failure to obtain the goods desired.

On this first excursion it is advisable for the buyer to keep complete notes as to prices, materials, styles, and the best offerings of each vendor. Before he makes his second trip, during which he will probably place orders, careful study should be made of these notes. This practice saves him the trouble of again calling upon *all* vendors and reviewing *all* their offerings.

Many buyers visit stores in the central market city either before or after exploring the offerings of vendors, to observe merchandise being displayed. Sometimes trips to certain cities may be made just to observe other stores. To illustrate, the fashion reputation of Neiman-Marcus of Dallas, Texas, is so great that its fashion expositions attract store buyers from all parts of the country.

2. Selecting vendors: many or a few? With full information concerning available merchandise, the buyer is ready to select the items he believes best adapted to the needs of his customers. Through a careful study of his notes, he is able to determine quickly the sources of supply with the goods he requires at the most favorable terms. These resources he visits for the second time to check more carefully on specific items, to negotiate prices and terms, and to place his orders.[14]

Because of the information the practice provides, the buyer should shop all vendors in the central market handling the type of merchandise in which he is interested. Such shopping, however, does not necessarily imply he will spread his purchases among many vendors.[15] In fact, by concen-

[14] In women's apparel there is considerable "crossing of lines" in the search for new resources. One publication reports that ". . . coat buyers are going to dress houses to get coats; dress buyers seek out coat resources to find dresses; and coat buyers shop dress firms to pick up . . . dresses to add to their stock." "Buyers are Crossing Lines to Find New Resources," *Women's Wear Daily,* August 19, 1969, p. 35.

[15] The discussion which follows is applicable to the selection of vendors in all markets and not in central markets alone. For a detailed analysis of this subject cf. E. W. Crooks, "The Case for Concentration of Purchases," *Journal of Retailing,* Vol. 42, No. 1 (Spring 1966), pp. 14–18; and Richard Rosenthal, "Concentration of Resources—the Retailer's Reactions," Part I, *Stores,* November 1969, pp. 33–36 and Part II, *ibid.,* December

trating his purchases, the buyer saves time, earns the goodwill of vendors, obtains better credit terms and improved deliveries, assures that his orders are filled more accurately, and that his claims are more cheerfully adjusted. Moreover, concentrating orders allows the buyer to secure larger quantity discounts.

The buyer should recognize, however, the benefits gained when spreading his orders among several resources.[16] This practice gives him a greater assurance of supply through reducing the risk of floods, fires, or strikes. Competition among several suppliers may result in getting better prices or terms of sale as each tries to enlarge his share of the buyer's order.

In brief, the retailer must weight the advantages of both concentrating and spreading his orders. Each specific situation should be weighed carefully, but as a rule retailers should confine their purchases to those vendors having the "best buys." Hence, when they find sources of supply which (1) have merchandise meeting their needs, (2) can be counted on as steady sources of supply, (3) are in sound financial condition, (4) have fair prices and terms of sale, (5) give good delivery service, (6) make adjustments promptly on all reasonable complaints, (7) are fair and honest in their dealings, (8) have progressive managements, and (9) deliver goods identical with their samples, they tend to concentrate their purchases with them.

3. *The resource file* Maintained by many buyers to help decide which vendors shall get the bulk of their orders, this file consists of a card record for each vendor with whom business has been done, with notations concerning past dealings. For example, the card will show discounts allowed by the vendor and whether or not the goods delivered were identical with samples. When a resident buying office is used, the resource file may be maintained in that office.[17]

Resident buying offices Resident buying offices have grown in importance in recent years and today are literally merchandising consultants for their client stores. They probably serve as many as 90 percent of the country's department and specialty stores as well as many discount houses.

Resident buying offices may be classified into two groups: *Independent offices,* including salaried or paid offices and merchandise brokers; and

---

1969, pp. 33–36. Rosenthal reports that of 317 retailers surveyed, 80 percent have maintained a concentration policy during the past decade with most of them finding it beneficial.

[16] Hess's of Allentown, Pennsylvania, follows a policy of working closely with key or "core" resources but also buying from a number of others. Thus, "if there are 10 or 12 shirt manufacturers . . . two will be our full-line core resource and we will buy what is fashion important from the rest." "A Hometown Store Takes to the Road," *Business Week,* June 20, 1970, p. 119.

[17] Cf. E. B. Weiss, "Collaboration vs. Confrontation between Major Suppliers and Major Retailers," *Advertising Age,* January 31, 1966, pp. 92, 95.

store-owned offices, including private offices, associated offices, and syndicate and chain offices.[18]

1. Independent offices The independent buying office is a private company with an ownership different from that of the several stores which it serves. In the salaried or paid type of office, contracts are usually written providing the use of the services offered to the buyer for a certain period, typically, one year. Some contracts set a minimum fee as low as $100 a month, with larger payments according to annual sales or the services rendered. Other contracts stipulate that the fee equal a certain percentage of the sales of the store or of the departments involved, commonly ¼ of 1 percent for large stores.

The merchandise broker, formerly known as a commission resident buying office, exists to serve smaller retailers who cannot afford the minimum cost of the salaried type. Whereas it is estimated that annual sales of at least $75,000 are needed to justify a contract with a salaried buying office, the merchandise broker can be used by much smaller stores. This is true because these offices are usually paid an average fee of 3 percent on all orders by the vendors with whom orders are placed. No contract exists between the store and the merchandise broker, with the result that shifts may often take place.

2. Store-owned offices The store-owned buying office is owned outright by a single large store or group of stores. When operated as a definite division of one organization, it is known as a "private" buying office. When it is owned and operated by several independent or ownership-group stores for their own benefit, it is known as an "associated" buying office. Probably the best-known offices of this type are the Associated Merchandising Corporation[19] and Frederick Atkins, Inc. The former serves some 30 major department stores including the Dayton-Hudson Corporation and Rich's of Atlanta, while the latter office has some 40 other department stores as members.[20]

The syndicate office, the third type of store-owned resident buying office, is best exemplified by the chain-store or ownership-group buying office, which purchases centrally or otherwise for the stores involved. It closely resembles the associated buying office but is able to force adoption of its recommendations to a much greater degree because of common

---

[18] This classification is based on J. W. Wingate, "Some Data on Resident Buying," *New York Retailer,* October 1962, pp. 2–6.

[19] In May 1970, the corporation discontinued its wholesale division doing an estimated $150 million annual volume. For details, cf. Harry Berlfein, "AMC to Drop Wholesaling," *Women's Wear Daily,* May 4, 1970, pp. 1, 20.

[20] Some of the changes being made and the problems encountered by resident buying offices are discussed in Carole Sloan, "Offices Restructuring for Total Service," *Women's Wear Daily,* September 9, 1970, p. 20; and in Samuel Feinberg, "From Where I Sit," *ibid.,* March 24, 1971, p. 41.

ownership of the stores. Examples of the syndicate type of buying office are Associated Dry Goods Corporation and the Allied Purchasing Corporation. The latter organization serves the more than 100 stores of the Allied Stores Corporation through buying offices in New York, Chicago, Los Angeles, Miami, and Dallas and a foreign-buying subsidiary which operates buying offices in several cities abroad. While the buyers within each store have considerable authority to make direct purchases to meet local market demand, even on these purchases the buyers are aided by the advice and recommendations of the resident buying office staff. Buyer committees for various lines of merchandise composed of both store buyers and those from the Allied Purchasing Corporation, also may select many items which must be carried by all stores.[21]

The various types of resident buying offices discussed have seen their greatest development in the New York market but some are located in such cities as Chicago, Los Angeles, and St. Louis. The majority of resident buyers operate in the women's and children's apparel trades, although many offer service in the purchase of furs, men's wear, millinery, home furnishings, jewelry, and other lines. Some are fairly small and serve only a limited number of stores in a few lines; others are organized to render service in a large number of fields.

3. *Services rendered buyers*[22] The services provided by buying offices enable store buyers to do a much better job than they could do without such assistance. Among these services are the following: They place orders upon request, check on deliveries, handle adjustments, and provide the store buyer with information as to goods available, fashion trends, prices, and the best sources of supply. The store buyer gets his information from experts, and he gets it quickly. When he is in the market a buying office representative accompanies him on visits to vendors so that both can pass judgment on merchandise offers and locate the "best buys". The office also may arrange for "showings" at which the offerings of many vendors are put on display, thus conserving the buyer's time; and it can provide facilities such as office space, stenographic aid, and sample rooms where vendors may display their goods. Finally, the resident buying office often plays an important role in making group buying arrangements.[23]

When the store buyer is not in the central market, the resident buying office may aid him through a constant stream of market information in the

---

[21] Cf. the comments on "individual store" and "central" buying in the Allied organization in Wingate and Friedlander, *op. cit.*, pp. 40–41.

[22] For an excellent discussion of the services rendered by resident buying offices, cf. Howard Eilenberg, "Resident Buying Offices: Key Links of Marketing Channels," *New York Retailer*, December 1968, pp. 8–11. Also cf. Herbert Koshetz, "Resident Buyers Staging Comeback," *New York Times*, November 15, 1970, p. F13.

[23] Cf. the next section.

form of letters, special reports, or regular weekly or monthly bulletins. Thus the buyer is kept informed concerning fashion and price trends and special buys. During recent years there has been a tendency for resident buying offices to broaden their services to the stores they represent. To illustrate, sometimes samples of new goods or of exceptional value are forwarded to the buyer. If he decides to purchase some of them, he may ask the buying office to place an order. This office also handles many fill-in purchases and may even consolidate shipment on a number of small orders placed with several vendors, thus reducing the cost of transportation. In some instances the buying office—aided by a unit-control system worked out between the store and the office—may make all the purchases of staple merchandise thus allowing the store buyers to concentrate attention on other goods. Some offices actually merchandise fashion departments in the stores they serve. While others, having foreign branches or working closely with similar groups abroad, purchase quite large amounts of foreign merchandise.

The resident buying office sometimes offers the store two other services which, although not directly related to buying, are very valuable. One is to suggest goods for promotional events, prepare advertising copy, and outline the whole campaign. The second is to operate as a clearinghouse for information from all the stores served. For example, data may be gathered on expenses, markdowns, training systems, and sales promotions and distributed to all the stores of the group.

Group buying Group buying involves joint purchasing by a group of buyers representing noncompeting stores.[24] Typically, samples are gathered from various vendors and placed on display at buying offices or, in some cases, in hotel sample rooms. Sometimes vendors' labels are removed so that buying may be as objective as possible. After the samples have been examined, the committee of buyers decides, by a majority or two-thirds vote, on the items to be bought. Each buyer usually takes at least a minimum quantity of the merchandise selected.

Although done mostly by department and departmentized specialty stores, group buying is also practiced by retailers of hardware, appliances, foods, drugs, and other merchandise lines. Because of the benefits realized, the practice is likely to spread.

1. Benefits of group buying Group buying yields at least six main advantages to the participating stores. First, it permits placing large orders on certain goods and securing substantial discounts. Second, it provides a pooling of knowledge as to what customers want, goods available, and fashion trends, thus enabling buyers to select items that will sell to better advantage. Third, it saves the buyer's time while he is in the market. Fourth, it makes

[24] When items are selected by a committee of buyers chosen to act for the buyers of all the stores, the practice is referred to as "committee buying."

possible the direct comparison of samples of merchandise from several vendors in one place and results in better buying. Fifth, in some cases, sufficient quantities are purchased to enable standards to be developed for certain items which can then be produced according to specifications. Sixth, it may also yield some sales promotional advantages. To illustrate: After buying certain goods, brand names may be chosen for them and then widely advertised. The resident buying office assists in planning these group promotions.

2. Limitations of group buying In addition to the objections raised by vendors—that it results in too many price concessions, causes pressure to reduce quality, and encourages style piracy while samples are on display—other difficulties with group buying are involved. Many store buyers consider such buying a step toward their elimination, with their buying function taken over by central buyers. As a result, they do not cooperate in "pushing" the goods selected by the group or they place minimum orders for the selected goods. In the latter case, their action makes it difficult for the group to present a united front in asking lower prices of the vendor. The practice is also time consuming; and not all groups have provided the better selection of goods expected.

Group buying probably is best suited to stores handling medium-priced lines. Low-priced stores find that most of the goods they buy are made by manufacturers for stock, and no production savings are available when a single large order is placed. Retailers of high-priced goods realize that the individuality of customers' demand precludes their participation in extensive group-buying arrangements.

Central buying Central buying implies that a large part of the authority over buying lies outside the individual retail store as is true in many chain-store organizations. Instead of the store manager choosing vendors this task is performed by headquarters executives. The central buyer is made responsible for purchasing, and the store manager for selling.

1. Growth of central buying Two authorities write that "perhaps the major trend in modern merchandising has been for two or more stores to unite to centralize their buying activities. Central buyers replace buyers for individual stores."[25] Even department stores have adopted some central-buying practices. For example, some ownership-group department stores—Allied Stores Corporation and Associated Dry Goods Corporation—have long used central buyers for some staples and lower-priced fashion merchandise.[26] But the loss of authority by the department store buyer should

[25] Wingate and Friedlander, *op. cit.*, p. 39.

[26] In 1970 Bullock's, Inc., of Los Angeles, a regional department store chain, instituted a limited program of central buying. Six all-store buyers were appointed and 39 buyers were switched to the new position of manager. Cf. Bill McNeill, "Six All-Store Buyers Named at Bullock's," *Women's Wear Daily,* September 16, 1970, p. 8.

not be overemphasized. The practice has not made much headway outside of staples, and some firms have returned to individual store buying after experimenting with central buying.

Many organizations with central buyers depend to a degree on store buyers, especially in regard to shopping goods. Even such large chains as W. T. Grant Company, F. W. Woolworth Company, and J. C. Penney Company let their store managers select much of their merchandise from lists supplied by headquarters. In other instances the managers meet and choose from the samples gathered by the central buyers, with blanket orders being placed on the items selected. In department store ownership-groups, store buyers may refuse goods selected by central buyers. Yet the trend toward central buying has taken away from many store buyers an appreciable part of their authority over purchasing.[27]

Central buyers require a constant stream of information concerning customers' demands. To obtain this information they use all of the methods discussed in a preceding section. Through perpetual inventory systems and unit inventory control plans—which increasingly are being made more complete, more accurate, and more up-to-date by the use of electronic devices—as well as through reports from the store to the central buyer as to how goods are moving and related information, many central buyers know as much or more about the wants of customers they never see as their store counterparts.

2. Advantages and disadvantages of central buying[28] In part, the advantages of central buying are similar to those of group buying such as the lower prices secured by quantity buying and the possibility of central planning of sales promotions. But other advantages also result. Since the central buyer spends his full time in buying, he becomes more expert in this task and often does a better job than the store buyer, for whom it usually is a part-time activity. Located in the central market, or at least closely in touch with it, the central buyer secures new merchandise immediately. Traveling expenses are reduced and inspection of goods, especially fashion items, is made easy. Finally, relieving the store buyer of considerable purchasing frees him to devote more attention to selling.

The benefits of central buying are greatest for staples. For fashion goods it is contended that, since the buyer must keep in touch with his store's customers whose wants may differ from those of other stores, he may be unable to buy in sufficient quantities to get important quantity discounts. There is sufficient truth in these contentions, perhaps, to justify the conclusion that fashion goods appealing to buyers for stores with upper-income clienteles

---

[27] For supporting evidence cf. "Manufacturers Accuse Retailers of Downgrading the Buyer's Role," *Merchandising Week*, March 7, 1966, p. 25.

[28] Also cf. the discussion of the merits and limitations of separating the buying and selling functions in departmentized stores on pp. 167–69, above.

will never be purchased in any quantity by central buyers. Yet methods of keeping these buyers informed as to what customers want are developing so rapidly that the future may well bring changes.

3. Ordering for specific stores in chain systems One main problem growing out of central buying by chain organizations is devising an adequate system to (1) inform store managers of the goods purchased by the central buyers and (2) to enable them to requisition stock for their stores from such merchandise. The food chains furnish a good example of the factors involved in this problem.

For many years it has been the practice of these chains to furnish their store managers with a list of the items carried in company warehouses. Usually these merchandise lists are on a printed form also used for placing orders. For dry groceries, the store manager takes his list and, at particular times, checks it against the quantity on hand for each item and enters the amount he wishes to order. This form is sent to the nearest company warehouse where the order is filled.

Today the food chains are speeding up this ordering process by the use of electronic equipment.[29] Many units of Safeway Stores, Inc., are equipped with an ordering machine which produces a tape listing the wanted merchandise. In turn, the symbols on this tape are transmitted electronically to a warehouse from which the order is filled. The National Tea Company system has store employees place the order on cards. These cards are sent to headquarters where they are "read" by an electronic machine which automatically transmits shipping orders to the warehouse. This company, however, has experimented with a telephone wire transmission system which reduces the time between placing an order and receiving the merchandise in the store from three days (when cards are mailed) to one day. Many chains in other fields—variety, drug, shoe, general merchandise, to mention a few—are also using electronic equipment to speed up the flow of orders to their retail units.

Not all chain systems depend on the store manager to decide on the merchandise that should be handled by "his" store. In other words, some firms "merchandise" individual stores from headquarters or a branch headquarters. Previously, Diana Stores Corporation and, for some lines, the J. C. Penney Company, have been cited as examples of this type of electronic operation.[30] Through a combination of model stocks, the flow of sales tags or

[29] The growth of EDP in food chains is evident from the fact that 63 percent of small chains and 95 percent of large ones now use this system. Among the latter, 76 percent use EDP to analyze shipments to individual stores and 67 percent use it for planning and evaluating merchandising and promotion programs. "37th Annual Report of the Grocery Industry," *op. cit.*, p. 65.

[30] Cf. pp. 241–42, above.

tickets to headquarters, and the rapid analysis of these tags, headquarters can quickly decide what merchandise is needed in the store.

□ Foreign markets as sources of supply

Significant fluctuations have taken place in the use of foreign markets as sources of supply. During World War II, the inflow of goods from foreign lands dropped abruptly. Recently, however, an increased interest in foreign-made goods has been manifested with some large stores featuring extensively imports from Mexico, France, Italy, Japan, and other countries.[31] Although reliable data on the ratio of sales of foreign merchandise to total sales in such stores are not available, it is probable that it seldom exceeds 5 percent. For Sears, Roebuck and Co. and for Montgomery Ward & Company imports probably account for from one half of 1 percent to 2 percent of sales; J. C. Penney Company 3–4 percent; and W. T. Grant Company about 5 percent.[32]

Many retailers believe that the goods obtained from abroad—laces from Belgium, furniture from Denmark, sporting goods and wood carvings from Switzerland, linen from Ireland, men's wear from England—give prestige to the store and, because of the high markup often taken, contribute to net profit. Moreover, in some lines the percentage of business done in foreign merchandise is high. An Atlanta retailer, for example, expects that one-third of his sales of handbags and jewelry will involve foreign-made products and Sears Roebuck sells more imported sewing machines than domestic machines. With the increasing variety of foreign merchandise available and the special promotions adopted to sell the items purchased, it is probable that the quantities imported will continue to increase in the foreseeable future.[33] Even supermarkets are interested in foreign-made merchandise.[34]

---

[31] Imports have been so large in some lines of merchandise that organized labor has taken steps to curb them. In May 1969, for example, the Amalgamated Clothing Workers of America began picketing Ohrbach's in New York City "protesting the store's selling imported men's and boy's apparel." This was said to mark "the beginning of a nationwide drive against imports. . . ." Cf. "Union Pickets Ohrbach's over Sale of Imports," *Women's Wear Daily,* May 20, 1969, p. 24.

[32] For an excellent analysis of the advantages, disadvantages, and sources of imported merchandise cf. J. D. Goodnow, *The Significance of Imported Consumer Goods in Indiana Retailing* (Indianapolis: Economic Research Division, Indiana Chamber of Commerce, 1969).

[33] It is of interest to note, however, that the K-Mart stores of the S. S. Kresge Company are buying fewer soft goods imports because of the competitive edge in fashion and quality existing in the United States.

[34] "New Supermarket Group Planning Orient Buying," *Merchandising Week,* January 5, 1970, p. 35.

However, special import duties and changes in the value of the dollar, announced during the summer of 1971 as part of President Nixon's price policy, may counteract the tendency toward increased importation.

Most foreign goods bought by retailers come through importers located in New York City, although a considerable quantity enters through those on the Pacific Coast. Many of these importers send catalogs and/or salesmen to retailers, but the latter often take the initiative and call on the vendors.

Other retailers make purchases from foreign sellers by correspondence or through resident buying offices. It is not uncommon for the larger retailers to send buyers abroad or to have foreign store-owned buying offices. Thus, the Associated Dry Goods Corporation maintains a buying office in London and the Great Atlantic & Pacific Tea Company has coffee-buying offices in Colombia and Brazil. Those who send buyers abroad often employ a foreign resident buying office which assists buyers in the same way they are aided in domestic central markets by similar offices.

■ SELECTING SUITABLE MERCHANDISE

Once the buyer has a knowledge of available sources of supply and of buying methods and arrangements, he must make preparations to judge the suitability of the merchandise for the purposes for which it is purchased. Fortunately he has certain rules to guide him in this process as well as the assistance of testing bureaus.

□ Some general rules

Judging the suitability of merchandise may be done by inspection of the goods, by means of a sample, or by a description. But, regardless of the procedure adopted, the buyer should know what his customers want and be able to recognize what he wants when available merchandise is examined. We have already discussed how the buyer may learn what his customers want. To make certain that he obtains goods that meet these requirements, he needs a broad, detailed knowledge of raw materials, of manufacturing techniques, of workmanship, and of possible finishes. Fashion trends, of course, also require continuous attention.

Despite the attention the buyer gives to customers' requirements when making purchases, he is often surprised by the rapidity of sale of some items he has bought with some trepidation. That is, at times customers will buy things that he does not consider to be in "good taste." This situation emphasizes two points: (1) The buyer should be open-minded in judging the advisability of purchasing the goods available to him, and (2) certain items should be bought in limited quantities on a "tryout" basis to test their acceptability by the store's customers.

In determining the suitability of goods the buying plan may also be of assistance. If laid out with care, so that the plan really reveals customers' wants, few bad choices will be made. The buyer should also make sure that the goods being bought do not compete too directly with other goods already in stock.

Quite obviously, suitability is also dependent on the probable "customer appeal" of the merchandise, including its physical features and its price. The significance of price, of course, varies from store to store. Whereas a discount store with a low-price reputation must rely largely on goods that will largely "sell themselves," an old-line department store can resell at a much higher markup. Yet, as concerns each item, the buyer will do well to ask himself: What price will *my* customers pay for this item? With this price in mind, the required markup can be deducted and the price the buyer can afford to pay be determined.

□ The role of testing bureaus

Testing bureaus furnish valuable aid to the buyer in judging the suitability of goods. The growth in the number of these bureaus and in the services they render makes it clear that retailers now recognize the necessity of providing their customers with (1) the highest quality of merchandise commensurate with the price, (2) accurate information about the goods offered for sale, and (3) adequate safeguards against unserviceable merchandise. In fact, it is the policy of one successful retailer—Sears, Roebuck and Co.—to require buyers to obtain laboratory approval before merchandise is purchased. Such a policy is exceptional, however, and that of the J. C. Penney Company is more typical. This firm places the final responsibility for purchasing decisions on the buyer with the laboratory's role restricted to advice on the quality of products and whether they meet manufacturers' claims.[35]

Testing bureaus are used (1) to test merchandise for fading, shrinking, and wearing ability before ordering; (2) to check uniformity of sizes in wearing apparel before commitments are made; (3) to conduct the planning and research necessary for developing products to meet the retailer's standards; (4) to devise purchasing specifications; (5) to check on the quality of goods delivered and their conformance to specifications; (6) to compare merchandise offered for sale in one store with that of competing stores; and (7) to suggest product innovations or improvements. But others than

[35] Matthew Kasten, "Penney's Testing Moving into Era of Expansion," *Women's Wear Daily*, March 11, 1970, p. 41.

buyers may also gain from such testing: Adjustment departments are provided with facts for dealing with customer merchandise complaints and management is assured that the claims presented in the store's advertising are valid.

Testing bureaus are of two main types: store owned and commercial, the latter offering their services to retailers and others on a fee basis.[36] Because of the expense involved in store-owned testing bureaus, they are usually operated only by large-scale retailers whereas the commercial bureaus are used by stores of all sizes.[37] In some instances groups of stores operate jointly-owned bureaus. As one would expect, however, large retailers are the chief users of testing as a means of determining the capacity of certain goods to meet customer wants.

Many retailers review the periodic bulletins published by such consumer-supported testing and reporting organizations as Consumers Union[38] and Consumers' Research, Inc., especially in the case of reports on their own brands of merchandise, and use the ratings (where favorable) in promoting sales.[39] Aware of the sharp increase in consumer-protection measures by governmental organizations and of the growing acceptance by consumers of the recommendations of testing agencies, retailers are making increasing use of all relevant information to judge the suitability of the goods they buy.

■ REVIEW AND DISCUSSION QUESTIONS

1 Distinguish among the major types of merchandise resources available to the retailer.

2 What general guidelines may be suggested to assist the retailer in choosing a particular resource(s)?

---

[36] Two of the better known "outside" laboratories are the United States Testing Company of Hoboken, New Jersey, and the Better Fabrics Testing Bureau of New York City. Product testing by manufacturers is also carried on through "independent" agencies; witness the testing by the Underwriters' Laboratories of the American Insurance Association.

[37] It costs Sears over $2 million annually to operate its Merchandise Development and Testing Laboratory, which employs 180 scientists and technicians. Consequently, even large-scale retailers find the store-owned bureau expensive. A few years ago, after three years of its own testing, The Kroger Co. shifted to commercial testing.

[38] In a development of interest Consumers Union in 1969 lost a court fight to force the Federal Government to release results of its tests to the public. The suit concerned tests conducted on hearing aids but was considered a test case on a wide range of products.

[39] Consumers Union and Consumers' Research do not allow their ratings to be used for advertising purposes, but store salesmen will often mention favorable ratings when selling major appliances and other "big ticket" items.

3 Explain briefly the reasons why many retailers prefer to buy directly from the manufacturer. In view of this preference, how do you account for the fact that wholesalers are used so widely as sources of supply?

4 When the vendor takes the initiative in finding buyers, under what conditions or circumstances is it advisable to use each of the two main methods employed?

5 Choose any five central markets for particular types of merchandise and discuss the factors responsible for their development in the specific areas of the country in which they are located.

6 How do you explain the fact that certain retailers frequently send buyers into central markets, whereas others send buyers quite infrequently?

7 Discuss resident buying offices with respect to type, services performed, and their probable future.

8 Differentiate clearly between group buying and central buying. In your judgment which form will enjoy the greatest growth under present conditions? Why?

9 Account for the increased attention given to foreign-made merchandise by American retailers and the buying methods they employ to obtain desired goods.

10 Explain the types of testing bureaus available to the buyer and the services they perform.

chapter 12

BUYING: NEGOTIATIONS WITH MERCHANDISE RESOURCES

When the buyer has decided that certain merchandise fulfills his customers' needs, he must negotiate on a number of factors before a purchase is made. A major element is the prices to be paid. This amount depends on the vendor's list price and the various discounts allowed. But the retailer is also interested in the period of time allowed for taking the discounts as well as the date when the bill finally becomes payable, *i.e.*, the dating. These two elements—discounts and dating—are known as the "terms of sale." Sometimes the retailer asks the vendor to guarantee prices against decline for a certain period; and the vendor may seek an "escalator clause," providing for upward price adjustments under certain circumstances. Finally, negotiations may also take place over transportation charges and the exclusiveness of the merchandise. In this chapter, attention is devoted to these various aspects of negotiations and, more briefly, to the transfer of title and vendor relations.

SOME BASICS OF NEGOTIATIONS

In negotiating purchases with vendors, the buyer should recognize that the *merchandise* is what his customers want, even if it has to be sold at a relatively high price. In other words, getting the *right* merchandise is more important than getting a price concession on the wrong goods. Moreover, he should not expect unreasonable price concessions from the vendor. "Stiff" demands often lose the goodwill of vendors; as a result, they retaliate by being less cooperative. Prompt delivery and information about special buying opportunities are more likely to go to those with whom the vendors are on friendly terms. Consequently, a valuable asset of a buyer is the ability to obtain and keep the friendship and respect of vendors.

The buyer, however, should not be "soft" in his negotiations. When he finds vendors giving concessions to other comparable buyers, he should insist on similar terms. Also, buyers should not purchase only from their friends. But, it is to the buyer's own long-run interest to not take unreasonable advantage of a seller. Negotiations should be based on a considered mutual understanding of each other's position.

The buyer will do well in his negotiations not to give the vendor the idea that he "knows all the answers." The buyer who attempts to impress everyone with his knowledge as to prices, quality of goods, and market trends usually ends up by incurring the vendors' ill-will. Most vendors have sufficient knowledge to pick out quickly the well-informed buyer from the uninformed one, and sometimes take pleasure in selling goods they should *not* buy to buyers who pretend to "know it all."

Before beginning his price negotiations the buyer should accumulate a considerable amount of price information. The sources of these data are too numerous to mention completely but include conversations with salesmen, newspaper items, trade journals, luncheon and telephone conversations with vendors and other retailers, past purchases, commodity market quotations, catalogs and price lists of vendors, and prices in other stores.

The buyer should also realize that the concessions granted from the asking price vary from vendor to vendor and from field to field. As a rule, when vendors are small and buyers are large, asking prices are subject to a considerable haggling. To illustrate, a buyer for a large department store may represent such an important outlet for a small dress manufacturer that the latter may be willing to grant a significant price concession rather than lose the account. The case for a price concession might be even stronger if the buyer represented a large chain store organization which was the sole outlet for the manufacturer. To a large food manufacturer, in contrast, the account of a small grocer is insufficient to warrant any price bargaining.

■ TERMS OF SALE: DISCOUNTS

A discount is any reduction in the list or quoted price of merchandise which is allowed the purchaser by the seller. Discounts may be grouped into six classifications: quantity, trade, seasonal, advertising or promotional, brokerage, and cash. Each of these discounts raises questions for the buyer concerning their legality under the Robinson-Patman Act. Consequently, after explaining their nature and use, a concise review of the legal implications involved for each is presented.

◻ Quantity discounts

A quantity discount is a reduction allowed from the invoice price because of the amount purchased and is based typically on the quantity ordered[1] at a given time—the noncumulative quantity discount. Thus, a vendor might quote a price of $9.75 per dozen with a discount of 25 cents per dozen for purchases of from 3 to 5 dozen at a time, 50 cents off for purchases of from 6 to 15 dozen, and 75 cents off for orders of over 15 dozen.[2] A cumulative quantity discount, on the other hand, also known as a "deferred discount" or a "patronage discount," applies to the total purchases made within a period. For example, a manufacturer of toothpaste may allow a discount of 5 percent if total purchases for the year amount to $10,000, 7 percent if purchases amount to $15,000, and 10 percent if they reach or exceed $20,000. The discount may also be based on the number of units purchased.

Closely related to the quantity discount, or, in fact, a variation of it, is the "free deal" or "free goods." This practice involves including in the shipment certain goods in excess of those ordered; that is, if six dozen of an item are ordered, an extra half dozen may be shipped without charge.

Why quantity discounts are granted Quantity discounts are granted, perhaps, for two major reasons. One is the economies made possible for the vendor. Salesmen's cost may be reduced when a retailer, who has formerly given a small order each week, adopts a policy of placing one large order every two months. The cost of billing and collecting may be little more on a large order than on a small one. The packaging and transportation cost per unit is less on large orders. If the vendor is a manufacturer, the large order may also aid him in cutting his cost of production through buying his raw materials and other supplies in larger quantities and operating his plant more steadily.

So far as the resulting economies are concerned, however, the cumulative quantity discount does not encourage the kind of buying which results in reducing the vendor's cost so much as does the noncumulative quantity

[1] Sometimes the "quantity ordered" refers to the quantity of a *single* item; at other times, it refers to the quantity of *all* items included in the order.

[2] For a mathematical approach to the construction of a quantity discount schedule, cf. J. F. Crowther, "Rationale for Quantity Discounts," *Harvard Business Review,* Vol. 42, No. 2 (March–April 1964), pp. 121–27.

discount. Under the former the goods may be shipped in small lots at various times, thus involving higher billing, packing, transporting, and collecting costs. Although the buyer's concentration of purchases with a single vendor may give the latter a more certain market which enables him (1) to reduce the frequency of calls by his salesmen, (2) to cut down his advertising somewhat, and (3) to plan his production schedule to better advantage, such savings are small at best and, in the majority of cases, probably do not exist. Even when buying is concentrated, discounts may be so high that the same result could have been obtained at a lower cost by some form of sales promotion.[3] But from the retailer's point of view, cumulative quantity discounts tend to prevent him from overbuying at any one particular time, except perhaps near the end of the discount period when he may be eager to qualify for a higher discount.

The second major reason for granting quantity discounts is pressure from buyers. Such pressure has even been exerted in cases where higher unit costs actually have resulted from the large order. For instance, many fashion goods, such as women's dresses, are produced by relatively small manufacturers whose costs are largely direct ones. In such cases, production economies are limited. When the larger order has to be filled by overtime work and the hiring of inexperienced help, unit production cost is likely to be increased.

The Robinson-Patman Act Quantity discounts are subject to limits other than those resulting from the bargaining ability of buyer and seller. Under the Robinson-Patman Act, passed by Congress in 1936, a vendor selling in interstate trade may *not* give a lower price to one buyer than to another under the following circumstances:

1. If the buyer takes commodities of the same grade and quality.
2. If the price difference
   a) Substantially lessens competition, or
   b) Tends to create a monopoly, or
   c) Injures, destroys, or prevents competition with vendor or buyer, or customers of either.
3. If the price difference is not one merely making "due allowance for differences in the cost of manufacture, sale, or delivery resulting from the differing methods or quantities in which such commodities are to such purchases sold or delivered," or one offered "in good faith to meet the equally low price of a competitor."

1. Overall appraisal of the act An excellent case can be made that the Robinson-Patman Act is inconsistent with the principles of a competitive

[3] Cf. the excellent analysis in C. E. Griffin, "When Is a Price Reduction Profitable?" *Harvard Business Review*, Vol. 38, No. 3 (September 1960), pp. 125–32.

economy. Through its emphasis (1) on cost as the basis of price differentials and (2) on "proportionately equal terms" for advertising allowances,[4] it inhibits a seller from achieving the best possible competitive "mix" of price and nonprice strategy and has "the effect of limiting the decision-making freedom of businessmen."[5] Another authority concludes that the Act, as interpreted by the Federal Trade Commission and the courts, has "rigidified price structures, deprived the economy of the advantages of free bargaining, prevented innovation in marketing techniques, and moved us in the direction of a cartelized distribution system."[6] And, as Professor Grether points out, action taken under the act has "often [been] contrary to the purposes of antitrust enforcement."[7]

It should also be emphasized that the Robinson-Patman Act has not achieved its real goal which was "to protect the small independent retailer ... (by curbing) the growth of multiunit retail operations."[8] In fact, the same authority suggested that effective support can be found for the conclusion that the act has resulted in "a strengthening of the market position of the large retailer."

In view of the foregoing implications it is not surprising that many voices have long urged a careful revision of the Robinson-Patman Act.[9] Congress has not heeded these suggestions, however, with the result that the original act is still the law: it must be taken into account in establishing discounts. Under it, once the Federal Trade Commission has established the facts that (1) the commodities are of "like grade and quality," (2) there is a price difference between buyers, and (3) the buyers are in competition, the burden of proof is upon the alleged violator; he is held guilty unless he can prove himself innocent.[10] In all cases in which price discrimination is found to exist, the buyer is equally guilty with the vendor if he "knowingly" receives the discount.

2. *"Like grade and quality"* For many years the Commission attempted to define "like grade and quality" by applying the test of physical likeness.

---

[4] Cf. pp. 285–86, below.

[5] L. X. Tarpey, Sr., "The Woman's Day Case and Cooperative Advertising," *Journal of Marketing*, Vol. 29, No. 3 (July 1965), p. 39.

[6] Milton Handler, "Recent Antitrust Developments," *Yale Law Journal*, November 1961, p. 98.

[7] E. T. Grether, *Marketing and Public Policy* (Englewood Cliffs, N.J.: Prentice-Hall, Inc., 1966), p. 59.

[8] L. G. Schiffman, " 'Like Grade and Quality': The Borden Case," *New York Retailer*, December 1965, p. 13.

[9] In 1966, revision of the act was recommended by the Report of the National Commission on Food Marketing, *Food from Farmer to Consumer* (Washington, D.C.: U.S. Government Printing Office, 1966), p. 107.

[10] The rule that the burden of proof is upon the alleged violator has been accepted by the courts in many cases under the Act. For an example, cf. *Bergjans Farm Dairy Co.* v *Sanitary Milk Producers*, D.C.E. Mo. (March 1965).

It decided that if the Borden Company sold chemically identical cans of evaporated milk, they were of "like grade and quality"—even though some of the cans were marketed under a national brand while others were distributed as private brands. But in a 1964 decision, the Circuit Court of Appeals, by accepting the market as its testing ground of likeness, had ruled otherwise, saying

> [We cannot] ignore the fact that a brand name product may be able to command a higher price than an unknown brand because of its public acceptance . . . [We] do not believe it was the intention of Congress that such clearly demonstrable consumer preferences should simply be ignored in determining when products may be priced differently . . . [When] labels are proven to have demonstrable commercial significance . . . they can change the grade of a product.[11]

In brief, for two commodities to be of "like grade and quality," the U.S. Court of Appeals held that they must be alike physically and have somewhat similar consumer acceptance in the market.

In March of 1966, however, the United States Supreme Court reversed the lower court by accepting the Commission's "identical composition" test and rejecting the market test.[12] Businessmen and economists alike have criticised this decision as being contrary to sound economic analysis and in conflict with the marketing policies and practices of many firms.[13] But this Supreme Court ruling may not have as much impact upon marketing practices as was anticipated, and feared, when it was handed down. The Circuit Court subsequently held, in a ruling so far unchallenged, that Borden's price differential between private and national brand milk would not have any harmful anticompetitive effect and consequently would not violate the Robinson-Patman Act so long as it only reflected and did not exceed the differences in prices that consumers were willing to pay for the two brands.[14]

Legality of quantity discounts Under the Robinson-Patman Act, most of the firms that have been called upon to defend their quantity discounts have done so under item 3. That is, they have claimed a cost differential as

[11] *The Borden Company* v. *Federal Trade Commission,* 339 F. 2d 133 (CA-5, December 1964).

[12] *Federal Trade Commission* v. *Borden Co.,* 383 U.S. 637 (1966).

[13] The decision in the Borden case is discussed by L. X. Tarpey, Sr., in the *Journal of Marketing,* Vol. 29, No. 3 (July 1965), pp. 67–68. Also cf. R. O. Werner, "Marketing and the United States Supreme Court, 1965–1968," *ibid.,* Vol. 33, No. 1 (January 1969), p. 17.

[14] *The Borden Company* v. *FTC* , 381 F.2d 175 (5th Cir. 1967). For a detailed description of the ten years of litigation involved, cf. M. L. Mayer, J. B. Mason, and E. A. Orbeck, "The Borden Case—A Legal Basis for Private Brand Price Discrimination," *MSU Business Topics,* Vol. 18, No. 1 (Winter 1970), pp. 56–63. The authors conclude that the Borden decision continues to permit price discrimination between private brands and well-known national brands that enjoy a high degree of public acceptance.

the basis of their discount schedule. In many of these instances the Federal Trade Commission, which has instituted most of the cases under the act, has decided that the evidence of a sufficient cost differential has been lacking and has held the discount schedule illegal. Moreover, based upon the cases which have been appealed to the courts, "the record shows that few firms have been able, in litigation, to justify price differences on the basis of cost."[15]

In view of the foregoing actions, it is now clear that, unless it can distinctly be established that the resulting lower price was made in good faith "to meet a competitor's equally low price," the Commission and the courts will throw out any quantity discount schedule not based on a careful allocation of costs (including overhead costs) in relationship to the quantity.[16] For example, a seller cannot assume that all his manufacturing overhead is allocated against his first 100,000 units of production, so that a price just covering direct costs plus a small profit can be granted to a large-quantity buyer. In addition, all sales costs involved in selling to a quantity buyer must be assigned to him, plus his share of all general selling costs.

Since the buyer who "knowingly" benefits from price discrimination is equally guilty with the vendor, the retailer must resist the temptation to bargain for a larger quantity discount than can be justified by the cost differential. To many authorities this section of the law, literally interpreted—which it probably would not be—makes the unrealistic assumption that the buyer knows the vendor's cost. In this connection, and partly to aid the buyer, one student of the subject suggests that (1) the seller's price schedule should contain a statement that it is based on cost differences and (2) the cost defense should be denied any seller who has not determined his cost savings *before* being called upon to justify his discounts.[17] But such is *not* the present situation, so the buyer must exercise restraint. He should be especially wary in urging vendors to give him cumulative quantity discounts, since such discounts are especially difficult to justify on a cost basis.[18]

---

[15] M. C. Howard, *Legal Aspects of Marketing* (New York: McGraw-Hill Book Co., Inc., 1964), p. 62.

[16] For an excellent study of the Commission's position and a summary of the court cases dealing with the cost defense, cf. R. A. Lynn, "Is the Cost Defense Workable?" *Journal of Marketing*, Vol. 29, No. 1 (January 1965), pp. 37–42. For the cost defense in a specific case cf. H. F. Taggert, *Cost Justification: Thomasville Chair Company* (Ann Arbor, Michigan: University of Michigan, Bureau of Business Research, 1964). Also cf. comments by Grether, *op. cit.*, pp. 63–64.

[17] Cf. D. J. Fennelly, "On the Judging of Mince Pies," *Harvard Business Review*, Vol. 42, No. 6 (November–December 1964), pp. 77–86.

[18] Cf. J. R. Grabner, Jr., *Legal Limits of Competition, Harvard Business Review*, Vol. 47, No. 6 (November–December 1969), pp. 12–13.

☐ Trade discounts

The trade (or functional) discount is a price reduction granted to various types of customers to meet their costs of performing specified trading functions. A manufacturer selling both to service wholesalers and independent retailers, for example, may offer a 50 percent trade discount to all service wholesalers and a 35 percent discount to the retailers. This discount bears no relationship to the quantity purchased and may be given in addition to a quantity discount.

Sometimes vendors who deal with several trade groups use a string or chain of discounts. Thus, a particular vendor might offer the wholesaler buyers a trade discount of 30, 20, 10 or, as it would usually be stated, "less 30, less 20, and less 10." When such a chain of discounts is used, the discounts are deducted from the list price shown on the invoice in the order stated; that is, 30 percent off the list price, 20 percent off the balance, and 10 per cent off the second balance. As a result the wholesaler would pay a price amounting to 50.4 percent of the list price. Such a percentage, known as the "on" percentage, may be applied to the list price to determine actual cost.[19] For sales to independent retailers the "on" percentage would be 70 percent.

The manufacturer's list price is often the suggested resale price at the consumer level and, when trade discounts are considered, also provides the resale price at the wholesale level. To illustrate: A drug manufacturer, selling through wholesalers for distribution to retailers, lists his product at $12 per dozen. His trade discounts are "less 33⅓ and less 15." Under these circumstances, the wholesaler would pay $6.80 per dozen. ($12.00 – $4.00 (33⅓ percent) = $8.00 – $1.20 (15 percent) = $6.80). He would resell to the retailer at $8.00 a dozen, realizing a 15 percent markup on his selling price and allowing the retailer a 33⅓ percent markup on his selling price of $1.00 each, or $12 per dozen.

Justification of trade discounts From the retailer's point of view the practice of offering trade discounts is well justified. As noted, often the manufacturer's list price is approximately the resale price. Therefore, if the goods are to be resold at this price a discount must be obtained to provide a margin to cover operating costs and profit.

But what is the retailer's reaction when a manufacturer offers trade discounts which vary according to the status of the buyer, for instance, 50 per-

---

19 Based on the figures given, this percentage is calculated as follows: Assume 100 percent represents the list price shown on the invoice. Thirty percent of 100 is 30, and this amount deducted from 100 is 70. Twenty percent of 70 is 14, leaving 56 as the balance. Ten percent of 56 is 5.6, leaving 50.4 percent as the "on" percentage.

cent to wholesalers and 35 percent to independent retailers? Such discounts are usually justified by one or both of two quite different reasons. First, there may be a significant variation in the vendor's cost of selling to the different trade groups. For example, it is less costly for a manufacturer to sell 5,000 dozen units of his product to a single wholesaler than it is to sell the same quantity to 200 independent retailers. Sales to the latter trade group would be especially expensive in terms of salesmen's time, number of shipments and invoices, and collection problems.

Second, different trade discounts may be justified by differences in the buyers' costs of operation. To clarify let us assume that it costs a vendor exactly the same to sell to wholesalers and cooperative chain retailers but that the latter have a lower operating cost as compared to the wholesaler-independent retailer channel. Under these conditions, if both buy at the same price, the wholesaler-independent channel can be undersold and may withdraw from the sale of the vendor's product. This possible step could be prevented by a larger trade discount to the wholesaler than to the cooperative chain retailer. In such a case the trade discount would be used to keep the product on sale in more retail outlets, that is, to broaden its retail distribution.

Legality of trade discounts Discounts based on trade status are not mentioned in the Robinson-Patman Act. To the layman, however, it would seem that, under item 3, page 279, vendors would have to justify the prices that result from their trade discounts on the basis of "cost of manufacture, sale, or delivery." But the Federal Trade Commission and the courts have not taken this position; instead, they have ruled that, as long as the various trade discounts are offered equally to all buyers in a specific grouping, they are legal. In other words, the present interpretation is that different trade discounts to various trade groups result in no injury to competition and therefore constitute no violation of the act. As long as the Commission and the courts take this position, the retailer should bargain for the best trade-discount classification he can get. But it should be emphasized that the trading groupings recognized by a seller must have a factual base.[20] In other words, a manufacturer could not arbitrarily classify one variety store as a

---

[20] For a case involving this principle cf. *General Auto Supplies, Inc.*, et al. v. *Federal Trade Commission,* CA-7 (April 1965). Also cf. the discussion of "Quality for the Functional Discount of the Wholesaler," in J. W. Wingate and J. S. Friedlander, *The Management of Retail Buying* (Englewood Cliffs, N.J.: Prentice-Hall, Inc., 1963), pp. 287–88. The situation becomes quite complicated if a manufacturer sells to, say, wholesalers, chain store central warehouses that perform many of the wholesaling functions, and independent retailers. A strict interpretation of the law holds that the chain store organization cannot qualify for the same discount as the wholesaler, but only for the retailer discount plus a cost-justified allowance for the services it performs. The chain store discount cannot include any allowance for profit on the wholesaling functions. Cf. Earl Kintner, *A Robinson-Patman Primer* (New York: The Macmillan Company, 1970), pp. 139–44.

"retailer" and give a "wholesale" rating to two other variety stores which have joined together for group buying.

□ Seasonal discounts

Seasonal discounts are percentage reductions in the billed price given to encourage ordering, and sometimes accepting delivery, in the so-called "off" seasons of the year. Vendors of toys may grant seasonal discounts to encourage buyers to place orders and to accept delivery in June, rather than to wait until August; and paint manufacturers may give such discounts to secure orders for spring stock in October, November, and December.

From the retailer's point of view, the seasonal discount should be large enough to compensate him for storing the goods purchased for several weeks or months and for the interest on the investment involved when he pays for the merchandise soon after delivery. The main justification for this discount, however, is the economies which may accrue to the vendor. These include (1) obtaining business during normal "slack" periods, thus keeping his factory in operation and enabling him to distribute his overhead costs more evenly; (2) reducing his storage costs; and (3) minimizing his risks due to price changes.

Under the Robinson-Patman Act a vendor may use seasonal discounts as long as the same reduction is given to all competing comparable buyers who purchase at approximately the same time. The discount may also be altered from time to time as the seasons change.

□ Advertising discounts or allowances

Sometimes retailers may obtain allowances for various forms of sales promotional effort. A manufacturer, for instance, may wish to have his product advertised in cities over the name of a local department store to benefit from the prestige of each store and to lower his advertising cost, since local advertising rates are substantially lower than national rates.[21] Other manufacturers want their goods to be adequately displayed and called to the customer's attention by salespeople. A promotional allowance may be used for securing these services.

Accounting for advertising allowances Retailers face the problem as to how advertising discounts should be handled. Should they be treated as reductions in the cost of merchandise or in advertising cost? On the one

[21] Cf. C. H. Sandage and Vernon Fryburger, *Advertising Theory and Practice,* 8th ed. (Homewood, Ill.: Richard D. Irwin, Inc., 1971), p. 665.

hand, it would seem logical to treat them as reductions in advertising cost since the manufacturer is paying the retailer to advertise for him, thus increasing the retailer's advertising cost. But, on the other hand, when the payment is really for promotional work, it is compensation for a trading function or service, like the trade discount. Consequently, both kinds of discounts should be, and in most cases probably are, treated the same way, that is, as reductions in the cost of the merchandise.

Impact of the Robinson-Patman Act For *competing* buyers the Robinson-Patman Act limits discounts for promotional purposes to those made available on "proportionately equal terms," but "proportional *to what* is not stated. . . ."[22] Various cases coming under this section of the act, however, make it clear that a vendor should not offer, nor should a buyer accept, a promotional allowance unless (1) it is a reasonable payment for the service; (2) it is made for a service which competing dealers in this product similarly and proportionately furnish to the vendor; and (3) it is proportionalized between the dealers furnishing a similar service. Likewise, a retailer should not accept a merchandising service, such as store demonstrators, from a vendor unless the service is similarly and proportionally furnished to competing dealers.[23] In some cases, however, the Federal Trade Commission has suggested that a "substitute service" rather than the "same service" might satisfy this requirement. For example, although the store demonstrators offered by some cosmetic manufacturers might be economical in large retail stores with a heavy traffic of customers, they would be impractical in small stores. In such a situation, therefore, the manufacturer could continue to use demonstrators in the large store but offer the smaller retailers a substitute service.

As a practical matter, the "proportionally equal terms" rule may not allow the seller buying a promotional service to pay what the services of competing buyers are really worth to him. "For example, a high-class store buying no more than a discount store performs a more valuable service in advertising the manufacturer's product, in that the high-class store's sponsorship carries more weight with the public and with the buyers of other stores who are considering the purchase of the manufacturer's line. But the lack of objectivity in such a concept of proportionality will in all probability make it unacceptable to the Federal Trade Commission."[24] The Commission and the courts have also placed restrictions on the advertising purchased in a publication owned by a buyer.[25]

---

[22] Howard, *op. cit.*, p. 52. Cf., however, the discussion of FTC guidelines on the following page.

[23] Cf. the discussion in Howard, *op. cit.*, pp. 69–73.

[24] Wingate and Friedlander, *op. cit.*, p. 326.

[25] L. X. Tarpey, Sr., "The Woman's Day Case and Cooperative Advertising," *op. cit.*, pp. 35–39.

In a landmark decision in 1968,[26] the United States Supreme Court held that a vendor who furnishes advertising or promotional assistance to retailers buying directly must also supply such assistance on "proportionally equal terms" to those who compete with the direct-buying retailers but who purchase the vendor's merchandise from wholesalers. Taking cognizance of this decision, the Federal Trade Commission issued the following set of guidelines on advertising allowances, merchandise payments, and services effective May 1, 1969.

(*a*) Payments or services must be made available on proportionately equal terms to all competing customers; (*b*) sellers should take action to insure that timely notice is given to all competing customers so that they all can take full advantage of the program; (*c*) if all competing customers cannot participate, alternatives must be made available; (*d*) the information provided should give a clear understanding of exact terms of the offer, including all alternatives and the condition upon which payment of services will be made; and (*e*) sellers must take reasonable precautions to see that the services for which they are making payment are actually being performed.[27]

□ Brokerage discounts or allowances

The brokerage allowance or discount is a reduction granted by the vendor because the retailer makes it unnecessary for the vendor to use a broker. Thus, the payment is to the retailer rather than to an independent broker.

The buying organization of the Great Atlantic & Pacific Tea Company indicates how a retailer may render a brokerage service to the vendor. This company has buying offices throughout the United States, each office more or less specializing in purchasing products raised or packed in its district. Thus the firm's San Francisco office buys (among other things) California canned fruits and vegetables, dried fruits, nuts, and fresh fruits. Buyers deal directly with the sellers, so that the packer need not pay a broker for selling his product. If this packer prices his goods on the assumption that he will pay a fee to an independent broker, it would seem logical that the A & P, which in this case performs the brokerage function, should receive either a lower price or the brokerage charge.

Legal aspects No matter how logical it may seem, however, a long line of Federal Trade Commission and court cases makes it clear that, *if a vendor uses brokers for part of his sales,* he may not grant lower prices to reflect the

[26] *Federal Trade Commission* v. *Fred Meyer, Inc.,* 390 U.S. 341 (1968). Cf., also, Werner, *op. cit.,* p. 19.

[27] D. M. Love, "FTC Guidelines on Advertising and Promotional Allowances," *The Marketing News,* May 1, 1969, p. 7. Also cf. the comments by L. X. Tarpey, Sr., in "Regulation of Competition-Price Discrimination," paragraph 2, *Journal of Marketing,* Vol. 33, No. 4, Part 1 (October 1969), p. 81.

nonpayment of brokerage to any sellers on direct sales.[28] And this statement is true even when the vendor can show that the performance of a brokerage service by the buyer resulted in a saving to the vendor. In other words, only those vendors who sell *all* their output directly to retailers may grant lower prices than they might ask if using brokers.

The conclusions of the preceding paragraph give rise to one of the paradoxical elements in the Robinson-Patman Act. The brokerage provision keeps "manufacturers and processors from turning over to voluntary and cooperative chain headquarters the selling commissions that they save on the large-scale direct orders they receive from these organizations. Thus an act that was intended to aid small merchants, particularly independent grocers, has served to eliminate a major potential support for the type of organization that seems necessary to the survival of many of these small merchants."[29]

□ Cash discounts

A cash discount is a reduction in price given by a vendor in return for prompt payment of his invoices. It is typically computed as a percentage of the amount that remains after other discounts have been deducted from the billed amount. Thus, the discount may be 2 percent for payment within 10 days of the date of the invoice. If such terms appear on an invoice dated April 1, the buyer may take this deduction if he pays not later than April 11. If payment is not made by April 11, it is customary for the buyer to wait 20 days longer and pay the total invoice price at that time. In other words, the terms are usually stated on the invoice as 2/10, net 30. When the net-payment day is not stated, it is assumed to be 30 days from the date of the invoice or whatever period is customary in the particular trade. If payment is not made within 30 days, the vendor has the legal right to add an interest charge, usually 6 percent, although this has increased in very recent years.

Other terms for cash discounts are also common. Under a bill with terms of 2/10–30 extra, the 2 percent cash discount is extended for a 30-day period in addition to the 10-day period, or a total of 40 days. Terms of 2/10 EOM mean that the cash discount period runs for 10 days following the end of the month in which the purchase was made. For example, for a purchase made on April 1 with terms of 2/10 EOM, the 2 percent discount could be taken at any time through May 10.

Significance and legality The retailer should take advantage of cash

[28] Cf. *Southgate Brokerage Company, Inc.* v. *Federal Trade Commission,* 150 F. (2d) 607 (4th Cir., 1945).

[29] S. C. Hollander, *Restraints upon Retail Competition,* (East Lansing, Michigan: Graduate School of Business Administration, Michigan State University, 1965), p. 37.

discounts even if he has to borrow the money to do so. Such action is a means of gaining the goodwill of vendors, and is immediately profitable from the retailer's point of view—so much so that one successful retailer refers to the cash discount as "a profit cushion."[30] Under the terms 2/10, *n*/30, the retailer who does not pay within 10 days is paying 2 percent for the use of the money for the remaining 20 days. Since there are approximately eighteen 20-day periods in a year, this is equivalent to about 36 percent interest. For terms of 3/10, *n*/60, the equivalent interest rate would be 21.6 percent;[31] and it would be even higher in those fields, like women's coats and suits, where the cash discount is as much as 8 percent.

As long as uniform cash discounts are granted to all competing comparable buyers, there is no danger that they will result in price discrimination and thus run afoul of the Robinson-Patman Act. In general, cash discounts have been used in a nondiscriminatory manner. But this has not always been true. One buyer may be given terms of 2/10, *n*/30, whereas a comparable buyer, after exerting sufficient pressure, may obtain 4/20, *n*/90. If both buyers take the cash discount, the second buyer gets his merchandise at a lower net cost than the first buyer. If the second buyer does not take the discount, he still gets the advantage of a longer credit period. In either case, we have an example of a price differential which is illegal. As a practical matter, however, "the difficulties in the way of apprehension and prosecution are so great that the Act tends to penalize the 'gentlemen' or 'ethical' buyer in his competition with the 'tough' buyer."[32]

□ Price negotiation still legal and essential in buying

Despite the limitations placed on price bargaining by the Robinson-Patman Act, the buyer still has ample opportunity to negotiate for lower prices and to obtain the lowest *lawful* prices that sellers are willing to offer or accept.[33] *The act neither requires nor prevents the use of discounts of any kind; it simply places limits on them when they are used.* Hence, a vendor may decide not to grant discounts. In such a case the buyer may need to bargain with the vendor to get even the discount that the law makes legal. In fact, some large buyers often do not receive discounts as large as the actual difference in cost, that is, as large as are legal. Moreover, in all

[30] J. M. Ney, writing in *The Buyer's Manual*, 4th ed. (New York: National Retail Merchants Association, 1965), p. 88.

[31] In figuring interest, the year is assumed to contain 360 days.

[32] Wingate and Friedlander, *op. cit.*, p. 293.

[33] Two of the best analyses of what *can* be done under the Act are Werner, *op. cit.*; and Grabner, *op. cit.*

cases in which competition does not exist, the buyer can negotiate for larger discounts. To illustrate: If the buyer takes the entire output of a vendor, there is no competition, so that any price or any discount he may obtain is legal. With the seller legally able to cut prices "in good faith" to meet competitors' prices, the buyer must frequently bargain to achieve the prices made possible by this provision.[34]

Many states have not adopted provisions similar to those of the Robinson-Patman Act; consequently, for buyers and vendors within these states, price differentials are not bound by cost differentials.[35] Also, by preparing his own specifications and obtaining a product that is not of "like grade and quality" with the vendor's other goods—the buyer opens the way for price concessions. In any case, as already suggested, he "has the right and obligation to seek the lowest prices given to competitors of his class . . . [For him] to assume routinely that quoted prices are standard and fixed merely because the vendor claims a one-price policy, is to be naive."[36]

TERMS OF SALE: DATINGS

The dating of an invoice refers to the time before which specified discounts may be taken and also to the time when payment of the invoice becomes due. As noted earlier, terms of 2/10, *n*/30 mean that a 2 percent discount may be taken within a 10-day period and that payment of the billed amount is due in 30 days from the date of the invoice. These periods of 10 days and 30 days make up the dating of the bill. Of course, when no discounts are granted, the dating refers simply to the length of the period before which full payment is expected. Since the retailer wants as long a period as possible during which discounts may be taken and/or final payment may be made and sellers usually want payment as soon as possible, datings are a subject of negotiation.

Datings are of two broad types, immediate and future. COD (cash on

---

[34] For cases upholding the principle of freedom to meet competitors' prices cf. *Federal Trade Commission* v. *Standard Oil Co.*, 78 S. Ct. 369 (1958); and *Utah Pie Co.* v. *Continental Baking Co. et al.*, 386 U.S. 685 (1967). Also cf. *Federal Trade Commission* v. *Mary Carter Paint Co.*, 382 U.S. 46 (1965).

[35] This exemption is, however, of limited applicability. It applies only when the seller and both the buyers who pay the higher prices and the ones who pay the lower prices are all located in the same state. And even under those circumstances, the Federal Trade Commission and the courts sometimes hold that the Robinson-Patman Act applies if the intrastate sales are part of an "interstate flow of commerce." The rules on the intrastate exemption for discriminatory advertising allowances and services are even more restrictive than those concerning the exemption of price differentials. Cf. Earl Kintner, *op. cit.*, 80–91.

[36] Wingate and Friedlander, *op. cit.*, p. 298.

delivery) is the only form of immediate dating. There are several kinds of delayed or future datings.

☐ Immediate dating: COD

When merchandise is sold COD, discounts must be taken and payment made on receipt of goods. COD datings are relatively rare. They are so disliked by buyers that sellers use them only when there is doubt concerning a buyer's ability and willingness to pay. For instance, a buyer may be in the central market and decide to place an order with a vendor not previously dealt with. The buyer may want the goods at once, but the vendor may refuse to extend credit until an investigation has been made. In such circumstances the buyer may agree to COD terms. Some buyers are in such poor financial position that they can buy only on a COD basis. In practically all other cases, however, future datings can be arranged.

☐ Future datings

Some illustrations of future datings already have been given. The *ordinary dating* of "net 30 days" is a good example. In *extra datings* the vendor allows added time before the ordinary dating period begins. Thus, if the terms are "2/10, 60 days extra," the buyer has 60 days before the ordinary dating of 2/10, *n*/30 begins. *EOM dating* means that the ordinary dating period begins at the end of the month in which the purchase is made. Consequently, on an invoice dated March 4, with terms 3/10 EOM, the 3 percent cash discount may be taken through April 10.[37]

Three kinds of future datings are used in which the invoice date is not the point from which either the discount or the due date of the invoice is calculated. *Advance dating* simply sets some date following the invoice date from which the ordinary dating period begins. Thus, an invoice made out on May 15 may be dated "as of September 1," so that the buyer does not have to make payment in full until 30 days following the advance date, or, October 1. *Seasonal dating* is similar except that the date from which the ordinary dating begins is related to the seasons. To illustrate: Many retailers may want to place orders for their Christmas merchandise during the summer months but do not wish to make payment until the goods have been sold. To accommodate these retailers, vendors may use a seasonal dating of December 1. *ROG* (receipt of goods) *dating* means that the ordinary dat-

[37] In practice, under EOM terms, purchases made on and after the 25th of the month usually go into the following month. Thus, on a purchase made on April 26 with terms of 2/10 EOM, the cash discount could be taken through June 10.

ing period begins on the date the goods are received by the retailer. Goods with a 2/10, *n*/30, ROG dating which are received on April 11 must be paid for on or before April 21 to obtain the cash discount; and the invoice becomes payable on May 11.

Reason for future datings Future datings are used because most retailers, especially the smaller ones whose finances are decidedly limited, need credit for a period long enough to allow them to turn at least a part of their purchases into cash. Since the turnover of groceries is fairly rapid, terms of 2/10, *n*/30 are satisfactory to the buyer. Many hardware items turn over very slowly, however, and 60- or 90-day periods are desirable. ROG datings are preferred by retailers located at some distance from vendors, since part or all of the credit period under ordinary dating would be gone before the goods arrived. These datings merely put these operators in a position comparable to that of retailers who get ordinary datings and are located nearer sources of supply. EOM datings are granted by sellers chiefly as a convenience to their customers.

Anticipation Most large retailers are financially able to pay their bills before the due dates. Such prepayments, made primarily to keep their funds "at work" by earning an extra discount, are referred to as anticipation. Computed at a 6 percent rate of interest for many years, the "tight" money situation and mounting interest rates during 1969 and 1970 may have sounded the death knell of this traditional rate. Many, perhaps most, firms advanced the anticipation rate to 7.5 percent with numerous retailers demanding—and receiving—as much as 9.5 percent to 11 percent.[38] Accompanying this demand was a slowdown in payments by consumers and a growing trend by retailers requesting extra time to meet their obligations. Interest charges on late payments were as high as 12 percent. As this is written it is impossible to predict how long this siuation will persist.

The general rule for anticipation taken before the end of the cash discount period is as follows:[39] The retailer may take the cash discount plus anticipation on the balance for the number of days remaining until the end of the cash discount period. For example, an invoice for $1,000 with terms of 2/10, *n*/30 is paid 5 days before the end of the discount period. The 2 percent cash discount is equal to $20, leaving $980 to be paid. But this $980 balance is subject to a reduction equal to 7.5 percent interest for 5 days, that is, $1.02.[40] Hence, the actual payment made by the retailer is

---

[38] J. F. Stack, "Retailers Use Suppliers as a Financial Crutch," *Women's Wear Daily*, September 9, 1969, p. 18; and by the same author, "Mills and Factors See Red on Slow Collection Ills," *ibid.*, February 17, 1970, p. 28. Also cf. "Slow Retail Pay Hurting," *ibid.*, August 19, 1970, pp. 1, 35.

[39] In rare instances anticipation may be allowed after the expiration of the discount period for the number of days by which the date of payment precedes the time the invoice falls due.

[40] Seven and one-half percent interest on $980 for a year is $73.54. Five days is 1/72

$978.98. Or again, an invoice with terms of 2/10–30 extra, paid in 10 days, is anticipated 30 days prior to the expiration of the cash discount period. In this case, both the 2 percent cash discount and the 7.5 percent interest for 30 days are deductible.

Many retailers consider anticipation good practice, in that it gains for them the goodwill of vendors; and they consider the interest received a fair return on their money. As a result, anticipating is more prevalent than is realized by most students of retailing, especially among department stores and departmentalized specialty stores. Whether or not a specific retailer can anticipate depends upon this rule: He has no legal right to take anticipation "unless it is part of the contract express[ed] or implied, that is, unless the right to take anticipation is noted on the invoice, or unless anticipation is an established custom of the trade, an established practice of the parties concerned, or otherwise a part of the agreement between purchaser and seller."[41]

Discount loading Far less common than anticipation is the practice of "loading," that is, charging to selling departments any excess in the amount of the cash discount arbitrarily set by the management above that actually received from the vendor. For example, a store may fix 6 percent as the cash discount which all buyers must receive from resources. If the buyer receives only 4 percent his department is charged, or "loaded," with the extra 2 percent. More specifically, assume that the amount billed before cash discounts was $100. After the 4 percent is deducted the actual cost is $96. But the buyer should have received 6 percent and the actual cost should have been $94. Consequently, the department is charged $102.13, arrived at as follows: $96 = 100 percent − 6 percent = 94 percent of the loaded cost. The loaded cost equals 100 percent, or $102.13.

Loading is practiced mainly for three reasons: (1) The large cash discount required induces the buyer to drive harder bargains; (2) all inventory and purchase figures are placed on a comparable basis; and (3) higher markups are obtained when based on inflated invoice costs, particularly in stores applying fixed percentage markups.

■ OTHER NEGOTIATIONS FOR MERCHANDISE

There are other items to be considered in negotiations with merchandise resources: price guaranties, transportation terms, and exclusiveness of goods.

---

of a year of 360 days, the number of days used for computing interest on anticipation. One seventy-second of $73.54 is $1.02.

[41] M. P. McNair, E. A. Burnham, and A. C. Hersum, *Cases in Retail Management* (New York: McGraw-Hill Book Co., Inc., 1957), p. 63.

□ Price guaranties

Sometimes a buyer seeks guaranties against possible future price declines. For placing orders early, he may ask for both a seasonal discount and a price guaranty. The vendor may agree that, if he lowers his price after the order is placed, he will refund to the buyer the difference between the price at which the order was placed and the price asked when the goods are shipped. If the price advances, there is no refund, the buyer paying only the price at which he placed the order. Thus, he is protected against both price rises and price declines.[42] The guaranty may apply against the prices of the vendor's major competitors as well as against his own prices.

The price guaranty is fairly common for seasonal items for which the vendor is especially eager to encourage early orders. It is also used to encourage buyers to place extra-large orders on staples during periods when the price structure is uncertain.

□ Transportation terms

Transportation terms offered by vendors may take any one of several forms. When prices are quoted f.o.b. (free on board) factory, the buyer pays all transportation charges from the vendor's delivery platform; when quoted f.o.b. shipping point, the vendor assumes the cost of transportation to his local shipping point but the buyer pays all further transportation charges, and when goods are sold f.o.b. store, the buyer has no transportation charges to pay. Sometimes, vendors quote prices f.o.b. certain cities, for example, f.o.b. Chicago or f.o.b. Detroit.

Transportation costs are high and continuing to increase.[43] Consequently, retailers should exert all possible efforts to control them. In addition to inducing vendors to absorb them, other measures may be taken. Carloads travel at lower unit rates than small shipments, so that the large buyer who concentrates his purchases has an advantage. Even when purchases are not concentrated, it may be possible for the buyer to have his representative or a private packing company consolidate purchases from several vendors in the city where the merchandise was bought, thus achieving a lower cost of transportation.[44] More careful planning of routes may

---

[42] Sometimes sellers insist on "escalator clauses," which permit them to advance prices under certain conditions.

[43] In August 1970, executives of major eastern and western railroads petitioned the Interstate Commerce Commission for a two-step 15 percent increase in rates designed to bring in an additional $13 million in revenue. Cf. John Osbon, "Rail Hike Plan Steams up Stores," *Women's Wear Daily,* August 19, 1970, pp. 1, 16.

[44] For example, freight-pooling cooperatives have been established to allow smaller stores to take advantage of volume rates on hanger shipments of apparel. Savings of 20–25

reduce this cost. Perhaps a cheaper method of transportation can be used. For goods not needed at once, a slower and less expensive method of delivery is often satisfactory. Moreover, the vendor may be induced to develop improved packages, perhaps reducing the weight and size of the package. And when the retailer pays the freight he should have all packages shipped in the cheapest possible freight classification. To insure this saving, all freight bills should be checked closely prior to their payment. Such auditing sometimes results in substantial savings on transportation bills.

□ Exclusiveness of goods

Often the exclusive right to handle certain goods is as important to the retailer as it is to buy them at low prices. In fact, many retailers of specialty goods are willing to pay higher prices for goods for which they act as exclusive distributors than for other merchandise of comparable quality. The retailer who desires an exclusive agency expects that it will yield the benefits of the good will the manufacturer has acquired and also eliminate all direct price competition, since no other retailers in his immediate area can undersell him. But the arrangement involves certain risks. The retailer may lose the agency through no fault of his own because the manufacturer may change his policy, or decide to use some other nearby retailer. And, since to get the exclusive agency, the retailer may have to agree not to carry competing products of other manufacturers,[45] his sales will be limited to those customers who are willing to buy the particular line he carries.

The retailer may also negotiate over the temporary exclusive distribution of certain goods, especially new fashion items, because it enables him to be ahead of his competitors with "the last word" in merchandise as well as obtain a higher markup on the new goods than would be possible otherwise.

■ THE PURCHASE ORDER

When negotiations have been completed, the buyer prepares a purchase order form. In the small store, however, the vendor's order form is usually used. Actually, many such stores depend upon the vendor's representative to make out the order, after which it is examined and signed.

---

percent have been achieved with faster deliveries and no unpacking and ironing problems.

[45] When exclusive contracts of this type (that is, which forbid the retailer from selling competitors' products) cover so many of the retail outlets in a given market that they tend "substantially to lessen competition," they become illegal. Cf. the discussion in C. F. Phillips and D. J. Duncan, *Marketing: Principles and Methods,* 6th ed. (Homewood, Ill.: Richard D. Irwin, Inc., (1968), pp. 636–37. Also cf. Grabner, *op. cit.,* pp. 21–24; and Werner, *op. cit.,* pp. 18–19.

Large retailers provide their buyers with order forms, an example of which is given in Figure 12–1.[46] This practice is advantageous to the store for the following reasons: (1) It permits developing an order form suited to its own requirements, including printing the desired information on the form and preparing sufficient copies for distribution to interested departments; (2) it provides protection against those vendors who enter on their own forms (usually in small type) certain conditions often unacceptable to the buyer; and (3) it furnishes an ideal medium for giving vendors shipping instructions and stating the conditions under which the merchandise ordered will be accepted.

□ Preretailing

Preretailing, practiced mainly by large firms, refers to the practice of placing the retail price of the items being bought on the store's copies of the purchase order (1) at the time the order is placed or (2) at least before the actual receipt of the merchandise. When the shipment arrives, price tickets may be attached without delay.

■ THE INVOICE

Frequent mention has been made in previous pages of an "invoice." Because of its close relationship to the purchase order, a few words concerning it may be in order. An invoice is simply an itemized statement (or bill) of merchandise shipped or sent to the purchaser by the vendor with the quantity, price, terms of sale, and other relevant data included. Since it is prepared following receipt of the purchase order, it corresponds closely to such an order.

■ TRANSFER OF TITLE

Transfer of title, the final major step in the buying process, usually takes place when the vendor releases the merchandise to a common carrier for delivery. Thereafter, responsibility for the merchandise lies with the buyer; if goods are damaged in transport, the buyer's recourse is against the common carrier, not the vendor. In dealing with certain vendors, however,

---

[46] Data-processing equipment is also used in the ordering process. For example, "optical scanning has enabled Von's Grocery Co. of El Monte, California to reduce its total ordering costs by 3 percent and its keypunch force by more than one-third." Cf. "Optical Scanner Cuts Costs for Von's," *Chain Store Age* (Executives Edition), September 1970, p. E44.

FIGURE 12–1 **Purchase order form**

DATE OF ORDER	DATE TO SHIP	CANCELLATION DATE	Merchandise will be returned collect if vendor deviates from these dates.	MERCHANDISE ORDER– VENDOR'S COPY	OUR DEPT. NO.	OUR ORDER NO. M 137976

ROUTING INSTRUCTIONS SEE TRANSPORTATION TERMS ON REVERSE.

F.O.B. POINT

TRANSPORTATION PAID BY VENDOR ☐ BY MACY*S ☐

MFR'S NO.

TRANSPORTATION ALLOWANCE

CONSIGNMENT (RIDER ATTACHED) ☐

NEW YORK OFFICE
Corporate Buying Division
151 West 34th Street
New York, N.Y.
10001

Macy*s California
P.O. BOX 7888 – PHONE (415) 397-3333
SAN FRANCISCO, CALIF. 94119
A Division of R.H. Macy & Co. Inc.

LOS ANGELES OFFICE
Arkin & Arkin
208 West 8th St.
Los Angeles, Calif. 90014

THIS ORDER IS GIVEN SUBJECT TO ALL OF THE TERMS AND CONDITIONS PRINTED ON THE FRONT AND BACK HEREOF.

TERMS OF PAYMENT
From receipt of invoice or goods, whichever is later. On shipments received on/or after the 25th of the month, terms begin as the first of the following month.

☐ EOM ☐ ROM
____%____DAYS

ANTICIPATION
☐ NO
☐ YES ____

TRADE DISCOUNT DEDUCT IF FOR ENTIRE ORDER

ADVERTISING ALLOWANCE
% OR TOT. $____

Ordered From:

Address:

City & State: Zip Code

All merchandise delivered hereunder and the label and labelling thereof shall be in compliance with all applicable federal, state and municipal laws, rules and regulations, including, but not restricted to those relative to fiber content, shrinkage and flammability.

SHIPPING INSTRUCTIONS TO VENDOR - Read Carefully
MACY'S CALIFORNIA RESERVES THE RIGHT TO RETURN ALL OR ANY PART OF THIS ORDER IF MERCHANDISE IS NOT SHIPPED AS SPECIFIED AND BY THE DATE SPECIFIED.

1. Show detail of size & color by style no. on invoice.
2. PACK and LABEL Merchandise for Each Store SEPARATELY.
3. Clearly Mark Carton Containing Invoice.
4. COMBINE ALL PACKAGES INTO ONE SHIPMENT.
5. MARK all Packages - Invoices - Bills of Lading with our DEPT. NO. - OUR ORDER NO. - OUR STORE OF DESTINATION.
6. INVOICING - Use ONE INVOICE to cover shipment.
   A. ENCLOSE ORIGINAL INVOICE WITH
      1. All Shipments by Air - Express - Parcel Post.
      2. All SF Bay Area and Los Angeles area shipments.
   B. AIR MAIL ORIGINAL INVOICE AND BILL OF LADING ON DATE SHIPPED, AND ENCLOSE DUPLICATE INVOICE WITH SHIPMENT ON
      1. All Shipments by Rail - Water - Truck other than SF Bay Area or Los Angeles Area.
7. SEND ENTIRE SHIPMENT AND INVOICE TO:
   ☐ Macy's California, 200 Paul Avenue, San Francisco, Ca. 94124
   ☐ Macy's California, 1556 El Camino Real, South San Francisco, Ca. 94080

SIDE MARK PKGS. FOR ____

Style No.	Class	GRAND TOTAL QUAN.	DESCRIPTION	UNIT COST	TOTAL COST	SIZES

MONTH DE-LIVERY DUE	GRAND TOTAL ORDERED	BUYER'S SIGNATURE	DATE / /	TOTAL COST $	MERCHANDISE ADMINISTRATOR'S SIGNATURE	DATE / /	COMPANY OFFICER'S SIGNATURE

F10-10 2/70

Courtesy: Macy's, California

buyers sometimes obtain physical possession of goods without taking title as explained in the following paragraphs.

□ Consignment buying

When goods are bought on consignment, title to the merchandise remains with the vendor and the retailer is relieved of such risks as those of price decline and obsolescence. These risks remain with the vendor, since he agrees to accept the return of any merchandise not sold. The retailer, however, is responsible for any neglect on his part such as the loss of merchandise through theft and fire or from physical damage from other causes.

It will be helpful in understanding the retailer's attitude toward consigned merchandise if we first examine the two main reasons why vendors engage in this practice. First, they find it necessary to get retailers to stock their goods. That is, consignment selling is adopted usually when no other sales strategy will work. Second, because it gives them the legal right to fix the resale price.[47] As a practical matter, however, this right is being increasingly restricted by court decisions.[48]

The retailer's attitude toward consignment merchandise Despite the fact that on consignment merchandise the retailer is freed from certain risks which go with outright ownership and additional funds are not tied up in inventory, most retailers hesitate to accept consigned goods. They are afraid that such goods may be inferior and that vendors are offering them on consignment because they cannot be sold by other methods. And, since the vendor accepts the risks of ownership, his prices may be advanced. Other retailers object to having their resale prices set by vendors. On returned goods the vendor may claim that the goods have been damaged or that they could have been sold with more aggressive merchandising. This attitude, which may be justified in many cases, may cause ill-will between vendor and retailer. Still other retailers may accept too many consigned items and use display space which might have been employed to better advantage for other merchandise.

In view of these disadvantages, retailers should scrutinize with care the merchandise offered them on consignment. Even though it may be wise to place the first order for a new item on this basis, it is probably best to purchase outright as soon as future sales potentialities warrant such action.

---

[47] Cf. the discussion of resale price maintenance in Chapter 17.

[48] For example, the courts have held that consignment selling cannot involve (1) coercion on the seller's part and (2) an agreement among buyers to fix prices. Cf. *Simpson* v. *Union Oil Company of California* (U.S. Supreme Court, 377 U.S. 13).

☐ Memorandum buying

The exact meaning of memorandum buying varies with the wording of the agreement between seller and buyer,[49] but, in general, it is a method of obtaining merchandise involving features of both outright purchase and consignment buying. As contrasted with consignment buying, title usually passes legally to the buyer; but, since the buyer retains the same privilege of returning goods as under consignment buying, most of the risk remains with the vendor. The retailer, therefore, as owner of the merchandise, is free to price it as he wishes. In other respects memorandum buying from the retailer's point of view is quite comparable to that of purchasing on consignment.

☐ Returns of merchandise to vendors

Returns of merchandise to vendors is quite common among retailers and the reasons for such action should be understood. Some returns, of course, are fully justified while others constitute a questionable practice. Among the former are the following: The goods received may not be as described in the vendor's catalog, may fail to conform to specifications or samples, or even prove defective when used by customers; merchandise may not have arrived on time, necessitating markdowns if the peak of demand has already passed; wrong quantities may have been shipped; or the terms of sale are different from those originally agreed upon.

Sometimes merchandise returns are attempted that are quite unjustified. Prices may have declined since the goods were ordered or placed in stock, and the retailer may wish to pass the loss from inventory depreciation back onto the vendor. Or an unexpected fashion change may result in an increase in refusals. Unless other factors exist, however, a vendor should not be expected to accept returns merely because the retailer did a poor job of buying. Price and fashion changes are part of the risks of buying and once the retailer has accepted title, these risks are his.

When making returns, such action should be taken promptly and vendors given a full explanation of the reasons.[50] This is particularly true for fashion goods; otherwise the vendor may suffer unnecessary loss. Harmonious relations with resources require mutual respect and understanding of each other's problems.

---

[49] Wingate and Friedlander, *op. cit.*, p. 319.

[50] For a more extensive discussion of cancellations and returns cf. D. E. Moeser, "Sound Buying Practices," in *The Buyer's Manual, op. cit.*, pp. 81–84.

□ Joint retailer-manufacturer agreements

To minimize disagreements between retailers and vendors on cancellations and merchandise returns, these subjects are sometimes dealt with in "basic trade provisions" prepared jointly by retailer and manufacturer trade groups. A good xample is the one established in the apparel trade some years ago, pertinent sections of which read, in part, as follows:

> Purchaser may not cancel this Order for any reason before date for completion of delivery; cancellation after date for completion of delivery shall be effective only upon Purchaser's written notice to Seller, but shall not be effective with respect to any shipments made by the Seller within three (3) working days after receipt of such notice.
>
> No returns of merchandise shall be made except for defects therein, or for non-conformity with some material provision of this Order. Where defects are discoverable upon reasonable inspection, or where non-conformity is claimed, such returns shall be made within five (5) working days after the receipt of the goods affected. The Purchaser shall send the Seller a separate written notice, setting forth the nature of the defects or non-conformity claimed, prior to or simultaneously with the return. Seller may replace such return merchandise, provided such replacement is made within five (5) days after the last permissible delivery date.
>
> In the event of the material interruption of the business of either the Seller or Purchaser by reason of fire, war, Act of God, governmental action, or strikes which materially affect the performance of this contract, the party so affected may cancel the order for such merchandise as has not been delivered, upon notice to the other party, notwithstanding any other provisions herein.[51]

The agreement also provides that "any controversy or claim rising out of or relating to any of the provisions of this Order shall be settled by arbitration in accordance with the rules of the American Arbitration Association." Both buyer and seller are automatically bound by the agreement unless they accept, in writing, some other terms.

■ REVIEW AND DISCUSSION QUESTIONS

1 Carefully evaluate three of the several guidelines for negotiations suggested on pages 276–77.

2 Explain what is meant by "terms of sale." Define each of its two major elements.

---

[51] Statement of the Apparel Industries Interassociation Committee, *Women's Wear Daily*, December 16, 1965, p. 35.

3 Distinguish among the various types of discounts and appraise the legality of three of them under the Robinson-Patman Act.

4 As a buyer you have been asked to explain to your new assistant why price negotiations are still important despite the limitations placed upon them by the Robinson-Patman Act and rulings of the Federal Trade Commission and courts. What particular points would you emphasize? State your reasons.

5 Explain briefly five kinds of future datings and the conditions under which each is commonly used.

6 Assume that merchandise shipped on June 15 was billed at $2,750 with terms of 2/10–30 extra, f.o.b. destination, and that the bill was paid on the day the cash discount expired. On what date was the bill paid and what was the amount of the check?

7 Assuming the same terms and figures given in the previous question, plus the fact that anticipation was allowed, what amount should be remitted to the vendor if the bill was paid on June 1?

8 What is meant by the following terms: (*a*) anticipation; (*b*) discount loading, (*c*) preretailing, (*d*) consignment buying, and (*e*) memorandum buying?

9 In addition to price, what other major forms of negotiation concerning merchandise may buyers and merchandise resources carry on? Discuss briefly.

10 Evaluate critically returns of merchandise to vendors by retailers, giving particular attention to their causes and the methods by which they might be reduced.

chapter chapter 13 chapter chapter

MERCHANDISE MANAGEMENT

Our discussion of retail buying in previous chapters should make it clear that effective purchasing requires adequate controls to insure a balanced stock and to minimize the investment in inventory consistent with the satisfactory fulfillment of customers' wants. The rapid growth of multistore operations has intensified the need for prompt, accurate, and complete data upon which to base merchandising decisions.

Finding satisfactory solutions to merchandising problems is not easy. Policies governing all aspects of merchandise management must be formulated and implemented with effective procedures adapted to the needs of the particular store, regardless of its size. In small stores, the desired relationship between stocks and sales is secured through the proprietor's inspection of his stock and study of his records. In larger ones, however, as the assortments of merchandise handled become greater, the problem becomes more difficult. Personal inspection becomes less practicable; and more records of various types are essential to sound decisions. These records constitute an important phase of merchandise control.[1]

[1] Merchandise management or control in most large stores is a joint responsibility of the merchandise manager and the controller. Therefore, it may be considered as a major function of either or both executives and is often discussed from the point of control as in the case of expense control or financial control. The present authors believe it advisable to examine the various aspects of merchandise management at this particular point because of its close relationship to buying.

■ THE NATURE AND GOALS OF MERCHANDISE MANAGEMENT

The general objective of merchandise management or stock control is the maintenance, in a store or a department, of assortments of merchandise that are adapted to the demands of customers and prospective customers. The balanced relationship which merchandise management seeks between stocks and sales is obtained through (1) an appreciation of its benefits by proprietors, buyers, and others; (2) the development and use of appropriate procedures, forms and equipment which will provide in usable form the information needed by buyers to know when, what, and how much to buy; (3) the revision of procedures and forms to meet changing requirements; and (4) the analysis and interpretation of the data collected and the actions taken as a result thereof. It is the *use* of the information gathered that makes control possible.

□ Specific goals of merchandise management

Once the basic objective of merchandise management—a well-balanced stock—is achieved, the retailer is able to realize the following purposes or goals.

To meet customer demands satisfactorily As the "purchasing agent" for his customers, the retailer should provide the merchandise his customers want, at prices they are willing and able to pay. Since customer demand will vary from day-to-day and from season-to-season, this task is not easy. But if proper merchandise control procedures are used, they will help the retailer attain this objective.

To improve profits Balanced stocks commonly result in greater sales and fewer markdowns, thereby increasing the dollar gross margin. And, if expenses remain the same or do not increase proportionately, profits will be increased. Methods and devices employed to control merchandise also contribute to improved profit by revealing trends and conditions that require attention by executives, by focusing attention on fast- and slow-moving items, by helping to keep stocks "clean" and "fresh," by assisting in the planning of advertising and sales-promotion events, and by enabling the buyer to reorder more frequently.

To provide buying information A good buyer needs a continuous stream of information if he is to know what, when, and how much to buy.[2]

[2] This task continues to become more difficult. Take the supermarket, for instance: As the product mix has increased and as stores become larger and more sophisticated,

These data should include sales of his department or store by types and prices of merchandise, returns by customers, markdowns taken to sell goods, and other information of a similar nature. Such information is helpful in making purchasing commitments, but plans should be made sufficiently in advance of buying commitments to insure maintenance of a balanced stock. Review of past experience is also essential if buying mistakes are to be minimized and fast-selling merchandise is to be reordered promptly.

To optimize investment in inventory The desirability of keeping the investment in merchandise inventory at a level consistent with the fulfillment of customer demand is evident. Such action, of course, results in a better rate of stockturn. But increasing the rate of stockturn should not be thought of as a major purpose of merchandise control; to repeat, the chief objective is to maintain well-assorted, balanced stocks in relationship to sales. If this is done the rate of stockturn will take care of itself; and the advantages of a satisfactory rate of stockturn will accrue to the management of the business.[3]

In addition to the major goals of merchandise control we have discussed, others may be mentioned very briefly: (1) To minimize the amount of slow-selling merchandise carried; (2) to make selling easier through improved assortments and cleaner stocks, thus reducing selling expense; and (3) to develop an appreciation of the fundamental continuing relationship between stocks and sales in achieving profit goals.

□ Some guidelines for effective merchandise management

When undertaking a program designed to provide a better balance between his stocks and his sales, the retailer should recognize certain guidelines that are essential to success. These are as follows:

1. Control methods are not an adequate substitute for knowledge, experience, and wisdom on the part of the buyer: They are aids to his judg-

---

demands on the buyer have grown rapidly. Among the factors causing him considerable concern are duplication of many items, numerous sizes, late deliveries, too much paperwork, and crass commercials. Cf. "What Bugs Buyers," *Chain Store Age* (Supermarket Executives Edition), March 1970, pp. 26–28.

[3] Note the statement of the chief executive officer of Montgomery Ward: "Our policy used to be not to be too critical if we lost business as a result of lack of inventory. Buyers were criticized only if they overstocked. So there was a trend toward preventing criticism by not stocking too much. Now we have a performance standard—both ways, for the store and the buyer. Not to have too much or too little." Robert Booker with John McDonald, "The Strategy That Saved Montgomery Ward," *Fortune*, Vol. 80, No. 5 (May 1970), p. 169.

ment and not substitutes for it. This statement is equally true for staple items and fashion goods. Regardless of the "automatic" nature of the procedures established, there still remains the necessity of analyzing and interpreting the information supplied.

2. Frequent appraisal of the systems adopted is necessary. Routines or procedures are set up to provide specific types of information under a given set of circumstances and need to be reviewed frequently to determine their suitability to new situations.

3. Merchandise information systems are costly to install and to maintain. The need for their frequent revision in our rapidly changing economy because of the increasing computerization of merchandise data, is evident.[4] Many retailers fail to recognize the technical knowledge of design, programming, and operation required for conversion to computers as well as the necessary retraining of their staff members. In any case, the advantages of the system must be measured against the cost involved. And the system adopted should provide the desired data quickly and accurately.

4. The word "control" is probably a misnomer. Control exists only when information is interpreted and translated into action. Despite improvements in recent years, effective control of merchandise inventories still constitutes one of the major problems of retail executives. Consequently, every suitable method and device should be employed to develop the information essential for sound decision making in balancing stocks and sales. Buyers cannot abrogate their responsibility for determining what, when, and how much to buy.

☐ Responsibility for merchandise management

Responsibility for merchandise management[5] varies among retail stores. The small retailer assumes this function himself; but in larger stores the task is more complicated and responsibility is divided among a number of people. In department stores the merchandise managers share it with their buyers. In fact, the job may be so great that a merchandise controller, under the direction of the merchandise manager or the president, may supervise these activities and work closely with the various buyers. Sometimes the controller governs stock control activities as part of his responsibility for all systems and records.

---

[4] Cf. "EDP and Merchandise Management," pp. 316–19, below.

[5] For excellent discussions of the buying function and of organization for buying and control of merchandise in single and multiunit stores, cf. J. W. Wingate and J. S. Friedlander, *The Management of Retail Buying* (Englewood Cliffs, N.J.: Prentice-Hall, Inc., 1963), chaps. 1 and 2.

In chain stores, responsibility for merchandise control is usually centered at headquarters under the controller or a special control executive who reports to the head buyer or merchandise manager. Considerable information on sales of important individual items and on the condition of stock is supplied by warehouse and store managers, who make frequent and detailed reports to merchandise managers in the headquarters city. Automation is of considerable assistance here.[6]

BASIC TYPES OF MERCHANDISE INFORMATION SYSTEMS

As has been emphasized, effective merchandise management requires accurate, timely, and complete information. To provide such data, two basic types of information systems—commonly referred to as dollar control and unit control—have been developed. *Dollar control* is exercised in terms of the amount of money at retail prices invested in merchandise. Control by physical units, or *unit control,* is usually accomplished in terms of individual items or pieces of merchandise. Dollar control answers the question "How much?"; unit control goes further and attempts to tell "What."

Either dollar or unit control may be very simple, as illustrated by the case of unit control exercised through personal inspection of the items in stock at various intervals in many small stores. Sometimes the retailer may rely upon the vendor's salesman to suggest what is needed to complete his stock, a common practice in the grocery, drug, and variety goods fields.

In somewhat larger stores, personal inspection is impracticable and salespeople are often assigned definite sections of the stock to watch. They report to the proprietor or buyer when the stock of an item is low or when sales are unusually heavy for specific merchandise. In some stores handling staple items—such as drug, grocery, and hardware stores—this reporting task is assigned to stockmen.

Such relatively simple methods of controlling stocks frequently prove unsatisfactory and more formal methods have to be adopted. Among larger stores, carefully designed procedures are essential because of the size and value of the merchandise inventory, the need for detailed information for buying purposes, and the element of fashion. The specific methods used will depend upon the size of the establishment, the methods employed by similar stores, the kind and amount of data desired, the use to be made of this information, and executive preferences. Let us now consider in some detail the two more formal merchandise information systems—dollar control and unit control.

---

[6] Cf. the discussion on pp. 317–18, below.

□ Dollar control

Dollar control[7] as an information system usually involves the maintenance of records designed to provide the desired data in terms of retail prices and the use of such data as a guide in buying. It may apply to the whole store as a unit, to departments, to classifications, to merchandise sections, and even to price lines.

Departmental control When control is exercised on a departmental basis, sales, returns by customers, purchases, returns to vendors, markup, gross margin, markdowns, rate of stockturn, and physical inventories are recorded for each department. It permits judging the profitableness of each department and the performance of each buyer. Strong and weak departments may thus be determined and measures be adopted to improve operations. It is not possible under this method, however, to detect points of strength and weakness within each department. Since effective merchandise management requires more than overall figures for each department, and since many departments have grown so large with such a variety of items that controlling them in total is meaningless, controls by classification and price-line have been developed.

Classification control Classification control, increasingly referred to as "classification merchandising," is that form of dollar control based upon classifications of related types of merchandise within departments. All the essential information recorded departmentally under departmental control is recorded by merchandise classification under classification control. Thus, in a men's furnishings department, data may be recorded separately for such classifications as shirts, neckties, hosiery, pajamas, underwear, robes, and sweaters.

No aspect of retailing, with the possible exception of EDP and its various applications, has received greater attention in recent years than classification merchandising.[8] Many retailers, dissatisfied with the negative connotation of "control," have adopted the new term and instituted programs placing emphasis on "the discovery of opportunities for increased sales" and a better "balancing of stocks in relation to sales."[9] As a part of these programs, there has been a tendency not only to subdivide broad classifications into smaller groups but also to reclassify them into categories of items "considered by the customer as essentially interchangeable from the standpoint of end

[7] For a detailed explanation of dollar control cf. C. S. Thompson, "The Dollar Merchandise Plan" in *The Buyer's Manual, op. cit.*, pp. 134–49. Also cf. J. S. Meyer, "Mathematics of Merchandise Control," *ibid.*, pp. 164–80.

[8] Cf. the discussion by C. C. Wilson and C. D. Greenidge, "Classification Merchandising: An Overlooked Opportunity for Increasing Merchandising Profitability," *California Management Review*, Vol. 12, No. 1 (Fall 1969), pp. 53–61.

[9] Hugo Frank, "Problems in Introducing Classification Programs Successfully," *Retail Control*, February 1966, p. 12.

use."[10] As individual firms have established classifications and categories suited to their particular requirements, an urgent need has developed for a common nomenclature for retailers as well as for their suppliers.

Standard Merchandise Classification In response to the urgent need mentioned, the Controllers Congress of the National Retail Merchants Association, after several years of effort, developed a Standard Merchandise Classification.[11] One close observer of the retail scene credits this development as one that ". . . shapes up potentially [among the] four great pathfinders in retail merchandising of the past half century."[12]

Standard Merchandise Classification seeks to provide a common nomenclature or universal language of "comprehensively researched guidelines" that will serve both the retail and manufacturing industries "as the foundation and basic structure of future merchandising information."[13]

> To attain this objective, the various standards established are implemented through a coding or numbering system in which all types of merchandise have unvarying identification in all stores, regardless of type, size, or geographic [or within the store] location, or whether the stores keep records manually or on a computer.
>
> Tied into a vendor punched ticket—*i.e.,* machine readable premarking—the codification into nine major areas of consumer demand from fashions to food and into numerous sub-classifications is visualized as a universal language understandable to retailers and manufacturers alike. [It meets an] urgent need for a scientific method of information in dollars to serve as the basis for planning and controlling [a balanced stock]. SMC tells the store in dollars how much business it does in each classification and sub-classification, how much inventory it needs to do that business, where to allocate promotional emphasis.[14]

Regarding the usefulness of this classification, the following comments by two investigators are of interest:

> The NRMA system can be used by a broad range of retailers—from small specialty stores to giant merchandise organizations. It is useful whenever the retail manager must plan and control a large number of . . . items of low- to moderate-unit value, and it is especially useful in multidepartment and multistore operations. Most

---

[10] Matt Wigginton, "Concerted Action Now," *Retail Control,* April 1965, p. 50.

[11] Cf. *NRMA Standard Classification of Merchandise,* 2d ed. (New York: National Retail Merchants Association, 1969).

[12] Samuel Feinberg, "Another Pathfinder in Retail Merchandising" in "From Where I Sit," *Women's Wear Daily,* February 6, 1968, p. 12. The others mentioned were MOR (the new Merchandising and Operating Results of Department and Specialty Stores published by the Controllers Congress of NRMA), Unit Control, and EDP (Electronic Data Processing).

[13] Sam Flanel, *Department Store and Specialty Store Merchandising and Operating Results of 1968, MOR,* Vol. I, (New York: National Retail Merchants Association, 1969), p. i.

[14] "Another Pathfinder in Retail Merchandising," *op. cit.,* p. 12.

importantly, classification merchandising systems provide profitability information for relatively narrow segments of merchandise investment; because of this they are well suited to dealing with today's adverse profitability trends in retailing.[15]

Despite the promising potential of Standard Merchandise Classification, retailers and manufacturers have been slow in adopting this more sophisticated system of control. A 12-city survey by a leading retail publication in March, 1968 revealed a strong need for more education concerning its uses, benefits, and limitations. And more than two years later—nine years following its introduction—"painfully slow progress" was being made.[16] Among the reasons for this situation, in addition to the broad educational problem involved, are the reluctance of retailers to change from individual systems used for many years and the costs involved in a change-over. Proponents of the new coding and numbering system continue to be optimistic, however, and expect the standards to become a "universal language" in the years ahead.

Price-line control This form of dollar control is based on price lines, *i.e.*, the particular prices at which assortments of merchandise are offered to the public. Just as departments may be divided into classifications to effect better control, so departments or classifications may be broken down into price lines to obtain more detailed information. But price-line control does not naturally follow classification control; rather, it is often used as a substitute for classification control. Price lines may also be broken down into classifications, such as material, size, and style.[17]

Dollar-control systems Department, classification, and price-line control may be operated either through a perpetual or a periodic inventory system.

Under the *perpetual inventory system* the accounting records "perpetually" show, as in the retail inventory method,[18] the retail value of the inventory which should be on hand. A physical count is conducted once or twice a year to verify the correctness of the "book" figure. Since detailed records are required, the major problem under the perpetual inventory system is to obtain complete and accurate information, a task made less difficult through the use of EDP equipment.[19] But whether handled by electronic equipment or by people, for merchandise to which it is applicable

---

[15] C. C. Wilson and C. D. Greenidge, *op. cit.*, p. 54. The authors also evaluate the potential of this system in a five-step analysis.

[16] Samuel Feinberg, "Merchandise Coding System Progresses Slowly but Surely," *Women's Wear Daily*, May 6, 1970, p. 26.

[17] Cf. Frank Burnside, "The Application of Taxonomy [the science of precise classification] to Retail Merchandise Data" in *Readings in Modern Retailing* (New York: National Retail Merchants Association, 1969), pp. 333–46.

[18] This accounting method is explained in Chapter 23.

[19] Cf. pp. 118–20, 239–40, 242, 270–71, above, and pp. 316–19, below.

the perpetual inventory method makes possible prompt adjustments through providing current, useful information.

The *periodic inventory system* involves the keeping of three important records—all at retail prices—inventories, purchases, and markdowns. From these records, sales data and other valuable information may be obtained for the period desired. To illustrate:

Retail stock on hand, August 1	$ 50,000
Retail purchases, August 1–January 31	100,000
Total retail stock handled	$150,000
Inventory at retail, January 31	60,000
Sales and markdowns, August 1–January 31	$ 90,000
Markdowns, August 1–January 31	10,000
Derived sales (including stock shortages)	$ 80,000

When an estimated amount for stock shortages is deducted, based on previous experience, actual sales may be determined.

The periodic inventory method may be extended beyond this simple illustration. By recording the opening inventory and the purchases both at cost price and at retail price, a markup percentage may be obtained; and by using the cost complement of this markup percentage (100 percent—markup percent = cost percent), the retail value of the stock on hand may be reduced to a cost basis. This procedure permits the calculation of the gross cost of merchandise sold, and the gross margin figures for any department, classification, or price line. The chief advantages of this system of control are its simplicity and its economy, but since information is provided only when inventories are taken its usefulness is considerably reduced. Moreover, the increasing sophistication of sales registers and terminals providing information at the point of sale has made the use of the system much less practicable. In other words, employing this "disappearance" method to obtain departmental, classification, or unit sales figures is advisable only when the desired data are not provided by the sales registers, sales checks, or other devices.

□ Unit control

Unit control,[20] the second basic type of merchandise information system, involves maintaining records in terms of physical units, rather than in terms of dollars. Such control commonly supplements dollar control. Both types are essential to keep stocks adjusted to customer demand.

[20] On this system of control in small stores cf. "Unit Stock Control," *Hardware Retailer*, June 1970, pp. 48–49.

Unit-control systems Unit-control systems vary widely among stores and departments, but they have a common attribute—provision of information quickly for any desired period. Such information may include, for instance, data on sales and stocks by style number, color, size, material, or any other characteristics of the merchandise. It may also include data on markups, markdowns, gross margin, and rate of stockturn, by price, merchandise classification, and vendor, depending on the store's needs. A major reason for the rapid growth of EDP is that it provides the required data quickly and accurately. Like dollar control, unit control may be effectuated through either a perpetual inventory or a periodic physical inventory system.

Perpetual inventory system Under this system each item is recorded when it arrives and when it is sold, permitting adjustments in stock to be made promptly to meet sales requirements. This system affords a check on stock shortages[21] by making possible their calculation when physical inventories are taken. It is used frequently for merchandise such as men's clothing, women's apparel, and shoes, where sales are easily recorded by units and reorders are common. It is not practicable where the unit is small and record-keeping costs are high as is true, for example, in drugs, cosmetics, and notions.

Physical inventory system This system is based upon periodic physical inventories: In other words, the only way to determine the quantity of an item on hand is to make an actual count. No attempt is made to record sales by units as they occur. A figure for sales—which also includes stock shortages—is obtained, however, by adding the beginning inventory of each unit to the purchases and then subtracting the ending inventory. Information for control purposes is obtained at the time of the physical inventory by analyzing the rate at which items are being sold and by comparing the goods in the previous inventory with those in the current inventory. Purchases, of course, must be analyzed in a similar manner.

Other systems of unit control Used with either the perpetual or periodic inventory system, or both of them, other forms have been developed to meet special requirements and conditions. They are designed chiefly to minimize lost sales caused by merchandise being out of stock and to maintain adequate assortments of goods in relation to customer demand.

1. Requisition or reserve stock control This system operates through the reserve stock, and provides needed control over goods such as drugs and cosmetics where unit control in the selling department is not feasible. Requisitions are drawn on the stock room by the selling department for

---

[21] Broadly speaking, a stock shortage is the amount of merchandise in terms of retail prices which has "disappeared" during a particular period. In other words, a shortage exists when the amount of merchandise on hand is less than the store records indicate should be on hand. Cf. the discussion on pp. 328–30.

groups of items known as "units," and such withdrawals are considered as sales. Over a period of time the withdrawals will be equal to the sales if the forward stocks are properly maintained.

2. Tickler control Under tickler control, periodic inventories, usually covering only certain sections of the stock, are taken at frequent intervals. The word "tickler" is used because the lists of items to be inventoried each day are placed in a tickler file, and the list for any particular day automatically comes to the attention of the buyer. This system may be used for forward stocks, reserve stocks, or for a combination of the two, depending on whether goods pass through a reserve stock room before reaching the selling floor. It is most useful for articles having a steady rate of sales.[22]

3. Checklist system In this system goods on hand are checked against a basic or model stock list[23] at regular, short intervals. Personal inspection of the stock is supposed to reveal the need for reorder but the effectiveness of this system depends on (*a*) the care with which the list is checked against the actual stock, (*b*) the maintenance of a uniform arrangement of the stock, and (*c*) the alertness shown by salespeople and other responsible persons in avoiding a complete sellout of any items.[24]

4. Warehouse control system Control over such "warehouse items" as furniture, stoves, refrigerators, and television sets—commonly sold from samples in the store, with delivery made from warehouse stock—may be exercised either in the store or in the warehouse, or in both places. When sales are made, sales checks are usually sent to a control operator who stamps the warehouse copy of the sales check to indicate that he has entered it. This step permits prompt entries in the control books, which are always accessible to department managers and assistants for review, and prevents overselling. These records necessitate, however, the maintenance of some records at the warehouse such as bin or shelf stock cards, or a visual

[22] The term "tickler control" is also used to refer to the practice of placing cards, slips, or gummed labels at certain places in the stock as reminders to the buyers. As goods are sold and the "reminders" are reached, the cards are removed and placed in containers provided for the purpose. At frequent intervals, the cards are collected and reviewed as to the advisability of reorder. It is apparent that these reminder cards should contain sufficient information to permit the prompt placing of orders. This form of control is also termed "reorder control" and "reminder control."

[23] A basic stock list represents the *minimum* assortment and quantities of items that should be on hand at a given time to meet reasonable demands of customers. A model stock list includes a complete, *well-balanced* assortment of merchandise designed to meet a specific sales volume. Automatic reorder quantities are frequently used with a basic stock list. Cf. the discussion on pp. 238–40, above.

[24] Closely related to the checklist system is the "never-out" list used by some stores. The "never-out" list contains only the name of items, usually staples, for which there is a large and steady demand and which the store must have on hand at all times or risk losing sales and customers. Items on the list are checked againt the stock on hand at frequent intervals.

index system to facilitate inventory taking and to assist stockmen.[25]

Benefits of unit control Unit control was developed to meet a need that remained unfulfilled by the use of various forms of dollar control. Specifically, it sought to provide information relative to physical characteristics of merchandise useful in buying and selling. It is logical, therefore, to summarize its benefits from the buying and selling points of view.

As a *buying* tool, unit control yields these benefits:

1. It reveals what merchandise is selling best, to the end that similar merchandise can be bought, with proper allowance being given to current sales and fashion trends.
2. It indicates the merchandise that is selling slowly and that should not be reordered. It furnishes a valuable guide, therefore, in reducing the number of price lines, styles, and colors which are carried.
3. It shows the proper time to buy merchandise, thus insuring a stock of goods to meet customers' requirements. In like manner, by showing goods on order, it tends to prevent unnecessary duplicate reorders.
4. It aids in establishing model stock plans, thus insuring complete, well-balanced stocks.
5. It reveals, where the perpetual inventory system is used, the quantity of stock on hand at any time without taking a physical inventory. Moreover, by comparing this book figure with that obtained when the physical inventory is taken, the stock shortage may be found. This comparison focuses attention on stock shortages and assists in controlling them.

As a *selling* tool, unit control provides assistance as follows:

1. It shows the age condition of the stock, thereby indicating the items requiring markdowns or special promotion. Losses are reduced when markdowns and other necessary actions are taken promptly.
2. It reveals the best-selling items and permits "playing the winners" and improving profits.
3. It minimizes "out-of-stock" situations.
4. It serves as a guide in planning special sales events by providing information on the goods available for promotion.
5. It often saves time for the customer by giving precise information on particular items in stock.

Reasons for limited use of unit control In view of the buying and selling benefits of unit-control systems just summarized, it would seem that all stores able to afford it would adopt this method. But many have failed to do so and it is advisable to inquire as to the reasons.

[25] On stock handling in warehouses of larger retailers, cf. *Warehousing and Merchandise Distribution for Mass Retailers* (New York: Mass Retailing Institute, 1970).

1. Many retail store executives believe that the cost of maintaining the necessary records exceeds the benefits derived from the information supplied. Frequently this is not a disadvantage of unit control but a fault of the system as planned and a reflection upon the judgment of those who make use of the data.
2. The publicity given to the elaborate systems used in large stores with their expensive forms, numerous recapitulations, and involved handling of records has instilled skepticism in the minds of proprietors of smaller stores as to the usefulness of similar, though less elaborate, systems in their stores.
3. The failure of some retailers to define the specific purposes and uses to which the information will be put prior to its collection often results in the gathering of data which are not useful and are consequently disregarded.
4. The opposition of some inexperienced buyers who believe that unit-control systems are established to furnish information to merchandise managers and the controller regarding the buyers' incompetence, rather than as a means of helping them to become better buyers.
5. The fear of many buyers that a unit-control system, by supplying detailed merchandise information, would supplant part of their function. Most buyers dislike the term "automatic buying."
6. The strong conviction of some buying executives that effective control over merchandise can be maintained only through study of the merchandise itself and not by placing dependence upon records.
7. The unhappy experience of some buyers with unit-control systems has caused them to look with disfavor upon such systems. This experience may have been caused by poorly planned systems, by expecting too much of the system installed, by attempting to make the records tie in completely with dollar control, or by failure to build an adequate organization to do the unit-control job. Frequently, the "unhappy experience" is exaggerated by the buyer because he is temperamentally opposed to the systematic records required for unit control. His major interests lie in buying and selling, not in accounting.

Instituting a unit-control system If a careful review of the advantages and disadvantages of unit control, supplemented by an investigation of the conditions under which such a system of control would operate, results in a decision to set up this type of control, the executive responsible should proceed as follows:

1. Make a complete list of all the information that it would be advisable to obtain from the system. In doing so, secure the opinion of other merchants and of employees . . . who understand the purposes of such control.

2. Examine the methods by which the desired information may be obtained to determine their suitability in his situation. Review such factors as the type of merchandise, including size, color, and variety handled; the unit price; the manner in which goods are purchased and stored, that is, the frequency of orders, their size, and whether regular use is made of the reserve stock room; and the rate of stockturn.
3. Devise the forms necessary to provide information of the kind and in the form wanted. The guides in this connection should be brevity, simplicity, and clarity. Detailed explanation of the use of the forms should accompany their distribution.
4. Take a physical inventory to determine what items are in stock and the quantities of each. This step furnishes a basis upon which records may be built and also permits the desired segregation to be accomplished without difficulty. When the goods are properly segregated, they are ready to be remarked.
5. Mark the goods to permit the recording of the necessary information. This step involves (*a*) preparing suitable price tickets with symbols, letters, or numbers to designate style, color, size, vendor, and the like; and (*b*) attaching the tickets to the mechandise.
6. Provide for the accurate recording of sales. Although there are numerous ways of doing this, the most common methods consist of price ticket stubs, copies of sales checks, sales register receipt stubs, salespeople's tallies, and reserve stock requisitions. Very recent years, however, have witnessed many changes in methods of recording sales, particularly by the more progressive firms, as technological improvements have enabled them to speed up transactions, obtain more complete information, and reduce the number of errors. New-type sales registers, for example, are now available that permits sales transactions to be recorded quickly as one of the first steps in a complete system of merchandise management.[26]
7. Maintain complete and accurate control records in such a manner that the unit-control information can be summarized, tabulated, and recorded promptly and fully, and checked frequently.

When a unit-control system has been set up in the manner outlined, control has been only partially accomplished. The data recorded must be analyzed, interpreted, and used. It is in this connection that the value of the system is tested. If the information provided is not translated into improved buying practices and better-balanced stocks in relationship to sales, the system is a failure.

---

[26] Cf. *The Values of Total System Reports for Retailers* (Dayton, Ohio: National Cash Register Company, n.d.). Procedures manuals are also available for installing the system in some kinds of stores.

■ EDP AND MERCHANDISE MANAGEMENT

In preceding chapters we have noted that many progressive stores have adopted EDP equipment to furnish information to decision-making executives on many aspects of retail operation.[27] At this point we need add but a few paragraphs to illustrate the use of such equipment in the control of merchandise inventories, an area for which EDP is particularly suited. It should be emphasized at the beginning, however, that satisfactory merchandise information systems require, in addition to suitable equipment, the use of properly designed price tickets marked to yield the desired data at the point of sale and determination of the kinds and sequence of the routines involved.[28]

The need is great among retailers for a continuous flow of relevant information to insure correct decisions on merchandise matters. The computer has helped fulfill this need.[29] Nevertheless, a considerable gap continues to exist between computer capabilities and their application to retail activities as well as a reluctance on the part of retailers to accept the discipline these devices demand.[30]

◻ EDP in department stores

The use and benefits of EDP for merchandise management in department stores are well illustrated by the experience of Woodward & Lothrop of Washington, D.C. This organization, a pioneer in the use of EDP among retailers, operates a main store and eight suburban branches with total annual sales exceeding $100 million. Its EDP setup, one of the country's most sophisticated systems, employs several million dollars worth of electronic computers and supporting ware that enables executives and buyers to main-

---

[27] Cf. the discussion on pp. 118–20, 239–40, 242, and 270–71.

[28] The marking of merchandise, together with the types of tickets currently employed, is discussed in Chapter 15. The newer forms of electronic sales-registering equipment are described and illustrated in Chapter 25.

[29] Both dollar and unit control of merchandise inventories are made possible through new electronic point-of-sale registers which capture data in forms suitable for computer input. Among the several firms which have developed such devices and systems are the National Cash Register Company, the Friden Division of Singer Company, Pitney-Bowes-Alpex, Inc., and American Totalisator. Cf. the discussion in Chapter 25 and "Cash Drawers that 'Talk Computer,' " *Business Week,* August 29, 1970, pp. 66–67.

[30] Cf. Tom Alexander, "Computers Can't Solve Everything," *Fortune,* Vol. 80, No. 3 (October 1969), pp. 126 ff.; and J. G. Bradley, F. K. Wodarsky, and P. F. Gundell, "Are You Willing to Accept a Computer's Discipline?" *Retail Control,* January 1970, pp. 3–16. But one source estimates that, in spite of these resistances, retailers will boost their data processing expenditures by 60 percent in the next five years (1971–76) from $500 million to $800 million. Cf. "Retail EDP Costs to Hit $800 million," *Chain Store Age* (Executives Edition), February 1971, pp. E17–E22.

tain close checks on the sale of specific product lines and on customer tastes.

Concentrating on "management and people disciplines" to make its EDP systems work, the company uses, among other equipment, two IBM 360 Model 40 computers in connection with three basic merchandise information systems as follows:[31]

1. A soft goods or fashion system using print-punch tickets to provide unit sales data by store, by date, by style and in some cases even permitting price, color, and size analysis. (Depending on a department's needs, other information may be added.)
2. A staples system called SMART (staple merchandise automatic reorder and transfer), designed to permit the automatic reordering of staple goods. This system now covers over 100,000 stockkeeping units with further aspects under development.[32]
3. A locator and status type system for big ticket hard goods, presently concentrated on furniture but expected to be broadened to include major appliances and home electronics. Every piece of furniture in the warehouse carries a record indicating its exact location and sales status plus other merchandise information.

□ EDP in chain stores

Chain stores also have been active in updating their methods and equipment to improve control over merchandise inventories. The J. C. Penney Company, Inc., S. S. Kresge, the Kroger Company, and The Food Fair of Los Angeles—to mention only a few—are among those employing the improved devices and systems new developments have made possible.

The distribution network of the Kresge organization, operated through a computer complex in Fort Wayne, Indiana, controls 25 percent of all merchandise sold by the company. The computer center inventories and updates stocks for the firm's distribution centers in Fort Wayne, Indiana, Atlanta, Georgia, and Sparks, Nevada.[33]

Another example of merchandising data resulting from EDP is afforded by the Kroger Company, a large food chain.[34] This firm has developed a

---

[31] Cf. Betty Morris, "Woodie's Puts EDP Where the Money Is," *Women's Wear Daily,* March 9, 1970, p. 26. The remainder of this discussion is based on the same source.

[32] *For related information on staple goods,* cf. S. B. Smith, "Automated Inventory Management for Staples," *Journal of Retailing,* Vol. 47, No. 1 (Spring 1971), pp. 55–62.

[33] For additional details cf. "Kresge Counts on Computer in Distribution," *Women's Wear Daily,* April 27, 1970, p. 32.

[34] Eighty percent of food chains employ EDP systems, with seventy-five percent of these firms analyzing shipments by items to individual stores. "Food Chain Performance and Trends," *Progressive Grocer,* April 1970, p. 61. Also cf. "Computer Use in Food Distribution," *ibid.,* June 1970, pp. 160–81.

Product Movement Index, a by-product of its computerized system. The Index furnishes grocery manufacturers with weekly data on shipments of branded goods from Kroger warehouses to its 1,300 stores in 20 states. Through the data supplied, manufacturers learn their weekly sales in Kroger stores, the sales of competing brands, their share of total market, and the prices paid by consumers. One result has been the removal of about 50 percent of the brands of a major company from the shelves of Kroger stores because of slow sale.[35]

In other supermarket chains, including the Food Fair of Los Angeles, a system called Marketron is used, providing benefits for both store management and customers. Current inventory information is furnished by a computer that keeps continuous records of stock movement at the store, warehouse, and chain headquarters levels and when inventories fall to a predetermined point, it prints out a reorder automatically. This can eliminate the need for backroom storage, overstocking that causes price-cut sales, and extra delivery charges.[36]

□ EDP in smaller stores

Again it should be emphasized that various arrangements are now available under which smaller stores can realize the advantages of EDP. In September 1970, for instance, the National Retail Merchants Association reports that some 270 to 310 of its affiliated smaller stores were actively using outside service bureaus for merchandise statistics, inventory control, and related purposes; another 21 were involved in negotiating contracts with service bureaus associated with the organization; and about 101 additional stores were planning or contemplating the use of a service bureau.[37] In this connection it is of interest to note that, as a result of their experience with outside service bureaus, as many as 200 stores have probably converted to their own in-store computer systems.[38]

---

[35] "Computer Control of Shelf Life Perils Slow Moving Items, Says Borden's Durrant," *Advertising Age*, March 24, 1969, p. 63. For an analysis of the relationships among sales of particular items and profit margins in connection with the space occupied in supermarkets, cf. "The Management of Merchandise," *Progressive Grocer*, April 1971, pp. 151–55.

[36] "Computers Reach the Checkout Counter," *Business Week*, June 13, 1970, p. 86.

[37] Data supplied by the Information Systems Division, National Retail Merchants Association.

[38] On the application of EDP to small stores in general, cf. Jake Fuller, "EDP Service Aimed at Small Stores," *Women's Wear Daily*, July 7, 1969, p. 31; and "EDP Helps Turnover, Shrinkage, and Family Peace," *Stores*, February 1969, pp. 24–25. On its use among hardware stores, cf. Ellen Hackney, "The Computer's Role in Retailing," a section of "The Computer Age in Merchandising," *Hardware Retailer*, October 1968, pp. 101–6; and Tom Jenkins, "The Computer's Role in Store Management," *ibid.*, pp. 107–9.

As to the future development of EDP in retailing, the following statement by the manager of the Information Systems Division of the National Retail Merchants Association is of interest: "[Very shortly EDP will enable stores to récord transactions] without too much human intervention; pick up credit and merchandise information in one pass; identify the availability of merchandise; update and keep current the customer's account; reduce drastically the time the customer spends taking her merchandise out of the store; and, finally, improve relations with customers."[39]

■ THE PHYSICAL INVENTORY

The physical inventory—an actual counting and listing of the goods in stock at a given time, together with the cost or retail price of each item—is considered a "necessary evil" by most retailers. Occurring once or twice a year, it is necessary to determine whether a profit has been made during the past fiscal period.[40] But in addition to this financial purpose, the physical inventory is an important aspect of merchandise control.

As of a specific date, the physical inventory shows the kinds, quantities, and values of the items in stock for the store as a whole and by departments. Moreover—depending on the store, the merchandise handled, and the information placed on the price ticket—the physical inventory makes possible the classification of items by sections or divisions of departments, by age groups, by price lines, by physical units, or by other desired groupings. It helps the retailer to improve his buying and selling methods, enables unit control and other stock records to be checked, and furnishes the figures to compare with book inventories to determine the amount of stock shortage or overage.

□ Taking the physical inventory

Accuracy and completeness are essential in taking the physical inventory. Consequently, it should be carefully planned, the required information listed by qualified personnel, the calculations and summaries checked, and the inventory reports issued promptly. A review of the methods employed in different types of stores is helpful in understanding the activities involved.

In chain stores selling standardized goods There is no standard procedure for taking the physical inventory in all chain stores. At one extreme, for example, is the monthly inventory of the grocery chain for which there

---

[39] Irving I. Solomon, as reported in Sandy Parker, "Computers A Way of Life," *Women's Wear Daily*, January 11, 1971, p. 34.

[40] Cf. "Inventory: Asset or Liability," *Hardware Retailer*, June 1970, pp. 45–47. For its significance in determining operating results of the business, cf. Chapter 23.

is little advance preparation. The inventory crew, usually consisting of at least two men, comes into a store quite unexpectedly. As one man goes through the stock, calling off the number of units at each price, the other records; or perhaps a tape or wire recorder is used, so that both men can count. Although headquarters may want to know the quantities on hand for a few specific items, in general all it desires is the total value of the goods in the store; consequently, only the price-quantity relationships are required. When the count has been completed, the sheet is sent to headquarters, where the value of the stock is computed.

In department stores At the other extreme in taking the physical inventory is the department store where advance preparation for the inventory is essential.[41] Commonly, the process covers the four stages referred to previously—planning, counting and recording of the goods on hand, calculation of the value of the stock, and issuance of inventory reports.

In the planning stage, the department buyer, working under the direction of the controller or an inventory supervisor, usually takes the following steps:

1. Classifies and groups merchandise by type, price, and style.
2. Adjusts prices so that they are market prices, and makes certain that all necessary information is on the price tickets.
3. If time is available before the inventory date, sometimes plans a sale to reduce stock to a minimum and to clear out any undesirable merchandise disclosed in step 1.
4. Prepares a layout chart of the department, showing the location of each fixture with merchandise. This chart enables the controller to issue inventory sheets or tags marked for specific sections in each department.
5. Obtains the necessary inventory sheets or tags from the controller.
6. Checks the salespeople's knowledge of inventory instructions.

After plans have been completed and the designated inventory date arrives, the actual counting and recording begin. The recording may take place on inventory sheets or inventory tags but the former are used by the vast majority of firms. When sheets are used, a number of items (including description, quantity, price, and other desired characteristics) are recorded on each sheet (see Figure 13–1); with tags or tickets only one item of a particular size or type appears on each ticket (see Figure 13–2). Since selling may be going on while the inventory taking is in progress, all sales are recorded either on the tags or on special deduction sheets, thus allowing computation of the stock on hand when the inventory taking has been completed. Since most large department stores use the retail inventory method, they maintain perpetual or book inventories and are thus able further to

[41] Cf. National Retail Merchants Association, *Inventory Taking Manual* (New York: The Association, 1965).

FIGURE 13–1 Example of a form for taking inventory

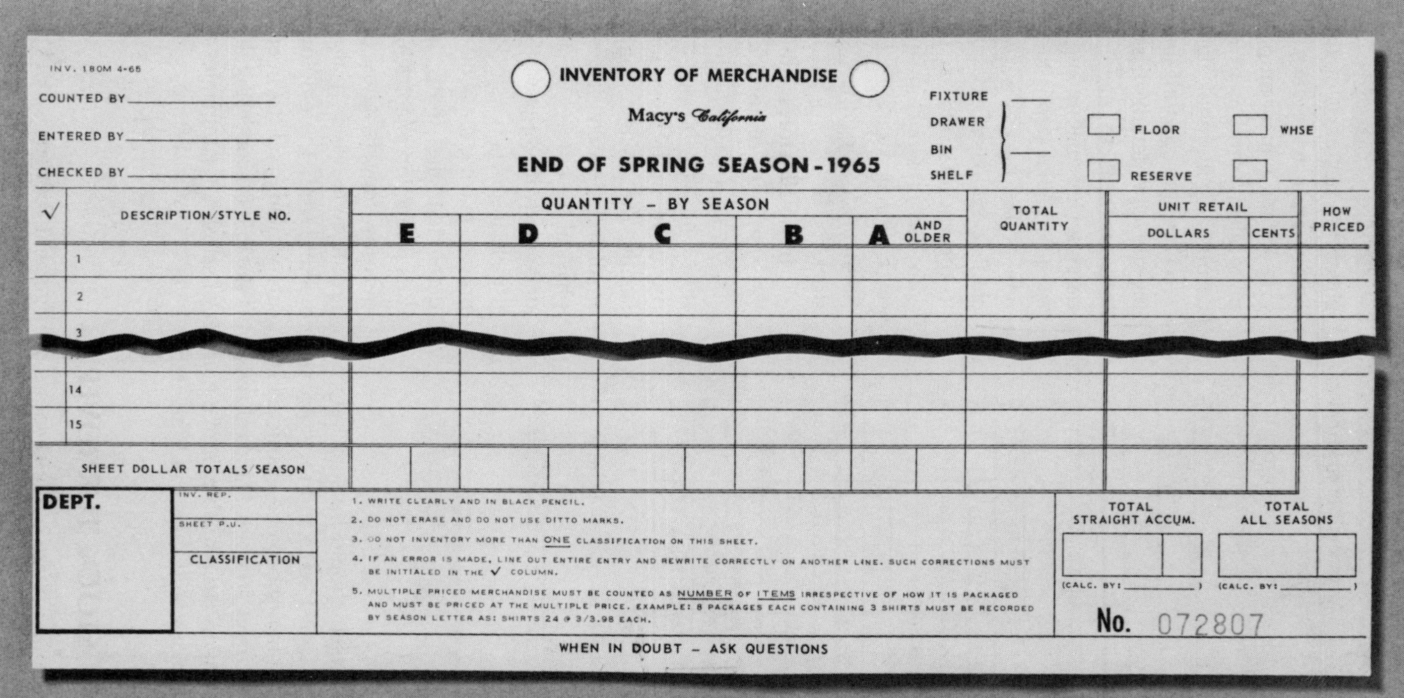

INV. 180M 4-65

INVENTORY OF MERCHANDISE

Macy's California

END OF SPRING SEASON - 1965

COUNTED BY ____________

ENTERED BY ____________

CHECKED BY ____________

FIXTURE ____ DRAWER BIN ____ SHELF

FLOOR WHSE RESERVE

√	DESCRIPTION/STYLE NO.	QUANTITY – BY SEASON E	D	C	B	A AND OLDER	TOTAL QUANTITY	UNIT RETAIL DOLLARS	CENTS	HOW PRICED
	1									
	2									
	3									
	14									
	15									
	SHEET DOLLAR TOTALS/SEASON									

DEPT.

INV. REP.

SHEET P.U.

CLASSIFICATION

1. WRITE CLEARLY AND IN BLACK PENCIL.
2. DO NOT ERASE AND DO NOT USE DITTO MARKS.
3. DO NOT INVENTORY MORE THAN ONE CLASSIFICATION ON THIS SHEET.
4. IF AN ERROR IS MADE, LINE OUT ENTIRE ENTRY AND REWRITE CORRECTLY ON ANOTHER LINE. SUCH CORRECTIONS MUST BE INITIALED IN THE √ COLUMN.
5. MULTIPLE PRICED MERCHANDISE MUST BE COUNTED AS NUMBER OF ITEMS IRRESPECTIVE OF HOW IT IS PACKAGED AND MUST BE PRICED AT THE MULTIPLE PRICE. EXAMPLE: 8 PACKAGES EACH CONTAINING 3 SHIRTS MUST BE RECORDED BY SEASON LETTER AS: SHIRTS 24 @ 3/3.98 EACH.

TOTAL STRAIGHT ACCUM. (CALC. BY: ________)

TOTAL ALL SEASONS (CALC. BY: ________)

No. 072807

WHEN IN DOUBT – ASK QUESTIONS

Courtesy: Macy's, California

FIGURE 13–2 An example of an inventory ticket in general use

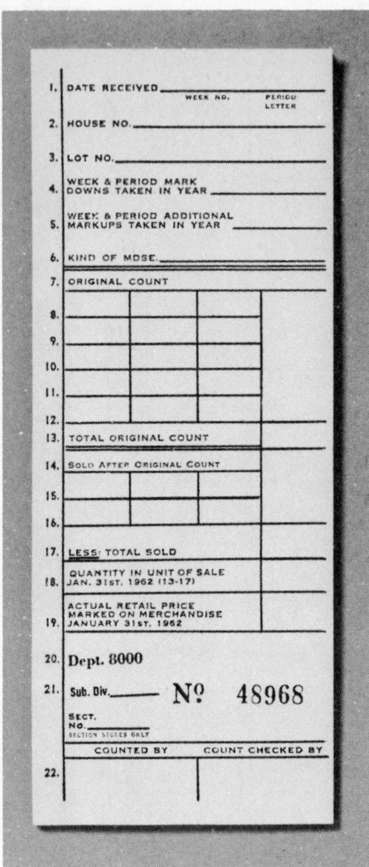

1. DATE RECEIVED ______ WEEK NO. PERIOD LETTER
2. HOUSE NO. ______
3. LOT NO. ______
4. WEEK & PERIOD MARK DOWNS TAKEN IN YEAR ______
5. WEEK & PERIOD ADDITIONAL MARKUPS TAKEN IN YEAR ______
6. KIND OF MDSE. ______
7. ORIGINAL COUNT
8.
9.
10.
11.
12.
13. TOTAL ORIGINAL COUNT
14. SOLD AFTER ORIGINAL COUNT
15.
16.
17. LESS: TOTAL SOLD
18. QUANTITY IN UNIT OF SALE JAN. 31st. 1962 (13-17)
19. ACTUAL RETAIL PRICE MARKED ON MERCHANDISE JANUARY 31st, 1962
20. Dept. 8000
21. Sub. Div. ______ No. 48968

SECT. NO. ______
SECTION STORES ONLY

COUNTED BY | COUNT CHECKED BY

22.

check the accuracy of their book figures against the physical inventory. In fact, a major purpose of the physical inventory is to check the accuracy of the book figures.

Once the counting and recording are completed, all sheets and tags are sent to the controller's office for calculating and summarizing. The final step is the preparation of the necessary reports, including, for instance, those relating to the age of goods as compared with the previous inventory, the stock shortages or overages by departments, and the warehouse stocks.

In small stores In between the simplicity of the physical inventory of the standardized chain-store unit and the rather complex procedure in the department store stands the system suitable for small independent stores. Since a physical inventory is taken only once (or twice) a year, the retailer usually inspects his stock carefully prior to making the actual count to determine the items on hand. This inspection enables him to sort out slow-moving items, or "sleepers," which should be sold before the inventory is taken. It also permits him to adjust costs and retail prices to market levels. The employees used to assist him should be instructed in inventory taking and the need for care and accuracy stressed. Standardized forms suitable for recording the desired information are available from a number of salesbook companies and trade associations, and their use is advisable.

■ STOCK TURNOVER

Another phase of merchandise management concern is stock turnover, or rate of stockturn, the number of times during a given period—usually a year—in which the average amount of stock on hand is sold. Usually computed on a yearly basis, it may be derived for any period desired.

□ Calculating the rate of stockturn

The rate of stockturn is most commonly determined by dividing the average inventory at cost into the cost of the merchandise sold. Quite frequently, however, it is computed by dividing the average inventory at retail into the net sales figure.[42] A much less common but equally satisfactory method is to divide the average inventory in physical units into sales in physical units.

These three methods of calculating the rate of stockturn may be illustrated by assuming certain figures. A clothing merchant begins the year with 100 suits costing $50 each and retailing at $75 each. During the year, other suits are purchased and at year's end 60 suits remain in stock which cost $40 each and retail at $60. For the year, net sales of the 360 suits were $24,975 and their cost $16,650. The annual rate of stockturn may now be found as follows:

1. Opening inventory at cost (100 × 50)	$ 5,000
Closing inventory at cost (60 × 40)	2,400
	2/$ 7,400
Average inventory at cost	3,700
Cost of goods sold	16,650

$$\frac{\$16,650}{\$\ 3,700} = 4.5 = \text{Stockturn rate}$$

2. Opening inventory at retail (100 × 75)	$ 7,500
Closing inventory at retail (60 × 60)	3,600
	2/$11,100
Average inventory at retail	5,550
Net sales	24,975

$$\frac{\$24,975}{\$\ 5,550} = 4.5 = \text{Stockturn rate}$$

3. Opening inventory in units	100
Closing inventory in units	60
	2/160
Average inventory in units	80
Net sales in units	360

$$\frac{360}{80} = 4.5 = \text{Stockturn rate}$$

[42] The *Hardware Retailer* recommends a sales-to-inventory at cost ratio "as a somewhat easier way to look at one's management efficiency and . . . [because it] helps establish a goal if an inventory reduction program is required." Actually this is *capital* turnover, rather than inventory turnover, and should be distinguished from the stockturn rate.

In computing stock turnover, two major cautions should be observed. First, sales and average stock figures must be comparable, *i.e.*, both of them should cover the same operating period and also be either in terms of cost or retail prices. Second, the average stock must be representative, that is, it should truly reflect the average size of the inventory for the period it covers.

□ Advantages of rapid stockturn

The advantages to the retailer of a rapid rate of stockturn are quite evident. By limiting his investment in inventory such expenses as interest, taxes, insurance on merchandise, and store and storage space are reduced. By having "fresher" merchandise on hand, greater sales may be achieved with a smaller stock than with a larger one made up of soiled and shopworn goods. Markdowns may be reduced. And retailers with relatively high stockturns find that their return on invested capital may rise.

Despite these advantages, the statistical evidence in Tables 13–1 and 13–2 reveal that successful retailers have wide variations in their rates of stock turnover. To understand the reasons for this situation, we need to examine the causes of such variations, the relationship of turnover to profits, and the possible disadvantages of a relatively high turnover rate.

□ Causes of variations in the rate of stockturn

Four main factors, among others, are responsible for the variations in stockturn rates among retail stores: the type of goods sold, store policy, store location, and the aid furnished by manufacturers.

Type of goods sold Table 13–1 shows the rates of stockturn for retail stores in a number of fields. At one extreme are supermarkets (groceries only) (19.7) and food (chain) stores (11.9); whereas at the other extreme, jewelry stores turned their stock only 1.2 times a year. Reasons for this wide variation lie both in the characteristics of the goods and in the buying habits of consumers. Supermarket and other food store customers prefer to purchase at frequent intervals, thus enabling this type of retailer to operate with a relatively limited stock in relation to his sales. In contrast, jewelry is bought less frequently than most other items, and a large and costly stock is usually necessary to meet customers' demands. The same is true for small shoe stores and hardware stores.

Store policy Differences in policies among stores cause variations in rates of stockturn. For instance, those which may lead to relatively high

TABLE 13–1

Rates of stockturn in selected retail stores

Kind of business	Rate of stockturn
Department stores (sales $1 million to $2 million)	2.6
Drug stores (prescription pharmacies) (sales $140,000 to $160,000)	3.5
Food stores (composite figure for chains)	11.86
Hardware stores (profit makers)	2.3
Jewelry stores (cash—sales $100,000 to $300,000)	1.2
Shoe stores (sales $25,000 to $50,000)	2.2
Specialty stores (sales $1 million to $5 million)	3.15
Stationery stores (office supplies and equipment)	3.62
Supermarkets (groceries only)	19.7
Women's specialty apparel (sales $25,000 to $50,000)	2.83

Source: National Cash Register Company, *Expenses in Retail Businesses* (Dayton, Ohio: The Company, n.d.). The food store figure is from the *Progressive Grocer,* April 1971, p. 79 and that for department stores is from Jay Scher, *Financial and Operating Results of Department and Specialty Stores in 1969* (New York: National Retail Merchants Association, 1970), p. 9.

rates of stockturn include the following, among others: hand-to-mouth buying; elimination of slow-selling items; fewer price lines; minimizing number of styles, sizes, and colors; promotional activity and low-margin pricing; and concentration on fast-moving national brands. In the drug field, for example, many cut-rate stores, including chains, limit their stocks to fast-moving items, engage in much promotional activity, and price their goods with a relatively small markup. In contrast, other drug retailers follow policies of full stocks and "regular" prices. These two groups of retailers will obviously have different rates of stockturn.

Location The location of a store or of a branch contributes to a low (or high) stock turnover. Some stores are so located—perhaps in small towns or in city neighborhood sections—that large sales are impossible. Since a certain basic stock is necessary, these stores have relatively low rates of stockturn. Stores located where customer traffic is heavy and large sales are possible, however, will show higher rates of stockturn; *i.e.,* their stocks will not increase proportionately with their sales.

Aid furnished by manufacturers As some retailers have limited their stocks to achieve a better stockturn, they have been criticized by manufacturers for failing in one of their major functions, that is, providing adequate assortments of goods to meet customer demand. Especially are manufacturers concerned because of the retailer's hesitancy to stock a new item until the manufacturer, through advertising, has created a demand for it.

TABLE 13–2

Rate of stockturn and profits in selected types of retail trade, 1970

Retail trade	Rate of stockturn*	Net profit as percentage of net sales
Clothing and furnishings stores—men's and boys'	5.9	4.02
	4.0	2.36
	2.8	0.60
Department stores	7.1	3.11
	5.6	1.91
	4.3	0.85
Discount stores	7.2	2.86
	5.3	1.63
	3.9	0.76
Furniture stores	6.2	4.38
	4.6	2.22
	3.6	0.64
Grocery stores	22.9	1.71
	16.8	0.99
	12.8	0.63
Hardware stores	5.4	4.35
	3.9	2.52
	3.0	0.98
Shoe stores	5.0	4.44
	3.9	2.10
	2.9	0.78
Variety stores	5.7	3.63
	4.5	2.12
	3.5	1.14
Women's ready-to-wear stores	9.4	3.71
	6.7	1.86
	5.2	0.44

* This column does not show true stockturn figures, since it is calculated by dividing net sales by inventory at cost.

Source: "The Ratios of Retailing," *Dun's*, September 1971, p. 77.

To meet this situation, some manufacturers, aware of the retailer's need for strict inventory control, have developed stock-control plans providing a reasonable display of their products and also yielding a good turnover figure to the retailer. One skirt manufacturer, for instance, helps the retailer set up a model stock, has his salesmen take a weekly inventory, and offers to replace slow-selling items with fast-selling ones. Such assistance is of particular value to smaller retailers who often lack the stock-control programs of larger firms.

□ Stock turnover and profits

It is often stated that there is a direct relationship between stock turnover and profits and that the retailer can enlarge his profits by increasing his rate of stockturn. To support this position, data such as those summarized in Table 13–2 are presented which indicate that firms of the same kind with the highest rate of turnover realize the greatest profit ratio to sales. It should be made perfectly clear, however, that there is no such causation between stock turnover and profits as these statistics might lead one to conclude. Mere improvement in stock turnover does not necessarily mean an increase in profits. *Whether or not profits increase with stock turnover depends entirely upon the methods by which the higher stock turnover is obtained.* To illustrate: A retailer may increase his stock turnover by reducing his average stock while maintaining the same sales volume. To this end, slow-moving items may be eliminated and some price lines or competing brands dropped. A hand-to-mouth buying policy may be adopted. The net result *may* be increased profits, since the smaller stock may decrease both markdowns and operating expenses.

Increased profits are not sure to result from reducing stock, however, even if sales hold even. Purchasing in small quantities may result in additional correspondence and clerical cost; greater expense in receiving, checking, and marking merchandise; and in the loss of quantity discounts which may more than offset the gains from a faster stock turnover. Moreover transportation costs on small orders are relatively greater than on larger orders. And, over a period of time, it may be impossible to maintain sales on the reduced stock because inadequate assortments may engender customer ill-will and sales and profits will eventually decline.[43]

In conclusion, it should be emphasized that a mere increase in stock turnover is not what the retailer wants. Rather, he wants increased profit. Sometimes this goal is achieved by steps that also lead to a higher stock turnover, but at other times the path lies in another direction. If the retailer will concentrate on such matters as careful buying, judicious pricing, a well-balanced stock, effective sales promotion, and properly trained personnel, he will not have to worry about stock turnover. Satisfactory stock turnover is a result of good merchandising and, therefore, a measure of the alertness and ability of the management.

■ STOCK-SALES RATIOS

Executives responsible for merchandise management are also interested in stock-sales ratios. Such ratios indicate the relationship that exists between

[43] Cf. George Baylis, "Are the Brakes Too Tight to Let the Train Roll?", *Retail Control*, October 1965, pp. 15–26.

the stock on hand at the beginning of a period (usually a month) in terms of retail prices and the sales for that month.[44] If, for example, the retail value of goods on hand in a department on October 1 was $50,000 and the sales for October were $25,000, the stock-sales ratio for the month would be 2 to 1.

Through a knowledge of his own past stock-sales ratios and those of other stores, a retailer has a good basis for planning the stock he needs to meet anticipated sales.[45] Like other merchandise statistics, however, they are an *aid to* the executive's judgment and not a *substitute for* it. Such ratios should not be considered mere formulae which answer all questions relating to stock and sales relationships.

■ STOCK SHORTAGES

A growing and continuous problem of merchandise management, already mentioned in Chapter 1, is the control of stock shortages—the unaccounted-for disappearance of merchandise expressed in retail prices. Such shortages may develop at many points in the operation of a retail store.[46] To illustrate: Merchandise may be sold for less than the price tag indicates, some breakage is inevitable, and mismeasuring plays a role. But the two chief causes of stock shortages are dishonesty and errors in records.[47]

□ Dishonesty as a cause of shortages

Stock shortages caused by thefts of merchandise by employees, customers, amateur and professional shoplifters, and even armed robbers have plagued retail stores for many years.[48] And the problem has been magnified

[44] It is possible, of course, to express this relationship in terms of the end-of-the-month stock rather than that at the beginning of the month, or even to use physical units.

[45] Stock-sales ratios for merchandise groups by sales volume and by the number of selling units in a company are given in two volumes—each volume containing different groups of merchandise—by Jay Scher, *Department and Specialty Store Merchandising and Operating Results of 1970* (MOR) (New York: National Retail Merchants Association, 1971).

[46] States a leading banker, "Stock shortages have become an increasingly important problem to retailers, and, so far, no ready solutions have been found to correct this situation." "Banker Rather Bearish on 1970 Retail Outlook," *Women's Wear Daily,* June 1, 1970, p. 16. Also cf. Samuel Feinberg, "Internal Shortages Major Factor in Lower Profits," in "From Where I Sit," *ibid.,* May 13, 1970, p. 22.

[47] One management engineering firm reports that employee dishonesty "at all levels" accounts for about 70 percent of stock shortages, shoplifting for 15 percent, and bookkeeping records for 15 percent. Cf. "Leary's High Pay Position at A & S Hailed as Pace Setter," *ibid.,* September 9, 1970, p. 6.

[48] States *Business Week:* ". . . Retail inventory losses across the country—pushing $3 billion a year—have jumped 150% since 1960 and reached the level where the FBI

in recent years with the growth of self-service and the increase in the number of supermarkets and discount houses.[49] Among department stores with sales of from $10 to $20 million in 1969 the stock-shortage figure was 1.66 percent of sales and among departmentized specialty stores with annual sales of from $1 million to $5 million during the same year the figure was 1.41 percent.[50] It is not possible to determine the exact proportions of these shortages caused by thefts.

To minimize stock shortages resulting from dishonesty, retailers take many steps. Burglar alarm systems and regular police protection supplementing security guards are important against professional operators. The careful selection, training, and constant supervision of employees is another essential aspect of an antishortage program. Shoplifting is fought by the use of human "spotters" and television "eyes" throughout the store, and instructing employees to recognize the characteristics of the typical shoplifter—the customer who (1) hangs around without buying, (2) carries a shopping bag, (3) has a large purse, and (4) wears a topcoat in mild weather. In many cities, retailers exchange information on shoplifters, and, in cooperation with the Better Business Bureau, Chamber of Commerce and the police department sometimes issue booklets dealing with the problem.[51]

Municipal and state laws designed to afford better protection to the retailer who brings about the arrest of the shoplifter are also encouraged by retailer groups. Such laws are necessary since, without them, the retailer who apprehends a shoplifter runs the risk of being sued for false arrest or false imprisonment. The Florida law, for example, minimizes this danger for the retailer by allowing him to take a suspect into custody for a "reasonable length of time" in an attempt to recover the goods. Even though the merchant has made a mistake, he cannot be sued successfully if he can satisfy a court that he had a "probable cause" for acting as he did. At least seven states now have such laws—Arizona, Pennsylvania, West Virginia, Ohio, Illinois, Florida, and Kentucky. Moreover, the courts are now taking a more

---

calls them 'the fastest growing larceny in the nation.' " "The Pinch That Hurts," June 27, 1970, p. 72. Also cf. L. E. Daykin, "Employee Theft—It Hurts the Worst," *Progressive Grocer,* November 1970, pp. 42–47.

[49] Among discount department stores in 1970, for example, stock shortages rose to a record 3.13 percent of total sales. Cf. "Shortages Peak for Year at Discount Department Stores," *Women's Wear Daily,* January 5, 1971, p. 75.

[50] Jay Scher, *Financial and Operating Results of Department and Specialty Stores in 1969* (FOR) (New York: National Retail Merchants Association, Controllers' Congress, 1970), pp. 32, 60. Results for 1970 will probably show a sharp increase in these figures.

[51] This action was taken, for instance, in Winston-Salem, North Carolina. Cf. "Pamphlet Gives N.C. Teens Message on Shoplifting," *Women's Wear Daily,* January 3, 1969, p. 96. Also cf. C. L. Wood, R. F. Van Pelt, and S. D. Astor, "Shortage Prevention Techniques," *Retail Control,* August 1969, p. 33.

serious view of shoplifting. In California a district court of appeals held, in effect, that a retailer no longer needs delay detention until the shoplifter leaves the store: if he carries merchandise through a check-out stand without paying, action may be taken to recover the goods without risking a suit for false arrest.

□ Errors as a cause of shortages

Honest mistakes made by employees which cause stock shortages are almost legion: errors in marking, in inventory taking, in handling returns, in delivering the wrong merchandise, in billing credit customers, in making change for cash customers, and in recording markdowns. While care in the selection and training of employees plus closer supervision of paper work and merchandise handling will minimize these errors, they will not eliminate them—any more than stock shortages caused by dishonesty can be eliminated. All the retailer can do, therefore, is to utilize all the techniques at his command to minimize these shortages and maintain constant vigilance to protect his earnings from further erosion.

■ REVIEW AND DISCUSSION QUESTIONS

1 Formulate in your own words a satisfactory definition of "merchandise management," taking into account recent developments.

2 Explain the nature and purposes of the new concept of "classification merchandising."

3 Summarize the essential differences between dollar control and unit control as information systems for merchandise management.

4 Discuss the use of perpetual inventory systems and periodic inventory systems under both dollar and unit merchandise control.

5 As manager of a men's clothing store you plan to institute a unit-control system. Explain the specific kind of system you would establish and how you would put it into operation.

6 Assume you were asked to speak for 10 minutes before your Retailing Class on the topic "Electronic Data Processing and Merchandise Management." What points would you cover and why?

7 Calculate the rate of stockturn based on the following figures: beginning inventory at retail $40,400, ending inventory at retail $32,800, and net sales $109,800.

8 Distinguish between the terms "stock turnover" and "stock-sales ratio."

In your judgment, why are not stock-sales ratios used more widely as a merchandise-control device as compared to rates of stockturn?

9 Explain the term "stock shortage," the chief causes of such shortages, and ways by which these shortages may be reduced.

10 Visit your school or local library and examine the newer two-volume annual compilation of merchandising and operating results by the Controllers Congress of the National Retail Merchants Association. Report on the general nature of the data included and the innovative highlights and refinements introduced as compared with previous years.

chapter 14

MERCHANDISE MANAGEMENT THROUGH THE BUDGET

In the previous chapter the general purposes of merchandise man-agement and control were emphasized and information systems employed to accomplish these objectives were discussed. In this chapter we consider the merchandise budget, one of the most effective tools available to the retailer for effectuating dollar control over his merchandise.

■ MERCHANDISE BUDGETING: MEANING AND OBJECTIVES

Broadly speaking, a merchandise budget or plan is a forecast of specified merchandise activities for a definite period of time. It usually involves setting down on paper the desired results (plan) for a specific period and the appropriate methods by which these results will be accomplished. Although variations exist among stores with respect to the factors included in the budget, the essential elements are sales, stocks, reductions—including markdowns, employee, and other discounts—and stock shortages, purchases, and gross margin. Other elements often included, however, are stock turnover, total and direct expense, net profit or controllable net profit, merchandise returns by customers, number of transactions, and average sales.

□ Purposes of merchandise budgeting

The fundamental purpose of a merchandise budget is to provide a clear-cut plan of merchandising operations for a specific period of time based upon careful study of existing needs and foreseeable conditions. Individuals or firms contemplating the expenditure of several thousand dollars for the construction or renovation of a building would never think of going ahead without drafting definite plans, reviewing these plans carefully, and then abiding by them. Yet proprietors of many small stores and a few large ones make substantial investments in merchandise without making definite plans or analyzing the factors involved. Such action means proceeding in the dark, not knowing what to expect or what lies ahead.

The merchandise budget provides both a definite course of future action and a yardstick for evaluating current performance. It enables the retailer to obtain sales by timely buying of merchandise, to adjust his inventories to meet sales requirements, and to plan promotional efforts more effectively. Moreover, it permits him to check the performance of merchandise executives and buyers and fix responsibility therefor, to coordinate all departments of the store into a profit-making entity, and assists the chief financial officer in planning the funds needed to buy merchandise.

The budget also provides a cumulative record of past results, both planned and actual, enabling the retailer to judge the accuracy of past estimates and to improve future ones. It develops a "planning consciousness" and a realization on the part of buyers of the need for facts rather than guesswork and hunches in buying and selling activities. Many retail executives believe that the planning involved in preparing the budget is more valuable to them than the formal budget itself.

□ Requisites of a good budget

To accomplish its purposes, a merchandise budget should: (1) be planned some weeks in advance of its effective date; (2) be as simple as possible and still include the elements that are considered necessary to successful merchandising operations; (3) represent the combined judgment of those whose activities influence its success; (4) cover a period not longer than that for which reliable estimates may be made; and (5) be flexible enough to permit necessary adjustments.

Most of the foregoing requisites of a good budget are self-evident and require little further explanation. It is clear, for example, that in the large organization advanced, careful planning is essential. Such planning should include a review of past years' experience, a reconsideration of the elements to be included, and the weighing of new factors influencing future results.

These steps are necessary to improve the accuracy of forecasts; and the more closely the plans approximate actual results, the more valuable are the budgeted figures.

In the small store where the owner is closely associated with all operations, relatively few elements need to be included in the budget.[1] It is perhaps enough to plan his sales, stocks, reductions, purchases, and gross margin; and this much can be done by reviewing past records, examining stock periodically, and by estimating future needs. As the store grows in size, however, and the owner becomes further removed from the details of his business, it will be increasingly difficult for him to make future plans on such a simple basis as that used in the small store.[2] A system must be established to provide him with a flow of useful information and additional aspects of his business must be included in the budget to increase its value to him.

A workable merchandise budget requires that, in the preparation of estimates, proper weight be given to the opinions of those individuals, such as the buyers and store manager, whose activities influence the success of the plan. This step makes it easier to obtain each executive's cooperation in securing the desired results. And, before the plan becomes effective, the budget should be reviewed by the merchandise manager and the controller. These men will usually suggest revisions to improve the reliability of the estimates; thus, the final figures will represent the composite judgment of a number of persons.

The longer the period covered by the budget the more difficult it is to make dependable estimates. Although the usual period covered is one season of six months, in practice this period often is broken down into monthly or even shorter periods. Sometimes preliminary estimates are made one year in advance and revised each month. The final figures should represent reasonable expectations in the light of prevailing conditions and other facts known at the time. But despite the care taken in preparing estimates, all possible contingencies cannot be foreseen; and it is inevitable that actual results will show deviations from those planned. As soon as these occur, revisions should be made promptly to maintain the value of the budget as a planning and measurement tool.

□ Form of the budget

The form of the budget depends mainly on the purposes for which the information is to be used, the kinds and amounts of data included, the

---

[1] Cf. Figures 14–1, 14–2, and 14–3, below.

[2] For a specific illustration of this point, cf. the Wayman Department Store case in C. H. McGregor and P. C. Chakonas, *Retail Management Problems*, 4th ed. (Homewood, Ill.: Richard D. Irwin, Inc., 1970), pp. 126–30.

period or periods covered, and the preferences of those collecting and using the information. For retailers of fairly comparable operations the forms used differ largely in the manner in which the data are presented rather than in the information itself.

Trade associations in the retail field often recommend the use of standardized forms by their memberships and prepare specific kinds for adoption. Figures 14–1, 14–2, and 14–3 show the profit-planning sheet and the business control form recommended by the National Retail Hardware Association and used by its members for several years.[3] Note that the profit-planning sheet explains the various steps involved in the budget, and the business control form emphasizes planned and actual figures, monthly and cumulatively, for the period covered but does not show those for the previous year. These latter figures, however, may be obtained easily from the comparable form for the previous year.[4] More elaborate forms used in a department store are shown later in this chapter.

■ BASIC ELEMENTS IN MERCHANDISE BUDGETING

Planned sales In most large stores, the first step in merchandise budgeting is to plan sales rather than expenses as recommended by the National Retail Hardware Association (Figure 14–1).[5] This planning is done either in units by price lines or in dollars for the period of time involved. Either approach is dependent on the availability of relevant information. Forecasting sales by units and translating these into total sales figures for the department or store, for instance, is impossible without records upon which to base estimates and to obtain the final results. Similarly, sales in dollars cannot be estimated without reliable data concerning (1) the long-term trend of sales reflecting the normal rate of growth of the business, (2) the conditions outside the business which affect its sales volume, and (3) the conditions within the business which influence future sales. Planning of sales in dollars is almost universally practiced.

Long-term trend of sales A review of past experience is of vital importance in planning sales. Sales by months for several years should be listed

---

[3] Please note that in Figure 14–1 (Profit-Planning Sheet) and in Figure 14–3 (Business Control Form) expense data are provided as well as merchandising data. Our discussion here is restricted to merchandise budgeting; expense budgeting is explained in Chapter 24.

[4] In most budgets, it is customary to include the previous year's figures in addition to planned figures for the budgeted period.

[5] States the controller of Bullock's Department Stores, "Everything is predicated on sales," lending emphasis to the fact that the real basis for all future plans and projections even with computerized systems is the sales figure. Cf. "Sales Figures Still Rated on Top of Retail Program," *Women's Wear Daily*, March 9, 1970, p. 14.

FIGURE 14–1 **Profit-planning sheet for business control**

Profit Planning Sheet

For Business Control

Devised by

THE NATIONAL RETAIL HARDWARE ASSOCIATION

Firm ____________________

Address ____________________

FIRST STEP: Plan expense for this year.

Enter actual expense for last year in each classification. If classifications do not agree with yours, change to agree with your records. **In no case include shop labor and freight with expense.** Then enter planned expense for this year.

Expense Item	Actual Last Year (Use nearest dollar figures)	Planned This Year	Expense Item	Actual Last Year (Use nearest dollar figures)	Planned This Year
A Salaries, Owner			M Depreciation, Delivery Equipm't		
B Salaries, Clerks			N Depreciation, Furniture and Fixtures		
C Salaries, Office			O Depreciation, Building		
D Office Supplies and Postage			P Rent		
E Advertising			Q Repairs		
F Donations			R Heat, Light and Water		
G Store Supplies			S Insurance		
H Telephone and Telegraph			T Taxes		
I Losses, Notes & Accounts			U Interest on Borrowed Money		
K Salaries, Delivery			V Association and Other Dues		
L Other Delivery Expense			X Unclassified		
			Y Total Actual Expense Last Year and Planned This Year		

SECOND STEP: Plan margin for this year.

Determine percentage of margin for the past five years by filling in columns below.

(Use nearest dollar figures)

	19__	19__	19__	19__	19__
1. Enter year for which figures are given.					
2. Enter under each year the amount of merchandise inventory at beginning of that year.					
3. Enter total amount of merchandise purchased each year. Include shop labor and freight.					
4. Add amounts on lines 2 and 3.					
5. Enter amount of merchandise inventory at end of each year.					
6. Subtract amounts on line 5 from those on line 4 giving cost of goods sold during year.					
7. Enter total net sales for each year. Merchandise returned by customers should be deducted first.					
8. Enter cost of goods sold from line 6, same column.					
9. Subtract amounts on line 8 from those on line 7. The result is the margin.					
10. Divide amounts on line 9 by those on line 7. The result is percentage of margin on sales.	%	%	%	%	%

11. Planned margin that can reasonably be expected, based on experience as shown on line 10 .... ______%

THIRD STEP: Find sales required to pay expenses and leave 5% for profit.

12. Deduct 5% for profit from planned margin (line 11) ______% which leaves percentage available for expense of ______%

13. Expense ______% (line 12) equals planned expense of $______ (Line Y, planned column)

14. 1% equals $______ 100% will then be the amount of sales necessary .... $______

Example: If expense is 20% of the planned sales and amounts to $10,000, 1% will be 1/20 of $10,000 or $500. 100% will equal 100 times $500 or $50,000, amount of sales.

Courtesy: National Retail Hardware Association

FIGURE 14–2 Profit-planning sheet, reverse side

FOURTH STEP: Plan monthly sales.

In the first three columns below enter net sales by months for the past three years.

In Column A, add the sales for each month for the three years. Thus line 15, Column A will be the total of January sales for three years. Line 27, Column A, will be the sum of the total sales for three years.

In Column B, enter the percentage of total sales usually obtained in each month. To find, divide total sales for each month, Column A, by the sum of the total sales for three years, line 27, Column A. Thus, if total sales for three years are $150,000 and total sales for three Januaries, $7,500, the probable sales for January will be 7,500 ÷ 150,000 or 5%.

In Column C, enter the planned sales for each month. First, enter in Column C, line 27, the planned sales for the year from line 14 in Third Step. Then multiply the planned sales for the year by the percentages in Column B. Enter result in Column C. Thus, if planned sales are $50,000 and it is found in Column B that 5% of the yearly sales result in January the planned sales for January will be $50,000 multiplied by .05 or $2,500.

(Use nearest dollar figures.)

	19 __	19 __	19 __	Column A Total of Months	Column B Mthly. Pctgs.	Column C Planned Sales	
15. January					%		January
16. February					%		February
17. March					%		March
18. April					%		April
19. May					%		May
20. June					%		June
21. July					%		July
22. August					%		August
23. September					%		September
24. October					%		October
25. November					%		November
26. December					%		December
27. Total					100 0 %		Total

FIFTH STEP: Determine the amount of purchases required to leave a desired investment in merchandise inventory at end of the year. Follow instructions below.

(Use nearest dollar)

28. Enter planned sales for this year (line 14, Third Step)	
29. Enter planned margin (planned sales as above, multiplied by per cent. of margin, line 11, Second Step)	
30. Deduct amount on line 29 from that on line 28. The result is the approximate cost of goods sold	
31. Enter amount of merchandise inventory desired at end of this year	
32. Add amounts on line 30 and 31	
33. Enter actual inventory at beginning of this year	
34. Deduct amount on line 33 from that on line 32. The result is planned purchases for this year	

SIXTH STEP: Plan monthly purchases. (Follow similar procedure as in Fourth Step.)

In the first three columns below enter net purchases by months for the past three years. The amounts should include freight paid, also shop labor. Merchandise returned to wholesalers or manufacturers and credited by them during a given month should be deducted from purchases for the month.

In Column D, add the purchases for each month for the three years.

In Column E, enter the percentage of total purchases usually obtained in each month. To find, divide total purchases for each month Column D, by the sum of the total purchases for three years, line 47, Column D.

In Column F, enter the planned purchases for each month. First, enter in Column F, line 47, the planned purchases for the year from line 34, Fifth Step. Then multiply the planned purchases for the year by the percentages in Column E. Enter result in Column F.

(Use nearest dollar figures)

	19 __	19 __	19 __	Column D Total of Months	Column E Mthly. Pctgs.	Column F Pl. Purchases	
35. January					%		January
36. February					%		February
37. March					%		March
38. April					%		April
39. May					%		May
40. June					%		June
41. July					%		July
42. August					%		August
43. September					%		September
44. October					%		October
45. November					%		November
46. December					%		December
47. Total					100 0 %		Total

FIGURE 14–3 **Business control form**

BUSINESS CONTROL FORM

Beginning Inventory $________________ Estimated Margin______%

	SALES				EXPENSE						PURCHASES						ESTIMATED		
	Planned		Actual		Planned		Actual		Percent of Sales (Cumulative Figures)		Planned		Actual		Percent of Sales (Cumulative Figures)				
19	A Monthly	B Cumulative	C Monthly	D Cumulative	E Monthly	F Cumulative	G Monthly	H Cumulative	I Estimated	J Actual	K Monthly	L Cumulative	M Monthly	N Cumulative	O Estimated	P Actual	Book Inven-tory Q	Profit or Loss R	LINE NO.
January																			1
February																			2
March																			3
April																			4
May																			5
June																			6
July																			7
August																			8
September																			9
October																			10
November																			11
December																			12

Courtesy: National Retail Hardware Association

and trends noted. Has growth been steady or have variations upward and downward occurred? What are the reasons? After past results have been examined, conditions affecting future sales possibilities should be investigated.

Outside conditions Among the major conditions outside the business which influence planned sales are the following:

1. The general business conditions expected during the coming period in the country as a whole and in the particular area where the store is located. Although such conditions usually cannot be forecast accurately, considerable information from a variety of sources is now available to the retailer which makes his estimates more reliable than formerly.[6]
2. The trend of population and its characteristics in the trading area in which the store is located.
3. Changes in the purchasing power of the store's customers and prospective customers caused by shifts in business activity in the particular trading area.
4. Differences in the competitive situation resulting from the addition of new stores, the modernization of existing ones, or through changes in sales promotional activity.
5. Evidence of broad fashion movements which affect merchandise of the type handled by the store. Recent emphasis on teen-age fashions, for example, should be evaluated in the light of the store's policies and practices.

Inside conditions Analysis of present conditions within the store, and those likely to prevail in the foreseeable future are necessary in any sales forecast. Examples of such conditions are the following:

1. Possible revisions of promotional and credit policies such as an increase or decrease in advertising expenditures, the addition or dropping of trading stamps, and liberalization of credit policies.
2. Shifts made in the location or size of space occupied by particular departments or in the arrangement of their physical facilities.[7]
3. Addition of new merchandise lines.
4. Possible expansion of parking facilities for customers.

---

[6] For an illustration of factors considered in making forecasts and how economic changes necessitate readjustments, cf. "Draw Bright Retail 1970s," *Women's Wear Daily*, December 10, 1969, pp. 1, 20, and "Predict Rising Economy, Clouds ahead for '70s," *ibid.*, June 4, 1970, p. 33.

[7] In food stores, for example, cf. K. K. Cox, "The Effect of Shelf Space upon the Sales of Branded Products," *Journal of Marketing Research*, Vol. 7, No. 1 (February 1970), pp. 55–58; and R. F. Frank and W. F. Massy, "Shelf Position and Space Effects on Sales," *ibid.*, pp. 59–66. In drug stores, cf. J. A. Kotzan and R. V. Evanson, "Responsiveness of Drug Store Sales to Shelf Space Allocations," *ibid.*, Vol. 7, No. 4 (November 1969), pp. 465–69.

5. Change in store hours, particularly night and Sunday openings.
6. Opening of new stores and branches, or the modernization of existing ones, and the effect of such actions on the "parent" store or other company stores operated in the area.

Beating last year's figures It is evident that estimating future sales requires considerable study and good judgment. Yet many retailers take the easy way out and set their goal as that of "beating last year's figures." Unfortunately, the solution as to "what lies ahead" for the sales of any retailer is not this simple. For some lines of merchandise and even for entire departments, consumer demand may be on an uptrend; but for others, demand may be leveling off or actually in the declining stage.[8] To illustrate: There is ample evidence that a "new customer" is developing—one with wants quite different from the customer of years past—who is interested in a higher standard of living, better quality merchandise, and in buying on credit to a degree never before experienced. It is essential, therefore, that every retailer, regardless of size, should analyze his sales outlook by his major lines of merchandise. As the late Kenneth Collins wrote, he must "roll with the punch . . . give up volume one place while making it up in another . . . [If he always tried] to beat last year's figures every place, . . . [he might] wind up beating them no place."[9]

Monthly sales estimates When sales for the budget period have been estimated, the next step is to break down this figure by months or some other short period. This step requires an analysis of past experience, weather conditions, seasonal variation, the number of selling days in each month, the special sales events planned for each month, and the dates of such important holidays as Easter.[10] Even so, certain developments may occur that are impossible to forecast and necessitate revisions in estimates. Recent newspaper strikes in such cities as Detroit, Pittsburgh, New York City, and San Francisco are illustrative of such happenings.

Sales forecasts for new stores The factors we have mentioned apply chiefly to established stores. New ones have no past-sales records on which to base future estimates. Therefore, they must rely on the sales volume of other comparable stores or departments in similar locations and make visits to other stores to observe customer traffic and talk with their potential com-

---

[8] Cf. 1967 *Census of Business, Retail Trade, Merchandise Line Sales, United States Summary,* Series BC 67–MLS (Washington, D.C.: U.S. Department of Commerce, March 1970).

[9] "Today and Yesterday in Retailing," *Women's Wear Daily,* April 19, 1957, p. 8.

[10] Some stores also forecast sales in terms of number of transactions, particularly during periods of price stabilization following periods of price increases. Through studying the trend in the number of transactions, an estimate may be made of the forthcoming period. The same is true of the average sale. By multiplying the two figures, the total sales figure for the budget period may be determined.

petitors. Other suitable means should also be employed to arrive at sound estimates of sales volume.[11] Despite the care exercised, the new retailer may find that his forecasts are subject to a substantial margin of error.[12]

□ Planned stock

In planning stock to meet expected sales, the objective is the same as we have emphasized previously—to maintain a balanced relationship between them. This means that the retailer should (1) maintain an assortment of sufficient length and breadth to satisfy the needs of his customers,[13] (2) adjust his inventory to conform to the forward movement of the selling season,[14] and (3) keep his inventory investment under such control that his stock turnover is satisfactory from a profit standpoint. As in planning of sales, it is advisable to estimate a season's requirements and then to divide these estimates into months or shorter periods.

Methods of planning stocks Four methods are commonly employed to plan needed stocks as follows:

1. The basic stock method Under this plan the beginning-of-the-month (B.O.M.) stock is determined for any particular month by adding planned sales for the period to the basic stock figure. Expressed as a formula in terms of retail prices—

$$\text{B.O.M. stock} = \text{Planned sales for the month} + (\text{Average stock at retail} - \text{Average monthly sales})$$

2. The percentage variation (or deviation) method Here the beginning-of-the-month stock is increased or decreased from the planned average stock by 50 percent of the sales variations from the average monthly sales. Or, in terms of retail prices,

$$\text{B.O.M. stock} = \text{Average stock} \times \tfrac{1}{2}\left(1 + \frac{\text{Sales for the month}}{\text{Average monthly sales}}\right)$$

[11] Cf. R. F. Kelley, "Estimating Ultimate Performance Levels for New Retail Outlets," *Journal of Marketing Research,* Vol. 4, No. 1 (February 1967), pp. 13–19.

[12] Among supermarkets opened in 1970, approximately 30 percent experienced sales above those estimated and 36 percent below. Only 34 percent obtained about the sales anticipated. Cf. *Facts about New Super Markets Opened in 1970* (Chicago: Super Market Institute, Inc., 1971), p. 6. How the computer may be used to estimate sales for a new retail development is suggested by D. L. Huff and Larry Blue, in *A Programmed Solution for Estimating Retail Sales Potentials* (Lawrence, Kansas: University of Kansas, 1966).

[13] Cf. H. B. Wess, "Merchandising Assortment and Items," *The Buyer's Manual, op. cit.,* pp. 240–47; and C. G. Taylor, *Merchandise Assortment Planning* (New York: National Retail Merchants Association, 1970).

[14] "There's Less Reason to be Jolly," *Business Week,* December 27, 1969, pp. 14–15; and "Caution Cue for Fall Buys," *Women's Wear Daily,* May 20, 1970, pp. 1, 75.

3. The weeks' supply method When this method is used the planned stock is based upon a predetermined number of weeks' supply as judged by the planned sales for this period. In practice, the planned stock is related specifically to a desired stock turnover.

4. The stock-sales ratio method In this case the planned sales volume for the month is multiplied by the planned beginning-of-the-month stock-sales ratio to ascertain the planned B.O.M. stock.

Regardless of the method or methods used, it is clear that stock planning involves a decision as to the merchandise required at the beginning of the period; that which is to be bought during the period; and that expected to be on hand at the end of the period.

It is important for the retailer to bear in mind that stocks and sales do not necessarily increase or decrease proportionately. As sales increase, for example, stocks may actually decrease, and stock turnover may increase. Moreover, some merchandise in which size is important, such as shoes and dresses, have minimum levels below which stock cannot go, regardless of volume. It is also evident that stocks should be adjusted to the forward movement of the selling season; and that the general business outlook, including availability of merchandise and price trends, needs to be considered.

□ Planned reductions

Planning of reductions is a third essential step in merchandise budgeting. Reductions include markdowns, discounts given to employees and certain types of customers such as clergymen, and stock shortages. Since discounts to special customers and to employees usually are included in markdowns, only planned figures for markdowns and stock shortages are shown on most budget forms. These figures, like others on the budget form, are stated in retail prices.

Markdowns[15] A retailer marks down his merchandise so that his prices will prove satisfactory to his customers and gain their patronage. In other words, the retailer does not *take* markdowns; rather, the markdown is merely his recognition and recording of something that has happened or in his judgment will take place. Markdowns are inevitable and failure to include them in the budget is a short-sighted policy. Careful planning is just as essential here as it is for sales and stocks. Actually, planning markdowns results in reducing their size and frequency because the buyer is made more conscious of them and takes steps necessary to minimize them.

Planning markdowns necessitates determination of their causes for the

[15] As a pricing problem, markdowns are discussed in Chapter 17.

benefit of buyers and others concerned. These causes may be grouped under four main headings: (a) Markdowns growing out of preventable causes, or errors in buying resulting from failure to analyze customer demand adequately and the purchase of wrong styles, sizes, colors, and the like; (*b*) those caused by price adjustments outside the buyer's control, such as declining price levels, changes in price lines, and competitors' prices; (*c*) those attributable to store promotional policies, such as special sales events and multiple pricing, which are also outside the buyer's control; and (*d*) normal operational markdowns, such as price reductions on soiled and damaged goods, sample cuts and remnants, and breakage, which are practically inevitable in buying and selling merchandise.[16]

In addition to understanding the causes of past markdowns, consideration should be given to other factors, both within and without the department or classification, which will probably influence markdowns in the budget period ahead. Among these are the sales promotional events planned for the period; the trend in business conditions, including prices; the nature of the merchandise and its condition at the beginning of the period; the markdowns of comparable stores and departments; and contemplated changes in policies and in the personnel of the department.

Stock shortages Like markdowns, stock shortages are inevitable in retail stores of all kinds despite efforts to prevent them. Consequently, to be realistic they should be included in the merchandise budget.

In planning the stock-shortage figure, which is commonly done on a percentage-of-sales basis, the past experience of the store or department and that of similar stores or departments of such stores should be reviewed.[17] Wide variations exist among different stores and departments selling different merchandise. To illustrate: Discount houses have larger shortages than jewelry stores and costume jewelry sections of department stores have smaller ones than those in self-service variety stores. Contemplated changes in price-change procedure, in checking incoming and outcoming merchandise, in the personnel of the department, and in the frequency of price reductions should also receive study. Moreover, planned "drives" by the management to make employees more "stock-shortage conscious" should be considered as well as efforts made to improve security. Based on such information, the retailer arrives at a budget figure for his stock shortages.

---

[16] For further details on the causes of markdowns, cf. Chapter 17.

[17] Stock shortages in 1970 were at an all-time high. For those experienced by department and specialty stores, cf. the annual reports on financial and operating results (FOR) published by the Controllers Congress, National Retail Merchants Association. Also cf. the discussion in Chapter 13, pp. 328–30, above.

□ Planned purchases

When figures for sales, opening and closing stocks, and reductions have been planned, the planning of purchases in dollars—the fourth major step in merchandise budgeting—becomes merely a mechanical or mathematical operation through the use of certain formulas. Those in common usage, both in terms of retail prices, are as follows:

1. Planned purchases = Planned sales + Planned reductions + Planned increase in stock, or − Planned decrease in stock
2. Planned purchases = Planned stock at end of period + Planned sales + Planned reductions − Stock at beginning of period

These formulas may be applied, as illustrated in Figure 14–4, to an entire store, a department, a classification, or a price line for the budget

FIGURE 14–4 Application of formulas in planning purchases

Formula 1, as applied to the month of September:			
Planned sales		$10,000	
Planned reductions		1,000	
Markdowns	$900		
Shortages	100		
Total			$11,000
Stock on hand, September 1		$20,000	
Planned stock, September 30		22,000	
Planned increase in stock			2,000
Planned purchases in dollars			$13,000

Formula 2, also applied to September:		
Planned stock, September 30	$22,000	
Planned sales	10,000	
Planned reductions	1,000	
Total		$33,000
Stock on hand, September 1		20,000
Planned purchases in dollars		$13,000

period or for any part of the period. Moreover, they are applicable to control in physical units as well as in dollars. Quite obviously, they are useful only when the figures upon which they are based are accurate, timely, and tempered with the buyer's judgment. Improved equipment and EDP have speeded up the availability of the information required for sound decisions and for prompt revisions in estimates. When such adjustments are made, then the computed purchase figure adequately fulfills its function—as a guide to the buyer's judgment, not a substitute for it.[18]

The open-to-buy The "open-to-buy" is that amount, in terms of retail prices or at cost, which a buyer is open to receive into stock during a certain period on the basis of the plans formulated. To illustrate, and using retail prices, assume that planned purchases for October are $1,000. On October 1, therefore, the buyer is open-to-buy that amount during the month. By October 20, he has spent $700 for merchandise already received or due to arrive before the end of the month, leaving $300 to be spent for goods to be received during the rest of the month. In other words, he is open-to-buy $300 on October 20. In practice, however, open-to-buy calculations are not so simple. Adjustments in inventories during the budget period, fluctuations in sales volume, markdowns, and goods ordered but not yet received—all serve to complicate the determination of the amount that still may be spent.[19]

As indicated above, open-to-buy figures may also be stated in terms of cost, although it is customary to state them at retail. Cost figures may be obtained by applying the cost complement of the initial markup percentage[20] to the retail figure. For example, if the initial markup is 40 percent on retail, then the open-to-buy figure at cost may be found by multiplying the retail figure by 60 percent (100 percent − 40 percent).

Many buyers make trips to market to examine offerings of manufacturers and to make purchases of needed merchandise. Prior to such trips they determine their open-to-buy for the remainder of the budget period. It is essential, therefore, that this information be available currently, a need increasingly being fulfilled by automated equipment of various types.

As an example, let us review how the open-to-buy figure may be determined for a store or a department in the middle of a budget period. Assume the following figures for the month of April:

Actual stock, April 1	$37,000
Planned sales for the month	75,000
Planned markdowns and shortages for the month	2,500
Planned stock, April 30	35,000
Planned initial markup	40 percent

[18] The amount and percentage of markup to be placed on goods purchased is an important phase of purchase planning, since the planned stock figures are at retail, whereas the store buyer is faced with cost prices in the wholesale market. Because the initial markup is discussed at some length in the following chapter, further attention is not given to it here.

[19] For illustrations of the problems in determining the open-to-buy, cf. Ed Kieta, "Inventory: Asset or Liability," *Hardware Retailer,* June 1970, pp. 46–47, and "Caution Cue for Fall Buys," *op. cit.*, pp. 1, 75.

[20] The initial markup is the difference between the cost of merchandise and the first retail price placed on the goods. The initial markup percentage is obtained by dividing the initial markup by the initial or first retail price.

Assume further that, during the first half of April, net sales were $28,000; markdowns and shortages, $900; and receipts of goods, $30,000. On April 15, goods on order for April delivery amounted to $20,000 at retail prices. The amount the department is open to buy may be calculated as shown in Table 14–1. If the available stock exceeded the needed stock, the department would be overbought.[21]

TABLE 14–1

Calculation of open-to-buy figures

Needed Stock		Available Stock		
Planned stock, April 30	$35,000	Stock on hand at present ($67,000–$28,900)		$38,100
Planned sales for remainder of month ($75,000–$28,000)	47,000	Actual stock, April 1 ...	$37,000	
Planned markdowns and shortages for remainder of month ($2,500–$900) ..	1,600	Receipts of goods	30,000	
		Total stock handled ...	$67,000	
		Markdowns and shortages to date	900	
		Sale to date	28,000	
		Total deductions	$28,900	
		Goods on order for April delivery		20,000
Total	$83,600	Total		$58,100

Needed stock ($83,600)—Available stock ($58,100) = Open-to-buy at retail ($25,500)
Open-to-buy at cost = $25,500 × 0.60 = $15,300

The open-to-buy form used need not be complicated or elaborate. In fact, simplicity is highly desirable. The best form is one that furnishes the needed information in the most concise manner possible. One store uses that shown in Figure 14–5.

The open-to-buy figure is a guide rather than a set amount which cannot be exceeded. Even though the amount budgeted for purchases during a given period has been spent, further purchases are not impossible if stock is needed to meet customers' requirements. A department may be overbought but still be in urgent need of staple, fast-selling merchandise. To refuse its buyer further funds to make purchases would only serve to intensify the problem, not solve it.[22] Causes of the overbought condition should be

[21] For other methods of calculating the open-to-buy, cf. Murray Krieger, *Merchandising Math for Profit* (New York: Fairchild Publications, Inc., 1968), p. 53.

[22] States one retailer: "To give buyers the greatest chance to do their best job . . . put the Open-to-Buy where the demand lies by recognizing that the traditional retail

FIGURE 14–5 A simple open-to-buy form which provides essential information

DEPT.	YOUR SALES LAST YEAR	ESTIMATED SALES SAME PERIOD THIS YEAR	INVENTORY	UNFILLED ORDERS	YOUR INVENTORY AND UNFILLED ORDERS TOTAL ON	IF YOU PURCHASED NOTHING MORE YOUR INVENTORY WOULD BE ON	HOWEVER YOUR INVENTORY SHOULD BE ON	THEREFORE YOU ARE OPEN TO BUY ABOUT	
	FROM______	TO______						RETAIL	COST

ascertained, however, and measures taken to prevent their recurrence. To condone such a situation without penalizing those responsible encourages the repetition of mistakes.

Small retailers do not collect information of the type described in as great detail or as frequently as large stores, but they do formulate definite buying plans and adhere to them rather closely. Since small operators make few trips to market, they must utilize their time and their finances while there to good advantage. Therefore, although they may not fix formal purchasing limits, they should have rather definite ideas about how much they will or may spend before going to market.

☐ Planned gross margin and operating profit

Determining gross margin is the fifth step in merchandise budgeting. Because net profit is ascertained by deducting expenses from the gross margin, the significance of the latter figure is obvious. The selling price, of course, may or may not be the price at which the goods are originally offered for sale to the public. In other words, the gross margin is the initial markup adjusted for price changes, stock shortages, and discounts to employees.[23] Once the initial markup and retail reductions have been planned, the gross margin may be found by the following formula:

$$\text{Gross margin} = [\text{Initial markup} \times (100 \text{ percent} + \text{Retail reductions})] - \text{Retail reductions}$$

Thus, assuming that the initial markup is 45 percent and the retail reductions are 15 percent, we calculate the gross margin as follows:

$$\begin{aligned}\text{Gross margin} &= [.45 \times (100 + 15)] - 15\\ &= .45 \times 115 - 15\\ &= 51.75 - 15 \text{ or } 36.75 \text{ percent}\end{aligned}$$

In practice, however, the gross margin is often determined from a table, which indicates gross margin percentage figures for inital markup, cash discounts, and retail reductions of various sizes.[24]

During recent years, a rising expense ratio has forced many retailers to

---

dollar Open-to-Buy by department often works to squelch action on the known factors of current interest. Free money for new adventures in merchandise by giving the buyers up-to-date tools for the efficient management of inventory." George Baylis, "Are the Brakes Too Tight to Let the Train Roll?" *Retail Control,* October 1965, p. 25.

[23] Cf. the discussion of the relationship between initial markup and gross margin in Chapter 16.

[24] In the formula given, gross margin and maintained markup are considered to be the same. When cash discounts received by the retailer and alteration costs are considered, the former is added and the latter subtracted from the result to obtain a true gross margin.

plan a higher gross margin to protect their net profit. This has been difficult to accomplish, however, with the result that some types of retailers have experienced a "profit squeeze"; that is, while their sales have increased, they have found it impossible to improve gross margin sufficiently to offset the advance in expenses. An analysis of the annual reports of eighty-six retail organizations for 1969 by a leading trade newspaper reveals a continuation of this trend with first quarter results in 1970 showing even sharper profit deterioration. While sales climbed 9.9 percent in 1969 over 1968, "the ratio of total net profits to total sales dipped to 3.1 percent from 3.3 percent . . . Only 26 firms, or 30 percent, were able to show higher ratios" in 1969 than in 1968.[25]

Whether competitive factors in retailing will allow still higher markups is for the future to determine. Meanwhile, the basic problem as related to budgeting remains—how best to forecast an attainable gross margin figure that will yield, after the deduction of expenses, a satisfactory and reasonable net profit.

■ MERCHANDISE BUDGETING PROCEDURE

A brief description of the budgetary procedure in a department store will illustrate the steps leading to the formation of the budget and show how the budget is used as an operating tool. But again it should be emphasized that the procedure followed, the information assembled, and the timing and use of the data should be adopted to the particular needs of the firm.

□ Initial planning of budget

About three months in advance of the date on which the budget is to become effective, a preliminary six-month merchandise plan for each department by the appropriate classification and showing the results of the previous year, is prepared in the merchandise manager's office.[26] This form, shown in Figure 14–6, is sent to each buyer for the season being planned who reviews past experience and, with the assistance of the divisional merchandise manager, inserts his estimates for the season ahead in the space provided. These estimates are then discussed with the general merchandise manager for approval.

In this discussion the estimates are reviewed carefully and comparisons

[25] Arthur Werfel, "Retail Profit Margins Continue Decline in '69," *Women's Wear Daily*, June 8, 1970, p. 2.

[26] Retailers using a thirteen-month year often replace the two six-month budgets with three budgets, two covering sixteen weeks each and one covering twenty weeks—the so-called 4-5-4 calendar.

FIGURE 14–6 **Preliminary six-months merchandise plan by department and classification** The form may be used for either the spring season beginning in February or the fall season beginning in August.

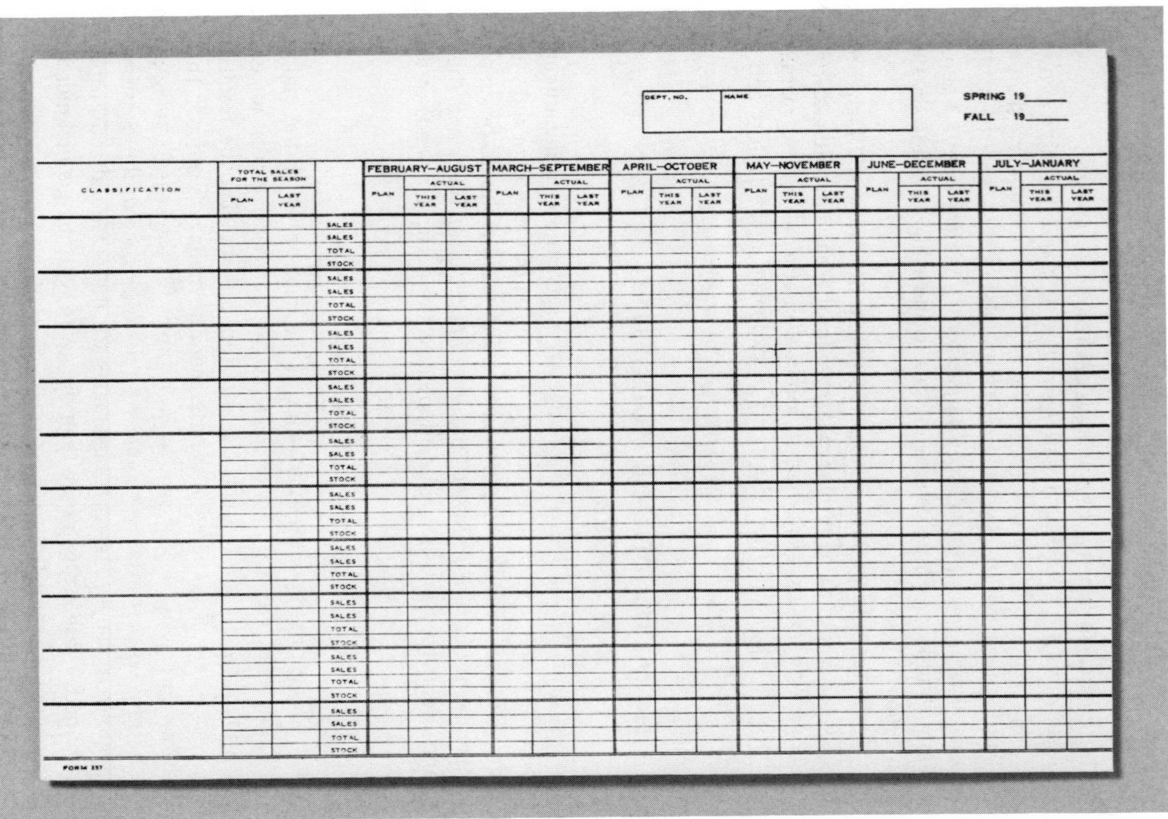

DEPT. NO. | NAME

SPRING 19______

FALL 19______

CLASSIFICATION	TOTAL SALES FOR THE SEASON			FEBRUARY–AUGUST			MARCH–SEPTEMBER			APRIL–OCTOBER			MAY–NOVEMBER			JUNE–DECEMBER			JULY–JANUARY		
					ACTUAL			ACTUAL			ACTUAL			ACTUAL			ACTUAL			ACTUAL	
	PLAN	LAST YEAR		PLAN	THIS YEAR	LAST YEAR	PLAN	THIS YEAR	LAST YEAR	PLAN	THIS YEAR	LAST YEAR	PLAN	THIS YEAR	LAST YEAR	PLAN	THIS YEAR	LAST YEAR	PLAN	THIS YEAR	LAST YEAR
			SALES																		
			SALES																		
			TOTAL																		
			STOCK																		
			SALES																		
			SALES																		
			TOTAL																		
			STOCK																		
			SALES																		
			SALES																		
			TOTAL																		
			STOCK																		
			SALES																		
			SALES																		
			TOTAL																		
			STOCK																		
			SALES																		
			SALES																		
			TOTAL																		
			STOCK																		
			SALES																		
			SALES																		
			TOTAL																		
			STOCK																		
			SALES																		
			SALES																		
			TOTAL																		
			STOCK																		
			SALES																		
			SALES																		
			TOTAL																		
			STOCK																		
			SALES																		
			SALES																		
			TOTAL																		
			STOCK																		
			SALES																		
			SALES																		
			TOTAL																		
			STOCK																		

FORM 237

are made with the previous year's operations and, in some cases, with the operations of several past years. Comparisons may also be made against standards previously set up and also against "outside" statistics, such as those issued by the Controllers' Congress of the National Retail Merchants Association, and Fairchild Publications. This review is designed to insure that plans are realistic and all relevant information is considered. Sometimes it is decided that the anticipated sales should be higher or lower than those estimated; that the ending monthly stocks should be "peaked" earlier or later; or that the timing of purchases should be changed. Adjustments are then made in the figures to represent the best judgment of the group.

☐ Monthly departmental merchandise plan

The second step is the preparation of a merchandise plan for each department. This plan is mainly a recapitulation of the approved figures shown on the initial or seasonal plan (Figure 14–6), but it is for the department as a whole rather than by classifications. The specific form used (Figure 14–7) also provides additional information on deliveries, average stock, rate of stockturn, cash discounts, cumulative markup, and markdowns.

☐ Merchandise statistics report

The third stage in merchandise planning involves preparing a merchandise statistics report for each selling department by classifications. This report (Figure 14–8) shows both planned and actual sales for the particular month and for the season (year) to date. Data are also provided on the end-of-month stock situation and outstanding commitments *on a cost basis.* To permit better control of markdowns, dollar amounts for each classification are shown monthly.

☐ Three-month summary and buyer's guide

Each month, following a study of the merchandise statistics report, projections of anticipated results and a record of current performances are made for each department—and sometimes each classification—for a three-month period. These forecasts are so closely related to current activity that the overall report (Figure 14–9) is known as "The Buyers' Bible."

Let us examine the eight figures in Figure 14–9 used to improve buyers' performance. (1) "Sales" refers to those planned for the current month; (2) "Model EOM" is the planned end-of-month stock taken from the prelimi-

FIGURE 14–7 Monthly departmental merchandise plan

FROM

TO

MERCHANDISE PLAN
(ALL FIGURES AT RETAIL)

DEPARTMENT

		ACTUAL LAST YEAR	PLANNED THIS YEAR	PLANNED % INC. - DEC.		ACTUAL LAST YEAR	PLANNED THIS YEAR	PLANNED % INC. - DEC.
SALES					DELIVERIES			
					AVERAGE STOCK			X X X
	TOTAL				STOCK TURN			X X X
% CASH DISCOUNT				X X X	% MARKDOWN		X X X	X X X

CUMULATIVE MARKUP	%	JANUARY / JULY	FEBRUARY / AUGUST	MARCH / SEPTEMBER	APRIL / OCTOBER	MAY / NOVEMBER	JUNE / DECEMBER	JULY / JANUARY
PLANNED THIS YEAR:	LAST YEAR							
	ACTUAL THIS YEAR							

SPRING / FALL			JANUARY / JULY	FEBRUARY / AUGUST	MARCH / SEPTEMBER	APRIL / OCTOBER	MAY / NOVEMBER	JUNE / DECEMBER	JULY / JANUARY
STOCK END OF MONTH	TOTAL	LAST YEAR							
		PLANNED THIS YEAR							
		ACTUAL THIS YEAR							
DELIVERIES	TOTAL	LAST YEAR							
		PLANNED THIS YEAR							
		ACTUAL THIS YEAR							
SALES		LAST YEAR							
		PLANNED THIS YEAR							
		ACTUAL THIS YEAR							
		LAST YEAR							
		PLANNED THIS YEAR							
		ACTUAL THIS YEAR							
	TOTAL	LAST YEAR							
		PLANNED THIS YEAR							
		ACTUAL THIS YEAR							
MARK DOWNS (DOLLARS)	TOTAL	ACTUAL LAST YEAR							
		ACTUAL THIS YEAR							

F288 BUYER | DIV. MGR. | GEN. MDSE. MGR. | CONTROLLER

nary six-months plan shown in Figure 14–6; (3) "Total Requirements" represents the total merchandise needed and is obtained by adding the planned sales to the planned EOM stock; (4) "Stock on Hand" is available from the merchandise statistics report (Figure 14–8); (5) "Retail Open-to-Buy" is determined by subtracting the stock on hand from the total requirements; (6) "Cost Open-to-Buy" is obtained by multiplying the retail open-to-buy by the cost complement of the cumulative markup; (7) the "Goods-on-

FIGURE 14–8 **Monthly departmental statistics report by classifications**

MERCHANDISE STATISTICS REPORT

Period __________ to __________

CLASS	SAN FRANCISCO SALES				OAKLAND SALES				TOTAL SALES				TOTAL PLANNED SALES		E.O.M. STOCK			OUTSTANDINGS AT COST			MARK DOWNS
	Period		Year to Date		Period		Year to Date		Period		Year to Date										
	TY	LY	TY	LY	TY	LY	TY	LY	TY	LY	TY	LY	Period	Year to Date	TY	LY	Plan				
1A Panels																					
2A Novelty Curtains																					
3A Drapes																					
4A Rugs and Bath Sets																					
5A Decorator Pillows and Chair Covers																					
6A Slip Covers																					
TOTAL																					

DEPARTMENT Draperies, Curtains, and Rugs

ALL FIGURES TO NEAREST HUNDRED $ RETAIL EXCEPT OUTSTANDINGS AT COST

FIGURE 14–9 **Three-months summary and buyers' guide**

DEPT. OR CLASSIFICATION

PERIOD									
ADJ. DATES									
1. SALES									
2. MODEL E. O. M.									
3. TOTAL REQ.									
4. STOCK O.H.									
5. RETAIL O.T.B.									
6. COST O.T.B.									
7. ON ORDER									
8. BALANCE O.T.B.									

REMARKS	DATE	ORDERS	BALANCE	DATE	ORDERS	BALANCE	DATE	ORDERS	BALANCE

Order" figure is easily found by referring to the "outstandings at cost" shown on the merchandise statistics report (Figure 14–8); and (8) the "Balance O.T.B." is simply the cost open-to-buy minus the cost of the goods on order.

To keep the buyer currently informed as to his open-to-buy, each purchase order is entered on the lower part of the form. Thus, by subtracting the amount of the order from the "Balance O.T.B." shown in number 8, the buyer knows exactly how much he may spend during the remainder of the month.

☐ Monthly operating statement

The final step in the merchandise budgeting process is the preparation of a monthly operating statement (Figure 14–10) for each department showing the actual results of the merchandising operations. It is cumulative or progressive in nature and furnishes the desired information for each month and for the season to date.

FIGURE 14–10 Monthly operating statement L.Y. refers to last year, T.Y., to this year.

MONTHLY OPERATING STATEMENT

MONTH: L.Y.	%	MONTH: T.Y.	%		YEAR TO DATE: L.Y.	%	YEAR TO DATE: T.Y.	%
				1 NET SALES - Increase or Decrease %				
				2 RETURNS - % to Gross Sales				
				3 NUMBER OF TRANSACTIONS				
				4 AVERAGE GROSS SALE				
				5 MARKDOWNS AND ALLOWANCES - % to Sales				
				6 EMPLOYEES' DISCOUNT - % to Sales				
				7 INVENTORY SHORTAGE AND SHRINKAGE				
				8 RETAIL PURCHASES - MARKUP %				
				9 CASH DISCOUNT - % to Cost Purchases				
				10 RETAIL STOCK E.O.M. - CUMULATED MARKUP %				
				11 NET WORKROOM COST				
				12 GROSS MARGIN - % to Sales				
				EXPENSES				
				13 SPACE CHARGE - STORE				
				14 SPACE CHARGE - WAREHOUSE				
				15 TAXES AND INSURANCE				
				16 INTEREST ON MERCHANDISE				
				17 MAINTENANCE				
				18 NEWSPAPER ADVERTISING				
				19 ADVERTISING PREPARATION				
				20 WINDOWS				
				21 SIGN SHOP				
				22 OTHER PUBLICITY - DIRECT				
				23 RECEIVING AND MARKING				
				24 DELIVERY				
				25 DIRECT SELLING				
				26 STOCK AND CLERICAL				
				27 MAIL AND TELEPHONE ORDERS				
				28 CASHIER WRAPPING				
				29 CRATING AND PACKING				
				30 BUYING EXPENSES				
				31 RETURN TO VENDOR				
				32				
				33 TOTAL CONTROLLABLE EXPENSE				
				34 INDIRECT EXPENSE				
				35 TOTAL EXPENSES				
				36 NET PROFIT				

DEPARTMENT________________

The data provided are available for the buyers' and their superiors' review and guidance. Comparable figures for the previous year and percentage changes in results between the two years are also entered on the form. When the expenses are entered, it is possible to determine the net profit for the department for the latest month as well as for the season to date. Thus the form furnishes a detailed picture of each department and corrective action is made possible.

LIMITATIONS OF THE MERCHANDISE BUDGET

Despite its widespread use as a tool of management, the merchandise budget has certain limitations. First, it is an aid to the judgment of those who use it and is not designed to control their thinking. Consequently, it does not provide an automatic control over merchandise inventories; it requires review at frequent intervals, and the information it contains must be complete and current. Otherwise the budget will be a failure.

Second, the planning and the operation of the budget involve considerable time, effort, and expense. The benefits derived from its use must be greater than the cost involved in preparing and maintaining it.

Third, some buyers claim that the budget often so restricts their actions that they are unable to take advantage of exceptional buying opportunities which may arise. Since the budget is designed to aid the buyer and not curtail his activities, this complaint deserves further examination. In practice, the buyer ordinarily has a voice in preparing the merchandising budget, so that the planned figures reflect his judgment as well as that of his associates. If he believes that some figures are unattainable or unreasonable in view of the facts as he knows them, then he should object strenuously to these particular items and attempt to convince others of the merit of his stand. At the same time, store officials should provide their buyers with merchandising data quickly and assist them to interpret and use it. After all, the responsibility of buyers and other employees is conditioned upon their knowledge and the authority given them.

Fourth, since the planned figures are based upon analysis and interpretation of known facts and probable future conditions, they are of value only as long as conditions closely approximate those anticipated. When changes occur, revisions in estimates should be made in the light of these conditions.

RESPONSIBILITY FOR THE MERCHANDISE BUDGET

Responsibility for the merchandise budget may be divided into two distinct parts: its formation and its supervision in operation.

Budget formation

In small stores the sole responsibility for developing a merchandise budget rests with the proprietor. The form the budget takes, the type of information collected, and the use made of it will depend upon the needs of the store and the proprietor's attitude toward merchandise planning. Before anything of a formal nature is undertaken, the retailer should appreciate the value of budgeting and be willing to expend the necessary time and effort to establish the system and afford it a chance to work. Too often, the fault with a budget system that fails to work lies not in the system itself but rather in the attitude of those affected by it.

Among large stores responsibility for budget formation is usually shared by the merchandise manager and the controller or treasurer. The actual formation of the budget, however, is based to a large degree upon estimates prepared by buyers or divisional managers in department stores and discount houses and by merchandise assistants, supervisors, and store managers in chain stores. These estimates, however, are submitted to their superiors for final approval. When approved, departmental, classification, or store budgets are commonly consolidated into divisions, and the divisions into a complete store or company plan. Sometimes sales plans or quotas are prepared by the major executives for the company as a whole, after which the sales are divided among stores or departments upon the basis of experience and reasonable future expectations.[27]

□ Budget supervision

Supervision of the budget includes more than mere checking of actual results against planned figures. It also involves follow-up to determine if information in the form desired is being promptly and accurately supplied; if purchases and markdowns are properly authorized; if the open-to-buy figure is frequently being exceeded and, if so, who has approved such action; and if the budgeted figures are being revised when necessary.[28] Furthermore, supervision involves the review of the budget at frequent and regular intervals by merchandise and control executives.

Here again responsibility for the activities described rests with the proprietor in small stores. In larger ones it is divided between the merchandise manager and the controller, aided by those who assist in formulating the merchandise budget. Wherever responsibility lies, supervision should be thorough, consistent, and continuous.

---

[27] Readers interested in computer-programmed merchandise budgets will find of considerable interest L. G. Olson and R. H. Olson, "A Computerized Merchandise Budget for Use in Retailing," *Journal of Retailing,* Vol. 46, No. 2 (Summer 1970), pp. 3–17, 88.

[28] States W. J. Wallis, vice-president of Macy's, New York: "Top management's most important instrument of control is performance reports that are obtainable under a proper system of budgeting." "Budget Follow-Through Stressed to Controllers," *Women's Wear Daily,* May 27, 1970, p. 41.

REVIEW AND DISCUSSION QUESTIONS

1 Explain the main objectives and requisites of a good merchandise budget.

2 Suppose you were told by a small retailer, following your explanation of the advantages of merchandise budgeting to the small store, that budgeting was useful only to large stores and that he had been successful for years without doing any budgeting. How would you reply?

3 Summarize the steps recommended by the National Retail Hardware Association in its Profit Planning Sheet for Business Control. How do you explain "expense planning" as the first step when department stores and specialty stores start with "planned sales"?

4 Based on your reading of the preceding chapter as well as the discussion in this one, what are the relationships between EDP and merchandise budgeting? That is, what specific benefits does EDP make possible in the budgetary process?

5 Explain briefly the major factors that should be taken into account in planning sales for a budget period. To what extent do these factors vary in importance among stores of different kinds and sizes?

6 Discuss the chief purposes of stock planning and the four main methods employed to attain these objectives.

7 How much is the department manager open-to-buy at retail for the month of May in the following situation?

Stock on hand April 1 at retail	$26,900
Outstanding orders for delivery in April at retail	3,650
Planned sales for April	9,600
Planned stock at retail May 1	19,300

8 How do you explain the decline in net profit for most retail stores in 1969 and 1970 despite the increase in sales volume? Be specific as to the reasons.

9 Visit a progressive retail store in your community and determine the merchandise budgeting procedure employed. Describe this procedure in detail, using whatever forms and illustrations are necessary to make your description clear.

10 Discuss critically the statement that "Top management's most important instrument of control is performance reports that are obtainable under a proper system of [merchandise] budgeting."

chapter 15

HANDLING AND CONTROLLING INCOMING MERCHANDISE

Merchandise that is purchased must be delivered to the store and made available for inspection by customers. This process involves the performance of the closely related activities of receiving, checking, marking, distributing, and traffic, all of which should be closely controlled and coordinated.

■ ACTIVITIES RELATED TO INCOMING MERCHANDISE

Receiving refers to the taking of physical possession of merchandise (and also supplies and equipment) at the store and moving it to an area for unpacking and checking. Checking includes a matching of the purchase order against the invoice, the opening of containers, the removal and sorting of merchandise, and the comparing of the quantity and quality of the goods with the specifications of the order. Marking consists of placing the desired information on the merchandise or on price tickets attached to or placed near the merchandise, to aid customers and salespeople in making selections, and to provide information for certain aspects of control. Distributing has to do with moving merchandise from the marking room to the stock room or to the sales floor. Traffic is concerned with the choice of routes for shipments, the filing and collection of damage claims, the auditing of transportation bills, and similar matters.

Adequate performance of these activities is significant both to the customer, who gains from the resulting better service, and to the retailer, who benefits from greater profits. Exclusive of inward transportation, they may cost as much as 1 percent of sales. Consequently, they afford many opportunities through mechanization and automation to reduce costs and improve results. Yet merchandise handling continues to receive insufficient attention by top management in many stores.

□ Requirements of effective performance

Although the methods used to carry out the activities mentioned will vary among stores, certain basic requirements for their effective performance are common, as follows: (1) use of specialized employees when the work is sufficient to justify the cost; (2) development (through work simplification programs) of standardized routines—or specialized ones in exceptional cases—to increase the speed and accuracy with which the activities are performed; (3) centralization of all receiving operations and provision of adequate space for this purpose; (4) the use of mechanical equipment to reduce cost wherever feasible; and (5) maintenance of adequate control records.[1]

Today, many retailers, forced to handle merchandise in unprecedented volume, are turning to the mechanization of receiving, marking, and related functions. Space shortages, higher labor and material costs, and keener competition are accelerating this trend.

□ Centralization of activities common

Except in smaller stores, where receiving, checking, and marking are often done on the sales floor or in a back storage room, centralization of these operations in a separate room is common for the following reasons: (1) It affords better control over incoming merchandise by lessening the danger of lost invoices and discounts. (2) It permits use of specialized employees, insuring more uniform and better quality of work at lower cost. (3)

[1] To this list, some retailers would add a sixth, that is, the use of special bonuses or incentive payments to encourage speed and accuracy on the part of personnel performing these activities.

It overcomes the objections of salespeople who dislike doing such work. (4) It avoids the confusion and congestion that result when goods are opened and marked on the sales floor.

Frequently, ready-to-wear merchandise is opened and checked in a separate room to facilitate its removal from containers, thus avoiding wrinkling, and to speed up its movement to the selling floors. These factors have become less important in recent years, however, because of the widespread practice of shipping apparel by truck and on hangers. As a precaution against theft, jewelry and other items of high value are usually checked in a separate room or in a special section of the main receiving area. Furniture and other heavy household items are customarily received and stored in warehouses or at subsidiary receiving points located near elevators leading to the furniture department. If a basement store is operated and the size of the store warrants it, a separate receiving room is sometimes used for merchandise going to this store. With these main exceptions, however, a centralized receiving room is superior to decentralized or sales floor receiving.

When branch stores first developed, goods were received, checked, and marked in a central facility—and, to a considerable degree this practice is still common. Increasingly, however, to hasten the movement of merchandise to selling floors, many firms have provided space, equipment, and personnel at the branches to perform these operations.[2]

☐ Factors determining location of centralized department

Value and adequacy of the space As a rule, receiving and related activities should be centralized in space that has a relatively low value for selling purposes. In small grocery, drug, hardware, and ready-to-wear stores, these activities may well be centralized in the back room. In the large multifloor store, receiving, checking, and marking activities are usually concentrated on an upper floor, although a receiving point will be located on the ground level. In such cases elevators connect it with the checking and marking room. The space must be adequate to meet the everyday needs of the store and also to provide room for handling merchandise at peak periods, such as Christmas and Easter.

Location in relationship to stock rooms It is customary to have some merchandise opened, checked, and marked on the same floor as the stockroom and adjacent to it. Such a location minimizes the handling of merchan-

[2] Cf. S. M. Huey, Eugene Roth, and Robert Wessel, "Central Warehousing versus Decentralized Receiving," *Retail Control*, November 1969, pp. 29–40. Questions and answers follow.

dise and therefore reduces costs. As a practical matter, moreover, general stock rooms are not so important as they were years ago; in part because of changes in retailers' buying habits,[3] and in part because many retailers now carry much of their extra stock along with their selling stock. Thus when Giant Foods, a supermarket chain, added nonfood items in some of its conventional-size stores, it did so by using former backroom areas. Furthermore, some of the more recently designed stores have many storage areas with each kind of merchandise stored next to or near its appropriate selling department. Thus, in the circular store that Macy's has built in Queens (Figure 5–4), stockrooms are on the periphery of each floor.

Location in relationship to the selling floor Since most merchants still place incoming merchandise on the selling floor as needed, it is desirable that the receiving room and the stock room be readily accessible to the selling areas. Such an arrangement brings savings in personnel, better customer service, and greater sales. Yet, as we have noted, as long as convenient mechanisms for transferring merchandise are available, the receiving room and the sales floor may be widely separated.

For merchandise sold by sample, such as furniture, radios, stoves, and refrigerators, warehouses are operated by large stores in relatively low-rent districts, often at some distance from the stores. Receiving, checking, marking (if any), and storage are performed in the warehouse, with delivery made direct to the customer's home.

■ RECEIVING ROOM LAYOUT AND EQUIPMENT

Efficiency in receiving merchandise, and the activities associated therewith, is dependent in part upon adequate space and its proper utilization, the equipment provided, and the work methods employed. And there are important differences among stores of various size and kind in dealing with these activities.

□ In small stores

Small stores, of course, usually do not require any special facilities or particular layouts in the receiving area since merchandise is commonly unloaded onto a sidewalk or is carried into the back room. It is unpacked and marked at the convenience of an employee or the manager. Some stores have stationary or double-deck, portable tables in the receiving area. As merchandise is unpacked, it is sorted, placed on these tables, checked, and marked.

---

[3] Cf. the discussion of hand-to-mouth buying on pp. 247–48, above.

☐ In larger stores

In larger stores the layout of the receiving area depends upon the system used in handling the merchandise received. Three methods are widely employed, while a fourth—which involves the use of mechanized conveyors—is increasing in use. Perhaps the most common one is the use of *stationary tables* or *check-marking tables,* as illustrated in Figure 15–1. These tables are

FIGURE 15–1 **Flow chart showing checking and marking operation with stationary tables**

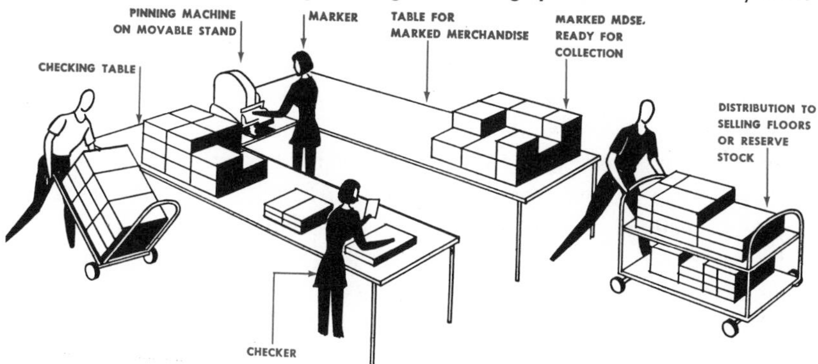

Courtesy: Dennison Manufacturing Co.

This method of operation is based on parallel stationary tables, with attaching machine on movable stand between them. Tables and machine stand are exactly the same height (about 36″) and space between tables is just wide enough for marker and machine. Overhead electric connection permits machine to move the length of the table. The operating method is as follows:

1. Receiver or stockman brings packages containing merchandise to be machine-marked to checking table.
2. Checker matches invoice to package, opens, piles merchandise on table, checks invoice, leaving retailed invoice with merchandise.
3. Marker moves pinning machine opposite merchandise, and machine-marks, piling marked merchandise on the table at her *right.* As piles of boxes are marked, she moves machine so that merchandise to be marked, and space to pile it after marking, always are right at hand.
4. Stockman collects marked merchandise from table, takes to forward or reserve stock.

This operating plan shows a single unit for one attaching machine. It is capable of indefinite expansion by increasing the length of the tables and adding more pinning machines. It is adaptable to portable table operation by using lines of portable tables in place of the stationary tables; or to a combination of the two systems by having the checking table stationary and the tables for marked merchandise portable.

frequently placed in a room large enough to allow cases to be brought in and unpacked. Merchandise is then sorted, and placed on tables. After being checked and marked, it is moved to the stock room or to the sales floor.

The second method used is the *portable table.* Goods are placed on tables with wheels where they are sorted and checked for quantity. Tables are then moved to another section for marking. This method minimizes a major disadvantage of systems employing check-marking tables, just described. When both checking and marking are performed in one location, buyers sometimes enter the receiving room to check the receipt of goods that they are eager to have sold and remove merchandise before the quantity check has been completed. When buyers are not allowed in the section where quantity checking is done, the danger of their removing merchandise prior to the quantity is minimized.

A third method used to facilitate the checking and marking of merchandise is known as the *bin method.* This involves dividing the receiving room into two sections, one for checking and one for marking, with a series of bins or openings dividing the sections. As merchandise is checked on tables in one section, it is shoved through the bins onto tables in the other section, where marking takes place. As with the portable-table system, this method tends to keep buyers from removing merchandise that has not been checked, since they are not allowed in the checking sections of the receiving room. But it necessitates an extra handling of all goods and may cause some confusion in marking if unlike goods are mixed in a bin.

Most large retailers use a fourth method—*mechanical* conveyor belts or

FIGURE 15–2 Use of conveyor in marking The picture shows the central conveyor and several spurs.

Courtesy: Rapids-Standard Co., Inc.

roller conveyors—to move merchandise from the receiving point through the checking and marking operations. At the appropriate checking point, for example, the merchandise may be moved off the central conveyor for examination and later moved on to the marking area. Here a conveyor spur detours it while marking is performed (Figure 15–2). Even the movement to the selling area or to the stock room may be by mechanical equipment.

■ RECEIVING PROCEDURE

To clarify our discussion of layout and the facilities required for the effective handling of merchandise, some methods employed in receiving and checking have already been mentioned. We now return to the actual receiving of merchandise and note the steps necessary to prepare the goods for sale.

□ Activities at the receiving point

At the receiving point—station, dock, or sidewalk—all boxes, cartons, and other containers should be inspected at time of delivery to determine their condition and any damage to merchandise. If there is no such indication, the receiving clerk signs the carrier's receipt; but, if damage is detected, the receipt will be signed only after the word "Damaged" has been written upon it. Such action facilitates the filing of damage claims later. This receiving point inspection does not involve any examination of the merchandise itself. Goods are then moved into the receiving room by means of trucks, elevators, chutes, and roller conveyors as soon as possible. If any damage, loss, or shortage is revealed when containers are opened and the goods are checked, a claim should be filed promptly against the transportation agency, the vendor, or others responsible.

□ Receiving records

Recording of incoming shipments is essential. The information commonly includes the date and hour of arrival; apparent condition of the shipment (e.g., any damage); weight; delivery charges (if paid by the retailer); shipper's name and location; form of transportation—such as railroad, express, or parcel post; person making the delivery (e.g., name of truck driver); number of pieces; amount and number of invoice;[4] and the

[4] Invoices from local vendors and, to an increasing extent, from those located at a distance when shipments are made by truck, usually arrive with the merchandise, so that they are available to the receiving clerk when he makes out the receiving record. On other out-of-town shipments, invoices come by mail and usually arrive before the mer-

FIGURE 15–3 A receiving record which permits attachment of the invoice

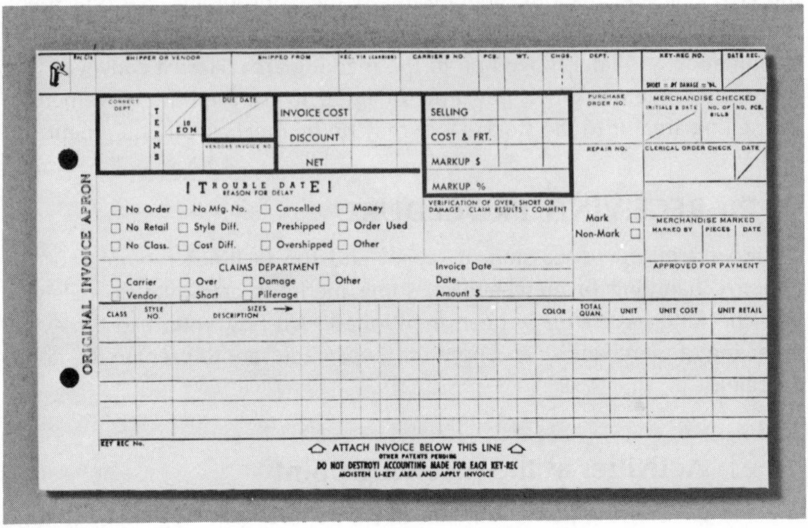

department for which the merchandise is intended. Figure 15–3 shows a typical receiving record. Currently, some large retailers are replacing or supplementing this type of receiving record with punched cards which can be "fed" directly into a computer.

Several benefits result from the use of a receiving record: It provides information useful in cases of disagreement between vendor and the store relative to the receipt of a particular shipment. By placing the invoice number on the receiving record, each invoice is associated with the proper merchandise. This action is especially important for partial shipments and when many shipments are received from one vendor. The receiving record also allows management to check on the length of time invoices and merchandise are held in the receiving room. Finally, by requiring that invoices be checked against receiving records before they are paid, the store avoids paying for merchandise not yet received.[5]

When the receiving records are completed and proper notations are placed on containers, the merchandise is moved to the checking and mark-

---

chandise. If so, they sometimes go to the receiving point, where they are held until the arrival of the merchandise. The receiving record number is placed on the invoice and on the receiving sheet or slip, if the latter is used.

[5] This requirement is not always fulfilled, especially in cases in which buyers are located at some distance from vendors. If past relationships have been satisfactory, goods are sometimes paid for before their receipt in order to take advantage of the cash discount. If discrepancies arise, adjustments are made without difficulty.

ing room. This movement may be by hand, by movable tables, by chutes, or by some mechanical means such as trucks, elevators, or roller conveyors.

■ CHECKING PROCEDURE

Checking consists of four quite distinct steps: First, the invoice is checked against the purchase order; second, the merchandise is removed from the shipping containers and sorted; third, the merchandise is checked for quantity; and, finally, the goods are checked for quality. Two or more of the steps may be performed by the same employee.

□ Checking invoice against purchase order

By comparing the invoice with the purchase order it can be determined (1) if the description and quantity of the goods billed are the same as those ordered and (2) if the terms of sale (dating and discounts) on the two forms are the same.

□ Unpacking and sorting merchandise

Despite the trend we have mentioned to ship wearing apparel by truck in garment bags,[6] most merchandise still arrives at retail stores in various types of containers and cannot be checked until unpacked and sorted. In some firms these tasks are not performed until invoices are available. This policy prevents removal of goods before they are checked in, thus causing a stock shortage. Or if the store makes a record of the merchandise removed from the container, places the goods in stock, and later finds a discrepancy when the invoice arrives, there is no way of rechecking the shipment. Although, as a general rule, it seems wise to avoid opening containers until invoices are available, it is probably best—if the goods are needed on the sales floor—to take the chances involved and unpack the merchandise at once.

□ Checking for quantity

The two main methods of checking incoming merchandise for quantity

[6] Dresses, blouses, coats, and similar items are frequently placed in garment bags and hung in trucks for shipment. Upon arrival at destination, the garments are easily removed, marked, and transferred to the selling floor. Problems of unpacking, eliminating wrinkles, and marking are simplified.

are the direct check and the blind check. Variations of these methods—the semiblind check and the combination check—are also used by some retailers. Basically, selecting the method for a particular store depends upon the attitude of management regarding the tightness of control and upon whom it places responsibility for careful checking.

The direct check Under this system incoming shipments are usually checked directly against the invoice. If the invoice is not available, the shipment is usually held unopened until the invoice arrives. If the checking room becomes crowded or if certain merchandise is needed on the selling floor, however, "dummy" invoices are made out; checking then proceeds as if these dummy invoices were the originals. In some firms the direct check is against the purchase order rather than the invoice.

The main advantages of the direct check are its speed and simplicity, its economy, and the ease of rechecking discrepancies between the checker's count and the invoice quantity. Probably its chief disadvantages are the possibility of careless checking and the piling up of goods in the receiving room to wait for invoices, thus delaying the movement of merchandise to the selling floor. This delay has been minimized in recent years, however, by the increased number of vendors enclosing duplicate invoices with their shipments. Despite these limitations, the direct check continues to be the most common method of checking for quantity in small stores, and probably in large ones.

The blind check This method consists of listing for each shipment the kinds and description of the merchandise, the quantities, the shipper, and other pertinent information about the merchandise received. The checker is furnished a blank prepared form or merely plain sheets of paper for this purpose. This procedure results in more careful checking, allows the task to be performed immediately and the merchandise placed on sale, cost figures are not divulged to checkers, and invoices are moved promptly to the accounts payable office.

As for disadvantages, the blind check is more expensive than the direct check since extra time is required to prepare the list and check it against the original invoice. In addition, if merchandise is removed from the receiving room before the list is checked against the invoice, a recheck is impossible. Here again, however, the practice of including packing slips in shipments has removed the uncertainty regarding their contents and has led some checkers to use these slips to make up their list to check against the invoice.

Other checking methods The *semiblind method* of checking saves time and cost as compared with the blind check. A checker is given a list of the items in a shipment but with the quantities omitted. He simply counts the merchandise and enters the quantities. The time saving is partially offset, however, by that required in the invoice office to prepare the lists for the checkers.

The *combination check* is a combination of the direct and blind checks. Its object is to obtain an accurate count of the goods received and speed up their removal from the receiving room. If invoices are available when the merchandise is received, the direct check is used; but if goods arrive and an invoice is not at hand, the blind check is used.

Regardless of the method or methods employed to check merchandise, most stores check quantities merely on the basis of the quantities listed on the outside of the packages included in the shipment. To illustrate: A shipment of nylon hosiery, packed three pairs to the box, would be checked for quantity simply by counting the boxes and multiplying by three. Checking each package is left to the marker when he attaches price tickets. This process is facilitated by marking machines which can print any specific number of price tickets. The use of such equipment is explained on pages 373–75 below.

Checking *bulk merchandise* presents a different problem from that of other goods. When this merchandise is received, both the number of bulk containers and the weight of the contents of each container must be checked. Care is needed in examining containers for substandard weights. Fruits and vegetables, for example, are often repacked by shippers and, in the process, loss of weight sometimes occurs; or the time element alone may be responsible for shrinkage.

Handling quantity discrepancies When the quantity check reveals a discrepancy with the invoice, and the merchandise is still in the receiving room—as it will be if the direct check is used—the checker calls a supervisor to make a recheck. In the small store, of course, the proprietor makes the recheck. If the merchandise has already been placed in stock and a recheck is not possible, the original count serves as the basis for a claim against the shipper, or against the carrier if it is his fault. When shipments contain less than the quantity shown on the invoice, it is customary for the retailer to make a compensating deduction from the billed amount when payment is made to the vendor. If an overage is revealed, however, the buyer is asked how to handle the situation. If he believes that the extra merchandise can be sold, payment will be made accordingly; otherwise, payment for the invoiced amount will be made, and the extra merchandise will be returned to the vendor.

□ Checking for quality

All too frequently the emphasis placed on the quantity check results in partial neglect of the quality factor. The usual basis of quality checking is the buyer's experience, his knowledge of quality and values, and his memory of the merchandise purchased. Increasingly, however, larger firms are providing their buyers with more objective standards for judging quality.

Some buyers purchase samples in showrooms and check merchandise received against these samples. Others are aided by standards and specifications established by the government, the trade, the vendor, or the retailer himself. The National Bureau of Standards, for instance, has established standards for some items and allows manufacturers to certify that their products conform to these standards. And the Fair Packaging and Labeling Act of 1966, commonly referred to as the "Truth-in-Packaging Act," contains certain provisions related specifically to product quality through listing of ingredients on labels.[7] A few of the large department stores, mail-order firms, and chain stores have testing laboratories in which samples of incoming merchandise are tested for quality.[8] The facilities of outside testing organizations are also available.

■ MARKING MERCHANDISE

Marking merchandise by means of price tickets, gummed stickers, an automatic imprinting system, or even by hand before placing it on sale is common practice among retailers. In very recent years significant developments in electronic and other equipment for recording sales, controlling inventory, authorizing credit and other purposes has revolutionized marking systems and sharply increased the types and varieties of tickets and tags used.[9] Yet some retailers handling highly standardized goods or merchandise marked by the manufacturer, or which is sold at a single price, dispense with price marking. Even in these cases, however, some marking may be necessary to provide better stock control and to facilitate the taking of inventory.

□ Some guidelines for marking

Certain basic principles guide the retailer in marking his merchandise regardless of the methods or devices he uses in the process.

1. Merchandise should be marked legibly, neatly, and as permanently as possible without damage to the goods. The use of rubber stamps and marking machines has helped to solve this problem.

---

[7] Cf. the discussion in Chapter 19, pp. 467–68 below. For additional details cf. C. F. Phillips and D. J. Duncan, *Marketing Principles and Methods*, 6th ed. (Homewood, Ill.: Richard D. Irwin, Inc., 1968), pp. 127–28.

[8] Cf. the discussion of testing bureaus on pp. 273–74, above.

[9] One business publication notes that for the retailer "the big trouble with price tags is that there are so many of them [and that while] keypunch systems dominate the tag field now . . . 'magic wands' are on the way [with] machines, not the clerk . . . [reading] the tag." Cf. "Retailers Search for the Right Price Tag," *Business Week*, January 23, 1971, pp. 52–53.

2. All necessary information should be placed on the price ticket, if one is used, at the time the goods are marked. These data should be limited to facts that supply needed information to those handling the goods, including customers, and to facts that are used by buyers for merchandise control purposes and for guidance in future purchasing. In small stores the cost of the item, in code, and the retail price will usually be given. The code may consist of some word or phrase which does not contain a duplication of letters.[10] In department and specialty stores, for instance, the information ordinarily includes the season letter and week in the season, department number, the size and color of the goods, the retail price, and sometimes the manufacturer and his style number.

3. Merchandise should be so marked as to minimize manipulation of prices either by employees of the store or by customers. This end is usually accomplished (a) by the use of marking machines and specially prepared ink and *(b)* by attaching tickets to merchandise so securely that their removal is difficult. Unused price tickets should not be allowed in selling departments.

4. When a record of articles sold daily is desired for control purposes, price tickets with perforated stubs should be used. The stubs furnish information as to the articles selling best as well as the most popular colors, styles, and sizes. They also enable the department head to maintain a perpetual inventory.

5. Certain items should be marked in some manner, usually in addition to the price ticket, which will prevent their wear or use by the customer before they are returned. To millinery, for instance, some retail stores attach a tag reading: "If this tag is removed, this merchandise may not be returned for credit." Other stores use specially printed price tickets indicating that certain goods cannot be returned for sanitary reasons.

6. Merchandise should be marked as quickly and economically as possible consistent with accuracy and the type of merchandise handled. The actual application of this principle is, of course, a matter of good management.

□ Some additional reasons for marking

Other reasons for marking merchandise other than those mentioned in the preceding section are apparent: (1) Listing the price, size, color, and other data aids salespeople in serving customers. (2) Marking creates customer goodwill since customers prefer to deal with retailers who treat all

[10] Among cost codes in common use are "trade quick," "blacksmith," "rusty nail x," and "young blade."

patrons the same, and marking is an indication (but not a guaranty) that the store does so. (3) The markings, especially the price, encourage the customer to serve herself, thus reducing sales effort. (4) Marking simplifies taking the physical inventory. (5) Marking the date the goods were received aids management in selecting items to be sold through price reductions, thus keeping fresh merchandise in stock.[11]

☐ Marking procedures

At least three procedures are followed in marking merchandise. *Immediate marking,* the one most widely used, involves the marking of each item of merchandise in the desired manner as promptly as possible after its receipt. A second method, known as *delayed marking,* refers to the practice of writing the retail price and other necessary information on the outside of the containers only. Then the merchandise is moved to a reserve stock room. When it is needed on the sales floor, the containers are opened and the individual items marked. This procedure is practicable for items such as canned goods and fast-selling staples and also advisable for merchandise on which prices change frequently; in such cases bulk marking,[12] saves the expense of re-marking. Perhaps its chief disadvantage is that insufficient information may be given by the markings to provide adequate control of merchandise.

Under the third procedure, *group marking,* containers are marked on the outside when received, as in delayed marking, and the goods moved to the reserve stock room. Later, they are moved to the selling floor *without* marking the individual items; instead, the merchandise is grouped in set locations and the price indicated by a nearby price tag. This procedure has developed primarily to reduce the cost of marking and re-marking goods and to speed up their delivery to the selling floor. It is widely used by food stores and those selling low-priced variety goods, drug accessories, and inexpensive automobile supplies. Supermarkets and other stores which operate on a self-service basis, however, find it necessary to mark the retail price on individual items; otherwise, the check-out is slow and often inaccurate.

---

[11] A very recent development is the adoption of "open dating" by food chains. This new service "consists of opening or sharing with the public their 'freshness' codes—the dates that they or their manufacturers stamp on food products so that store clerks know when to pull them from the shelf. [Formerly these codes were] numbers, letters, and tricky combinations of both. Under the new system, the shopper . . . can now" determine when the particular item was purchased. Cf. "Chains Woo Consumers with Open Dating," *Business Week,* January 16, 1971, pp. 48–49.

[12] The term "bulk marking" is used by some retailers, however, to denote other practices. When a grocer, for example, places a large box of soap chips on his sales floor and writes "80¢ per pound" on the box, he considers such action to be bulk marking.

☐ How and where merchandise is marked

The desired information may be placed on the merchandise or its container in several ways—by writing, using a rubber stamp, or by attaching labels or tickets or tags of various kinds to the merchandise by hand or by using a machine designed for this purpose. Some stores attach a print-punch tag to each item, part of which may be detached at the point of sale and fed into an electronic data processing system for automated information feedback. Whatever kind of ticket or tag is used, it must be adapted to the system of merchandise control employed and to the type of sales registering equipment used. This is particularly true for the newer electronic devices discussed in a later chapter.[13]

Hand and rubber-stamp marking Hand marking, of course, is most common in small retail stores. In the hardware and paint store, for example, the salesperson may write "$3.98" on each quart can of paint as he places it on the shelf; or he may enter the price on a gummed label which he attaches to the merchandise.

Rubber stamps have largely replaced gummed labels, pin tickets, and string tickets for marking a wide variety of merchandise. In stores selling packaged foods, drugs, and cosmetics, for instance, the retail price is often stamped on the top of each package prior to removal from the bulk container.

Price tickets Since marking by hand and rubber stamps is time consuming, often results in errors, and the markings may be blotted out before the merchandise is sold, many small retailers and practically all large ones currently attach price tickets to merchandise. Many kinds are used, even within a single store. Some of the common types of tickets are shown in Figure 15–4.

It is customary to employ electric or hand-operated equipment to print the designated information on the price tickets and often to attach the tickets to the merchandise. Recent improvements in equipment permit the use of all kinds of paper stocks—gummed, ungummed, heat-seal, pressure-sensitive as well as heavy tag or board stocks. The hand-operated Kimball Stamp-It (Figure 15–5) prints on a fast-peeling label which is easily attached to the items by being hand-pressed against it. Another hand-operated machine, the Monarch Model 116—Senso Ply (Figure 15–6), both prints and applies the label as the operator squeezes the handle. Figure 15–7 shows the electrically operated Monarch Model 28 Dial-A-Pricer which provides 7 characters for stock control and prints 200 tickets, tags or labels a minute. For the retailer who wants a more automatic operation, the Kimco 2000 (Figure

[13] Cf. Chapter 25, "Sales Transaction Systems."

FIGURE 15–4 Some forms of price tags and tickets in common use

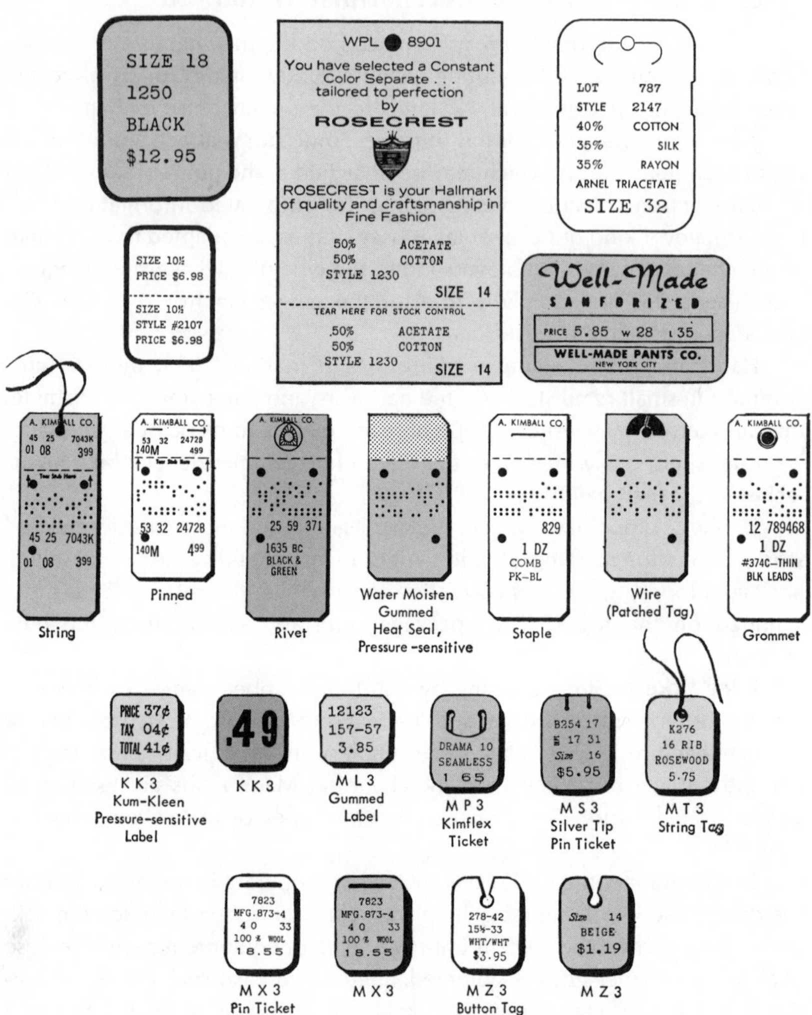

Courtesy: Kimball Systems, a Division of Litton Industries

15–8) imprints and applies pressure-sensitive labels to conveyorized or hand-fed merchandise at the rate of 150 per minute; while the Kimball PM 75 (Figure 15–9) both prints and punches tags with detailed information in machine language which is automatically converted for processing in any conventional or computer system. Most of these machines turn out such complete price and inventory tickets that the stubs are picked up by

FIGURE 15–5 **A low-cost, hand-operated labeling machine, the Kimball Stamp-It**

Courtesy: Kimball Systems, a Division of Litton Industries

mechanical or electronic means and the resulting tabulations are used for stock control purposes.

Where merchandise is marked Small retailers frequently have salespeople do the marking on the selling floor in their spare time. This should be done only as a last resort because any cost saving that results is usually more than offset by frequent errors, slower marking, and less legible price entries or tickets. It is advisable, therefore, to have marking concentrated in the receiving room or in a checking and marking room. Such a location also facilitates the use of marking machines.

Authorizing marking Regardless of who does the actual marking of merchandise or where it is done, proper authorization is necessary to ensure that it is done correctly and promptly. In the small store, the proprietor may do this by entering the proposed price on the invoice. In the large store the usual practice is to instruct the markers through the invoice (or a copy of it) after it has been entered for payment, checked against a

FIGURE 15–6 **The Monarch Model 116—Senso-Ply—for printing and applying labels**

Courtesy: Monarch Marketing Systems: A Subsidiary of Pitney Bowes

copy of the purchase order, and the goods are examined (a quality check) and priced by the buyer.

Some stores use a priced sample to instruct the markers. Under this plan the buyer takes a sample of the merchandise when he makes his quality check and places on it a ticket that contains the information desired on all the items. The sample is then turned over to the markers.

Numerous other stores now authorize marking through a process known as *preretailing*. This practice, which requires that the buyer place the retail prices of the items being bought upon the store's copy of the purchase order at the time the order is placed, affords two main advantages. First, it forces the buyer to consider the retail price at the time of purchase, thereby discouraging purchases which do not seem likely to provide the desired

FIGURE 15–7 Monarch Model 28 Dial-A-Pricer provides seven characters for stock control

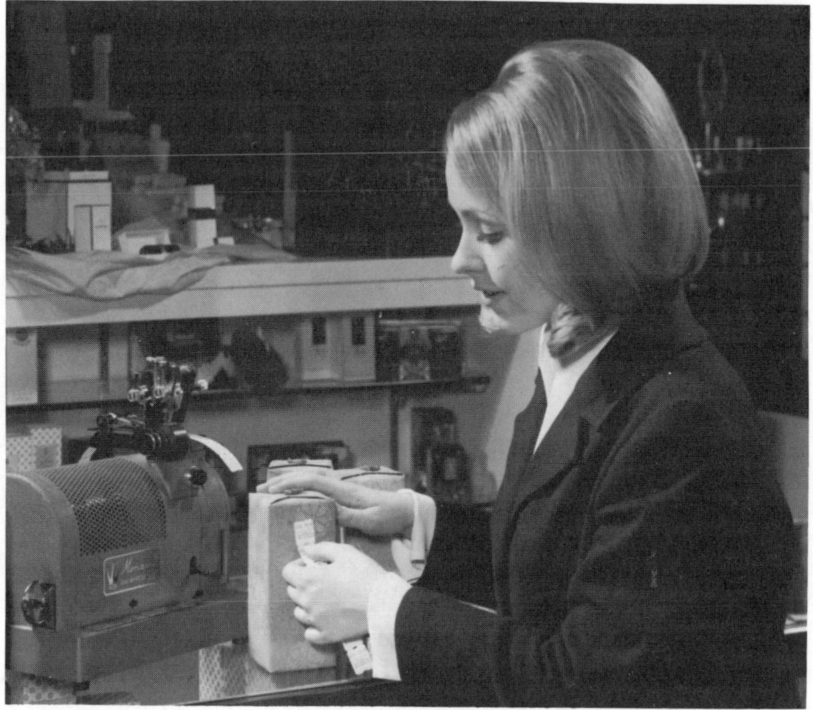

Courtesy: Monarch Marketing Systems: A Subsidiary of Pitney Bowes

mark-on. Second, marking is expedited because it can begin as soon as the goods arrive. In addition, some retailers have discovered that preretailing, by allowing practically all records to be maintained at retail (rather than both at retail and at cost) prices, simplifies and speeds up their accounting systems.

Source marking Some large retailers, to reduce marking expenses and to move goods more quickly to the selling floor, have induced vendors to mark merchandise prior to shipment,[14] a practice known as source marking.[15] In some cases the stores prepare price tickets and send them to vendors for attaching to the goods; in other cases, vendors furnish the price

[14] An address by the Director of National Standards Programs of Kimball Systems entitled "The 'Why' and 'How' of Source Marking" is available from offices of that organization. Also cf. "Source Marking—An Answer to Out-of-Stock Conditions," *Department Store Economist*, November 1967, pp. 22–23, 57.

[15] Where manufacturers have placed fictitious prices (that is, relatively high prices to mislead customers) on the tickets, the Federal Trade Commission has opposed the practice.

FIGURE 15–8 The Kimball Kimco 2000 for imprinting and applying pressure-sensitive labels

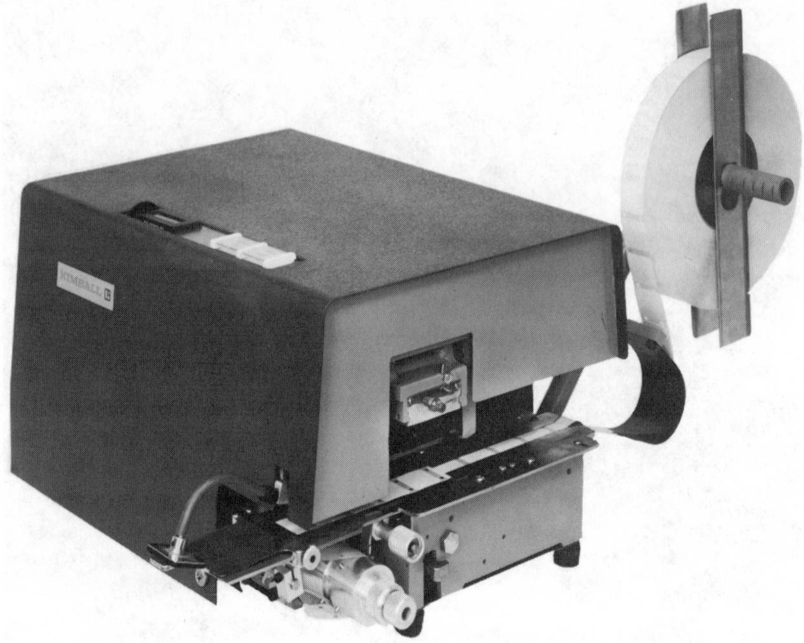

Courtesy: Kimball Systems, a Division of Litton Industries

FIGURE 15–9 A highly automatic machine that prints and punches up to 29 columns of information into tags, the Kimball PM75

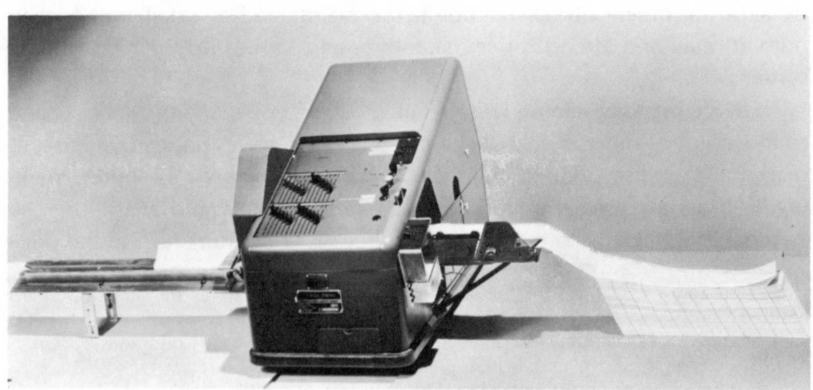

Courtesy: Kimball Systems, a Division of Litton Industries

tickets, enter the information supplied by the retailer, and affix them to the merchandise.[16] Although staples and fair-trade goods, because of their greater price stability, are the best candidates for source marking, men's clothing, women's hosiery, and greeting cards are also frequently source-marked. Source marking makes it easier for the retailer to utilize EDP more effectively, thus improving the feedback of information to the manufacturer and enabling him to promptly adjust his production to the popularity of specific items or lines. For some goods a standard tag code and format has been developed. (See Figure 15–10.)

FIGURE 15–10 Source marking standard tag code and format

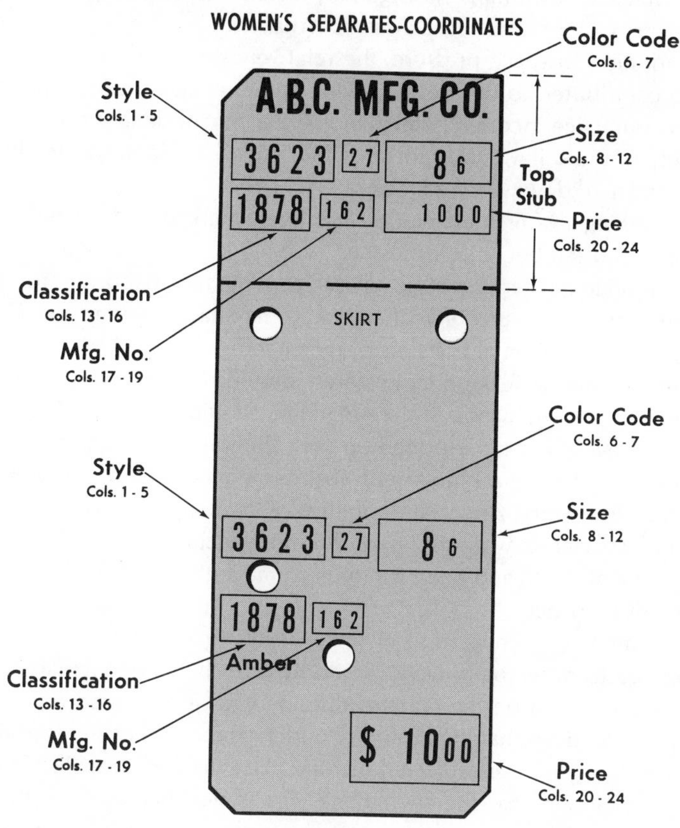

Courtesy: National Retail Merchants Association

[16] The relationship of this practice to inventory control is discussed in James Anderson, "Source Marking and Inventory Control," *Retail Control*, February 1969, pp. 33–39; and *ibid.*, April–May 1969, pp. 17–24.

It should be noted, however, that manufacturers marking merchandise for their retailer customers must let all competing customers know that the service is available; otherwise they will run afoul of the Robinson-Patman Act.[17] Practically all retailers agree that a further extension of source marking should be encouraged to reduce retail costs.

Outside marking of fashion merchandise A growing trend in marking practice is the hiring of outside carrier firms to mark fashion goods. Stimulated by the opening of new stores or branches and the inability of the central location to expand its processing space fast enough to permit prompt movement of merchandise to the other stores, many retailers now engage in this practice, including Montgomery Ward, Gimbels, Marshall Field, Alexander's, Goldblatt's, and Davison's (Atlanta).

In addition to space pressure, the relatively short life of fashion items has also contributed to this development. Some retailers believe that, since under this practice incoming merchandise can be checked and moved immediately to the selling floor, three or four days are added to the "life" of an item and markdowns are reduced.

Re-marking After merchandise has been marked and placed on the sales floor, it often becomes necessary to re-mark it. Price rductions (markdowns) or price increases may be advisable; some merchandise returned by customers must be re-marked; price tickets may have become soiled, torn, or lost; and departmental transfers of merchandise may call for re-marking. Since *all* marking (at least in large stores) should remain under the control of the marking-room manager, all re-markings should also be done under his supervision even if it is performed on the selling floor or adjacent thereto. Specialized marking machines are available for this purpose. As previously suggested, by centralizing responsibility for marking, this activity is performed by specialists who are faster and more accurate; control over price tickets is maintained; and there is more assurance that all price changes will be properly recorded.

In re-marking merchandise to lower levels (markdowns), retailers follow two quite different policies. Some believe that the original (former) price should remain on the merchandise, perhaps just crossed out and the new price added, so that the customer understands a "bargain" is available. Other retailers prefer to replace the entire price tag and show just the new price. They reason that the re-marking cost is not increased by this procedure, the resulting price tag is clearer and more attractive to the customer, and the pricing psychology is better—they want to avoid the implication of:

---

[17] Cf. the discussion on pp. 279–82, above. Section 2(e) of the Robinson-Patman Act outlaws discriminatory furnishing of "services or facilities connected with the processing, handling, sale or offering for sale" of commodities.

"We tried to get you to pay $19.95 for it; you didn't fall for that high price, so we'll now try a lower one."

■ DISTRIBUTION OF MERCHANDISE

After incoming merchandise has been marked, it is ready for distribution[18] to the reserve stock room or to the selling floor. Information as to where the merchandise shall go is supplied by the proprietor in the small store, by the store manager in the chain store, and by the buyer or department head in the large store. Usually, the receiving-room manager knows from past experience and the type of merchandise where to move the goods. In some large stores, however, the buyer may give distributing instructions at the time he "retails" the merchandise. If the merchandise is placed in the stock room, it is released only on requisition from the buyer. In smaller stores employees marking the merchandise know what is to be done with the goods. And all employees of these stores are usually allowed in the stock room to obtain merchandise when it is needed on the sales floor.

■ TRAFFIC DEPARTMENT

Our discussion thus far has pertained largely to the movement of merchandise *after* it reaches the store. But the retailer is also vitally interested in its transportation from the vendor to his store, *i.e.*, in obaining faster deliveries and in reducing costs. Since "no buyer can, in addition to his other duties, be familiar with the everchanging transportation field, nor can the average vendor know or employ a traffic expert who knows the best routes and schedules to . . . which the company's product is shipped,"[19] large-scale retailers have established traffic departments to fill this gap.

The functions of a traffic department include the selection of the best routes for shipments and tracing them when necessary; the checking of freight classifications and rates, including the auditing of transportation bills; the payment of transportation charges; the placement and collection of loss and/or damage claims; and other activities associated with the physi-

[18] On the complex problems involved in handling merchandise in large stores, cf. R. S. Crumme, "Materials Handling Systems in the Downtown Store," *Stores,* April 1969, pp. 16–18. How conveyors are used to move goods to and from the selling floor in a two-level store is explained in D. X. Feinstein, "Conveyors Solve Handling Problems in Two-Level Illinois Store," *Progressive Grocer,* January 1970, pp. 51–58.

[19] E. H. Wabler, "Traffic, Receiving, and Marking," in *The Buyer's Manual,* 4th ed. (New York: National Retail Merchants Association, 1965), p. 378.

cal movement of the merchandise. Savings and benefits realized usually far exceed the cost of performing these functions.[20]

Since the routing of merchandise affects transportation cost, speed of delivery, and the care with which the merchandise is handled, the traffic manager should work with buyers to instruct vendors as to how merchandise should be shipped. Some traffic departments hold classes for buyers to make them "transportation conscious." When overcharges result from failure to follow instructions, vendors should be billed for the amounts involved. It is also advisable to audit all freight bills at regular intervals, to make certain that merchandise has been shipped in the correct classification, at the proper rate, and that computations on the bills are correct.

The tracing of delayed shipments is also important. Usually, this means maintaining contact with the carrier until the shipment is located. Filing of claims for loss or damage against the vendor or the carrier should be done promptly and full information supplied to support them.

■ HANDLING INCOMING MERCHANDISE IN CHAIN STORES

Among chain-store firms operating their own warehouses, there is a considerable variation from the procedures so far discussed. Receiving and checking are performed at two points—in the warehouse and again in the store. In the former, special facilities are employed to handle the large volume of goods, such as pallets moved by highlift trucks, overhead track towveyor systems, towline arrangements, roller conveyors, and electronic controls.[21] The location, size, and layout of distribution centers or warehouses are also very important in the control of merchandise handling costs. Consequently, much time, effort, and expense are devoted to these problems.[22] The magnitude of the undertaking is illustrated in Figure 15–11.

But not all chain organizations find distribution centers desirable. States the chief executive officer of Montgomery Ward:

> Ward had been structured for small stores supplied by *distribution centers*. We had to eliminate the distribution centers and go to big stores. We also had to reorganize to get away from some department store concepts . . . being practiced. . . . The big thing here was a new procurement policy, which would be part of a complete mass

---

[20] Cf. David Breedon, "Controlling the Costs of Merchandise Transportation," *Stores*, April 1969, pp. 30–34.

[21] Cf., for example, "Towveyor System Solves Warehouse Handling Woes," *Stores*, October 1969, pp. 37–38.

[22] Cf. "Ten Factors in Siting A Distribution Center," *Stores*, April 1969, pp. 16–18.

FIGURE 15–11 J. C. Penny's distribution center complex in Buena Park, California In addition to warehousing and shipping selected lines of merchandise to Penney stores nationwide, it serves as a common stockroom permitting economical distribution of merchandise in Southern California. An automated fashion distribution facility is also provided for fast dispatch of such items to 348 stores throughout the West. Supplementing these services, among several others, is a West Coast Data Center in which computers process tickets for computer written reordering of merchandise in 800 stores, process data for central mechandise and fashion distibution, and handle all charge account records and billing as well as complete payroll records for area stores and field offices.

merchandising system extending from the suppliers at one end to the customers at the other. . . .[23]

At individual chain stores, receiving typically consists of having a truck back up to a rear door (or a front one) to unload the goods. They are then moved by conveyor or by hand inside the store. Before the unloading starts, the truck driver hands the manager an invoice. He checks for quantity and returns the invoice to the driver or sends it back to headquarters by mail. The driver is usually required to sign for shortages. Checking for quality is performed at the warehouse.

In some of the large retail units operated by chain organizations, the handling of merchandise within the store is substantially mechanized. One

[23] Robert Booker with John McDonald, "The Strategy That Saved Montgomery Ward," *Fortune*, Vol. 8, No. 5 (May 1970), p. 169.

firm, for instance, uses 1,200 feet of overhead conveyor track which electrically moves aluminum carriers from loading dock to 8 different stock areas. Since the merchandise has already been received, checked, and marked at a warehouse, it is ready for sale within 30 minutes after reaching the store.

In organizations with relatively small units, prices are set at headquarters; and each store manager is notified of those to be used. Actual marking is usually done in the store, although there are many exceptions to this practice. In chain supermarkets a wide variety of methods are employed. Prices may be marked on cases at the warehouse or after reaching the store. Individual items may be marked when received at the store, in the backroom as needed, or when placed on the shelves.

Women's apparel chains quite typically place price tickets on garments before shipment from their warehouses. Many of the drug, variety, and hard-lines chains have installed the latest type of pricing devices at their warehouses, where they pre-mark some merchandise, thus decreasing cost and increasing accuracy. Grocery, drug, hardware, and variety chains depend largely on group marking—writing prices on large containers and bins for floor displays and using shelf tickets—while self-service stores commonly write or stamp the price on the individual item. Store employees usually perform whatever re-marking is necessary.

Merchandise shipped directly to the individual chain stores by vendors is received, checked, and marked by methods somewhat comparable to those used in independent stores. But checking for quality is frequently under the control of headquarters employees, who will make spot checks. Prices are usually set at headquarters, but the actual marking is done in the store. Vendors generally send invoices directly to headquarters for payment.

■ ORGANIZATION FOR INCOMING MERCHANDISE

Although in small stores the proprietor, perhaps assisted by a sales person, handles incoming merchandise, in larger ones responsibility for receiving, checking, marking, distributing, and traffic is commonly centralized in the operations manager or superintendent, with a receiving or a traffic manager exercising day-by-day control.[24] Some large and medium-size organizations, however, place these activities under the controller or the merchandise manager. Both of these arrangements may be entirely logical. Yet other firms are now appointing distribution managers (some-

[24] Cf. R. C. Bond, "Department Store Organization," in *The Buyer's Manual, op. cit.*, pp. 14–15.

times with the rank of a vice president) with broad responsibility over traffic, warehousing, and inventory control. In deciding where to place responsibility, probably executive personalities and previous experience are the major factors considered.

■ REVIEW AND DISCUSSION QUESTIONS

1 Discuss concisely the basic requirements for handling of incoming merchandise. In view of their importance, how do you explain the fact that top management has not given more attention to the activities involved?

2 Summarize the merits and limitations of centralizing receiving, checking, and marking activities. In your judgment is centralization advisable when branch or suburban stores are operated by the company? Why?

3 Visit the receiving departments of two of the following kinds of stores: (*a*) a small neighborhood grocery; (*b*) a supermarket; (*c*) a men's shop; or (*d*) a discount house. Prepare a report evaluating the layout of this department in each of them.

4 Explain the procedural steps necessary to properly check incoming merchandise.

5 Differentiate clearly among the chief methods of checking merchandise (*a*) for quantity and (*b*) for quality.

6 Formulate five currently useful guidelines for marking merchandise in large and medium-size stores.

7 Visit a department store and a supermarket in your area and determine the methods each employs to mark its merchandise and the reasons therefor.

8 Explain the current status of mechanization in the receiving, checking, and marking of merchandise.

9 Discuss the major functions of the traffic department.

10 How do the receiving, checking, and marking activities of chain stores differ from those of single-unit retail establishments? What significant current trends are evident?

chapter 16

JUDICIOUS PRICING

Judicious pricing decisions are essential for two reasons: (1) The retailer depends upon his prices to (*a*) cover the cost of his merchandise, (*b*) pay most of his expenses, and (*c*) provide most of his profit. He often receives some funds from other sources, such as service charges to customers, rental of space for leased departments, and income from outside investments. But he normally obtains most of his revenue from merchandise sales. (2) The customers' opinions concerning his prices—whether they consider the store to be an expensive or inexpensive place to shop—will help determine whether they patronize him or someone else. Thus he will want to have prices that will appeal to his customers, cover his expenses, and maximize his profits.[1]

■ CONSIDERATIONS INFLUENCING PRICING DECISIONS

To achieve his objectives, a retailer must exercise sound judgment in making two types of decisions. The first group of decisions concerns his general price policy. First, he has to decide on the general relationship of his prices to his competitors; whether he will follow a "one-price" policy; and

[1] Of course, the retailer (like every other businessman) also has other goals in mind, such as the growth of his company and the firm's prestige in the community.

whether he will organize his prices into "price lines." Then he (or his employees) must price the individual items he carries in conformance with these general policies. Sometimes the supplier establishes the retail price for a product, as discussed in the next chapter, and in such cases the retailer can only decide whether or not he is willing to handle the item at the specified price.[2] In most instances however, the retailer is the one who sets the final resale price. In so doing, he must keep the following points firmly in mind.

☐ Consistency

The retailer's price policies should be consistent with the rest of his basic operating decisions. If he plans to charge relatively high prices, he will have to offer the merchandise, convenience, and/or services that will make those prices acceptable to his potential customers. In contrast, one recent study suggests that customers will not believe that a store is inexpensive, no matter how low its prices may actually be, if its atmosphere seems too luxurious.[3]

☐ Long-run point of view

The retailer should also always maintain a long-run point of view in pricing. For example, when he opens his business he may plan to sell at very low prices for the first few months in order to build up his clientele. His short-run profits will suffer as a result of this policy, but it may attract enough customers and build sufficient repeat business to maximize profits in the long run.

☐ Price level and maximum profits

Even in the long run the retailer may want to keep his prices at a fairly low level. Selling at high prices does not necessarily produce maximum profits. Profits result from the relationships among sales, prices, costs of merchandise, and expenses of operation. Sometimes these factors will indicate maximum profits with prices higher than those now being charged, but they may also indicate that profits will increase if prices are reduced.[4]

To illustrate: Retailer A follows a high-price policy and consequently only attracts those customers who find his location or merchandise especially appealing. His total annual volume is $200,000, merchandise cost

---

[2] Cf. the discussion of resale price maintenance, pp. 418–24, below.

[3] F. E. Brown, "Price Image versus Price Reality," *Journal of Marketing Research*, Vol. 6, No. 2 (May 1969), pp. 185–91.

[4] Cf. also, the discussion of policies of pricing below competitive levels on pp. 389–91, below.

$140,000, operating expenses $52,000, leaving $8,000 as net profit. But Mr. A decides to experiment with lower prices. This policy proves so attractive that his sales gradually expand to $300,000 a year. Since he receives greater discounts on his larger purchases, his merchandise cost expands at a somewhat lower rate than sales, becoming $204,000 and leaving a gross margin of $96,000. Although some expenses also increase as a result of the added sales, others such as rent, heat, light and power, remain relatively unchanged. His present employees handle part of the additional work, so payroll increases at a lower rate than sales. As a net result, operating expenses only rise to $58,000. Thus in spite of selling at lower prices, Mr. A's profit increases from $8,000 to $28,000.

□ Pricing as an art

Successful retail price setting is an art as well as a science. Formulas and general price policies provide a basis for price making, but any experienced merchant will then use judgment, intuition, and trial and error to adjust the resultant prices. Even so, he cannot be absolutely certain as to how his customers will react to any specific price. Sometimes raising the price will make the item more appealing to the customers, in other instances a reduction may be needed to move the goods.[5] But over time a successful merchant develops a "feel" or judgmental sense for the prices that are appropriate to his cost, market and competitive situation.

■ GENERAL PRICE POLICIES

The retailer must make a number of fundamental decisions about his general pricing policies and practices. The most basic pricing decision concerns the relationship between his prices and those of his competitors.

□ Competitive position

As one might expect, most retailers tend to set their prices at about the same level as their major competitors. But this statement needs two qualifications: (1) Most retailers tend to think of merchants of the *same type* as their major competitors. Thus a small independent grocer will usually consider other nearby independent grocers, rather than large supermarket chains, as the competitors whose prices he has to meet. Similarly, a neighborhood druggist will usually try to match the prices in other neighborhood drugstores rather than those in discount house pharmacy departments. (2)

---

[5] Benson P. Shapiro, "The Psychology of Pricing," *Harvard Business Review*, Vol. 46, No. 4 (July–August 1968), pp. 14–25 ff.

Retailers, such as supermarket operators, who sell wide assortments of convenience and non-shopping goods, usually will not try to match their competitors' prices item for item. They expect to be higher on some items, lower on others, and are more concerned with the general price image or impression their store reflects.

Many shopping goods retailers, on the other hand, give item-by-item price comparisons a great deal of attention. Today practically every department store and most large specialty store organizations employ comparison shopping staffs that check their store's prices, merchandise, and service against its competitors'. Some department store firms have decided that they will run such competitive departments as drugs and toiletries and small electric appliances at a loss, if need be, in order to match discount house competition. At times those stores have even advertised that they will give a refund to any customer who finds the same item at a lower price in any other store in town.

Pricing below competitors' level Some merchants go one step beyond simply meeting competition and actually try to undersell their competitors. Many chain store, mail order, supermarket, and discount house organizations, among others, believe in seeking their profits through the use of relatively low prices to attract a large volume of sales. The net result, of course, has been a rise in their customers' standard of living, as well as an advance in the firms' profits.

Underselling retailers usually have certain definite characteristics. They are "hard" buyers, since they must acquire their merchandise at low cost to permit the profitable use of low prices. They often operate with relatively low-cost physical facilities and they may dispense with many of the services that other stores offer. They frequently limit their stocks to the fast-moving items; customers may be expected to assist themselves to some degree; and credit and delivery services may be either curtailed or entirely eliminated. These retailers are often strong advocates of private brands whose prices cannot be directly compared with competitors' offerings. And these underselling stores generally devote their advertising to announcing price "specials."

In other words, retailers who adopt a low-price policy must use consistent policies in the other aspects of their business. Those who do not will soon find themselves characterized by the sign in the window of a vacant store: "We undersold everybody."

1. Discount house pricing Discount houses illustrate many of the low-price retailing characteristics cited above.[6] Some discount store firms are now "trading up" and offering more elaborate facilities and services, but

[6] Cf. the discussion of discount houses in Chapter 1, pp. 20–23.

many have been able to keep their operating costs at relatively low levels. One study of 42 discount store firms reported a weighted average expense rate of about 21.3 percent of total sales in 1969–70, considerably below the 32 percent typical of similarly sized department stores.[7]

Consequently, discount stores can cover their total operating expenses and earn satisfactory profits with prices below those of many competitors. Although few careful price studies are available, the concensus is that discount store nonfood prices range from 5 to 15 percent lower than those of competing stores, and that discount food prices are about 5 percent below conventional supermarket levels.[8]

2. Price wars A price war may develop when a number of competing retailers try to undersell each other. The participants in such a war keep reducing their prices drastically in efforts to attract each others customers. The war will often be confined to a few fast-moving items, such as milk, cigarettes, gasoline, or bread, but those items may be reduced to one-half or one-third their normal price before the battle is over.

These wars end in various ways. All of the competitors may simply withdraw from the struggle when they find that their rivals quickly match their price reductions. In other cases, the retailers or their suppliers may have to take some form of joint action before prices move upward. Sometimes the retailers hold a meeting and, in effect, agree upon a truce. In other cases the suppliers have used various methods to stop the retail price cutting. Major oil companies have terminated some local gasoline price wars by supplying their gasoline to the service stations on consignment and thus retaining the right to fix final selling prices.[9]

Legislative action has often been suggested as a means of eliminating price wars. But one careful student of the subject—with whom the present authors concur—concludes that such a program would cause further reduc-

---

[7] Earl Brown and Panna Kulkarni, *Operating Results of Self-Service Discount Department Stores 1969–70* (New York: Mass Retailing Institute, 1970), p. 15. The discount and department store figures are not directly comparable, however, since the two types of stores handle somewhat different merchandise assortments with the discount stores receiving a greater portion of their sales in relatively low expense lines. Also leased departments (whose expenses are only partially included in the store expense report) play a much more important role in discount than in department stores.

[8] Cf. Rachel Dardis and Louise Skow, "Price Variations for Soft Goods in Discount and Department Stores," *Journal of Marketing* Vol. 33, No. 2 (April 1969), pp. 45–50; Eugene Beem, "Turmoil in the Supermarket Industry," in *Retail Management Strategy: Selected Readings,* David Rachman, ed. (Englewood Cliffs, N.J.: Prentice-Hall, Inc., 1970) pp. 240–48; Robert Minichiello, "Comparative Prices in Discount Food Stores and Conventional Supermarkets," *Journal of Retailing*, Vol. 46, No. 3 (Fall 1970), pp. 57–67.

[9] Some courts have cast doubt on the legality of this technique, especially when there is any evidence (1) that dealers were coerced into accepting the new program or (2) that dealers were brought together in groups, thus implying horizontal price-fixing. *Sun Oil Co.* v. *Federal Trade Commission,* CA–7 (August 1965). Also see *Simpson* v. *Union Oil Co. of Calif.,* 377 U.S. 21 (1964).

tions in "competitive activity in an era in which competition is, if anything, too soft."[10]

Pricing above competitors' level Other retailers regularly follow a policy of selling some or all of their merchandise at prices above their competitors. Retailers who follow this policy recognize that many nonprice considerations, such as those outlined in the following paragraphs, may attract customers to their stores. These merchants often find that they can operate their businesses successfully, in spite of charging higher prices, if they offer some of the following features.

1. *Satisfactory services* Many customers are willing to pay somewhat higher prices in order to receive desired services. They will trade with the store that provides more helpful personal attention or that has more generous delivery, credit, and returned goods policies, even if its prices are slightly above those of its competitors. By way of illustration, many of the conventional, older department stores offer such services more liberally than do the new stores that have been opened by Sears, Roebuck & Company or Montgomery Ward & Company. Consequently the operators of the conventional stores can charge somewhat higher prices without losing too many of their customers to the lower-priced outlets. Similarly, a recent study suggests that small retail stores are more likely to build profitable trade with such service elements as "speed of service," "satisfaction of customer complaints," "management and employees' knowledge about their merchandise," and "helpful and friendly attitude of employees," than by offering low prices.[11]

2. *Prestige* A store that has historically set the standard for quality in its community may have acquired considerable prestige in the eyes of its customers. This prestige helps remove the store from direct price competition with its competitors, and often enables it to charge a higher price than other stores. Thus a woman's coat carrying a label from Saks Fifth Avenue, Neiman-Marcus, I. Magnin, or Marshall Field is "different" in the customer's view, and might command a higher price than a similar coat sold by a less prestigious firm.

3. *Convenient location* Some people will pay a premium for the convenience of being able to shop at a handy location. Neighborhood grocery, drug, and hardware stores, for example, tend to have higher prices than the big shopping center supermarkets and discount stores, but some customers

---

[10] Ralph Cassady, Jr., "Price Warfare—A Form of Business Rivalry," in *Theory in Marketing,* 2d. ed., Reavis Cox, Wroe Alderson, and S. J. Shapiro, eds. (Homewood, Ill.: Richard D. Irwin, Inc., 1964), p. 379. For another of Professor Cassady's valuable analyses of price war behavior, cf. his "The Price Skirmish—A Distinctive Pattern of Competitive Behavior," *California Management Review,* Vol. 7, No. 2 (Winter 1964), pp. 11–16.

[11] Hal Pickle, Royce Abrahamson, and Alan Porter, "Customer Satisfaction and Profit in Small Business," *Journal of Retailing,* Vol. 46, No. 4 (Winter 1970–71), pp. 38–49.

will pay a few cents extra per item rather than travel to the lower-priced outlets. A drugstore or giftshop in an airport terminal, a hamburger stand in a football stadium, or a store in an isolated community may have a virtually "captive" market because of its location, and thus be able to command unusually high prices.[12]

4. Extended store hours A retailer who keeps his store open when the other shops are closed may be able to charge higher prices than his early-closing competitors. Many small neighborhood shops have done a large share of their business in the evening and on Sunday. Chains of "convenience stores" and "bantam superettes," that sell a limited assortment of the most popular items but that stay open very long hours, have become an important part of the grocery trade.[13]

The price advantage that comes from long hours tends to disappear, however, as more and more supermarkets, discount houses, and shopping centers stay open evenings and Sundays.[14]

5. Exclusive merchandise An assortment of items or brands that are not available in competitive stores will also give a merchant some freedom from direct price competition. Sometimes a retailer will obtain an exclusive agency for a certain manufacturer's products so as to make certain that none of his immediate competitors can get the same goods. A letter from a cosmetic manufacturer to his exclusive dealer in Passiac, New Jersey illustrates this type of arrangement: ". . . yours is the only outlet for XYZ products in the entire city. In the entire state of New Jersey, we have no city in which more than three stores handle XYZ products, and we sell to no store known as a price cutter or with a history of price cutting. We therefore believe that you will have no problem maintaining the full retail markup in XYZ products." Similarly, a fashion goods retailer will often try to get vendors to agree that no other store within a certain radius will be allowed to purchase the same styles.

The difficulty of escaping price competition Businessmen generally prefer nonprice competition to price competition for two reasons: (1) They believe that customers who are attracted by nonprice factors will prove more loyal than those who shop around for low prices; and (2) competitors may encounter more difficulty in matching nonprice factors than in meeting price changes.[15]

---

[12] A few airport shops, catering only to international travelers, feature luxury merchandise at low prices because of special exemptions from domestic taxes and import duties. The shops at Shannon, Ireland, and Amsterdam, Holland, are especially famous in this respect.

[13] "Growth Continues as Key Word for Convenience Stores," *Progressive Grocer*, April 1970, pp. 114–18.

[14] See Chapter 21.

[15] Cf. Jules Backman, *Advertising and Competition* (New York: New York University Press, 1970), p. 3.

But a merchant can seldom completely escape price competition even though he might prefer to engage in nonprice rivalry. A store may be able to charge somewhat higher prices as a result of its prestige, services, location, and hours, but too broad a difference will drive customers away. In fact, any price difference causes a store to lose some customers, since there are some who have little regard for a store's services or prestige. The wider the price differences become, the more customers leave and go over to the lower-priced store. Of course, customers sometimes become suspicious of quality if prices seem too low. This is one of the reasons why pricing calls for skill and judgment.

Moreover, it is particularly difficult to escape price competition on staple items and well-known brand merchandise. The thriftier buyers of these items can go from store to store and learn the prices that various retailers are asking for comparable goods. Retailers who sell style items are somewhat less likely to be affected by competitive prices since customers cannot always make direct price comparisons on these items.

Finally, most stores find that they have some competitors who have about as much prestige and offer as many services as they do. Hence, even a relatively minor price differential between such stores may cause a fairly rapid shift of trade to the lower-priced establishment. A retailer must keep the prices of such comparable stores in mind when he is pricing his own goods, since he may not be able to charge any higher prices than they do.

Private brands Some retailers gain a certain amount of freedom from direct price competition by displaying their own "private" brand or label, rather than the manufacturers' "national" brand, on some or all of the items they sell.[16] A consumer making an ordinary shopping trip cannot compare and rate the values of two different private brands sold by two different retailers with anywhere near the precision that she can compare the same two merchants' prices for a specific national brand product. Some prestige stores are able to command fairly high prices for private brands that have won consumer acceptance. For example, S. S. Pierce & Co., a famous grocery firm in Boston, has successfully sold a premium-priced line of packaged, gourmet foods under its own label for many years. The line has become so popular with consumers throughout the country that Pierce now sells the line to other stores.

But most private label grocery, toiletry, electric appliance, staple clothing, and similar lines are normally sold at lower retail prices than comparable national brands. Chain store organizations and other leading users of private brands follow this policy for several reasons. (1) Consumers usually

[16] A & P's Red Circle coffee and Anne Page jellies, Sears' Allstate tires, and J. C. Penney's Towncraft shirts are examples of retailers' private brands; Maxwell House coffee, Goodyear tires and Arrow shirts are examples of manufacturers' brands. Also see the discussion of retailers' and manufacturers' brands on p. 27 above.

will not pay as much for a store-brand product as for a well-known, well-advertised national brand. In fact, many customers will select the national brand in preference to a private brand in spite of a price differential. A & P, one of the most enthusiastic private branders in the grocery trade, obtains only about one-fifth of its sales volume from private brand products, and private brands probably account for only about 12 percent of all chain store grocery sales.[17] (2) Low prices for the store's own brands, not available in competitive outlets, help build strong ties with the store's customers. One chain store merchant who features low-priced private brands says: "I think our private label mix has helped to reinforce our fair price-quality image. It strengthens our overall identity with the public."[18] (3) Private label merchandise usually costs the retailer substantially less than comparable nationally branded goods. Consequently he often receives a much greater margin from the private brand item in spite of its lower selling price. One chain sells its own brand of paper towels for about 5 cents less per roll than comparable national brands and still obtains a 30 percent markup (difference between cost and selling price) as compared to 10 or 12 percent on the national brands.[19]

□ One-price policy

Most American retailers claim to follow a one-price policy. A retailer who adheres to this policy charges the same price to everyone who buys the same item in comparable quantities under similar conditions. Thus, if his price for a particular brand of men's socks is $1.50 a pair, every customer who comes into the store, regardless of who he may be, will be charged $1.50 per pair for that brand.

This policy builds up customer confidence in the store, since the customer never has to worry whether he is being charged more than someone else. It also saves a great deal of time and skill that might otherwise have to be spent in bargaining with customers. The one-price policy helps rou-

---

[17] "Trends in Share of Private Label," *Progressive Grocer,* July 1968, pp. 56–57. In contrast, Sears, Roebuck and Co. and Montgomery Ward & Co. report that private brands produce more than 90 percent of their total sales of branded merchandise.

[18] "Behind the Private Label," *Chain Store Age* (Supermarket Executives Edition), August 1968, p. 57. Also cf. "Who Will Buy My Beautiful Label?" *Supermarketing* (August 1970), pp. 7–8.

[19] "Trends in Share of Private Label." *op. cit.* Many private brands, of course, are manufactured by firms selling nationally advertised brands. For example, cf. the packaging of physically identical evaporated milk under private labels and its own label by the Borden Company. "Legal Developments in Marketing," *Journal of Marketing,* Vol. 29, No. 3 (July 1965), pp. 67–68. While sometimes the merchandise sold under the two kinds of brands is quite comparable, in other instances there are significant quality differences.

tinize sales transactions, and thus facilitates large-scale retail operations.

We are so accustomed to the one-price policy today that we usually overlook the possibility of a retailer's following a varying price policy under which he charges different customers different prices for the same item. However, bargaining and haggling is still common, particularly in small shops and open marketplaces, in many of the less economically developed countries of the world, and was the general practice in this country until the latter part of the 19th century.[20]

Actually, even in this country, deviations from the general rule of the one-price policy are more frequent than we sometimes realize. Store employees are often allowed a discount or favored price on the merchandise they buy, as noted in Chapter 9. Some druggists give physicians and nurses a special "professional" discount.[21] Occasionally, a merchant may set up a special discount arrangement for a particular group, such as the members of a sport club or the workers in a nearby factory, whom he hopes will concentrate their purchases with him.

But such systematic discounts affect only a very small portion of all retail sales. Individual bargaining over "trade-in allowances," a very common practice in the sale of automobiles, electric refrigerators, radios, television sets, fine cameras and other consumer durables, is a more important deviation from the one-price system. Bargaining and haggling often occur in the sale of durables, particularly in the automobile trade, even when no trade-in is involved.[22] Some small and medium-sized merchants dealing in other nonconvenience goods will also occasionally "shade the price" or give the customer a discount in order to close a difficult sale.

Some retailers maintain that a reduction in the quoted price is all right if it can be disguised. Perhaps the customer can be talked into buying two items for less than the sum of the two usual prices, thus making the reduction appear to be a quantity discount. Or the retailer may explain that he was planning to reduce the price in the very near future and thus is merely taking the markdown a few days sooner than planned. The customer may be told that this is an exceptional case, not to be repeated. Or perhaps, the retailer may agree to make a certain amount of alterations at no charge. However, the risks of becoming known as a retailer who is willing to bargain argue against the use of such practices. A one-price policy builds confidence and successful retailing is built on confidence.

---

[20] See, W. A. Tonning, "The Beginnings of the Money-Back Guarantee and the One-Price Policy in Champaign–Urbana, Illinois, 1883–1880," *Business History Review,* June 1956, pp. 196–210.

[21] Thomas E. Coleman, *Profitable Drugstore Management* (Englewood Cliffs, New Jersey: Prentice-Hall, Inc., 1970) pp. 84, 86, 98.

[22] Cf. "Do Auto Prices Mean What They Say?" *Business Week,* September 6, 1969, pp. 60–65.

□ Price lines

Price lining consists of selecting certain prices and carrying assortments of merchandise only at these prices, except when markdowns are taken. For example, men's ties may be carried at $2.50, $3.50, and $5.00; and women's dresses at $22.98, $29.98, and $39.98.

Reasons for price lining It is easy to see why price lining developed. Customers desire a wide assortment when buying shopping goods (to which price lining is especially applicable) but become confused if there are small price differences among the various items. This confusion is reduced when the assortments are confined to certain specific price levels.

Salespeople who sell at only a few price lines become well acquainted with their prices and make fewer mistakes. This facilitates selling and improves customer goodwill. Price lining may also reduce the size of the store's inventory, increase turnover, decrease markdowns, simplify stock control, and reduce interest and storage costs. It also helps the department buyer select merchandise, since it enables him to concentrate on items that can be sold profitably at the pre-set price levels.

Establishing price lines Price lines[23] are usually established through a careful analysis of past sales, picking out those prices at which the bulk of the sales were made. In some cases, however, past sales are disregarded: The retailer simply selects new price lines which he then expects his sales people to "push." Although it is unwise to be too definite as to the number of price lines needed, a merchant will usually want at least three to provide low-, medium-, and high-price groups. One popular-priced women's sportswear chain has selected four price lines;[24] and a large store may find that it needs half a dozen or more price lines for such merchandise as hosiery to satisfy its customers' requirements.

Some of the advantages of price lining are lost if the price lines are not far enough apart to indicate definite differences in quality. Otherwise, the customer will still be confused with several goods selling at fairly comparable prices. The retailer should have full assortments at each price line to serve the customers attracted by that line.

He must also frequently check his competitors' price lines to make sure that they have not found lines with greater customer appeal than the ones he has established. One retailer expresses the need for constant reappraisal of price lines in these words: "The price line picture can seldom be con-

---

[23] On this subject, also cf. the discussion of "Principles of Price-Line Determination," in J. W. Wingate and J. S. Friedlander, *The Management of Retail Buying* (Englewood Cliffs, N.J.: Prentice-Hall, Inc., 1963), pp. 382–83.

[24] *Women's Wear Daily,* October 13, 1965, p. 52.

sidered static; testing and checking are always helpful—above and below and in between the established price lines."[25]

Price lines in periods of general price change The retailer may want to shift his price lines somewhat if either wholesale prices or his customers' incomes change. Some retailers follow a policy of maintaining the same price lines and lowering the quality sold at each price as prices rise, whereas others think that the quality should be maintained with the price rising to reflect significant increases in wholesale prices. Still other retailers feel that both the quality and the price should be raised during periods of prosperity. They feel that, during such periods, people usually have the desire and the funds for better things. These retailers point out that a 5 percent rise in total income will enable customers to spend more than an additional 5 percent on shopping goods, since many other expenditures will be relatively fixed in amount. Although there is some truth in this argument, it would seem better policy for the store to maintain the quality of its price lines and try to "step up" some customers to its next higher price line.

Stores tend to lower both price lines and quality during depressed periods. This policy is tempting when the stores find that their customers want to "trade down" because of reduced incomes. Yet it is also dangerous, since it breaks down whatever quality standards a store has built up for each of its price lines. The wiser policy seems to be to lower the price line so long as this can be done without sacrificing quality, but not to go beyond that point. Customers who demand lower quality merchandise should be encouraged to drop to the next lower price line.

In brief, during periods of price and income changes—whether rising or falling—a retailer will do well to change his price lines only when he can or must do so to maintain quality. Customers demanding higher or lower qualities should be traded up or down to other price lines.

Limitations of price lining Price lining does reduce the buyer or merchandising executive's range of alternatives in selecting goods for the store. The buyer must secure merchandise that will provide a profit when sold at the store's established price lines. This requirement sometimes hampers his efforts to obtain adequate assortments and more than offsets whatever advantages he receives from only having to consider those items that fit his store's price lines. Price lining also limits the store's ability to meet competitive prices.

Still other disadvantages include (1) the danger that the price lines selected will not be suited to the preferences of customers and prospective

[25] F. S. Hirschler, "Price Lines and Price Lining," *The Buyer's Manual*, 4th ed. (New York: National Retail Merchants Association, 1965), p. 125.

customers, (2) the difficulty of maintaining price lines and uniform quality during periods of changes in price levels, (3) the likelihood that price lines will multiply over a period of time, and (4) the tendency to focus attention on price rather than on the merchandise. In spite of these drawbacks, the advantages of price lining have resulted in a widespread use of the practice in the retailing of apparel and other shopping goods. It is not as useful, however, in selling staples such as foods and toiletries, where customers generally do not want to compare an assortment of styles, colors, and sizes at one price.[26]

Single-price policy A single-price policy is the extreme version of price lining. Under this policy a store sells all of its merchandise of a given type at the same price. Generally stores that use this approach feature their single price in their advertising and sales promotion. Thus a specialized men's necktie store might advertise that its entire stock of ties are priced at $1.50. This approach is usually only suitable to stores with inexpensive merchandise, since it forces emphasis upon price, and it is a difficult policy to maintain whenever general price levels are changing substantially. The single-price policy, which is concerned with uniformity of prices among items, should not be confused with the one-price policy, which involves uniformity of prices among customers.

■ MARKUP

The concept of markup will play an important role in the retailer's thinking, both as he decides on his general price policies and as he goes about setting the prices of specific, individual items. Markup formulas are often used to compute prices, and to help determine whether prices will cover operating costs. But we must remember that the marketplace provides the final test for any pricing decision. The decision is wrong, regardless of what the formula indicates, if the customers aren't willing to pay the amount requested for the item.

□ Meaning of markup

"Retail markup" means the amount that is added to the cost price to arrive at the retail price, a relationship which is frequently stated in the phrase "cost plus markup equals retail." This amount may be expressed in dollars or as a percentage of the *retail price*.[27] For instance, an item costing $.80 and sold for $1.20 carried a markup of $.40, or 33⅓ percent. Markup

[26] Wingate and Friedlander, *op. cit.*, p. 382.

[27] Some retailers still follow the older practice of expressing this difference as a percentage of the cost.

may refer to a single item, as in the preceding sentence; or it may be used concerning a department, a store, or a chain of stores. Thus, if a toy department operating merely during the Christmas season places prices totaling $10,000 on goods costing $6,000, the markup is $4,000 or 40 percent.

Initial markup versus gross margin It is essential to distinguish between the initial markup and the maintained markup or gross margin. The initial markup, also known as the "original markup" or the "markon," is the difference between the cost and the first retail price placed on the goods. Using the same figures as those of the preceding paragraph, an item costing $.80 and originally priced at $1.20 carried an initial markup of $.40, or 33⅓ percent. However, perhaps customers refused to buy this item at $1.20, and it was finally cut to $.98 before it was sold. The difference between the cost and the actual selling price, $.18, or 18.4 percent in this case, is called the "maintained markup" or "gross margin." In other words, whereas the initial markup is the amount by which the original retail price of goods exceeds their cost, the maintained markup or gross margin is the amount above cost realized when the goods are sold. It should be evident that, from the point of view of profitable operation, the maintained markup is more important than the initial markup. In the preceding case, the store lost money on that particular item if its selling cost was more than 18 cents.

Cost of merchandise Exactly what do we mean by "cost," when we say that markup is the difference between the cost of merchandise and its selling price? To clarify: A supplier charges $100 for an item. However, this $100 is subject to a quantity discount of 7 percent, a cash discount of 3 percent, and a freight charge of $5. Is the cost of merchandise $100 (face of invoice), $105 (invoice plus transportation), $90.21 (all discounts deducted),[28] or some other figure? Since we want to know exactly what the item cost the retailer delivered to his store, we find the cost figure as follows: $100 minus $7 (quantity discount), minus $2.79 (cash discount), plus $5.00 (freight), or $95.21. In other words, "cost of merchandise" means the invoice cost of the goods minus discounts plus inward transportation paid by the retailer. If the merchant wants an initial retail markup of 40 percent on this item that had a net cost of $95.21, he would price it at $158.68.[29] (In practice, of course, he would normally round that figure to $159.00, $159.50, or $160.00.)

Some retailers, however, prefer to overstate the cost of their merchandise when making this sort of calculation. Then, if they use the same initial markup percentage as other retailers, they will wind up with a higher initial selling price. The merchants who want to do this determine their cost of

---

[28] Seven percent from $100 leaves $93. Three percent from $93 leaves $90.21.

[29] The difference, or dollar markup, between $95.21 and $158.68 is $63.47, which is 40 percent of the $158.68 retail price. Note that the markup is calculated as a percentage of the *retail* price.

merchandise without regard to cash discounts. Using this method in the preceding case, the cost of goods would be stated at $98.00 and the 40 percent markup would produce a price of $163.33 (which probably would be rounded to some more customary figure between $162.50 and $165.00).

Anyone who uses this latter method is, in a sense, "fooling himself," much like someone who puts his alarm clock ahead at night so as to make certain that he gets up at the right hour in the morning.[30] The modern approach is to think of the item's true cost as being $95.21, and to consider the higher price ($163.33) as providing a markup of approximately 41.7 percent. Nevertheless, at least a few storekeepers feel that they set more profitable prices through this device of thinking of the cost of goods as being higher than it actually is.

Markup calculations It might be thought that the markup can be used as a simple mechanistic method of setting prices, as follows: The proprietor of a store determines from his past records that his operating costs equal 29 percent of sales and his profit is 3 percent on sales. Thus, by pricing his goods so that a gross margin of 32 percent on sales is secured, he will be able to meet his costs and make a profit. However, this procedure demands more than a 32 percent initial markup; after being put into stock, some goods may be subject to markdowns or lost through pilferage. In addition, stores commonly have a policy of selling to employees at a discount. Perhaps the total reductions (markdowns, shortages, and discounts to employees) are estimated as 6 percent of sales. Using the formula

$$\text{Initial markup percentage} = \frac{\text{Gross margin} + \text{Retail reductions,}}{100 \text{ percent} + \text{Retail reductions}}$$

the proprietor arrives at the following initial markup percentage:

$$\frac{32 \text{ percent} + 6 \text{ percent}}{100 \text{ percent} + 6 \text{ percent}} = \frac{38 \text{ percent}}{106 \text{ percent}} = 35.85 \text{ percent}$$

Thus to get a gross margin of 32 percent, an initial markup of approximately 36 percent is needed.

Buyers and merchandising executives frequently have to calculate retail prices from the following two pieces of information: (*a*) the cost of the goods, and (*b*) the desired markup, expressed as a percentage of the retail price. A typical problem might be: What retail price will give us an initial

[30] A more dignified way of putting it is that some store executives prefer to treat the cash discount as a financial earning, and enter it as part of "other income" on the operating statement. This is a fairly widespread practice in manufacturing industry, where cash discounts received tend to be small and cost of goods is usually only a small part of selling price. But most modern retailers consider the cash discount to be a reduction in the cost of merchandise, as shown in the first method.

markup of 36 percent (of retail) on an item that costs us \$.96? The formula that answers this question is:[31]

$$\text{Retail price} = \frac{\text{Cost}}{100 - \text{Desired markup percentage}} \times 100$$

$$\text{Retail price} = \frac{.96}{64} \times 100 = \$1.50$$

■ PRICING INDIVIDUAL ITEMS

A retailer has only begun to solve his pricing problems when he has determined the *average* markup needed or desired for the entire store. He will seldom want to apply a uniform markup percentage throughout the store as a whole. Markups considerably below average may be advantageous or necessary for some departments and some items; correspondingly, other departments and items may support substantially-above-average markups.

□ Factors limiting use of a single markup

Many factors normally prevent the use of a single markup percentage on every item in the store. Goods having the same cost may differ greatly in customer appeal and consequently will permit or require very different markups. Competitors' prices and markups, which will normally vary from item to item, will influence the markup a store may take on any particular product. Some high style and perishable products may require large initial markups to offset severe markdown rates. Higher-than-average markups may be needed for some items that involve extra handling or selling costs. Even though a single average markup percentage is often a useful starting point in price calculations, determination of the actual prices for the indi-

---

[31] Instead of using this formula, some retailers prefer to convert the markup on retail (36 percent in this case) to a markup on cost, and then go through the following two additional steps: (*a*) the cost is multiplied by the cost-percentage markup to obtain the dollar markup, and then (*b*) the cost and the dollar markup are added together to determine the retail price. Retailers who follow this method often use prepared tables that show the equivalent markup percentage on cost for any given markup based on retail. However, the following formula can also be used to convert the percentage from one base to the other:

$$\text{Markup on cost} = \frac{\text{Markup on retail}}{100 - \text{Markup on retail}} \times 100$$

$$\text{Markup on cost} = \frac{36}{100 - 36} \times 100 = 56.25 \text{ percent}$$

56.25 percent of \$.96 = \$.54. \$.96 + \$.54 = \$1.50, the same result as in the other method.

vidual items will normally require many upward and downward deviations from that average.

Using several markups Some retailers divide their stocks into several groups and apply different markup percentages to each group. This practice is one step beyond the use of a single markup for the whole store. A food retailer will realize that markdown and spoilage costs are much greater for perishable fresh fruit and vegetables than for canned goods. His competitors, who have the same spoilage problem, normally take a higher markup on fresh produce than on canned goods, and, consequently, his customers expect and are willing to pay prices that include higher markups for the fresh fruits and vegetables. He may decide that a 30 percent initial markup is necessary in the produce section, whereas 20 percent will be satisfactory for canned goods. Similarly, a shopkeeper who sells various types of women's apparel may use different markups for different product groups. Perhaps an initial markup of 50 percent is needed for dresses and other products most subject to markdowns; the more staple goods might be carried profitably on a 30–40 percent markup.

Individual item pricing But increasingly, retailers are recognizing that even this practice of dividing the products into different markup groups is not flexible enough to produce maximum profits. The more skillful merchants try to mark each item with the price that will have the most beneficial effect on the store's total profits, even though some of the individual markups that result from this process may be above or below the desired average percentage for the store as a whole.

Some large-scale retailers have undertaken careful (and costly) studies of the turnover of various items when sold at different markups. Voluntary chain wholesalers prepare price guides which suggest to their retailers the "most profitable" markups for each item they carry.[32] Some retail trade associations offer a similar service to their members.[33] These guides help the retailer develop more flexible and more effective pricing practices.

□ Some factors influencing markup

A retailer has to consider many factors in determining the most profitable price and markup for each item in his stock. A number of the more significant factors are outlined in the following paragraphs.

Customer appeal of the goods If one is realistic, he will recognize that the cost of an item sometimes has little relationship to how much an item

---

[32] An illustration of such a guide for food retailers is given in "A Pricing Program for Profit Makers," *Voluntary and Cooperative Groups Magazine*, April 1969, p. 28.

[33] Cf. The National Retail Hardware Association's *Stock Selection Guide*, as described in R. R. Mueller, "Shortest Route to Increased Profits," *Hardware Retailer*, December 1965, p. 15.

appeals to customers. A merchant may purchase two dress styles at $8.75, and find that one moves readily at his regular $16.75 price; the other may hang on the rack even after being marked down to $9.75. One of the most difficult aspects of pricing is recognizing what products and prices will or will not appeal to the customers.

One successful retailer strongly urges that: "Buyers should spend enough time in the receiving room properly appraising goods in terms of *what prices they will bring*. They should also examine the merchandise in their departments rather than rely on stock figures or unit control records exclusively. They must develop a 'feel for merchandise' that tells them almost instinctively what items and styles will sell at a profit."[34]

Customer response to lower price Different items vary in their basic appeal to customers, and they also vary in the extent to which their sales can be increased through the use of lower prices and markups. For example, a retailer may handle two electric appliance items, both of which cost him $60 per unit and which he might normally price at a 40 percent markup or $100. One is a rather new specialty item that will sell in small but satisfactory quantities to a limited market consisting of his upper income customers. Reducing his markup and offering the item at a lower price will not increase sales substantially. The other product has a wider market and is subject to some price cutting in competitive stores. It may be more profitable to sell this item at substantially less than his customary markup.[35] In other words, the increased sales may provide enough total dollar margin to offset both the reduction in margin per unit and the extra operating costs of increased sales.

To illustrate: He might be able to sell only two units of the second item per week at the $100 price. His gross dollar margin on that product would then be $80 per week ($100 − $60 = $40 × 2 = $80). If his weekly sales increase to six units when he drops the price to $79, his *total* dollar margin will increase to $114 ($19 each × 6 units) even though his percentage margin falls to approximately 24 percent ($19 on a selling price of $79). His net profit will increase unless the extra costs of selling the four additional units are more than $34 (the increase in dollar margin).

The profitability of this approach depends upon the rate at which sales grow in response to lower prices, and the extent to which the increase in operating costs lags behind the growth in sales. Retailers sometimes underestimate the sizable addition to sales that is needed to offset a reduction in margin. In the example above, a 200 percent addition to sales produced only a 42.5 percent increase in total dollar margin ($34 is 42.5 percent of $80). And some, perhaps all or more, of that additional dollar margin would

---

[34] Morey Sostrin, "Merchandising to a Profit," *The Buyer's Manual, op. cit.*, p. 282.

[35] Economists call the first item "relatively price inelastic," and the second one, "relatively price elastic."

be absorbed by the extra costs of selling the increased volume. Similarly, a 66⅔ percent increase in sales is needed simply to maintain dollar margin in the case of a 10 percent price reduction on an item that normally carries a 25 percent markup. Sales may have to double or more before the reduction becomes profitable in view of the extra expense involved in increased sales.

Leader merchandising The primary motivation for the markup reductions we have just discussed is the hope of increasing sales and profits *on the items offered at low margins*. But many retailers will also price some items at very low markups for the primary purpose of attracting customers who will also buy *other products* that carry higher markups. Items intentionally sold at low prices for the purpose of drawing trade to the store are often called "leaders" or "specials." Some people apply the term "loss leader" to any such item priced at less than the store's acquisition cost; other people use the same term for all trade-attracting specials offered for less than the sum of acquisition cost and the cost of handling the items.[36]

Some merchants who believe in using leaders select a few items from various departments for this purpose; others may operate an entire department, such as the food department in a discount store or the restaurant in a department store, as a leader.

But in either case the theory is that the leaders will attract a large number of customers who then purchase enough other items carrying sufficiently large markups to increase the retailer's total profit. Although many stores have used leader pricing successfully, it does require considerable skill. Even such an outstanding firm as R. H. Macy & Company, which for many years used cigarettes to attract customers to its New York store, finally discovered that most of the people who bought its cigarette specials left without making any other purchases.[37]

The retailer who uses price leaders should make certain that the prices of his other products are consistent with this policy. His specials will attract price-conscious customers. Consequently, he cannot raise the prices of other items to the point where these customers become disenchanted with his nonleader merchandise. He should also recognize that a very large price reduction for some kinds of merchandise may repel, rather than attract, customers. As we have already noted, customers sometimes consider the price of an item to be an indication of its quality.[38] Consequently, too large a reduction may suggest damaged or inferior goods.

---

[36] Legal limitations on loss leaders will be discussed in the next chapter. Cf. pp. 424–25, below.

[37] "Take Me to Your Leader," *Wall Street Journal*, February 7, 1966, p. 14.

[38] In this connection, cf. J. Douglas McConnell, "The Price-Quality Relationship in an Experimental Setting," *Journal of Marketing Research*, Vol. 5, No. 3 (August 1968), pp. 300–303.

Advertising value of an item or department As the last paragraph suggests, some items are better suited than others for use as leaders. From the retailer's point of view, the most effectve leader products (1) appeal to most of the store's customers and potential customers; (2) are purchased frequently, so that at any given time most of the customers will need or want the items; (3) are not so costly that they will use up most of the customer's current purchasing ability, even when sold at a reduced price, and thus discourage sales of other merchandise; and (4) have easily recognizable values. Easily identified, well-known branded products are thus often very effective as leaders. Similarly, frequently visited departments that sell relatively low-unit cost items are often most suitable for leader use.

New departments and items Relatively low markups are often used to attract customers when a store expands its merchandise offerings by adding groups of items or departments that it has not handled previously. Thus a supermarket that adds a health and beauty aids department to its merchandise mix may feature some very striking "introductory specials" and may also take a relatively low markup for the entire department.

On the other hand, rather high markups may be taken on expensive items that are truly new, in the sense of their first appearance on the market, that involve a great deal of risk of nonacceptance, and that will appeal, if at all, only to non-price-conscious buyers. High fashion items and major technical innovations such as color television and the Polaroid camera tend, when they first appear, to fall in this category.

Seasonal and fashion goods The initial markup for seasonal goods is influenced by the time and weather of the season. Early in the season, there is a tendency to place higher markups on goods than when the season is advanced, the assumption being that early buyers are less price-conscious than those holding off, since the early shoppers are buying to take advantage of a better selection. Also, especially on fashion goods, the retailer realizes that he may later have to close out part of his stock by heavy markdowns; consequently, he needs a larger markup on early sales.

Cost of merchandise It might be thought that the cost of merchandise would have no influence on the markup that a product might carry; however, it does. As a result of a special "buy," the retailer may be able to place a high markup on certain goods and still meet or "beat" the prices of competitors. In contrast, a high cost of merchandise may force a store to operate on a smaller markup than it deems advisable. One drug manufacturer has even urged retailers of his products to place substantially smaller markups on high-cost items than on those having a lower wholesale cost—his theory being that customers for expensive drugs now pay a disproportionate share of the retailer's total operating expenses.

Customary prices We noted earlier that a retailer who calculated a price of $158.68 for an item through the use of his traditional markup percentage would be extremely unlikely to offer the item at that price. Some prices and price endings have become customary in some trades, and most retailers will adjust their markups to fit these customary prices. $158.68 is simply not a customary price and few retailers would use it.

The extreme form of customary price is found among those products that are usually sold at only one or two specific price points. Thus many stores sell candy bars at the conventional points of 10 and 15¢ per bar, and the candy manufacturers themselves set wholesale prices that will facilitate this sort of retail pricing. Standard price lines, such as $5, $6, and $9 in the case of men's shirts, also shape many pricing and markup decisions. However, customary prices naturally tend to lose some of their influence on both consumer and retailer decisions during periods, such as the late 1960s, when price levels and costs were changing rapidly.

Odd prices Prices that end in the digits 5, 7, 8, and especially 9, such as 29¢, $6.89, $12.97, and $29.95 are often used in the retail trade instead of round number or "even" figures such as 30¢, $7.00, $13.00 and $30.00. Many explanations have been advanced for this custom of using odd prices. Some people claim that it forces the customer to wait for change, during which time she may look around and make additional purchases. Also, the fact that the salesperson has to make change encourages the use of the sales register, so that the sale is recorded and the risk of employee theft is thereby reduced. However valid these arguments may have been at one time, they have much less significance today when many stores use check-out lines separate from the sales counters; when sales taxes in many states convert practically all transactions into odd amounts; and when more and more customers regularly charge most of their purchases.

The argument most frequently voiced for odd prices concerns their supposed psychological effect. It is often claimed that a price of 49¢ will move many more units of an item than a 50¢ price, either because people subconsciously consider 49¢ much smaller than 50¢ or because they believe that any item sold at 49¢ has been subject to a deep price cut while 50¢ seems to be a "regular," full price. Modern research, however, suggests that these odd prices have very little effect upon sales rates.[39] Many department stores and many manufacturers who preticket their products are now shifting towards the use of even prices.

---

[39] Andre Gabor and C. W. J. Granger, "Price Sensitivity of the Consumer," *Journal of Advertising Research,* Vol. 4, No. 4 (December 1964) pp. 40–44; Robert J. Holloway, "Experimental Work in Marketing," in F. M. Bass, C. W. King and E. A. Pessemeir, eds. *Applications of the Sciences in Marketing Management* (New York: John Wiley & Sons, Inc., 1968) pp. 393–94; David M. Georgoff, "The Effect of Odd-Even Retail Pricing on Value Determination, Product Perception and Buying Propensities," unpublished Ph.D. dissertation, Michigan State University, 1970.

Multiple pricing The practice of quoting a special price for a number of units, for example: 25¢ each, 6 for $1.39, is called "multiple pricing." Many retailers find that this technique, when used either as a regular practice or during special sales, builds up the quantity sold and increases dollar margin per transaction. Nevertheless, considerable caution should be exercised in utilizing multiple pricing. It is only appropriate, as a general rule, for items that the customer will use in considerable quantities. And some customers resent the technique because they feel forced into buying more than they really want at any one time.[40]

Operating cost As has been suggested at several points in this chapter, the freedom of a retailer to vary his markup is determined, in part, by his operating cost. That chain food stores, in general, have long undersold independent food retailers as a well-established fact.[41] While several factors are responsible for the chains' price advantage, it is quite clear that relatively low operating cost plays a major role. Departments with low expense rates can be operated profitably at a low markup; similarly departments and items that require substantial handling, service, or selling costs need larger markups.

Competition As has also been indicated at several points, competitive prices will often determine the markup that a store may place on some items or classifications of merchandise.

Price level adjustments The retailer will find it necessary to vary his markup on goods according to whether the general price level is declining or advancing. Consider the situation when the general price level is falling. Men's hose purchased at $8 a dozen pairs and sold at $1 a pair for a markup of 33⅓ percent yield a gross margin of $4. If the store's operating expenses absorb $3 of this gross margin, the store has $9 in place of the $8 it had before the hose were bought and sold. Now, as a result of a fall in the general price level, the retailer is able to replace the dozen pairs of hose in stock at a cost of $7 a dozen. In addition to the $1 profit realized, the store has an extra $1 with which to buy goods. In such circumstances the retailer might well consider using a markup of less than 33⅓ percent. If competition is keen, he may have little choice in the matter, since he will be forced to sell his hose for less than $1 a pair.

In a period of rising prices, the retailer will have to take a higher-than-usual markup or else his working capital will decrease. This situation may be illustrated by assuming that the hose which cost $8.00 a dozen pairs cannot be replaced for less than $9.50. But the $1 per pair leaves only $9, after deducting operating expenses, to replenish the stock. In view of the higher

[40] Cf. "Multi Methods for Dual Pricing," *Supermarket News*, March 23, 1970, p. 14.

[41] C. F. Phillips and D. J. Duncan, *Marketing: Principles and Methods*, 6th ed. (Homewood, Ill.: Richard D. Irwin, Inc., 1968), p. 226.

replacement cost, the store has lost money on the transaction. Sound pricing would lead the retailer to take a larger markup during periods of rising prices or to consider his cost as the replacement cost. Unfortunately, from the retailer's point of view, competition usually keeps him from advancing his prices as rapidly as wholesale prices rise; consequently his working capital may decrease during such periods.

CONCLUSIONS ON MARKUP

On the basis of our discussion, it seems reasonable to formulate the following conclusions concerning the markup policies of retailers:

First, a retailer may aim at prices which are (1) at, (2) below, or (3) above those of his competitors.

Second, some retailers find it possible to solve most of their pricing problems by using an average markup which they apply to practically everything they sell. This situation is most likely to exist in the small specialty shop.

Third, a larger number of retailers handle their pricing problem by dividing the goods they sell into a number of classes and applying a set markup to all goods falling into a particular class. These classes may be based on differences in the cost of handling the goods, variations in markdowns, differences in cost of merchandise, or some other factor. As the number of classes increases, the retailer approaches a policy of individual-item pricing.

Fourth, the great majority of retailers find it necessary to deviate widely from any rule of a set markup, even for a limited class of goods. Factors of customer appeal, competition, price lining, time of season, customary prices, odd prices, cost of merchandise, considerations of turnover, the advertising value of an item, operating cost, price maintenance by manufacturers, and government price laws,[42] play a part in the determination of actual markups. The retailer should always remember that he is interested in *total profits*, not in profits on any particular item. Markups on specific items should be in a process of constant adjustment in an effort to reach this goal.

It should be noted that this constant process of adjusting markups involves the retailer in trying to forecast results and that such predictions may not be very accurate. Among other things, the retailer must try to estimate the effect on turnover of a certain price reduction, the effect on cost if sales increase, and how markdowns will be affected by a higher or lower initial markup. All of these forecasts are subject to correction when the change is actually put into effect. In other words, adjustments on a trial-and-error basis are a "must." If a certain reduction in markup does not bring the expected increase in turnover, the retailer should try some other markup. Cor-

[42] Price maintenance and price legislation are discussed in Chapter 17.

rect retail pricing involves a willingness to experiment. The retailer who tries to simplify his pricing by the mechanistic use of a single markup will usually find that he is losing out to more aggressive merchants.

■ REVIEW AND DISCUSSION QUESTIONS

1 Distinguish between the short-run and the long-run points of view in pricing at retail. Provide several illustrations of situations in which short-run and long-run points of view might lead to different price decisions.

2 What problems does a retailer face if he tries to price below competition? What are some of the operating practices and policies he may use to solve or help solve those problems? (Try to provide specific examples to illustrate those solutions.) Similarly, what are some of the problems and policies associated with pricing above competitive levels?

3 List and evaluate the advantages and disadvantages of a one-price policy. How suitable is such a policy for *(a)* a discount drugstore, *(b)* a sporting goods store, *(c)* a dress shop, and *(d)* a department store?

4 What are the major advantages and disadvantages of using price lining in (a) a ready-to-wear shop? *(b)* a hardware store?

5 Visit some local stores, or watch their advertising, and compare their prices for private and national brands. What factors seem to cause the price relationships that you have discovered?

6 Eighteen coats are purchased at $57 each. If a 40 percent markup is desired, what is the retail price per coat? What is the total retail of the purchase?

7 How much can a buyer afford to pay for a dress to retail at $65, if he desires a markup of at least 45 percent?

8 Select one specific type of store, such as supermarkets or department stores, and try to judge which items in those stores would usually be priced at less than the stores' average markup, and which would usually be priced above. What factors explain the difference?

9 State the various arguments for the use of leaders; appraise each from the point of view of (a) the exclusive women's apparel shop, *(b)* the service food store, (c) the neighborhood drugstore, and *(d)* the discount house.

10 List the prices quoted for (a) dry cereals, *(b)* men's shirts, (c) women's dresses, *(d)* automobile tires, and (e) shampoo, in various retailers' advertisements in one or more issues of your local newspaper. Which of these are "odd" and which are "even" prices? Can you find any "customary" prices?

chapter 17

JUDICIOUS PRICING (continued)

In this chapter, we continue our discussion of retail pricing with emphasis on: (1) Price adjustments and reductions, and (2) Legislation affecting pricing policies and practices.

■ PRICE CHANGES

Prices are constantly on trial, and often must be adjusted to meet changing conditions. Most price changes are decreases, referred to as "markdowns," but there may also be some advances or "additional markups."

□ Markdowns

Retail accounting usually expresses total markdowns as percentages of net sales. Consequently, for purposes of *internal control and analysis,* a price reduction on an individual item is usually also stated as a percentage of the new and lower (actual selling) price. To illustrate: When a dress priced at $50 is reduced to $40, the reduction is considered to be a 25 percent markdown.[1] Markdown percentages are thus computed through use of the following formula:

[1] Of course, from the customer's viewpoint, this is only a 20 percent reduction and it should not be advertised or announced to customers as more than a 20 percent price

$$\text{Percentage markdown} = \frac{\text{Dollar markdown}}{\text{New (or actual) selling price}} \times 100 \text{ percent.}$$

Some reasons for markdowns Some markdowns result from buying and pricing mistakes on the retailer's part. Buying mistakes are illustrated by the men's clothing merchant who added a line of male cosmetics that did not appeal to his particular customers, and by the womenswear dealer who reordered many items too close to Easter—an error often described as "going to the well once too often." Pricing mistakes also occur because it is impossible to set exactly the right price on every item flowing through the store. The original prices are really only estimates of what the customers will pay for the merchandise. If experience proves that the original estimate is too high, markdowns are necessary.

However, a markdown does not necessarily indicate that the original asking price was too high from the store's point of view, or that the store buyer was at fault. Perhaps wholesale prices have declined, so competitors who bought later have lower costs for the merchandise and are charging lower prices. Newer, more stylish, or more acceptable products may have come on the market since the goods being marked down were purchased. Other markdowns must be taken because the goods have become shopworn. Even more importantly—in fact, it is one of the major reasons for markdowns—products may be reduced in price to provide attractive promotional or "sale" merchandise.

Some markdowns result from a policy of deliberately purchasing more items than the store expects to sell at full price in order to have a good assortment on hand throughout the selling season. Often the retailer is not sure which particular items in a shipment of fashion goods will sell well. Consequently he may decide to place a fairly high initial markup on all the dresses, for example, and later use a markdown to clear out those that remain. Likewise, retailers of seasonal goods often find that they must mark down the stocks of those goods remaining at or near the end of the season. Perhaps a large number of summer suits have been purchased, but because the weather has been cold and rainy, most are still in stock at the end of July. A drastic markdown may be the only way to move them.

Salespeople sometimes cause markdowns when they take the line of least resistance and merely show customers what they ask to see. As a result, other goods lie in stock until it is too late to sell them at regular prices. Other salespeople may be too aggressive and get customers to take several

---

cut. This figure, which expresses the relationship of the reduction to the *former* retail price, is called "the off-retail percentage," and represents the way in which the consumer looks at the price change. The markdown percentage, which expresses the relationship of the reduction to the *new* price, is only used for the retailer's own analytical and recordkeeping purposes.

items home "on approval." Markdowns may be necessary when some of these goods are returned to the store, especially if the customer has not taken proper care of the merchandise or if sales have been lost while the goods were out of stock.

Every retailer gradually accumulates "odds and ends." If he handles men's shirts, he may sell most of his blues while many of the grays remain in stock, or his customers may purchase the 14½ and 15½ collar sizes, and leave the 15's and 16's. If he handles piece goods he will accumulate a large number of small pieces of cloth that remain on each bolt. Substantial markdowns are usually required in order to sell these odds and ends.

Finally, poor stock control also causes markdowns. Unless the retailer keeps proper records and uses them conscientiously, he will not have adequate warning of items that have become "slow sellers" or of seasonal stocks that are not selling according to plan. Some large retailers now use electronic equipment to provide such information quickly and economically and thus reduce the markdowns that are attributable to inadequate recordkeeping.[2]

Markdowns as a merchandising tool The foregoing paragraphs demonstrate that markdowns are inevitable and not necessarily totally undesirable. Indeed, the successful retailer looks upon them as an indispensable tool for keeping his stock composed of attractive, currently salable merchandise, for promoting sales, and for meeting competition. And since they are unavoidable, markdowns are planned for in the store's budget.[3]

Timing of markdowns Merchants disagree as to the best time to take markdowns. Some retailers delay taking markdowns in the hope of additional sales at the original prices. This policy can be more suitable to a downtown store that attracts a transient (and hence, less frequent) trade than for a suburban store that relies on frequent visits from its regular customers. Other retailers only take markdowns during two or three large sale events each year; these yearly clearance sales become established in the minds of economy-conscious customers and serve to unload the shelves of the least desirable merchandise. Exclusive shops may delay taking markdowns to discourage bargain hunters and to preserve the store "image." Alternatively, they may take markdowns early and still avoid large numbers of bargain hunters by placing the garments in the next lower price line without indicating that reductions have been made.

But most successful retailers believe that markdowns should be taken early. This policy makes room for a steady flow of new goods to the store and thus keeps stocks fresh. It reduces the size of the markdowns needed to move the merchandise, since the goods will lose more of their appeal or

---

[2] Cf. the discussion of electronic data processing on pp. 118–20, 239–40, 270–71, 316–19 above and 604–7 below.

[3] Cf. "Planned Reductions," pp. 342–43, above.

become more shopworn as time goes on. It also avoids the cost of special sales. Thrifty buyers are encouraged to visit the store regularly if some marked-down goods are always available.

1. *Some general rules on timing* Because of these advantages of early markdowns, some large-volume retailers have adopted certain general rules that speed up decisions to take such reductions. These retailers maintain that a markdown should be taken as soon as sales of a fashion item begin to fall off; that is, as soon as the peak of the fashion cycle has been reached, *if* the store has any appreciable quantity of the item on hand. Staples are marked down before they have been in stock long enough to become shopworn. Seasonal fashion goods must be sold before the end of the season. The rule requires that the retailer take inventory as soon as the season's first rush of business ends and judge whether his stock will sell out at the original prices; if not, markdowns are in order. For instance, although many men's winter suits are sold in the months after Christmas, the majority of clothing stores reduce prices on such goods immediately after the first of the year.

But even aggressive retailers disagree about markdown policy for seasonal goods of a staple nature. Toys not sold this Christmas may be sold next year. Marbles not moving this spring may find buyers next spring. Is it better to clear these goods out at markdown prices and begin with a new stock next season, or is it better to carry the merchandise until the next selling season? There is no one "correct" answer to this question. Holding the goods may be profitable if the retailer has available space. He must realize, however, that this practice ties up some of his funds, that it involves storage costs, that his employees must spend time packing the goods away, and that the merchandise may suffer some breakage or other damage. In view of these disadvantages, it is often better to sell the goods out if this can be accomplished by means of a moderate reduction.

2. *Automatic markdowns* There is a tendency today toward taking markdowns earlier than ever before. Fashion merchandise retailers, who must keep their goods moving out of their stores, may follow a policy of lowering the price of any garment in stock for four weeks. A few of them have even adopted an automatic markdown plan which controls both the amount of the markdowns and the time when they take place. This policy is illustrated by the basement store of William Filene's Sons Company of Boston, where all merchandise that remains unsold after 12 selling days is repriced at 75 percent of its original price; after six more days, at 50 percent; after another six days, at 25 percent; and after a final six days, is given to charity.[4] The Ohrbach store in New York City follows a somewhat similar policy, and begins a series of 10 percent reductions after any garment has been in stock for two weeks.

---

[4] Cf. "The Boston Supershoppers," *Time*, December 26, 1969, p. 27.

While the Filene and Ohrbach plans have apparently proven successful for these particular retailers, they have not been adopted by many merchants. Typically the retailer prefers to adjust both the amount and timing of the markdown to the specific situation, rather than have these two elements set by an inflexible rule.

Size of the markdowns The data of Table 17–1 make it evident that markdowns vary widely from one line of merchandise to another. For individual items, of course, the range would be much more than that indicated by the table.

TABLE 17–1

Typical markdown percentages for selected departments of department stores and departmentalized specialty stores, 1970 (net sales = 100 percent)

NRMA departmental classification number	Department	Upstairs store	Downstairs store
1100	Women's, Misses & Juniors' Coats & Suits	16.9	12.7
1500	Women's, Misses' & Juniors' Dresses	14.9	11.3
2711	Millinery	11.9	n.a.
2911	Women's Footwear	15.0	14.0
3100	Men's Clothing	12.5	10.0
3400	Men's Furnishings	6.0	7.3
5612	Apparel Fabrics	10.4	n.a.
5911	Cosmetics, Drugs & Toiletries	2.0	n.a.
7100	Furniture & Bedding	8.0	8.8
8400	Major Appliances	6.0	n.a.

(n.a., not reported due to the small number of stores with basement departments in these classifications.)

Source: Jay Scher, *Departmental Merchandising and Operating Results of Department and Specialty Stores in 1970* (New York: National Retail Merchants Association, 1971).

To be effective, a markdown must be large enough to induce customers to buy the merchandise. Marking a skirt down from $16.75 to $15.75 is probably not adequate, since most people who are willing to pay $15.75 will usually also pay $16.75. Perhaps a reduction to $12.75 is needed to reach the desired number of people. The retailer should remember the old retail adage that "the first markdown is the least expensive." Put another way, when the merchant wants to clear stock, he should not nibble away at the price by small successive reductions; the major correction should generally be made in one step.

Of course, the ideal markdown is the one that is just enough to sell the goods under consideration. But defining the "ideal" markdown is quite different from deciding what it is in a specific case. The retailer's decision must take into account not only tangible factors such as quantity of merchandise on hand and rate of movement but also those intangibles such as how competitors will respond to a price cut and how customers who bought at the higher price will react.

The size of the markdown necessary to sell the merchandise involved is also related directly to the promotional effort put forth by the retailer and the selling effort made by sales personnel. A "p.m."[5] with a moderate markdown may move more merchandise than a larger markdown without an incentive to the sales staff.

Markdowns under price lining Two general policies are used for handling markdowns on price-lined merchandise. The usual policy is to reduce the item to at least the next lower-price line.[6] This policy keeps the price structure simple, so that the customer is not confused; and it also automatically determines the extent of the markdown.

The second policy consists of having special price lines, for marked-down goods only, located between the regular price points. It is argued that this policy reduces the size of the reductions that the store has to take. The marked-down merchandise is also more clearly distinguished from the regular-priced goods, and consequently may sell out rapidly. Furthermore, segregating the price-reduced merchandise from the regular lines helps build up the idea that each price line stands for a certain quality. Adding marked-down items to an established, regular price line reduces that line's homogeneity.

Publicizing markdowns The amount of promotional attention that will be given to a markdown will depend upon (*a*) the quantity of goods involved, (*b*) the reason for the markdown, and (*c*) the image the store wishes to have its advertising reflect.[7] Normally advertising and window display space will not be used to announce markdowns that have been taken on isolated odds and ends of merchandise that have become soiled, shopworn, or somewhat out-of-date. The space is too expensive to use for this purpose and customers might be mislead into expecting the store to have more reduced-price merchandise than is actually available. However, a catalog-type listing of these items may be used, particularly in the clothing and furni-

---

[5] A "p.m." is a small cash payment or bonus given to salespeople for selling specific items.

[6] Some retailers state this general rule as "the next lower *active* price range." What they mean is that the merchandise must go into a price line where goods are selling in considerable volume.

[7] Cf. the discussion of promotional advertising at pp. 435–37.

ture trades, if a considerable quantity of miscellaneous reduced-price merchandise is being offered during a clearance sale. In contrast, markdowns taken for leader purposes will be vigorously publicized in order to attract the largest possible customer traffic. Also, some advertising may be necessary if the store has a considerable inventory of any marked-down items. Beyond this, merchants vary in the extent to which they want to feature price in their advertising, since this will strongly influence the way in which customers think of the store. Some retailers want to develop reputations for low prices and aggressive price cutting, others feel that emphasis upon marked-down items will detract from their image of quality and style leadership.

1. *Coupons* Some retailers and many manufacturers, particularly in the grocery trades, stimulate sales through the use of coupons that entitle the holder to a special price reduction when presented in the store. These coupons are sometimes included in newspaper or magazine advertising or they may be distributed by direct mail. Usually they are valid only on purchases of specific items, and in most such instances the manufacturers of those items reimburse the stores for the coupons they have redeemed.

2. *Sale prices on price tickets* As noted, one technique for demonstrating markdowns to the customers is to draw a heavy line through the original price on the price ticket and enter the new one above it in different colored ink. Some merchants oppose this practice and, for two reasons, insist that new tickets be made out for each price change. (1) They feel that the altered tickets detract from the store atmosphere and give it a cheap image, particularly when goods have been through two or three successive reductions. (2) Some degree of control will be lost and some markdowns will go unrecorded if price changes can be made right on the selling floor. Insisting that new tickets be attached by marking room personnel insures that a record will be made. The markdown price tickets can be printed on different colored paper if the store wants to draw attention to its sale items.

Recording markdowns There are several reasons for maintaining a record of all markdowns. Perhaps most important, a knowledge of past markdowns is essential for intelligent decisions about initial markup. The formula for initial markup, as noted in Chapter 16, is:

$$\text{Initial markup percentage} = \frac{\text{Percent gross margin} + \text{Percent retail reductions}}{100 \text{ Percent} + \text{Percent retail reductions}}$$

A retailer may estimate that he needs a 30 percent gross margin to cover estimated operating expenses of 26 percent and a desired 4 percent net profit. But he cannot determine the initial markup needed to provide this gross margin until he is able to calculate a figure for retail reductions. And the markdown rate is a major component of the retail reduction figure.

Information on markdowns is also important as a check on pilferage. Assume that, in the case mentioned in the preceding paragraph, 7 percent is allowed to cover these retail reductions (markdowns, stock shortages, discounts to employees, and others) making the initial markup 34.58 percent. Of this 7 percent figure, 2 percent is intended to cover stock shortages. However, net profit at the end of the period is only 2 percent rather than the desired 4 percent. With records of markdowns and discounts available, the cause of the lower profit ratio can be determined. If the markup was 34.58 percent, expenses have been held to 26 percent, markdowns to 3 percent, and discounts to 2 percent, then the lower profit ratio must be a result of a larger-than-expected stock shortage. Without records of markdowns and discounts, the retailer could locate his problem only in a very general way; that is, he would know that his retail reductions were too large, but he would not know whether he had a markdown, a discount, or a stock-shortage problem.[8] Finally, a knowledge of markdowns on various types of goods and on goods of specific manufacturers is an important managerial and buying aid. The retailer may discover that certain types of goods require unprofitably large markdowns. Or, he may find that goods purchased from some suppliers lead to larger markdowns than merchandise from other sources.

□ Additional markups

Additional markups—the amount by which the existing retail prices are advanced to new prices—are usually limited to periods of rapidly advancing prices. Whenever a retailer discovers that he cannot replace his present stock except at higher prices, he should not hesitate—if competition makes it possible—to advance his prices. Otherwise, he will find that he does not achieve the inventory gain needed to offset the inventory loss which will come if prices fall.

Once in a while a retailer may find that an item will sell better if its price is advanced. It may happen that the original price was so low that customers hesitated to buy, believing that the low price indicated low quality. In such cases, additional markups are advisable.

■ RETAIL PRICE LEGISLATION

Various laws influence the retailer's pricing practices or, in some cases, allow the manufacturer to set the prices the retailer must charge. The most

---

[8] The importance of markdown information for use in controlling inventory and analyzing retail reductions is discussed more fully in Chapter 14, pp. 342–43.

controversial laws of this type, generally known as resale price maintenance, are discussed in the paragraphs immediately below.

□ Resale price maintenance

Resale price maintenance (also called "fair trade" by its proponents) is an arrangement under which a manufacturer specifies the prices (or the minimum prices) retailers must charge for his products. The laws relating to this arrangement have a long and complicated history, and we will only note the most essential facts here.

Legal aspects The passage of the Sherman Antitrust Act (1890) made resale price maintenance contracts and arrangements illegal in interstate commerce.[9] In 1937, however, Congress passed the Miller-Tydings Enabling Act, which allowed manufacturers to set the retail prices for their products *in any state that enacted a resale price maintenance law*. Forty-six states—the exceptions being Alaska, Missouri, Texas, and Vermont plus the District of Columbia—passed such laws.[10] These so-called "fair trade" laws contained a "nonsigner's clause" which provided that the prices the manufacturer established became binding upon all retailers within the state, whether they signed a contract or not, upon notification that one retailer had signed such an agreement.

But in the Schwegmann decision of May, 1951, the U.S. Supreme Court ruled that this nonsigner's clause was illegal under federal law.[11] As a result of this decision, a manufacturer who wanted to fair trade his product had to obtain signed contracts from all of his dealers, which was a highly impractical procedure unless his firm sold its goods directly to a limited number of retailers.

The Schwegmann-decision limitation on fair trade did not last long. The McGuire Amendment to the Federal Trade Commission Act, enacted in 1952, removed the federal legislative restriction on the nonsigner's clause in interstate commerce. Nevertheless, a series of adverse court rulings concerning the validity of the nonsigner's clause under the federal and state constitutions, and various legislative actions (the fair trade laws have been repealed in Hawaii, Kansas, Mississippi, Nebraska, Nevada, and Rhode Island) have greatly reduced the number of states in which resale price maintenance is now legally effective.

---

[9] Bona-fide consignment sales, in which the manufacturer retains ownership of the goods and the retailer acts as his agent, are sometimes an exception to this rule. Cf. the discussion of consignment transactions, pp. 297–98, above.

[10] Some had passed the laws prior to 1937, California being the leader in 1931. But until the Miller-Tydings law was enacted in 1937, the state laws were only applicable when both the manufacturer and the retailer were located within the same state.

[11] *Schwegmann Bros.* v. *Calvert Distillers,* 341 U.S. 384 (1951).

During the mid-1960s, Congress considered, and for a while seemed favorably disposed toward, a so-called Quality Stabilization Bill that would have established national resale price maintenance. This bill, if enacted, would have permitted a manufacturer of a branded item to establish resale prices anywhere in the United States by merely notifying wholesalers and retailers of those prices through advertising or price labels attached to the goods. The bill was ultimately defeated, in part because of strongly voiced opposition from many government agencies, economists, businessmen, and consumer representatives.

Current legal situation As indicated above, there has been considerable fluctuation in the legal status of resale price maintenance, and new judicial decisions or legislative enactments may further change the number of states in which price maintenance is legally permissible. As of the time of writing, only 17 states allowed suppliers to control dealer prices by notification without the complicated procedure of signing contracts with every retailer. Three of these states—Ohio, North Dakota, and Virginia—use a new approach that substitutes the doctrine of "implied consent" for the old nonsigner's clause. In these three states the law says that a retailer has automatically "contracted" to resell at the stated price if he accepts goods from a manufacturer who has notified him of the price maintenance program.[12] In all 17 states the required notification may be performed relatively simply by stating the resale prices in price lists, sales contracts, invoices, trade paper advertising, or bulletins sent to the dealers. Approximately 19 more states permit the manufacturer to control resale prices if he can obtain individual price maintenance contracts from each of his dealers in the state.

Products generally must carry the manufacturer's or wholesaler's "trademark, brand, or name" to be eligible for price maintenance.[13] Close-out sales, sales of damaged and deteriorated merchandise, sales to charitable and educational institutions, and sales of items from which the trademark identification has been removed are often exempted from the manufacturer's price controls, although the various state laws place different restrictions and limitations upon these exemptions. Mail-order firms in nonfair trade states have complete pricing freedom, even when selling to customers in fair trade states, since the transactions are governed by the laws of the place where the goods are transferred to a common carrier for delivery.[14]

---

[12] The North Dakota law is reported in Commerce Clearing House *Trade Regulation Reporter*, sec. 33,720; the Ohio law, secs. 33,820, 33,821; and the Virginia law, sec. 35,120.

[13] A further requirement of the Miller-Tydings Act, that the products be in "free and open competition with commodities of the same general class produced or distributed by others," has been invoked in a few instances.

[14] Cf. the discussion of "Transfer of Title," pp. 297–98, above; and *General Electric Co. v. Masters Mail Order Co.*, 335 U.S. 824 (1957).

The price maintenance laws do not permit "horizontal" price agreements, that is agreements among manufacturers, among wholesalers, or among retailers. Competing retailers may not agree on prices among themselves nor may they legally act together to force a manufacturer to set minimum resale prices. Moreover, an integrated firm that operates at several levels, for instance a drug manufacturer who is also a drug wholesaler or retailer, cannot set resale prices for the firms that buy from him and compete with his own wholesale or retail branches.[15]

Manufacturers' problems Some manufacturers who have used fair trade have sincerely desired to control resale prices because they felt such action was necessary: (1) To protect their products' reputation; (2) to obtain widespread distribution; or (3) to encourage their dealers to provide adequate service and display for their products. Other manufacturers, probably a larger group, have adopted price maintenance reluctantly and only in order to placate their dealers' demands. Both groups of manufacturers have found that price maintenance programs involve serious enforcement and marketing problems.

1. Enforcement depends upon private action As we have noted, state law determines whether price maintenance is legal. And in states where price maintenance programs are permitted, manufacturers may use the courts for lawsuits against retailers who cut the prices of fair-traded goods. But these two factors constitute the usual limits of government support for or involvement in such programs.[16]

The manufacturer who fair trades his products sets the prices on his own, without approval or review by the state authorities. Moreover, those authorities will not take action against or prosecute a retailer who sells those goods for less than the fair trade prices. The manufacturer must police and enforce his price maintenance program himself, through business decisions such as refusal to sell and through private lawsuits against the price-cutting dealers. This enforcement activity may consume much executive time and involve considerable legal expense. The W. A. Sheaffer Pen Company once spent $2 million dollars over a two-year period in a futile attempt to enforce its price maintenance contracts. Furthermore, court decisions have increasingly limited the actions that firms may take to police their fair trade agreements.[17] Consequently, many manufacturers have been unable to obtain rigorous compliance with their programs and many retailers complain bitterly about the lack of adequate enforcement.

---

[15] *United States* v. *McKesson-Robbins,* 76 S.Ct. 937 (June 1956); *Janel Sales Corp.* v. *Lanvin Parfums, Inc.,* 396 F2d 398 (CA–2, 1967), *cert. denied,* 1968.

[16] Some exceptions to this statement exist in special situations, such as the alcoholic beverage trade where some states require price maintenance.

[17] These decisions are outlined in considerable detail in Commerce Clearing House *Trade Regulation Reporter,* secs. 6320–6374.

2. Competitive problems Many manufacturers have also found that price maintenance programs can create serious competitive handicaps for both themselves and their regular dealers. The establishment of a high price and a wide margin for the branded product encourages the growth of private brands that undercut the manufacturer's trademarked line. It also tempts discount houses and other retailers to "discount" the manufacturer's line, that is, to sell it on a price-cutting basis. Enforcement becomes even more difficult as such discounting spreads, since any dealer who is ordered to maintain prices is likely to lose sales to his price-cutting competitors.

The spread of discounting and the legal and enforcement difficulties of price maintenance caused many firms, who formerly used the practice extensively, to abandon it for some or all of their products. These firms included General Electric Company, Sunbeam Corporation, Eastman Kodak Company, Bell & Howell, Schick, Inc., Royal McBee Corporation (Royal typewriters), Ronson Corporation, International Silver Company, E. Ingraham Company (clocks and watches), and Revere Copper and Brass. Some of these companies, however, have sought to minimize resale price cutting on certain products through such arrangements as consignment selling and franchise agreements.

The impact of price maintenance on retailing Some retailers strongly favor resale price maintenance, while others strongly oppose it.

1. In the short run Small merchants who lack buying advantages and whose operations require relatively high markups often desire price maintenance. These retailers consider it as a shield against competition from the low-price store. A few typical price comparisons indicate how severe that competition may be: Clairol Shampoo listing at $2.25 advertised at $1.12; $1.20 box of Hershey candy bars for 76 cents; Dupont's $7.99 Lucite wall paint at $4.99; 79 cent Colgate Instant Shavecream 3/79 cents; $1.80 Sylvania photographic Flashcubes at 86 cents; and a $10.00 set of 8 AC Sparkplugs at $4.99.[18]

Retailers favoring fair trade reason that if such price differentials on well-known brands are abolished, a large part of the "pull" of the low-price store will be lost. As a result, "regular-price" retailers, especially those in the drug field, have lobbied for fair trade laws. Then they and their trade associations have induced manufacturers to put their products under price maintenance. These retailers are the active proponents of fair trade; they have literally forced many manufacturers to become at least apparent advocates of the practice.

The retailers who oppose fair trade laws claim that their lower prices result from such factors as lower operating costs, lower cost of merchandise, and willingness to accept lower profit margins, and not from loss

[18] Advertisement, *Washington Post*, October 11, 1970.

leaders or predatory price cutting. They point out that some chain organizations have been able to operate profitably and efficiently while selling broad lines of well-known goods for less than what many independent merchants charge.

Studies by disinterested groups show wide variations in operating and merchandising costs for different sizes and types of stores. The existence of these cost differences suggests that many retail price differences are economically sound. Yet some regular-price retailers denounce all price-cutters as "chiselers." This denunciation is so typical that one wit has defined a "chiseler" as anyone who is able to sell at a lower price than his competitors.

2. In the long run The opponents and proponents of resale price maintenance argue whether the practice increases prices in general. In 1969, the President's Council of Economic Advisers quoted, and apparently endorsed, estimates that price maintenance resulted in a net price increase of about $1.5 billion per year.[19]

But even with such increases, it is questionable whether price maintenance can provide higher profits for the regular-priced retailers. As we have already noted, the lower-priced outlets will continue to use private brands, nonprice-controlled manufacturer's brands, and unbranded merchandise to attract customers away from the higher-priced stores. The price-maintained items will also often continue to be subject to some price cutting, and this will place the retailer who tries to observe the established price at a disadvantage.

More extensive nonprice competition, such as increased advertising, additional services, or broader stocks, can increase expenses and absorb profits even if price cutting is abolished. More commonly, the higher margins may attract new competition that will substantially reduce the established merchants' profits. To cite only one illustratlion, many supermarkets added health and beauty aid products during the 1950s and early 1960s because of the large margins that resulted from price maintenance for those products. Consequently, fair trade laws may not provide the long-run profitability that their sponsors anticipate. A careful analysis of retail failure rates in states with and without fair trade concludes:

> The best data available do not support the contention that the enactment of fair-trade laws lessens the number of retail failures or bankruptcies or increases the number of retail stores. Whatever effect they have apparently had has been slight and in an opposite direction to the one claimed by proponents of fair trade.[20]

---

[19] *Economic Report of the President together with the Annual Report of the Council of Economic Advisers.* (Washington, D.C.: U.S. Government Printing Office, 1969), p. 108.

[20] S. M. Lee, "The Impact of Fair-Trade Laws on Retailing," *Journal of Retailing,* Vol. 41, No. 1 (Spring 1965), p. 6.

Outlook for fair-trade laws Resale price maintenance has been increasingly under attack during the last two decades and more, both in this country and abroad. It is now specifically prohibited in Canada, Denmark, Finland, France, Great Britain, Italy, Norway, Spain, and Sweden, although in many of those countries various government bodies can grant exemptions from this prohibition under some special circumstances. The Austrian, German, and Irish governments have prohibited price maintenance in some trades where they thought it had unduly restrictive effects. The Japanese government, however, relegalized fair trade in 1953, after banning it in 1945.[21]

Numerous government agencies and study commissions in the United States, including at various times the Department of Justice, the Federal Trade Commission, the Attorney General's National Committee to Study the Antitrust Laws, and the President's Council of Economic Advisers, have urged repeal of the fair trade laws.[22] During the mid-1960s, many of these agencies joined with the Departments of Agriculture and Commerce in opposing the proposed Quality Stabilization Bill that would have permitted national resale price maintenance. Much of the legislative drive for price maintenance seems to have ended after Congress defeated that bill in 1965.[23]

On the economic front, as we have already seen, the growth of discount houses and widespread price reductions have led many manufacturers to abandon fair trade or to question the wisdom of all-out efforts to enforce resale price contracts. Even before resale price maintenance's recent legal and economic defeats, its use was largely confined to such products as drugs, toilet goods and cosmetics, household appliances, photographic supplies and equipment, books, sporting goods, and liquor. Probably no more than 5 to 10 percent of all U.S. retail volume has ever been in fair-traded merchandise and certainly even these figures are too high for the current situation.

Nevertheless, it seems unlikely that resale price maintenance will be completely eliminated. Abandoned by many manufacturers, it is still strongly supported by others. Some of the firms that have abandoned it occasionally decide to give it another trial.[24] Never adopted by 4 states and severely limited or made ineffective in 29 others, it is still fully permissible in 17

[21] *Guide to Legislation on Restrictive Business Practices* (Paris: Organization for Economic Co-operation and Development), looseleaf; B. S. Yamey (ed.) *Resale Price Maintenance* (Chicago, Ill.: Aldine Publishing Co., 1966).

[22] For an example of these recommendations, cf. *The Report of the Council of Economic Advisers, 1969*, pp. 108–9.

[23] Irving Scher, *Manual of Federal Trade Regulations Affecting Retailers*, new ed. (New York: National Retail Merchants Association, 1969), p. 90.

[24] Cf. "Price Protection Is Snowballing," *Home Furnishings Daily*, July 17, 1968; "GE Adopting Fair Trade in So. California," *ibid.*, June 25, 1970.

states, including some of the most heavily populated ones. Moreover, if economic conditions should ever become sufficiently depressed, many retailers will undoubtedly undertake a strong campaign for restoration and extension of this form of price protection.

Suggested prices and preticketing A manufacturer may try to influence his dealers' prices, aside from resale price maintenance, by suggesting retail prices for his products. He may even mark the goods with the price he expects the dealers to charge. Thus a shirt manufacturer might have a $7 price printed on the plastic envelopes in which he packs one of his branded shirts. This practice of pre-marking is called "preticketing."

But he cannot legally make the dealers observe those recommendations except through the use of resale price maintenance, where valid, or through the device of consignment selling, which is usually impractical. Moreover, his preticketing may actually tempt some dealers into price cutting, since the pre-marked price provides dramatic evidence of the reduction the store is offering. To further complicate matters, the Federal Trade Commission holds that a preticketed price is "deceptive" if any substantial number of retailers sell the item for less than the pre-marked price, even though the manufacturer may not be able to stop their price cutting. Consequently a manufacturer should be reasonably certain that his dealers will follow his recommendations before preticketing his products.

□ Unfair-sales and unfair-trade practices acts

About 29 states have unfair-sales acts, unfair-trade practices acts or sales-below-cost laws that aim at protecting the retailer from competitors who might sell leader items at less than cost. Whereas fair trade laws are permissive[25] and apply only to brand merchandise, these laws are mandatory, and apply to all goods. Twelve other states have special unfair practices or sales-below-cost laws that apply to specified commodities, mainly cigarettes and milk.

Minnesota's Unfair Sales Act, which is fairly typical of the general statutes, requires retailers to charge a margin of at least 8 percent above invoice cost for all goods except damaged or deteriorated items. Lower prices may be charged, however, if necessary to meet the legal prices of competitors. A law such as this does forbid deep price cutting, but the minimum required price is low enough to enable a retailer to give his customers all of the benefits of low cost operation. Since the minimum costs of retailing practically any item involves a margin of more than 8 percent, this law does

---

[25] As noted above, the liquor laws of some states provide for compulsory price maintenance.

not force a retailer to raise his prices above what his own costs would normally require.

Some of the other state laws may have less desirable effects. The Arizona statute requires a markup of at least 12 percent.[26] Since this is in excess of the markup required in retailing some goods it may result in higher prices to the consumer.[27] In California, the law forbids sales below cost except to meet competition, but then defines cost as invoice or replacement cost, whichever is lower, *plus the dealer's cost of doing business.*[28]

The California type of statute has at least two serious faults: an administrative difficulty and an economic fallacy. The administrative problem involves the difficulty of determining operating costs when a retailer is accused of violating the law. The economic fallacy is that the law seems to require the markup on each item to be at least equal to the merchant's average cost of doing business. Many items can be profitably sold at margins considerably below the store-wide average cost of doing business, and there is no sound reason for raising the prices of such merchandise.

In practice, although violations are statutory offenses and subject to action by the attorneys general of the various states, very few of these laws have been aggressively enforced. As a consequence, in certain states wholesalers and retailers have formed associations partly for the purpose of bringing alleged violations to the attention of the attorneys general and of encouraging the enforcement of the laws. In some instances these associations have themselves been prosecuted on the grounds that they were being used to encourage horizontal price fixing contrary to both state and federal laws.[29]

■ OTHER PRICE REGULATIONS

Retailers are affected by several other forms of price regulations from the federal, state, or local level.

□ Price ticketing and price posting

Clear, legible price tickets, signs, or other markings that enable the customer to note the price of an article at a glance are usually highly desirable for many sound business reasons and are a feature of most modern retail

---

[26] This markup is required unless the retailer can affirmatively prove a lower cost of doing business.

[27] For criticism of the Arizona law, cf. Robert L. Knox, "Competition and the Concept of Sales below Cost," *Arizona Business Bulletin,* Vol. 16, No. 9 (November 1969), pp. 227–32.

[28] *California Business and Professions Code,* Division 1, Part 2, Chap. 4, Sec. 17026.

[29] Cf. S. C. Hollander, *Restraints upon Retail Competition* (East Lansing, Michigan: Bureau of Business and Economic Research, Michigan State University, 1965) p. 39.

operations.[30] Federal, state, or local legislation now requires price signs in the case of a few commodities. State and local laws generally specify the way gasoline prices must be shown or posted at the service station pumps. Federal law requires a label or "window sticker" showing the list price, cost of accessories, and freight and preparation costs on every new automobile sold at retail.[31] The Federal Consumer Credit Protection Act, discussed in Chapter 22, is somewhat similar legislation in that it outlines the information that must be communicated to the customer concerning the charges for (price of) credit service. In contrast, the advertising of prices is sometimes prohibited in fields where, it is claimed, such promotion might lead to undesirable practices. Thus most states forbid advertisement of the retail prices of prescription pharmaceuticals or compounded prescriptions.[32] But most observers of the consumer movement and of recent legislation believe that future laws are likely to require more, rather than less, display of price information.

□ Unit pricing

One type of information that some consumer advocates would like to see required is called "unit pricing." Under this system, the price per standard unit of weight or measure (ounce, pound, pint, quart, gallon), as well as the per-package price, is displayed or marked on goods sold in odd-sized packages. The unit pricing proponents contend that only an expert in mental arithmetic can make a meaningful comparison of prices and values between two packages of a grocery product if, for example, one contains 2 4/11 ounces and sells for $.78, while the other contains 3 7/15 ounces and sells for $1.04. Consequently, the advocates of unit pricing legislation want mandatory price marking that would show that the cost of the first package equals 33¢ per ounce, and the second one equals 30¢ per ounce. (This system is sometimes called "dual pricing," since two prices—the actual package price and the per ounce equivalent—are displayed for each item.)[33]

---

[30] See the discussion of price marking pp. 370–80, above.

[31] But the Federal Trade Commission now complains that the list prices usually shown on the window sticker are considerably higher than the prices at which automobiles are usually sold (cf. our discussion of bargaining in the automobile trade, p. 395) and consequently are deceptive. The FTC wants the manufacturers to post more "realistic" list prices. Cf. "Do Auto Prices Mean What They Say?" *Business Week,* September 6, 1969, pp. 60–65.

[32] Cf. "Drug Makers Recant and Support Pharmacists in Opposing Ads," *New York Times,* December 23, 1968, p. 18.

[33] Readers who may be confused by the similarity of the terms, "one price," "single price," and "unit pricing" will find that businessmen and writers often use these words interchangeably. Consequently, one is forced to look at the context to determine how these words are being used. Strictly speaking, however, "one price" refers to the

Such legislation is now under discussion in many areas and has been adopted in Massachusetts.[34]

Many supermarket operators claim that it would be prohibitively expensive to post and constantly update unit price information for the thousands of items they offer for sale. If and where such legislation is adopted, small merchants will probably be exempted from unit pricing requirements, because of the clerical labor and time costs involved. However, several chains are voluntarily experimenting with unit pricing with mixed customer reactions; some liking the practice while others report that very few shoppers seem interested in such information.[35]

□ Price advertising

Truth-in-advertising standards and controls, discussed more fully in the next chapter, are being applied increasingly to the price information offered in retail advertising. The Federal Trade Commission, for instance, has issued a helpful set of "guidelines" as to what it considers deceptive statements about retail prices. Essentially, a merchant cannot claim or imply that a price has been reduced from some former level unless the former price quoted was an actual, *bona fide* one at which he offered the product to the public on a regular basis for a reasonably substantial recent period of time. For example, he cannot take an item regularly selling for $7.50, mark it up to $10.00 for a day, then reduce it back to $7.50 and advertise it as "a big bargain—marked down from $10.00." If the retailer claims his price is lower than either the manufacturer's list or suggested price—or the price prevailing in other stores—he must make certain that the quoted prices are those at which substantial sales are being made in the principal stores in his area. He must clearly state all the terms and conditions in any special offer, such as "Buy one—get one free," or a "Half-Off Sale."[36] The Better Business Bureaus, voluntary business organizations, have also issued guides and suggestions on price claims. Such standards for price advertising help protect responsible merchants from unscrupulous competition and, at the same time, help provide consumers with meaningful information.

---

practice of charging *all customers* the same amount for the same item purchased under the same conditions; "single price" refers to the practice of selling *all of the items* in a store at the same price; and "unit pricing" refers to the provision of information about the price *per standard unit* of weight and measure.

[34] "New York State Retailers in Dual Price Switch," *Supermarket News*, October 19, 1970, p. 14.

[35] Cf. "Label War: Inflation Hot Issue," *New York Times*, February 1, 1970, Sec. 3, p. 14; and "Unit Pricing Chalks Up Some Surprises," *Business Week*, October 31, 1970, pp. 80–81.

[36] Bureau of Industry Guidance, Federal Trade Commission, "Guides to Deceptive Pricing," January 8, 1964.

RESTRICTIONS ON PRICING FREEDOM

Fair trade laws and unfair-sales acts are examples of laws which restrict the pricing freedom of retailers. Yet competitive pricing, which requires pricing freedom, is the very heart of the free-enterprise system. How far we can limit that freedom and still retain our type of economy is one of today's major questions. At some point—if we want the advantages of freedom and the high standard of living which our system offers—we must be willing to accept the rigors of price competition and not try to protect everyone from its impact. And there is a very encouraging aspect of these restrictive laws: A careful evaluation of their history indicates that over a long period of time, these restraints seem to lose much of their force. Apparently (and fortunately) it is difficult to remove the impact of competitive factors in the retail field.

Emergency controls

During periods of national emergency, the government sometimes finds it necessary to suspend the normal operations of the marketplace. During the depths of the Great Depression of the 1930s, the NRA (National Recovery Administration) program was instituted to reduce price-cutting and to place floors under prices and wages. During World War II and the Korean crisis, the government imposed an elaborate system of price ceilings and other economic controls designed to curb price inflation. Similarly, in August, 1971 President Nixon announced a temporary price and wage "freeze" as an anti-inflationary measure. Such measures represent the extreme degree of government control over pricing. But even in more "normal" times, as our foregoing discussion has indicated, a variety of laws and regulations affect retail pricing. Both as a merchant and as a citizen, the retailer should become thoroughly familiar with these laws and understand their effects and the obligations they impose.

REVIEW AND DISCUSSION QUESTIONS

1 Define "markdowns." Using a hypothetical example, compute the dollar and percentage markdown.

2 "A markdown does not necessarily indicate that the original price was too high." Do you agree? Explain your answer.

3 Explain fully why markdowns are referred to as "an effective merchandising tool."

4 Analyze the advantages and disadvantages of an automatic markdown policy for (a) the used-car dealer, (b) the exclusive women's apparel shop, and (c) the basement operation of a department store.

5 "There are two general policies in use for handling markdowns on price-lined merchandise." What are these policies, and which one do you think merchants should use? Why do you prefer this policy?

6 What is the current legal situation regarding resale price maintenance?

7 Analyze the advantages and disadvantages of retail price maintenance from the point of view of a *(a)* neighborhood drugstore, *(b)* supermarket chain, and *(c)* department store.

8 If you were operating a men's furnishing store, would you want the manufacturers to mark their suggested selling prices on the merchandise you handle? Would your answer differ if you were operating a discount-house chain? Explain the reasons for your answer in both cases.

9 What are the objectives of the unfair practices acts? What are their weaknesses and limitations?

10 A chain of sporting goods stores advertises: "Special sale—35 percent reduction—X Brand sets of matched clubs only $65." What facts must be true if that advertisement conforms to the FTC rules on price advertising?

PART VI

Sales promotion and customer services

chapter 18

RETAIL ADVERTISING AND DISPLAY

Once a store has been properly equipped and well-balanced assortments of merchandise have been assembled to meet the needs of prospective customers, measures must be adopted to attract these customers into the store and to induce them to make purchases. Such measures—to be really effective—should build good will for the store to insure continuous patronage from satisfied customers. When this is done, sales volume will be maintained on a profitable level. The function of sales promotion is to accomplish these purposes.

Sales promotion efforts are of two major types: (1) Those of a nonpersonal nature—the presentation of goods, ideas, or services to individuals, singly or in groups; and (2) those of a personal nature—offering such goods and services on a personal or face-to-face basis. The first type is illustrated by advertising, display, and mail-order catalogs; the second type by "personal salesmanship."[1] Both forms should be effectively coordinated to maximize profits. In the present and next chapter, the nonpersonal forms of sales promotion are considered. Personal salesmanship is discussed in Chapter 20.

---

[1] For other explanations of these terms, cf. C. H. Sandage and Vernon Fryburger, *Advertising Theory and Practice* 8th ed. (Homewood, Ill.: Richard D. Irwin, Inc., 1971), pp. 3–7; Otto Kleppner, *Advertising Procedure*, 5th ed. (Englewood Cliffs, N.J.: Prentice-Hall, Inc., 1966), chapter I; and J. S. Wright, D. S. Warner, and Willis Winter, Jr., *Advertising*, 3d ed. (New York: McGraw-Hill Book Co., 1971), pp. 4–5.

RETAIL ADVERTISING: ITS USES AND GOALS

Advertising is "any paid form of nonpersonal presentation and promotion of ideas, goods, or services by an identified sponsor."[2] It is used by the retailer to stimulate desire for the different kinds of merchandise and services he has for sale, to tell people what goods and services he has available, to keep people interested in his store between visits, to encourage customers to fulfill all their needs in his lines at his store, and to develop goodwill for his business. In other words, its main job from the retailer's standpoint is to create in the minds of his customers the image he desires; and this image is the composite of many factors.

Retailers who a decade ago used very little advertising now employ this medium extensively. Take F. W. Woolworth as an example. After relying mainly on window displays for many years, in 1958 the company embarked on an ambitious newspaper advertising program with highly successful results. Today it uses radio, television, and magazines to supplement its millions of lines of newspaper advertising and special promotions at the local level, all designed to acquaint the public with its upgraded lines, wider assortments, and new merchandise that contribute greatly to Woolworth's new image.[3]

To achieve its goals, advertising should conform to sound management policies and be carefully planned, prepared, tested, placed in appropriate media at the right times, and reviewed frequently. Moreover, if maximum benefits are to be realized, it must be coordinated with other activities of the store.

Advertising is not a panacea for the management deficiencies of the retailer. Actually, those retailers who recognize the limitations of advertising programs and plan their programs accordingly will derive the greatest benefit from such efforts. They should keep in mind the warning voiced by two students of advertising more than a decade ago that:

1. Advertising cannot sell merchandise that people do not want to buy;
2. Advertising cannot sell merchandise in profitable quantities without the backing of every other division of the store; and

---

[2] This definition was formulated by the Definitions Committee of the American Marketing Association. Cf. the report of this Committee in the *Journal of Marketing*, Vol. 13, No. 2 (October 1948), p. 205. It continues to be widely accepted.

[3] One critic notes the ineffectiveness of "image" advertising by many firms. Cf. E. B. Weiss, "Most Corporate Image Advertising Couldn't Pass These Ten Simple Tests," *Advertising Age*, November 3, 1969, pp. 78, 80.

3. Advertising cannot succeed to the fullest extent unless it is used continuously.[4]

This clear warning emphasizes the fact that advertising, to be most effective, must serve the customer as well as the store.[5]

□ Main types of retail advertising

For purposes of analysis two types of retail advertising may be distinguished: (1) promotional or direct action, and (2) institutional or indirect action. Most advertisements represent a blending of both types.

Promotional or direct-action advertising The main purpose of this type of advertising is to bring customers into the store to purchase specific items of merchandise. Advertising with this emphasis constitutes the greater proportion of total retail advertising. It may take one of three forms: (1) regular-price advertising, where the appeal is based on the desirability of the goods (Figure 18–1); (2) "bargain" advertising, which features price appeal in relation to value[6] (Figure 18–2); and (3) clearance-sale advertising, whose main

FIGURE 18–1 **A regular-price promotional advertisement for fashionable women's shoes**

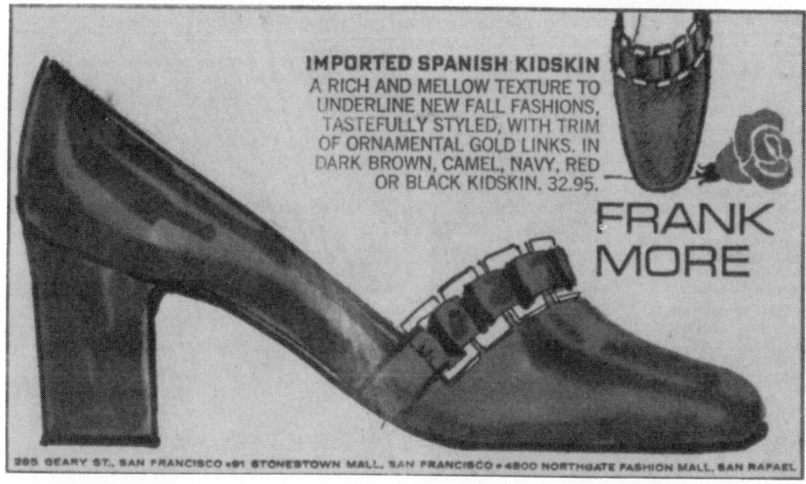

IMPORTED SPANISH KIDSKIN
A RICH AND MELLOW TEXTURE TO UNDERLINE NEW FALL FASHIONS, TASTEFULLY STYLED, WITH TRIM OF ORNAMENTAL GOLD LINKS. IN DARK BROWN, CAMEL, NAVY, RED OR BLACK KIDSKIN. 32.95.
FRANK MORE
285 GEARY ST., SAN FRANCISCO • 91 STONESTOWN MALL, SAN FRANCISCO • 4800 NORTHGATE FASHION MALL, SAN RAFAEL

---

[4] C. M. Edwards, Jr., and R. A. Brown, *Retail Advertising and Sales Promotion*, 3d ed. (Englewood Cliffs, N.J.: Prentice-Hall, Inc., 1959), p. 14.

[5] What customers expect from advertising is discussed by L. P. Bucklin, "The Informative Role of Advertising," *Journal of Advertising Research*, Vol. 5, No. 3 (September 1965), pp. 11–15.

[6] Cf. "Getting the Most from Avertised Specials," *Discount Merchandiser*, March 1970, p. 126.

FIGURE 18–2 A promotional advertisement featuring assortment with emphasis on copy

Yes! $1,000,000 worth of fabulous home furnishings now up to 50% off.

TEN BREUNER STORES TO SERVE YOU!

During the recent transportation tie-up more than 100 freight cars and truck-loads of quality home furnishings were undeliverable to Breuner's. In the past three weeks this merchandise has been received into our warehouses. As a result our ten stores are packed with fresh, new merchandise and we must make room for the additional shipments that are arriving daily. We are staging the biggest sale in our recent history — a Million Dollar Sale! Yes, Breuner's are offering more than $1,000,000.00 worth of fine quality home furnishing to you at very important savings!

SAVE ON UPHOLSTERED FURNITURE ★ BEDROOM FURNITURE ★ OCCASIONAL FURNITURE ★ BOX SPRINGS AND MATTRESSES ★ DINING ROOMS ★ SOFA SLEEPERS ★ LAMPS AND ACCESSORIES

SOMETHING EXTRA! 25% OFF

Stunning Allan Keith "decorator chairs" with savings of 25% and more. Be early!

BE HERE WHEN THE DOORS OPEN! It's first come first served! Look for hundreds of GREEN "GO" TAGS to show the savings! Use your Breuner's charge account. Hurry!

BREUNER'S
Complete Home Furnishers
SINCE 1856

FIGURE 18–3 A clearance-sale promotional advertisement Note brevity of copy.

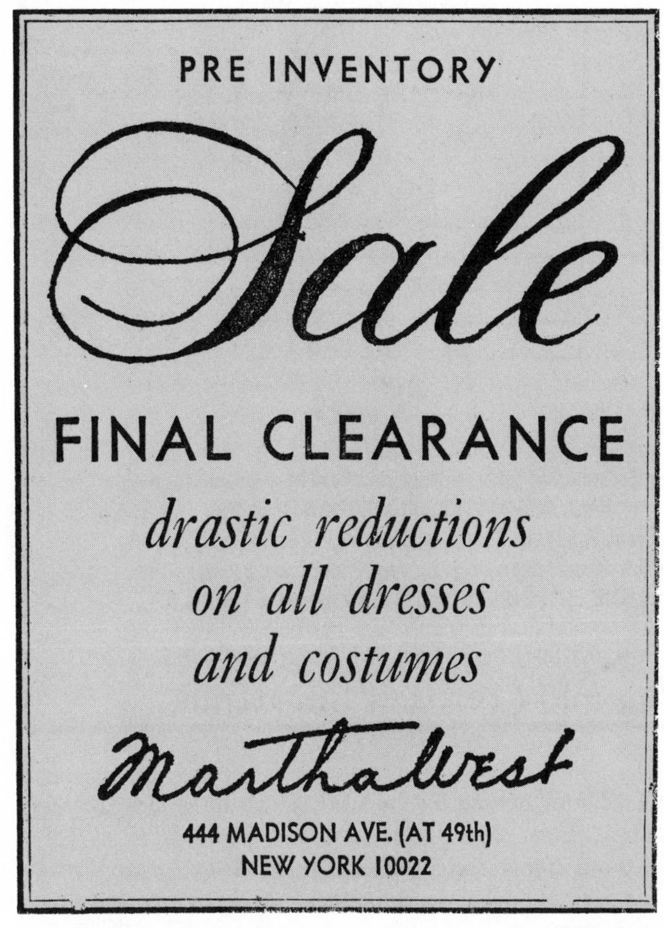

purpose is to close out slow-moving items, broken assortments, and remnants at reduced prices (Figure 18–3).

Institutional or indirect-action advertising Designed to develop goodwill for the store—to build confidence in its merchandise and services (Figure 18–4) and thus to build permanent patronage—institutional advertising is of two main kinds, prestige advertising and service advertising. The former aims to lend "atmosphere" to a store by acquainting present and prospective customers with the retailer's progressiveness in assembling adequate varieties of merchandise embodying the newest ideas in style, design, and material. Service advertising seeks to attract patronage by stressing the vari-

FIGURE 18–4 **An institutional advertisement stressing a showing of bridal fashions**

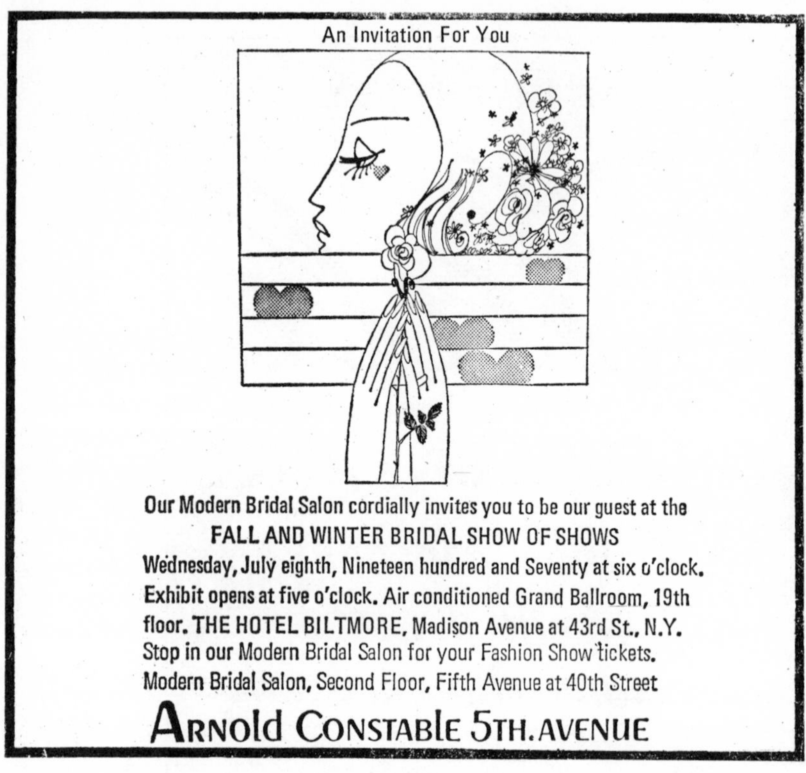

ous services and facilities offered by the store which make it a desirable place in which to buy.

An Invitation For You
Our Modern Bridal Salon cordially invites you to be our guest at the
FALL AND WINTER BRIDAL SHOW OF SHOWS
Wednesday, July eighth, Nineteen hundred and Seventy at six o'clock.
Exhibit opens at five o'clock. Air conditioned Grand Ballroom, 19th
floor. THE HOTEL BILTMORE, Madison Avenue at 43rd St., N.Y.
Stop in our Modern Bridal Salon for your Fashion Show tickets.
Modern Bridal Salon, Second Floor, Fifth Avenue at 40th Street
ARNOLD CONSTABLE 5TH. AVENUE

Blending of promotional and institutional advertising Many advertisements combine promotional and institutional appeals. By weaving a considerable amount of store character into his promotional advertising, one prominent retailer has sought to build traffic, reflect the store's personality, and sell the item advertised—in that order.[7]

Food-store advertising, often cited (incorrectly) as strictly promotional in nature, well illustrates a combination of the two main types of retail advertising. A study of the advertisements of four competing food chains in Philadelphia some years ago concluded that they were used to create a favorable image so that customers would visit the stores—not necessarily for the items mentioned but for the general classification of products in stock. As a result, the typical advertisement contained three general classes

[7] Cf. Samuel Feinberg, "From Where I Sit," *Women's Wear Daily*, November 12, 1965, p. 8.

of items, with the first two classes greatly predominating: (*a*) those used to differentiate the advertiser from competitors, *i.e.*, items not stocked or not featured by other chains; (*b*) those serving as a reminder list—to inform customers of the breadth of stock; and (*c*) a few priced to neutralize the previous advertisements of competitors, *i.e.*, items on which competitors' advertised prices were met.[8]

□ Cooperative advertising

Typically, the retailer assumes complete responsibility for the preparation and cost of his advertising. At times, however, he engages in cooperative advertising, in which he shares responsibility and cost with a manufacturer or wholesaler. To illustrate: The product is advertised over the retailer's name with the resource paying part—typically, 50 percent—of the cost up to a maximum amount, commonly 5 percent of the retailer's purchases. Perhaps as much as $2 billion is spent each year by manufacturers on cooperative advertising, although this amount has probably declined recently.[9] In return for this expenditure, the resource gains from the added interest shown by the retailer in his product, from the retailer's prestige, and from the lower local advertising rates obtained. Despite these advantages, however, many manufacturers dislike cooperative advertising. They are dissatisfied with the return they obtain from the advertising allowance, and often prefer to deal directly with the media. Consequently, the trade press sometimes publishes stories of manufacturer dissatisfaction with the arrangement.

To the retailer, cooperative advertising yields benefits such as assistance in preparing his advertisements, the tie-in posters and displays supplied for use in the store, and in the increase in the total space he can afford. He should be sure, however, that the product is one with which he wants his reputation associated, and be fully aware of the obligations he assumes. On balance, the retailer should probably engage in some cooperative advertising, but be careful to select the best deals offered to him.

---

[8] Wroe Alderson, et al., *The Structure of Retail Competition in the Philadelphia Market* (Philadelphia: Wharton School of Finance and Commerce, 1960), p. 32. Cf., however, "Grocers' Ads Seen Shifting from Item Stress to Selling Store's Personality," *Advertising Age*, August 11, 1969, p. 83.

[9] The Federal Trade Commission pursues an active program designed to eliminate any discriminatory use of cooperative advertising. The guidelines issued following the Fred Meyer decision by the Supreme Court (see Chapter 12, p. 287) caused some firms to drop the cooperative arrangement. A major reason was the difficulty of legally administering a program under the guidelines established. Cf. "Motorola Reminds Distributors That It's Dropped Coop.," *Women's Wear Daily*, January 7, 1970, p. 50 and; "Shakeup in Coop. Ad Practices Seen," *ibid.*, April 8, 1971, pp. 1, 2. Also cf. Irving Scher, "Cooperative Advertising Guidelines Tend Only to Confuse," *New York Times*, January 24, 1971, p. F15.

☐ Expenditures for retail advertising

The total amount of money spent for advertising in the United States is large and continues to grow even larger. The 1969 annual total exceeded $19 billion—and in 1970 reached $20.8 billion—with local advertisers (mainly retailers) increasing their expenditures at a faster rate than national advertisers.[10] One investigator reports that "retail advertising is currently running at the rate of about $7 billion per year . . ."[11] This amount includes the limited amounts spent by small retailers who prepare their own advertisements—often with the advice and assistance of a local printer or newspaper publisher—as well as the large expenditures of discount houses, department, and chain stores, which operate extensive advertising departments often working in cooperation with advertising agencies. Thus, in the course of a year, the small neighborhood food store may spend less than a hundred dollars for the printing and distribution of a few hand bills, while the J. C. Penney Company spends $75 million for newspaper advertisements plus approximately $2.3 million in 75 market areas for television.[12] Its radio expenditures are also substantial.

Reliable figures showing the percentage of net sales spent for advertising by retailers as a group are not available. We do know, however, that the proportion spent varies widely among both large and small stores because of such factors as the type of store, its size and location, and the competitive situation. Among department stores, for example, which are large and consistent advertisers, advertising expenditures in 1969 varied from 2.18 percent of net sales for stores with sales under $500,000 to 2.84 percent for those with sales from $10 to $20 million.[13] For specialty stores the range for the same year was 2.29 percent for those with sales under $1 million to 3.14 percent for those with sales over $5 million.[14] For self-service discount department stores the combined dollar average is 2.31 percent of sales.[15] Among food chains the amount spent for advertising is 1.2 percent of sales.[16]

---

[10] Seymour Banks, Ronald Reisman, and C. Y. Yang, "Ad Volume Rises 1.6% in 1970 to $20.8 Billion, but U.S. Production Dips, Prices Increase," *Advertising Age*, June 7, 1971, p. 27.

[11] J. O. Whitney, "Better Results from Retail Advertising," *Harvard Business Review*, Vol. 40, No. 3 (May–June 1970), p. 111.

[12] P. H. Dougherty, "Penney Unit Looks like Agency, but Isn't," *New York Times*, June 14, 1970, p. F12.

[13] Jay Scher, *Financial and Operating Results of Department and Specialty Stores in 1969* (New York: National Retail Merchants Association, Controllers' Congress, 1970), pp. 3, 36.

[14] *Ibid.*, pp. 57, 70.

[15] Earl Brown, Panna Kulkarni, and Robert Day, *Operating Results of Self-Service Discount Department Stores 1969–70* (Ithaca, New York: Cornell University, 1971), p. 47.

[16] "Highlights of Chain Operations in 1970," *Progressive Grocer*, April 1971, p. 78. Based on Internal Revenue Service data, corporate retail food stores spent $677 million

■ PROGRAMMING RETAIL ADVERTISING

In practice, retail advertising involves determining the advertising appropriation, planning the advertising, preparing the actual advertisements, testing the advertising, and selecting appropriate media. These steps should be coordinated into a complete advertising program, perhaps with the aid of an advertising agency. To assist their members, retail trade associations prepare helpful materials at frequent intervals. Among those performing this service are the National Retail Furniture Association and the National Retail Hardware Association.

□ The advertising appropriation

The amount a store *needs* to spend for advertising will depend upon the objectives it is seeking to accomplish, together with such factors as the store's age, policies, size, location, trading area, competition, and its past success in attracting customers. It will also be influenced by the rates and circulation of media, by business conditions, and by what is done by similar stores.

What the retailer *needs* to spend for advertising, however, and what he can *afford* to spend are not always the same. In deciding how much to spend for advertising during a given period he should (1) analyze his situation carefully, (2) define his objectives, (3) decide upon the methods he will follow in attaining these objectives, and (4) set aside the money required—provided he can afford to do so. His success is influenced also by such factors as the right merchandise and selling appeals, proper timing, judicious pricing, effective presentation, and coordination of the program among different media. These factors strongly influence the productiveness of his expenditure.

□ Effective planning

The care with which advertising plans are made will determine the usefulness and value of the results they produce. Careful planning yields the following benefits: (1) It provides a definite concrete plan based on facts rather than indefinite, last-minute decisions based on opinions and guesswork; (2) it forces a review of past experience, thus focusing attention on past mistakes and successes; (3) it requires looking ahead—adopting a long-

---

for advertising in 1968 or 1.3 percent of sales. Large firms spent 1.5 percent and small firms 1.2 percent. Leland Southard, "Advertising Expenditures by Corporations Marketing Food," *Marketing and Transportation Situation,* November 1969, p. 19.

range perspective; (4) it takes into account all phases of the advertising program, thus insuring attention to each and its relationship to others; (5) it insures proper attention to the needs of each department and each store in departmentized and chain stores; (6) it anticipates new developments through projecting plans into the future for a specific period of time; (7) it considers probable changes in the status of competitors and their policies; and (8) it facilitates coordination of the advertising activities with those of merchandising, store management, and control.

Advertising should be planned in stores of all sizes, even in the small shop where the proprietor exercises direct supervision over all promotion. As in the merchandise plan or budget, the advertising plan may cover a period of several months and be further subdivided into months, weeks, or shorter special promotions. It should set forth programs for various types of promotions, including selection of merchandise to be advertised and choice of advertising media; and it should also provide for the coordination of advertising and special forms of sales promotion, as well as for adjustments to meet unforeseen conditions.

Proper timing Proper timing is vital in the planning of advertising efforts. Food retailers in some cities, since Thursday, Friday, and Saturday of each week are the days when customers usually make large purchases, concentrate their advertising in Wednesday afternoon and Thursday morning papers. Department and specialty stores often advertise heavily on Sunday on the assumption that Sunday newspapers are read more thoroughly than those published on weekdays. But the growing number of stores open five or six nights a week and on Sunday[17] may well result in "a tremendous shift" from the traditional heavy Sunday advertising to Saturday editions.[18]

For retailers of high-fashion goods, timing in terms of weather is particularly important. A large amount spent on advertising fall fashions during a warm spell may produce few sales. Likewise, the promotion of lightweight summer dresses during a summer cold spell may result in a large outlay with little customer response. In an effort to improve their timing, some retailers study the monthly weather forecasts of the United States Environmental Services and adjust their promotions accordingly. Others go far beyond this and subscribe to weather forecasting services.[19]

Here, again, many leading trade associations, such as the National As-

---

[17] Cf. Chapter 21, pp. 510–12 below, on this development.

[18] This opinion is expressed by the vice president of Foley's (Houston, Texas). Cf. "See Sunday Sales Saturday Ad Spur," *Women's Wear Daily,* January 27, 1970, pp. 1, 39.

[19] The *American Investor,* the magazine of the American Stock Exchange, reports a study that revealed a loss of retail sales of 1 percent for every degree of temperature below normal any day in the spring or above normal any day in the fall. It was found, also, that "every one-tenth inch of rain that falls between 7:00 and 11:00 A.M. on any day inevitably depresses sales by 1 percent." *Time,* "Economic Theory," March 19, 1965, p. 98.

sociation of Retail Druggists and the National Retail Merchants Association, recognizing that their members require assistance in developing advertising plans and timing these plans most effectively, prepare promotional calendars and guides for various months and events throughout the year.[20] Trade publications offer a similar service.

Suitable merchandise Perhaps the greatest waste of retail advertising dollars is promoting the wrong merchandise. The best advertisements cannot sell goods the customer does not want. In contrast, relatively poor advertising is often effective in moving *wanted* merchandise. A major purpose of retail advertising, therefore, is to increase the sale of such merchandise and every effort should be directed toward this objective.

In selecting goods to advertise, the retailer should be guided by past experience regarding proven best sellers; by the merchandise that is selling well in other stores; by pretesting goods to determine their probable rate of sale; by his desire to promote private brands; by the advice of his salespeople (and by department heads in larger stores); and by considerations of timeliness, buying habits of the community, variety, and frequency of purchase.

Finally, in selecting merchandise to advertise, a word of caution is in order. Too often retailers advertise certain items without first making certain that adequate quantities are on hand to meet reasonable sales expectations.[21] When quantities are exhausted, customers unable to buy the goods advertised are annoyed and encouraged to make their purchases elsewhere. Many alert retailers, aware that their stocks may be inadequate to meet customer demands, specify limited quantities or broken sizes and colors in their advertising copy.

□ Preparing the written advertisement

When the overall advertising plan has been completed, the retailer can turn to the three factors involved in preparing the actual advertisements: developing and writing the copy; choosing the illustration; and making the layout.

---

[20] These aids are illustrated in *Attracting and Holding Customers* (Dayton, Ohio: National Cash Register Company, n.d.), pp. 13–16.

[21] The prevalence of this practice among food retailers led the Federal Trade Commission to propose a rule requiring stores to stock ample supplies on all advertised items. Its surveys had shown that "outages of advertised specials run as high as 20 percent in some chain outlets in . . . Washington and Baltimore." The proposed rule was strongly opposed by the National Association of Retail Grocers and the National Association of Food Chains who contended that "outages . . . result from transportation and planning problems which are generally beyond control." Cf. "Retailers Urge FTC: Tone Down Food Ad Rule," *Advertising Age*, April 6, 1970, p. 24. As this is written no final action had been taken.

The copy The term "copy" refers to the reading matter of an advertisement, including both the text and the headline. Copy may be said to be the heart of a retail advertisement, although color, illustrations, and typography must be coordinated with it to obtain the desired results.

Since human wants and needs are the basic influences motivating behavior, the retailer's advertising copy should reflect a close familiarity with them. That is, copy should "interpret the want-satisfying qualities of [the retailer's offerings] . . . in terms of the consumer's [needs and desires]."[22] The retailer should also bear in mind that "efficiency in advertising seems to depend on the use of simple language—simple direct presentation of sales arguments—and the avoidance of tricky attention-getting devices unrelated to the product itself."[23] Unless these guiding principles are followed results are certain to be disappointing.

When the copy has been written, it should be subjected to certain tests to determine its value. Kleppner mentions the following qualities that should be examined:

> Does it present the benefits that the product offers to the reader? Is it clear? Is anything in it liable to be misunderstood? Is the most important benefit given the most prominence? Does it give adequate information? Is it accurate? Is it plausible? Can it be made more specific? Can the story be told in fewer words, in shorter words, or in fewer sentences? Does it make the reader want the product advertised? As to the headline, does it attract attention and create interest in the rest of the copy?[24]

The illustration There is an old saying that one picture is worth a thousand words. Although it is not essential that the advertisement contain an illustration—effective food advertising, for example, often contains no picture—retailers use illustrations frequently to attract attention, to show the merchandise and/or its use, to lend "atmosphere," and to confine the reader's attention within the advertisement. Small retailers find the advice and assistance of the local printer and the manufacturers whose products they handle of much value in choosing illustrations. Large retailers have their own specialists who, singly or in cooperation with advertising agencies or newspaper artists, devise appropriate illustrations to suggest the effect desired.

The illustration should be simple, clear, and appropriate; focus attention on the points desired; contribute to the value of the advertisement more than would an alternative use of the space; and "face" into the ad-

---

[22] Sandage and Fryburger, *op. cit.*, p. 249.

[23] Alfred Politz, "The Dilemma of Creative Advertising," *Journal of Marketing*, Vol. 25, No. 2 (October 1960), pp. 1–2. Also cf. "A & P's Own Brand of Consumerism," *Business Week*, April 11, 1970, p. 32.

[24] Otto Kleppner, *Advertising Procedure*, 5th ed. (Englewood Cliffs, N.J.: Prentice-Hall, Inc., 1966), pp. 108–9.

vertisement and toward the copy if possible. Otherwise the reader's "gaze motion" may be directed toward the advertisement of a competitor in an adjoining column.

The layout The layout usually consists of a sketch showing the location of the text, headline, and illustration in the advertisement. It enables the advertiser to visualize the complete advertisement and to provide instructions to the printer for setting up the advertisement. How detailed the layout will be depends upon the preferences of the person in charge of the advertising and the instructions required by the printer.

Just as there are certain guidelines for the retailer in other phases of his advertising plans, the retailer has similar ones in connection with layout. Specifically, the layout should (1) have attention value, presenting a complete and balanced picture pleasing to the reader; (2) provide the desired emphasis through focusing attention on the more important parts of the advertisement; (3) reflect the character or image of the store; and (4) make effective use of type faces and sizes, white space, slogans, and photoengravings in conformity with the best standards of advertising practice.[25]

□ Testing retail advertising essential

In recent years it has become necessary for retailers to check or test the effectiveness of their advertising. Tests commonly take one or both of two forms: (1) checking the advertisement prior to its insertion in chosen media —the precheck;[26] and (2) checking of the results produced—the aftercheck.

To insure proper coverage of all essential points in the precheck, checklists have been developed. The advertising department of the *Chicago Tribune* has long used the following and variations of it:

1. Has the advertisement maximum attention value?
2. Is it "in character" for the store it represents?
3. Does it dramatize the offer? This point includes the appeal to the reader's emotions.
4. Does it satisfy the sense of value of the prospective purchaser? This point could be elaborated to ask: Does it give conviction that price is right, that quality is good, that the merchandise will be beneficial and useful?
5. Does it inspire confidence in the advertiser?
6. Have necessary details been included as to size, color, style, price, address, phone, store hours, time of sale, free parking?
7. Has it a selling "hook" or unusual inducement for direct action?

---

[25] On trends in supermarket advertising, with emphasis on layout, cf. "Big, Bold Look Dominates Ad Layouts," *Supermarket News*, July 21, 1969, p. 4.

[26] In the words of one advertising man, "An ounce of copy pretesting is worth a pound of presumptions."

The aftercheck of advertising is equally important. Sales results should be compared with those expected, for the particular item, department, and the entire store. Such action permits analysis of the reasons for the results and helps the retailer to repeat past successes and avoid previous mistakes. Numerous difficulties, however, are encountered in measuring accurately the effectiveness of the advertising. Writes one economist: "It is almost impossible to measure the effects of past sales promotion efforts. And it is even more difficult to predict the effects of any combination of sales promotion devices in the future."[27] Although "keyed" advertisements are employed and offerings of certain merchandise are restricted to particular media, for example, other relevant factors cannot be held constant. Thus, a customer entering a store to purchase one item may see another advertised item on display and purchase it.

□ Selecting appropriate advertising media

In choosing the media[28] for his advertisements, the retailer should carefully evaluate all those available to him. Each medium should be evaluated in terms of (1) the store's present and prospective customers—their location, buying habits, reading habits, and income; (2) its cost in relationship to the money the retailer can afford to spend; (3) the advertising media used by competitors; (4) the trading area of the store; (5) the size of the store; and (6) the kind of message to be sent—whether it shall be of limited or general interest, or whether it shall be institutional or promotional. No medium is "correct" for all retailers under all conditions.

The more important media for retailers, each of which may be divided into several forms, are as follows:

1. Newspapers.
2. Magazines.
3. Direct mail.
4. Radio.
5. Television.
6. Outdoor.
7. Public vehicles.
8. Personal distribution.
9. Classified.
10. In-store.

Newspapers Newspapers constitute the main medium for large retailers and for many small stores with a trading area fairly comparable to that

---

[27] A. R. Oxenfeldt, *Pricing for Marketing Executives* (Belmont, Calif.: Wadsworth Publishing Company, 1961), pp. 11–12.

[28] For a concise explanation of the main factors governing the choice of media by small retailers and other businesses, cf. H. R. Cook, *Selecting Advertising Media: A Guide for Small Business* (Washington, D.C.: U.S. Government Printing Office, 1969).

covered by the local papers.[29] Among supermarkets newspapers are the predominant medium. Ninety-six percent of them advertised in newspapers in 1968 with 87 percent spending more money in this medium than any other.[30] The S. S. Kresge Company, which operates both variety stores and discount houses spends almost all of its advertising budget in newspapers. The J. C. Penney Company, as noted previously, spent about $75 million in this medium in a recent year. Perhaps 65 percent or more of the department and specialty stores' advertising budgets are spent for newspaper advertising. In contrast, newspaper advertising is too costly for the small retailer—the grocer, for example—whose market is very limited.

Many retailers of fashion merchandise seek publicity on the women's pages of newspapers. Since the editors of such pages wish to provide readers with newsworthy developments in fashions, buyers who furnish such information have little difficulty in obtaining recognition for themselves and for their stores.

Newspapers are popular among retailers because of their low cost per reader, market coverage, readership, quick response, quick check on results, availability for regular and frequent advertising, flexibility and speed, fewer size restrictions, and acceptance.[31] Despite these advantages, however, they possess obvious limitations such as the following: the waste circulation in certain areas and among people who are not potential customers; their numerous editions with "home coverage" not proportionately large; their short life, often an hour or less; the large number of advertisements they contain, with keen competition for the reader's attention; and their reproduction problems caused by the quality of paper used.

National magazines An interesting development in media usage by large retailers is the trend toward national magazines. Although specialty stores such as Saks Fifth Avenue, I. Magnin & Co., and Neiman-Marcus have used them for some time, only recently have department stores, chains, and mail-order companies begun their use on an extensive scale.[32] The reasons

---

[29] The Bureau of Advertising reports that in 1969 "retail advertising in newspapers had its best year [passing] the $3 billion mark." Cf. "Retail Looks Rosy," *Advertising Age*, April 20, 1970, p. 96. Another source states that "[1970] saw retailers pour about $150 million more into newspapers . . . than in 1969, for a total investment of $5.9 billion . . ." Cf. Denis Sheahan, "Stores Increased Print Ad Monies $150 M Last Year," *Women's Wear Daily*, January 11, 1971, p. 1.

[30] *The Supermarket Industry Speaks 1969* (Chicago: Super Market Institute, 1969), p. 19. Comparable data were not given in this publication in 1970 or 1971.

[31] Cf. C. J. Dirksen and Arthur Kroeger, *Advertising Principles and Problems*, 3d ed. (Homewood, Ill.: Richard D. Irwin, Inc., 1968), pp. 399–411.

[32] Cf. "Montgomery Ward Is 'Unexpected' in $2,000,000 Nationwide Magazine Push," *Advertising Age*, February 3, 1969, p. 3; and "Sears Moves Heavily into Magazines; Then Ward Gives It a Whirl," *ibid.*, October 20, 1969, p. 200.

for such a move are, in general, those given by Montgomery Ward: improvement of image, achievement of a more permanent impact, development of more enthusiasm among employees, increased consumer awareness of the firm's stores, wider interest in various merchandise lines, and higher interest.

Direct mail Direct mail[33] is the major form of advertising in some small stores. A Pennsylvania shop specializing in women's sportswear, for instance, found that five direct-mail pieces each year were sufficient for its purposes, so that no newspaper advertising of any kind was used. And a small fur store on Long Island, while inserting some advertisements in a local paper, relies heavily on three or four direct mailings each year to a list of 5,000 names, plus more frequent mailings to 500 to 1,000 persons. Even among department stores and specialty stores, direct mail is used extensively.

Properly used, direct-mail advertising enables the retailer to select his audience and to make his message personal in nature; it obtains concentrated attention without distraction from competing advertisements; it makes possible a more accurate check of results; and it permits choice among several methods of conveying a message. But it also has definite limitations. Its effectiveness is dependent on a mailing list the cost of which may be high, specialized skill is required to prepare the material, and the cost per unit is rather large for materials, printing or typing, postage, and preparation for mailing.[34]

Radio and television The universal use of radio in homes, places of business, passenger cars, and elsewhere makes it an advertising vehicle of significance to many retailers.[35] Likewise, television has become an important medium for a growing number of retail organizations, some devoting as much as 50 percent of their advertising dollar to this vehicle.[36]

The retailer using the radio or television may choose from a wide variety of programs and vary his appeals so as to reach all members of the family. He may reach them at times when they are receptive to suggestions of merchandise suited to their needs, and he may make last-minute changes

[33] On this topic cf. National Retail Merchants Association, *Direct Mail Advertising by Retail Stores* (New York: 1967).

[34] On the effective use of direct mail, cf. the section of this title in Irvin Graham, *Encyclopedia of Advertising,* 2d ed. (New York: Fairchild Publications, Inc., 1970).

[35] Cf. "Retailers Using 'Marconi Message,'" *Supermarket News,* November 10, 1969, p. 5. Highlights of a report by the Radio Advertising Bureau are presented. Also cf. John Osbon, "Chicago Retailers Pouring Their Ad Dollars into Radio," *Women's Wear Daily,* November 10, 1970, p. 36.

[36] Cf. "Allied [Stores Corporation] Members to Devote 33–50% of Ad Budget to TV," *Women's Wear Daily,* October 1, 1969, p. 18; and Ben Cohen, "Roos/Atkins Cuts Print Ads, Stepup in Radio, TV Planned," *ibid.,* February 9, 1970, p. 13. But also cf. "Newsmen Feel TV Has Far to Go for Retail Ad Dollar," *ibid.,* January 19, 1970, p. 2.

which appear advisable. Finally, radio and television advertising lend prestige to some types of retailers and create confidence and enthusiasm among employees.[37]

Perhaps the major disadvantage of radio and television is the fact that, because of their cost, their use is restricted mainly to large- or medium-size stores, or to combinations of small stores, although spot announcements are often within the cost possibilities of the small retailer. Also, many retailers do not appreciate the fact that these media demand special talents; some programs are ineffective because they are developed without professional aid.

Personal distribution The shopping-news type of publication, one form of personal distribution, is typically owned cooperatively by the retailers who advertise in it, but some are nonretailer controlled. Usually published once or twice a week, each issue consists of retail advertisements and brief articles on matters such as fashions and recent developments of interest to prospective customers. These papers are distributed free to homes and apartments in the city or within designated boundaries.

Some stores, especially those in small cities, often use hand bills or dodgers. Even some large stores such as Sears and Penney's make extensive use of dodgers in the form of circulars. Properly prepared, these media are quite effective in stimulating the sale of general merchandise, household items, foods, and other goods. They are especially useful for special sales events discussed in a subsequent section.

■ TRUTH IN ADVERTISING

The effectiveness of retail advertising is dependent upon the confidence of readers in the honesty of the advertiser. As two students have written: "If advertising does not have the confidence of most consumers, it will lose its influence and surely die. If people grow to disbelieve a substantial percentage of the advertising messages that come to them, they will soon tend to reject most or all advertising."[38] Yet some retailers continue to be guilty of misleading and exaggerated claims in their advertising, thus bringing discredit to themselves and making readers skeptical of advertising in general.[39] Consequently, leading retailers, manufacturers, advertising men, the govern-

[37] Among supermarkets, for example, cf. "TV: Chains Picture of Prestige," *Supermarket News,* May 12, 1969, p. 1 ff.

[38] Sandage and Fryburger, *op. cit.,* p. 79. For a critical exposure of some advertising practices and techniques that are misleading, cf. S. S. Baker, *The Permissible Lie: The Inside Truth about Advertising* (Cleveland, Ohio: World Publishing Company, 1968).

[39] Cf. B. W. Becker, "The Image of Advertising Truth: Is Being Truthful Enough?" *Journal of Marketing,* Vol. 34, No. 3 (July 1970), pp. 67–68; and E. J. Kottman, "Truth and the Image of Advertising," *ibid.,* Vol. 33, No. 4 (October 1969), pp. 64–66.

ment, and others have long been active in curbing the unfair advertising practices of this minority group. Among other ways, this program has been furthered through the work of Better Business Bureaus, the *Printers' Ink* model statute against unfair advertising, which has been adopted in whole or in part by 44 states[40] and the District of Columbia, the Uniform Deceptive Practices Act developed by the Council of State Governments; the work of the Federal Trade Commission including its "little FTC Act"; and such federal acts as the Wheeler-Lea Act of 1938 and the Food, Drug and Cosmetic Act of 1938.[41] And in November 1969, the "Consumer Protection Bill of 1969" was introduced in Congress listing, among other factors, 11 specific sales practices the federal government planned to expose through action by the Justice Department and the Federal Trade Commission.[42] Among these were "bait and switch" selling, failure to make appropriate refund of deposits, recommending unneeded goods and services, misrepresenting brand and quality, and guaranties.

Each merchant owes to his fellow retailers his full support of activities looking toward the elimination of untruthful advertising.

■ SPECIAL SALES EVENTS

An important part of the retailer's advertising program is the planning and execution of special promotions or special sales events—that is, the heavy promotion of merchandise at reduced prices for a limited period of time. Most retailers believe these events contribute significantly to sales and profits, and that they maintain the customers' interest in the store. As one successful retailer has said: "Store business is show business."

Three kinds of special sales events may be distinguished: (1) Distress sales—those designed to raise money quickly regardless of their effect on future business; (2) turnover sales—those conducted to sell slow-moving merchandise or to close out a line, brand, or department; and (3) promotion sales—those used to attract new customers, introduce new goods, or secure favorable publicity. Illustrative of the many forms which these events may

---

[40] In 1968 the American Advertising Federation proposed a Model State Deceptive Practices Act for submission to state legislatures for enactment. Certain provisions applied directly to advertising. Text of the proposed act is given in *Advertising Age*, November 25, 1968, pp. 26–28. It is difficult to provide accurate information regarding the action taken in the various states since the model acts serve primarily as spring boards for legislative action. It can be reported, however, that some 24 states are considered not to have adequate legislation in this area by the Federal Trade Commission.

[41] For details, cf. C. F. Phillips and D. J. Duncan, *Marketing: Principles and Methods*, 6th ed. (Homewood, Ill.: Richard D. Irwin, Inc., 1968), pp. 119–31.

[42] These practices are detailed in "Eleven Criteria for False Advertising Specified in Bill," *Advertising Age*, November 24, 1969, p. 3.

take are the following: clearance sale, anniversary sale, white-goods sale, back-to-school sale, Mother's Day sale, one-cent sale, and fire sale.

The types of special sales events used by a retailer, and their frequency will depend upon his past experience, the competitive situation, group efforts undertaken with other retailers as in a shopping center, aid obtained from manufacturers, the seasonableness of the weather, the accumulation of slow-moving merchandise, and similar factors. Many large stores use special sales extensively to obtain a satisfactory sales volume,[43] but when used too frequently, they undermine customer confidence in "regular" prices. In addition, customers become indifferent to such events, employees lose their enthusiasm, accounting and control problems are complicated, and merchandise returns are increased.

□ Joint promotions

Special sales events are often organized by groups of retailers. This practice is not new. But the growth of shopping centers has brought group promotional activities to a new peak. Retailers in these centers have long engaged in joint promotions, often organized around the visit of a celebrity, a circus, an outdoor party on the parking lot, an art exhibit, a concert, or a beauty contest. As shopping centers grew in size and number, and as they became competitive with one another, special sales events became even more desirable as a means of drawing customers to a particular center; and this trend was furthered as free-standing discount houses became more numerous and gave the centers formidable competition for customers. In turn, the special events of shopping centers and discount houses have forced downtown merchants to undertake joint events of their own.

□ Planning special sales events

Regardless of whether the special sales event is used by an individual retailer or by a group of retailers, it must be planned with care so that all activities are effectively coordinated. Store-wide sales, for instance, are often planned three to six months in advance. To obtain the best prices, buyers should approach resources in ample time to arrange for price concessions, which are frequently made possible through production in dull periods or because of vendors' overstocks. When these arrangements are completed, time is required for production, delivery to the store, receiving,

[43] Sears, Roebuck and Co., for example, commonly features such events during the last four days of each week and often supplements them with extra specials on Saturdays, Sundays, and Mondays.

and marking. Time is necessary, also, for the preparation and release of advertising—a task superimposed on the regular daily activities of the advertising staff—and for the securing of additional selling and nonselling employees to meet anticipated requirements. Otherwise, the value of the advertising in bringing customers into the store is diminished, since sales are lost and customers become disgruntled because of poor service.

■ STORE DISPLAY

The growth of self-service has brought increased emphasis on display in stores of all kinds and sizes. Both window and interior displays have undergone a renaissance and more attention is being given to their coordination with advertising and personal salesmanship to build a balanced sales promotion program.[44] Yet many retailers still continue to misdirect the talents of their display people, fail to criticize displays constructively, and neglect fashion emphasis. In other words, "the greatest shortcoming in many stores is management's lack of interest and desire in building good-looking displays."[45]

□ Window displays

Importance as a sales producer Window displays have long been recognized as a builder of sales volume because of their emphasis on specific merchandise, their attractiveness, and the prestige they create for the store.[46] As the authors have noted for many years, their primary purpose is to stop passersby from passing by and induce them to enter and (hopefully) purchase the merchandise shown.

Since windows are at the front or side of a store, the space they occupy is among the most valuable footage in the building. Recognition of this fact has served to make management continuously aware of the importance of window displays and the need for care in planning and evaluating them. Evidence that many retailers manifest such an awareness is furnished by the considerable expense they assume to prepare their window displays. Some of the chains even have headquarter experts set up the forthcoming displays,

---

[44] The close relationship between store layout and display has already been discussed in Chapter 6. Cf. pp. 138–40, above.

[45] Bob Vereen, "Why Worry about Competition?" *Hardware Retailer,* September 1969, p. 13. Also cf. "Special Display: Key Weapon in the Period Ahead," *Progressive Grocer,* May 1970, Part II, pp. 193 ff.

[46] Cf., as illustrations, Trudy Prokop, "Wanamaker Windows Stop Traffic Like a Red Light," *Women's Wear Daily,* April 24, 1969, p. 22; and Peter Ainsle, "Saks Blazing New Trail in Display," *ibid.,* September 8, 1970, pp. 1, 49.

and then send photographs and complete instructions for their reproduction to their store managers. In the department store field, also, it is the belief of some display directors that "display headquarters away from the central downtown store location is the trend of the future."[47] Usually, however, window display experts are part of the regular staff, sometimes supplemented with outside professionals who provide ideas and materials for such special occasions as the Christmas season.

Perhaps most display money is still allocated to windows despite the growing emphasis on interior displays, a trend evident for more than a decade. As one Sears, Roebuck and Co. executive stated in 1960: "Show windows to display merchandise were justified when people rode buses and streetcars. Now most of our customers come by automobile. They enter the stores through the rear parking lot. Advertising, not display windows, brings them in."

Effectiveness of window displays Most retailers consider display windows vital to successful operation yet, unfortunately, they neglect to plan them properly, to "dress" them effectively, and to change them frequently. Too many merchants still consider window dressing as a necessary evil, delegate the responsibility to employees uninterested in such work, and refuse to spend money on fixtures and supplies necessary to do the job properly. The inevitable result is that sales are lost because the store is looked upon as unprogressive. Such a situation is more common among small retailers than among large ones. Large stores, as a rule, plan their window displays several weeks in advance, carefully select merchandise to be displayed, arrange definite time schedules for each window, and assign display space to various departments upon the basis of need, prevailing conditions, and other similar factors.[48]

A good window display can usually convey effectively only one message. This message, of course, may relate to any one of a number of ideas—the variety of values offered; the fashion leadership of the store; or the tie-in with holidays such as Easter, Independence Day, Thanksgiving, and Christmas, or with special occasions such as Mother's Day.

The value of window displays is determined by the frequency with which they are changed. Although much depends on the location of the store, both as to size of the city and the site occupied as well as shopping centers, probably stores in small cities *should* change their displays more frequently than stores in the central shopping areas of the large cities or

---

[47] Kathleen Warren, "Parisian's Display Headquarters Kept apart from Stores," *Women's Wear Daily*, May 5, 1970, p. 40.

[48] Cf. Suzy Farbman, "Hudson's Top Display Men Change Signals Faster than a Traffic Light," *Women's Wear Daily*, August 12, 1969, p. 46.

those in regional shopping centers. In practice, however, the reverse is likely to be the case, but small city retailers are now changing displays more often than in past years.

□ Interior displays

Interior displays constitute practically the only method of inside sales promotion other than window displays in some stores—particularly supermarkets, variety stores, and many small grocery, drug, and hardware stores. Other retailers coordinate such displays with newspaper advertising featuring the same kinds of merchandise. Or they use them to induce their customers to purchase additional items: Perhaps one-half or more of the purchases made in some types of stores are the result of decisions made by the customer *after* entering the store. And with impulse buying so prevalent in many stores, the correct use of interior displays requires continuous attention.[49] Among food chains, for example, where self-service is so common, the number and use of special displays continues to increase. Whereas in 1969 35 percent of such stores reported using more displays at one time than previously, by 1970 this percentage had increased to 44.[50] In this connection it is interesting to note that during the same period the proportion of displays given to private brand items gained from 35 to 40 percent.

Types of interior displays Interior displays may be conveniently classified into three groups: (1) merchandise displays, (2) dealer displays, and (3) store signs and decorations. These classifications are rather arbitrary and overlappings among them are inevitable.

1. Merchandise displays Merchandise displays constitute the main type of interior displays. Three forms may be distinguished: open, closed, and architectural displays.

Open displays are those that make merchandise accessible to customers for examination without the aid of a salesperson. Their variety is legion—shelf displays, as in self-service food stores; counter-top displays, as in drugstores; island displays and mass displays, as in supermarkets; and table-top displays and rack displays, as in department stores. Open displays permit customers to handle merchandise, are readily adjustable to meet variations in customers' demands, are simple and inexpensive to set up, and employ advantageously space that otherwise might not be used. Interestingly enough, some experiments have concluded that "jumble" (rather than

---

[49] For excellent discussions of the importance of displays in food stores, cf. "How the Basics of Special Display Affect Sales and Profits," *Progressive Grocer,* January 1971, pp. 34–45; and "How to Make Displays More Sales Productive," *ibid.,* February 1971, pp. 34–45.

[50] "Trends in Special Display," *ibid.,* April 1971, p. 88.

neatly stacked) displays encourage the customer to handle, and to buy, more merchandise.

Closed displays consist of merchandise shown inside a wall case or showcase and inaccessible to customers without the aid of a salesperson. Their chief advantages are protection against theft and maintenance of merchandise in salable condition. For example, merchandise such as jewelry, fur coats, silverware, and expensive cosmetics is so valuable that close control must be exercised. Men's and women's clothing needs protection from excessive handling to prevent soiling and wrinkling.

Architectural displays provide an appropriate setting showing various articles of merchandise in use, such as model homes or complete kitchens or complete bathrooms.[51] Their main advantage is that they dramatize the merchandise by showing it in a realistic setting.

2. Dealer displays Dealer displays, also known as point-of-sale (or point-of-purchase) advertising, consist of signs, banners, display racks, and other selling aids provided by the manufacturer, including those used in windows. Levi Strauss & Co., for instance, furnishes an "Instant Window Trim Kit" to its dealers. Dealer displays encourage sales in two ways—by reminding salespeople of the product and its merits, thus encouraging suggestion selling, and, more significantly, by informing the shopper of a product at the very moment she is in a buying mood. From the manufacturer's point of view, dealer displays can present the advantages of his product pictorially and dramatically. And this presentation is made to the very people most interested in his product since they are in a store where such products are sold.[52]

Although many valuable displays are furnished retailers by manufacturers either as a gift or at a moderate charge, the increasing volume of point-of-sale display material, coupled with the much slower expansion of available space in the store where this material may be placed, has created problems both for the retailer and the supplier. The manufacturer encounters greater difficulty in getting his displays used and retailers find that many of the displays are too large, poorly designed, and ineffective as sales tools. It is evident, therefore, that the retailer must consider each display piece on its own merits and find satisfactory answers to such questions as: Is the display suitable to my type of operation? Does the merchandise concerned justify the area occupied by the display? Does the attached sign, taken in

[51] A comparable concept is "shop merchandising" in which related groups of merchandise are displayed together in the proper setting. Thus, in a hardware store might be found a Bath Shop, a Gourmet Shop, and a Bridal Shop. Cf. "Shop Merchandising: New Dimension in Housewares," *Hardware Retailer,* January 1970, pp. 119–27; and Ellen Hackney, " 'Shop Merchandising' Opens New World of Housewares Display," *ibid.,* July 1970, pp. 45–53.

[52] The effective use of dealer displays is discussed in Kleppner, *op. cit.,* p. 410 ff.

conjunction with the merchandise, tell the customer the full sales story, or is the salesperson still needed? What is the cost of the display rack or case?

3. Store signs and decorations The term "store signs" includes counter signs, price cards, window signs, hanging signs, posters, elevator cards, flags, banners, and similar devices. These selling aids are used by all retailers, but mostly by stores making frequent use of special promotions and sales events. They are helpful in directing customers to items being featured and in calling attention to particular merchandise values.

Decorations refer to distinctive displays and other related preparations for such occasions as Christmas, Halloween, and for anniversary and birthday sales. Seeking to generate a spirit that will be conducive to buying, retailers probably devote more attention to their Christmas decorations than to those of any other time.

■ RESPONSIBILITY FOR ADVERTISING AND DISPLAY

Regardless of store size, responsibility for advertising and display activities carries with it the obligation to originate and to appraise such activities and to combine them effectively to attain the desired results. In small stores the responsibility rests with the proprietor. In larger ones this responsibility is delegated to qualified individuals, so that the proprietor may devote his attention to coordinating all activities of the business.

In department stores responsibility for sales promotion is centered in the publicity director or the sales promotion manager, who may have the assistance of an advertising agency in planning and carrying out his assignment. Under him may be a display manager who is responsible for window and interior displays; an advertising manager who directs the work of the advertising department—including copy, art work, and production for various media; and an individual in charge of miscellaneous methods of promoting sales of the types mentioned in the previous section. Sometimes this person may be called the "fashion coordinator." And the growth in use of television has led some stores to create the position of "broadcast coordinator."[53]

Among chain stores, problems are encountered unlike those in single-store operation. For example, traveling window-display crews may be employed, and advertisements in the form of matrices or proofs, television spots, and radio tapes may be sent to individual stores for use. The J. C. Penney Company, for instance, takes the latter step some 30 days before a

---

[53] Cf., for example, W. G. Peck, "L. S. Ayres Establishes Post of Ad Broadcast Coordinator," *Women's Wear Daily*, July 25, 1969, p. 40.

particular program goes into operation. Items that are "newsworthy and will create a response" are selected jointly by buyers and by sales promotion specialists—who are located in New York City—about four or five months in advance of the use of the advertisements. The New York office employs some 250 "communicators" organized into three departments—production, media, and broadcast. This office works closely with an advertising agency in performing its various functions.[54]

In chain organizations the lines of responsibility are similar to those in department stores, and, depending upon the size of the firm and its policies, an advertising agency may or may not be used in carrying out the activities involved.

■ REVIEW AND DISCUSSION QUESTIONS

1 Explain the term "sales promotion" and the factors that determine the part played by advertising in a retail store's sales promotional program.

2 Distinguish among the main types of retail advertising and indicate the considerations that influence the use of each type. Under what conditions is a combination of the types advisable?

3 Define "cooperative advertising" and point out some of the recent developments in connection with its use.

4 Account for the wide variations among different types of stores in the amounts spent for advertising.

5 Explain briefly the main steps to be followed in programming retail advertising.

6 Assume that you have been asked to prepare an advertisement for a small retail store of your own choosing in your particular community. How would you proceed and what information would you want to fulfill this assignment?

7 Precisely how should a retailer proceed in evaluating the various advertising media available to him? What basic determinants govern his final choice?

8 Explain the chief characteristics of "special sales events" and the steps involved in planning and executing them.

9 Discuss the importance of store display and the need for coordinating it with the store's overall sales promotional program.

10 Suggest desirable guidelines for the retailer in planning (*a*) his window displays and (*b*) his interior displays.

---

[54] P. H. Dougherty, *op. cit.*

chapter 19

RETAIL SALES PROMOTION BY OTHER NONPERSONAL METHODS

In addition to advertising and display as discussed in the previous chapter, other nonpersonal methods of retail sales promotion are used by retailers. Among those of importance today are telephone and mail-order selling, packaging, labeling, and consumer premiums, including trading stamps.

TELEPHONE AND MAIL-ORDER SELLING

Soliciting purchases or accepting orders by telephone or mail on the part of retail stores is not a new development.[1] As long ago as 1905, Strawbridge and Clothier of Philadelphia used a full-page advertisement to tell potential customers that it was "The Telephone Store."[2] But not until the depression of the 1930s did a substantial growth in telephone selling take place. In contrast, mail-order selling by retailers has long been accepted as

[1] As used throughout this section, "mail orders" refer to such sales made by retailers who predominantly sell over the counter.

[2] *Philadelphia Bulletin*, June 3, 1905.

an easy and convenient method because customers could buy needed merchandise and have it delivered.

☐ Extent and importance

Today both large and small stores actively encourage telephone or mail orders in their advertising.[3] The extent of this practice is evident from the advertisements in the Sunday issues of metropolitan newspapers many of which contain the statement "Mail and Phone Orders Filled" (some mentioning "within five days of receipt of order," and others noting the minimum-size order that will be accepted). In many cases reply coupons are used to facilitate ordering by mail (see Figure 19–1). In fact, the practice of

FIGURE 19–1 Coupon used by department store to facilitate ordering by mail

ALEXANDER'S MAIL ORDER DEPT. ST-6-28-70
P.O. Box 107, Fordham Station, Bronx, New York 10458
Enclosed please find check or money order for $________.
Please send the following knit dresses:

STYLE	QUANTITY	SIZE	COLOR 1st choice 2nd choice

Name________
Address________
City________
State________ Zip Code________

Add 60c for delivery of each knit. Add 6% sales tax within N.Y.C. No phone orders. No C.O.D.'s.

ordering by telephone and by mail has become so prevalent that on occasions customers must be reminded that no mail or telephone orders will be accepted for special merchandise offerings.

In addition to the solicitation of telephone and mail orders through newspapers, a growing number of retailers periodically issue small catalogs or booklets, especially just prior to the Christmas season, to emphasize fashion, seasonal, and other merchandise.[4] In fact, the tremendous growth of

---

[3] A Michigan State University study reveals that mail and telephone shopping has doubled in recent years despite the expansion of suburban shopping centers. Cf. P. L. Gillett, "An Analysis of Demographic, Socioeconomic and Attitudinal Characteristics of the Urban In-Home Shopper" (unpublished Ph.D. dissertation, Michigan State University, 1969), p. 5.

[4] Marshall Field & Co.'s *Fashions of the Hour* and I. Magnin & Co.'s Christmas Catalog are good examples of this practice.

mail-order selling is one of the most striking retailing developments in recent years. States one close observer: ". . . Americans today are being inundated by some 19 billion pieces of direct mail and by an estimated 100 million catalogues this year [1970]. And much of this sale-by-mail explosion has been ignited by those innocent-looking plastic credit cards that lie so quietly ready in the man's wallet."[5]

Many other illustrations of telephone and mail-order selling by retailers are readily available. In 1966 the J. C. Penney Company purchased a small mail-order firm and placed order desks in many of its stores in order to ultimately provide a nationwide mail-order service. Sears, Roebuck and Co. attributes a substantial part of its post-World War II increase in sales to the growing popularity of its telephone selling. Sales of this type have grown so rapidly in recent years, now accounting for an estimated 5–10 percent of total sales,[6] that the company's retail promotion manager terms the development to be the result of "a telephone class of customers." To serve this customer the company has installed telephone sales service in each of its stores, mail-order plants, and catalog, retail, and telephone sales offices. In 1969 alone the company added 197 catalog, retail and telephone sales offices and units operated by independent catalog merchants.[7] Favorable results from telephone selling are also being shown by such other firms as Montgomery Ward & Company,[8] Spiegel, Inc., and Aldens, Inc., each providing telephone service through telephone offices, catalog offices, and retail stores.

In the department store field, many firms now sell 5 to 13 percent of their volume by telephone.[9] Carson Pirie Scott & Co. of Chicago; T. Eaton Company, Ltd. of Toronto, Canada; The J. L. Hudson Company of Detroit; and numerous others have long promoted sales by this medium. The same is true for many small and large retailers of other types in all parts of the country; many neighborhood and downtown drug and food stores, for instance, have long depended on the telephone to bring in many of their

---

[5] Isadore Barmash, "Credit Cards Ignite Explosion in Sale-by-Mail," *New York Times*, August 16, 1970, p. F1. This is an excellent source of information on present and prospective sale-by-mail trends.

[6] The company does not publish sales figures revealing telephone business as distinct from order desk and catalog sales office business. Our 5–10 percent estimate is based on various statements made by Sears' executives.

[7] Cf. *1969 Annual Report*, p. 15.

[8] In Montgomery Ward's Fort Worth, Texas, store a staff of 72 telephone "shoppers" provide 24 hours per day service. Cf. Hildred Barber, "Say Catalog Chains Will Be TV-Phone Shopping Leaders," *Women's Wear Daily*, November 13, 1969, p. 26.

[9] National Cash Register Company, *Attracting and Holding Customers* (Dayton, Ohio, n.d.), p. 27.

orders. Among specialty stores, telephone selling is also an effective sales tool.

☐ Factors contributing to growth of telephone and mail-order selling

In analyzing the growth of telephone and mail-order selling we need to consider the points of view of the customer and the retailer.

Customer's point of view The telephone has come into widespread use in homes[10] and business because buying by telephone is convenient and is demanded by many buyers as a customer service. The inconveniences of shopping are avoided, and there is no tiresome walking to do and no driving and parking problems to solve. A survey of 52 major department stores in 7 cities conducted by students at the Harvard Graduate School of Business Administration a few years ago led to these conclusions:

1. Telephone sales are plus sales. They do not replace floor sales. Half of the women interviewed shop by phone in one store and in person in another.
2. Half of the women interviewed stated they shop by phone for many items not advertised in the newspapers.
3. The average sales check on phone orders is 40 percent higher than on floor sales.
4. Other factors, like distance from the store, inclement weather, lack of babysitter, illness, and sundry other problems favor telephone shopping in many instances.[11]

Retailer's point of view The telephone offers the retailer an easy method to contact customers and point out especially advantageous purchases of merchandise. Improved telephone-selling equipment closely adapted to the retailer's needs is also available. As for mail-order selling, it is easy for the store to insert a few words in advertisements indicating that the same merchandise can be purchased by mail. Customers, therefore, can avoid the traffic and congestion in downtown shopping areas. And progres-

---

[10] On December 31, 1969 about 56,663,000 households in the United States (90.3 percent of the total) had telephones. (Information supplied authors by Pacific Telephone.)

[11] Cf. Fred Eichelbaum, "Bells Are Ringing up Extra Sales in Best's Campaign," *Women's Wear Daily,* March 29, 1966, p. 48. But also cf. footnote 1 in Chapter 10, p. 235, above.

sive retailers have found that mail-order and telephone selling enables rather close contact to be maintained with their customers.

Many large stores also feature a "Shopping Service" designed to assist telephone or mail-order customers in finding suitable merchandise for all types of occasions. Some of them use special names to identify this service. In San Francisco, for example, the Emporium has its "Barbara Lee" and I. Magnin and Company its "Kitty Steele."

□ Telephone selling as a business builder

The telephone can build business for the retailer in the following ways.

1. Customers can be notified of the receipt of merchandise which was not in stock at the time of their visit to the store or which has been ordered especially for them. Such service prevents lost sales and builds customer goodwill.

2. As the business grows and each of the employees builds up a personal following, there is an increasing opportunity to make use of the telephone to get business by personal calls to customers who are pleased to be notified when some new merchandise arrives.

3. New residents can be tactfully solicited on the telephone, although this practice should be followed carefully. Some shop owners do not approve of it, as they claim that a blind solicitation by telephone often annoys a customer; if she is a busy housewife any interruption of her duties may be considered a nuisance. Therefore, it is often better to build customers' confidence by securing their permission to telephone them.

4. The telephone can be used in an effort to revive inactive credit accounts. With friendliness and a desire to obtain facts, one can:

(*a*) express regret over the decreasing volume of business from such credit customers;

(*b*) ascertain any cause for dissatisfaction;

(*c*) make what commitments you feel are deserved by the circumstance; and

(*d*) solicit an increase of future business.[12]

□ Limitations of telephone and mail-order selling

Despite the growth of telephone and mail-order selling, and despite some evidence to the contrary, many retailers are still reluctant to employ these forms of sales promotion because they fear customers will be kept from visiting their stores. Consequently, some of them still run the line "no

[12] *Attracting and Holding Customers, op. cit.*, p. 27.

mail, no phone, no COD" in their advertisements, hoping this will induce store visits and result in other purchases being made. Other retailers object to this type of selling because the merchandise sold is more likely to be returned than that bought in the store, resulting in increased costs and reduced profits. Of course, if a retailer trains his telephone staff to say, "Let us send you several dresses from which you can select one or two," high returns on telephone sales are to be expected. A similar result follows the sending out of merchandise—for instance, fruits and vegetables—which over-the-counter customers refuse to purchase. If the store makes an honest effort to treat telephone and mail-order customers as well as it treats those who come to the store, there is no reason for excessive returns on such sales.

Some practical operating disadvantages must also be overcome. Sufficient stock should be maintained to permit fulfillment of all orders, thus avoiding customer disappointment when goods are unavailable; delivery service must be provided; and arrangements made to collect on COD transactions and/or to extend credit to telephone customers who desire to purchase on this basis. The telephone salesperson also is at a disadvantage in that she cannot see the customer[13] and thus note facial reactions to suggestions made. Moreover, some expense and trouble is involved in training and maintaining a telephone and mail-order staff.

☐ The future of telephone and mail-order selling

Disagreement exists among retailers concerning the future importance of this business. Those who have obtained satisfactory results from these sales promotion methods are convinced they have a bright future, but those who have not obtained the benefits expected often reach an opposite conclusion. On balance, it seems to the authors that the current sales increases from these methods of selling are in line with fundamental trends, and that further gains may be expected. But each retailer must determine the extent to which he will utilize these sales promotional devices based on his judgment of their effect on his sales volume, the costs involved, and their relationship to other forms of selling effort he is employing.

In conclusion, it should be emphasized that sales by telephone and mail order do not just happen; they are the result of proper planning and the continuous, effective execution of these plans. Successful telephone selling, for example, depends in no small degree upon (1) proper selection and training of personnel; (2) a satisfactory wage scale, which will attract the desired

---

[13] The recent development of the Picture Phone may overcome this objection in the years ahead. By 1976 this service is planned for 27 cities.

type of employee; (3) proper working conditions, including the provision of adequate facilities; and (4) competent supervision.

■ PROMOTING SALES THROUGH IMPROVED PACKAGING

The past two decades and more have witnessed a sharp increase in the attention given to packaging by manufacturers and by retailers. Today, well-conceived packages are essential both in stores where displays must carry a major part of the sales task and in retail outlets which rely mainly on salespeople.[14] Packaging also influences both store layout and display, since the maximum effectiveness of packages cannot be obtained without good display techniques and appropriate fixtures. Assuming that manufacturers and retailers combine these elements into well-conceived programs, packaging should become even more important over the years just ahead.

□ Current emphasis on packaging

Four main factors have led to the growing interest in packaging by manufacturers and retailers: their desire to meet their customers' wishes, the realization that the package is an effective tool of sales promotion, the growth of the self-service and self-selection store, and various technological and environmental changes. All of these factors are interrelated; each factor is partly cause and partly effect of the others.

So far as customers are concerned, they have favored the "packaging revolution" since it aids them in buying convenient amounts, assures a higher degree of sanitation, protects fragile items, provides convenient containers for the storing of items while being used in the home, and offers a way to communicate product differences and information.

In addition to pleasing his customers, the manufacturer or the private-branding retailer who packages his product discovers he has gained a valuable sales promotion tool.[15] In fact, some marketing experts rate package appeal as the main reason why a consumer buys one product rather than another. Although the authors are not in agreement with this statement, because in the long run it is the customer's satisfaction with the contents of

---

[14] For a unique explanation of the major aspects of package evaluation based on the word "View"—visible, informative, emotionally appealing, and workable—cf. D. W. Twedt, "How Much Value Can Be Added through Packaging?", *Journal of Marketing,* Vol. 32, No. 1 (January 1968), pp. 58–61.

[15] For illustrations of this point, cf. W. P. Margulies, "Plan Packages to Fit into Their Retail Environment," *Advertising Age,* February 2, 1970, pp. 51–53.

the package which results in repeat purchases, there is little doubt but that the appeal of the package—including its style, color, utility, and attractiveness—plays a role in the product's salability. Consequently, the manufacturer who devises an attractive package often finds he has increased his competitive advantage over his competitors.[16] This competitive factor has been especially significant in self-service stores, where there are no salesmen to extol the merits of the less distinguished package or the unpackaged merchandise.[17]

Technological changes have made possible the greater emphasis on packaging. To illustrate, when the packaging of fresh meat was first attempted the available materials led to discoloration. Gradually the research laboratory turned out today's plastics, including transparent trays, which allow the meat to "breathe" and retain its natural color, thus increasing its salability. Similar technological changes in the wood, paper, metal, and glass industries have produced an almost unbelievable variety of containers.[18]

Two other developments are also bringing significant shifts in packaging. One is the growing acceptance among consumers for foods originating abroad, *i.e.*, ethnic foods, which has stimulated new packaging strategies.[19] Second, and perhaps more important, is the sharply increased interest in ecology on the part of consumers and retailers alike. Improved packaging and the disposal of used containers and packages are matters of growing concern and the recycling of such waste is gaining in all areas of our country.[20]

□ Retailer preferences in packaging

Retailers want packages that attract customer attention, protect the product, make the product available in proper amounts or sizes, reflect the

---

[16] One major supplier of gift packaging for retail apparel departments and stores emphasizes the fashion aspects involved and the need to redesign packaging to cover the complete store image. Cf. "Susan Crane Proves Packaging for Stores Can Be Fashion," *Women's Wear Daily*, September 9, 1969, p. 48.

[17] In the opinion of one marketing research director: "An effective package can be the most efficient mass selling medium that marketing management can employ. It is worth much more attention and money than are now devoted to it by most companies." D. W. Twedt, *op. cit.* Also cf. "Trends in Supermarket Packaging, 1970," *Chain Store Age* (Supermarket Executives Edition), August 1970, p. 29 ff.

[18] Cf. "The Sophisticated Materials," *Dun's Review and Modern Industry*, November 1966, pp. 144–47.

[19] W. P. Margulies, "Booming Ethnic Food Market Spurs New Packaging Strategies," *Advertising Age*, April 19, 1971, pp. 59–60.

[20] Consumer attitudes concerning the disposal problem are discussed in "What Consumers Think about Packaging Waste," *Modern Packaging*, March 1971, pp. 38–41.

nature and use of the product, offer convenience in handling and placing on the shelves and in customer use, make effective displays, are moisture-proof, and are easily identified so that the customer is aided both in the selection process and in the rejection of substitutes. They also want packages which are not deceptive to the customer, such as results from slack filling. Many customers believe deception through packaging still exists, a condition substantiated by their buying experiences.[21] Manufacturers and private-branding retailers who engaged in this practice had only themselves to blame when the late President Kennedy urged a government program looking toward "improving packaging standards and achieving more specific disclosure of the quantity and ingredients of the product inside the package. . . .[22]

LABELING TO PROMOTE RETAIL SALES

Labeling is the placing of text or pictorial material upon a product or attaching such information to its container. It is illustrated by the gummed paper sheet on the package, the printed material placed inside the container, and the tag attached to the product itself.

Labeling has long been used for such purposes as identifying the manufacturer or distributor of a product, disclosing the quantity of product in the package and the materials from which it is made, and informing the customer as to how the product should be used. In recent years—with the expansion of self-service stores and federal legislation requiring certain product information on various consumer goods—labeling has become an important tool of sales promotion. On a tag attached to a television set appears a brief listing of the set's special features. Directions on a tag attached to a woman's Orlon sweater emphasizes the ease with which the sweater can be washed. The gummed label on a package of cake mix employs both text and picture to convey the message that in a few minutes the customer can produce a cake superior to that "which mother made." And legislation now makes mandatory the listing of ingredients in foods as well as the composition of textile products.[23]

---

[21] Cf. James Antone, "Charge Consumer Is Confused by Unfair Packaging Methods," *Women's Wear Daily*, May 27, 1969, p. 33; and Pat Barnes, "Charges Cosmetic Packaging Disguises Hike in Prices," *ibid.*, June 6, 1969, p. 83.

[22] Message to Congress of March 15, 1961, as reported in full in the *New York Times*, March 16, 1962.

[23] How the "Fair Packaging and Labeling Act" has affected labels and packages in food stores is discussed in "Packaging," *Chain Store Age* (Supermarket Executives Edition), July 1969, pp. 30–46.

☐ Retailers' interest in labeling

Retailers have much to gain from the awakened interest in labeling. Labels may promote additional sales and reduce selling costs by requiring less aid from salespeople. Since the added information helps customers select merchandise better suited to their needs, their goodwill is gained and fewer returns of merchandise result. As with packaging, however, the retailer suffers if the labeling is misleading. Consequently, regardless of whether the manufacturer or the retailer does the labeling, accuracy on all labels is essential.

☐ Truth in packaging and labeling

Governmental efforts are also being directed toward better-labeling practices: witness the 1966 enactment of the "Fair Packaging and Labeling Act," commonly referred to as the "Truth-in-Packaging Act."[24] The Act became effective July 1, 1967, and called for expanded responsibility by the Federal Trade Commission and the Food and Drug Administration in areas covered by the Act's title. Among the provisions are those authorizing the Commission and the FDA to move against the following actions, among others: (1) misleading pictorial matter on labels; (2) packages or labels not listing the ingredients, the net quantity, and the size of serving when the number of servings is specified; (3) the use of such words as "jumbo" or "giant" quart; and (4) the employment of "cents off" deals other than on a short-term basis. Specific regulations were issued governing compliance after public hearings and comments from those affected, but numerous problems were encountered in this process.[25]

Despite the need to eliminate deception in packages and labels, there is real concern among some retailers and manufacturers that government regulations in this area may result in unnecessary restraints on private business. Specifically, they "fear that negative rules against misrepresentation and deception may lead into detailed, positive regulative requirements and standards" which will weaken the competitive positions of honest companies. Consequently, it is important that Congress "strike a proper balance

---

[24] Some of the conditions which the Act sought to correct are suggested in E. T. Grether, "Sharp Practice in Merchandising and Advertising," *Annals of the American Academy of Political and Social Science*, Vol. 363 (January 1966), pp. 108–16.

[25] Cf., for instance, M. C. Howard, "FTC Faces New Experience," *Marketing News*, September 1, 1969, p. 7; Isadore Barmash, "Truth in Labeling Proves Elusive," *New York Times*, June 8, 1969, p. F1; and "U.S. to Step up Lagging Enforcement of Packaging Law, Congress Is Told," *Advertising Age*, March 30, 1970, pp. 10, 71.

so that only packaging and labeling that in fact do confuse and deceive consumer are proscribed."[26]

PROMOTING SALES THROUGH CONSUMER PREMIUMS

The use of consumer premiums[27] as traffic builders and as sales stimulators for retailers, particularly those in the food field, has assumed boom proportions in recent years. Used to some degree since the early years of this century, today an increasing number of companies are "devoting special sales efforts to the premium field, sometimes setting up separate divisions." Currently the premium business approximates $3.5 billion annually,[28] of which grocery retailers do an estimated 20 percent.[29] The retailer may use premiums to induce his customers to pay their bills on time, to watch demonstrations, to sell specific merchandise identified by his own brand or that of the manufacturer, and to promote continuous customer patronage.

Types of consumer premiums

From the continuous customer-patronage point of view, a premium may be defined as a tie-in arrangement in which a product (the premium) not part of a seller's regular sales assortment is sold at a discount or given away in return for purchases made in the regular sales assortment. From the point of view of the retailer, two major types of such arrangements may be distinguished: (1) the single transaction offer in which the customer may obtain the premium with a single purchase either as a gift or for the payment of a small additional amount; and (2) the continuity offer involving a series of purchases to accumulate coupons, cash register tapes, trading stamps, or the like to obtain a premium.[30] Illustrations of the first type are: (*a*) a miniature fire boat for $1 and two Kellogg's Rice Krispies box tops, and (*b*) the gift of the *Encyclopedia of Sports* with a Gillette Razor. As already

[26] E. T. Grether, *Marketing and Public Policy* (Englewood Cliffs, N.J.: Prentice-Hall, Inc., 1966), p. 47.

[27] Although many manufacturers use premiums to promote the sale of their merchandise, the present discussion is restricted primarily to activities of retailers. Cf., however, "Redemption of Manufacturers' Coupons" in a later section of this chapter.

[28] Estimated in a special report of the *Grocery Manufacturer* entitled, "How the Industry Uses Premiums," September 1969. The same report quotes the president of the National Premium Sales Executives as stating that "premium activity exerts some influence on more than $100 billion in sales."

[29] *Ibid.*

[30] Another classification of consumer premiums used by grocer manufacturers is as follows: (1) self-liquidators, (2) in-pack premiums, (3) coupon plans, (4) on-pack premiums, (5) free mail-in premiums, and (6) container premiums. "How the Industry Uses Premiums," *op. cit.*

suggested, an example of the continuity offer is provided by the trading-stamp plans which are discussed in the next section of this chapter.

Careful planning and proper execution of a premium program is essential, including establishing guides for selecting products to use as premiums, providing adequate publicity, arranging operating details, and maintaining close cooperation with the manufacturer.

□ Trading stamps

For many years trading stamps have been used by retailers to promote sales. The percentage of total retail sales accounted for by retail stores offering trading stamps is not currently available. One source reports that in 1970, however, sales of stamp services declined 5.81 percent to $773 million.[31] Among supermarkets, which have long been leading users of trading stamps, their use continues to decline. This decline began, perhaps, in 1966 when food prices started to increase and stores started dropping stamps in favor of lower prices. Whereas 78 percent of supermarkets distributed stamps in the 1961–1963 period, by 1970 only 37 percent did so. And in 1970 but 31.2 percent of local and regional chains and 22.4 percent of independent supermarkets and superettes were using this promotional tool.[32]

Reports one careful researcher

> . . . The inroads made by the discounters, the near saturation level in the use of stamps by competitors in many markets, and the declining shopper interest in stamps have all set the stage for supermarkets to discontinue stamps and return to lower-price merchandising. As a result, several thousand supermarkets have discontinued stamps and the share of market held by stamp-giving stores has decreased, on the average 25% from the peak year 1962. In markets where price competition has been particularly severe . . . the market share of stamp-giving supermarkets has fallen by as much as 75% to 100% from their highest market penetration.[33]

Stamps appeal to many customers Despite the decline in the use of trading stamps among supermarkets and the negative reaction of some customers to this promotional device, many retailers continue to offer them to satisfy the preferences of their other customers. A study in four midwestern cities in 1965 revealed that "trading stamps were saved by 90 percent of

[31] "Trading Stamps in a Decline," *Incentive Marketing,* March 1971, pp. 57–63. Yet, in the long run, they remain "the most effective retail traffic building promotion ever devised."

[32] "38th Annual Report of the Grocery Industry," *Progressive Grocer,* April 1971, p. 65; *The Super Market Industry Speaks 1971* (Chicago: Supermarket Institute, 1971), p. 12.

[33] F. C. Allvine, "The Future for Trading Stamps and Games," *Journal of Marketing,* Vol. 33, No. 1 (January 1969), p. 52. Also cf. B. J. LaLonde and Jerome Herniter, "The Effect of a Trading Stamp Discontinuance on Supermarket Performance: A Panel Approach," *Journal of Marketing Research,* Vol. 7, No. 2 (May 1970), pp. 210–15.

all the respondents" and, in general, "respondents in all four cities had favorable attitudes toward trading stamps."[34] Many factors probably contributed to this favorable response.

To some customers, stamps are a relatively painless way of saving. To others, they offer certain psychological satisfactions: a reputation for being thrifty, a response to the collecting instinct, and a sense of accomplishment in filling one's stamp books and redeeming them for merchandise. But the basic answer is economic in nature: The belief that the store offering trading stamps gives them more per dollar spent (when both the merchandise purchased and that obtained through the stamps are considered) than does the nonstamp store.

It is not feasible here to present evidence supporting customers' beliefs in the real value obtained from trading stamps or whether higher prices are paid because of their use.[35]

Requirements for successful use of trading stamps Trading stamps are not a panacea for all retailers. Competitive conditions will not usually allow a retailer to raise his prices to compensate for the cost of stamps, and the discontinuance of stamps involves many serious problems. Before adopting them the retailer should be reasonably sure that he can increase his sales or reduce his other operating costs. These goals can be achieved only if he has some or all of these characteristics: (*a*) sufficient excess capacity to permit absorbing a 10 to 20 percent increase in sales without an appreciable change in total overhead costs; (*b*) a location in reasonably close proximity to a group of stores in various fields using the same brand of stamp to facilitate stamp accumulation by consumers; (*c*) a willingness to promote the stamps, *i.e.*, he must encourage customers to take them, save them, and redeem them; and (*d*) the ability to meet his competitors in terms of convenience of location, prices, selection and quality of merchandise, courteous and friendly service, cleanliness of housekeeping, and type and quality of services. In the words of one supermarket executive: "Whether stamp or discount, the *best operated* store is the one which succeeds."

Since not all retailers have these four characteristics, or do not have them in the same degree, the success they have achieved with stamps varies widely. Some have so increased their sales that their profits have advanced, despite the cost of the stamps; others have suffered lower profits.

---

[34] J. G. Udell, "Can Attitude Measurement Predict Consumer Behavior?," *Journal of Marketing*, Vol. 29, No. 4 (October 1965), p. 50.

[35] The interested reader will find such evidence in the following sources: F. E. Brown and A. R. Oxenfeldt, "Price and Quality Comparisons between Stamp and Nonstamp Food Stores," *Journal of Retailing*, Vol. 45, No. 3 (Fall 1969), pp. 3–10; F. E. Brown, "Price Movements Following the Discontinuance of Trading Stamps," *ibid.*, Vol. 43, No. 3 (Fall 1967), pp. 1–16; H. L. Vredenburg and H. H. Frisinger, "The Value of Trading Stamps as Measured by Retail Prices," *ibid.*, Vol. 41, No. 3 (Fall 1965), p. 31; and Udell, *op. cit.*, p. 50.

What of the future? As to the future of trading stamps, present trends are not very favorable. We have noted (page 469), the share of market held by food stores offering them has declined sharply in recent years. And this has occurred despite multiple-stamp days, the use of coupons in advertisements providing double the stamps usually given on purchases, and similar attractions.[36] A survey by the Super Market Institute found 37 percent of the respondents believed that stamps are "here to stay," 24 percent thought they "were on their way out," and 39 percent were "uncertain" as to their future. Moreover, the answers disclosed that of the stores which had dropped stamps, 66 percent reported the move was a wise one for the store, 3 percent found the results disappointing, and 31 percent stated "it was too early to say."[37]

Turning to the conclusions of the researcher quoted previously, we find still another unfavorable forecast of the use of trading stamps in food stores.

> The evidence studied revealed no reason to suspect that the pressures giving rise to the dropping of stamps will abate . . . Over the next five years the rate at which stamps will be dropped will at least equal, if not exceed, that of the past five years. . . .
>
> The synergistic benefits by the non-competitive stores giving a particular stamp are seriously reduced when a food chain ceases to distribute a stamp. Thus, as fewer food chains distribute stamps, a corresponding decline in the issuance of stamps by other types of retailers can be expected. . . .[38]

In these days of constant change in retailing it is more difficult to forecast developments, perhaps, than ever before. Each retailer, therefore, needs to analyze his particular operations with great care, and review thoroughly his customers' preferences and his chief competitors' policies before deciding whether to use trading stamps in his sales promotion program.

□ Factors in growth of premium merchandising

Some attempts have been made to interpret the current widespread use of premiums by retailers "merely as a phase of a cycle entirely comparable

---

[36] On the Pacific Coast in 1970 some gasoline service stations were offering as many as 15 times the usual number of stamps to their customers. Yet in other areas stamps have been discontinued. Also cf. "Hundreds of Midwest Gas Stations Revolt and Give up Trading Stamps," *National Observer*, November 24, 1969, p. 6; and "The Games Oil People Play," *Business Week*, April 19, 1969, pp. 132–38.

[37] "What Is the Future of Trading Stamps," in *The Super Market Industry Speaks, 1970, op. cit.*, p. 19.

[38] Allvine, *op. cit.*, p. 52.

with the past." More than a decade ago, however, an authority in this field emphasized several causal factors that indicated such an interpretation was not justified. These factors, which are still pertinent and bear repeating, are as follows:

1. The dominance and increasing trend toward limited service distribution of food and allied products at retail. . . . Consequently, (*a*) manufacturers of grocery products can expect little help from dealers through personal selling efforts and (*b*) shelf positions, display, and price are much more important relatively in influencing purchases by consumer-buyers.
2. Paralleling this trend is that toward one-stop shopping by consumer-buyers at single enterprises or in integrated shopping centers. Consequently, (*a*) competition among manufacturers for consumer attention is focused more sharply and (*b*) endeavors to find relief by seeking distribution through unorthodox outlets run into increasing resistance.
3. The high degree of concentration of volume in the hands of chains, supermarkets, voluntary chains, cooperatives, and large-scale or organized groups, together with the preceding two influences has made it increasingly essential for manufacturers to focus their promotional efforts more sharply and more effectively, especially in the food field. It is much simpler relatively to hold the whip-hand over an army of unorganized small dealers. . . . The bargaining position of large-scale and organized dealers has been greatly improved by their demonstrated capacity to sell products under their own private labels.
4. Sales promotional difficulties and necessities have been accentuated in recent years by three developments in brand promotion: (*a*) the rather complete knowledge and acceptance of the commodity as such by consumers in many product fields involving heavy consumer expenditures (that is, the pioneering, learning phase of market promotion is past); (*b*) the general acceptance of several brands of such products as almost entirely interchangeable (for example, the lack of recognition by many consumers of basic product differentiation, as among the major brands of gasoline); and (*c*) the growing importance of chain and other controlled brands. This latter expansion in itself, of course, reflects to a considerable extent the previous two factors.
5. An exceptional opportunity for premium selling directed at children has been created by (*a*) the increasing proportion of the population in the lower age levels arising out of the increase in the birth rate during and since World War II, and (*b*) the enormous increase in the number of TV sets in American households.
6. Finally, the widespread presence of fair trade, unfair practices, unfair sales, and anti-discrimination laws on the statute books of the states and the evolving code of fair competition in federal law and regulation have raised legal issues quite different from those prior to World War I. Among these issues, perhaps the most interesting and as yet unresolved one is just what a nonusing seller may do lawfully in good faith in meeting the competition of competitors offering premiums, trading stamps, and similar inducements. Under about half of the fair trade laws

such practices are supposed to be prohibited. Under the other fair trade laws and the unfair practices acts, and under special forms of legislation, the legal issues are greatly beclouded.[39]

Recent years have not only brought considerable proliferation in premiums and other forms of incentive merchandising, but consumers have become more sophisticated in their attitudes toward such promotions. One prolific writer notes that "the bulk of . . . incentive promotions have a strong appeal to only about 15% of the market (in number of adults) . . . and that by far the majority of [them] achieve only a temporary increase";[40] such promotions, therefore, are losing their effectiveness.

Redemption of manufacturers' coupons For years many retailers have been concerned about their role in handling the coupons used by manufacturers to induce consumers to try new products. These coupons are made available to the consumer in a variety of ways, most commonly through newspapers, Sunday supplements, and magazines, by direct mailings, and in or on packages. The face value of the coupons ranges from 3 cents to 50 cents, with a 10-cent coupon being used most frequently, so that they are attractive to value-conscious shoppers. A survey conducted by the A. C. Nielsen Company revealed that 17.5 billion coupons to promote drug and food products were distributed by advertisers in 1969, an increase of 1 billion over 1968. Redemption rates vary from some 3 percent for newspapers to 15 percent for direct mail. Current data showing the dollar savings they represent off the regular prices of the products affected are not available, but probably far exceed the $100 million figure of 1965.[41]

With the large number of manufacturers presently using coupons, the retailer faces a heavy task in redeeming them and returning them to the issuing manufacturers for credit. In April 1969, 10 large manufacturers increased the coupon-handling fees they paid to retailers from 2 cents to 3 cents. This action followed a study by Arthur Andersen Company, sponsored by seven food industry associations, which revealed that retailers handling costs were 2.1–2.7 cents for chains and 3.2–4.6 cents for independents.[42] Many other manufacturers, however, failed to take similar action but were expected to follow eventually. The benefits derived from this increase were a matter of considerable conjecture on their part.

---

[39] E. T. Grether, "External Product and Enterprise Differentiation and Consumer Behavior," in R. H. Cole, ed., *Consumer Behavior and Motivation* (Urbana, Ill.: Bureau of Economic and Business Research, University of Illinois, 1956), pp. 91–93.

[40] E. B. Weiss, "Today's Sophisticated Consumers Are Killing off Incentive Promotions," *Advertising Age,* December 1, 1969, p. 98.

[41] Data supplied by the Promotion Department of the A. C. Nielsen Company.

[42] "Mixed Reaction Greets Raising of Coupon Fees." *Supermarket News,* April 14, 1969, p. 1.

PROMOTING SALES THROUGH OTHER METHODS

In addition to the methods and devices described, retailers use numerous other ways and means to attract customers to their stores and to retain their permanent patronage. Merchandise stunts, such as inviting a star baseball or football player to a sporting-goods store or department to meet customers and assist them in their purchases or to autograph goods purchased, afford a type of showmanship which often stimulates sales. Fashion shows, in which the newest designs in women's ready-to-wear are featured on live models, are widely used by department stores and by some specialty and limited-line stores. Flower shows, such as those held by Macy's of San Francisco and the May Company in its Denver store, attract numerous "observers" and undoubtedly many buyers. Contests of various sorts—related to cooking, photography, and craftsmanship—are sometimes used by retailers.

In many communities, retailers cooperate in the planning and execution of an annual "Bargain Day" to attract customers to the shopping district and thus to increase sales. Some stores sponsor parades to advertise the store and promote business. R. H. Macy & Company's parade inaugurating the Christmas season and using mammoth balloon animals and comic strip characters is probably one of the best known.

Still other illustrations of techniques used to encourage sales include games of various kinds of supermarket chains—Bonus Bingo and Let's Go to the Races, for example.[43] And, a Bonus Gifts program, operated as a joint venture by the Rexall Drug and Chemical Company and the Glendinning Companies which gives consumers the option of taking cash or trading stamps in promotional redemptions, "threatens to be the largest on the horizon in its field."[44] In addition, many stores provide a sampling of foods and candy; and still others conduct demonstrations, either in the store or in the home, to promote the sale of appliances.

Although there is no question that all of these methods attract crowds and stimulate sales, recent consumer opposition, the proliferation of consumer protection laws, and the boycotting of stores have forced users to reevaluate their programs. Numerous people are attracted merely to observe rather than to buy, and the resulting congestion may interfere with regular business and increase the stolen-goods problem. Yet, used with discretion, these sales promotion methods can prove very effective. Above all, they

[43] In 1970 Safeway Stores, Inc. was featuring dinnerware and stainless flatware at reduced prices, in most cases requiring a $5 purchase to obtain each piece.

[44] "Consumer Laws and Coupons on Upswing, Premium Users Hear," *Advertising Age*, December 1, 1969, p. 6.

should be carefully planned in the light of the store's standing in the community and should denote originality and distinctiveness in the minds of customers.

■ GOVERNMENTAL CONCERN OVER SALES PROMOTION PRACTICES

Besides actively seeking the improvements in packaging and labeling referred to previously,[45] the federal government has evidenced its concern for the consumer in many other ways. To cite one prominent example: In 1964 President Johnson, motivated by the increasing disparity in the prices received by farmers and the prices paid by consumers in retail stores, appointed a National Commission on Food Marketing to examine the causes of this development. The report of the Commission[46] contains certain suggestions or proposals related to sales promotion methods and devices which are of particular interest to the student of retailing. Considerable controversy was provoked by the report and a strong dissent to various findings of the Commission was issued by 6 of its 15 members. They deplored the summary presented in the "overview and appraisal" as well as the "conclusions" of the majority because they considered them "unsupported and unsupportable."[47] The advertising industry also was highly critical of the Commission's analysis.[48]

It is not possible here to analyze in detail either the Commission's proposals or the arguments against them. Let it suffice at this point, therefore, to note that the report contained material related specifically to grade labeling and standards, packaging, trading stamps, and to the difficulties encountered by the consumer in buying foods, all pertinent to the previous discussion in this chapter.[49]

In other areas both the federal and state governments have been active in their efforts to protect the consumer from misleading sales promotional materials. Among activities of the former are the work of the Federal Trade Commission attacking in-package coupon usage[50] and "free" offers as well

---

[45] Cf. pp. 467–68, above.

[46] National Commission on Food Marketing, *Food from Farmer to Consumer* (Washington, D.C.: U.S. Government Printing Office, 1966).

[47] *Ibid.*, p. 126. For statements by the minority members cf. pp. 125–89.

[48] Cf., for example, W. H. Chase, "How Can the Food Industry Answer that Damning Report?," *Printers' Ink*, July 22, 1966, pp. 21–24, 29; and "First Toll of a Death Knell," *ibid.*, p. 26.

[49] Cf. the report, especially pp. 77, 101, 109, 130–31, and 150–51.

[50] Cf. "FTC Attacks In-Package Coupon Use," *Supermarket News*, December 22, 1969, p. 1.

as its rules to prohibit games "rigging";[51] the ban on the use of cyclamates in foods by the Food and Drug Administration—with the resultant questioning concerning other additives—causing a furor among manufacturers using them and consumers alike;[52] and President Nixon's message to Congress calling for a "Buyers' Bill of Rights" in November 1969.

Concerning state efforts, of chief interest, perhaps, is the formation of consumer advisory councils in many states[53] and the growing awareness of consumers of their need for protection against the deceptive practices of some manufacturers and retailers. The revelations of Ralph Nader and his associates have contributed to this awareness.

■ REVIEW AND DISCUSSION QUESTIONS

1 Explain the present and probable future status of (*a*) telephone selling and (*b*) mail-order selling as forms of retail sales promotion.

2 Discuss these statements:
   a) "An effective package can be the most efficient mass selling medium that marketing management can employ."
   b) "Packages should be planned to fit into their retail environment."

3 Based on observations in local stores, give four examples of labeling used to promote sales. In at least two of these examples, suggest how the labeling could be improved.

4 Explain the nature and meaning of the Fair Labeling and Packaging Act with particular reference to its implications in the field of retailing.

5 Summarize in sufficient detail to make your meaning clear the main types of consumer premiums and the steps necessary to insure their success by users of them.

6 How do you account for the growth of trading stamps as a sales promotional tool and their recent discontinuance by many stores?

7 Visit three stores in your community which now use or have discontinued using trading stamps and obtain the views of executives concerning their value and the problems connected with their use.

---

[51] These rules on games of chance currently (January 1971) apply among food stores and gasoline service stations. Cf. 16 CFR Part 419, August 4, 1970 (*Commerce Clearing House Trade Regulation Reporter*, paragraph 7, 975).

[52] Cf. J. J. Schrogie, "A Decision on Cyclamates" in *FDA Papers* (Washington, D.C.: Food and Drug Administration, Bureau of Medicine, November 1969), p. 28 ff.; and "FDA Asks Relabeling on Cyclamate Limit," *Supermarket News*, April 1, 1969, p. 1.

[53] Cf. "Consumer the Queen Bee as States Buzz to Protect," *Supermarket News*, January 27, 1969, p. 4.

8 Review the special forms of sales promotion (other than trading stamps) which have been used recently in your community. Appraise the results of these efforts.

9 Explain briefly the meaning and purposes of premium merchandising and the main factors responsible for its growth.

10 What evidence can you present to indicate the growing concern of the federal government regarding sales promotional practices?

chapter 20

PERSONAL SALESMANSHIP

Except for self-service stores and purchases from vending machines or by mail, a customer-salesperson relationship is essential to consummate a retail sale. The importance of this relationship is evident when it is realized that the impression the customer receives from the salesperson often forms her opinion of the store.[1] The attitude and actions of the salesperson in dealing with the customer can even nullify the sales-promotion efforts which are responsible for the latter's presence in the store. Stated positively, the customer should be treated in a manner that will please her, that will assist her to make purchases suited to her needs, and that will secure her continuous patronage. These are the purposes of retail salesmanship; it should be the goal of every salesperson to aid in their accomplishment.[2]

CURRENT SIGNIFICANCE OF RETAIL SALESMANSHIP

Someone has defined salesmanship as "selling goods that won't come back to customers who will." If articles of merchandise sold to customers

[1] Cf. "Customer Is Created at Point of Purchase," *Stores*, February 1969, pp. 33–34.

[2] All phases of personal selling are discussed in O. P. Robinson, W. R. Blackler, and W. B. Logan, *Store Salesmanship*, 6th ed. (Englewood Cliffs, N.J.: Prentice-Hall, Inc., 1966).

meet their needs adequately, if the prices paid represent good values, and if customers are satisfied with the services rendered by the store, then these customers will continue to patronize the store. This regular patronage is necessary for stores to operate successfully and is based upon goodwill—the disposition of a pleased customer to return to the store where she has been well treated. The importance attached to customer goodwill by one retail organization is indicated by these lines which are constantly reiterated to all store personnel: "Let no man and no woman leave this store at night without being able to say, 'I have done something today to preserve and increase the goodwill of Rich's.' "[3]

This Customer-is-King concept of salesmanship—to look at everything from the customer's point of view—is relatively new. For many years the doctrine of *caveat emptor* (let the buyer beware) prevailed. Under this doctrine the forces of persuasion and cunning were brought to bear upon the prospective customer, so that she would buy regardless of her intentions or the suitability of the goods for her requirements. Today, however, in marked contrast to the early concept of salesmanship, the idea is to help people to buy. The preference of satisfied customers for particular stores and particular salespeople is built upon the faith they have in the honesty and the sincere desire of management and salespeople to serve the customers' interests.[4]

☐ Personal salesmanship still necessary

During recent years some observers have contended that the era of informed, creative personal selling in stores has passed and that we are now in the age of impersonal selling. As a discount house operator has said within the hearing of one of the authors: "We don't want salesmen in our organization. Our people are educated order-takers. . . . Our clerks are trained to be courteous, to answer his (customer) questions, and give him what he wants, but not to waste time trying to sell him anything. I believe this is the coming pattern of retailing—for every kind of merchandise—cars, motor-boats, everything. Selling has become an unnecessary vocation."

Those who take this "personal salesmanship is unnecessary" point of view are influenced by a number of developments, such as the pre-selling of customers by national advertising; the growing part of the selling task as-

---

[3] F. H. Neely, *Rich's: A Southern Institution since 1867* (New York: The Newcomen Society in North America, 1960), p. 14.

[4] "It is no exaggeration to appraise pleasing, cordial attention and service as being the prime factors in making people want to patronize a store." *Attracting and Holding Customers* (Dayton, Ohio: National Cash Register Company, n.d.), p. 24.

signed to merchandise displays, packaging, and labeling; the rise of self-service and self-selection stores as illustrated by the supermarket and the discount house; and by the thought that the automated store lies just ahead. A few of them even see the end of the retail store as we know it, with the customer "shopping" at home over a television set or ordering by telephone from a "warehouse with no floor traffic" establishment.

Although the foregoing factors have lessened the importance of personal selling in *some* stores, most observers still consider personal salesmanship essential in the vast majority of retail stores and, despite its shortcomings, the great need is for improvement rather than curtailment. Actually, executives in *service* stores of all types recognize the need for such improvement, especially in view of the growing competition among retailers and the continued expansion in the variety and supply of merchandise available. Moreover, shorter hours and higher wages have forced management to give more attention to increasing the productivity of employees.

☐ Effectiveness of retail salesmanship

The quality of retail salesmanship today still leaves much to be desired. Too many salespeople are either uninformed about the merchandise they sell or too uninterested to tell the customer what they do know. Discourteous treatment of customers is much too common.[5] Slow service is *not* the exception. Chatting among salespeople while customers wait is so prevalent that ". . . even in full-service stores, customers are not approached by salespeople within a reasonable period of time in from 10 to 50 percent of the instances and . . . discourteous, uninformed, unintelligent floor selling is common . . ."[6]

For many years the Willmark Service System, Inc., of New York City has analyzed the selling efforts of salespeople in retail institutions of various types. Until quite recently it prepared a retail "selling quotient" for the United States: With 100 percent representing the ideal sales performance, its studies rated actual performance as about 75 percent—thus suggesting ample room for improvement. Moreover, the current situation has changed little from that described by the late Pierre Martineau more than a decade ago:

---

[5] Rudeness among salespeople is so prevalent that a growing concern about it is being manifested by retail executives in all parts of the country. Cf. "Salesclerks Stir Counter Warfare," *Women's Wear Daily,* September 23, 1969, pp. 1, 16.

[6] E. B. Weiss, quoted in Herbert Koshetz, "The Merchant's View," *New York Times,* November 11, 1965, p. F11. Of course slow service is also a result of too few salespeople in some stores. For a technique of determining the number needed cf. C. J. Stoker and Philip Mintz, "How Many Clerks on a Floor?" *Journal of Marketing Research,* Vol. 2, No. 4 (November 1965), pp. 388–93.

It is ironical that at the very time when a better educated and discriminating shopper expects more from the store and the clerk, management is dragging its feet in upgrading salespeople. The stores are more beautiful and interesting; they have escalators, air conditioning, and improved fixtures; they have buyers ranging far and wide to offer the broadest merchandising selection. But what about the salespeople?[7]

□ Vital need for improving retail salesmanship

In view of the conditions described, it is apparent that retail salesmanship should be improved and it is management's pressing obligation to adopt whatever measures are necessary to accomplish this objective. Self-selection and self-service have been widely adopted but such action merely dodges the problem by substituting impersonal sales methods for the salesperson. Moreover, all too often self-selection and self-service, instituted to reduce selling costs, have resulted in poorer rather than better customer service.

In stores where retail salespeople are necessary, measures may be taken by management to obtain better productivity by salespeople. Probably the most important is the selection, training, and supervision of the sales staff. Qualified personnel cannot be hired without carefully prepared job descriptions and tests to determine if applicants possess the required characteristics. And they cannot perform adequately without proper training in their duties, including emphasis on proven sales techniques.

Supervising and evaluating salespeople is essential to the attainment of sales goals.[8] The basics of sound sales supervision have been summarized by one authority as follows:

1. Know what you expect the salesman to do.
2. See that he knows what you expect him to do.
3. Know that he does what you expect of him.
4. Let him know you know that he has done it.
5. Let him know you appreciate what he has done.[9]

Although these points apply to salesmen in general, they have equal relevance to retail salespeople. Numbers (1) and (2) have been covered in the previous paragraph. Concerning numbers (3), (4), and (5), it is evident that everyone deserves recognition of his accomplishments, encouragement in seeking continued improvement, and adequate rewards when the desired results are achieved.

---

[7] Cf. his "The Personality of the Retail Store," *Harvard Business Review*, Vol. 36, No. 1 (January–February 1958), pp. 52–53.

[8] Cf. "Management's Responsibility for Personal Salesmanship," pp. 493–94 below.

[9] J. C. Aspley, *The Sales Manager's Handbook* (Chicago: Dartnell Corp., 1968), p. 708.

Many firms have adopted an "engineering approach" to improve sales efficiency. Essentially, this approach refers to the use of mechanical equipment, store layout improvements, scientific grouping of merchandise, and the better planning of the flow of work so that the salesperson has more time to devote to selling. Automation in its various forms has reduced substantially the time required to perform *nonselling* activities. The use of mechanical devices has speeded up the movement of merchandise from receiving areas and stock rooms to the selling floor; electronic equipment has decreased the time that sales personnel must give to recording sales transactions; and inventory-taking has been facilitated through the use of various sophisticated devices. But the adoption of such measures is only a good beginning; future years are certain to bring many more significant developments as competition forces the need for greater sales productivity and makes more urgent the need to reduce selling costs.

Some manufacturers and trade associations provide retailers with the means of evaluating the productiveness of their salespeople in relation to selling cost. For example, the National Cash Register Company has pre-

FIGURE 20–1 Form for evaluation of salespeople in retail stores

SALARY COST PERCENTAGES

WEEKLY SALES	$72.50	$75.00 (6)	$77.50	$80.00	$82.50	$85.00	$87.50	$90.00 (1)	$92.50	$95.00	$97.50	$100.00
$ 150	48.3	50.0	51.7	53.3	55.0	56.7	58.3	60.0	61.7	63.3	65.0	66.7
160	45.3	46.9	48.4	50.0	51.6	53.1	54.7	56.3	57.8	59.4	60.9	62.5
170	42.6	44.1	45.6	47.1	48.5	50.0	51.5	52.9	54.4	55.9	57.4	58.8
180	40.3	41.7	43.0	44.4	45.8	47.2	48.6	50.0	51.4	52.8	54.2	55.6
190	38.1	39.5	40.8	42.1	43.4	44.7	46.1	47.4	48.7	50.0	51.3	52.6
200	36.2	37.5	38.7	40.0	41.3	42.5	43.8	45.0	46.3	47.5	48.8	50.0
210	34.5	35.7	36.9	38.1	39.3	40.5	41.7	42.9	44.0	45.2	46.4	47.6
220	32.9	34.1	35.2	36.4	37.5	38.6	39.8	40.9	42.0	43.2	44.3	45.5
230	31.5	32.6	33.7	34.8	35.9	37.0	38.0	39.1	40.2	41.3	42.4	43.5
240	30.2	31.2	32.3	33.3	34.4	35.4	36.5	37.5	38.5	39.6	40.6	41.7
250	29.0	30.0	31.0	32.0	33.0	34.0	35.0	36.0	37.0	38.0	39.0	40.0
260	27.9	28.8	29.8	30.8	31.7	32.7	33.7	34.6	35.6	36.5	37.5	38.5
270	26.8	27.8	28.7	29.6	30.6	31.5	32.4	33.3	34.3	35.2	36.1	37.0
280	25.9	26.8	27.7	28.6	29.5	30.4	31.3	32.1	33.0	33.9	34.8	35.7
290	25.0	25.9	26.7	27.6	28.4	29.3	30.2	31.0	31.9	32.8	33.6	34.5
300	24.2	25.0	25.8	26.7	27.5	28.3	29.2	30.0	30.8	31.7	32.5	33.4
325	22.3	23.1	23.8	24.6	25.4	26.2	26.9	27.7	28.5	29.2	30.0	30.8
350	20.7	21.4	22.1	22.9	23.6	24.3	25.0	25.7	26.4	27.1	27.9	[illegible]
375	19.3	20.0	20.7	21.3	22.0	22.7	23.3	24.0	24.7	25.3	26.0	[illegible]
400	18.1	18.8	19.4	20.0	20.6	21.3	21.9	22.5	23.1	23.8	24.4	[illegible]
425	17.0	17.6	18.2	18.8	19.4	20.0	20.6	21.2	21.8	22.4	22.9	23.5
450	16.1	16.7	17.2	17.8	18.3	18.9	19.4	20.0	20.6	21.1	21.7	22.2
475	15.3	15.8	16.3	16.8	17.4	17.9	18.4	18.9	19.5	20.0	20.5	21.1
500	14.5	15.0	15.5	16.0	16.5	17.0	17.5	18.0	18.5	19.0	19.5	20.0
525	13.8	(5)	14.8	15.2	15.7	16.2	16.7	17.1	17.6	18.1	18.6	19.0
550	13.2	[illegible]	14.1	14.5	15.0	15.5	15.9	16.4	16.8	17.3	17.7	18.2
575	12.6	13.0	13.5	13.9	14.3	14.8	15.2	15.7	16.1	16.5	17.0	17.4
600	12.1	12.5	12.9	13.3	13.8	14.2	14.6	15.0	15.4	15.8	16.3	16.7
625	11.6	12.0	12.4	12.8	13.2	13.6	14.0	[illegible]	14.8	15.2	15.6	16.0
650	11.1	11.5	11.9	12.3	12.7	13.1	13.5	(2)	14.2	14.6	15.0	[illegible]
675	10.7	11.1	11.5	11.8	12.2	12.6	13.0	13.3	13.7	14.1	14.4	[illegible]
700	10.4	10.7	11.1	11.4	11.8	12.1	12.5	12.9	13.2	13.6	13.9	[illegible]
725	10.0	10.3	10.7	11.0	11.4	11.7	12.1	12.4	12.8	13.1	13.4	[illegible]
750	9.7	10.0	10.3	10.7	11.0	11.3	11.7	12.0	12.3	12.7	13.0	[illegible]
775	9.3	9.7	10.0	10.3	10.6	11.0	11.3	11.6	11.9	12.3	12.6	[illegible]
800	9.1	9.4	9.7	10.0	10.3	10.6	10.9	11.3	11.6	11.9	12.2	12.5
[illegible]	8.8	9.1	[illegible]	[illegible]	[illegible]	[illegible]	10.6	10.9	11.2	11.5	[illegible]	[illegible]

WEEKLY SALES	$160.00	$165.00	$170.00	$175.00	$180.00	$185.00	$190.00	$195.00	$200.00	$205.00	$210.00	$215.00	$220.00	$225.00	$230.00
$ 150	106.7	110.0	113.3	116.7	120.0	123.3	126.6	130.0	133.3	136.6	140.0	143.3	146.6	150.0	153.3
160	100.0	103.1	106.3	109.4	112.5	115.6	118.8	121.8	125.5	128.1	131.2	134.3	137.5	140.6	143.7
170	94.1	97.1	100.0	102.9	105.9	108.9	111.7	114.7	117.6	120.5	123.5	126.4	129.4	132.3	135.2
180	88.9	91.7	94.4	97.2	100.0	102.7	105.5	108.3	111.1	113.8	116.6	119.4	122.2	125.0	127.7
190	84.2	86.8	89.5	92.1	94.7	97.4	100.0	102.6	105.2	107.8	110.5	113.1	115.7	118.4	121.0
200	80.0	82.5	85.0	87.5	90.0	92.5	95.0	97.5	100.0	102.5	105.0	107.5	110.0	112.5	115.0
210	76.2	78.6	81.0	83.3	85.7	88.1	90.4	92.8	95.2	97.6	100.0	102.3	104.7	107.1	109.5
220	72.7	75.0	77.3	79.5	81.8	84.1	86.3	88.6	90.9	93.1	95.4	97.7	100.0	102.2	104.5
230	69.6	71.7	73.9	76.1	78.3	80.4	82.6	84.7	86.9	89.1	91.3	93.4	95.6	97.8	100.0
240	66.7	68.8	70.8	72.9	75.0	77.1	79.1	81.2	83.3	85.4	87.5	89.5	91.6	93.7	95.8
250	64.0	66.0	68.0	70.0	72.0	74.0	76.0	78.0	80.0	82.0	84.0	86.0	88.0	90.0	92.0
260	61.5	63.5	65.4	67.3	69.2	71.1	73.1	75.0	76.9	78.8	80.7	82.7	84.6	86.5	88.4
270	59.3	61.1	63.0	64.8	66.7	68.5	70.3	72.2	74.0	75.7	77.7	79.6	81.4	83.3	85.1
280	57.1	58.9	60.7	62.5	64.3	66.0	67.8	69.6	71.4	73.2	75.0	76.7	78.5	80.3	82.1
290	55.2	56.9	58.6	60.3	62.1	63.8	65.5	67.2	68.9	70.6	72.4	74.1	75.8	77.5	79.3
300	53.3	55.0	56.7	58.3	60.0	61.6	63.3	65.0	66.6	68.3	70.0	71.6	73.3	75.0	76.6
325	49.2	50.8	52.3	53.8	55.4	56.9	58.4	60.0	61.5	63.0	64.6	66.1	67.6	69.2	70.7
350	45.7	47.1	48.6	50.0	51.4	52.9	54.2	55.7	57.1	58.5	60.0	61.4	62.8	64.2	65.7
375	42.7	44.0	45.3	46.7	48.0	49.3	50.6	52.0	53.3	54.6	56.0	57.3	58.6	60.0	61.3
400	40.0	41.3	43.0	43.8	45.0	46.2	47.5	48.7	50.0	51.2	52.5	53.7	55.0	56.2	57.5
425	37.6	38.8	40.0	41.2	42.4	43.5	44.7	45.8	47.0	48.2	49.4	50.5	51.7	52.9	54.1
450	35.6	36.7	37.8	38.9	40.0	41.1	42.2	43.3	44.4	45.5	46.6	47.7	48.8	49.9	51.0
475	33.7	34.7	35.8	36.8	37.9	38.9	40.0	41.0	42.1	43.1	44.2	45.2	46.3	47.3	48.4
500	32.0	33.0	34.0	35.0	36.0	37.0	38.0	39.0	40.0	41.0	42.0	43.0	44.0	45.0	46.0
525	30.5	31.4	32.4	33.3	34.3	35.2	36.1	37.1	38.1	39.0	40.0	40.9	41.9	42.8	43.8
550	29.1	30.0	30.9	31.8	32.7	33.6	34.5	35.4	36.3	37.2	38.1	39.0	40.0	40.9	41.8
575	27.8	28.7	29.0	30.4	31.3	32.1	33.0	33.9	34.7	35.6	36.5	37.3	38.2	39.1	40.0
600	26.7	27.5	28.3	29.2	30.0	30.8	31.6	32.5	33.3	34.1	35.0	35.8	36.6	37.5	38.3
625	25.6	26.4	27.2	28.0	28.8	29.6	30.4	31.2	32.0	32.8	33.6	34.4	35.2	36.0	36.8
650	24.6	25.4	26.2	26.9	27.7	28.4	29.2	30.0	30.7	31.5	32.3	33.0	33.8	34.6	35.3
675	23.7	24.4	25.2	25.9	26.7	27.4	28.1	28.8	29.6	30.3	31.1	31.8	32.5	33.3	34.0
700	22.9	23.6	24.3	25.0	25.7	26.4	27.1	27.8	28.5	29.2	30.0	30.7	31.4	32.1	32.8
725	22.1	22.8	23.4	24.1	24.8	25.5	26.2	26.8	27.5	28.2	28.9	29.6	30.3	31.0	31.7
750	21.3	22.0	22.7	23.3	24.0	24.6	25.3	26.0	26.6	27.3	28.0	28.6	29.3	30.0	30.6
775	20.6	21.3	21.9	22.6	23.2	23.8	24.5	25.1	25.8	26.4	27.1	27.7	28.3	29.0	29.6
800	20.0	20.6	21.3	21.9	22.5	23.1	23.7	24.3	25.0	25.6	26.2	26.8	27.5	28.1	28.7
[illegible]	[illegible]	[illegible]	20.6	21.2	[illegible]	[illegible]	[illegible]	[illegible]	[illegible]	24.8	[illegible]	[illegible]	[illegible]	[illegible]	[illegible]

Source: *Expenses in Retail Businesses* (Dayton, Ohio: National Cash Register Company, n.d.), p. 45.

pared the chart shown in Figure 20–1. To understand its use, let us assume that a salesperson receives $90 per week in a store whose salary cost percentage is 15.0. To determine how much he should sell to earn his salary we proceed as follows:

> Under the column headed $90 (1), find the figure 15.0 (2). To the side in the "Amount of Weekly Sales" column, you will find that he should sell $600 (3) worth of merchandise to justify his salary.
>
> But suppose at the end of the week he has sold but $500 worth of merchandise. Obviously, he is below quota. Now locate this figure (4) in the weekly sales column and then follow along the line to the left until you reach 15.0 (5). At the top of this column . . . a weekly salary of $75 (6) is indicated. This means that the salesperson's efforts for the week have earned only $75 in salary—$15 less than he is being paid! This difference must be advanced to the employee from the store's earnings or from those of other profitable employees. . . .[10]

In brief, retail management must recognize that the need for better salesmanship exists throughout the entire structure of retailing wherever salespeople are employed. Retailers must move quickly to meet this need if their profit margins are to be maintained.

■ FUNDAMENTAL ELEMENTS IN A RETAIL SALE

The basic elements in any retail sale are (1) the store and its policies, (2) the customer, (3) the merchandise, and (4) the salesperson.

□ The store and its policies

Policies of the store in which the sale takes place govern the selling methods pursued and the actions of salespeople. For example, in mass-selling stores, little individual attention is given the customer: one salesman may be serving three shoe customers at the same time. In contrast, many stores place so much emphasis on their standards of salesmanship that they prepare booklets covering the procedure to be followed in the selling process for the detailed guidance of their salespeople. In small stores, reliance is placed on verbal instructions from the proprietor.

□ The customer

The customer is the very heart of the sale, a fact which the famous retailer, Marshall Field, recognized in his phrase, "Give the Lady What She

[10] *Expenses in Retail Businesses* (Dayton, Ohio: The National Cash Register Co., n.d.), p. 46.

Wants." And Jack I. Straus of R. H. Macy & Company stated a few years ago: "We are embarking on a major effort to demonstrate that we care that the customer finds what she wants, gets the help she desires, and derives satisfaction from every contact with Macy's."

Unless the customer is pleased with her reception in the store, unless she is completely satisfied with the merchandise she purchases and the services rendered in connection with it, the sale has not been successful.[11] And today, ". . . an era characterized by a continual stream of innovation, it is not surprising to find a renewed emphasis on the old adage that 'Your best salesman is a satisfied customer'."[12] Salespeople should be guided by this understanding, and sell from the customer's point of view. To do so, they should know something about consumer psychology and about buying motives—what pleases or irritates customers, what considerations motivate their buying, and recognize their growing sophistication.[13] They should also have a thorough knowledge of the merchandise they are selling and of the fundamental principles of salesmanship—how to bring customers and merchandise together effectively as well as recognize the importance of getting along with people—customers, associates, and superiors.

A moment's reflection will bring an awareness of the fact that in the long run the interests of the customer, the salesperson, and the store are identical, since successful operation is impossible without continuous satisfaction of customers.

□ The merchandise

The third important element in a retail sale is the merchandise. A thorough knowledge of the lines offered is essential to successful salesmanship. The information needed will vary with the type of merchandise sold and the clientele served, but, in all stores, the salesperson should be able to give a clear picture of the sizes, styles, designs, finishes, patterns, qualities, and colors of the merchandise. He should know, also, how to bring out points of superiority such as durability, utility, service, safety, prestige, satisfaction, and comfort, and possess the facts pertinent to the uses and care of

---

[11] "A satisfied customer is the businessman's unpaid partner actively working to convince his associates of the excellence of his choice. The dissatisfied customer is an active force in reducing sales and profits." W. G. Kaye, "Take in a New Partner—the Consumer," *Nation's Business,* February 1970, p. 4.

[12] J. F. Engel, R. J. Kegerreis, and R. D. Blackwell, "Word-of-Mouth Communication by the Innovator," *Journal of Marketing,* Vol. 33, No. 3 (July 1969), p. 15.

[13] "To sell Mrs. Smith what Mrs. Smith buys, you must see what's seen through Mrs. Smith's eyes." Ralf Shockey, "Selling Is a Science," Part IX, *Department Store Economist,* December 1965, p. 88. Also cf. "How Housewives See the Discount House Today," *Discount Merchandiser,* March 1970, pp. 77 ff.

the merchandise. He should also be aware of the offerings of competing stores.

The knowledge of merchandise required for effective selling may be obtained in many ways: experience; handling goods; asking others, including wholesale salesmen, the head of stock, and the buyer; learning from other salespeople and from customers; through manufacturers' representatives and printed material; trade journals, home and fashion magazines, advertisements, newspapers, and books; and also by reading information on tags and labels that come on the product.[14]

Despite the wide range of information available to them, the fact remains that many retail salespeople still lack knowledge of the merchandise they are attempting to sell. Responsibility for this condition is twofold: First, salespeople are to blame for failing to prepare themselves adequately for the selling task. Second, store management—either through the proprietor in the small store or the training division in the large store—sometimes fails to impress employees sufficiently with the importance of knowing merchandise, neglects to provide proper instruction concerning it, and does not offer the supervision and follow-up necessary to determine how the selling job is being done.[15]

□ The salesperson

The final essential element in a retail sale is the salesperson.[16] Good appearance, the right attitude, and courteous treatment of customers are fundamental to success in selling. The salesperson can easily nullify other forms of sales promotion, as well as his own knowledge of customer traits and merchandise, by failing to demonstrate a sincere interest in determining and filling satisfactorily the customers' wants.[17]

In general, the qualifications of a successful salesperson are much the same as those necessary for success in any line of business: hard work; confidence in oneself, one's company, and one's merchandise; courage to meet

---

[14] Selling guides for 21 merchandise lines are given in A. E. Zimmer, *The Strategy of Successful Retail Salesmanship* (New York: McGraw-Hill Book Co., Inc., 1966), pp. 165–209.

[15] Cf. "Management's Responsibility for Personal Salesmanship," pp. 493–94 below.

[16] States one keen observer of the retail scene: "The worst thief in the store is the employee who figuratively beats up the customer, not the employee or shopper who actually steals the merchandise. The worst thief is one who, by not doing a proper job of selling goods and services, hurts volume and net profit, darkens the future of more efficient and effective fellow workers, and endangers the company's continued existence and the community's economy." Samuel Feinberg, "From Where I Sit," *Women's Wear Daily*, September 25, 1970, p. 13.

[17] On the part played by store personnel—and the salesperson is most important here—in attracting retail patronage, cf. P. R. Stephenson, "Identifying Determinants of Retail Patronage," *Journal of Marketing*, Vol. 33, No. 3 (July 1969), pp. 57–61.

disappointment and defeat; judgment; discrimination and good sense; creative imagination or the capacity to develop ideas; a talent for getting along with one's associates and superiors; and knowledge of the job to be done. If the salesperson also possesses or develops such qualities as a genuine interest in people, enthusiasm, the ability to instill confidence, and some flair for showmanship, his chances for success are enhanced.[18]

Since the salesperson should be able to overcome the customer's natural causes for hesitation, he must be positive, active, creative, and self-confident. He should also be a good loser. It is not possible to close every sale attempted; but if the salesperson does his best and closes with a smile, it is likely that the customer will come back either after she has shopped around or the next time she is in the market for the type of merchandise in question.

In summary, it is apparent that the responsibility of the salesperson is a vital one in retail selling. Much of this responsibility may be summed up in one word: *courtesy*. One of the most effective "courtesy platforms" which has come to the attention of the authors is that of Marshall Field & Company. Because of its comprehensiveness, and because it has proved so effective in building highly satisfactory customer-employee relationships for many years, it is presented in full, as follows:

Courtesy Platform—Marshall Field & Company[19]

We, the members of the Marshall Field & Company organization, recognizing that courtesy is an essential part of every job in this business, endorse the following platform and pledge our united efforts to carry out the policies stated therein. We are convinced that true courtesy is important to the continued growth and success of Marshall Field & Company and to each of us as individuals. We subscribe to the proposition that courtesy is not only warmth and friendliness—not only seeing the other person's point of view—but also DOING THINGS RIGHT AND DOING THEM RIGHT THE FIRST TIME. Therefore, we pledge to work together to achieve our most important goal—100% SERVICE TO 100% OF OUR CUSTOMERS AND 100% COURTESY TO EACH OTHER.

Bearing in mind that all of our relationships with other people—customers, fellow workers, and supervisors—should be based on co-operation and understanding:

we will— I. Show a real interest in every customer through an attitude of friendliness and genuine helpfulness. Give every customer, no matter how small her purchase or how simple her request, the same courteous service we like to receive when we are customers;

we will— II. Make certain that communications by telephone and letter reflect the

---

[18] The difficulties faced by retailers in securing and keeping good salespeople are discussed in "Wanted: Someone to Watch the Store," *Business Week*, September 19, 1970, pp. 52, 57.

[19] Reproduced by permission of Marshall Field & Company.

same considerate and courteous service which we attempt to give in face-to-face contacts;

we will— III. Practice the principles of courtesy until courtesy becomes a habit;

we will— IV. Handle difficult situations (complaints, exchanges, emergencies), as willingly and pleasantly as we handle easy ones;

we will— V. Make no promises which we cannot keep. Follow through on every promise we do make. When disappointments or unavoidable delays occur, let the person involved know where he stands;

we will— VI. Make a sincere effort to give accurate answers whenever information is requested. Remember that no question is so simple that it does not merit a helpful answer. Never hesitate to admit we don't KNOW, but always GET the answer;

we will— VII. Make a special effort to be helpful to all new employes—make them feel welcome and at home, take time to answer their questions and to give them the information they need. Show them our high standards by our own example;

we will—VIII. Remember that true courtesy extends to the employe across the aisle, to the fellow in the other department, to the person on the other end of the phone, to the person whose work we supervise, to the supervisor for whom we work. Giving consideration to the feelings and rights of the other person helps him in turn to understand our problems and respect our rights. Show our understanding in actions as well as in words;

we will— IX. Give every employe-customer the traditional Marshall Field & Company service;

we will— X. Take a personal responsibility for maintaining an error-free record for ourselves and for our sections;

we will— XI. Make our own jobs and those of other people easier by proper care of equipment necessary to the performance of our jobs, and by respect for the property of others. Create a pleasant atmosphere for customers and employes by maintaining high standards of housekeeping;

we will— XII. Live up not only to the letter but to the spirit of all our policies and rules. By doing so, we make our business run more smoothly, our work easier and things more pleasant both for ourselves and the other person;

we will—XIII. Compliment a job well done. Make it a habit to recognize the good things people do;

we will—XIV. Never criticize or complain unless we have something constructive to offer about the thing of which we complain.

■ THE SELLING PROCESS

Once the salesperson has an appreciation and understanding of the four major elements of a sale, he is in a position to proceed with the selling process.[20] This process may be thought of as involving seven steps, as follows: (1) approach and greeting, (2) determining the customer's needs, (3) presenting the merchandise effectively, (4) meeting objections, (5) closing the sale, (6) suggestion selling of additional items, and (7) developing goodwill after the sale.

In discussing these steps certain qualifications should be recognized at the outset. First, any classification of steps must be arbitrary and all of them are unnecessary in consummating some sales. Second, the sequence of the steps performed will often vary, depending upon the customer and the skill of the salesperson in defining the customer's wants. Third, the salesperson should remember that his major task is to serve the customer in a courteous, intelligent manner. If too much attention is devoted to the sequence of steps in a sale, the sale may be lost. The successful salesperson is one who develops the ability to analyze each selling opportunity and adapts his approach and his tactics to the particular situation.

□ Approaching and greeting the customer

A proper approach to the customer is a matter of skill and judgment. It requires friendly interest and a sincere desire to be of service, balanced by proper reserve and self-confidence. The customer should be welcomed with a genuine smile and a pleasant greeting and made to realize that the opportunity to serve her is appreciated by the salesperson and by the store. If this is done properly the sales transaction probably will be successful.[21]

In many stores customers are greeted by name and given a hearty welcome. Most people like recognition and because they wish their patronage to be appreciated, they are pleased when these are evidenced as they enter the store. The number of customers served by salespeople in large stores makes it difficult to remember names, but this practice should nevertheless be encouraged.

Alertness and promptness on the part of the salesforce are essential to an effective approach. Yet all too often salespeople gather in groups to converse and neglect customers. Occasionally, customers are deliberately avoided for fear of delayed lunch hours or prompt departure at closing time. This condition can be corrected through proper instructions and effective supervision.

---

[20] The persuasive and perceptive aspects of the selling process are discussed in R.M. Baker, Jr., and Gregg Phifer, *Salesmanship: Communication, Persuasion, Perception* (Boston: Allyn and Bacon, Inc., 1966), pp. 240–415. Also cf. Lawrence Leemaster, "Sales Improvement with Psychology," *New York Retailer,* May 1969, pp. 11–13. The examples given all deal with a summer tourist in a souvenir store.

[21] Cf. "First Impressions Vital to Success," *Hardware Retailer,* June 1969, p. 126.

□ Determining the customer's needs

After the customer has been properly greeted, her needs should be defined as quickly as possible. This task is easy for such staple, branded items as groceries and toilet articles but more difficult for women's ready-to-wear, gloves, and hosiery. Careful sizing up of the customer and a few well-phrased questions are very helpful in this connection. Her dress, speech, manner, and her reaction to the merchandise first shown, furnish valuable guides to the salesperson. By eliminating quickly those articles which do not meet her requirements, attention can be concentrated on those that appear to suit her needs.

A common mistake made by salespeople in defining a customer's needs is to judge the desirability or suitability of the merchandise being shown by their own tastes and purchasing power. This mistake should be avoided since it serves to irritate and confuse the customer and often results in lost sales.

□ Presenting the merchandise effectively

No sharp line of demarcation exists between determining the customer's needs and presenting merchandise, since proper demonstration usually is necessary to ascertain her requirements. It is true, nevertheless, that an effective presentation can be made only when the customer's needs are known.

Presenting merchandise to customers in a manner that will induce them to purchase involves the following: (1) knowledge of its location in the store or department, (2) wise selection of what is shown or demonstrated, (3) proper display of the merchandise, and (4) careful selection of its chief selling points and their effective presentation.[22] The importance of these factors should be obvious, thus requiring no further discussion.

□ Meeting objections

Meeting objections satisfactorily is probably the most difficult step in the selling process. Although they should be anticipated and answered as much as possible in the sales presentation, all of them cannot be foreseen.

---

[22] "An electro-mechanical-optical system that permits a woman to see how she looks in a dress without trying it on will soon be found in department stores in various sections of the country." Cf. "How Does the Dress Look? Fashion Mirror Can Tell," *Women's Wear Daily*, January 26, 1970, p. 22. Also cf. " 'Fashion Mirror' Boon to Bridal Gown Sales," *ibid.*, April 8, 1970, p. 40.

Objections may be divided into two groups: (1) genuine objections, constituting honest and sincere reasons for failure to buy; and (2) mere excuses, usually designed to conceal the real reason for failure to take action. Since genuine objections are definite obstacles to consummating a sale, they should be met squarely and without evasion. In contrast, excuses may often be ignored, although they may be recognized and answered by the salesperson. Sometimes excuses are more difficult to handle than genuine objections, since they do not really reflect the opinions of the customer and, consequently, furnish no solid basis for answering them.

Some general rules for meeting objections Certain "proven" general rules are helpful in meeting customer objections.

1. Never argue with a customer. An argument may be won but a sale and a customer lost.
2. Learn to anticipate objections and incorporate answers to them in the presentation.
3. Deal with objections fairly and completely, making sure not to belittle the customer's opinions.
4. Inspire confidence on the part of the customer and contribute to her self-esteem by the tactful handling of her questions.
5. Avoid, if possible, mention of competitors and their merchandise. If the customer mentions them, speak well and briefly of them.

Knowledge of, and conformance to, these rules, supplemented by the experience gained in handling specific reasons customers give for failing to buy, will enable the salesperson to meet successfully the large majority of selling situations that arise.

Handling the price question Because of the many and varied wants of *all* people and the limited incomes of *most* people, the fundamental objection to purchase for nearly all people is price. "I cannot afford it" and "I like it very much, but the price is too high," are common customer expressions with which salespeople are constantly faced.[23]

In most cases, perhaps, price should not be mentioned until the suitability of the merchandise to the customers' needs has been demonstrated. When this has been done, the price factor becomes less important to the customer. Many customers, however, inquire about prices at the outset. In such instances, the salesperson should not hesitate in stating prices; but he should immediately stress the values at these prices. It is often advisable to show higher-priced merchandise of better quality to demonstrate the difference between the various items. Some firms have their salespeople fol-

---

[23] One women's shoe store has this sign—"10% Discount on shoes purchased in 10 minutes."

low a practice of "trading up"—of attempting to induce customers to buy better-quality merchandise at higher prices.[24]

☐ Closing the sale

If the transaction has been properly handled, closing the sale[25] will come naturally and without particular notice by the customer. But many sales are not closed, and the best way to avoid such occurrences is for salespeople to analyze each sale they lose, try to determine the mistakes made in their presentations, and to correct these errors in subsequent contacts with customers. Among the more common avoidable errors are the following: "pushing" the customer into making a decision before she has evaluated all aspects of the purchase; not meeting her questions or objections fully and truthfully; failure to emphasize important characteristics of the merchandise because of inadequate knowledge concerning it; evidencing irritation and making caustic comments as a result of the customer's delay in choosing the item to buy; and failing to provide the courteous and considerate service the customer deserves as a guest of the store.

Knowledge of the reasons why sales are lost, however, is insufficient preparation on the salesperson's part. He must translate this knowledge into improved salesmanship and do all he can to minimize the mistakes that cause sales to be lost. In this connection, his own experiences should prove a valuable guide, since he will tend to use more frequently those methods he has found effective and to avoid using those he has found ineffective. In all instances, however, he should attempt to close the sale in a manner pleasing to the customer.

☐ Suggestion selling

Once the sale has been closed on the merchandise desired by the customer, the salesperson has an excellent opportunity further to serve the customer and promote his own interests through suggestion selling. This may take any of the following forms, among others:

1. Increasing the amount of the sale by suggesting better quality merchandise and pointing out the advantages of buying the better item, a form of the trading-up process referred to previously.

---

[24] A study of the bargaining on price and other factors which takes place between the customer and the salesman of appliances is reported in A. L. Pennington, "Customer-Salesman Bargaining Behavior in Retail Transactions," *Journal of Marketing Research,* Vol. 5, No. 3 (August 1968), pp. 255–62.

[25] Factors governing the close of a sale are explained and illustrated in C. A. Pederson and M. D. Wright, *Salesmanship, Principles and Methods,* 5th ed. (Homewood, Ill.: Richard D. Irwin, Inc., 1971), pp. 442–60.

2. Increasing the amount of the sale by suggesting the larger sizes and explaining the saving they represent and by selling larger quantities or groups of the same item. For example, the $1.00 size of an item may contain three times the quantity of the 50-cent size, or three men's shirts may be sold at $11.50 instead of one at $3.95.
3. Suggesting related, associated, or companion items. To illustrate: The woman buying shoes may need hosiery, gloves, or a bag. Similarly, the man buying razor blades may need shaving cream or soap.
4. Suggesting seasonable, timely merchandise in demand by customers. During the winter season, cold remedies and vitamin tablets are required by many people. At Easter, millinery, spring clothing, and flowers are appropriate.
5. Suggesting special values or bargains being offered in the department or the store. These values may represent substantial reductions in the prices of regular goods for a limited period or may be caused by particularly advantageous purchases which permit lower-than-usual prices for such merchandise.
6. Suggesting new merchandise which has just arrived. Since some women (and men) like to be the first to wear or to exhibit something new, such a suggestion ordinarily arouses interest and may result in a sale if the goods appeal to the customer.

The current emphasis placed on suggestion selling by Edison Brothers Stores, Inc., a large retail footwear chain, is indicated by this statement by a company executive: "Edison does not believe in selling one pair of shoes. . . . A sale is not complete until two or three pairs are sold. [Other stores] now advocate this but Edison was the first to develop the principle and do a really scientific training job." The shopper also is invited "to look at matching handbags, hosiery, and other accessories that account for about one-fifth of [our] volume."[26] These combined efforts, along with others, resulted in increasing suggestion sales to about 30 percent of total sales, and stock turnover and sales per store also increased sharply.

Since most retail salespeople dislike the additional mental and physical effort required, and since training and supervision are frequently lax in this direction, suggestion selling is not widely practiced. And, although some customers resent suggestions, others welcome them. The customer's attitude toward this practice depends upon the manner in which it is made, upon the merchandise offered, and upon the situation in which she finds herself. Suggestions are useless unless they are appropriate, definite, and helpful in the light of the customer's needs. While they constitute a valuable

[26] "New Shine for a Master Retailer," *Business Week*, April 16, 1966, p. 112.

method of increasing sales when used properly, if used incorrectly they may lose sales and customers.

□ Developing goodwill after the sale

When the customer makes her original purchase or even when she has bought additional goods as a result of suggestions made by salespeople, the selling process still has not been completed. The goods purchased must be carefully wrapped for carrying by the customer or for delivery when promised, and correctly billed if credit has been extended. She should also be satisfied with her purchase, and recall favorably the store and the department as a desirable place to trade. These goals call for effective action on the salesperson's part even after the customer has said, "I'll take it."

A cheerful and sincere expression of gratitude for the purchase will be remembered by the customer, and she will remember favorably her dealings with the salesperson and the store. For example: "Thank you very much, Miss Jones. I hope you will enjoy this article and that you will come in again. It was a pleasure to serve you." The words used when the customer departs are just as important as those used in greeting her.

Even if no sale is made, the customer should be thanked for her interest. By doing so, the salesperson builds goodwill and makes friends for the store and for himself. By failing to do so, or by expressing resentment at the customer's inability to decide on a purchase at that time, he creates ill-will and loses customers for the store.

In some small stores, salespeople are often responsible for seeing that the merchandise is placed on a delivery cart or truck as soon as possible, for wrapping the goods for mailing or for gifts, and for checking on the performance of articles such as washing machines or carpet sweepers after they have been used for several days. The interest evidenced in performing these activities is a mark of good salesmanship and builds patronage for the store.

■ MANAGEMENT'S RESPONSIBILITY FOR PERSONAL SALESMANSHIP

Successful personal salesmanship in retail stores involves more than the development of proper attitudes, knowledge, and practices on the part of salespeople and other employees. It is the responsibility of management, through alert leadership and adequate supervision, to provide the direction and the type of selling atmosphere throughout the store which is conducive to effective selling. When this is done, customers will be pleased with the surroundings in which they shop; employees will be congenial in their relationships with each other and their supervisors, and satisfied with the conditions under which they work.

Retail management also has major responsibilities in the guidance, supervision, and energizing of the people who make up the sales force, including, for example, fair distribution of work among employees, assignment of definite responsibility to each worker, and even-tempered supervision involving interest in and encouragement of the sales force. Executives should recognize that the maintenance of high standards in selling efforts necessitates rather close and constant observation of the selling process carried on in the particular store or department; that it requires detailed study of performance records; and that it demands correction of sales methods as a result of such observation and study.[27] Moreover, skill and judgment should be shown in the conduct of meetings: An attitude of superiority should be avoided and employees should be encouraged to participate. When these responsibilities are met, personal selling efforts will be improved and profit possibilities enhanced. Fortunately, there are signs that management is increasingly aware of its obligations in attaining these goals.[28]

■ REVIEW AND DISCUSSION QUESTIONS

1 Define salesmanship in your own words and explain its significance in retail stores today despite the growth of self-service operations.

2 "Rudeness among salespeople is so prevalent that a growing concern about it is being manifested by retail executives in all parts of the country." Discuss the factors you believe to be responsible for such rudeness and suggest what actions should be taken by management to correct the situation.

3 Explain briefly the measures management should adopt to improve the quality of personal salesmanship in general. How would you determine if actual improvement results from such measures?

---

[27] Reports one investigator: "Two issues are at the bottom of most selling problems: (1) Failure of retail management to appreciate the real contribution that creative personal sales effort can have on the final sale; and (2), management's lack of interest in scientifically determining the causes of salesmen's behavior in situations where various forms of salesman-customer interaction, such as bargaining and negotiation, are important in the final sale." J. C. Cotham, "Case for Personal Selling: Some Retailing Myths Exploded," *Business Horizons,* Vol. 6, No. 2 (April 1968), p. 81.

[28] "Sales management at the retail level is on the threshold of determining, with some certainty, the real determinants of successful selling performance." *Ibid.*

4 Discuss concisely the four major elements in a retail sale. Indicate their interrelationships.

5 Comment on the statement that "A satisfied customer is the businessman's unpaid partner actively working to convince his associates of the excellence of his choice. The dissatisfied customer is an active force in reducing sales and profits."

6 Assume that you are an executive of R. H. Macy & Company and have been asked to outline a program designed "to demonstrate that we care that the customer finds what she wants, gets the help she desires, and derives satisfaction from every contact with Macy's." How would you proceed and what information would you develop in connection with this assignment?

7 Prepare a critical evaluation of the Courtesy Platform of Marshall Field & Company detailed on pages 486–87.

8 Summarize the major steps in the "Selling Process." Of what value to a salesperson is knowledge of these steps? If possible, base your answer on your own selling experience.

9 Since meeting objections satisfactorily probably constitutes the most difficult step in the selling process, what general guidelines or rules can you suggest to insure that this step is handled properly?

10 Discuss (*a*) the salesperson's responsibility for effective personal selling, and (*b*) management's obligations in connection with this activity.

chapter 21

CUSTOMER SERVICES

The retailer's most basic function or service consists of assembling a satisfactory assortment of desirable merchandise and offering it for sale, at reasonable prices, in an attractive, conveniently-located store. But often this is not enough. His customers may expect many traditional additional services, such as clothing alterations, gift wrapping, merchandise delivery, and assurances of complete satisfaction with the merchandise they have bought. Such services are normally offered at cost, less than cost, or free of extra charge, and are intended to encourage customer purchases. Competent, prompt, cheerful, and courteous performance of the appropriate services is a significant form of nonprice competition and a necessary element in developing a favorable store image.

Many retailers are now also offering an increasing number of "income producing" services, such as tool and equipment rental or insurance sales, to meet their customers' changing demands. These activities also contribute to the store image, since their availability suggests that the store is trying to satisfy all of its customers' desires. The income services may also lead to sales of related merchandise, as, for example, when golf instruction leads to the sale of clubs or other equipment. But while the traditional services represent expenses that the store incurs in order to sell its wares, the income services are undertaken to produce their own direct profits or contribution to overhead. Large retailers, who are seeking additional ways to serve their customers profitably, will probably offer an increasing number of income services in forthcoming years.[1]

SCOPE OF THE CHAPTER

Although we will consider both traditional and income-producing services, we cannot and need not examine every possible service in detail in this chapter. The customer services that result from having an attractive and well-designed store, including air conditioning, good lighting, and convenient vertical transportation, have already been discussed in Chapter 5. Similarly, the services that a helpful and attentive sales force can provide have already been noted in Chapter 20. Some other services, for example "piped-in" background music, present relatively few managerial problems, and only require brief mention here. In contrast, credit activities are so important to so many retailers, are so complex, and have been subject to so many recent changes that a separate chapter is needed for adequate discussion.[2]

Consequently, we will first look at some basic service policies. We will next examine some traditional "extra" services in detail, and then consider the rising market for income-producing services.

SERVICE POLICIES

Decisions concerning number and variety of services Considerable judgment must be exercised in deciding on the number and variety of services to be provided, and on the policies, procedures, and conditions under which they will be offered. Overly elaborate and inappropriate services may create a false image and make the customers *think* that the store is expensive even though its actual prices are competitive with other establishments. And inappropriate extra services that do not generate suitable extra sales volume will increase costs and absorb profits inordinately. Moreover, customers' expectations concerning service are often difficult to judge, and, in many instances, experimentation is needed to provide the answer. Yet the retailer must provide the services that his clientele needs and expects. Fortunately, he has certain guides, as follows, that will help him decide on the "bundle" of services he will offer:

Guides to services offered (1) Competitors' policies and practices are important guides since the retailer's customers will expect him to meet competitive standards or to offer compensating advantages. (2) The type of

[1] E. B. Weiss, "New Retail Services Push Skyward," *Advertising Age*, September 23, 1968, pp. 84–86.

[2] Chapter 22, "Retail Credit and Collections."

merchandise he handles will influence the services he will render. Heavy merchandise, such as electric refrigerators, stoves, washing machines, and furniture usually requires delivery service. Moreover, some form of deferred payment is essential for these high unit value items. In contrast, customers can readily carry cosmetics, shoes, and hosiery, and may not desire credit when buying these products. (3) The customers' income, location, and buying habits influence the services that must be rendered. Generally speaking, the higher the income group, the greater the number of services expected and offered. (4) The type of store is important. Customers may expect more personalized service in a small specialty store than in a large establishment; and more service in a traditional department store than in a mail-order company branch. (5) The store's pricing policy affects the nature and extent of its services, since customers expect less service in a "bargain" outlet. (6) Store location also plays a role as in the case of the downtown retailer who has to offer delivery service while his suburban competitor may rely on customers carrying their own purchases. Similarly, a hardware retailer in a suburban area, where "do-it-yourself" is common, is often expected to rent tools and equipment to his customers.

Realistic service standards The retailer should remember that the services he offers are intended to contribute to the store's *long-run* profitability. An attempt to satisfy every possible customer would be both costly and futile. A few people will make demands that are impossible to fulfill. The retailer should take all reasonable steps to minimize unpleasant situations. He will normally avoid offending a good customer just to win a small argument, and he should carefully investigate all complaints, no matter how unwarranted they may seem. But if such investigation shows that his policies and procedures are sound, he should not be discouraged at losing an occasional unreasonable customer. The important thing is to be certain that the store's merchandise and services will satisfy the great majority of its present and potential customers—the people who can provide the repeat business that is essential for ultimate success.

Service charges Decisions must be made, not only as to the number and variety of services to be offered, but also as to whether fees will be charged for any of them, and if so, how much. In some cases, the decision is obvious. Some traditional services must be offered without any extra charge. A merchant could hardly request a fee for listening to customer complaints, or for telling customers where to find goods in his store!

In contrast, charges will naturally be imposed for the income-producing services that are instituted to earn profits.[3] And some of the customer-convenience services are so costly to the store that no one expects them to

[3] A store-operated travel agency may be an exception to this generalization, since some or all of its revenue will consist of commissions paid by hotels, carriers (airlines, steamship companies), and tour operators.

be available without charge. Department stores, for example, often operate their restaurants as a service that will attract people to the store and induce them to spend more time there. In such cases, the meals may be priced so low that the restaurant inevitably loses money. But none of the patrons expect the meals to be totally free.

Policy with regard to certain other services varies from store to store or from community to community. But today an increasing number of merchants charge at least partial fees for services once included in the price of the merchandise. A number of stores now charge for delivery service, especially on small orders. Many retailers now charge extra for alterations to women's—and to an increasing extent, men's—clothing.

The tendency to reduce the number of totally "free" services results in part from rising labor and supply costs and in part from increased competitive pressure. The store that offers services without extra charge must recover the costs of those services in the prices it receives for its merchandise. Competition from self-service or self-selection stores, such as discount houses, has forced many traditional merchants to reconsider the services that they offer and the price levels they must charge to provide those services. Retailers are also increasingly aware of the fact that many customers are willing to pay directly for many of the services that they use.[4]

But competition among retailers is a competition of services as well as merchandise. Many factors must be considered in deciding to add or to reduce services. What do customers expect? What will the service cost? Can the store charge for the service, or offer it "free," and still retain its existing price policies? Are the customers of the type and income group that requires the service? What are competitors doing? Is the service well adapted to the store's merchandise? The retailer should evaluate each service he currently offers in view of these same questions. Without doubt, a careful analysis will lead certain merchants to the conclusion that they are offering too many services, whereas others will decide to add still more.

Some especially important services are discussed on the following pages.

■ ALTERATIONS

Alterations are widely expected and required in selling clothing. Women's dresses often need to be shortened, made longer, or taken in at the hips. Men's clothing and even children's garments often also require

---

[4] This arrangement is more equitable, since customers who do not want and do not use a particular service do not share its costs. Cf. "Conclusions and Recommendations of the Committee on Distribution" in Paul W. Stewart and J. Frederic Dewhurst, *Does Distribution Cost Too Much?* (New York: The Twentieth Century Fund, 1939), pp. 351–52, for a "classic" marketing study that recommended the use of separate service charges to pay for individual services.

various adjustments. The clothing retailer must provide facilities for making these alterations.

Originally alteration was usually a "free" service, but this practice has changed considerably in the last four decades. Even now, though, the charge sometimes fails to cover the full cost of the alteration. Charges are typically made for alterations on women's clothing, but not for minor adjustments (cuffing trousers, lengthening or shortening sleeves, altering waistlines) on men's clothing. An increasing number of retailers now charge, however, for major alterations to menswear, such as recutting trousers or adjusting the degree of fullness across the back of the coat. Many small retailers oppose this policy and claim they would prefer to raise their prices rather than charge for alterations on men's and boy's clothing. Both large and small retailers often charge, nevertheless, for any adjustments on men's clothing sold at special sales prices.

■ WRAPPING MERCHANDISE

Practically all retailers in this country expect to wrap or bag[5] their customers' purchases,[6] although the amount and kind of wrapping service varies widely from store to store. The high-fashion store, for example, utilizes far different wrappings than does the drugstore or supermarket. Attractive paper and plastic shopping bags have become popular with many customers. These bags, which are available in many sizes, shapes, colors, and designs, tend to give the store's name or insignia very effective display on the street, and in buses and suburban trains, at very low cost. But the individual items still must be wrapped in many cases, even though the customer is carrying a shopping bag. This may be desirable as a security measure, to show that the merchandise has not been shoplifted, as well as a customer convenience.

□ Wrapping systems

Three major types of wrapping systems are in common use—clerk wrap, department or floor wrap, and central wrap.

Clerk wrap The salesperson who waits on the customer also does the wrapping under a clerk wrap system. The customer usually prefers this system since one person carries out the whole transaction. This saves the customer's time and gives her a feeling that she has really received service—a

---

[5] The term "wrapping" includes "bagging," (that is, placing the merchandise in bags) as generally practiced in supermarkets, discount stores, and self-service outlets.

[6] This statement would not always be true of other countries. In some European supermarkets, customers bundle the purchases themselves after they have passed the check-out cashier.

feeling she does not get if she has to go to a wrapping station and wait in line for her package. The clerk wrap system is by far the most practical and most widely used system for small and medium-sized service (as distinguished from self-service) stores. It is also used by large stores for departments, such as handkerchiefs, hosiery, and toilet goods, that do not require special packaging arrangements.

Department wrap Under the department or floor wrap system, each department or group of departments has a conveniently located station where specialized employees wrap all the merchandise sold in those departments. Sometimes, especially during busy seasons, the station may employ one or several full-time wrappers; in other cases one individual may act as both cashier and wrapper. The salesperson may carry "take-with" merchandise to the wrapping desk, wait until it is wrapped, and return it to the customer; or she may excuse herself and leave the customer to wait for the package. In some stores the customer is expected to carry her "take-with" purchases to the wrapping desk. The salesperson usually takes "send" merchandise to the station.

Central wrap Central wrap localizes the store's wrapping service in one or a few places, thereby achieving the advantages of greater specialization. It also permits the use of wrapping machines which can handle as much as 70 percent of the merchandise in some stores at substantial savings in both space and wages. The wrapping department is usually placed in the basement of the store, but large stores that require two or three wrapping centers will locate them on various floors adjacent to selling departments. In a sense, the check-out counter in a self-service store is a central wrap system. In such cases, the cashier or a "bagger" typically performs the wrapping—placing the items in a large bag or in a box—at a point near the exit from the store.

□ Prepacking

Some manufacturers assist the retailer by placing their goods in packages that contain the number of units the customer usually purchases. This practice is called "prepacking" or "prepackaging." Lamps, china, glassware, and other breakable items are often prepackaged to reduce damage and handling costs.

□ Gift wrapping

A large number of stores offer gift wrapping throughout the year, but it is most important during the pre-Christmas season. It is a fairly expensive service. Good quality gift boxes range in cost from relatively small sums to as much as $5 each. Specially expert wrappers will be assigned to this service, if the volume is sufficient, since customers want their gift packages to look especially well. Some customers will buy gifts in a low-grade store and then bring them to a higher-grade one for wrapping. Because of these factors, some stores make a charge for gift wrapping service. But most department and specialty stores that are eager for gift business continue to provide some free gift packaging the year round, charging only for specially elaborate wraps.

■ DELIVERY SERVICE

Despite customers' increased willingness to carry goods home and the growth of self-service "cash and carry" stores, merchandise delivery remains one of the most important services rendered by many retail stores. Such service is practically universal for many large or heavy items—including furniture, stoves, refrigerators, washing machines, television sets, rugs, mattresses, and mirrors. Delivery service can even be arranged in some supermarkets and chain stores where "cash and carry" is the standard practice. Moreover, many people who are unwilling to cope with the traffic problems of metropolitan shopping areas now buy increasing amounts by mail and telephone order and have the purchases delivered to their homes.

Delivery costs, already high, are increasing rapidly, largely because of rising labor costs. Per-package cost for delivery now approximates 75 cents in the larger cities[7]; and among department stores delivery costs probably range from 0.75 to 1.0 percent of net sales.[8] Nevertheless, delivery is usually performed on a "free" basis. Some retailers require a minimum purchase of $2 to $5 for free delivery and levy a small charge (such as 50 to 75 cents) when the minimum is not reached. Likewise it is common practice to charge for express or parcel post deliveries to addresses outside the store's normal delivery service area.

☐ Delivery systems

Retail delivery systems may be divided into five categories: (1) individual-store system, (2) mutual system, (3) consolidated system, (4) express, and (5) parcel post.

Individual-store system Under this system the individual store uses its own personnel and equipment to provide delivery service. The proprietor of a small store may make the deliveries himself, using his car or a handcart. A delivery boy may be employed part- or full-time to make deliveries by

---

[7] Information received from a major delivery company.

[8] Jay Scher, *Financial and Operating Results of Department and Specialty Stores in 1969* (New York: National Retail Merchants Association, 1970), pp. 27, 35, 43, 51.

bicycle or truck if volume warrants. Regular delivery routes are not maintained; and, when necessary, deliveries may be made immediately. Otherwise, the employe making deliveries waits until a few orders have accumulated. No special system is used to check out goods for delivery or to check in returned goods.

Much more highly organized systems are used in medium-sized and large stores. The delivery department becomes responsible for all goods as they leave the wrapping department. It is usually also responsible for collecting goods from the selling floors if clerk wrap or department wrap systems are used. The merchandise is sorted in the delivery department and transported along carefully laid-out routes.

The individual-store delivery system is the most flexible one any store can use. The store can arrange routes and schedules to meet its own requirements. Furthermore, the deliveryman is a store employee who can be trained to serve its interests, for example, in reporting customer complaints and messages to the proper store authorities. Furthermore, the store receives some advertising through display of its name on its trucks. And if the volume of work is sufficient to keep the department fully utilized, the cost of a store-owned system may be nearly as low as that of any alternative arrangement.

Mutual delivery system In some cities the retailers have formed mutual or cooperative delivery systems. They usually set up a separate delivery company whose shares they then own. The expenses are divided among the various shareholders according to some agreed basis. The delivery company picks up the goods for delivery from each retailer, takes them to its own sorting station, sorts the merchandise, makes delivery, collects COD accounts, and returns goods that cannot be delivered or that customers do not want.

The mutual delivery system has two main advantages over the individual store system: (1) combining packages of all cooperative stores permits better delivery service through more frequent deliveries; and (2) savings in space, personnel, equipment, and management supervision result in lower costs to the stores.

But certain problems arise when mutual delivery systems are used. These include: (1) building the necessary organization and providing the essential equipment to accomplish the objective; (2) determining an equitable basis for allocating expenses among the members of the group; and (3) maintaining effective control over the system to insure customer satisfaction. Consequently, mutual delivery systems are not spreading rapidly at present, although they have been very successful in some cities.

Consolidated delivery systems Consolidated delivery systems operate much the same way as mutual ones. But instead of being owned by the stores they serve, the consolidated systems are formed and operated by independent firms that hope to make a profit out of the fees they charge the stores. The United Parcel Service, which has facilities throughout the country, is an illustration of these systems. Its rapid growth in recent years is strong evidence of the need for such services.

The consolidated system has the same advantages as a mutual system and avoids some of the problems that can arise in joint or cooperative activities. Moreover, management often prefers having an independent outside company handle delivery activities since retail unions frequently gain their first toehold among the drivers in store-owned delivery departments. Consequently, United Parcel Service and similar organizations seem likely to continue to grow in the future.

The difficult problem of determining delivery charges arises whenever either a consolidated or a mutual system is used. Three principal methods are employed in both systems: (1) a per-package charge (which may vary with either or both the size or weight of the package), (2) a flat weekly rate based roughly on the number or value of orders delivered for each merchant over a period of time, and (3) a combination of the flat weekly rate and a charge per package.

Parcel post and express delivery The delivery systems already discussed handle most retail deliveries. All large stores, however, use express companies and parcel post service to some extent, especially for mail orders and gift shipments sent to points outside the store's delivery area. A small store that has few packages to deliver may also find these services very suitable to its needs. Greyhound and other bus package services are sometimes used for intercity shipments.

The rates for parcel post and express shipments tend to become quite high if the packages are heavy or bulky. Parcel post rates, package size limitations, and other rules have been subject to several changes in recent years. The fact that total parcel post shipments have actually declined somewhat during the last two decades, in spite of the economic expansion of the period, indicates that current rates, rules, and services are not competitive with alternative delivery services.[9]

CUSTOMER COMPLAINTS AND ADJUSTMENTS

No retailer, no matter how skilled, can completely eliminate customer complaints. The retailer should not be upset by an occasional complaint; in fact he should welcome them as a source of information about things that

---

[9] 1955 *Annual Report of the Postmaster General,* (Washington, D.C.: U.S. Government Printing Office, 1956), table 201, p. 51; and 1969 *Annual Report of the Postmaster General,* (*ibid.,* 1970), table 203, p. 197.

may be wrong in his operations. He should make certain that complaints receive attention and are investigated. Moreover, he should try to adjust them satisfactorily from both the customer's and the store's point of view and, if practical, rectify whatever causes the complaints.

□ Major causes of complaints

In general, complaints may be traced to one or more of four factors:

Improper buying The purchase of goods unsuited to customers' needs is an important cause of complaints. The store's buyers may lack experience; they may not know what the customer wants; or perhaps they are simply careless in their buying. Whatever the reason, poor buying cannot help but result in customer complaints.[10]

Inefficient store system A weak store system results in many complaints. If a delivery order fails to specify the number of packages, the driver may leave a certain address after having delivered one package instead of two. The result is a complaint that the delivery is "short."

Inadequately trained and careless personnel Salespeople who do not know the proper procedures for preparation of sales checks and credit slips, who do not dispatch "sends" to the delivery department promptly, and who fail to give all customers courteous service, contribute to the number of complaints. Likewise, some retailers have inadequately trained repairmen to service the appliances and television sets which they sell.

Carelessness and mistakes can produce complaints even in the store that has developed an adequate system and has given its employees detailed training. Incorrect addresses may be placed on "sends," wrong sizes may be delivered, and another account credited when goods are returned. Better supervision of employees can minimize much of this carelessness.

Habitual complainers Some customers are habitual complainers: They always seem to assume that they should have received even better merchandise or better service. If an automobile tire shows wear at the end of 25,000 miles, the customer feels that it should have gone 30,000. The $5 shirt which begins to fray on the cuffs after repeated washings is returned as being defective. In brief, every store has a few customers who will complain even though everything possible has been done to give satisfaction.

□ Handling complaints

Maintaining goodwill A customer who feels that her complaint has not been settled satisfactorily is likely to turn to some other retailer. She may

[10] Frequently, it is unfair to place all blame for unsatisfactory merchandise upon the buyer. For example, variations in sizes of ready-to-wear among manufacturers are an important cause of complaints and returns.

also voice her grievance to her friends, who may follow her advice and give their business to a "more responsible" merchant. This can be very damaging to the store. There is no point in spending large sums on advertising to develop goodwill and then lose it through inadequate attention to customer complaints and adjustments. The personnel who handle complaints should recognize that they have an important part to play in building goodwill for the store and should appear friendly and sympathetic to the customer's point of view.

In an effort to turn complaints into goodwill many retailers have very liberal adjustments policies.[11] Typical of these policies is that of Sears, Roebuck and Co.; "Liberal and prompt adjustments to our customers, *even if we may think they are wrong,* are desirable as a matter of policy. . . . The Sears motto, *Satisfaction guaranteed or your money back,* is a real policy, to be faithfully observed." Some retailers who follow such policies quite automatically make the adjustment the customer requests. Others quickly make any adjustments called for by a failure on the part of the store; but otherwise they try to distinguish between (1) customers who honestly feel they have a legitimate complaint, and (2) those who are merely taking advantage of the store's "the-customer-is-always right" policy. While adjustments are made in the first case, they may be refused in the second instance.

Minimizing complaints In addition to building goodwill, the adjustment of complaints should provide basic data that will enable the store to reduce future complaints. A careful analysis might indicate, for example, that many complaints arise because of delayed deliveries, because of improper handling of charge transactions, or because of defective merchandise sold in a certain department. This information can be very valuable for the control of future complaints. All too often, however, executives fail to take prompt and effective action upon the basis of such data; therefore the complaints continue.

□ Systems for dealing with complaints

The proprietor or manager usually deals with most of the complaints in a small store, although the salespeople may handle some minor matters directly. Some other arrangement is needed for medium-sized and large stores, where the chief executive could not possibly handle all of the

[11] Throughout the discussion that follows, an *adjustment* refers to the action taken by the retailer in an effort to satisfy the complainant. Sometimes the adjustment consists of making an *exchange,* that is, the merchandise returned by the customer is exchanged for other goods. Such exchanges may be even or uneven. Cf. the distinction between even and uneven exchanges in Chapter 25, pp. 596–97, below.

complaints. Any one of three systems may be adopted: (1) a centralized system or adjustment department, (2) a decentralized system, or (3) a combination of certain elements of both.

Centralized system Under this plan, every complaint, regardless of its nature, is referred to the adjustment department. This procedure has two major advantages from the customer's point of view: (1) Her grievance is handled by people who are trained to hear complaints and to make adjustments, and (2) she is more likely to receive a satisfactory adjustment since an impartial adjuster, rather than the salesperson involved in the transaction, hears her complaint.

The store also gains several advantages. Skilled adjusters, selected on the basis of their patience, tact, and ability to deal wtih all types of aggrieved customers, can handle difficult situations uniformly and build goodwill for the store. Salespeople and buyers are relieved of the task of handling complaints and consequently can devote more time to their other duties. Complaints are discussed in at least semiprivacy in the adjustment department, instead of being debated in front of other customers on the selling floor. Finally, centralized adjustments make it easier to keep records of all complaints and to analyze them, so that the data may be used as a means of reducing future complaints.

But most customers dislike being sent to an adjustment department. They naturally expect that the salesperson, or at least the department, that sold the goods should adjust the complaint. They resent having to take the time and effort to go to the adjustment department, possibly having to wait in line to be heard, and having to explain the whole matter to a third party. The presence of other customers, also complaining, contributes to a negative impression of the store. Moreover, it is difficult to arrange merchandise exchanges in the central adjustment department since the goods are not readily at hand. Instead, the customer may insist upon a full refund.

Decentralized system In this system, the department head or floorman has authority to settle complaints. Some stores also authorize head salespeople to make adjustments, especially in instances where the store is obviously at fault. Only executives, however, are allowed to refuse adjustments. This system eliminates the disadvantages of the centralized adjustment department, but it also eliminates the advantages of using specialized, skilled, well-trained, impartial adjusters to handle complaints.

Combination system Many medium-sized and large stores usually try to gain the advantages of both systems by combining the two. The decentralized system, which the customers prefer, is used for the great majority of complaints. Only the difficult complaints, that is, those that seem unreasonable to the department head and those that involve fairly substantial amounts of money, are referred to the specialists in the adjustment department. This seems to be the most satisfactory arrangement for the bigger stores.

■ RETURNED GOODS

The returned goods problem is closely related to the problem of complaints and adjustments. Few customer services are as widely used, and abused, as the return privilege. To cite but one example, returns by and allowances to customers ranged from 5.37 to 8.71 percent of sales in department stores of various sizes in 1969.[12] Some departments, such as toilet articles, books, and groceries naturally have very low return rates, perhaps 1 to 3 percent of sales; but returns of women's dresses, furniture, rugs, and some electrical appliances may range from 8 to 25 percent.

□ Cost of handling returns

The customer seldom appreciates all the costs and difficulties involved in handling returns. In many cases, the store may be required to deliver the merchandise and then pick it up, incurring double expense without sales revenue. Additional recordkeeping is required. The goods have to be reinspected, re-marked, and placed in stock again. Salespeople must devote additional time to resell returned merchandise. Markdowns are often required; probably more than 50 percent of returned goods must be sold at a reduced price. Also, the store has a considerable sum invested in goods that are in the hands of customers but that will be returned to the store. The interest on this investment is another cost of handling returned goods. All of these costs mount up to a significant expense for the retailer.

□ Causes of returns

The great bulk of all returns are due to merchandise problems, inadequate store service, and store policies that foster returns. Still other returns result from irresponsible practices on the part of the customers. But some returns are inevitable and will always be part of the retail business.

Unsatisfactory merchandise Items may be returned because of poor workmanship and manufacturing defects, incorrect size designations, or inadequate informational labeling. Poor assortments and overpricing also lead to returns when the customer finds a better "buy" in another store.

---

[12] Jay Scher, *Financial and Operating Results of Department and Specialty Stores in 1969* (New York: Controllers Congress, National Retail Merchants Association, 1970), pp. viii, ix.

Faulty store service Delayed deliveries, delivery of incorrect items, poor alterations, and damages during delivery also result in returns.

Store policy Store policies can cause many returns. The salespeople may be encouraged to use high-pressure methods that force sales of items the customers are unwilling to keep. Salespeople may also urge customers to take items home for further consideration, with assurance that whatever is not wanted may be returned without obligation. Such a sales policy usually results in large returns. Easy credit policies encourage credit purchases, and returns are higher from credit customers. A very liberal return policy, accepting the great majority of returns without question, also induces a high return rate. Some merchants, however, feel that such a policy is necessary to build customer confidence and encourage purchases.

Customer responsibility for returns The customer may change her mind about price, color, quality, or style. Other returns result when she buys gifts that do not completely suit or please their recipients. Some customers "buy" merchandise for some special occasion, such as a wedding or a football weekend, and then return it after use. The blame for such returns is obvious.

Returns cannot be totally stopped. People will change their minds; and if one store refuses to accept returns they will take their business to other retailers who extend this privilege. The customer often needs to see how furniture and other items will look in her home, and expects to return whatever is unsuitable. But the store is not without fault. Delays in delivery often occur with resultant customer dissatisfaction. Hence, except for special events in which he specifies that "all sales are final," the retailer must expect to allow some returns. The best he can do is to minimize unnecessary ones.

□ Minimizing returns

Retailers are not overly concerned when merchandise is returned within a three- to ten-day period, undamaged, with the price ticket intact, and accompanied by the sales check. The main problems involve merchandise that has been "out" for some time, that has to be re-marked because the price ticket is gone, or for which there is no sales check. Even some of these returns are inevitable. But retailers have tried to minimize returned goods and still retain customer goodwill through two approaches: (1) individual store action and (2) cooperative action by retail groups.

The individual store approach The individual store's attempt to reduce returns should start with analysis of what causes excessive returns. If merchandise defects and overpricing are responsible for disproportionate returns, the buying operations should be improved. If unsatisfactory service causes returns, then steps should be taken to improve the service—for example, to decrease damage, delays, and errors in delivery. Employees should be kept "return-conscious." The store's overselling practices and policies of urging "on approval" sales should be modified if they lead to a very high rate of returns. A policy of charging for picking up returns may replace a free pickup policy.

A store may impose a "no return" policy for some wearable and personal items, such as hats and millinery. Most customers will actually welcome this rule on sanitary grounds. Some well-entrenched stores may be able to set strict return limits that would not be feasible for most establishments. To illustrate, cash customers may receive less than full refunds or be required to accept merchandise certificates. Other stores use certificates when merchandise is returned without sales checks, on the theory that the certificates lead to the purchase of other items in the store while cash may be used to make purchases elsewhere. But rigid rules of this sort usually break down over time, and can easily engender serious ill-will while in operation.

The group approach The retailers of a community, as a group, can afford to do many things that the individual store cannot undertake. By joining together, the merchants can activate educational campaigns on the costliness of returns, provide material for publicity drives, frame sanitary provisions and seek local ordinances establishing sanitary controls over returns, exchange information about customers with records of excessive returns, and exchange return-ratio data.

Merchants also sometimes use group action to remove the competitive pressures against stricter return policies. The stores may agree on uniform time limits for returns, set a standard policy of refusing to pick up certain merchandise, or standardize pickup charges for returned merchandise. But attempts to reach such agreement may fall apart in disputes over what the policies should be. This problem is aggravated if the group is large and includes stores of different types offering a variety of services. Moreover, suspicion may arise among the members as to whether every one is complying with the stated policies, or whether some are seeking competitive advantages through more liberal practices. In such case the agreement is likely to lose its effectiveness very quickly.

■ STORE HOURS

The days and hours of the week the store should be open to serve its customers is an increasingly important problem. Although customer preferences are probably the chief determinant, competitors' policies, employee attitudes, and government regulations are also basic considerations.[13] The retailer's desire to serve his customers has lead to long hours of business for retail stores in comparison to other firms. However, the present trend toward night and Sunday openings has extended current store hours substantially beyond the practices of 20 or 30 years ago.

□ Night openings

Probably beginning with supermarket operators in Southern California, the movement toward night openings has spread rapidly throughout the United States. Faced with the inroads of discount houses and other competitors, many stores have reluctantly added evening (and in numerous cases, Sunday) openings. Today almost all kinds of stores in all sections of the country are open some evening or evenings each week. Downtown retailers have adopted evening hours as a competitive tool to weaken the pulling power of shopping centers, and in many cities, are open one, two, or three nights per week.[14] Shopping center merchants consider evening hours essential, and are usually open five or six nights. Many retailers make 25 to 35 percent of their sales during evening hours, and this figure rises to 60 percent in some stores.

The individual retailer faces some major questions in deciding on night openings, including the following:

1. Do the potential customers prefer this time for shopping? Since the retailer exists to serve his customers this question is the key one.
2. Are night openings profitable? That is, do they result in increased sales without a proportionate increase in expenses, or do they merely shift part of the volume to the night hours with no overall sales gain?
3. Are night openings necessary to meet competition from other stores, whether downtown or in suburban centers?
4. Do night openings impair or improve customer service?
5. Do night openings raise or lower personnel standards? Does the practice aid or retard the retailer's ability to obtain qualified personnel?
6. What combination of staggered hours, part-time employment and "shift" schedules will be needed to remain open at night and still give the employees the shorter hours they now demand?
7. Two additional questions must be answered if a policy of night openings is adopted:
   (*a*) How many nights will the store be open?
   (*b*) What night or nights and what hours shall be chosen?

---

[13] The impact of wage and hour regulation is covered on page 229, above.

[14] But in some cities the downtown stores have suffered from very low customer traffic and sales volume during the evening hours. Cf. "Downtown Areas: Night Sales Slow," *Women's Wear Daily*, October 23, 1969, pp. 1, 14.

☐ Sunday openings

Some stores, such as drug and food retailers, newspaper shops, and service stations, have long operated on Sunday, but many other types of stores have now adopted this practice. The rapid expansion of shopping centers and highway stores is a major factor in this development. The roadside and shopping center retailers quickly found that night and Saturday hours were especially important because of the opportunities for family shopping. When they tried Sunday hours, they experienced another substantial increase in sales.

State and local ordinances have often been used, usually unsuccessfully, in attempts to prevent stores from opening on Sundays. Retail trade unions oppose Sunday selling, even if overtime wages are paid and a 40-hour week is maintained through "staggering" of employees' hours. Some retailers, strongly opposed to Sunday retailing, have sponsored joint advertisements condemning the practice and urging customers to stay out of stores on Sundays. Opinions differ regarding the effectiveness of the plea. In practice, however, increasingly stores are yielding to competitive pressures and remaining open on Sundays.[15]

The widespread adoption of Sunday openings by retail stores of almost all types has raised questions for management similar to those already mentioned for night openings and need not be repeated here. These questions should be carefully considered, however, before a decision is made.

■ SOME OTHER SERVICES

Many other services are also useful in attracting and holding customers. Some of these services are briefly discussed in the following paragraphs.

☐ Personal shopping

Many large department stores and departmentized specialty shops, as well as some smaller specialty shops, offer personal shopping services. These stores will select merchandise for their customers in response to mail or telephone requests. In some stores, representatives of the shopping department will go out and find the merchandise elsewhere if the desired items are not in the store's stock. Sometimes the name of a fictitious individual is used to personalize this service. For example, Marshall Field & Co. promotes its services under the names Pauline Shaw (P for personal, S for shopping)

[15] "The Turn to Sunday Shopping," *U.S. News and World Report,* January 5, 1970, p. 7; and E. B. Weiss, " 'Never on Sunday' Retailing Rule Loses out after Long, Hard, Battle," *Advertising Age,* November 17, 1969, p. 117.

and Mary Owen (M for mail, O for order) even though it actually has a large staff of shoppers. Numerous retailers also employ a number of especially well-trained salespeople, either year-round or during the pre-Christmas peak, to accompany customers from department to department and to assist in making selections. Some stores call these persons "escort shoppers" to distinguish them from "personal shoppers" who shop in response to written and telephone communications. Both escort and personal shopping business is growing rapidly in many establishments and stores are seriously competing for this business.

□ Helping customers to find merchandise

Most small retailers find it unnecessary to do more than provide salespeople to help the customer find what she wants. But the problem of helping customers locate what they want becomes more complicated in large stores. The merchandise may be on several floors, or the sales floor may be so large—as in the modern supermarket and discount house—that all the merchandise cannot be seen from any one spot. Under these conditions, several steps may be taken to aid customers. The salespeople may be trained to answer customers' questions about the location of goods; signs can be placed over each department or category of merchandise, as is done in most variety stores and supermarkets; store directories may be placed near the store entrances or in and near the elevators; elevator operators may be trained to direct customers to the various departments; and floormen and information booths may be provided to direct customers.

□ Providing merchandise information

Many retailers are intensifying their efforts to give their customers more information about merchandise. Some grocery chains are providing increased information about the packaging date and freshness of grocery products.[16] Some large firms can obtain merchandise data from their own testing bureaus. Thus, R. H. Macy & Company has its Bureau of Standards, and Sears, Roebuck and Co. has its merchandise laboratory. Smaller retail organizations are making greater use of commercial testing firms; and both

---

[16] Customers seem to pay relatively little attention to this information, (sometimes called "open dating") but they seem to appreciate the fact that the store has made the information available. "Chains Woo Consumers with Open Dating," *Business Week*, January 16, 1971, pp. 48–51. For discussion of an experiment which found department store customers paying little attention to information on electrical appliances, cf. Frank Mayans, "Preliminary Conclusions on Buying Guide Tag System," *Retail Overview*, Vol. 3, No. 3 (Fall 1970), pp. 30–34. Also cf. n. 11, p. 372, above.

large and small retailers are asking their suppliers to furnish more detailed information on such factors as color fastness, shrinkage, and washability. These data are passed on to the salespeople to improve their selling efforts. In an increasing number of cases, at least part of this information is placed on labels attached to the merchandise.

☐ Accepting COD orders

Many retailers sell some merchandise on a COD basis. Buying COD is especially convenient for the customer who places an order by mail or telephone and who does not have a charge account at the store. But because of the problems involved in handling such transactions many stores now add an extra fee for this service.

In addition to the expense of handling them, COD's also result in a high percentage of returns—almost double that of cash and charge sales. Because of this fact some stores now refuse to accept COD orders unless a down payment is made or unless the total order is in excess of a specified amount.

☐ Still other miscellaneous services

Many other services may be offered to induce customers to patronize the store. Some stores employ interior designers to advise on selection of furniture and home furnishings. This service may be offered without extra charge, or the charge may be waived if the customer buys a certain amount. A few stores have established playrooms, where children may be left during a shopping trip. Others provide auditoriums for use without charge by women's clubs. Beauty parlors may be operated at a loss to attract customers, and "free" educational classes may be conducted in knitting and sewing. The store may offer a check-cashing service or it may provide a branch post-office to accommodate its customers. Through a personal service bureau, theater and transportation tickets may be purchased. Or a lost-and-found department may be operated.

Adequate and convenient parking facilities attract many customers. As parking has become more difficult, some retailers have provided their own facilities or made arrangements for their patrons to park in nearby garages or parking lots; others offer bus service at frequent intervals from parking lots to their stores; and still others have placed their stores in locations (1) where there is ample parking room in the streets, (2) where the store may operate its own parking lot, or (3) where several retailers may join together to offer parking facilities, as in a shopping center.

■ INCOME PRODUCING SERVICES

The services previously mentioned, and numerous others that could be mentioned, are usually primarily intended to increase the sale of the store's merchandise. But, as we have already noted, many retailers are now adding services that produce their own direct revenues. A statement in Montgomery Ward & Co.'s 1968 annual report exemplifies this trend among large retail firms.

> The business of providing more and better services for the convenience of customers has quadrupled in dollars and more than doubled as a percent of total sales in the past 10 years. . . . Wards is continuing its leadership in providing specialized services for customers of all ages. Wendy Ward charm and self-improvement courses now are taught in 178 stores and graduates of these courses, mostly teen-age girls, exceed one million. A new series of eight 1½ hour classes in home decorating was introduced in March of 1968 and will be offered in 90 stores by year end. . . . Wards also offers advisory services for planning and remodeling of kitchens and bathrooms, installation of central heating and air conditioning and other home improvements. . . . Ward's one-stop customer accommodation centers in approximately 200 stores provide a variety of services that include utility bill payment, check cashing, money orders, licenses and photocopying. The company attracts many new customers through these service centers in metro district stores. More than 500 Ward stores provide tire and auto service, in addition to sales and installation of tires, batteries and accessories. Ward stores in Los Angeles, Phoenix and Orlando offer rent-a-car services and credit customers can use their Charg-all cards for car rentals or leases. Patrons of Wards auto service centers there can rent a car while theirs is being serviced. . . . Other services include beauty salons and floral services; snack bars, coffee shops, cafeterias and buffeterias serve 150,000 customers daily.[17]

□ Rentals

Renting of merchandise to customers is another example of an income-producing service that has grown rapidly during the past decade. The customer can now rent power mowers, floor polishers, electric power tools, stapling guns, ladders, chain saws, and a host of other items. Many stores have established separate rental departments to meet the needs of their customers; while other retailers, such as those selling hardware, believe that they already carry virtually every item that a prospective rental customer might request.

Hardware retailers, and others who have entered the rental business,

---

[17] *Annual Report,* Marcor, Inc., 1968, p. 29.

have been motivated by at least five basic factors: (1) the high profit potential when the operation is controlled effectively; (2) the absence of strong competition, since many chain and department stores continue to neglect the potential of renting; (3) the additional sales produced by purchases of tools, both used and new; (4) the sales of related items—those designed to be used with the equipment rented; and (5) the overall store growth generated by new customers with needs for other merchandise and services.[18]

But a rental service is not an automatic source of easy profits. Those operators who are considering a rental department should carefully weigh all relevant factors including the following: (1) The size of the inventory investment required to provide a balanced stock of suitable merchandise; (2) the difficulty of displaying effectively a variety of used and unrelated items; (3) the setting of equitable rental rates; (4) the provision of adequate insurance protection for the retailer, the customer, and the equipment or tools rented; and (5) the establishment of proper controls over the insurance, care, and return of the rented items.

■ PUBLIC SERVICES

The retailer's social contributions have already been discussed, in Chapters 2 and 3[19]. But it is only fitting to conclude this discussion of retail services with mention of the wide and increasing variety of public service activities that socially conscious retailers are rendering. These activities range from parades, civic celebrations, and art festivals to efforts to encourage disadvantaged and minority citizen enterprises. They include, among many other endeavors, voter registration drives, community health programs, scholarships and charitable efforts in depressed areas, consumer education conferences for home economics teachers, vocational training seminars, employment of the handicapped and mentally retarded, fund raising for a working boys' home, and maintenance of a cultural center in the store for exhibitions of local talent in the arts.

■ REVIEW AND DISCUSSION QUESTIONS

1 Summarize the main guides that the retailer may use in establishing his customer service policies.

---

[18] Cf. "Rentals . . . If the Market Is There, Tap It and Watch Customers Buy, Too," *Hardware Retailer,* June 1969, pp. 54–57.

[19] Pp. 40–41, 45 and 56 above.

2 Discuss the statement: "It is foolish to argue the wisdom of charging or not charging for customer services. In our present affluent society customers are able and willing to pay for the services they receive and expect to do so. The rapid growth of 'income-producing' services is evidence of this fact."

3 Three major methods of wrapping merchandise are used in retail stores. Summarize the merits and limitations of each and indicate the conditions under which it should be used.

4 Distinguish among the major types of delivery systems and indicate the conditions under which each one might be used to advantage.

5 Prepare a list of the chief causes of customer complaints in retail stores, classifying them into logical groups that will aid in finding solutions.

6 Discuss the relative merits of handling complaints in both small and large stores (*a*) by the salesperson and (*b*) in a central office.

7 Suggest several methods by which the percentage of returns may be reduced. Which methods do you believe have the best chances for success?

8 What are some of the major problems retailers encounter if they stay open nights and Sundays? Do you feel that these problems are similar for all retailers, or that they vary in nature and importance with the size, location, and type of store? Explain.

9 In your judgment, what factors are responsible for the growing interest of retailers in "income-producing" services? Explain.

10 Discuss the pros and cons of establishing a rental department in a hardware store.

chapter 22

RETAIL CREDIT AND COLLECTIONS

As noted in the previous chapter, an ever-growing number of customers now demand credit service. Buying on credit has become such a well-established practice in American economic life that our society is sometimes called "a credit economy." And with good reason in view of the current high level of consumer credit.

VOLUME OF RETAIL CREDIT SALES

Total consumer credit outstanding at the end of the year, aside from cash loans which were also often used to finance purchases of goods and services, grew from approximately $4 billion in 1945 to $86 billion in 1970. Of this latter amount, $70 billion was installment credit (including $35 billion automobile debt) and $16 billion noninstallment. In addition, consumers had about $42 billion worth of personal loans outstanding at the close of 1970.[1] The University of Michigan Survey Research Center estimates that 51 percent of all American families owed some installment debt

[1] *Federal Reserve Bulletin,* Vol. 57, No. 7 (July 1971), p. A56. The installment figure for 1970 includes approximately $4 billion in home modernization and repair loans.

at the beginning of 1969, and that during the previous year, some 40 percent used some credit cards other than gasoline and oil cards.[2]

Exact figures are not available, but we can safely estimate that about one-third of our total retail sales are transacted on credit. Probably about one out of every three retail firms offers to sell on credit but the importance of credit varies widely between different types of stores. More than two-thirds of all furniture, household appliance and jewelry store sales are made on credit. Almost 60 percent of department store sales and 67 percent of specialty store sales involved credit in 1963; comparable figures for 1969 are 55.44 percent and 59.67 percent, which constitute very substantial amounts.[3] Discount stores, which originally operated on a cash basis, now increasingly offer credit. The supermarket is the most important type of retailing to resist the trend toward widespread credit. The supermarket chains that have experimented with credit card and other plans have generally found those plans too expensive for profitable implementation.[4]

Credit is now widely used by consumers in all income groups and for most kinds of merchandise and services. Even income tax payments and church donations may be charged by means of credit cards in some communities. An indication of how deeply some people have gone into debt is shown by the fact that the number of individual wage-earner bankruptcies increased by about 600 percent between 1950 and 1967.[5]

Some retailers are concerned over the growing tendency to offer charge accounts to teenagers and young adults, but others are finding that the practice helps build sales and the losses are not excessive. Moreover, studies show that consumers generally use their credit fairly cautiously. Apparently only about 11 percent of all American families commit 20 percent or more of their *disposable* (after tax) *income* to installment debt. And approximately 70 percent of the families keep their installment debt-disposable income ratio below 10 percent.[6] All credit-conscious retailers, however, believe that close supervision and control over their credit accounts is essential in our highly dynamic economy.

---

[2] George Katona *et al., 1969 Survey of Consumer Finances* (Ann Arbor, Mich.: University of Michigan, 1970), p. 21; *1968 Survey of Consumer Finances* (University of Michigan, 1969), pp. 21–22.

[3] Jay Scher, *Financial and Operating Results of Department and Specialty Stores 1969* (New York: National Retail Merchants Association, 1970), pp. iii, v.

[4] "Chains Eye Credit Cards but Many Cite Drawbacks," *Supermarket News,* March 9, 1970, p. 1.

[5] Administrative Office of the United States Courts, *Tables of Bankruptcy Statistics,* published annually. The bankruptcy rate declined somewhat in 1968 and 1969, but increased again in 1970. Cf. Isadore Barmash, "Going Broke," *New York Times,* December 6, 1970, p. F2.

[6] Katona, *1969 Survey of Consumer Finances,* p. 25.

WHY RETAILERS SELL ON CREDIT

Retailers offer credit service because it helps increase their sales. Some of them have achieved very rapid growth as a result of featuring and intensively advertising their "easy credit terms." And some of these firms rely so heavily on credit account earnings that they might be called "finance companies that also have merchandise for sale."[7] But many retailers who place less emphasis upon credit terms also find that their customers expect and demand credit services. Moreover, retailers who operate their own credit departments can use those departments as a point of contact with their customers, as a means of developing mailing lists, and as a sales agency.

Customer preference and demand for credit

Customers desire credit for several reasons. It makes their shopping more pleasant and convenient. When credit services are available, the customer does not have to carry sizable sums of money on shopping trips or limit her purchases to planned items. Most stores will let credit customers take goods on approval, and items bought on credit can be returned more easily since the store merely credits the customer's account. Credit facilitates telephone and mail order sales. Children may be sent to the store to make credit purchases without the risk of entrusting money to their care.

Individuals who receive their income periodically or irregularly, such as employees who are paid monthly and farmers with annual crops, often require credit for a part of their purchases during the period between paychecks or income receipts. A large portion of the customers who want to buy television sets, electric refrigerators, and expensive clothing either do not have sufficient liquid funds to pay in full or do not want to deplete their bank accounts for that purpose.

Competitive pressure

A retailer who does not offer credit, when faced with these customer desires and needs, will drive much of his potential business to competitors.

---

[7] Some of the major finance companies have purchased interests in retail organizations, in part as a means of expanding their investments in consumer credit. Thus Beneficial Corporation (formerly Beneficial Finance Co.) now controls Western Auto Supply Co. (an automotive supply, sporting goods and hardware chain) and Spiegel's, Inc. (a large mail order firm). Household Finance Company owns a large number of furniture, hardware, appliance, variety, and grocery stores.

In many fields, such as the sale of furniture, household appliances, and television sets, competition practically forces the retailer to extend credit or retire from business. Some well-known firms that once were famous for their "cash-and-carry" policies, are turning to credit selling. For example, in 1958 the J. C. Penney Company introduced selling on credit in a few of its stores; today credit is available in all Penney stores and accounts for over 36 percent of the firm's annual business.[8]

☐ Credit provides continuous contact with customers

Many retailers are convinced that the credit customer is likely to be a steadier patron and, hence, to buy a greater proportion of his goods from one source than the cash customer.[9] Although it is difficult to prove this statement satisfactorily, the experience of many retailers has convinced them that it is true. The case of a small hardware retailer in Dayton, Ohio, is illustrative. An analysis of his charge accounts revealed that the average credit customer spent with him $205 annually, far above the average for his cash customers.[10] On an annual basis, Aldens' typical credit customer purchases three times as much as does the cash buyer. Aldens (the fourth largest mail-order company in the United States) reports that new credit terms, which encouraged its customers to utilize their borrowing capacity fully and to purchase bigger ticket items, helped produce the best sales and earnings in the company's history during 1969.[11]

☐ Aids in building a mailing list

Credit also helps produce sales by providing a selected mailing list of persons who have thought well enough of the store to have opened a charge account there. The retailer who has such exact information about the people trading at his store can get advertisements and announcements of special sales into their hands at minimum expense. Well-planned and consistent use of this list can result in appreciable additional business.

---

[8] Annual Report for the year ended January 31, 1970, p. 30. The Company is currently making a strong appeal to "young moderns" as users of its credit facilities. It says, in a recent announcement, "In our present economy of abundance it is more important than ever for young people to learn thrift and sound money management. A good reputation for financial responsibility, established early, will be a valuable asset all their lives . . ."

[9] Cash customers, of course, often resent the implications of this fact and make protests against the superior treatment accorded the credit customer.

[10] Cf. "How Much Is a Credit Customer Worth?" *Hardware Retailer*, December 1965, p. 48.

[11] Annual Reports, Aldens, Inc. year ending January 31, 1964, p. 7 and Gamble-Skogmo, Inc. (of which Aldens is now a part), year ending January 31, 1970, p. 11.

□ The credit department's role as a sales agency

In addition to the general sales-increasing advantages of credit extension which have been discussed in the preceding paragraphs, the credit department itself should be a valuable sales agency. The department should adopt a marketing philosophy and constantly ask: "How can credit be used to increase the store's sales?"

The department's effectiveness as a sales agency will depend upon (1) the imagination and judgment exercised in opening new accounts, (2) the wisdom shown in handling active accounts, and (3) the ingenuity and skill demonstrated in reopening inactive accounts. Tactful telephone calls and well-designed letters may persuade former customers, whose accounts have become inactive, to return to the store.

■ PROBLEMS OF SELLING ON CREDIT

Although selling on credit has its advantages, it does create some major problems for the retailer. These problems center around the costs of providing credit and the consequent need for skillful management of the credit function.

□ Credit costs

Credit selling creates some costs that are not incurred when the store sells for cash. The three major costs are: (1) credit, billing, and collection department payroll, (2) losses from bad debts, and (3) interest on the funds tied up in accounts receivable. Credit activities also involve extra space, equipment, supplies, postage, and communications expense. (Stores that use outside agencies, such as bank credit card plans, to handle their credit function pay most of these costs indirectly, through the fees or discounts they pay to those agencies.) Different types of stores, and stores with different annual sales volumes experience various credit expense rates, but the typical rate for department stores in 1969, not counting interest costs, was about 1.89 percent of *total sales.*[12] Since credit sales only accounted for about 55 percent of *total sales,* the credit expense really amounted to 3.5 percent of *credit volume.* Automation of some credit operations may eventually reduce this cost ratio somewhat but probably not by any significant amount.

---

[12] Jay Scher, *op. cit.,* p. x. Handling or service charges received by the stores amounted to about 2.24 percent.

Despite the care with which credit is extended, some bad debt losses are inevitable. In the smaller store, where the proprietor's personal relationship with his customers may lead him to be less careful in granting credit and less willing to apply pressure in making collections, losses of from 0.5 to 2 percent on credit sales are common. Bad debt losses in department stores may average about 1 percent of *credit* sales, or about 0.5 percent of *total* sales.

The interest cost on funds tied up in credit accounts varies with (a) the interest rate the firm pays for the capital used to finance its accounts and (*b*) the amount of time customers take to pay for their purchases. However, a very conservative estimate for this cost in large department stores would be about 2.5 percent of credit sales.[13]

Credit extension probably also adds to operating cost by stimulating merchandise returns. Customers are more willing to take home several items "on approval" for selection purposes when they do not have to lay out the cash for them. Consequently, part of the cost of handling returns should be considered as a cost of extending credit.

Installment credit is even more costly than open-account credit. Since open-account customers are likely to keep their accounts active for several months or years, one credit investigation may result in the opening of an account that produces a considerable volume of business. In contrast, installment credit customers tend to be less loyal so that more accounts must be opened and more investigation undertaken per dollar of sales. Bad debt losses on installments run even larger than for open-account credit. The General Finance Company reported that the delinquency rate (*i.e.*, overdue accounts, some of which would eventually be paid) on the installment contracts it handles for furniture, appliance, and television dealers had increased to 4.07 percent in January, 1970.[14] Moreover, the tracing of goods to be repossessed involves considerable expense, and the period over which payments are made is longer for installment sales, so that additional expense is involved in carrying the account.

□ Impact on prices and profits

In spite of the extra costs involved in credit selling, one cannot say that a store will necessarily have higher prices, an increased total expense rate (expenses as a percentage of net sales), or a lower profit rate if it switches from cash to credit selling. Credit may generate sufficient additional business,

---

[13] Cf. *Economic Characteristics of Department Store Credit* (New York: National Retail Merchants Association, 1969), p. 55.

[14] "Delinquents Forcing Retail Credit Curbs," *Women's Wear Daily*, March 12, 1970, p. 7.

without a proportionate increase in other expenses, to lower the total expense rate. Or it may raise the expense rate somewhat, and thus lower the profit *percentage* if there are no increases in prices; but if sales grow at a greater rate than the profit percentage declines, the net result will still be an increased *dollar* profit. In spite of the many possibilities, however, credit selling is probably generally accompanied by somewhat higher expense rates, higher prices, greater sales, smaller net profit percentages, and larger total dollar profits than would result from operating the same stores on a cash basis.

■ TYPES OF RETAIL CREDIT

Retail credit, one form of consumer credit, may be defined as present purchasing power based upon the seller's confidence in the buyer's willingness and ability to pay his bills as they mature. Historically, retail credit took two forms: open account and installment. However, additional forms such as revolving credit, option terms credit, and other variations in the two basic types have evolved and become important during the past 30 years or so.

□ Open-account credit

Under "regular charge account" or open-account credit, the customer (1) receives the goods he buys without any down payment and without pledging either those goods or any other asset as specific collateral for the debt; (2) is billed for the full amount of his charged purchases at the end of the billing period (usually one month); and (3) is then supposed to pay that bill in full within a conventional period (usually 30 days) from the time the bill is mailed. Most of the stores that offer open-account credit consider the costs involved as an operating expense to be covered by the price of the goods they sell and do not make a separate charge for this service. Some retailers, however, now impose a "service" charge when payments are delayed beyond the due date. They do this both to encourage prompt payment and to cover part of the extra costs that result from slow payment.

The retailer receives little or no credit charge revenue from open-account credit. He also has minimum formal security, since he receives no down payment and he cannot repossess the merchandise if the customer fails to pay his bill. He basically depends upon the customer's financial capacity and personal character, although expensive and complicated legal procedures can be used as a last resort in case of nonpayment. Open-account credit is the traditional form extended by department stores and at one time was offered only to well-to-do customers. Many credit men believe that more conservative and stricter standards should be followed in approving open-account credit than for other types of accounts.

□ Installment credit

Under installment credit[15] the customer's payment obligation is divided into parts, or installments, which come due at set intervals in the future. It thus differs from open-account credit where the customer is normally expected to make a single, full payment for goods bought following receipt of the first bill. Along with this basic difference, installment credit usually, although not invariably, differs from open-account credit in the following ways: (1) A down payment is usually required when the item is purchased or delivered; (2) the seller often requires some security that may be repossessed in case of nonpayment, as discussed in the next paragraph; (3) a written contract is used; and (4) a separate "finance" or credit charge is usually imposed for the installment service. To illustrate, the Sears, Roebuck catalog "payment table" shows that customers who want to divide purchases of $290.01 to $310.00 (after down-payment) into 18 monthly installments have to pay a finance charge of $48.10 for this arrangement.[16]

Secured transactions The installment seller often retains security rights in the merchandise sold, particularly if expensive or durable items are involved. In most states those rights are now specified in a standardized contract, called a Security Agreement or a Retail Installment Sales Contract. This contract has eliminated many complicated technical and legal questions that formerly arose when the security arrangements were embodied in conditional sales, chattel mortgage and bailment lease contracts.[17] The Security Agreement allows the seller to repossess the merchandise if the purchaser fails to make the required payments as they come due.[18] The seller may also sue the buyer for any remaining deficiency if the full balance owed cannot be recovered by reselling the repossessed item.[19] Or, instead of repossessing, the seller may sue for the entire unpaid balance in case of default.

---

[15] Installment contract terms are subject to a considerable amount of state regulation. Each retailer selling on installment should become familiar with his state laws.

[16] Spring 1971, catalog, p. 619; rate applicable in Illinois, Indiana, Iowa, Kentucky, and Wisconsin.

[17] Ernest A. Rovelstad, ed., *Credit Manual of Commercial Laws 1971* (New York: National Association of Credit Management, 1970), pp. 16–21, 131–35, 160.

[18] In practice, of course, delayed payments are usually accepted in lieu of other collection action.

[19] The Uniform Consumer Credit Code, adopted in some states and discussed on p. 549, below, modifies the right of repossession and generally prohibits suit for the remaining deficiency after repossession. A number of practical business considerations, discussed on p. 532, also limit the protection the seller receives through the right of repossession.

□ General credit contracts

The general credit contract, another type of installment agreement, does not give the seller the right to repossess. If the buyer defaults on his payments, the seller has only the same recourse as under open account credit, that is, the right to sue.

□ Revolving credit

Installment credit originally developed as a means of enabling customers to use and enjoy large items, such as furniture, major electrical appliances, and automobiles, while paying for them out of future income. But during the last 20 years or so, many major retailers have also developed plans that: (1) permit the purchasers of smaller items to divide up their payments if they so desire, and (2) involve a service charge to set against the costs of extending liberal credit. The principal plans they created, "revolving credit" (discussed in this section) and "option terms" (discussed in the following section) combine many of the aspects of installment and open-account credit.

Under the revolving credit plan the customer agrees to pay a fixed amount, for example $25 per month, during any month that he has an unpaid balance outstanding at the store. The store then agrees to provide a "line of credit" or credit limit, which in this case might be $300. Whenever the customer's debt to the store drops below the $300 limit he is entitled to charge additional merchandise up to that figure. A "service charge," often at the rate of 1.5 percent per month on the unpaid balance, is usually imposed and will be included in the regular monthly payment.[20]

The customer has the convenience of being able to purchase miscellaneous items (up to his limit) without having to sign a separate contract for each purchase as he normally would in the case of installment credit. Yet he is able to spread his payments out over a number of months. The fixed maximum credit line gives the store relatively tight control over the amount the customer is allowed to charge (although some stores will relax the limit for approved customers during peak buying periods such as Christmas and Easter) in contrast to the vague and indefinite limits usually associated with open-account credit.

---

[20] In approximately 30 states, specific legislation establishes the maximum rate, usually 1.5 percent per month, that may be imposed as a service charge on revolving credit accounts. In some of the other states, the courts have recently held that, in the absence of specific legislation, credit account service charges may not exceed the state's maximum legal rate of interest for cash loans. Service charges will be limited to 1 percent per month in some of those states if higher courts uphold these rulings. Cf. Stuart M. Rosen, "The Wisconsin Decision: Implications for Retailing," *Stores*, Vol. 53, No. 1 (January 1971), pp. 28–29.

□ Option-terms

The option-terms plan allows the customer to choose between paying the bill in full during the option period (generally 25 to 30 days after the billing date) or, if he prefers, only paying some minimum portion (usually one-tenth or one-twelfth) of the amount at that time. No service charge is imposed if the bill is completely paid during the option period, but a charge (often 1.5 percent of the unpaid balance per month) automatically goes into effect if the customer chooses the deferred payment arrangement.

This plan, sometimes called "option-terms revolving credit," is much more flexible than the basic revolving credit plan discussed above. The dollar amount of the monthly payment is fixed under the basic plan, while it varies under option-terms in proportion to the size of the customer's unpaid balance. Option-terms gives the customer a wider choice of payment alternatives than open-account does. The automatic service charge is easier to collect and induces much less customer resentment than might result from imposing the same fee as a penalty for late payment of open-account bills. Many retailers feel that the option-terms plan is the "ideal" credit arrangement and they think it will ultimately be the most widely used of all credit plans.

□ Other types of retail credit

Several other credit plans should be mentioned briefly. The "90-day" or "3-pay" plan used for men's and women's clothing typically requires a one-third down payment with the balance split into three equal amounts payable over a period of three months. A service charge may or may not be added. "Ten-pay" and "twenty-pay" plans are also in use, but they are paid off in ten or twenty weeks, not months.

Under "coupon book" plans the customer receives her credit limit in the form of a book of coupons which she spends as cash in the store. Advertised as providing "instant credit" to their users, these coupon books appeal chiefly to consumers who cannot qualify for other types of credit or who like the convenience of the coupon. Books are available in denominations of $25, $50, and $100, with individual coupons valued at 50 cents, $1, $2, and $5, and payments are made on a monthly basis.

■ BANKS, FINANCE COMPANIES, AND CREDIT CARD COMPANIES

This chapter deals primarily with the techniques and problems involved in the granting of credit by retail stores. But we should recognize that consumers also sometimes finance their purchases with credit from non-store institutions and agencies. To cite a few examples: Credit unions—cooperatives organized to extend small loans to members—have become a source of funds for many persons who wish to buy on credit. Increasingly, banks are advertising their small-loan services, and many of these loans are arranged for repayment on an installment basis. The sales finance company, which provides so much of the credit for sales of automobiles and other consumer durables, is still another example of a non-store source of credit.

□ Assistance from finance companies and banks

Although retailers *originate* most of the installment credit extended to consumers for the purchase of goods, most merchants do not hold their installment contracts to maturity. Instead, they sell some or all of them to banks and finance companies. This step provides cash at once and the finance company may also assume responsibility for collections. In return for this immediate cash, the retailer accepts something less than he would receive if he carried the contract until all payments are made. In other words, the finance company takes over the retailer's "paper" at a discount.

□ Credit card plans

Credit card organizations have become a major nonretail source for consumer purchasing credit in recent years. Banks, gasoline companies, travel and entertainment card firms, and independent credit card companies have sponsored credit card plans, but the bank plans have by far the greatest significance for general retailing.

Travel and entertainment cards, such as American Express, Carte Blanche and Diners' Club, are used primarily for hotel and restaurant bills and simi-

TABLE 22–1

Credit card plans, December 31, 1969 (amounts outstanding in billions of dollars)

Bank credit cards	2.6
Oil companies (consumer accounts)	1.5
Travel and entertainment (consumer accounts)	.1
Other (including "independent retail credit card companies")	less than .2

Source: Andrew F. Brimmer, "Statement to Congress," *Federal Reserve Bulletin*, Vol. 56, No. 6 (June 1970) p. 504.

lar travel services and are also accepted in some gift and souvenir shops and other stores that cater to travelers. The cardholders, who are mainly in the upper income brackets, pay an annual fee for the service. The card companies, however, receive most of their revenue from commissions paid by the hotels and other suppliers who honor their cards. Airlines and hotel and motel chains also issue cards and sometimes arrange to have those cards accepted in cooperating establishments.

The gasoline company cards are mainly intended for use in stations that sell the company's brand of gasoline, and thus are of greatest significance to the petroleum, tire, battery and accessory industries. The gasoline cards are also accepted in many motels, hotels, and other establishments that serve motorists. Both the gasoline companies and the travel card firms try to sell some general merchandise to their cardholders through direct mail solicitation along with their monthly bills.

Bank credit cards The bank card plans have grown meteorically in recent years. Two Federal Reserve Board studies show that the number of banks offering credit cards increased sixfold, from approximately 200 to a little more than 1,200, between September, 1967, and December, 1969.[21] Most such banks are members of either the Interbank (Master Charge) or the BankAmericard system.

The various bank plans are basically similar to each other, although they vary somewhat in details. Essentially, the sponsoring bank acts as a "collective credit department" for all the merchants who join the plan.[22] Customers may apply for credit either at the bank or at one of the cooperating retailers. In either case, however, it is the bank—rather than the retailer—who passes on the merits of the application. Once approved, the customer gets a credit card which serves to identify him and is valid at any cooperating store. The retailer who participates in the plan can make small sales without special authorization, but may call the bank if someone he does not know wants to make a large purchase. The merchant sends the salescheck to the bank, where the amount involved is entered to his account after deduction of a charge of about 3 to 5 percent, depending upon store volume.

The bank handles collections, usually without recourse to the merchant, and the customers typically have the option of paying their bills in full monthly or shifting into a revolving-credit plan with a monthly service charge on the unpaid balance. The banks and stores that participate in in-

---

[21] *Bank Credit-Card and Check-Credit Plans* (Washington, D.C.: Board of Governors, The Federal Reserve System, 1968) p. 1; Andrew Brimmer, *op. cit.*, p. 499.

[22] Some merchants belong to more than one plan and/or also maintain some individual store charge accounts along with the bank plan(s). In such cases, of course, each bank system acts as the "collective credit department" only with regard to its own accounts.

terchange systems, such as Master Charge and BankAmericard, agree to accept cards issued by any member bank. Their cards thus acquire national acceptability.

The so-called independent (*i.e.,* nonbank) retail credit card companies operate in very much the same way as the bank plans. In fact, the two firms that were the largest organizations in this category, Uni-Serve of New York and Central Charge Service of Wilmington, Delaware, and Washington, D.C., have recently become subsidiaries of major banks.

Benefits and limitations The bank and independent credit card plans are especially advantageous to the small retailer, who normally finds it difficult to compete with the large retailer's credit service. All of the details of investigation at the time of opening an account, the subsequent maintenance of up-to-date credit information and of accounting records, the collection of accounts, and the credit risk itself are carried by others. The retailer's cash is not depleted by the growth of accounts receivable. Since the same credit card is valid in several stores, he may also gain business from the customers of other participating retailers.

The major limitations of the plans are found in the store's loss of "personal hold" on the customer, the charge for the credit service, and the losses from fraudulent use of credit cards. The customer's loyalty to any one store is reduced since his credit relationships are largely with the organization issuing the card and since that card is usually valid at several competing stores. Whether the usual 3–5 percent charge is excessive or not depends largely upon the individual retailer. Some merchants are able to handle their credit costs, including losses, on a lower ratio to sales; but many others would reduce their costs if they used an outside plan. Many department and chain store firms believe that maintenance of their own credit departments, with all of the attendant advantages, is no more costly and may even be less expensive than the use of an outside credit card plan. In some instances the banks and credit card companies have offered special rates or rebates to attract the larger retailers, but most major department stores and many national chains continue to operate their own credit services.[23] Nevertheless, an increasing number of smaller chains and independent stores are using outside credit card plans to compete with the larger firms.

■ CREDIT MANAGEMENT

When a store sells on credit, accounts must be solicited; and someone must decide who is to get credit, what amount is to be granted, the time

[23] Cf. Theodore N. Beckman and Ronald S. Foster, *Credits and Collections,* 8th ed. (New York: McGraw-Hill, Inc., 1969), pp. 134–35; and "Can the Stores Trump Bank Credit Cards?" *Business Week,* January 30, 1971, pp. 62–64.

during which it is to be extended, and how collections shall be handled, including delinquent accounts and those involving customer bankruptcies. Specialized procedures have to be established for the activities of (a) opening accounts, (*b*) maintaining credit information, (c) identifying customers for whom accounts have been opened, (*d*) authorizing credit purchases, (e) billing customers, and (*f*) collecting past due accounts. Credit extension also creates problems in providing the necessary additional working capital, in deciding on the extent to which credit operations will be computerized, and in conforming to credit regulations established by the government.

□ Promoting credit accounts

Most retailers who regularly extend credit actively solicit new accounts, since the cost of obtaining each new account will normally be returned several times over in profit. Salespeople may be instructed to suggest the advantages of a charge account to their cash customers, and they may be rewarded for every new account they obtain. The retailer may use telephone or direct mail to solicit prospective credit customers chosen from membership lists of women's clubs, telephone directories, lists of new arrivals in town, taxpayers' lists, and similar sources. Stores also use newspaper, radio, television, and direct-mail advertising to emphasize the benefits of credit accounts and the ease with which such accounts may be secured. Many retailers are now actively soliciting student accounts with very satisfactory results.[24]

□ Setting credit standards

Decisions on accepting or rejecting credit applications involve two closely related questions. First, management must set standards; that is, it must decide on the credit standing (degree of creditworthiness) needed to obtain an account at the store. Second, prospective credit customers must be evaluated, as part of the account-opening procedure discussed on pp. 532–37, to determine whether they qualify under the store's standards.

The credit manager (or the proprietor in a small store) faces a dilemma in setting those standards. If he establishes low standards, the store will probably obtain greater sales than would result from a more conservative credit policy. But low standards also entail greater bad debt losses, heavier collection expenses, and the use of more personnel in the credit department. High standards reduce these cost elements but, as we have just noted, check the expansion of sales. The credit manager's task is to find the proper bal-

---

[24] Irving Penner, "The College Credit Market," *Stores*, Vol. 52, No. 9, September 1970, pp. 14–16.

ance between sales stimulation and expense reduction in order to maximize the store's net profits.

Standards for installment credit Installment sales agreements often give the seller some lien or claim on the merchandise sold, so that he may repossess it in case of nonpayment.[25] Because of this, some retailers feel that they can set lower standards for installment credit transactions and that they can safely omit scrutinizing installment credit applications with the care they use in approving open-account and option-terms credit.

But several factors have reduced the protection the retailer receives from the right of repossession. First, and most obvious, is the extension of installment selling to soft goods and services, such as travel, which usually have little or no repossession value. Second, even for durable goods, repossession value has become less certain. Fashion is becoming more important, and the market values of durable as well as soft goods are influenced by unpredictable changes in fashion. Third, some durable goods, such as automobiles and television sets, may be wrecked or damaged. Finally, competition on installment terms which has tended to stretch out the payment period has further weakened the security afforded by repossession and has increased the potential number of reclaiming actions.

Moreover, the long-term nature of the installment contract can create special collection problems since the customer's financial circumstances or his willingness to pay for the item in question may change before the contract is completed. Consequently, the establishment of installment credit standards and the evaluation of installment applications call for as much skill and judgment as in any other type of credit.

□ Account-opening procedures in the small store

The close personal contact between the proprietor of the small store and his customers makes it quite easy for him to decide to whom he should extend credit. He usually knows something about his customers, hence, he does not feel the need of the "red tape" through which the large stores go before extending credit. But this personal contact will prove detrimental if he permits his sympathies and emotions to influence his business judgment. It is difficult to refuse credit to friends, to impose a reasonable credit limit upon them, and even more difficult to pursue sound collection policies.

The large credit losses of many small stores indicate that their proprietors need to exercise better judgment in evaluating the credit qualifications of their customers. Although they do not require the formal credit-

---

[25] Cf. the discussion of secured transactions, p. 525, above.

granting organization of the large store, they should use the same techniques. Data should be gathered from references and from the local credit bureau. When a credit bureau does not exist or is considered too expensive, the local banker may be a good source of information.

The small retailer will find it a good practice to adopt a credit limit even though it may be quite flexible. And, like his larger competitor, he should explain to each customer the general rules governing credit extension, when bills will be rendered, and when payments are expected.

□ Account-opening procedures in the medium-sized and large store

Five basic steps are usually followed when the customer asks the store to open his account. These are: the credit interview, obtaining outside information, approving the credit application, establishing the credit limit, and informing the customer.

The interview The credit interview with the customer is conducted by personnel from the credit department. Through questions and a credit application (Figure 22–1) information is secured about the applicant's character, capacity, and capital. The interview is also used to educate the customer in the proper use of the credit account which may be opened for him and to "sell the store" to him.

Obtaining outside information Some stores extend credit solely on the basis of information obtained during the interview—especially when the customer desires to make an immediate purchase. Most stores, however, gather additional data and check the information received in the interview before opening the account. In areas where such an organization exists, the local retail credit bureau is probably the retailer's most valuable source of outside information. The majority of these bureaus are cooperatively owned by the stores that use them. Each participating store furnishes the bureau with detailed data on each of its credit customers, including the amount of credit extended and the promptness with which payments are made. When a member requests a report on a person, the complete data are given, but the sources are not disclosed. Hence, any store may supply full information to the bureau without having its competitors become aware of its credit problems. An illustration of such a report is shown in Figure 22–2. When an individual moves to another area also served by a credit bureau, a copy of this record may go to the new location.

Approving credit applications The credit manager decides whether or not to approve credit on the basis of the interview and outside information. Usually this decision is not difficult, since the majority of applicants easily meet the store's requirements. The evidence may indicate that credit exten-

FIGURE 22–1 **Application for a charge account**

PLEASE DO NOT WRITE TO THE LEFT OF THIS LINE →
IF MR. & MRS. PLEASE FILL OUT BOTH LINES
PLEASE PRINT FIRST NAME | MIDDLE NAME | LAST NAME
ACCT. NO. | MR. | MAIL BILL TO
C/R | P/H | N/C | YR | M/C | MRS.
LIMIT | MISS. | BUS. | RES.
OPENING LETTER | RESIDENCE NUMBER & STREET | CITY | STATE | ZIP CODE
APPLICATION BY | LENGTH OF RESIDENCE YRS. MOS. | OWN | RENT | HOME PHONE NO.
MO. | DAY | YEAR | FORMER RESIDENCE NUMBER | STREET | CITY | STATE | LENGTH OF RESIDENCE YRS. MOS. | OWN ☐ RENT ☐
AMOUNT PENDING | EMPLOYED BY | BUSINESS ADDRESS
PICKUP DATE | POSITION | BUSINESS PHONE NO. | HOW LONG YRS. MOS.
AMOUNT RELEASED | FORMER EMPLOYER | BUSINESS ADDRESS | POSITION | HOW LONG
RELEASE OK'D BY | SPOUSES EMPLOYER HUSBAND ☐ WIFE ☐ | BUSINESS ADDRESS
DOWN PAYMENT | POSITION | BUSINESS PHONE NO. | HOW LONG YRS. MOS.
AUTHORIZED BUYERS | PLEASE PRINT NAMES & RELATIONSHIP
NEAREST RELATIVE NOT LIVING WITH YOU | NAME | NUMBER & STREET | CITY & STATE | RELATIONSHIP
MY BANK | BRANCH | CITY | CK'ING | SAVING
OTHER STORES WHERE I HAVE ACCOUNTS | FIRM | ACCOUNT NUMBER | FIRM | ACCOUNT NUMBER
FIRM | ACCOUNT NUMBER | FIRM | ACCOUNT NUMBER

I UNDERSTAND MY ACCOUNT MAY BE PAID IN FULL AT ANY TIME AND THERE WILL BE NO SERVICE CHARGE ON ANY BALANCE PAID IN FULL BEFORE MY NEXT BILLING DATE. IF I CHOOSE TO PAY ACCORDING TO THE MONTHLY PAYMENT SCHEDULE I AGREE SERVICE CHARGES NOT IN EXCESS OF THOSE PERMITTED BY LAW WILL BE CHARGED ON THE OUTSTANDING BALANCES FROM MONTH TO MONTH. I UNDERSTAND THE MONTHLY SERVICE CHARGE WILL BE 1½ PER CENT ON THE BALANCE NOT EXCEEDING $1,000.00 AND 1 PER CENT ON ANY EXCESS; THAT SERVICE CHARGES WILL BE COMPUTED ON THE BEGINNING BALANCE; AND THAT MY ENTIRE BALANCE BECOMES DUE AND PAYABLE IMMEDIATELY IF ANY PAYMENT IS NOT MADE WHEN DUE. IF LEGAL ACTION IS NECESSARY TO ACCOMPLISH COLLECTION I AGREE TO PAY REASONABLE ATTORNEY'S FEES AND COURT COSTS.

REMARKS OR INSTRUCTIONS

CUSTOMER'S SIGNATURE(S) ______ SIGN YOUR NAME IN FULL AS YOU WILL SIGN YOUR SALES CHECKS
STORE WHERE OPENED

ROOS/ATKINS
CHARGE ACCOUNT APPLICATION
798 MARKET STREET, SAN FRANCISCO, CALIF. 94102
FORM 3030 7-[illegible]

Courtesy: Roos/Atkins

sion is clearly undesirable for a small percentage of the applicants, and the credit manager may have difficulty in deciding about another relatively small group. Additional information or a second interview may be required in these latter cases.

1. The "three 'C's" Credit decisions are usually made on the basis of three criteria, called the "three 'C's." These are: character, capacity, and capital. Character, the most important of the three, means willingness to pay obligations when due. It is evidenced by the prospective customer's payment record with other retailers and the community's judgment as to his honesty. Capacity refers to the ability to pay out of current income. Information received concerning the applicant's (or the applicant's spouse's) job, years of employment, and income indicate credit capacity. Capital, that is, financial resources or assets, provides another indication of ability to pay.

FIGURE 22–2 Confidential credit report

NAME AND ADDRESS OF CREDIT BUREAU MAKING REPORT

Credit Bureau of Anytown
2309 Fair, Anytown, Anystate 11003
Telephone CApitol 4-1234 (246)

☐ SUMMARY REPORT ☐ SINGLE REFERENCE ☐ TRADE REPORT
☐ SHORT REPORT ☒ FULL REPORT ☐ PREV. RES. REPORT

DATE RECEIVED	DATE MAILED	CBR REPORT NO.
11-25-69	11-27-69	
DATE TRADE CLEARED	**DATE EMPLOY VERIFIED**	**INCOME VERIFIED**
11-26-69	11-26-69	☐ YES ☐ NO

CONFIDENTIAL *Factbilt*® REPORT FOR: First National Bank of Anytown — IN FILE SINCE: 1-63

This information is furnished in response to an inquiry for the purpose of evaluating credit risks. It has been obtained from sources deemed reliable, the accuracy of which this organization does not guarantee. The inquirer has agreed to indemnify the reporting bureau for any damage arising from misuse of this information, and this report is furnished in reliance upon that indemnity. It must be held in strict confidence, and must not be revealed to the subject reported on.

REPORT ON (SURNAME):	MR., MRS., MISS:	GIVEN NAME:	SOCIAL SECURITY NUMBER:	SPOUSE'S NAME:
DOE	Mr.	Robert Thomas	123-44-5678	Betty Lynn

ADDRESS:	CITY:	STATE:	ZIP CODE:	SPOUSE'S SOCIAL SECURITY NO.:
921 Third Avenue,	Anytown	Anystate	77066	135-77-8910

COMPLETE TO HERE FOR TRADE REPORT AND SKIP TO CREDIT HISTORY

PRESENT EMPLOYER AND KIND OF BUSINESS:	POSITION HELD:	SINCE:	MONTHLY INCOME:
Anytown Morning Herald – Newspaper	Circulation Manager	1-66	$ 715

COMPLETE TO HERE FOR SHORT REPORT AND SUMMARY REPORT AND SKIP TO CREDIT HISTORY

DATE OF BIRTH: 5-15-32 — NUMBER OF DEPENDENTS INCLUDING SPOUSE → 2 — ☒ OWNS OR BUYING HOME ☐ RENTS HOME

FORMER ADDRESS:	CITY:	STATE:	FROM:	TO:
606 Grove Street	Thattown	Thatstate	12-62	1-66

FORMER EMPLOYER AND KIND OF BUSINESS:	POSITION HELD:	FROM:	TO:	MONTHLY INCOME:
City Publishing Co – Book Publisher	Manager – Bindery	12-62	1-66	$ 575

SPOUSE'S EMPLOYER AND KIND OF BUSINESS:	POSITION HELD:	SINCE:	MONTHLY INCOME:
Anytown Oil Company – Branch Office	Secretary	11-64	$ 350

CREDIT HISTORY (*Complete this section for all reports*)

KIND OF BUSINESS	DATE ACCOUNT OPENED	DATE OF LAST SALE	HIGHEST CREDIT	AMOUNT OWING	AMOUNT PAST DUE	TERMS OF SALE AND USUAL MANNER OF PAYMENT
O	---	11-65	--	53	53	0-9
D	1-66	9-69	181	23	00	0-1
C	9-68	6-69	68	00	00	0-1
S	2-69	2-69	48	00	00	0-2
C	3-66	9-67	200	60	00	I$5-1
A	10-67	10-68	2,200	00	00	I$72-2
H	11-68	8-69	260	156	00	R-1
J	9-68	9-69	85	85	00	0-0
B	3-66	Med 3 fig ckg				
B	8-66	Low 4 fig savs				
The following trade was reported 7-69						
O	--	3-69	--	56	56	0-5

PUBLIC RECORD AND/OR SUMMARY OF OTHER TRADE INFORMATION:

Trade from Thattown, Thatstate 1-66: 6 accts HC $97, 0-1
2 accts HC $1,800, I-1
P & L acct M 0-9, $34 3-66; pd 1-69

Public Record: Thattown District Court #12, Thatstate, Case No. 54857
XYZ Dept. Store vs Robert Thomas and Betty Lynn Doe,
$275.00, Judgment 3-12-66, satisfied 4-8-66

AFFILIATED WITH

Associated Credit Bureaus, Inc. *Credit Bureau Reports, Inc.*

Courtesy: Credit Bureau of San Mateo & Burlingame, California

Information about bank accounts, real estate, and ownership of securities is used to judge capital.

2. *Scoring techniques* Some large retailers employ a rapid, semi-automatic credit application evaluation procedure called *numerical* or *point scoring*. This technique, sometimes called statistical scoring, is based upon

a rather elaborate statistical analysis of large samples of the firm's customers with good and poor payment records. The aim of the analysis is to find those objective characteristics that distinguish one group from the other, and to assign a precise weight to each such attribute.

Such an analysis may show that the good-risk group includes higher percentages of people who are married, who own their own home, who own their own car, who have lived for three years at the same address, and so on. Moreover, it will indicate that being married adds a certain score, perhaps 10 points, and that owning an automobile adds another grade, perhaps 7 points, to the evaluation of a credit application. The various points are added to obtain a total score. Management can then set cut-off points that depend upon how anxious it is to add new credit accounts. Perhaps all applications scoring below 40 points will be rejected automatically and all above this figure accepted; or an intermediate zone may be established, for instance, 40 to 50 points calling for individual appraisal of the applicant. The basic statistical analysis has to be repeated periodically since the relative importance of the different characteristics seems to vary considerably from time to time.[26]

Establishing the credit limit The next step after approval is to set a limit on the amount of credit which will be granted. In fact, approval is commonly granted with a limit in mind. A fairly conservative rule is that the limit should be set at about twice the estimated weekly income of the customer. But other factors, such as general business conditions, the existing unemployment rate, and the individual's credit reputation have an important bearing on the limit.

The credit limit is not an absolute maximum that cannot be exceeded. Usually, it is set for control purposes: If a customer reaches his credit limit, the facts of the case are reviewed. Under revolving credit, the use of partial payments and service charges make it possible to be quite flexible regarding the credit limit.

Informing the customer The customer should be informed promptly of the credit department's decision. When it is unfavorable, every effort should be made to avoid antagonizing the customer. Letters are useful devices in this connection since they avoid involving the credit manager in an argument. Probably no specific reason should be given for the refusal, since this also provides a point for controversy, but a brief paragraph stress-

[26] William P. Boggess, "Screen Test Your Credit Risks," *Harvard Business Review*, Vol. 45, No. 6 (November–December 1967), pp. 113–22. Point scoring has also been discussed in the recent annual volumes of *Credit Management Yearbook* (New York: National Retail Merchants Association). Some credit analysts feel that point scoring is too rigid and arbitrary since it deals with average behavior and makes no allowance for the individual whose payment potential may be significantly better or worse than that of most people with the same set of objective attributes.

ing the advantages of trading at the store on a cash basis may help retain some goodwill.

If the store has decided to extend credit, a letter still seems the best medium for informing the customer. Not only does it save time for both customer and credit manager, but it enables the store to provide the customer with a written statement of the store's credit rules. For example, information concerning billing dates and when payments are expected may be included as well as a description of the system used by the store to identify customers.[27] The necessary coin, card, or "Charga-Plate" may also be enclosed in the envelope. Some stores inform the customer of his credit limit, although this is not the usual practice.

Opening an account at the store's initiative Although most credit accounts are opened at the request of the customer involved, retailers sometimes want to take the initiative in establishing accounts for potentially good-credit customers who have not requested credit privileges. This is done by sending letters to them stating that an account has been opened in their names. The J. C. Penney Company used this plan when it introduced its credit services in the late 1950s; many banks and oil companies have also used this approach.

The accounts that the store establishes on its own initiative can be profitable and create relatively little risk if sufficient information about the individuals involved can be obtained from outside sources—such as the files of the local credit bureau or through local banks. Many firms, however, formerly included credit cards and credit plates in the promotional letters sent to these invited customers, thus causing considerable resentment on the part of people who feared liability for lost or stolen cards that they had never requested and did not want. The Federal Trade Commission now prohibits the mailing of unsolicited credit cards.

□ Maintaining current credit information

Unfortunately for the retailer, a person's credit standing is subject to rapid change. Financial reverses, a death in the family, and sickness with its attending expenditures are only a few of the factors responsible for this change. As a result, retailers must keep their information on credit customers up to date. Maintenance of current information is seldom difficult in the small community or neighborhood store, where "everybody knows what everybody else is doing."

---

[27] Federal law requires a written statement of much of the information if credit or service charges are imposed. See pp. 549–50, below.

The large store finds this problem more serious, but periodic review of the store's own records will reveal which accounts are gradually deteriorating. "Revolving credit" and service charges may prove to be useful in dealing with such accounts. Some stores subscribe to rating books issued by local private credit bureaus to determine changes in ratings. Local newspapers also need to be scrutinized for information on day-to-day happenings such as accidents, divorces, deaths, and bankruptcies.

☐ Identifying credit customers

The installment customer will normally sign a contract for each purchase, and in the process will naturally identify himself. But open-account, revolving credit and option-terms customers require some means of identification that will permit them to make frequent purchases against their accounts.

Personal identification Identification presents no problem in the small store. Even in the medium-size store, many customers become known by name to the salespeople, while others may identify themselves by means of a driver's license or a similar device. But in the large store the identification problem is a real one.

Identification devices carried by the customer Most large retailers give their credit customers plastic cards or metal plates that show the customer's name, address, and account number. When the customer makes a credit purchase, she hands the card to the salesperson, thereby both establishing identity and providing much of the information needed in preparing the salescheck. Many stores use small hand-operated machines that will imprint the sales slip with the customer's name and address as recorded on the "Charga-Plate" or credit card. Stores in some cities have cooperated in establishing a group "Charga-Plate" plan under which only one plate need be carried for use in several stores.

The plan of having the customer carry some means of identification suffers two serious disadvantages. First, many customers do not carry the plate or card all the time, although the habit of carrying the identification device is growing steadily. Second, the device may be lost. This involves the store in the relatively minor expense of replacing it; but more importantly unless the store is promptly informed of the loss, the token may be found and used by an impostor.

Signature identification Another identification plan involves comparing the customer's signature with the signature obtained during the course of the credit interview. Under this plan, the clerk asks the customer to sign the sales slip which is then forwarded to the credit department for comparison. This method avoids the defects of the card or metal-plate method, although it involves a short wait on the customer's part—perhaps a minute or two—to establish identification.

□ Authorizing credit purchases

"Charge-take" transactions Credit customers often desire to take their purchases with them. The proprietor or manager of a small store will usually allow anyone who is recognized as a customer to do this without waiting for a formal check on his or her credit standing. In such cases, the steps of identification and authorization are combined.

Large stores that use "Charga-Plate" or credit card systems normally permit customers to take credit purchases involving less than $25 without waiting for specific approval from the credit department. Sales of larger amounts, however, must be authorized by this department. Two methods are commonly used for this purpose: (1) sending the sales slip to the credit department by means of some form of conveyor or tube system, or (2) calling the authorizer by telephone to get his approval.

The credit department usually provides its authorization within a very short period, ranging from about thirty seconds to, at the most, three minutes. Large stores employ several authorizers, each of whom handles the records of customers whose names fall in a certain part of the alphabet. The authorizer extends an immediate approval if the customer's record is clear. If the customer has exceeded her credit limit by a relatively large amount or if some other irregularity is evident, the authorizer may request that the customer be referred to the credit office; or the authorization may be granted and the irregularity taken up with the customer by letter. New mechanical and electronic systems which decrease the time required for authorization still further are now coming into greater use.

"Charge-send" transactions The need for speed in authorizing these sales is not so great, since authorization can be handled at any time before the goods leave the store. Yet, although authorization may not take place immediately upon sale of the goods, the majority of stores use the same system for authorizing charge-sends as for charge-takes.

□ Billing the customer

The final step in most credit sales is billing the customer for purchases made during the previous month.[28] For many years, all stores did this at the end of each calendar month, although those with a large number of ac-

[28] The billing and payment arrangements, either weekly or monthly, for installment contracts will be specified at the time the sale is made.

counts adhered to a "cutoff" date near the end of the month to facilitate the preparation of bills for mailing on the first of the following month.

Cycle billing Today, although most small stores probably still bill all of their customers on or near the first of the month, many large stores and some medium-size ones have adopted cycle billing. In this form of billing the names in the credit files are divided alphabetically and statements are sent to a different group on a fixed billing date within the month. Thus, customers in the alphabetical group "A-B" may be billed on the second of the month; those in group "C" on the fifth day; and so on throughout the month.

"Country club" billing One method of preparing monthly bills, still

FIGURE 22–3 **Recommended form for descriptive billing, showing information required by the Consumer Credit Protection Act**

Any Store U.S.A.

MAIN STREET—ANY CITY, U.S.A.

(Customer's name here)

AMT. PAID $

TO INSURE PROPER CREDIT RETURN THIS PORTION WITH YOUR PAYMENT

PREVIOUS BALANCE	FINANCE CHARGE 50 CENT MINIMUM	PAYMENTS	CREDITS	PURCHASES	NEW BALANCE	MINIMUM PAYMENT

FINANCE CHARGE IS COMPUTED BY A "PERIODIC RATE" OF % PER MONTH (OR A MINIMUM CHARGE OF 50 CENTS FOR BALANCES UNDER $) WHICH IS AN **ANNUAL PERCENTAGE RATE** OF % APPLIED TO THE PREVIOUS BALANCE WITHOUT DEDUCTING CURRENT PAYMENTS AND/OR CREDITS APPEARING ON THIS STATEMENT.

NOTICE

PLEASE SEE ACCOMPANYING STATEMENT(S) FOR IMPORTANT INFORMATION.

PAYMENTS, CREDITS OR CHARGES, RECEIVED AFTER THE DATE SHOWN ABOVE THE ARROW, WHICH IS THE CLOSING DATE OF THIS BILLING CYCLE, WILL APPEAR ON YOUR NEXT STATEMENT. TO AVOID ADDITIONAL FINANCE CHARGES PAY THE "NEW BALANCE" BEFORE THIS DATE NEXT MONTH.

ANY STORE, U.S.A. MAIN STREET, ANY CITY, U.S.A.

Source: Board of Governors, Federal Reserve System.

used by many small stores, involves recording each sale on the customer's ledger card or record when the sales slip is received by the accounting department, and then, at the end of the month, preparing a detailed, itemized statement to mail to the customer. Many larger stores have switched to a labor-saving method called "country club" billing. Instead of making ledger entries, the sales slips are simply filed in folders or dockets prepared for each customer. Microfilm copies of these slips are made for the store's records at the end of each billing period, and the original sales slips, plus a simple statement of the total outstanding, is mailed to the customer.

Descriptive billing An increasing number of large stores now use "descriptive billing," an even more efficient and economical method based upon utilization of electronic data-processing equipment. Sales slips are not sent to the customer; instead the store retains them for examination if a customer questions a particular charge. The monthly bill is a machine-produced statement (see Figure 22–3) that shows (1) previous balance, (2) a dollar figure for each purchase together with an indication of the department selling the item (if the customer wants to know the specific item covered by each figure she refers to her original copy of the sales slip), (3) total purchases and credits, (4) service charges, (5) amount due currently, and (6) the due date. This system of EDP billing results in significant labor savings and eliminates many human errors.

Sales promotion and the monthly statement Sales promotional material is often enclosed with the monthly statements. Inserts announce dates for special sales, colorful pamphlets promote specific items, gift certificates are suggested, and customers using revolving credit are informed as to the dollar amounts which can be added to their accounts without an increase in the monthly payments. These steps again emphasize the opportunities that credit accounts provide for sales promotion.

□ Automating the credit function

As the foregoing discussion indicates, many credit department activities involve highly repetitive procedures and involve the accumulation and use of vast amounts of standardized data. Alert credit managers, particularly in the larger organizations, are constantly seeking ways to speed service and to reduce costs through the use of computers and electronic data-transmission equipment. A shift from manual operation to EDP can be a major problem for the credit department of a large store, involving careful planning, the cooperation of many people, and the utmost detail in scheduling various activities. Often two complete credit systems, one manual and the other electronic, have to be maintained side-by-side until the "bugs" or difficulties are eliminated from the electronic system. Customers' accounts become confused and considerable customer irritation seems to be an inevitable element, along with substantial overtime work, in any conversion to credit EDP.[29]

In the long run, however, computer-based systems can provide faster service; improve the quality of floor authorization for credit sales; strengthen financial control; help in collection follow-up; and also provide useful sales information for soliciting credit accounts, reviewing inactive accounts, and analyzing departmental sales. In addition, they often permit substantial reductions in personnel expense through elimination of many manual operations. And the benefits of computerized credit operation need not be restricted to the large retailer. Smaller firms can have their data processed quickly and at a reasonable cost through the use of commercial computer service centers.

Automation in the future The longer-run implications of computers on present-day techniques of extending credit are suggested by the following quotation:

> Though speculation about developments in the future are sometimes unrealistic, it now appears certain that by 1980 very few American shoppers will be carrying bulky checkbooks in their purses or large amounts of cash in their wallets. The present proliferation of credit cards of all sizes, shapes, and colors will also be largely a thing of the past. Money will still serve as a unit of accounts, a standard of value, and a store of wealth. However, money as we know it today (in terms of cash and checks and a variety of credit card charge accounts) will take on a new appearance when used as a medium of exchange involving most consumer transactions. . . .
>
> Instead of paying for groceries at the supermarket check-out counter by cash (acquired by cashing a check at her bank or elsewhere), the housewife of the future will simply hand the store clerk a unique "funds identification card" which she alone can use. The clerk, before ringing up the amount of her purchase, will insert this identification card into an electronic apparatus which "reads" the card and establishes immediately and automatically an electronic communication to the customer's bank account. If sufficient funds are held in her account to cover this transaction, or if the customer has an established line of credit with her bank large enough to cover the transaction, an indicator on the card-reading apparatus will inform the clerk accordingly. The clerk will then activate the device, causing the amount of the purchase to be automatically deducted from the customer's account and added to the account of the supermarket. . . .[30]

The authors of the foregoing statement go on to point out that for "the emergence of a checkless society," no major technological breakthroughs are required; rather, "only a refining of present knowledge" is necessary.

---

[29] Robert M. Grinager, "What about Conversion," *Credit Management Yearbook, 1968–1969* (New York: National Retail Merchants Association, 1970), pp. 60–64.

[30] A. H. Anderson *et al.*, *An Electronic Cash and Credit System* (New York: American Management Association, 1966), p. 15.

They suggest further that these developments will increase the competitive ability of small retailers as compared with large-scale firms, and that retailers of all sizes will benefit as a result of a reduction in the cost of extending credit and through a reduction of their working capital requirements.

■ COLLECTION MANAGEMENT

Retailers who sell on credit[31] need to understand the collection function and the merits and limitations of various collection policies, as analyzed in the following pages.

□ The collection function

The collection function includes more than just obtaining cash from the negligent credit buyer. It begins with careful preparation of sales checks by the salesperson, since they are the first record of the amount due the store; proceeds through the maintenance of records of the customer's debits and credits; includes all activities associated with trying to collect actual cash from the customer—sending statements, letters, and making telephone calls; and does not end until cash has been received and a receipt given or until the account has been deemed uncollectible.

The collection function should maximize sales and minimize losses, while retaining the highest possible level of goodwill. Sound policies and procedures are required in order to achieve this objective.

The collection problem and credit policies The difficulties encountered in collecting overdue accounts are related directly to the store's credit policies. A store that gives credit to practically all applicants must expect to spend more money in trying to collect its accounts and also suffer more credit losses than the store that grants the credit privilege to a more carefully selected group. The collection problem of a given store is also influenced to some degree by the credit policies of other stores. A store that tries to be substantially stricter than other stores will simply drive its customers to competitors. This inability to escape the consequences of competitors' policies has fostered attempts to develop uniform community credit programs. These programs are usually channeled through the local credit bureaus.

Advantages of early collections The advantages of prompt follow-up on past-due accounts are readily apparent. Such action saves interest charges

[31] Strictly speaking, collection management is a part of credit management, as evidenced by the fact that the credit department manager normally supervises the store's collection manager. The collection function is of sufficient importance, however, to warrant discussion as a separate section of this chapter.

on funds tied up in accounts, reduces payroll expenses for employees making out collection notices, and lowers the cost of stationery and postage. The longer an account is outstanding, the harder it becomes to collect. Some people become more and more reluctant to pay as time elapses from the receipt of the merchandise and their initial enjoyment of it increasingly diminishes. Early collections also lead to increased sales. Many customers hesitate to go near a store when their accounts are overdue; but, once the account is paid, they again become regular customers.

Granting the desirability of early collections, the retailer should handle collections with tact. In some cases, this means putting pressure on the debtor as soon as his account becomes overdue. But, in the majority of instances, accounts can be collected with less loss of customer goodwill if the store reserves its pressure until it has tried a few gentle reminders of the overdue account. Apparently, most credit customers mean to pay their obligations; but many of them sometimes find that some delay is necessary. Collection procedures should aim to reduce this delay as much as possible while retaining the customer's patronage.

Similarly, installment sellers will normally make every effort to help the customer complete his payments, even after default on a contract, rather than reclaim the goods. Merchants feel that they are better off to increase the length of the payment period, either by decreasing the size of each payment or by skipping a payment and adding it on at the end, rather than to take back the article. To minimize the number of defaulters, however, a charge is usually made when any such extension of payment is arranged.

□ Collection policies

Retailers differ as to the collection policies they follow. Unfortunately, many small retailers follow no carefully worked-out collection program; and this deficiency is responsible in no small measure for their low collection ratios.[32] Yet some small retailers have worked out effective collection programs. In general, collection policies may be classified either as uniform (that is, applying uniformly to all customers) or as nonuniform (that is, treating customers differently according to their past records and the facts of the present situation).

Uniform collection policy Although it is difficult to generalize about the uniform collection policies of various retailers, the usual steps seem to be as follows: On or soon after the first of the month—or, if cycle billing is used, on a specified date during the month—each open-account debtor is

[32] A collection ratio expresses the amount collected during a month as a percentage of the uncollected amount at the end of the previous month.

usually sent a statement of his account at the store, together with a request for payment within ten days. On installment contracts the buyer has already been informed of the various payment dates and the exact sum due, so that a reminder is rarely used.

1. *Past-due statements* If payment is not made and if the debtor makes no move to explain his situation to the collection manager, a second[33] statement (usually not itemized) is sent out. If the retailer follows a policy of placing an interest charge on past-due accounts, this action may be evidenced on the second statement—which is usually accompanied by an appropriate

FIGURE 22–4 Effective inserts for use with statements on past-due accounts These forms are used interchangeably.

Penneys NOTICE OF PAYMENT DUE

ACCOUNT NUMBER

DATE

AMOUNT DUE

Penneys

PERHAPS ITS HAPPENED AGAIN...

NOW AND THEN WE SEND CUSTOMERS A REMINDER ABOUT THEIR OVER-DUE ACCOUNT . . . ONLY TO RECEIVE A CHECK IN THE VERY NEXT MAIL. SO IF YOUR PAYMENT IS ON ITS WAY, PLEASE DISREGARD THIS FRIENDLY NOTICE. OTHERWISE, WON'T YOU SEND IT TO US . . . BEFORE IT SLIPS YOUR MIND.

J. C. PENNEY COMPANY, INC.

Penneys

CUSTOMERS SAY THEY APPRECIATE...

BEING INFORMED WHEN THEIR ACCOUNTS BECOME PAST DUE, SO WE HOPE YOU WILL ACCEPT THIS FRIENDLY REMINDER IN THE SAME SPIRIT. IF YOU HAVE JUST SENT US YOUR CHECK, PLEASE DISREGARD THIS NOTICE AND ACCEPT OUR THANKS.

J. C. PENNEY COMPANY, INC.

Penneys

DID YOU FORGET US?

WE KNOW HOW BUSY ONE CAN GET THESE DAYS AND WE FEEL PERHAPS THAT'S WHY YOU MAY HAVE FORGOTTEN THAT YOUR ACCOUNT IS NOW OVERDUE. IF YOUR PAYMENT IS ALREADY ON THE WAY, PLEASE ACCEPT OUR THANKS.

J. C. PENNEY COMPANY, INC.

Courtesy: J. C. Penney Company

insert as illustrated in Figure 22–4. The time that elapses between the sending of the first statement and subsequent follow-ups will vary from retailer to retailer and from field to field; it also depends upon whether the account is open-account or installment credit. In general, retailers selling goods consumed rapidly (for example, food) will mail reminders within a week after

[33] First, if an installment account.

the account is past due; whereas department stores and furniture stores may wait from 30 to 60 days unless, of course, revolving credit is used. On installment contracts the notice will go out within 10 or 30 days following the due date.

2. *Letters and telephone calls* When a customer fails to respond to the reminders enclosed with his statements, the retailer may send a letter that, although mild in tone, requests prompt action by the customer. As an illustration, the text of the letter used by the J. C. Penney Company for accounts overdue from 60 to 90 days is as follows:

To retain your good will . . .
is always of first consideration. That's why we have to be so patient . . . even though you haven't replied to any of our reminders that your account is long over due. Naturally, when customers don't get in touch with us, we can only assume that they are no longer interested in this convenient way to shop. And, obviously, that means it might be necessary to restrict future purchases. Of course, you don't want this to happen . . . and neither do we. So won't you please mail us a check at once . . . or get in touch with us within the next five days?

Sincerely,
Collection Department

AD:GW
Amount Due $________
Account No. ________

If there is still no response, most credit men feel that the time has arrived to use pressure. Of course, the installment seller can sometimes repossess; but the open-account seller must use other tactics. More demanding letters may be sent. They may point out that the customer will lose her credit rating if she does not pay. She may be told that the past-due account will be reported to the local credit bureau, where the information will become common knowledge of all the local credit managers. Legal proceedings may be threatened. Sometimes a telephone call to the debtor will bring a response when a letter fails, or the store may have a letter written by its attorney.

3. *Collectors* If the store has been reasonably careful in extending credit, the preceding steps will collect most of the accounts. For those that are still outstanding, the personal collector is the next step. Depending upon the size of the store, the collector may be employed on a part-time or a full-time basis. Some stores use salesmen for collecting during periods when they are not needed in the store; or in the small store, the proprietor may make the necessary calls. Another plan is for several noncompeting stores to cooperate—usually through the local credit bureau—and employ a full-time collector. If personal collection fails, legal action is about all that re-

mains, unless the store desires to turn the account over to a collection agency.[34]

4. *Legal action and garnishment* Legal action may be too expensive if only a small account is involved, so the account may be closed out as a bad debt. In other cases the merchant may find it advisable to sue. He sometimes may obtain a garnishment order that may be served on the defaulting debtor's employer. This court-issued order requires the employer to pay a portion of the employee's wages directly to the seller to satisfy his debt.[35] The federal "Truth-in-Lending" law,[36] limits the portion of an employee's wage that may be subject to garnishment.

Nonuniform collection policy Some retailers believe that the collection program should be varied in accordance with the delinquent customer's past payment record and present situation. They hesitate to put the store's collection machinery into immediate operation if a customer who has a long record of prompt payments should fall behind in meeting one bill. Some special situation or circumstance probably explains the delay, and they do not want to send overly hasty collection letters that might offend a good patron.

Some other customers may withhold payment because they feel they have a valid, unsettled grievance or claim against the store. And still others may be classified as "slow pay, but sure," in that they are frequently tardy in making payments but always eventually settle their bills in full.

Many other factors may also cause delayed payments. Consequently the store faces many different types of collection problems. Although the large store cannot treat each account individually, it can classify accounts and submit comparable accounts to similar collection methods.

This does not imply that the store should be lax in its collections.[37] Rather, it means recognizing that differences do exist and that successful collections and the holding and building of customer goodwill demand that

---

[34] Many credit bureaus also act as collection agents. Apparently, fees for this service equal 15–25 percent of the amount collected. An increasing number of stores are able to employ lawyers to perform this service at fees of 10–15 percent of the sums collected.

[35] A wage assignment is a similar arrangement negotiated directly with the buyer at the time of making the installment sale and attached to or embodied in the installment contract for purposes of providing additional security. A number of states forbid, and others strictly limit the use of, wage assignment contracts.

[36] Cf. pp. 549–50, below.

[37] "I have found it almost impossible to ruin the business by making people pay their bills. Once in a while I stir up a hornet's nest, of course, and wonder whether the gain was worthwhile. But usually the man who is forced to pay me the bill he owes gets over it. In the long run the results are either that I get rid of a bad customer for good, or he gets over it and forgets." R. E. Gould, *Yankee Storekeeper* (New York: McGraw-Hill Book Co., Inc., 1946), p. 91.

these differences be recognized. But once customers have been grouped according to their similarities, the store should have a definite collection routine which operates quite automatically. Persistence and promptness are two great virtues in a sound collection policy.

□ Credit counseling services

Many major retailers, banks, finance companies, and chambers of commerce have joined together to set up credit counseling service bureaus, designed to improve consumers' ability to handle credit problems and to help reduce the large number of personal bankruptcies. About 110 such bureaus are already in existence in the United States and Canada, most of them on a nonprofit basis, and others are in the planning stage.

The counseling bureaus do not lend money, are not collection agencies, and do not sell anything. Their major function is to provide professional guidance and budgeting advice to families who have overextended their use of credit or are having trouble managing their debts. The bureaus also help set up prorating plans, under which the debtor pays off the same percentage of his outstanding debts to all creditors in cases where acute difficulties make this the most satisfactory solution to all concerned. Some bureaus also maintain educational programs dealing with the economics of credit and try to distribute sound credit advice as widely as possible.

Since both credit-grantor and credit-user have a mutual long-run interest in the maintenance of sound credit relationships, counseling bureaus fulfill a real need in our "credit economy." They are helping reduce the number of consumer bankruptcies and at the same time affording protection to creditors. Their services are either free or offered at a very nominal charge. They should not be confused with the commercial profitmaking debt-adjustment organizations that operate in some parts of the country.

■ GOVERNMENT REGULATION OF CONSUMER CREDIT

State laws As we have noted, state laws affect many phases of credit operations. Installment sales of practically all types of merchandise are subject to special laws in approximately 34 states and 13 additional states regulate installment sales of automobiles. These laws cannot be easily summarized here, since they vary widely and some are likely to be changed in the near future. However, most state laws affecting installment purchases require written contracts; many specify the information that must appear on the contract (cash price, down payment, credit charges and fees, *etc.*) and the form in which it appears; some establish maximum rates for finance charges; and a few (Connecticut, Florida, Hawaii, New Hampshire, Rhode Island, and Vermont) give the buyer the right, subject to some exceptions, to cancel the contract within two or three days after signing. Other provisions often control the creditor's remedies in case of default.[38]

All of the states have "bad check" laws and also establish bankruptcy procedures. Many of them regulate other phases of collection work. Debt adjustment and prorating services are subject to special laws in numerous others. Moreover, legislation has been enacted quite widely that parallels, supplements, or replaces the federal "Truth in Lending" law discussed later in this section.

Uniform Consumer Credit Code Since credit sellers who operate in more than one state often have difficulty in adjusting to the state-by-state differences in credit legislation, the National Conference of Commissioners on Uniform State Legislation (a semi-official body whose members are appointed by the state governors) has proposed a standard law for adoption in all 50 states.[39] This proposed Uniform Consumer Credit Code, or "U3C" as it is often termed, establishes uniform limits on finance charges, provides that installment contracts can be cancelled within three days after signing, and recommends the regulation of many other aspects of credit. It has encountered considerable criticism, however, and so far has been adopted in only a few states. Despite these attacks it seems likely that many of its provisions will become law in additional states in the reasonably near future.

□ The "Truth-in-Lending" law

Practically all retail credit sales that involve a finance charge, service charge, time-price differential or similar charges, are now subject to the federal Consumer Credit Protection Act of 1968, often called the "Truth-in-Lending" law; and also to Regulation Z of the Board of Governors of the Federal Reserve System issued under the provisions of the 1968 Act.[40]

Under this legislation, when a new credit account is opened, the seller must provide the customer with a written statement that shows, among other things, exactly how much payment time he is allowed before the

---

[38] Ernest A. Rovelstad, ed., *Credit Manual of Commercial Laws, 1971* (New York: National Association of Credit Management, 1970), pp. 160–72.

[39] For an excellent summary of this law, see Robert W. Johnson, "Uniform Code for Consumer Credit," *Harvard Business Review*, Vol. 46, No. 4 (July–August 1968), pp. 119–25.

[40] Public Law 90–321; 82 Stat. 146; *Code of Federal Regulations*, Title 12, Chapter II, Part 226. The Federal Reserve Board may exempt credit transactions from Regulation Z in any state where the Board finds that state laws impose substantially similar requirements and are effectively enforced.

finance charge is imposed; to what balances (end of the month or beginning of the month) the finance charge will be applied; exactly how the charge will be calculated; the minimum payment that must be made on each statement submitted; and any additional charges or penalties that may be imposed in connection with the account. The customer's statements must also show similar information, including the specific amounts involved. Purchases made on the installment basis are subject to some additional disclosure requirements.

The most controversial element of the law is its requirement that the equivalent annual percentage rate must be shown for all finance charges.[41] To illustrate: If the store's service charge is 1.5 percent per month on the unpaid balance, the customer's notice and bills must indicate that this charge represents an annual percentage rate of 18 percent. Many firms that use "option-terms" plans consider this requirement unfair because (a) they are not allowed to reduce the annual rate figure shown to reflect the 25 or 30 days of free credit before the service charge goes into effect, and (b) customers who settle their bills in less than a year don't actually pay such a rate. Advocates of the law claim, however, that consumers require a uniform system of describing credit charges (the annual rate method) to facilitate comparison of the costs of using different sources of credit.

Credit card controls The Federal Reserve Board has also issued several regulations, under the Truth-in-Lending Law, governing the distribution and use of credit cards. Credit grantors are now prohibited from sending unsolicited cards to lists of prospective customers, a method many companies formerly used in hopes of obtaining new credit patrons. The cardholder's liability, in case of a lost or stolen card, is now limited to $50 and even that limited liability is waived if the card-issuer has not provided him with a special, postpaid form on which to report the loss or theft.[42] Both federal and state laws provide very severe penalties for fraudulent or unauthorized use of a credit card.

□ The "Fair Credit Reporting" act

This federal law,[43] which became effective on April 25, 1971, controls credit bureau practices in compiling and distributing consumer credit ratings. The law gives the consumer an opportunity to examine his file in the bureau's records, if he so desires, and to rebut any erroneous adverse informa-

---

[41] Computation of the "equivalent annual percentage rate" becomes somewhat complicated in the case of installment contracts; consequently many retailers use rate tables that have been prepared by the Federal Reserve Board and other organizations.

[42] *Federal Register,* Vol. 36, No. 15 (January 22, 1971) pp. 1040–42.

[43] Public Law 91–508, October 26, 1970.

tion contained therein. Any merchant who rejects a credit application because of an adverse report from a credit rating bureau must notify the applicant of the name and address of the bureau that supplied the report. (But the merchant does not have to reveal the specific reason for rejecting the account.) The consumer may inspect his file at the credit bureau, may insist upon reinvestigation of any statements that he claims are inaccurate, and if not satisfied with the reinvestigation, may prepare a brief rebuttal statement to be included in the file. Except in specified circumstances, the bureau may not use any adverse or derogatory information that is more than seven years old, and most adverse information that is more than three months old must be re-verified before being used. The consumer must be notified in writing before interviews are conducted with friends, neighbors, or associates to collect information about his character, reputation, or mode of living, and he must also be notified if certain types of derogatory credit reports are likely to affect his chances of securing a job for which he has applied.[44]

Other legislation regulating credit is likely to be enacted in the near future. Several states and the federal congress have been considering legislation, for example, concerning the installment customer's rights and obligations if a dispute arises concerning the value or quality of the merchandise involved in the transaction. This increase in credit-related legislation testifies to the constantly growing importance of credit in our economy.

■ JUDGING THE EFFICIENCY OF THE CREDIT DEPARTMENT

All retailers, large or small, are vitally interested in the effectiveness with which their credit and collection activities are being performed. A variety of yardsticks are available for judging this effectiveness, including the following: (1) the number of new accounts opened in a given period; (2) the number of credit applications refused; (3) the number of delinquent accounts—usually obtained through a process of "aging" accounts; (4) the overall service rendered, as reflected in the number of complaints received and the time required for authorizing purchases on credit; (5) the percentage of delinquent accounts collected; (6) the writing off of uncollectible balances, *i.e.*, losses from bad debts; (7) the cost of credit department operations; and (8) the department's knowledge of, and full compliance with, the relevant laws and government regulations. In no other part of his business is it more necessary for the retailer to keep in touch with develop-

---

[44] "Retailers, Credit and the Law," *Retailing Today*, February 1971, supplement. Also cf. "New Credit Law Goes into Effect," *The New York Times*, April 25, 1971, p. 65.

ments than in the credit department; and for the large retailer a well-trained and able credit manager or executive is a "must."

REVIEW AND DISCUSSION QUESTIONS

1 Summarize the main points you would cover in explaining to a fellow student the importance of credit sales to retailers.
2 Explain how you would proceed in finding an answer to the question, "How much is a credit customer worth?"
3 "Credit selling inevitably raises the retailer's cost ratio and his prices." Evaluate this statement.
4 Point out the essential differences between open-account and installment credit. Precisely what is meant by "revolving credit"?
5 Discuss recent developments concerning credit cards sponsored by banks, independent organizations, and the general credit card companies.
6 What are the favorable and unfavorable factors of the following credit applications? Would you accept or reject them?
   a) An application is made by Mrs. A, age 50, in the name of her husband. Mr. A, age 55, has been selling encyclopedias, soliciting from door to door for the past 15 months. There is no bank account except a small inactive savings account. In 1969, Mr. A bought furniture for $150, paying promptly in 18 monthly installments. He has had no charge accounts since. An account is desired so that a coat costing $29.50 may be charged.
   b) An application is made by Mr. B, age 30. He has been unemployed for five years. He has no bank account. His wife receives $300 per month from her brother. Mr. B wants to charge a man's wrist watch, valued at $50.
7 Visit a retail credit bureau in your community or in a nearby city and prepare a description of its organization and functions.
8 Explain briefly the methods retailers use (*a*) to identify credit customers and (*b*) to authorize purchases on credit.
9 Review the major credit laws of your state with particular emphasis on developments during the last five years.
10 Discuss briefly the major changes now taking place in retail credit and collection practices and procedures. In your discussion point out the factors responsible for these changes and indicate if you expect them to continue.

PART VII

Accounting controls

chapter chapter 23 chapter chapter

SOME FUNDAMENTALS OF ACCOUNTING CONTROL

In previous chapters, attention has been given to important activities and problems with which the management of modern retail stores must deal. Unless these activities are coordinated properly and the problems encountered are solved, satisfactory profits cannot be realized.[1] But it is impossible to determine the results of operations without complete, accurate records of merchandise transactions, including purchases and sales, and of the expenses associated with the performance of these and related activities.

In this chapter, therefore, attention is devoted to the need for and purposes of financial records, to some of the basic types of these records required for appraising results—including comparisons with similar stores, and to the determination of profits or losses under the cost and the retail inventory methods of accounting. Brief mention is also made of other accounting concepts. More precisely, the aim of this chapter is to develop certain fundamental principles of retail accounting without attempting to discuss the variety of equipment used in performing accounting activities. It should be emphasized, however, that the newer electronic equipment is employed in this area just as it is for other purposes.[2]

---

[1] Cf. Chapter 26, "Coordination and Retailing Management."

[2] Cf., for example, B. L. Carter, *Data Processing for the Small Business* (New York: Macfadden-Bartell Corp., 1966).

WHY ACCOUNTING RECORDS ARE NECESSARY

Some small merchants believe they know enough about their businesses through day-to-day contacts to make the keeping of formal books unnecessary. These retailers proceed on the assumption that, if there is any money left over after bills are paid, they have made a profit. Unfortunately, however, court records are filled with cases of bankrupt retailers who "thought" they were making a profit until it was too late.[3] A retailer's accounting system should provide the facts required to judge the effectiveness of his various financial activities and to make logical decisions about future courses of action. These facts, to be most useful, must be made available promptly to permit corrective action without delay.[4]

Accounting records continue to increase in importance because of frequent revisions in federal and state income taxes and changes in the social security laws. Regulations affecting the valuation of inventories and the extensive use of sales taxes have further emphasized the need for complete and accurate records.

Although records are essential to successful operation, it should be noted that a retailer can have too many of them. In fact, some retailers maintain such elaborate systems of records that they neglect their major function —buying and selling merchandise. In other words, they become keepers of records rather than merchants.

Accounting knowledge required of retailer

It is unnecessary, under normal circumstances, for the proprietor of the one-man store to have any extensive knowledge of accounting methods, but it is essential for him to know enough about them to maintain a satisfactory system and interpret properly the information it provides.[5] Large retailers require competent staffs to handle their accounting problems, but, like the small retailer, they should be able to appraise their results intelligently. Otherwise, sound management is impossible.

---

[3] In 1970 there were 4,650 retail failures compared with 4,070 in 1969. Cf. Rowena Wyant, "Business Failures," *Dun's*, February 1971, p. 91.

[4] ". . . Lacking timely records, the businessman is all too often unable to see the direction in which his business is moving, the trouble spots that may be developing, and area of serious weakness that possibly already exist." Carter, *op. cit.*, p. 131.

[5] Organizations have been formed to assist small merchants in handling their accounting problems. The Accounting Corporation of America, for example, has developed extensive services along this line. Its bookkeeping-by-mail service, known as "Mail-Me-Monday," is used by many small firms.

□ Purposes of accounting records

Accounting records serve six main purposes as follows:

To determine financial results of past operations Without adequate records, it is impossible to determine the precise financial results of past operations or to ascertain if the business is reaching what should be its constant goal—maximizing its profit potential. But keeping records does not insure the making of a profit; the records merely indicate the results of the operations—whether the risks inherent in the business have been recognized and met successfully. As was stated so well some years ago:

> Profit and loss are inevitably associated with risk and uncertainty; there is no sure or guaranteed profit. Economists and statisticians may not always agree on theoretical definitions of profit, and their definitions may differ from the ordinary business usage. Among accountants and businessmen, however, there will be general agreement on the ordinary meaning of "net business profit" as a residual amount after the payment of all costs and expenses and after all taxes, and they will not be disturbed by the fact that such a figure from the point of view of the economist consists of a mixture of pure profit, interest, possibly some rent, and, on occasion, some wages of management. But whatever its theoretical content, profit essentially constitutes a reward for the successful management of business risks [6]

Profits, of course, result from the maintenance of a satisfactory relationship among sales, the cost of the goods sold, and total operating expenses. Otherwise, losses occur. As we shall see, these three elements are important parts of the operating statement. But balance sheet accounts such as cash, accounts receivable, merchandise inventory, and accounts payable are likewise significant. All of these are involved in the numerous risks which must be successfully undertaken by the retailer if profits are to be realized.

To provide information for appraising current results and making future plans Suitable accounting records also make possible the analysis of these past results and comparisons with previous periods. Studies of this nature, when supplemented with day-to-day information, provide data helpful in evaluating results of current operations and in making future plans.

To furnish information upon which credit lines may be established From time to time, most retailers must borrow money from banks to finance their operations. Before making loans, bankers require complete and up-to-date financial statements from applicants. Without records that supply this needed information in proper form, chances of favorable action upon the application are considerably reduced. Vendors, likewise, require ample

---

[6] M. P. McNair, E. A. Burnham, and A. C. Hersum, *Cases in Retail Management* (New York: McGraw-Hill Book Co., Inc., 1957), p. 37.

evidence of financial soundness before credit will be granted. Proper accounting records are evidence of good management, and merchandise resources are favorably inclined toward merchants who submit current and accurate statements. Likewise, a prospective purchaser of a retail business reviews accounting records in appraising the worth of the firm.[7]

To safeguard company assets Proper accounting records are invaluable in protecting the retailer's assets. Through summarized statements and reports at frequent intervals, attention is centered on these assets; any changes are noted and investigated; and everything of value—tangible and intangible—is safeguarded.

To meet governmental regulations Today, more than ever before, retailers must make detailed reports to various local, state, and federal governmental agencies. These include, among others: reports on taxable income; old-age pensions and unemployment insurance; withholdings of federal and state income taxes; and sales or retailers' occupational taxes collected. They must be filed promptly to avoid penalties.

To facilitate comparisons with standard figures Providing information that may be used for comparing results against a standard and/or to exchange comparable information with other stores is another function of accounting records.[8] To make possible comparisons against standard figures published by government agencies, university bureaus of business research, and retail trade associations, it is not necessary that records be maintained in the same forms used by these organizations, but it is essential that the retailer make proper adjustments in his figures to make them comparable with the standard figures. Similar precautions should be taken when operating and merchandising results are exchanged with other stores.

THE COST METHOD OF DETERMINING PROFITS AND LOSSES

To achieve the foregoing purposes of accounting records, the large majority of retail stores, including practically all small ones, use what is

[7] The significance of this statement can be illustrated by one instance. After Montgomery Ward & Company purchased a group of Chicago stores for $9 million, it discovered it had also assumed an unexpected liability of $3 million because of the group's unfunded pension plan. Cf. T. A. Wise, "Those Uncertain Actuaries," *Fortune*, Vol. 73, No. 1 (January 1966), p. 184.

[8] Note, however, the statement of a member of a leading accounting firm: "I've been in public accounting for 35 years, and I've never seen one company that's completely comparable with another as far as motivations, products, or results as percentages of totals [are concerned]," Cf. Kurt Kron, "Accountants Crack down on Financial Statements," *Women's Wear Daily*, May 14, 1969, p. 42.

known as the cost method.[9] In practice, this method requires that the retailer record the cost of all items entering the store, usually marking the unit cost in code and the retail price upon each item, and taking physical inventory on a cost basis with adjustments to make it conform to the axiom "cost or market, whichever is lower."[10]

Two important accounting statements, the operating statement and the balance sheet, are vital instruments in connection with determining the profits and the financial responsibility of the retailer. Since most readers, perhaps, will have had a basic course in accounting, it is unnecessary to treat each of these statements in detail here.[11] Emphasis on a few of the major factors involved in each, however, together with illustrations, may prove helpful to the reader.

□ The operating statement

Stated concisely, an operating statement (also known as an income statement and a profit and loss statement) is a summary of the results of operations carried on during a specific period of time, such as a month, six months, or a year. It shows the relationship that has prevailed for the period among sales, cost of goods sold, and expenses, and indicates the amount of the resulting profit or loss. As suggested by the highly simplified operating statement of Table 23–1, this relationship is as follows: net sales minus cost of goods equals gross margin; gross margin minus operating expenses equals net profit before income taxes.

Net sales A close look at each element in the operating statement of Table 23–1, shows that the term "net sales" is used. This phraseology implies that there may be a "gross sales" figure, and this is true. To illustrate: When a customer buys a $75 coat, a sale of $75 is recorded. If the coat is returned for full credit, the store's net sales will be $75 less than its gross sales. But, if the customer discovers the coat has a bad spot before he purchases it and receives a reduction in the sales price of $15, gross and net sales would both be $60. Stated simply, gross sales are the total of all the prices initially charged the customers on goods sold, whether sales are for cash or on some

[9] As used here, the term "cost method" refers to the use of the periodic inventory procedure described in Chapter 13, pp. 310–11.

[10] For a more precise statement of this rule cf. the discussion of inventory valuation, p. 560, below. Also cf. R. S. Lindbeck, "Conventional Retail—Lower than Cost or Market," *Accounting Review*, April, 1966, pp. 335–38; and M. A. Hartman, "A Simplified Solution to Cost or Market Problems," *ibid.*, January 1966, pp. 127–29.

[11] Others not possessed with such knowledge should consult any of the standard textbooks on accounting principles or the section on "Basic Financial Statements" in *The Values of Total System Reports for Retailers*, pp. 4–10, and its companion *Reference Supplement*, pp. 2–5. (Dayton, Ohio: National Cash Register Co., n.d.).

TABLE 23–1

Operating statement, January 1–June 30, 1971 (cost method)

	Dollars	Ratio to sales
Net sales	$100,000	100.0
Cost of goods sold	65,000	65.0
Gross margin	$ 35,000	35.0
Operating expenses	30,000	30.0
Net profit before income taxes	$ 5,000	5.0

form of credit. Net sales equals the gross sales figure minus any returns from and adjustments to customers. The net sales figure of Table 23–1, therefore, was obtained as follows: Gross sales ($110,000) minus returns and allowances (which in this case, happened to be $10,000) equals net sales ($100,000).

Cost of goods sold The $65,000 cost of goods sold figure in Table 23–1 represents what the retailer paid for the merchandise sold during the period covered by the operating statement.[12] When he inventoried his stock at the *close* of business on December 31, 1970, he discovered his cost for the merchandise on hand totaled $22,500.[13] During the period January 1–June 30, 1971, his purchases of merchandise totaled $66,000. On these purchases his cash and quantity discounts came to $6,000 and he paid $950 to have the goods delivered to his store. His net cost of purchases, therefore, was $60,950 ($66,000 − $6,000 + $950). When he inventoried the stock remaining in his store on June 30, 1971, he found it had a cost value of $18,450. From these figures the cost of merchandise ($65,000) shown in Table 23–1 was obtained, as follows:

Opening inventory at cost, January 1, 1971	$22,500
Purchases at cost (less discounts)	60,000
Freight and express	950
Total cost of goods handled	$83,450
Closing inventory at cost, June 30, 1971	18,450
Cost of goods sold	$65,000

Earlier in this chapter the need to adjust the closing and opening inventory figures so that they represent actual cost value at the time they are taken was mentioned. (See p. 559.) Some items may have become soiled or

[12] Such action is necessary to establish correct operating results.

[13] Cf. the discussion in the next paragraph on the method of obtaining this inventory figure.

deteriorated or fashion changes may have lowered the value of other goods in stock. Whatever the reason, whenever the typical retailer takes a physical inventory he discovers some merchandise of less value than he paid for it. Therefore, he does *not* value his stock at the total of all his cost figures, but adjusts these figures so they reflect the current situation. In brief, he applies the rule: Stock should be valued at actual cost or current replacement cost (within certain limits) whichever is lower—a rule which is usually shortened to "cost or market, whichever is lower." In the illustration given, this rule was applied to both the opening and closing inventory figures.

Operating expenses Chapter 24 deals at some length with the elements included in the "operating expenses" item of Table 23–1. At this point it is sufficient to note that "operating expenses" includes all the costs of running the store, such as payroll, rent, advertising, insurance, supplies, and taxes (other than income taxes). When all these expenses are deducted from the dollar gross margin, the balance represents net profit before income taxes.

□ Preliminary evaluation of the cost method for computing profits and losses

Although the merits and limitations of the cost method will be more evident following the discussion of the retail inventory method later in this chapter, a few words should be added here. Relative simplicity of records and ease of understanding are evident in the cost method. Since profits cannot be computed without a physical inventory,[14] however, and since most retailers find it too time-consuming to "cost their stock" more than once or twice a year, the cost method does not provide a profit figure as often as may be desired by many retailers. Moreover, it does not provide data on stock shortages. Despite these limitations, the great majority of retailers find the cost method suited to their needs and continue to rely upon it.

□ The balance sheet

Learning the outcome of his operations for a given period through the operating statement is but the first major step for the retailer. He should also determine his financial position from data supplied by the balance sheet.[15]

---

[14] This statement is not valid for retailers who can maintain a perpetual inventory figure. Cf. pp. 309–10, above.

[15] Whereas "the income statement can be thought of as a 'moving picture' of [the] business *over a specific period of time* . . . the balance sheet may be thought of as a 'snapshot' of [the] business *at a given moment of time.*" *The Values of Total System Reports for Retailers, op. cit.*, p. 4.

The capital he has invested in the business and the distribution of this investment among such items as cash resources, accounts receivable, merchandise inventories, and fixtures and equipment are known as assets. His indebtedness—the nature and amount of claims against his assets—are his liabilities. Net worth—the amount by which his total assets exceed his total liabilities—is especially important, as are the changes in the nature and amount of the assets and liabilities during the period. The simplified balance sheet of Table 23–2 shows some of these elements.

TABLE 23–2

Balance sheet, December 31, 1970 and June 30, 1971

	June 30, 1971	December 31, 1970
Assets		
Cash	$12,000	$10,000
Customers' accounts receivable (less reserve for bad debts)	8,000	8,000
Inventory (at actual or current cost, whichever is lower)	42,000	38,500
Fixtures and equipment (after depreciation)	15,000	15,600
	$77,000	$72,100
Liabilities and Net Worth		
Accounts payable	$28,000	$27,000
Loan from bank	7,000	6,000
Owner's net worth	42,000	39,100
	$77,000	$72,100

Here again, because of many readers' knowledge of accounting, it is unnecessary to explain further each of the elements in Table 23–2 or to discuss the desired relationships among them.[16]

◻ The cost method and large retailers

The discussion in the preceding paragraphs has been deliberately oversimplified to emphasize the point of view of the small retailer. Larger retailers operating under the cost method must maintain more detailed records. To illustrate: Their records are usually designed to provide operating statement data of the type described for each department or classification and

---

[16] For studies of balance sheet ratios for retailers of various types cf. "Ratios of Retailing," which appears each year in the September issue of *Dun's*.

gross margin figures are estimated monthly. Since physical inventories are not taken at such frequent intervals, book inventory figures are determined from the estimated gross margin. This procedure becomes more difficult as the number of departments or classifications within a store increases.

To secure current information not available under the cost method and to obtain closer approximations to the gross margin realized without the necessity of taking a physical inventory, almost all large stores and many medium-size ones use the retail inventory method of accounting which we now examine.

THE RETAIL INVENTORY METHOD

The retail inventory method of accounting derives its name from the fact that its procedures rely heavily on records at retail prices rather than on cost. The concept is not new but its widespread adoption came following its qualified approval by the Bureau of Internal Revenue in 1920.

Basic principles of the retail inventory method

Costing the retail inventory The essential ingredient of the retail inventory method is that it provides a procedure for reasonably estimating at any desired time the cost value of a closing inventory that is stated at retail value. For example, if the closing value of the inventory at retail prices is $10,000, it is possible through the retail inventory method to ascertain a cost figure for the goods on hand. Moreover, the cost value of the closing inventory can be computed regardless of whether the inventory figure is obtained by taking a physical inventory at retail prices, or by using the book record of the retail inventory. Actually, one of the major advantages of the retail inventory method is that it can be used with the book record of the inventory to determine operating results more often than is possible when a physical inventory is required. In practice, the retail inventory method is used to compute operating results several times a year based on book inventory figures. Physical inventories at retail prices are taken once or twice a year mainly to check the accuracy of the book inventory.

The retail inventory method requires the recording of both inventory and purchase figures at retail and at cost. Any additional markups are included in the retail figure. Physical inventories are taken at retail prices, and it is not necessary to place cost information on the tickets attached to the merchandise.

As noted, the closing inventory at retail may be converted to a cost value by using either the physical or book inventory figure. Let us illustrate both methods of conversion.[17]

1. Conversion based on physical inventory Based on the cost and retail records of his opening inventory and his purchases, and also on the figures for his closing physical inventory taken at retail prices, a retailer finds his position as follows:

	Cost	*Retail*
Opening inventory	$ 6,100	$10,000
Purchases	17,900	30,000
Total merchandise handled	$24,000	$40,000
Closing physical inventory at retail		$ 8,000

The cost of the merchandise handled during this period is 60 percent of the retail for this merchandise, that is, $24,000 ÷ $40,000 = 60 percent. Assuming the same relationship exists in the closing retail inventory, its cost value is 60 percent of $8,000 or $4,800.

In brief, a closing physical inventory at retail may be converted to a cost figure by using the formula—Cost value of inventory = retail value of inventory x cost percentage.

2. Conversion based on book inventory The basic facts needed to determine the cost value of the closing book inventory at retail are as follows:

	Cost	*Retail*
Opening inventory	$ 41,000	$ 65,000
Purchases	128,000	183,000
Total merchandise handled	$169,000	$248,000
Sales (from records)		$150,000
Markdowns (from records)		12,000
Shortages (estimated)		8,000
Total merchandise deductions		$170,000

The cost percentage is computed exactly as in the preceding illustration, that is: total merchandise handled at cost ($169,000) ÷ total merchandise handled at retail ($248,000) = 68.1 percent.

Since we do not have a physical retail inventory figure to which this cost percentage can be applied, we must create one. This is done by subtracting from the total merchandise handled at retail everything which has

[17] Both of the following examples are taken from J. W. Wingate, E. O. Schaller, and Irving Goldenthal, *Problems in Retail Merchandising*, 5th ed. (Englewood Cliffs, N.J.: Prentice-Hall, Inc., 1961), pp. 121–22.

decreased the value of this merchandise during the period covered—sales, markdowns, and shortages. Assuming these items amount to $170,000 ($150,000 + $12,000 + $8,000), we deduct this figure from the retail value of all merchandise handled ($248,000) and obtain a book inventory figure of $78,000 at retail. By multiplying this amount by the cost percentage—68.1—we arrive at the cost value of the inventory, $53,118. Any additional markups are included in the retail column of figures before the cost-retail percentage is calculated.

Summary of steps in the retail inventory method The foregoing illustrations suggest that six basic steps are involved in the retail inventory method: (*a*) charging merchandise to a department or to an entire store at both cost and retail prices; (*b*) keeping complete and accurate records at retail prices of all additions to and deductions from this stock; (*c*) determining the markup percentage and through this the cost percentage on the total merchandise handled; (*d*) calculating from the records the closing retail book inventory, that is, the retail value of the merchandise at hand in the closing inventory; (*e*) applying the cost percentage to the retail book inventory; (*f*) taking a physical inventory at retail prices, usually semiannually or annually, to check the accuracy of the retail book inventory. If this check reveals that the retail book inventory exceeds the physical inventory, which is the usual situation, a stock shortage exists; if the physical inventory is larger than the book inventory, there is an overage.

□ The operating statement

Except for fairly obvious deviations, the remaining steps necessary to prepare an operating statement under the retail inventory method are similar to those under the cost method. Referring to the data given in the preceding section, sales were assumed to be $150,000. The cost of goods sold is $115,882, that is, the difference between total merchandise handled at cost ($169,000) and the computed cost value of the closing inventory ($53,118). Operating expenses for the period are taken directly from the appropriate records: in the present case they are assumed to total $26,618. Consequently, the operating statement will show

	Dollars	*Ratio to sales*
Sales	$150,000	100.0
Cost of goods sold	115,882	77.3
Gross margin	$ 34,118	22.7
Operating expenses	26,618	17.7
Net profit before income taxes	$ 7,500	5.0

☐ Advantages and limitations of the retail inventory method

With a knowledge of the fundamental concepts involved in the retail method, let us evaluate its usefulness to the retailer and review the reasons for its growth.

Advantages of the retail method The main advantages of the retail method are seven in number as follows:

1. *Provides effective control over profit* Adequate retail management under the highly competitive conditions of today involves close and continuous review of the merchandising activities of the business. Assuming that expenses are known and controlled, profits depend upon the gross margin realized. Gross margin, in turn, depends upon the initial markup obtained and the markdowns taken. When full and accurate information is available at frequent intervals on these two factors, as it is under the retail method, prompt action may be taken to guard the planned or desired profit margin. Moreover, operating statements can be prepared frequently so that the profit trend can be observed and appropriate courses of action be determined.

2. *Permits valuation of inventory on conservative basis* The retail inventory method permits a conservative valuation of the closing inventory without taking a physical inventory. As noted, this result is achieved by applying the cost percentage to the book inventory at retail. But the question arises: Why does this procedure yield an inventory valuation on a conservative or "cost or market, which ever is lower" basis? The general answer lies in the fact that the cost percentage is calculated *after* additional markups but *before* markdowns. Further explanation will clarify this point.

Assume that a retailer purchases a man's suit at $60 and marks it to sell for $100, the cost percentage being 60 percent. Assume, further, that the retail price is increased to $120 by taking an additional markup of $20, so that the cost percentage drops to 50 percent. It is evident that the new cost percentage, 50 percent, will have to be applied to the new retail price, $120, to obtain the actual cost of the suit, $60. If the old cost percentage, 60 percent, were applied to $120, the cost of the suit would be shown as $72, which is clearly in error.

Now let us make another assumption. Suppose that another suit costing $60 is marked to sell for $100 but fails to do so and a markdown of $10 is taken, the cost percentage advancing from 60 percent to 66⅔ percent with this change. While the new cost percentage of 66⅔ percent will reduce the suit marked down to $90 to its original cost of $60, the question arises: Does

$60 represent a fair valuation of a suit which had to be marked down $10 to be sold? If the accounting maxim—anticipate losses but never profits—is adhered to, the loss caused by the markdown will be taken in the current period rather than in the following one. Consequently, the original cost percentage, 60 percent, will be applied to the reduced price of $90, yielding a book value of $54. Thus, the fundamental rule is that the cost percentage should always be calculated by including the additional markups but excluding the markdowns.[18]

3. *Facilitates taking the physical inventory* Because the physical inventory is taken at retail prices under the retail inventory method, it may be taken more easily and at less expense. There is less chance of error because no decoding is necessary, and entries on the inventory cards or sheets are made more rapidly. Moreover, it is possible to use personnel unfamiliar with the stock to list it and count it. Since it is easier to take inventories, they may be taken at more frequent intervals; thus, slow-moving items and irregularities in the stock may be detected more quickly.

4. *Aids in controlling stock shortages* By providing a book inventory figure, the retail inventory method makes possible the determination of stock shortages. Once determined, their causes may be studied and corrective measures adopted to minimize them. Presently stock shortages constitute a major problem in many retail stores.

5. *Furnishes equitable foundation upon which to base insurance coverage and adjust claims* When accurate and reliable records are kept, it is comparatively easy for retailers to establish proper insurance coverage and to obtain satisfactory adjustments on their insurance claims more quickly. These records, since they consist of irrefutable evidence, provide a sound and equitable basis for settling arguments.

6. *Reveals weaknesses in procedures and brings improved results* A chief benefit of the retail inventory method is the necessary and careful follow-up and appraisal of procedures and methods. This follow-up—including marking and re-marking of goods, proper recording of markdowns, and the like—is essential to insure the accuracy of the figures upon which the retail method depends.

7. *Provides basis for dollar control* A final significant advantage of the retail inventory method is the valuable aid it furnishes in the control of merchandise on a dollar basis.[19] By placing continued emphasis on the fundamentals of this accounting method and by concentrating the atten-

[18] For a comparison of inventory valuation under the cost method and the retail method cf. *The Values of Total System Reports for Retailers, op. cit.*, pp. 11–16; and *Reference Supplement, op. cit.*, pp. 6–7, 10–11.

[19] Cf. the discussion of dollar control on pp. 307–10, above.

tion of department managers and others on their accountability for merchandise in terms of dollars, a "merchandise consciousness" is developed which results in better stock control and improved profits. As emphasized previously, the value of the retail inventory method as a means of merchandise control is one of the causes for its widespread use.

Limitations of the retail method The retail inventory method has certain important limitations which the retailer must recognize.

1. An averaging method Probably the major disadvantage of this system of accounting can be traced to the fact that it is an averaging method. That is, in obtaining the cost percentage, the total *cost* of the merchandise handled and its total *retail* value are used (see page 564). Since low-markup merchandise tends to sell faster than high-markup goods, the former is represented in the total dollar purchases to a greater degree than it is at any time in the stock on hand. Consequently, when the closing book inventory at retail is reduced to cost by applying the cost percentage, the resulting valuation is higher than would be obtained by tabulating the specific costs of the items on hand. This disadvantage is particularly significant for stores and departments having (*a*) wide variations in markups and (*b*) many special sales events featuring merchandise at lower-than-usual markups.

2. Great care needed in recording of price changes Since the heart of the retail method consists of the maintenance of a book inventory figure which may be reduced to a cost or market basis at desired intervals, it is essential that this figure be accurate. Such accuracy depends upon the care exercised in recording all charges for merchandise delivered to the department, price changes such as markdowns and additional markups, transfers of goods to and from the department, and sales. Some unscrupulous buyers, however, may manipulate records—for example, markdowns—to their own advantage, with the result that the final figures are incorrect. This manipulation, of course, will result in higher stock shortages if the buyer is unable to alter the physical inventory figures. Only close supervision by management can overcome this danger.

3. Unsuited to some stores and departments The retail inventory method is not suitable for certain kinds of merchandise—such as bakery goods, soda fountain sales, and prescriptions—where composition or manufacturing takes place. Moreover, drapery and furniture workrooms, devoted to preparing merchandise for use by customers, need to be operated on a cost, rather than a retail, basis. Since many retailers have encountered little difficulty in operating the large majority of their departments on a retail basis and the remaining small number on a cost basis, however, this disadvantage is not serious.

4. Costly to operate Finally, the retail inventory method is costly to operate satisfactorily. The expense involved is greater than for the cost method because of the numerous records required to maintain complete and accurate book inventories for departments, classifications, and the store as a whole. In the final analysis, of course, these costs must be more than offset by the benefits gained. That this is the case is evidenced by the very large number of retailers who continue to use this method of accounting.

■ OTHER RETAIL ACCOUNTING CONCEPTS

Two additional accounting concepts—LIFO and merchandise management accounting—have particular application to retailing and deserve mention. Discussion of them must be brief, however, since a full explanation of their nature and use is outside the scope of this volume.

□ Inventory valuation under LIFO

As most retailers and informed students know, it is customary in the retail business to attempt to sell "old" stocks first and "new" stocks last. The established practice for many years, therefore, has been FIFO (first-in, first-out), with the inventory accounting following the physical movement of goods.

Following 1939, however, many retailers, led by the control executives of department stores who recalled their experiences in previous war periods, sought methods of minimizing the effects of inflation on their profits. This problem has continued to be of vital concern in recent years. Under the FIFO method of inventory valuation, larger profits result during periods of rising prices because higher values are placed on ending inventories than on beginning-of-the-year ones and the difference is added to profits, often termed "paper profits," upon which taxes must be paid. To remedy this situation, the LIFO (last-in, first-out) system was proposed and after much debate was approved by the Bureau of Internal Revenue in 1947.

LIFO illustrated The following illustration, showing how LIFO works, has been reproduced from *Fortune* and used with that publication's permission.

Rising prices Suppose a retailer of mechanical pencils buys 5,000 pencils at 50 cents each in January of a given year; by the latter part of the year his inventory is running low and he buys 5,000 more pencils, but the price has risen to 75 cents each. During the complete year he sold 5,000 pencils, 3,000 of them at $1 each and 2,000 of them at $1.50 each (the latter price being established when he learned that the price to him was going up). In order to simplify this example, assume he has no other costs of doing business. Here's how it works out:

		FIFO (First in, first out)		LIFO (Last in, first out)
Sales		$6,000		$6,000
Cost of goods sold	(5,000 @ 50¢)	2,500	(5,000 @ 75¢)	3,750
Reported profit before taxes		$3,500		$2,250
Federal income taxes (assumed arbitrarily at 50%)		1,750		1,125
Net profit		$1,750		$1,125
Ending inventory valuation (5,000 @ 75¢)		$3,750	(5,000 @ 50¢)	$2,500

The obvious results of going to LIFO in a period of rising prices are pretty clearly shown—(1) lower federal income taxes, (2) lower reported net profit, and (3) lower ending inventory valuation. . . .

Falling prices Suppose the retailer finds that the cost of pencils goes back down to 50 cents each early in the following year. He then sells at $1 apiece again. Then later in the year he reorders and finds the cost 40 cents each. At that time he cuts his selling price to 80 cents. Assuming

Purchases	3,000 @ 50¢	$1,500
	2,000 @ 40¢	800
Sales	3,000 @ $1	3,000
	2,000 @ 80¢	1,600

his profit and loss statement might look like this:

	FIFO		LIFO
Sales	$4,600		$4,600
Cost of goods sold (5,000 @ 75¢ = $3,750; reduction of inventory to market—3,000 from 50¢ to 40¢ = $300)	4,050	(2,000 @ 40¢) (3,000 @ 50¢)	2,300
Reported profits before taxes	$ 550		$2,300
Federal income taxes	275		1,150
Net profit	$ 275		$1,150
Ending inventory valuation (5,000 @ 40¢—result of reduction to market price)	$2,000	(5,000 @ 50¢)	$2,500

The results of being on LIFO in a period of declining prices are clearly shown: (1) higher federal income-tax payments, (2) higher net profit, and (3) higher ending inventory valuation. . . .

Steady prices If costs are constant over a long period, it makes no difference whether you are on FIFO or LIFO.[20]

LIFO has made substantial progress as a method of inventory valuation among large retailers and professional accounting firms in the past 25 years.

[20] "The Facts of LIFO," *Fortune*, Vol. 44, No. 6 (December 1951), p. 198.

The smaller firms and even the majority of large retailers, however, have continued with the more traditional methods of inventory valuation. As to the future, continued inflation of retail prices, which has accelerated since the late 1960s, is certainly a strong incentive toward the use of LIFO by more retailers. On the other hand, the added complications which LIFO introduces into the accounting system and the fact that, when a retailer adopts this valuation procedure, he must continue it even if the price level turns down, may act as deterrents. After weighing the advantages and disadvantages, two authorities conclude:

> Although any final assessment of virtues and demerits will have to wait on a longer accumulation of experience, it is reasonable to conceive that Lifo inventory accounting will have a substantial future in retailing. That Lifo will ever fully supplant Fifo-cost-or-market for retail business seems doubtful, however, unless indeed the two concepts are some day amalgamated. . . .[21]

☐ Merchandise management accounting

Just as the limitations of the cost method stimulated the growth of the retail inventory method, so has awareness of the shortcomings of the latter system encouraged the search for a new approach that would yield more positive benefits to the retailer under conditions existing today. Merchandise management accounting is one result of this search. Strictly speaking, merchandise management accounting is more a method of merchandising and pricing than it is a form of accounting. Since it relies so heavily on accounting records and demands some accounting information not required for other purposes, however, a few paragraphs concerning it are advisable here.

Merchandise management accounting seeks, among other objectives, to improve *dollar* profit (rather than *percentage* profit) through better determination and interpretation of costs by individual items. In other words, merchandise management accounting attempts to determine the total dollar cost which is quite closely associated with the handling and sale of each item in stock and to so price each item of merchandise that, after taking turnover into consideration, it yields the maximum dollar contribution to overhead. Its proponents claim that the retail inventory method places too much emphasis on department or store-wide gross margin percentages and deplore "the fixed habit of looking at departmental expenses, both direct and allocated, as applying across the board to all the goods sold in the de-

---

[21] McNair and Hersum, *op. cit.*, p. 379.

partment."[22] They point out that this traditional approach discourages retailers from purchasing merchandise which might move in great quantity if priced with a lower-than-normal markup.

Despite management's recognition of the need for more information of the type furnished by merchandise management accounting and the strong advocacy of this concept by certain accounting firms and students of retailing, only a relatively few stores have adopted the system. Adherence to traditional methods, unavailability of the required cost data and unwillingness to provide it, and lack of understanding of the techniques involved, among other reasons, are responsible.[23]

It seems certain, however, that the future will continue to bring frequent and critical evaluations of all accounting systems used by retailers as well as constant search for improved methods and devices to strengthen control. Such actions are necessary in view of the numerous current technological developments having particular application to retailing,[24] the growing competition among retailers for consumer patronage, the continuous pressure of personnel for higher wages and better working conditions, and the need to control prices and costs to insure a reasonable profit.

■ REVIEW AND DISCUSSION QUESTIONS

1 Explain fully the chief purposes of accounting records in the retail business.

2 "Recently, accounting records have assumed increased importance because of frequent revisions in federal and state laws." What state and/or federal laws have particular significance to the retailer from the accounting point of view and necessitate his continued familiarity with their provisions?

3 Distinguish between the operating statement and the balance sheet. What major information does each one furnish the retailer?

4 Discuss the problems involved in inventory valuation under the cost method. In view of these difficulties, and others, why do so many small retailers continue to use this accounting method?

5 Visit a local banker and report on the kinds of financial information he

---

[22] M. P. McNair and E. G. May, "Pricing for Profit: A Revolutionary Approach to Retail Accounting," *Harvard Business Review,* Vol. 35, No. 3 (May–June 1957), p. 111.

[23] For an analysis of these reasons, cf. Roger Dickinson, "Marginalism in Retailing: The Lessons of a Failure," *Journal of Business,* Vol. 39, No. 3 (July 1966), pp. 353–58. This source contains an excellent explanation of the fundamental concepts of merchandise management accounting.

[24] Some of these are discussed in Chapter 25 "Control of Sales Transactions."

requires from retailers before extending them credit. What particular type(s) of information has assumed special significance in recent months?

6 Define and illustrate the meaning of the terms "gross sales," "net sales," "cost of merchandise sold," "gross margin," and "net profit."

7 Explain the meaning of the term "retail inventory method" in your own words and describe the main factors responsible for its growth and widespread use.

8 Specifically, what information of importance to management does the "retail method" provide that is not available under the "cost method"? State concisely three chief limitations of the retail method.

9 Explain and illustrate how a closing physical inventory *at retail* can be converted to a *cost* basis.

10 What are the essential features of FIFO and LIFO? Illustrate with the use of hypothetical figures the effects on profits of adopting the LIFO system during (*a*) a period of rising prices and (*b*) a period of declining prices.

chapter 24 chapter

EXPENSE CONTROL: A REQUISITE OF PROFITABLE OPERATION

To an increasing extent in recent years, effective control of his ex-penses is both urgent and vital to the retailer's existence. Expense permeates every phase of his business, necessitating continuous attention to every item contributing to his operating costs. Without such attention, reasonable profits cannot be realized under the present profit squeeze.[1] Although expenses of retail stores vary with such factors as the type of store, *i.e.*, grocery, jewelry, or department store; with the annual volume of sales; with the size of city in which the store is located; and during the course of a business cycle, consideration of these factors is outside the scope of this volume.[2] Here we shall concentrate chiefly on the methods by which expenses may be controlled.

---

[1] Cf. "Gamble Starts Cost-Cutting Programs to Increase Profits," *Women's Wear Daily*, November 5, 1969, p. 36, and "Retailers Economize by Cutting Labor Costs," *ibid.*, June 22, 1969, pp. 1, 25.

[2] Cf. the discussion in C. F. Phillips and D. J. Duncan, *Marketing: Principles and Methods*, 6th ed. (Homewood, Ill.: Richard D. Irwin, Inc., 1968), pp. 162–64; and the statistics assembled in *Expenses in Retail Businesses* (Dayton, Ohio: National Cash Register Co., n.d.).

THE NATURE OF EXPENSE CONTROL

As we have noted in the previous chapter, profits result from a satisfactory relationship among sales, gross margin, and total expenses. They may be improved, for example, by increasing the gross margin dollars without a proportionate rise in expenses, by reducing expenses without a commensurate reduction in gross margin, and by a combination of these two methods. Since competitive influences often make it difficult to increase gross margin, constant vigilance over expenses is common practice among successful stores. When this is done, expenses are "controlled."

In the process of reducing expenses, however, it is noteworthy that instances are rare in which sizable savings are effected through major economies in one phase of operation. Cases are rather numerous, however, in which small savings have been realized in a variety of store activities through close and continuous scrutiny of all expense items, with the aggregate of such savings being substantial.

Expense control does not always mean expense reduction. On the contrary, by increasing certain expenses the retailer may so increase his sales that he adds to his profit despite higher costs. Certainly this is the aim of all advertising expenditures and of customer services. Hence, expense control should be thought of as deciding upon and limiting actual expenses to those that are necessary for the maximization of profit.

To effectuate the desired control over expenses it is necessary (1) to classify them properly and define each item of expense; (2) to distribute or allocate the expenses to departments and to functions; (3) to scrutinize, analyze, and compare them with budgeted figures; and (4) to take the corrective action necessary to effect whatever changes are suggested by this analysis. Let us first consider the classification of expenses.

EXPENSE CLASSIFICATION

Expense classification divides all the expenses of retailing such as rent, advertising, and salaries into a number of clearly defined groups. Its purposes are (1) to provide a detailed breakdown that can be used year after year and permit noting of expense trends for each classification and (2) to furnish bases allowing comparisons with other stores. These comparisons reveal expenses that are "out of line" and enable remedial action to be taken.

Expenses are classified in various ways among different types and sizes of stores, both multi- and single unit. These variations are clear when the expense classifications used in different types of stores are examined. It is in department stores and departmentalized specialty stores, however, that the greatest amount of attention has been given to expense classification, distribution, and analysis. Consequently, our discussion of these topics emphasizes the terminology and procedures used in these institutions.

□ Expense classification in hardware stores

Although the majority of small independent retailers employ a simpler expense classification, the one recommended to its member stores by the National Retail Hardware Association is shown in Table 24–1.

TABLE 24–1

Classification of expenses in hardware stores

I. Salary expense
   1. To owners and managers
   2. To salespeople, office and others

II. Other costs of doing business
   1. Office supplies and postage
   2. Advertising
   3. Donations
   4. Telephone and telegraph
   5. Losses on notes and accounts
   6. Delivery expense (other than wages)
   7. Depreciation—Delivery equipment
      —Furniture, fixtures and tools
   8. Rent
   9. Repairs to building
   10. Utilities
   11. Insurance*
   12. Taxes* (excluding federal income tax)
   13. Interest on borrowed money*
   14. Unclassified—including store supplies

III. Total expense (not including interest on investment)

* Not including amounts paid in connection with real estate ownership.

Source: "Compare Your Operational Costs with NRHA's Cost-of-Doing-Business Survey," *Hardware Retailer,* August 1971, p. 87.

□ Expense classification in chain store organizations

How chain store organizations classify expenses may be illustrated by those listed for food stores in Table 24–2. This classification, which is based

TABLE 24–2

Classification of expenses in food chains
Payroll
Supplies
Utilities
Communications
Travel
Services purchased
Promotional giveaways
Professional services
Donations
Insurance
Taxes and licenses (except on income)
Property rentals
Depreciation and amortization
Repairs
Unclassified
Interest

Source: Earl Brown, N. E. Payne, and Robert Day, *Operating Results of Food Chains, 1969–70*. (Ithaca, N.Y.: Cornell University, 1970.)

on *The Standard Manual of Accounts for the Food Chain Industry*, is quite similar to that used by hardware stores, although there are some differences in terminology. In practice, a number of subgroups may be used to identify further the nature of the expense.

☐ Expense classification in department stores

The National Retail Merchants Association suggests two types of expense classification—by natural divisions for smaller stores and by expense centers for larger ones.

Natural classification For smaller department stores a 16-point natural classification of operating costs is recommended as shown in Table 25–3. Along with these basic, natural divisions of expense, four additional category groups are provided for redistribution and offset purposes. Together, they constitute "the backbone of the system of expense classification" recommended by NRMA.[3] This grouping is referred to as a natural classifi-

[3] *Retail Accounting Manual* (New York: National Merchants Association, Controllers' Congress, 1962), p. III–1.

TABLE 24–3

National Retail Merchants Association natural division of expenses

	Expense division	Illustrations of costs included
01	Payroll	Salaries, wages, commissions, bonuses, prizes for contests, *etc.*, received by all employees.
02	Fringe benefits	Not in itself a pure natural division, but provided to permit optional redistribution of fringe benefits from expense center 630 to other expense centers.*
03	Advertising	Space costs in newspapers, radio and television time, direct mail, and other media.
04	Taxes	Federal (excluding income taxes), state, county, city, unemployment, social security, disability.
06	Supplies	All items consumed in operation of business such as stationery and wrapping, packing, and cleaning materials.
07	Services purchased	Nonprofessional services by outsiders—delivery, repairs, armoured cars, collection agencies, *etc.*
08	Unclassified	All expenses not included in other natural divisions—net cash shortages, policy adjustments, want ads., *etc.*
09	Traveling	Out-of-town travel expenses for all employees.
10	Communications	Postage, telegrams and cables, telephone service and rental of communications equipment.
11	Pensions	All payments to retired employees in nature of pensions, retirement allowances, and contributions to pension funds.
12	Insurance	All typs of insurance coverages—fire, liability, and others.
13	Depreciation	Depreciation of book value of buildings, furniture, fixtures and equipment, rolling stock, *etc.*
14	Professional services	Services of a highly specialized and professional nature such as legal fees, public accountants' fees, and appraisal fees.
15	Donations	Contributions to welfare, charitable, and educational institutions.
16	Bad debts	Bad debts, bad checks, and fradulent purchases less recoveries.
17	Equipment costs	Costs of all equipment rented or leased (except communications equipment)
20	Real property rentals	Expenses incurred or rent paid for real estate used in the business, less any income received from sub-rentals.
91	Expense transfers	Expenses transferred from one expense center to another to reflect actual operating costs of each center.
92	Outside revenue and other credits	Transactions involving credits related to such items as advertising and cost of merchandise in workroom departments as well as outside revenue not classified as gross or other income.
93	Multiple-store distribution	Designed to provide a vehicle for redistribution of accumulated central organization expenses to individual selling units.

* Expense center 630—Supplemental Benefits—is shown in Table 24–4.
Source: *Retail Accounting Manual* (New York: National Retail Merchants Association, Controllers' Congress, 1962), pp. III–1 to III–5.

cation because it assigns expenses on a simple, understandable basis that most retailers have used for many years.

Expense centers For the larger stores, the Association recommends that the natural division of expenses be assigned to 23 so-called expense centers, with each center designating a particular activity or service essential to the operating of the store such as management, sales promotion, and delivery. These 23 centers are shown in Table 24–4. Expenses are classified under both

TABLE 24–4

National Retail Merchants Association Expense Centers	
110	Management
120	Property and equipment
210	Accounting and data processing
310	Accounts receivable
320	Credit and collections
410	Sales promotion
510	Service and operations
550	Telephone and other utilities
570	Cleaning
580	Maintenance and repairs
610	Personnel
630	Supplementary benefits*
720	Maintenance of reserve stock
740	Receiving and marking
750	Shuttle service (Transfer Hauling)
810	Selling supervision
820	Direct selling
830	Customer services
860	Wrapping and packing
880	Delivery
910	Merchandising
920	Buying
930	Merchandise control

* See special explanation for Expense Division 02 in Table 24–3.
Source: *Retail Accounting Manual, op. cit.*, p. IV–1.

the appropriate natural division and the expense center. Thus, top management salaries (a part of natural division 01–payroll) and traveling expenses (natural division 09) are also charged to expense center 110 (management), while buyers' salaries (a part of natural division 01) and traveling expenses (09) are also charged to expense center 920 (buying).[4] Stores using the ex-

[4] It is not practicable here to discuss all aspects of expense classification covered in the *Retail Accounting Manual, ibid.* Readers interested in a more comprehensive

pense center classification can study their cost trends and also make comparative analyses with other firms for each center and each expense item within a center.

DISTRIBUTION (ALLOCATION) OF EXPENSES

Once a suitable classification of expenses has been adopted, the retailer is prepared to distribute or allocate them to selling departments within a store, to branch stores, or to all stores in a chain organization—an essential second step in expense control. This task is difficult because not all retail expenses can be clearly traced to specific departments, branches, or to individual units of a chain.[5]

Direct and indirect expenses

To permit a sound allocation of expenses, most retailers classify their cost items into two groups—direct and indirect. Generally speaking, direct expenses are those occasioned by the existence of a particular department, and which would disappear if the department were dropped. Such costs are illustrated by a department's payroll or by the supplies it uses. In contrast, indirect expenses are those not occasioned solely by a particular department, such as rent paid by the store and office overhead, and would not disappear if a particular department were discontinued. It is generally agreed that all direct expenses should be carried by the department causing them, but opinions differ concerning the allocation of indirect expenses.

Methods of allocating expenses

Three methods are employed to distribute retail expenses as follows:

The net profit plan Under this plan all expenses, both direct and indirect, are divided among the departments of the store. Direct expenses are assigned directly to the selling departments causing them, and indirect ones are distributed to these departments on a predetermined basis. For example, general management expense may be divided up in ratio to the net sales of the various departments, accounts payable cost may be assigned in ratio to the number of invoices involved, and checking and marking expense

---

treatment should consult that source, especially Chapter VI, "Elements of Reports and Statistics."

[5] The discussion which follows refers to distribution of costs among selling departments, but the reader can easily transfer the basic ideas to the units of a chain or to a branch organization.

allocated on the basis of the number of pieces marked. In general, net sales are used as the base for indirect cost distribution only when some other logical base cannot be found.

When the total expenses assigned to a specific department are deducted from the departmental gross margin, the net profit is determined. In brief, each department is considered as a separate profit-making entity and is judged on its ability to produce profit.

The chief merits of the net profit plan are that it furnishes a basis for judging the merchandising capacity of the department head, fixes responsibility for the overall performance of the department, provides a basis for rewarding exceptional performance through salary increases or bonuses, and makes the department head conscious of the need to control both direct and indirect costs (although in many cases he will have little, if any, control over indirect costs). Its major limitations are the lack of control by department heads over certain expenses (as just mentioned), the arbitrary allocation of many indirect expenses to departments, the time consumed and the costs involved in distributing the expenses, and the fact that the final figures do not reveal the true "profit" of the selling department.

Widespread dissatisfaction with the net profit plan, particularly the allocation of indirect expenses, led to the development of the contribution plan.

The contribution plan This plan of expense distribution was probably first enunciated by the late Carlos B. Clark of the J. L. Hudson Company in 1933 under the title "Reservoir Concept."[6] Currently, however, the "contribution plan," as it is now known, is used by many large retailers. This plan is designed to overcome the arbitrariness of allocating indirect expenses to selling departments by providing that only the direct or escapable expenses be so assigned. That is, each department is charged with the expenses directly incurred by it and which would disappear if it were discontinued;[7] all other expenses are placed in a general bracket with no attempt at departmental distribution. The department expense budget shows only estimates for various direct expenses and a balance that is contributed toward the store's indirect expenses and profit.

Besides its simplicity, the contribution plan forces selling departments *and* people performing such services as credit, delivery, and accounting to concentrate on those expenses over which they have some control. Its major disadvantages are two: (1) It does not provide a total expense figure for the department, so it is of little aid in pricing; and (2) selling department heads may make inordinate demands for credit, delivery, and other services for which they are not assigned a share in the cost.

---

[6] " 'Reservoir Concept' is Keynote of Future Profits," *Retail Ledger*, December, 1933, p. 13.

[7] For example, selling, delivery, and newspaper and direct mail advertising expenses.

Combined net profit and contribution plan Some retailers desire more detailed information than gross margin, controllable expenses, and "contribution" in weighing the results and value of various selling departments. Although interested in such facts, they want additional data on departmental expenses so that they can improve their control and increase profits. Consequently, they prepare reports for selling departments which show both the department's "contribution" and its "net profit." When all direct expenses are deducted from dollar gross margin a "contribution" figure is obtained which can be compared with that of other departments and stores. The principles of the net profit plan are then applied under which the "contribution" is decreased by the deduction of the indirect expenses allocated to the department.[8] These steps may be illustrated as follows:

Net sales	$60,000
Cost of merchandise sold	40,000
Department gross margin	$20,000
Direct expense of the department	9,000
Contribution of the department	$11,000
Indirect expenses distributed to the department[9]	8,400
Department net profit	$ 2,600

EXPENSE COMPARISONS AND ANALYSES

After expenses have been classified into groups and properly allocated to assure comparability both over time and with other firms, the important task of analyzing them may begin. This analysis usually involves three steps: (1) a review of the retailer's own expense trends over a period of time; (2) a comparison of his expenses with those of other retailers;[10] and (3) their analysis through an expense budget.

Reviewing expense trends and making comparisons with similar firms

Dollar and percentage-of-sales reports One effective way for the retailer to review the long-run trends in his costs is through a five- or ten-year

[8] For suggestions of a desirable procedure to be followed in establishing a combination plan, cf. *Retail Accounting Manual, op. cit.*, p. VIII–4.

[9] In some cases, these indirect expenses would be classified into two groups: (1) those assigned to departments in ratio to net sales and (2) those assigned on other bases.

[10] Cf., for example, "Compare Your Operational Costs with NRHA's Cost-of-Doing-Business Survey," *op. cit.*

expense table. Consisting of dollar figures for each item in the expense classification, together with these figures expressed as a percentage of sales, this table is a constant reminder of expense trends and calls for frequent study. Some cost ratios may be rising and others falling. What are the reasons? For example, are more customers demanding delivery service or are salespeople failing to encourage customers to carry their purchases? Has enough been spent to keep store fixtures and equipment up to date? Is more advertising being done or more expensive media being used? By answering these and other questions the retailer decides on the steps he should take to control his expenses.

Our emphasis on long-run expense trends does not imply that a retailer should analyze his expenses only once each year. Many large retailers prepare daily, weekly, and monthly reports to improve their control over expenses of all kinds.

Comparisons of a retailer's expenses with those of similar firms are made possible through reports expressing each cost as a percentage of sales. On page 620 average net profits for hardware stores are given as well as those for the "most profitable one-third" of the group. By comparing his own detailed expenses with those in the latter group, available from his trade association, the retailer can learn where his expenses are "out-of-line." Similar comparisons are now possible in most retail fields.[11]

Production unit accounting Some department, specialty, and chain stores use *production unit accounting* as a means of reviewing their own long-run expense trends and of making expense comparisons with other firms. This accounting concept differs from expense center accounting in that it involves making *use* of the data accumulated in many, but not all, of the expense centers to improve operations and enhance profits. Essentially, its goal is to secure a unit cost figure for as many of the store's activities as possible.[12]

Production unit accounting defines three chief elements involved in any activity: (a) the "work load" or amount of work to be done; (*b*) the speed or rate at which it can be done, termed "productivity"; and (c) the labor cost per hour of performing the job, called the "effective pay rate." These elements or factors are applied to each expense center where feasible, *i.e.*, where there is a payroll account and where the job can be measured. Their relationships may be expressed in a simple formula as follows: Work load (units) ÷ Productivity = Hours used × Pay rate = Payroll Expense.

[11] Cf. *Expenses in Retail Businesses, op. cit.* Also cf. the expense data published by trade associations listed for this chapter in the "Annotated Supplementary Readings."

[12] The details involved in production unit accounting are too complex for presentation here. Interested readers will find it advisable to consult the literature available on this subject. Especially recommended is Chapter XII in the *Retail Accounting Manual, op. cit.*

☐ The expense budget

No management tool, perhaps, is as effective for analyzing and controlling retailing costs as the expense budget. A somewhat detailed examination of the basic principles involved in preparing and using this management aid, therefore, is advisable.

Nature and purposes An expense budget is simply a series of estimates or a forecast in dollars of the various expenses a store will incur in a designated period. This period, as with the merchandise budget, normally consists of one season or six months; but it is usually broken down into months, or even weeks or days, depending on the needs of the store. The primary purpose of the budget is to make a careful forecast of expenses of all kinds, so that adequate provision can be made to meet them and the store's profits can be safeguarded.[13] Besides providing a definite goal and fixing responsibility on certain individuals in the store for attaining this goal, the budget stresses management's need to coordinate all of the store's activities. Moreover, at the close of the budget period, it is possible to analyze the extent of and reasons for any variations between planned and actual expense figures. In other words, the expense budget provides a means of analyzing each expense classification both *before* and *after* the actual expenditure takes place.

Desirable requisites To accomplish its purposes, an expense budget should be planned carefully, constructed with discrimination and judgment, and judiciously administered. It should be simple and still provide the necessary information to permit effective control. To maximize its benefits, each executive should understand its purposes and uses and participate in its formation.

The budget should also be flexible. If business conditions change suddenly and sales fall or rise more rapidly than was expected when the budget was constructed, changes should be made promptly to insure its effectiveness as an instrument of control. But there must be reasonable certainty that business conditions (including competitive changes) are responsible for the variations shown, and that they are not caused by poor management. After all, the budget is a mechanism for control; it sets a goal (a definite amount of profit) and permits measurement of the progress toward this goal. If the goal is changed too frequently and if disagreement exists regarding the necessity of such changes, confidence in the budget is lost. Original estimates should be formulated with care and require few significant revisions.

The budget should be an effective device for localizing responsibility

[13] The expense budget, together with the merchandise budget, is incorporated into an overall store financial budget.

and authority. In most large stores, the general manager is responsible for the entire budget, with heavy reliance on the controller both for preparing it and using it. He also delegates responsibility to others—for example, to each department manager to hold expenses within the limits set for his department. But responsibility of seeing that the store remains within its budget should be centralized in one person. Along with this responsibility must go authority—approval or rejection of any particular expenditure. Otherwise, it is impossible to give credit or to fix blame when actual results are compared with those planned.

Some objections to expense budgets Despite the foregoing commendable purposes, some executives still object to using a budget. They claim that it may make the organization so penny-conscious that sufficient outlays for its growth and development will not be made; that it is based upon overoptimistic sales estimates, with resulting large totals for operating expenses, and these latter sums will be spent even if the estimated sales fail to materialize; and, finally, that it lacks sufficient flexibility because of the difficulty of acting quickly when conditions change.

The foregoing contentions have some validity, although they are directed more at misuse of the budget than at the budget itself. If the aim of the budget—to serve as a tool for maximizing profits from a long-run point of view—is understood by all executives, they should not become too penny-conscious. Likewise, if those responsible for the budget consistently overestimate sales, the moral seems to be to let someone else do the estimating, not to throw out the budget. Moreover, if adequate checks are maintained during the budget period, all budgeted funds need not be spent if sales are below expectations. After all, a budget sets reasonable expenditures, not minimum ones. It is a guide, not a straitjacket; and it is an aid to the judgment of management, not a substitute for it.

Budgeting procedure In setting up an expense budget, at least three important steps are necessary:

1. Setting control figures or estimates based on all pertinent, available information. Basic data of two kinds are required for this purpose: (*a*) An over-all total expense figure, and (*b*) a control figure for each major expense account, adjusted to the overall control figure. These estimates, however, should be broken down by months.

2. Setting departmental budgets (or individual store budgets in the case of a chain). This step requires the following actions: (*a*) Each department head prepares a budget for his department. Unless the contribution plan is used, indirect cost must be prorated to the departments before this budget can be constructed. Under the expense center concept attention is focused on each center; and budgeting, so far as selling departments are concerned, relates only to planning direct expenses. (*b*) Department budgets

are adjusted to conform to the control figures. These adjustments are made by the merchandise manager, by the controller, or by the budget committee, often working closely with department heads.

3. Breaking down the control and department budgets into monthly or even shorter-period budgets.

Further explanation will serve to clarify these steps.

Store-wide control figures Variations are found among stores of different types and sizes, but the majority of retailers obtain an overall expense figure by combining two methods: (1) through estimating planned sales for the budget period and (2) by using the total expense figure for the previous year adjusted for changes anticipated during the budget period. When the first method is used, the cost of merchandise must also be estimated to secure a dollar figure for gross margin.[14] By deducting his desired net profit from this gross margin figure, an overall expense figure is obtained. This amount is then adjusted on the basis of previous expense experience and the retailer's judgment of conditions that will prevail in the budget period.

When the overall expense figure estimate is based on past experience, adequate records are required. This represents a real problem for many small retailers who do not have adequate accounting systems: They could not prepare accurate budgets by this method even if they wished to do so. But where records are available, they provide a sound basis for planning expenses. In this process, many stores start with "fixed" expenses—those that do not vary much with total sales, such as taxes, property rentals, and insurance. These costs yield a figure to which the "controllable" accounts can be adjusted.

Actually, such fixed costs as taxes, property rentals, and insurance are not so predetermined as one might expect. Take property rentals, for example. Perhaps the size of the store should be expanded, thus increasing the total charge for the period; or perhaps a part of the building may be sublet, thus reducing the total amount charged against the store. Again, this amount may be reduced by negotiating with the landlord.

Turning to expense items over which the retailer has relatively more control, each should also be reviewed regarding a possible increase or decrease over the preceding comparable period. Possibly some full-time employees may be replaced by part-time ones. Or a new method of compensating employees may result in increased productivity, thus reducing the number needed and decreasing payroll costs. On the other hand, close analysis may convince the retailer that he has too few employees and that better service to customers with more employees will increase his sales.

---

[14] How the retailer obtains his planned sales figure has already been discussed, cf. "Planned Sales," pp. 335, 339–41, above.

Considerable care is essential in building the estimates for each expense center. Methods of cutting costs and the consequences of such reductions, as well as the possible advantages gained from increasing expenses in certain areas, require study. The net result of such action is a careful estimate for each kind of expense which, when totaled, furnishes the overall expense figure.

Here again, let us note that despite the care exercised in constructing overall and major account expense figures, adjustments are often necessary to accommodate unforeseen developments.

Departmental and chain-unit budgets In departmentized stores or in chain organizations, the control figures previously set up are commonly broken down by departments or by individual stores.[15] The best approach, probably, is to have department heads or individual store executives participate actively in the formulation of the budget.[16] These individuals may even prepare preliminary estimates of their own based on their previous experience and the conditions expected during the budget period.[17]

To obtain realistic departmental budgets, however, the firm's budgetary officer or committee should provide the department head with all available pertinent information. This is necessary because no budget is better than the information upon which it is based. In addition to the data needed from within the store, similar information for comparable departments in other stores is also necessary, plus that concerning the outlook for general business, price trends, competition, and contemplated changes in store policy. The total number of transactions in relation to number of employees is likewise important. And, where feasible, the department head should be told how much of the general store overhead will be charged against his department and the bases upon which it will be allocated.

With the data suggested, the department head can make estimates of the direct expenses for his section for the budgeted period. This process requires a careful review of the exact needs of his department in consultation with his assistant and others in whose judgment he has confidence. Since wages and salaries typically constitute one-half or more of total operating costs, sound judgment is necessary in estimating the payroll figure. It is instructive, therefore, to review briefly the procedure followed in establishing such a

[15] In chain organizations the manager may break them down further by departments.

[16] Although the practice of budgeting probably is more highly developed among industrial firms than among retailers, a lower level of management is used by retailers in making up and using the budget than in industrial firms.

[17] To facilitate the discussion, the following analysis is expressed in terms of department budgets. However, the same analysis applies to the individual store in the chain-store system, with the store manager building the budget rather than the department buyer.

figure. Similar care is essential with respect to other major items in the expense budget, for instance, advertising.

1. Constructing a department payroll figure In performing this task a logical approach is as follows: (1) Set a control figure; (2) consider the work to be done; (3) estimate the number of employees needed to perform this work; (4) determine the total payroll needed; and finally, (5) adjust this "total-payroll-needed" figure to the control figure.

In a selling department, the payroll control figure may be obtained by taking the payroll-to-sales ratio of previous years. For example, this ratio may be 8 percent of sales for salespersons. This figure should be compared with the payroll ratio of comparable departments in other stores and also adjusted to the overall payroll figure for the entire store.

The work to be done may be expressed in terms of the number of transactions expected during various weeks of the budget period. To illustrate: Assume that the estimated sales for the first week of the period are $6,000. Based on past experience, the average sale may be estimated at $3.35. Dividing this average sale into the total estimated sales, we arrive at 1,800—the number of transactions expected during that week. Those for other weeks in the budget period may be calculated in a similar manner.

These estimates of weekly transactions must now be put in terms of employees. Again, we turn to past experience and find that, in comparable periods, each employee has been able to handle about 360 transactions. By dividing this figure into the number of transactions anticipated in the week under consideration, *i.e.* 1,800, we find that five salespeople will be needed in the department. If wages per salesperson average $110 per week, the total weekly payroll will be $550. In making these estimates, however, it should be held in mind that a minimum number of employees is required in each department. Irrespective of the number of expected transactions during a certain period, it takes some employees to provide service to customers, to keep merchandise arranged, and to prevent shoplifting.

The final step is to adjust the built-up payroll estimate to the control figure. As has been suggested, the control figure was put at 8 percent of sales ($6,000); consequently, the payroll for this week must not exceed $480. Our built-up payroll results in a total cost of $550. Necessary adjustments may be made by increasing the total sales without increasing the number of employees; by increasing the transactions per employee-hour, thus handling the estimated sales with fewer employee-hours; and by shifting employees among departments.

2. Adjusting department or store budgets to control figures After each department or chain-store manager has prepared *his* budget, it is reviewed with the merchandise manager, the controller, or the budget committee (if one exists) and checked against the control figures. If any expenses are found to exceed (or to be below) those provided for in the control budget for the whole store, adjustments must be made. These may include a reduction (increase) in estimates or a revision of the control figure for the store as a whole, or both. Changing the figures for the store as a whole, however, should be a matter of last resort and be done only after all means of adjusting the various department expense budgets have been exhausted.

Breaking down the budget period into smaller divisions The third major step in setting up an expense budget is to divide the six-month budget into shorter periods, *i.e.*, months or weeks. This division applies to departmental and individual chain-store budgets as well as to the overall control figures. Through this procedure, every person responsible for holding expenses within the limits of the six-month budget is able to follow his success from month to month or from week to week, as the case may be. And making the division is not difficult if records of past expenditures are available. Although total expenditures may change annually, the timing of the various expenditures is more constant. Delivery expenses, for example, will show little variation among similar months over a period of years.

Analyzing expenses through the budget At the beginning of our discussion we emphasized that the expense budget permits analysis of each expense classification *before* and *after* the expenditure of funds. The ensuing explanation has illustrated the kind of analysis necessary to build an adequate budget. To complete the picture a few comments need to be added regarding the importance of reviewing the results at the close of the budget period.

A well-planned expense-budget form provides space for entering both planned and actual figures for each expense item included. At the close of each budget period, these planned and actual figures should be scrutinized to determine the reasons for any variations. Take advertising, for example: Why did actual advertising cost exceed the planned figure? Did we use too many media rather than concentrating on the more productive ones such as newspapers? Was the budget figure unrealistic in the light of unexpected developments? It is through this kind of diagnosis that the retailer secures the information he needs for corrective action.

■ TAKING CORRECTIVE ACTION

Classifying, distributing, and analyzing expenses—although essential steps in the control of expenses—are just means to an end: the corrective action they make possible. In other words, expense control does not actually take place until someone does something about the expenses which the analyses show are out of line.

A main advantage of the expense budget is that it permits early remedial action. Even in small stores where budget preparation is limited, monthly reports comparing actual expenditures with those budgeted enable the proprietor to keep in close touch with the store's progress in remaining within its budget. In larger stores, where expenses are controlled by a large number of individuals, a tighter rein over actual expenses must be kept. Consequently, more attention is given to budget figures and to deviations from them. Some retailers, for instance, require that *before* any significant item of expense is undertaken, even if it is within the limits of the budget, the expenditure must be approved by an expense controller. Suppose that a department manager needs additional supplies and submits a requisition to the expense controller. If the latter finds that the cost involved is within reasonable limits of the departmental budget, he authorizes the expenditure. Otherwise, he refers it to the controller for approval. All expenses, of course, should not require requisitions, since some of them are indirect costs over which the department heads have no control. But it is advisable that all important direct expenses be subject to this kind of control.

In conclusion, we need to emphasize once again that records are a step to control, and not control. Some retailers, in the mistaken belief that records alone will provide the necessary control of expenses, have piled form on top of form and analysis on top of analysis. For one English retailer this situation became so absurd that it was necessary to junk 80 tons of record-keeping forms, thus saving an estimated $14 million in the cost of filling them out and substantially adding to his net profits.[18] While many small retailers still need additional data as a basis for improving operations, many large ones need fewer forms and more executive action.

■ REVIEW AND DISCUSSION QUESTIONS

1 "No problem facing the retailer today is more urgent, more continuous, and more vital to his existence than effective control of his expenses." Discuss.

2 Explain the two main goals of expense classification. Why do different kinds or types of stores classify their expenses in different ways?

3 Consult in your library the latest copies of *Financial and Operating Results of Department and Specialty Stores* and *Departmental Merchandising and Operating Results of Department and Specialty Stores,* published annually by the Controllers' Congress of the National Retail

---

[18] "The English Unorthodoxy of Marks & Spencer," *Dun's Review and Modern Industry*, October 1966, p. 128.

Merchants Association. Compare and contrast the type of information provided and the form in which the data are presented.

4 What are the chief differences between the natural classification of expenses in department stores and the expense center concept?

5 (*a*) Define the term "expense allocation" and summarize its main objectives.

(*b*) Comment on the statement: "The *net profit plan* of allocating expenses distributes all expenses to revenue-producing departments whereas the *contribution plan* centers its attention on each department's gross margin and direct expenses."

6 What are the most logical bases, in your judgment, on which to allocate the following expenses to selling departments in a department or large specialty store? (*a*) General management; (*b*) customers' returns of merchandise; (*c*) credit and billing; (*d*) checking and marking; and (*e*) personal shopping service. State your reasons in each case.

7 Discuss the purposes and methods of expense comparisons in retail stores.

8 (*a*) Explain the term "expense budget" in your own words including its purposes and requisites.

(*b*) What steps are necessary to establish one in a small or medium-sized store?

9 Describe the process by which a budget figure covering a specific period is constructed for payroll expense in a departmentized store. Use illustrations to make your meaning clear.

10 "Classifying, distributing, and analyzing expenses are just means to an end: the corrective action they make possible." Discuss, being sure to indicate specifically the kinds of corrective action this process makes possible.

chapter 25 chapter

CONTROL OF SALES TRANSACTIONS

All retail stores must perform several activities in making sales to their customers such as furnishing them with a sales check or a sales register receipt, receiving and safeguarding money, and recording the transaction in a manner that will provide the information desired. To perform these activities properly, suitable equipment should be obtained and effective procedures or routines established incorporating the new, improved techniques continuously being developed. When these steps are taken, the retailer can adequately control his sales transactions. Responsibility for establishing such a control system may be centered in the proprietor, the controller, a systems committee or department, or a research department.

THE NATURE AND GOALS OF SALES TRANSACTIONS SYSTEMS

A sales transactions system consists of the procedures, methods, and devices established to handle the various types of sales. Basic to its determination is a decision on the kinds of sales the retailer will make, and the types of equipment he will use to implement the procedures adopted. These decisions are practically inseparable since the equipment chosen depends on the uses to which it will be put. The main goal of the system, quite obviously, is to insure smooth functioning of this aspect of the business, thus helping to generate regular patronage by satisfied customers. Other purposes include the provision of accurate information of the type desired in a form suitable for use and at the proper intervals, the reduction of errors by making their causes more obvious, and the minimizing of losses from employee dishonesty. An adequate and efficient sales transactions system is the foundation stone of automation in the field of retailing.

Even in a small "family" store the proper system yields valuable benefits. Once established, information in the precise form desired flows smoothly and regularly to the places designated, thus requiring less time for direction and supervision by management. Moreover, efficiency is increased because more work can be performed with less effort in the same period of time.

The importance of carefully planned sales transactions systems is greater today perhaps than ever before. All types of sales transactions are being closely scrutinized because of the developments in electronics and automation which have brought far-reaching changes in methods, devices, and equipment. An essential task for the retailer under present competitive conditions, therefore, is to make a thorough study of the alternative methods of handling sales transactions now available to him, particularly—if his financial resources permit—those handled through the newer point-of-sale registers recently developed.[1] Careful planning should include an evaluation of his present system and may well lead to the adoption of another that is simpler, less expensive to operate, and better adapted to his requirements.

□ Requisites of an effective system

The basic requirements of a satisfactory sales-information system are as follows:

1. Simplicity to insure understanding and conformance. Instructing employees in new procedures is difficult at best and a relatively simple system minimizes this task.
2. Adaptability to the needs of the particular firm. Sometimes retailers, impressed with the success of a competitor, attribute his success to the system he uses. Although a suitable system does influence a store's success, no retailer should adopt another store's system without a survey of his own needs and recognition of possible essential differences between the two stores. A thorough analysis of the needs of the business is essen-

[1] Some of these newer forms of equipment are discussed in a later section of this chapter, "Selecting and Evaluating Sales-Handling Equipment."

tial prior to installing any system, and, once installed, it should be subjected to frequent review and possible revision.

3. Reasonable cost of installation and maintenance. The cost of the system should be reasonable in the light of the benefits to be derived from its use.
4. Provision of prompt customer service. Regardless of the adaptability of the system to the store's other requirements, it must permit satisfactory customer service. Customers want and expect prompt, courteous attention and rapid completion of the transaction once their decisions to buy have been made.
5. Furnishing of desired information quickly and accurately. The importance of having needed information in the form desired furnished quickly and accurately is obvious under today's competitive conditions. Its value frequently depends on its timeliness.
6. Adequate protection of assets. Providing adequate safeguards for the company's assets, particularly cash and merchandise, is an essential requisite of all sales transactions systems. Such safeguards are necessary to afford protection from customers, employees and shoplifters. Some unscrupulous customers attempt to take advantage of stores in such matters as refunds, exchanges, and adjustments. Employees, also, sometimes appropriate cash and merchandise for their own benefit and for the benefit of relatives and friends in the role of customers.[2] The system used should minimize these temptations.

■ TYPES OF SALES TRANSACTIONS

As already mentioned, the retailer's decision on the kinds of sales he will make is a basic consideration in planning the system adopted to handle them. Ideally, this decision should be made even before a store is opened, since it will govern largely the kinds of sales-handling equipment required. This equipment, in turn, may necessitate physical changes in the store necessary to permit its full utilization. In fact, one relevant factor in choosing a particular site for locating a store is the suitability of the building for the activities contemplated and for the types of equipment that will be required. It is easier and less expensive to install equipment as the store is being built or remodeled than at a later date.

In about one-half or more of all retail stores sales transactions are of two basic types—cash and credit. The other stores sell for cash only. There

[2] A common statement in retail stores is that "employees are 99 percent honest—the system must be designed to protect the store from the 1 percent."

are many variations of these two types, however, and knowledge of them is necessary to understand their influence on the procedures established to perform them.

☐ Cash sale

A cash sale is one in which the consumer pays for the merchandise at the time of purchase. It consists of two main forms: the *cash-take* (*"take-transaction"* or *"take-with"*) and the *cash-send* (or *"send-transaction"*). In the former the customer carries her purchase; and in the latter the goods are delivered.

☐ COD sale

The COD transaction, usually treated as a form of cash sale, is one in which the customer pays for the merchandise when it is delivered to her home. The amount collected may be either the full amount of the sale or the balance that remains after partial payment has been made at the store. The latter type of transaction is frequently referred to as "part-pay COD." Some stores make an extra charge for COD service.

☐ Charge sale

A charge sale is one in which the amount of the purchase is charged to the customer's account with payment expected in 30 days. Wide adoption of cycle billing, however, has brought variations in payment dates; while the revolving credit plan permits payment over a longer period than the normal 30 days.[3] As with cash sales, there are two kinds of charge transactions, the charge-take and the charge-send.

☐ Budget, on-contract, or installment sale

Originally limited to sales of high-value items, the budget or installment transaction has been extended to many other types of merchandise. The customer signs a Retail Installment Sales Contract or Security Agreement, promising to make weekly or monthly payments of a specified amount until the total amount of the sale, plus a carrying charge, is paid. The store retains

---

[3] On cycle billing, cf. p. 540, above; on revolving credit, cf. p. 526, above.

title to the merchandise and may repossess the goods in case payments are discontinued.

□ Will-call (layaway or deposit) sale

In the will-call sale the customer pays a percentage of the selling price of an item, usually 10–20 percent, to reserve it for an indefinite period—during which time payments are continued until the merchandise is fully paid for and released. Merchandise purchased under this plan is held in the department or moved to a "will-call" office, where it is always available on customers' calls. The will-call sale is really a variation of installment selling with one important exception—the store holds the merchandise until payments are completed. Many stores have discontinued this kind of transaction in recent years.

□ Discount sale

A discount sale takes place when a discount or reduction from the regular price is granted the purchaser. Such reductions are given store employees and certain types of customers such as clergymen, medical doctors, and dentists, depending on the type of store. Some stores classify sales to employees as E.D. (employee discount) transactions. Although employees may pay cash for their purchases and still receive the discount, it is common practice to charge the goods to their accounts and to deduct the amounts from their wages at monthly intervals.

□ Budget-book sale

The budget-book transaction, resembling both a cash sale and a budget or on-contract sale, is one in which merchandise certificates, purchased upon a definite contractual basis, and often bound together in a "budget book" are used as cash when goods are bought. The budget book contains certificates of various denominations aggregating $10, $15, or $25 in value. The customer ordinarily pays a small carrying charge, as in the case of budget or on-contract sales; and she agrees to make payments for the certificates on specified dates.

□ Exchange sales

Exchange sales transactions occur when customers return merchandise and purchase additional items. They are of two types—even and uneven. An even exchange is one in which the retail price of the goods returned is the same as that of the new selection, whereas in an uneven exchange the price of the goods returned is different from that of the original purchase.

■ RECORDING SALES

When policy decisions have been made regarding the types of sales transactions to use, the retailer is ready to choose the methods and equipment to record and control these transactions properly. This task is not easy because of the variety of procedures involved and the sophisticated electronic equipment continuously being developed to improve the sales-transaction process.[4] In fact, these developments have revolutionized sales-recording methods in recent years.

Typically, point-of-sale recording is achieved through (1) handwritten sales checks—or sales slips, as they are also called—and (2) sales register receipts and tapes. Most small stores probably rely solely upon sales (cash) registers, although those selling on credit make some use of sales checks. Larger stores use sales registers in some departments and sales checks in others, but the typical supermarket, drugstore, and variety store—regardless of size—rely entirely on the sales register. In some stores, however, both registers and sales checks are required in all departments; the sales check providing a "shipper" for delivery purposes and also information for controlling merchandise.

□ Increasing use of sales register receipts

Sales register receipts are increasing in use because the mechanism of the sales register has been improved so much that the receipt can now fulfill several of the functions formerly assigned to the sales check. In fact, current equipment provides for the recording of such a variety of information regardless of the type of transaction that the term "cash register" is being superseded by the term "sales register."[5] Even when charge-send transactions are involved, the sales register permits the recording of the desired data by inserting the sales slip in the slot provided on the register.[6] On the other hand, rising wage rates have encouraged many retailers to forgo some information which could be furnished by the more expensive sales check.

In view of the foregoing, and even though the current rapid develop-

---

[4] Cf. "The Battle of the Cash Registers," *Business Week,* April 21, 1971, pp. 67–68.

[5] The newer electronic equipment is discussed on pp. 604–7, below.

[6] Cf. the discussion on pp. 598–600, below.

ment of electronic equipment may render the handwritten sales check and the sales register receipt less necessary in future years, it is advisable to examine the purposes and uses of sales checks under present conditions.

□ The sales check

Functions and uses The major purposes of the sales check are: to provide a definite record of sales transactions; to make it possible to analyze sales and to allocate them among departments, salespeople, and classifications of merchandise; to furnish a receipt to the customer as well as a record of monies turned in to the cashier by the salespeople; to provide a "shipper" for merchandise deliveries; and to furnish a record upon which merchandise returns and adjustments may be adjudicated.

The foregoing functions are accomplished by having the salesperson write upon each check the necessary data. In large stores, this information commonly includes the date; salesperson's number; department number; the kind of sale, *i.e.* cash, charge, or COD for example; name and address of the customer and/or name and address of the person to whom the goods are to be delivered; and a brief description of the merchandise sold. For transactions other than "cash," additional data such as disposition of the merchandise, *i.e.*, whether "taken" or "sent," and the purchaser's signature are required. In smaller stores much less information is required. To facilitate sales auditing, adjustments, and similar matters, sales books are numbered serially; and sales checks are numbered 1–50 inclusive. A sales check used by one large retailer is shown in Figure 25–1.

It is customary to make out sales checks in triplicate. The original copy constitutes the store's record of the sale and in many stores continues to be used for analyzing and classifying sales, for preparing reports, and for similar purposes. The duplicate or customer's copy accompanies the merchandise, regardless of its disposition. The triplicate (tissue) copy remains in the sales book. Sales books containing these copies are filed and are helpful in tracing and investigating inquiries and complaints. Some stores use specially designed sales checks for sales of "warehouse" merchandise and for telephone orders.

It is advisable to maintain close control over sales books by recording the serial numbers of books issued to departments and to salespeople. All sales checks should be accounted for when the original copies pass through the sales audit department.

Recent changes in sales checks Many changes have been made recently in the forms of sales checks to accommodate the improvements in sales-registering equipment. These newer forms furnish pertinent information quickly and eliminate the necessity of salespeople entering details on

FIGURE 25–1 "Take" sales check

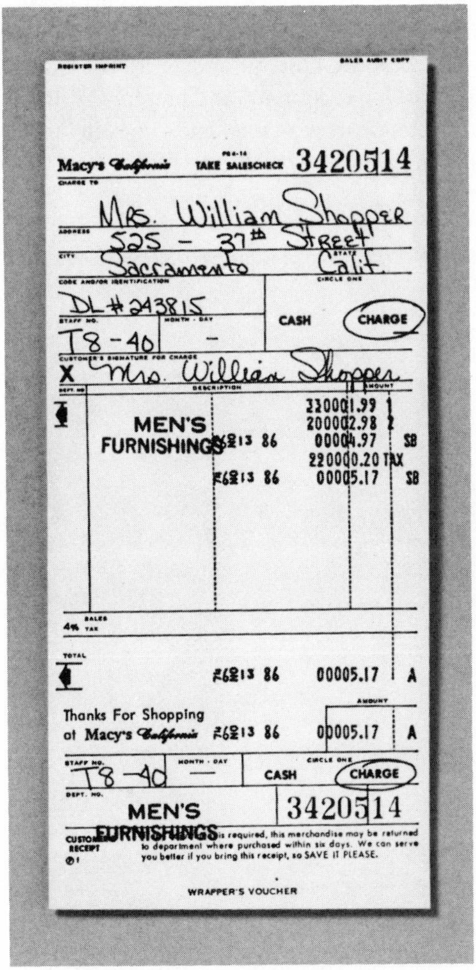

REGISTER IMPRINT

SALES AUDIT COPY

Macy's California TAKE SALESCHECK 3420514

CHARGE TO
Mrs. William Shopper

ADDRESS
525 – 37th Street

CITY
Sacramento

STATE
Calif.

CODE AND/OR IDENTIFICATION
DL # 243815

CIRCLE ONE
CASH CHARGE

STAFF NO.
T8 – 40

MONTH - DAY
–

CUSTOMER'S SIGNATURE FOR CHARGE
X Mrs. William Shopper

DEPT. NO. | DESCRIPTION | AMOUNT

MEN'S FURNISHINGS

3300001.99 1
2000002.98 2
613 86 0000004.97 SB
2200000.20 TAX
613 86 0000005.17 SB

4% SALES TAX

TOTAL
613 86 00005.17 A

AMOUNT

Thanks For Shopping
at Macy's California 613 86 00005.17 A

STAFF NO.
T8 – 40

MONTH - DAY
—

CIRCLE ONE
CASH CHARGE

DEPT. NO.
MEN'S FURNISHINGS

3420514

CUSTOMER RECEIPT

… is required, this merchandise may be returned to department where purchased within six days. We can serve you better if you bring this receipt, so SAVE IT PLEASE.

WRAPPER'S VOUCHER

Courtesy, Macy's, California

the sales check. One firm has devised a punch card form for all charge-take sales which account for over 80 percent of its total sales. Consisting of but a single check with a perforated customer receipt stub, it can be completed in four steps in contrast to the eleven operations required for the tri-part sales check used previously.

Other firms are employing new automatic equipment which permits the recording of all basic sales data on the sales register in a single "pass" across the keyboard by the salesperson. Automation also permits the economical use of separate sales checks for major types of sales transaction. Thus, Macy's of California has different sales checks for these kinds of transactions: "take" and "send" for both cash and charge sales, "COD," and "returned merchandise vouchers" covering cash refunds and credits to accounts. The "take" and "send" sales checks are used both for customers' and employees' transactions and also, with appropriate notations, for "even" and "uneven" transactions. One of the newer printed forms made available by recent electronic developments is shown in Figure 25–2.

FIGURE 25–2 Newer form of printed sales check made possible by electronic equipment
Name of store and customer are fictitious.

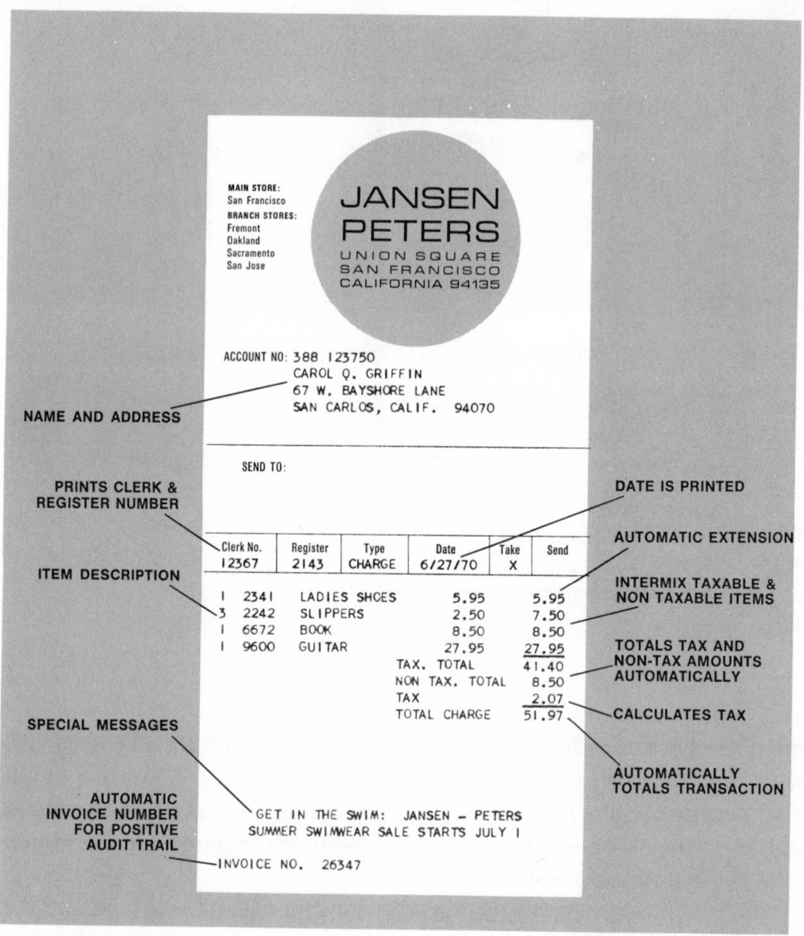
MAIN STORE:
San Francisco
BRANCH STORES:
Fremont
Oakland
Sacramento
San Jose

JANSEN
PETERS
UNION SQUARE
SAN FRANCISCO
CALIFORNIA 94135

ACCOUNT NO: 388 123750
CAROL Q. GRIFFIN
67 W. BAYSHORE LANE
SAN CARLOS, CALIF. 94070

SEND TO:

Clerk No.	Register	Type	Date	Take	Send
12367	2143	CHARGE	6/27/70	X	

1	2341	LADIES SHOES	5.95	5.95
3	2242	SLIPPERS	2.50	7.50
1	6672	BOOK	8.50	8.50
1	9600	GUITAR	27.95	27.95
		TAX. TOTAL		41.40
		NON TAX. TOTAL		8.50
		TAX		2.07
		TOTAL CHARGE		51.97

GET IN THE SWIM: JANSEN – PETERS
SUMMER SWIMWEAR SALE STARTS JULY 1

INVOICE NO. 26347

Courtesy: American Regitel Corporation

■ SELECTING AND EVALUATING SALES HANDLING EQUIPMENT

Major steps involved The complementary tasks of selecting the proper sales-handling equipment and continuing to evaluate its suitability to his needs following its installation, are difficult ones for the retailer. He must carefully define his requirements, investigate the equipment available at a cost he can afford, and, where feasible, thoroughly test the equipment that the investigation reveals will probably meet his requirements. The latter step is most common among large firms.

Defining requirements In defining his requirements, the retailer should first determine the data desired. Much of this information will be dictated by accounting needs, some by the type of store and type of clientele, and some by the desires of the owner or executives. Next, he should inquire how the characteristics of the specific store or department will affect the system and the equipment: Will there be a great volume of small transactions, where the customer is in a hurry; or will there be a more leisurely atmosphere, with a comparatively small number of large sales? Will the business be mostly cash or largely charge? Will the number of salespeople be fairly constant, or will a great number of "extras" be required on certain days of the week or in certain months of the year? Will close supervision of salespeople be required?

Investigation of equipment available With a full understanding of his needs, the retailer is ready to investigate the merits and limitations of the equipment available. Particular attention should be given to the newer types made possible by electronic advancements. But all forms having applications to his sales transactions should be studied. In this process original cost and economy of operation require special study. In some cases several types of equipment may provide the same information, the same control, and approximately the same customer service; but one will cost less than the others. Although cost alone should not be the decisive factor, it should certainly be given constant attention.

Testing equipment Large retail firms, desiring to protect themselves against choices of equipment that do not adequately meet their needs, consider it essential to test that which careful investigation indicates may satisfy their requirements. This testing prior to purchase, and continuous evaluation thereafter, are certain to increase as the variety of equipment multiplies and decisions become more difficult to make. States the Director of Technical Services of the J. C. Penney Co.: "We have a high level point-of-purchase committee that is constantly evaluating these devices and also a man whose full-time responsibility is to keep abreast of such developments."[7] Recently the firm, after testing the product of a well-known manufacturer, found it unsatisfactory for its purposes.

Let us now turn to an examination of some of the traditional types of sales-handling equipment in use. Following this we shall give attention to two of the newer electronic devices being employed in many stores.

☐ Traditional equipment

The two main types of traditional equipment which continue to be widely used are (1) sales (or cash) registers and (2) carrier systems—including the overhead conveyor and the pneumatic tube. As already noted, sales registers of various kinds are universally used in retail stores and significant improvements in them have been made in recent years. But some stores in smaller communities still use overhead conveyors, such as metal baskets and small carriages. In view of the improvements in sales registers to meet increasing demands for accurate, complete data at a moment's notice, manufacturers of pneumatic-tube systems have attempted to meet the challenge by making improvements of their own.[8]

Because of their extensive use, it is of interest to summarize the benefits which sales registers and pneumatic tubes yield to retailers.

Advantages of sales registers The major arguments favoring the use of sales registers are as follows:

1. They provide a fast and efficient method of serving customers who expect and demand prompt courteous service. Registers make this possible by enabling salespeople to give customers receipts and change without a delay.
2. They are sufficiently flexible to permit handling peak periods of activity without confusion. This flexibility also extends to their location, permitting movement of most types of registers to places where needed to accommodate special situations.
3. They are economical in the use of supplies as compared with the use of sales checks.
4. Their use tends to reduce the number of packages delivered. Experience

---

[7] "Penney Studies Other P-O-P Gear Despite G-E Reject," *Women's Wear Daily*, August 3, 1970, p. 18.

[8] In the retail trade, the term "decentralization" is used to describe that method of handling transactions in which sales are consummated locally in departments by means of sales registers. Frequently, also, the term is applied to those instances in which floor cashiers or inspector-cashiers are used. The term "centralization," on the other hand, refers to that method under which all sales—cash, charge, and others—are handled in a central location or locations (1) by means of a conveyor or tube system or (2) when the customer brings all her packages to one point as under a check-out system in self-service operations.

reveals that when a salesperson handles the complete transaction, including wrapping of the merchandise, the customer usually takes the package with her, especially small-bulk items.

5. They, *i.e.*, the newer machines, furnish a record of sales which may be audited quickly and economically, and provide other kinds of information required for improving departmental operations. The National Cash Register Company model 53, for example, supplies the customary receipt and validates sales checks in the conventional manner and also records on tape all basic sales data in computer language. Among other facts, these sales data include the department number, the class of merchandise and unit control number shown on the price ticket, amount of the transaction, and the sales-person's code number. If the transaction is a charge sale, the customer's credit card is inserted in the credit-card reader on the sales register. As the register operates, the account number shown on the card in punch-hole code is automatically recorded on the register's tape in optical-type font that can be read electronically.
6. They provide a speedy and effective method for handling "cash-send" as well as "cash-take" transactions. When the sales check is completed by the salesperson, it may be placed in a slot of the register before the amount of the sale is recorded. Then, through the use of a special key on the register, the sales check is stamped or authorized, thus eliminating the receipt and making it unnecessary for floor or central cashiers to be used.

The sales register and the self-service store check-out In Chapter 6 the development and present-day significance of self-service in retailing was reviewed.[9] At this point in our discussion its relevance relates to the use in supermarkets and other stores utilizing a centralized system of handling sales transactions[10] with the sales register playing an important role. In contrast with the centralized system used in some stores, however, where sales slips may be transported to a central desk by a conveyor or pneumatic tube, the customer brings her package to a check-out stand. Here the checker "rings up" the sale, "bags" the items purchased, and supplies the customer with a sales register receipt. In some types of stores, such as the large discount house, there may be a check-out operation for the "fenced-off" food area and perhaps still another for the drug area, with the remaining departments having their own sales registers. Regardless of the exact arrangement, sales registers are used for the reasons given in the preceding section.

To meet the specialized needs of stores using check-out operations, various sales-register systems, some incorporating devices for issuing trading stamps where these are given, have been devised to simplify and speed up

[9] Cf. pp. 142–47.
[10] Cf. footnote 8, p. 602.

this process. Other developments in check-out fixtures and equipment are taking place almost continuously, but the basic emphasis remains on the training and supervision of the checker.

Advantages of pneumatic tubes Despite many improvements in sales-registering equipment, most of them correlated with increasing automation of retail operations, and despite the growth of self-service and the use of check-outs in supermarkets and other stores, some retailers find it advantageous to use carrier systems. When pneumatic-tube systems—which we shall use to illustrate the general classification of carrier systems—are employed, sales checks are commonly made out to record the sale and are dispatched to a central cashier. The main benefits resulting from the use of tube systems are as follows:

1. They provide a maximum form of control by requiring the making out of sales checks for each transaction, by centralizing the handling of cash by qualified cashiers, and, when cashier-inspectors are used, by providing a check of the goods wrapped against those listed on the sales check.
2. They are particularly suited to the handling of peak sales periods since they can absorb a large number of carriers simultaneously and permit salespeople to do interdepartmental selling in rush periods.
3. They afford greater opportunity for suggestion selling during the time the tube is in transit, thus tending to increase the average sale.
4. They avoid the technical training necessary for salespeople in the use of sales registers as well as the mental strain on salespeople of "balancing out" their cash receipts each day.
5. They require the use of sales checks, thus providing the customer with an itemized receipt of her purchases.
6. They facilitate the authorization of charge sales, because of the ease and speed with which sales checks may be dispatched to the credit authorizer for approval.
7. They serve as mechanical messengers in the distribution of reports, requests, and messages among various departments of the store.

□ Electronic sales-recording equipment

Previous reference has been made to the increase of automated devices in retailing operations, particularly merchandise control, credit authorization, and the registering of sales.[11] Judging by current trends, as evidenced by the equipment illustrated in Figure 25–3, even more of tomorrow's sales-handling equipment will be electronic in nature.

[11] Cf. pp. 316–19, 541–43, and 597–98, above.

FIGURE 25-3 The NCR-280 point-of-sale recorder

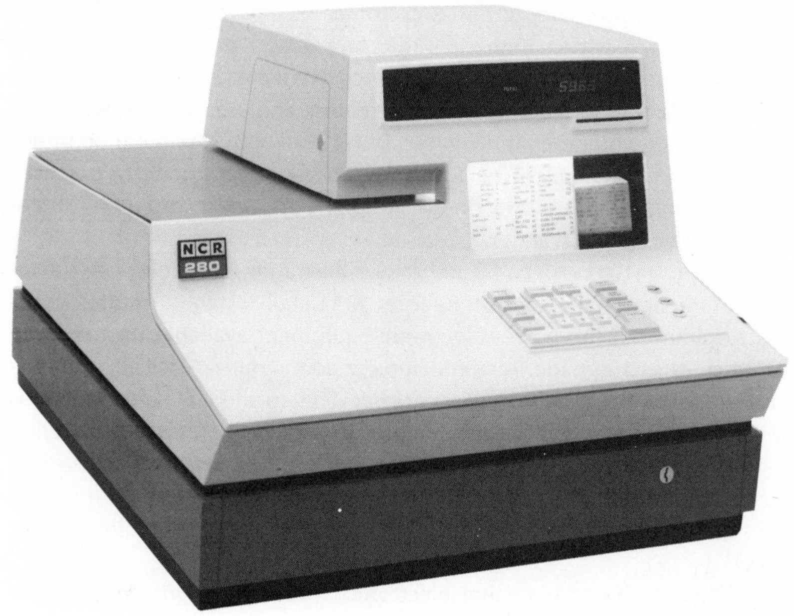

Courtesy: The National Cash Register Company

Actually, the variety of computerized systems now being offered the retailer often leaves him in a state of confusion. This confusion is confounded by the fact that the cost factor is of such magnitude to the merchant that "the wrong choice could put [even the] chain on the brink of bankruptcy."[12] But the confusion and concern of the merchant do not end with the purchase of equipment. In addition to the installation problem and the programming of the operation to yield the desired information in the form wanted, personnel must be trained to operate the equipment properly.

The question naturally arises—why are so many types of computerized point-of-sale equipment being offered to retailers in such a relatively short time? The answer is not difficult: Retailing is the least computerized of all industries and "the stakes" are large, probably in the billions of dollars. The basic aim of the manufacturers appears to be the development of a record-

---

[12] "Point-of-Sale Registers—A Dilemma," *Women's Wear Daily*, January 12, 1970, p. 34. Also cf. "A Point-of-Sale Register Decision—A Look Back and a Look Ahead," *Department Store Management*, January 1970, pp. 20–21.

ing instrument that will ". . . fuse the cash register and the computer into one electronic supermachine that will check credit cards, list items purchased, compute the sale, furnish a customer receipt, control inventory by automatically reordering items in short supply and provide management with regularly updated business and financial statements."[13]

It is not feasible here to describe the nature and use of the newer—and often complex—equipment now in use, but it is of interest to mention briefly two electronic machines in particular which are contributing importantly to the handling of sales transactions—the point-of-sales recorder or counter device and the optical scanner.

Point-of-sale recorder Figure 25–3, illustrating the point-of-sale recorder of the new National Cash Register 280 Retail System, furnishes an excellent example of the newer electronic equipment available for capturing data when sales are made. As the company points out—"Basically, the system consists of point-of-sale recording devices located at selling stations throughout the store and a data collector that writes complete transaction information on . . . magnetic tape for subsequent processing by a central EDP system." The keyboard consists of only 20 keys, 10 numeric and 10 function. Its design reduces the decisions required of salespeople and results in fewer errors.[14]

Another device, the Regitel electronic sales register shown in Figure 25–4, supplies similar information and also checks the credit of the customer within seconds after the account number is entered on the keyboard, accepts any automatic credit card reader or merchandise tag reader, enables shipping labels to be printed, and can handle markdowns, exchanges and returns accurately. Moreover, since this electronic device guides the salesperson through each step of the process and verifies entries, fewer mistakes are made. It may also be used to provide the basic inventory control data desired under any existing system.

Some types of counter devices contain perforated or sensitized tape on which all the desired data are recorded. Periodically, perhaps at the close of business each day or more frequently if desired, these tapes are removed and "fed" into a computer maintained at a central point within the store or mailed to the headquarters of the chain system. It is hoped that this type of counter device will also be of value to the medium-sized retailer, since his

---

[13] Irving Geller, "The Master Machines of Retailing," *Dun's Review*, October, 1969, p. 107. This is an excellent source of information on the newer sales-recording devices made by leading firms. More recent data may be obtained from the companies listed in the Annotated Supplementary Readings for this chapter. *Women's Wear Daily* also features at frequent intervals a page devoted to "The New Technology" which contains current developments of significance.

[14] For additional details cf. the brochure entitled "NCR 280 Retail System," available from any of the offices of the company.

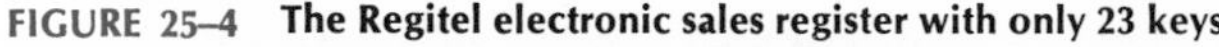

FIGURE 25–4 **The Regitel electronic sales register with only 23 keys**

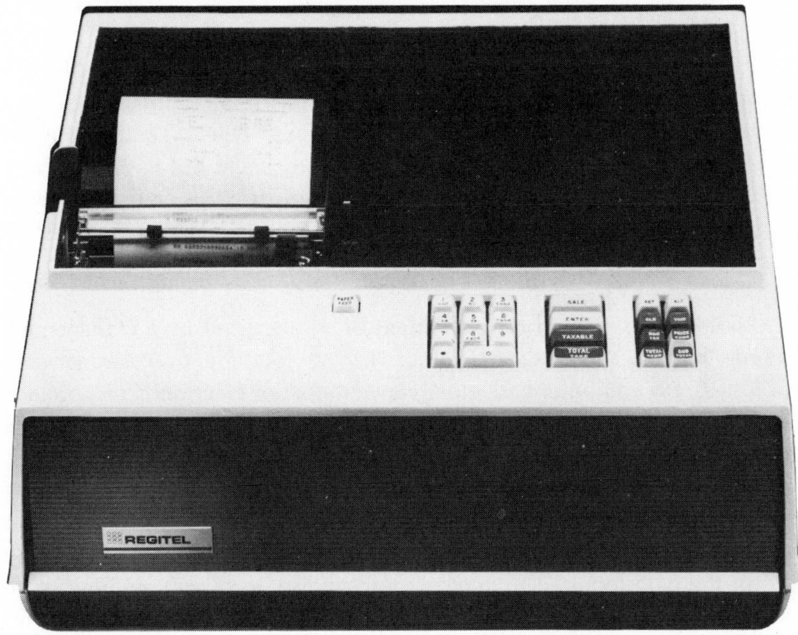

Courtesy: American Regitel Corporation

investment could be limited to the device itself, relying upon the computing centers available on a fee basis to process the tapes for him. Other counter devices are connected directly with the central computer. Obviously, use of this latter type of equipment is limited to the larger firms.

Optical scanner The optical scanner or reader, like the counter device, is another means of activating the computer. It moves rapidly across typed or handwritten letters and numbers, translating them into "machine language" or electrical impulses.[15] So far as sales transactions are concerned, the speedy and accurate "reading" of sales register slips and sales checks by the optical scanner permits prompt forwarding of data to the computer with resultant savings in both time and money. And in supermarkets, where such records are not available, electronic scanners are now being tested which "read" the code numbers of items as they are placed on the check-out counter and automatically calculate the total amount of the sale as the checker "bags" the purchases.

---

[15] "Optical Scanner Speeds up Controls," *Chain Store Age* (Executives Edition), May 1970, pp. E76–81.

□ Final comments on choice of equipment

All types of equipment for handling sales transactions are used by different kinds of stores and are providing satisfactory service. Sometimes complaints and arguments for or against a particular type of equipment are based on prejudice, on personal preference and belief not based on facts, and on experience with poorly operated equipment. Frequently, the equipment is blamed for poor service when the particular model or type does not meet the store's needs; and equipment may be blamed when the layout is at fault.

Poor service blamed on equipment often is caused by a management attitude of cost-consciousness rather than an attitude of customer-consciousness. No equipment, whether conventional or electronic, can provide satisfactory service unless it is properly selected, operated by knowledgeable personnel, and is adapted to the particular needs of the store or department.

Finally, it should be kept in mind that the equipment comprises but one part of the sales transactions system designed to provide fast and courteous customer service at the lowest cost to the store, to protect cash receipts, to furnish the data required to control merchandise, to permit auditing of all kinds of sales, and to prepare the necessary statistical and managerial reports. It is imperative, of course, that the sales transactions system should be related to other systems of the store to provide overall operating efficiency.

■ REVIEW AND DISCUSSION QUESTIONS

1 Explain the meaning, goals, and desirable requisites of a "sales-transactions system."

2 Comment constructively on the statement: "An adequate and efficient sales-transactions system is the foundation stone of automation in the field of retailing."

3 As the proprietor of a drug store in a city of 100,000 people, which of the types of sales-transactions explained in this chapter would you use? Why?

4 Discuss the functions and uses of the handwritten sales check in the recording of sales transactions. Include recent changes in it which are designed to increase its usefulness.

5 In the light of your answer to Question 4, how do you account for this increasing trend toward sales register receipts as opposed to handwritten sales checks among retail stores?

6 Explain briefly the main steps in selecting and evaluating suitable sales-handling equipment.

7 What are the chief advantages to the retailer of using each of the two main kinds of traditional sales-handling equipment?

8 Survey the retail stores in your community or a nearby one to determine the extent to which automation is being used in the handling of sales transactions. Try to learn the major problems that have been encountered and also the benefits derived from its adoption.

9 Explain the meaning, method of operation, and purposes of the counter device or point-of-sale recorder and the optical scanner. What is their relationship to the computer?

10 As a consultant to a retailing organization, what general advice would you give its executives regarding the selection of sales-handling equipment? Be as precise and complete as possible.

PART VIII

Coordination and management

chapter 26

COORDINATION AND RETAILING MANAGEMENT

Management's prime responsibility is to operate profitably. Without a profitable business the retailer cannot provide jobs at competitive wages, engage in research activities designed to improve operations, support community projects, or adapt his policies and practices to a changing environment.

■ COORDINATION ESSENTIAL TO PROFITABLE OPERATIONS

Coordination of all store activities is one essential step to profitable operation. Every retail firm needs some individual, or a very small group of individuals, to keep the various departments or divisions functioning as well-integrated units. Moreover, the whole organization should be continuously reviewed to make certain that it is (1) well adjusted to present conditions, and (2) flexible enough to meet conditions which may exist in the future. The purposes of this chapter are to discuss the factors involved in this process of coordination, explain some of the methods employed in making adjustments to current and future conditions, and indicate some of the problems that arise in connection therewith. Also included are some of management's responsibilities related to developments in management science which have made possible new approaches and techniques in operating retail stores. Moreover, the social responsibilities of retailing management are briefly examined.

□ Adjustment to present and changing conditions

To discover the adjustments called for by current conditions the retailer should possess an inquiring, critical mind and consult associates continuously to find answers to such questions as the following: Are our merchandising and sales promotional activities adequate to hold our place in the community or communities in which we operate? Would it be better, considering the competition of a nearby discount house, to "trade up" in services and merchandise or to reduce prices? Do we have enough salespeople to give the degree of service expected by our clientele? Is it desirable to appoint a fashion coordinator for wearing apparel and one for home furnishings to insure greater uniformity of quality and prices in the offerings of the various selling departments? Are there new techniques and equipment which might help us improve our customer service and increase annual sales? What innovations have been adopted recently by our chief competitors? Which, if any, of these should we adopt to preserve or strengthen our "image" in the minds of our customers? The coordinator must also be responsible for the adjustment of his organization to changing conditions, a difficult task because the rate of change today is constantly accelerating.

As suggested in the first chapter of this book, the outpouring of consumer's goods, the rise in population and in consumer purchasing power, shifts in consumption patterns, and the suburban movement have caused progressive retailers to make many adjustments in location, size of store, hours of operation, merchandise lines, services rendered, promotional methods, and equipment used, to mention but a few. The decade ahead will probably call for even more adjustments. To quote one close observer of the retail scene: "The future has had a way recently of sweeping down upon us and becoming part of today—or tomorrow, at the latest. It is not enough to discern the dimension of change the future will bring, we must also be able to appreciate when that future, as fashioned by change, will arrive."[1]

In brief, only by a continuous adaptation to changing conditions can retail organizations render satisfactory customer service and achieve maxi-

[1] Robert Beyer, "Top Management in the 1970's and Beyond," *Retail Control*, March 1966, p. 56.

mum profits. Indeed, unless the retailer looks ahead, notes the trends, plans *his* adjustments carefully, utilizes the newer management tools available to him, and coordinates his entire organization to effect the necessary changes, he may find that *he* is no longer in business. Retailing history is filled with examples of retailers, both large and small, who have failed at this task.

■ RESPONSIBILITY FOR COORDINATION

Since the function of coordination, or the harmonious adjustment of parts, is necessary and, in view of constantly changing conditions, is a continual process, we should next ask: Who in the retail organization should be responsible for this function? The answer is clear, and it is one concerning which there is little dispute among students of retailing: Coordination is a function of the general manager of the organization or of a small executive committee of two or three men. In practice, one man responsibility for coordination seems desirable; and in the majority of retail organizations the general manager bears such responsibility.

In the large retail organization the general manager finds that day-to-day contact even with the more important activities of the business is impractical; consequently, he must rely upon numerous individuals to whom authority and responsibility are delegated. The personnel manager, for example, must coordinate all activities relating to the employment, training, compensation, and welfare of employees. The merchandise manager, likewise, must assume responsibility for the maintenance of well-balanced stocks of goods in all selling departments. These individuals and others should report to the general manager either orally or in writing as frequently as warranted by the importance of the particular function or combination of tasks over which they exercise control. After all the facts are assembled, however, it makes for speed of action and centralizes responsibility if one man "has the final word."

□ Executive leadership in coordination

Since the human element is so important in retailing, it is difficult to overstate the need of executive leadership in achieving coordination.[2] Unless the personnel is convinced of the ability of its leader or leaders and un-

[2] Cf. the discussion of "The Retail Executive's Personal Qualities," in Chapter 2.

less the leader becomes the driving force of the whole organization, success will be limited at best. As a matter of fact, the quality of a store's leadership determines what the store is or is not. The type of executive who issues orders without explanation, commanding execution from a "scared-to-death" staff, and who strong-arms his way to results without proper consideration of his employees and of the factors that motivate them, is being less frequently placed in positions of ultimate responsibility.

◻ Major tools of coordination

The job of coordinating the varied activities in retail stores is a difficult one. Consideration and understanding of the problems associated with human relationships tempered with an objective and inquiring mind, plus a willingness to assume authority and meet issues as they arise are essential to managerial success.

Some retailers, in assuming the responsibilities involved, rely heavily on what they term "instinct." Said one chain-store executive to the writer: "I believe I run my business by feel. I instinctively know when a thing is wrong and realize its value when it is good, but to sit down and enumerate these things is rather difficult to do." By no means are all those who follow this procedure failures in business; in fact, the executive just quoted built a food chain which was a financial success. Based on many years of daily contact with his growing organization, he could sense trends and make adjustments without being conscious of the thought processes through which he passed.

Typically, however, the retailer needs more than "instinct"; and, fortunately, there are a number of tools available to him in carrying out the coordination function. Four of these tools are especially important—internal standards, comparisons of operating and merchandising results with those of other retailers, the budget, and research.

■ INTERNAL STANDARDS

In common usage, standards are considered to be measuring sticks, the basis upon which something may be judged. In business, however, they are thought of as scientifically determined measures of performance in which "at least two conditions are implied in setting the standard. (1) Standards are the result of careful investigation or analysis of past performance, and take into consideration expected future conditions. (2) Standards may need review and revision from time to time [since they are based] on certain conditions [which] change . . ."[3] Standards constitute valuable managerial instruments. Yet setting standards or goals is not enough. Some form of "control" is needed by which management can promptly discover the quality of performance in terms of these standards.[4]

☐ Types of internal standards

Retailers commonly use three types of internal standards: physical standards, operating and merchandising cost-ratio standards, and unit-cost standards. Each type has its place in coordinating *every* retail organization, although the degree to which each will be used varies from one firm to another.

Physical standards Physical standards are those that serve as yardsticks for quantity factors. The stock turnover ratio is a good example. A retail jeweler may conclude that he operates satisfactorily if his average stock on hand does not exceed his annual sales; a gift shop operator, on the other hand, may find that his average stock should be about one-third of his sales. These stock turnover figures of 1 and 3 are physical standards, relating one physical factor (average stock on hand) to another (goods sold in the course of a year).

Some organizations devise standards for the division of their business among various departments. Such standards, although they involve physical elements, are usually expressed in terms of sales. Thus, a food chain may decide that 55 percent of its business should be in dry groceries and dairy products; 12 percent in fruits and vegetables; 28 percent in meats; and 5 percent in nonfood items. Or a small department store may find that its main floor should account for 60 percent of its business, with the basement and second floor accounting for 20 percent each. Whenever the main floor's percentage of sales falls below this figure of 60 percent, the management is warned that some department or departments on that floor are not operating as planned.

Many other physical standards are used by various retailers. Among supermarkets, for example, "with wages moving upward at an accelerated pace, and at a rate exceeding the advances in sales per man hour, increased productivity is a 'must.' "[5] To determine what was being done to meet this

---

[3] J. B. Heckert and J. D. Willson, *Controllership,* 2d ed. (New York: Ronald Press Co., 1963), pp. 157–58.

[4] On the relationship of performance to objectives cf. "Management by Objectives," pp. 637–38, below.

[5] "Unit Productivity Standards," *The Super Market Industry Speaks 1970* (Chicago: Super Market Institute, 1970), p. 31.

problem, the Super Market Institute queried its members regarding how extensively four specified unit productivity standards of work performance were being used "to evaluate the productivity and efficiency of their store personnel beyond the universally used measure of wage percentage . . . and the widely used measure of sales per man hour." Of the four standards, dollars checked-out per man hour was employed by 56 percent of the companies, cases stocked per man hour by 19 percent, cases price-marked per man hour by 11 percent, and cases unloaded per man hour by 11 percent.[6]

Operating and merchandising cost-ratio standards Operating and merchandising cost ratios are in wider use than either of the other kinds of standards. These standards merely relate particular costs of retailing—rent, wages, advertising, taxes, and insurance—and the merchandising results achieved in a given period to total retail sales. For example, in chain store operations a standard relating rent to expected sales is of the utmost importance in locating a new store. Knowing that in cities comparable in size to the one under consideration, rent does not exceed 5 (or 2, or 4, depending upon the kind of business) percent of sales, estimates of sales for each of several possible locations can be made and the corresponding rents asked can be expressed as a percentage of the estimated dollar sales. If it does not seem possible to achieve a ratio as low as 5 percent in any of the locations, there must be some compensating advantage in having a location in this city, or a lease will not be considered. One food chain has classified all cities in its operating area according to population, using intervals of 500 people, and has set up rent standards for each population class. These standards are religiously applied in deciding where to establish new stores; the end result is that the firm has experienced exceptionally good results in its store expansion campaign.

As another example of the use of operating cost-ratio standards, it is common practice for retail stores to compare their results with those of "typical" stores operating under comparable conditions. These typical figures are available from a variety of retail trade associations and from such publications as the *Progressive Grocer* and the *Hardware Retailer*.

Unit-cost standards Some operators make considerable use of unit-cost standards, that is, standards which set forth the cost of performing a specific act. Frequently the standard for wrapping is of this variety, the department store calculating that its cost of gift wrapping during the Christmas season should be $0.35 per package; its wage cost per average sale should be $0.50; its delivery cost per package, $1.25; and its cost per prospective employee interviewed, $5.00.

---

[6] *Ibid.*

☐ Using internal standards

Establishing standards Most retailers use standards based on their past experience. The variety chain which adopted a standard of 4 percent of sales for rent did so because its past operations had proved profitable when this 4 percent figure was obtained. This procedure was also used by the firm in deciding that its wage cost for salespeople should not exceed 12 percent of sales since a study of company records revealed that such a figure was both obtainable and profitable.

Considerable care should be exercised in establishing standards. To illustrate: Two authorities have suggested five steps in setting effective cost standards, as follows:

1. Classify the costs according to functions and activities expressive of individual responsibility.
2. Select units or bases of measurement through which the standards can be expressed.
3. Analyze past experience relative to the cost of the functions and specific activities involved with a view to selecting the best experience and indications as to the best procedure.
4. Consider the effect on costs of expected changes in internal conditions and of the sales program as planned.
5. Summarize the judgment of those . . . whose experience and training qualify them to judge the measures of satisfactory performance.[7]

Standards not applicable in all areas It is not possible, of course, to set up objective standards for all areas in which the retailer is interested. For such matters as the courtesy with which his salespeople treat customers, the quality of wrapping done by the personnel performing this task, and the honesty of his employees, the retailer has to rely on such devices as his own observation, complaints of customers, and reports of hired shoppers. Yet standards can be devised for so many important matters that they become an essential device in the successful coordination of retail activities.

Written standards advisable Too many merchants (especially small ones), decide to set standards, and then fail to put them in writing. As a result, the standards are seldom used. Without a close examination of his written yardsticks, the retailer may, for instance, minimize the effects on profitable operation if his wage ratio exceeds his standard. In other words, if standards are to fulfill the purposes for which they are intended, they should be in written form, compared with actual results, and prompt action initiated when significant differences are revealed.

---

[7] Heckert and Willson, *op. cit.*, pp. 240–41.

COMPARISON OF RESULTS WITH THOSE OF OTHER RETAILERS

The second major tool of coordination for the retailer is the comparison of his operating and merchandising results with those of comparable retailers. Perhaps he is trying to run his store with poorly-trained employees, a fact that would be reflected in comparatively low sales per salesperson, a high returned goods ratio, and a low ratio of actual buyers to the number of people entering the store. Or perhaps he is not advertising enough—a situation reflected in a low advertising ratio and stationary or declining sales as compared with other retailers. Direct comparisons are needed to detect unfavorable trends and enable management to adopt measures to correct them. Illustrations of the comparisons made possible are found in the detailed financial and operating data published by such organizations as the Controllers Congress of the National Retail Merchants Association for both department stores and specialty stores as illustrated for the former in Table 26–1, and by Dun & Bradstreet, Inc., for several kinds of stores presented in Table 26–2.

To cite one further example, among hardware retailers the average net profit before taxes in 1969 was but 2.25 percent of sales; yet one-third of those reporting had earnings of 7.35 percent.[8] If the hardware retailer com-

TABLE 26–1

Selected operating results for department stores with annual sales of \$5–\$10 million in 1967, 1968, and 1969

Item	1969	1968	1967
Net total company sales—percent change this year/last year	4.1	4.0	5.1
Average gross sale (\$)	6.67	6.07	6.31
Gross margin*	39.10	38.24	37.90
Net operating expenses*	32.11	32.48	31.85
Pre-tax earnings*	4.11	3.37	4.01

* Percent of sales. Pre-tax earnings represent income from merchandising operations adjusted for net other income or deductions but before federal income taxes.

Source: Jay Scher, *Financial and Operating Results of Department and Specialty Stores in 1969* (New York: National Retail Merchants Association, Controllers' Congress, 1970), p. 23.

[8] *Management Report—A Report of Retail Hardware Store Experience—1969* (Indianapolis: National Retail Hardware Association, 1970), pp. 8, 18.

TABLE 26–2

Median financial ratios in selected lines of retail trade, 1970

Lines of retail trade	Current assets to current debt (times)	Current debt to tangible net worth (percent)	Inventory to net working capital (percent)	Net profit on net sales (percent)	Net Profit on net working capital (percent)
Clothing and furnishings, men's and boys'	2.84	57.9	94.2	0.60	7.29
Department stores	2.82	40.7	80.2	1.91	7.69
Discount stores	1.87	88.1	157.9	1.63	15.67
Furniture	2.81	52.4	63.0	2.22	6.46
Groceries	1.66	58.3	136.1	0.99	23.12
Hardware	3.81	25.3	82.7	2.52	8.80
Jewelers	3.09	36.0	82.4	2.98	6.88
Lumber and other building materials	3.03	37.1	69.8	1.43	6.19
Shoe stores	3.52	33.2	102.3	2.10	7.55
Women's ready-to-wear stores	2.38	54.5	71.1	1.86	9.98

Source: "The Ratios of Retailing," *Dun's*, September 1971, p. 77.

pares his own experience with that of stores in both groups he will obtain valuable information concerning points of strength and weakness in his operations.

□ Some sources of comparative data

In addition to the sources just mentioned, many others are available to the retailer. Only a few need be mentioned. The United States Department of Commerce releases information from time to time on such matters as credit, collections, and monthly sales for several types of stores. The Small Business Administration of the federal government also prepares helpful booklets containing comparative data.[9] And, as noted many times in our discussion, the National Cash Register Company publishes several compilations of expenses and other operating results based on various sources. The annual *Fairchild's Financial Manual of Retail Stores* reports, among other things, capital, surplus, assets, liabilities, and ten-year comparisons of sales and profits for over 200 publicly owned retail organizations.[10] Even more detailed data on a limited number of fields will be found in the reports released by the bureas of business research of such institutions as the University of Michigan and Cornell University. The Cornell data, for example, cover the operating and merchandising aspects of food chains and discount department stores.

At various times the *Journal of Retailing* publishes operating ratios, retail sales, and profits of selected kinds of stores. And for certain purposes—such as determining whether a store is holding a desired percentage of business in a community—the releases of the Bureau of the Census are of interest.

In addition to the National Retail Merchants Association, valuable data are available from many other trade associations such as the National Retail Furniture Association and the National Association of Retail Druggists. *Discount Store News, Chain Store Age, Women's Wear Daily, Supermarket News* and other trade papers are still other sources of information.

In some cases, especially in ownership and chain groups of department stores, it is possible for a retailer to work out a system whereby operating results of various stores are exchanged directly among the operators involved. Thus the representatives of the various stores in groups such as Federated Department Stores and Associated Merchandising Corporation, organizations such as Allied Stores Corporation and Gimbel's, and buying

[9] Cf., for instance, *Guide to Ratio Analysis for Small Businessmen* (Washington, D.C.: 1970).

[10] Also cf. E. B. Weiss, "Retail Statistics Warrant More Careful Inspection from Management," *Advertising Age*, October 6, 1969, p. 76.

offices such as Frederick Atkins, Inc., have periodic meetings at which cost and other comparisons are made.

■ THE BUDGET

The budget is a third major tool used by retailers to achieve an effective degree of coordination of activities.[11] As previously indicated, the steps involved in setting up the budget force the various executives of the store to plan and to coordinate and integrate their activities, even before effort is expended in the actual buying and selling of merchandise. Each official in the organization is given a goal in very specific terms—some in terms of goods to be handled, others in terms of sales to be achieved, and still others in terms of advertisements to be prepared and media to be used—and a definite amount of money is allocated for the attainment of these goals. Day by day, week by week, and month by month, reports on actual operations should be checked against the planned goals.[12] This checking demands a constant stream of reports covering all aspects of the organization's operations: monthly profit and loss statements; daily, weekly, and monthly sales; gross margin data; expense figures; reports on purchases, stocks on hand, and goods in transit; original markups and markdowns by various departments and classifications; turnover data; and others. Deviations from the desired goals at which the firm is aiming are noted by the general manager, and prompt explanations of them are demanded. Only through such action can the full benefits of the checking process be realized.

Because of detailed discussions of the budget in previous chapters,[13] it is unnecessary to devote more attention to it here. Its importance as a coordinating device, however, cannot be overemphasized and it is advisable for the reader to restudy these sections from this point of view.

■ RETAIL RESEARCH

Research, the fourth important tool used to coordinate activities, may be defined as the organized search for, and the analysis of, facts related

---

[11] Cf. J. B. Heckert and J. D. Williams, *Business Budgeting and Control*, 3d ed. (New York: Ronald Press Co., 1967).

[12] As one authority stated a few years ago, "In the modern, progressive business of today, the budget provides the target—and yardstick—for business to measure the efficiency of . . . operations against desired results. Budgeting has been described as precise planning—committing a plan of operations to quantitative terms." L. P. Neely, "Trends in Budgeting and Budgeting Techniques," *Budgeting*, March, 1965, p. 1. Also cf. R. L. Jones and H. G. Trentin, *Budgeting: Key to Planning and Control—Practical Guidelines for Managers* (New York: American Management Association, 1966).

[13] Chapter 14, "Merchandise Management through the Budget," and Chapter 24, "Expense Control: A Requisite of Profitable Operation."

to problems in the field of retailing. It includes, also, recommendations by the researcher designed to solve the problem being investigated and the essential follow-up to determine the results of their adoption.

Currently, many retailers are failing to recognize the benefits that the use of this valuable instrument can yield and consequently use it very little. This situation is especially acute among small and medium-sized independent stores.[14] One might go so far as to say that one of the dominant reasons for the slow progress of many small stores and some larger ones lies in the fact that their proprietors lack the time (or, at least, refuse to take the time) and ability to undertake research.[15] Clearly, it is an important advantage—and, as already suggested, one by no means yet used to its full possibilities—of the large retail organization that it can employ qualified personnel to carry on necessary research activities.

□ Main steps in retail research

Assuming that the problem upon which information is desired has already been recognized and defined, four steps are involved in retail research: (1) Gathering and summarizing the data; (2) analyzing and interpreting the data; (3) preparing a report containing recommendations for improvement; and (4) following up to see that the recommendations, when endorsed by management, are actually put into effect and noting the results of their adoption.

Some large retailers perform all four of these steps in a research department or research bureau; in other stores, only the first two or three steps are handled there, with the general manager taking care of the fourth step. Among smaller firms the proprietor or general manager is usually closely associated with all four steps.

Retail research cannot be carried on effectively unless management is research-minded. Specifically, management must recognize the importance of developing information to aid in making decisions; it should not be so impatient for results that studies are hurried and conclusions lack full support; and it should recognize and appreciate the costs involved. Moreover, research should be conducted by qualified personnel under the direction of one whose experience and knowledge justify management's confidence in his recommendations. Just as essential is the raising of provocative questions for consideration by top management. The qualifications of

[14] For suggestions on the conduct of research in small firms, cf. H. M. Anderson, "Managing Applied Research in a Small Company," *Management Review,* January 1970, pp. 31–35.

[15] Of course, this research does not have to be of the formal type, nor does it even have to be thought of as research by the executive. A good manager can recognize many problems and sense their solution through day-by-day contact with his business.

a good research director are reviewed in a later section of this chapter.[16]

☐ The nature and scope of retail research

An understanding of retail research can best be provided by a brief examination of some of the areas to which it is currently being applied.[17]

Customer research In recent years no subject in the field of marketing, perhaps, has received more attention from social scientists and practitioners than consumer motivation and behavior. Retailers need information regarding consumers as a means of improving their decisions on the goods and services to provide. And they continue to seek ways to create favorable images of their stores and merchandise as inducements to continuous patronage.

Broadly speaking, customer research refers to studies that are focused on customer attitudes, beliefs, buying habits, and motives.[18] It is designed to build favorable public relations, enabling customers to express their views with respect to such matters as merchandise carried, prices charged, and services rendered as well as bring about the changes necessary to better fulfill customers' wants. The actual research is usually carried out by telephone calls, mail inquiries, and personal and group interviews, although a few retailers make use of consumer panels.

A good illustration of consumer research is afforded by that recently conducted by Federated Department Stores. For a specific division of the firm, answers were sought to two main questions: (1) What is our present customer mix (income, age, occupation) and what should this mix be ten years hence? (2) If the division wants to increase its share of consumer purchases among important market segments (such as women working downtown, higher price-line customers, blue-collar customers) what should be done? Among other matters, the study revealed that the division had its strongest appeal to upper-middle income families, a "group expected to grow tremendously in the next decade." Furthermore, the research made it possible "to compute how much added business the store would have simply on the basis of the customer mix of the future as people's income rose."[19]

---

[16] See p. 631, below.

[17] Some of the illustrations were prepared by Robert Arkell and are used here with his permission. For another classification of areas where research is important cf. Frank Mayans, "Research in Retailing," *Retail Control,* May 1966, pp. 33–44.

[18] Cf., for instance, "What You Can Learn about Customers with a Telephone Survey," *Hardware Retailer,* October 1969, p. 88; and "What Stores Do Customers Think of First?," *ibid.,* p. 87.

[19] Mayans, *op. cit.,* p. 36.

Sales projections In our discussion of the merchandise budget in Chapter 14 it was pointed out that "the first step . . . is to plan sales."[20] While some retailers do their sales planning "by guess and by gosh," others recognize that considerable research is necessary to establish reliable estimates. Sears, Roebuck and Co. projects its sales five years in advance, correcting those forecasts from time to time as conditions warrant. About six to nine months prior to a specific selling season (for example, in January for the following fall season), this forecast is "firmed up" for that season.

Product and assortment research Research concerning the products and assortments to handle in the light of expected sales and available floor space involves customer studies as well as a review of information obtained from other sources. In view of the increasing variety of products offered by resources,[21] such research becomes even more essential for profitable operation.

A recent development of some significance in this research area is the formation of a marketing research organization known as SAMI which reports annually on the movement of 68 major groups of grocery products representing some 400 product categories through 67 of the nation's largest distribution centers. In 1971, tabulations during a three-month period covered 3.35 billion units, with a retail sales value of $1.12 billion.[22]

Management research Research having to do with the overall management of a retail organization is illustrated by a study of the responsibility and authority of all key management positions. Such a project may involve a comparison of the organization structure of the firm in the light of defined goals with that of its competitors. Another example is a study of the various reports flowing to top management for its guidance. One study of this type recommended that some reports be dropped or consolidated, that others be added, and that the timing and methods of preparation for others be changed.

Merchandising research This type of research, is concerned primarily with the problem of gathering, summarizing, and interpreting merchandising statistics. It is assuming greater significance because of three main factors: (*a*) the tremendous volume of merchandising data becoming available, (*b*) the mounting complexity of the information required to make valid merchandising decisions, and (*c*) the "speed virtually beyond comprehension

---

[20] P. 335, above.

[21] The number of items handled in A & P supermarkets, for example,—some 8,000 grouped into over 500 product categories—reflects the growing problem of selection by the supermarket shopper. Cf. "How Merchandise Moves in the Modern Super Market," (The A & P Study, Part VII), *Progressive Grocer,* September 1970, pp. 38–62.

[22] For details concerning the results, cf. "Fourth Annual Report on Grocery Product Movement," *Progressive Grocer,* August 1971, pp. 38–47.

by which this volume of data can be collected, transported, stored, retrieved, and processed."[23]

As a specific illustration of merchandising research, one store was on the verge of notifying a prominent manufacturer of men's clothing that his line would be discontinued because it carried a lower markup than competing brands. When the research department found that alteration costs, markdowns, and other cost aspects were lower on the brand in question than on directly competitive lines, however, it was concluded that the lower markup was more than offset by these savings. Consequently, a profitable item was retained rather than discarded.[24]

Advertising and display research A few illustrations will indicate the nature of this form of research. In one store the jewelry department was showing unsatisfactory results. Investigation revealed (*a*) that sales volume had declined; (*b*) that unimpressive unit displays were used with most of the stock in drawers behind the counter; and (*c*) that a competitor, whose volume was rising, had extensive counter displays of jewelry with spotlights focused on them. Steps to improve displays were taken; volume gained 15–20 percent immediately and remained at a satisfactory level. Another retailer made a specific study of direct-mail pieces to be sure the recipients were not those already being reached by the firm's newspaper advertisements. And a food chain has used advertising and display research to test the effectiveness of special displays in the sale of specific food products, to determine how best to group products on the shelves of a self-service operation, to analyze a number of special promotions, and to measure the sales effectiveness of various product labels.

Personnel research Today the significance of the human factor in the success of a business is widely recognized. Yet,

> No part of the productive resources of industry operates at lower efficiency than the human resources. The few enterprises that have been able to tap this unused reservoir of human ability and attitude have achieved spectacular increases . . . management of men should be the first and foremost concern of operating management rather than the management of things.[25]

In the light of the foregoing situation, the importance of personnel research is obvious.

Personnel research covers human relations problems involving both rank-and-file employees and executives. It is a broad and constantly expand-

---

[23] Cf. Robert Beyer, *op. cit.*, pp. 57–58.

[24] For specific studies of product profitability, cf. R. D. Buzzell, *Product Profitability Measurement and Merchandising Decisions* (Boston, Mass.: Harvard Graduate School of Business Administration, 1965).

[25] Peter Drucker in *The New Society*, quoted by Matt Wigginton, "Responsibility in Decentralized Multi-Unit Operations," *Retail Control*, April 1966, p. 38.

ing area of study embodying activities associated with selecting, training, compensating, motivating, and appraising employees at all levels. Research is now underway in many stores to obtain answers to such questions as the following: Are aptitude tests desirable in the selection of employees? What is the degree of correlation between results of aptitude tests and the demonstrated ability of employees under actual working conditions? Is our store competitive in training methods, salaries, and promotional schedules with other stores in the city? How effective is our follow-up when transfers and separations are involved?

Operating research This type of research involves the investigation of problems related to operating activities of the store.[26] It includes such matters as store layout; maintenance of the building; all forms of customer service; and receiving, marking, and warehouse operations. High service standards may be set by top management, but careful follow-up through research studies is essential to determine whether they are being maintained. For example, one establishment, concerned over its high marking room costs, investigated the problem and found that checkers were opening each box of hosiery to determine the total quantity in the shipment. By changing to an outside-of-box count only, and relying upon markers' tickets and the number of price tickets attached to goods to reveal the total figure, costs were reduced and goods moved through the marking room more rapidly.

Systems research The increasing complexity of business, accompanied by the growing demand for prompt and accurate data upon which to base decisions, has generated the need for improved information systems based on such technological advances as the vastly improved sales registers and EDP. And the role of systems in store management is certain to expand still more in the future as advances in equipment technology continue.

The need for research in the systems area is emphasized by an existing paradox. In the words of a public accounting executive: "While the time available for reaction in business [to the urgent need for systems work] is being shortened, the preparation time required in the systems area is being lengthened significantly. With today's methods and . . . level of systems training . . . we can look forward to years of preparation. . . ."[27]

Despite this paradox, the "information revolution" is resulting in an accelerating search for better retailing methods. Systems research will render valuable assistance in this search through developing data concerning customer behavior patterns and preferences regarding styles and prices. It

---

[26] The term "operations research" is often applied to all forms of scientific research in retailing, particularly operational problems and customer studies. We shall use the term in its more limited sense as defined in the text.

[27] Robert Beyer, *op. cit.*, p. 64. This source presents nine basic steps in applying systems planning to the retail organization.

will aid also in evaluating alternative advertising programs and relieve buyers of the trouble of making repetitive and routine decisions regarding staple items. These and other benefits are likely to be accomplished, at least among the larger organizations, through a centralized "Information Management Facility."[28]

Correspondence research Research of this type involves studies of a store's correspondence with its customers and merchandise resources for the purpose of improving relationships with them. By setting up tests and applying results to the store's correspondence, research may also increase the store's reputation and prestige in the community.

Basic retail research As indicated by the foregoing paragraphs, most of the current retail research deals with day-by-day operating problems. Such research draws "upon a reservoir of existing ideas and techniques—psychological, managerial, and technological. It is directed at meeting current competition, but not through innovation; it strives to increase sales, but only through customary inducements; it looks to more efficient customer services, but only within the framework of traditional procedures."[29]

Certainly research on day-to-day operating problems is necessary and needs to be expanded, but there is a growing opinion that more basic research leading to further innovations in retailing, should be undertaken. This type of research might study such problems as the following:

1. What are the predictable changes in consumer tastes, wants, and satisfactions deriving from the single fact that twice as many youngsters are going to college now as did a decade ago?

2. Are our stores properly organized to capture more and more consumer dollars? Do traditional department and classification breakdowns we have lived with for years parallel what the consumer thinks of when she comes in to buy? How can these classifications be flexible?

3. How much do we really know about the potentials of after-hours, Saturday night, and Sunday selling, of merchandising geared to convenience?

4. Have we really thought through the automobile revolution that General Wood (retired head, Sears, Roebuck) foresaw? Are we even now meeting more than a fraction of the customer's needs centering around the auto?

5. Have we given adequate thought to the tremendous field of services of all kinds—insurance, travel, gift shopping, perhaps using our mailing lists effectively to sell the services of other businesses?

6. Have we really learned the full lesson that the discount house taught us about how appliances can be sold more cheaply if one sells them according to clearly defined services or the lack of them?

7. Are we right in assuming that the millions of dollars we spend year after

---

[28] *Ibid.*, pp. 61–63.

[29] H. F. Clark and H. S. Sloan, quoted by Samuel Feinberg, "From Where I Sit," *Women's Wear Daily*, February 14, 1962, p. 4.

year in taking markdowns is really the only way to move slow merchandise? Would premiums, such as the soap people use, perhaps move them faster?

8. Are we keeping close watch on the fact that children are getting bigger in planning our stocks to predictably "popular" sizes? Or are we losing a lot of sales because we do not have big enough sizes—or big enough shoes, for example? Who really knows?

9. What sort of systems and equipment, designed especially for our needs, are we developing to reduce the delays, errors and monumental foul-ups in our so-called customer services, merchandise handling methods, and office procedures?

10. What are we doing to develop simpler, more effective, less costly information and communications systems, to replace the frightful ones we have to live with simply because we have failed to demonstrate how unproductive, misleading and expensive they really are?

11. Who has started an experimental store simply to try out and pilot new ideas? If not, why not?[30]

While some basic research may be carried out by the research departments of individual firms, in university bureaus of research, and through trade associations, further joint efforts by many retailers may offer the best approach. Perhaps the retail field needs a Retailing Science Institute to develop fundamental knowledge and to make its findings widely available.

□ Conducting retail research

It has been pointed out that productive research activities necessitate proper management attitudes and qualified personnel to carry them out. Assuming "research mindedness" on the part of management, where can the needed knowledgeable personnel be found? Shall an independent research agency be employed or shall a company build its own department? In answering these questions the size of the organization, the nature of the problems currently demanding executive attention and the availability of relevant information concerning them, and the research interests and capabilities of present staff members are indicative of the considerations that are decisive.

An independent agency or a salaried research department? It is easy to conclude that an independent agency should be employed to conduct research in small firms and a full-time, salaried research department established in larger ones. In practice, however, this conclusion does not receive wide support. Some large retail organizations maintain that the use of independent research men reduces their cost, since their own research is not continuous. Such a policy allows the firm to employ a research counselor who

[30] H. S. Landsman, quoted in Samuel Feinberg, "From Where I Sit," *Women's Wear Daily*, February 9, 1966, p. 12.

is especially well equipped to handle the particular problem to be investigated, and who has a completely objective point of view. Lacking close personal friends in the company, he can be thorough in his investigation and make the recommendations he considers advisable without fearing that a friend will lose his job.[31]

At the same time, it can be argued with validity that a large retail organization should be conducting research at all times, and doing so through independent agencies is too expensive. Also, a full-time department can acquire a vast amount of information about the firm for which it is working —information on policies, clientele, and competitors—which enables it to do its work in a shorter period of time and with less bother to the executives of the firm.

The advantages of continuous research are so great that many large firms employ full-time research directors on a salary basis. This is true, for instance, in the department store, chain, and mail-order fields. For special research jobs requiring skills that the director or his staff do not possess, or for investigations that directly touch the security of the positions of certain close friends of the director, however, it is probably wise to make use of an independent agency.[32]

Qualifications of the research director Irrespective of whether the research director is independent or a full-time employee of the retailer, he needs to be well trained in the principles and methods of research and to have had experience both in research and (preferably) in retailing. Without retailing experience his recommendations are likely to be looked upon by some of the firm's executives as "theoretical"; and they probably will be less sound than those a more experienced man would make. He should have the confidence of the firm's executives so that they will cooperate with him in gathering data, be objective and thorough in analyzing and interpreting data, understand the current subjects requiring practical research in his company, and have the capacity to raise pertinent questions regarding future plans. Finally, he should possess the abilities to write and to present orally short, convincing reports.

The research report The report made to management should be con-

[31] One very successful retail organization reports to the authors that a shift from a company owned to an independent research organization resulted in uncovering many facts not previously known. Of course, much depends on the quality of the outside researcher; some companies have discovered to their sorrow that the methods of some market researchers leave much to be desired.

[32] Some firms follow the policy of assigning particular problems demanding study to young men in their organizations, especially to young college men. Such a plan enables the employee to acquire a vast amount of information about the company in a short time, gives the company an objective analysis of the problem, and provides an opportunity for the employee to demonstrate his ability to organize and present his findings effectively.

cise and yet complete enough to provide the essential data required to interpret properly the findings. Clearly it should avoid terminology unfamiliar to its readers. Effective organization and presentation are necessary to bring into focus the important conclusions. Since many executives are not "figure-minded," they dislike detailed statistics. They are concerned primarily with the results of studies made, their significance in connection with the problem at hand, and the reasons for and the recommendations concerning future action. These facts should guide the report writer.

Research assignments The research director in the large store should both report to and be considered an "arm" of the general manager, by assisting the latter to coordinate the activities for which he is responsible. Thus, a large number of the projects handled by the research department will originate with the general manager. But if the research director is capable and succeeds in winning the confidence of the various department executives, he will find these executives constantly coming to him with problems. The merchandise manager needs assistance in evaluating the type of sales-recording equipment that will be most helpful in controlling inventories in various departments. The operating manager is concerned with the causes of an increase in customers' returns of merchandise. The sales manager of the automotive accessory chain wants to know how to get better cooperation from store managers in carrying out suggestions from headquarters.

In some organizations, all research assignments originate in the two ways suggested; that is, either from the general manager or from another executive. In contrast, although the approval of the general manager is usually necessary before the actual investigation can begin, some firms allow the research director to originate many projects of his own. There is some evidence that this is being done to an increasing degree. But if this practice is followed, it is essential that the research director be a man of broad background in retailing and familiar with current developments in the field.

KEEPING "CURRENT"

As suggested early in this chapter, all retailers, regardless of size, should keep abreast of changing conditions and adapt their policies and practices to these changes. In the present highly dynamic era this two-fold obligation is difficult to fulfill. How, then, does the retailer learn about the developments taking place so that he may adjust his internal operations to them?

Among small retailers, this knowledge may be secured through the efforts of the proprietor or his chief assistant. A vast amount of information can be acquired by watching competitive developments in the immediate vicinity; reading trade papers; traveling; attending conventions; and talking with salesmen, manufacturers, and competitors.

Even among large organizations executives rely heavily upon these same sources, although in a minority of firms they are supplemented in various ways. The director of research may investigate and report on all changes which come to his attention. Perhaps the firm subscribes to some advisory services which provide forecasts as to inventories of manufacturers, the business situation, and wholesale and retail prices. Or it may employ an economist to keep executives informed regarding external changes and to suggest what might be done in the light of these conditions. The use of such an expert by large retailers seems highly advisable since he is not so close to day-by-day operations that he "cannot see the forest because of the trees."

It should be emphasized that, whether it is formally recognized or not, making adjustments to changing conditions always involves forecasting or projecting operations into the future. Such forecasts are made in the various budgets—merchandise, expense, and financial.

□ Looking ahead on automation

In concluding this section on keeping abreast of changing conditions, stress should again be placed on the area of automation. Since retailing tomorrow may be affected so much by this factor, management has a special responsibility to be informed about it. One authority suggests this responsibility includes the following:

1. Management should become familiar with all the latest developments in the mechanization and automation of retailing operations, including the current status of electronic data processing.[33]

2. It should make a careful evaluation of the company's needs and requirements and the suitability of the available equipment or processes in the light of the firm's needs.

3. Assuming that investigation reveals the need and value of mechanization, make plans for installation of the proper system and anticipate the problems likely to arise. At least two major areas will require study: (a) choosing the activities to be covered such as classification control, control at the item level, accounts receivable, and promotion; and (b) making the organizational changes necessary to carry out the installations.

---

[33] Cf. "Retail EDP Costs to Hit $800 Million," *Chain Store Age* (Executives Edition), February 1971, pp. 17–20, and "Computer Use in Food Distribution," *Progressive Grocer*, June 1970, pp. 159–81. By no means are all retailers advocates of EDP. Although growing in use and yielding benefits to many, its glamour and pretentious promise are losing their luster for some stores. Reports of experience with it in various cities are given from time to time, for instance, in *Women's Wear Daily* and *Chain Store Age*.

4. Scheduling the conversions involved in the application of the new system to the various activities to be included.

5. Review the new installations continuously to discover unanticipated developments in operation and to improve their usefulness as tools of management.

6. Look to the future, constantly preparing to meet the challenges and the opportunities our growing economy will provide. "The stores of the 1970s and beyond are taking shape today."[34]

THE FOLLOW-THROUGH IN COORDINATION

Once again, it should be stressed that effective coordination of retail activities requires continuous attention and follow-through by top management. Far too many organizations have established research departments which have turned out recommendations which management has accepted in principle but failed to put into operation. This reflects bad management besides being costly and harmful to morale. Unless the chief executives are actively interested in implementing the recommendations of the research department, or have good reasons for not doing so at the time of their approval, the department should be abolished, no matter how good it may be. Otherwise, it is just "going through the motions," and needless costs are being incurred.

We have pointed out that one of the duties of the research department is to submit a follow-up report on all of its adopted recommendations. In the smaller store this task is the direct obligation of the proprietor. But regardless of the size of the firm, the follow-up report is so important that it should be made the definite responsibility of someone in the organization.

Communication essential

The "follow-through" aspect of coordination requires an adequate system of communication within the retail organization, since the desired adjustments cannot be made unless the personnel is fully informed regarding their responsibilities. In the small store the proprietor can inform his employees either individually or in a group of the plans he has in mind. In larger ones, however, contacts between proprietor and employee becomes less frequent and a more formal communication arrangement is necessary. Meetings should be scheduled; and written statements of plans and the reasons for them should be disseminated at appropriate times.

The task of communication is especially difficult for the chain store organization with widely scattered units. Although also relying heavily upon written material, such firms as J. C. Penney Company still like to have their

---

[34] Robert Beyer, *op. cit.*, p. 65.

people "talk things over." To this end, planned meetings are held throughout the organization: the headquarters operating committee of seven key executives meeting twice a week; all zone managers as a group coming to the New York headquarters several times a year and for a period of a week once a year, together with all district managers; district managers gathering each week with their zone manager; store managers being visited in their stores periodically by their district manager and meeting once a quarter with him in a group; and, finally, each store manager consulting daily with his staff.

In addition, management conventions are held every three or four years at leading eastern and western resort centers. In 1970 two of these were held with some 4,000 executives and their wives—a few hundred at a time—attending for a two-day period. Corporate officers were present throughout. Summaries of the meetings are placed on film and video tape and also in written form for distribution to managerial personnel at lower levels.

Although communication has been strengthened by these meetings and others, W. M. Batten, Penney's Board Chairman, still remains dissatisfied. Recently he stated: "Despite efforts considerably more comprehensive than a few years ago, communications is one of the biggest areas still needing improvement. Problems of trying to keep people tuned in is a monumental task. We're not satisfied that people are listening and understanding."[35]

It is evident that effective communication is an essential ingredient of coordination and profitable management in retailing. Vital in its implementation, however, is recognition of the fact that communication is a "two-way street." Unless lines are kept open in both directions—from the bottom to the top as well as vice versa—communication will suffer and dissatisfaction exist throughout the organization. All well-managed retailing institutions are ones in which mutual confidence and respect among employees and management have been engendered by sound lines of communication kept open at all times.

■ THE "NEW MANAGEMENT" AND THE SOCIAL RESPONSIBILITIES OF BUSINESS

The "new management" At several points throughout this volume we have mentioned in various stages of detail a number of techniques, types of equipment, and management methods used to conduct and to control retailing operations. Spawned by technological advances and the growth in applications of management science to retailing, these developments have

---

[35] Quoted by Samuel Feinberg in "Penney—Always in Transition," *Women's Wear Daily*, July 30, 1970, p. 20.

included, among others, greater emphasis on analysis of consumer behavior, improved employment and training methods, computerized information systems including such equipment as sales register terminals, credit authorization, and operations research. Employment of these newer techniques and devices, many of a highly sophisticated and technical nature beyond the scope of this textbook, increasingly is being termed the "new management."

Stated more simply in terms of retailing usage, the "new management" refers to those executives in organizations who are well-acquainted with the newer computerized techniques and management science tools and consequently are in a position to apply them effectively. This management, however, even employing the most advanced knowledge and tools at its disposal, should not be thought of as mechanical in nature.[36] Judgments must continue to be made on the basis of all the relevant information available, whatever its source, and in the light of present circumstances and probable future conditions.

Management's primary function always has been, and will continue to be, the production of optimum results with the resources available. Fulfillment of this responsibility requires a skillful blending of all resources—physical, financial, human, and others—varying the mixture as conditions and circumstances warrant.[37] Tough-minded management, new or old, carefully examines the nature and causes of its company's problems, critically evaluates alternative courses of action, and chooses that considered most desirable from the point of view of the company, its employees, and the customers it serves.

Furthermore, it should be emphasized that, just as management decisions are no better than the information upon which they are based, so the productiveness of executives is dependent upon the full utilization of their knowledge, energy, and abilities. If there is anything a retailing organization—or any other business enterprise for that matter—". . . cannot afford, it is to waste the time and talent of its executives."[38] On the other hand, it

---

[36] The former administrator of the National Aeronautics and Space Administration, James E. Webb, warns of this "myth" although recognizing that such knowledge and tools have resulted in accomplishments that would have been impossible otherwise. Cf. his statements in "The 'New Management' Finally Takes Over," *Business Week,* August 23, 1969, pp. 58–62.

[37] For a general discussion of the main "categories of change which will have an important impact on managers" in the future as well as "the salient characteristics of future management," cf. H. I. Ansoff and R. G. Brandenburg, "The General Manager of the Future," *California Management Review,* Vol. 11, No. 3 (Spring 1969), pp. 66–68. Also cf. E. N. Cole, "Managing for Progress in the 1970's," *MSU Business Topics,* Autumn 1969, pp. 7–11.

[38] D. E. Zand, "Executive Defenses: They Cost Plenty," *Dun's,* October 1969, p. 63. Also cf. G. J. Berkwitt, "The Big New Move to Measure Managers," *ibid,* September 1971, pp. 60–62ff.

is a fact of business life that too many companies continue to "carry" executive personnel (and others at lower levels) whose productiveness is minimal. Consequently, one of top management's essential but often unpleasant tasks is the "weeding out" of such individuals, commonly known as "deadwood." As one writer points out—"Many a chief executive is discovering that one small spot of decay can grow into full-scale disaster."[39]

□ Management by objectives

One phase of the "new management" philosophy is the present stress placed on management by objectives.[40] Broadly speaking, such a management technique or philosophy refers to the establishment of clearly defined objectives for all levels of management in the light of the goals set for the company as a whole. In other words, management by objectives seeks to improve company profitability through better managerial performance based on a clear understanding of each individual's responsibilities and their relationship to those of other executives.

Before one can manage by objectives, of course, these objectives must be formulated,[41] understood, and supported by company executives. Without detailing them in all areas of management responsibility, let it suffice to note briefly the criteria for effective objectives in any situation. One close student of this subject notes that "good objectives should meet [the following] tests:"

1. The people responsible for carrying out the objectives have had a role in setting them.
2. Senior management has participated in setting the objectives.
3. The objectives have some 'reach' [since] many people work better when there is a reasonable challenge.
4. The objectives are realistic in light of internal and external environmental constraints and trends.
5. The objectives in different parts of the company have been examined to see if they are mutually consistent.
6. The objectives are contemporary [based on recognition of the fact] that they must be updated and revised [from time to time].

---

[39] Cf. G. J. Berkwitt, "Dry Rot: The Most Elusive Enemy," *Dun's Review*, October, 1969, pp. 57–59.

[40] On this topic cf. G. S. Odiorne, *Management by Objectives* (New York: Pitman Publishing Corp., 1965) and also his *Management Decisions by Objectives* (Englewood Cliffs, N.J.: Prentice-Hall, Inc., 1969).

[41] "Simply having an objective doesn't lead to sound decisions. The objective must be stated in terms which lend themselves to measurement of results. When all of the effort has been expended, the logic applied, the measures of results expected provide the only means of specifying a route for the accomplishment of the decision." *Management Decisions by Objectives*, *op. cit.*, p. 24.

7. The key objectives are stated simply [to insure their] being borne in mind constantly by people responsible for carrying them out.
8. The objectives are innovative [especially in periods of rapid change] such as we are experiencing today.[42]

If the tests mentioned are met, management performance in retailing institutions of all types should be improved and better results achieved.

□ Social responsibility of retailing management

In the judgment of the authors, the responsibilities of modern retailing management go far beyond those advocated by many spokesmen for the "new management" and the emphasis placed on "management by objectives." They should (and to an increasing extent do) also encompass a strong sense of social responsibility and community involvement. In fact, states one authority, "it has become imperative for business to undertake social responsibilities on a major scale."[43]

Abundant opportunities exist for retailing's participation in the broad area of social responsibility. To mention a few: employment and training of minority groups to alleviate unemployment and reduce the number of welfare recipients; providing management assistance to minority businesses, particularly in their initial operations; furnishing advice and counsel on consumer credit uses and abuses; and serving on community committees and boards seeking solutions for both urban and suburban problems prevalent in all sections of our country.[44]

That businessmen in general, and retail executives in particular, are aware of their opportunities and obligations and are doing something about them is evident from their widening response. Only three examples need to be mentioned. First, is the formation of the National Alliance of Businessmen, an organization whose efforts have brought many thousands of un-

---

[42] C. H. Granger, "How to Set Company Objectives," *Management Review,* July 1970, pp. 3–5.

[43] W. C. Stolk, Chairman of the Committee for Economic Development, as reported in the *Management Review,* Vol. 57, No. 12 (December 1968), p. 43. Another qualified observer shares this opinion but emphasizes the fact that the "initial and primary responsibility [of business enterprises large and small] is to produce and distribute goods and services in competition, taking full advantage of advancing technologies . . . [They] meet the test both of social performance and of competitive market performance when they first fulfill the requirements of the open competitive market system." E. T. Grether, "Business Responsibility toward the Market," *California Management Review,* Vol. 12, No. 1 (Fall 1969), pp. 40, 41.

[44] Cf. A. T. Demares, "Business Picks up the Urban Challenge," *Fortune,* Vol. 79, No. 4 (April 1969), pp. 103–4, ff. Also cf. the special report entitled "The War That Business Must Win," in *Business Week,* November 1, 1969, pp. 63–74.

employed and under-privileged individuals into productive and rewarding endeavors. Second, is the creation of the Executive Volunteer Corps sponsored by New York City and designed to provide free advice to small businesses of all kinds. Its worthiness is manifested by the fact that during the first half of 1971 more than 3,000 "applicants" received assistance, almost as many as during all of 1970. Third, is the increasing number of executives who have "retired" early or simply resigned their positions to devote their time and energies to the solution of our social and environmental problems.[45] This movement seems certain to grow as our problems increase in number and complexity and satisfactory solutions become more difficult to find.

In closing our discussion of the social responsibilities of business, the following editorial comments by *Business Week* appear appropriate:

> While the effectiveness of [businessmen's] efforts cannot yet be measured, it is clear that the contribution of business to such critical areas as employment of minorities, air and water pollution, and urban rehabilitation has been enormous. . . .
>
> At the same time, it is now clear that far too much was expected—far too fast—by many of those who rallied business to take on new responsibilities in the critical areas. These are not simple problems and they do not yield to simple, cheap solutions. . . . Involvement with the great social problems of our times is not an ordinary business proposition . . . race relations, urban decay, and environmental deterioration are threats to the whole structure of U.S. society, including the U.S. business community. To deal with these problems, the nation must draw on the resources and skills of business. And business has no choice but to make its resources and skills available . . .[46]

■ REVIEW AND DISCUSSION QUESTIONS

1 Explain the meaning of the word "coordination" as a major responsibility of retailing management.

2 Discuss concisely the major tools of coordination available to the re-retailer. Of these tools do you consider any one of particular importance today? Why or why not?

3 Why are operating and merchandising cost standards used more frequently by retailers than other types of internal standards?

4 Obtain from your library or a local retailer copies of the most recent annual reports on merchandising, operating and financial results (known

---

[45] For specific examples, some in the field of Retailing, cf. Isadore Barmash, "Executives Retire to Work," *New York Times*, October 18, 1970, pp. F1-F2.

[46] November 1, 1969, p. 136. Also cf. the special report, "The War That Business Must Win," *ibid.*, pp. 63–74.

as MOR and FOR) issued by the Controllers Congress of the National Retail Merchants Association. Summarize the main types of information given in MOR and FOR.

5 Explain precisely how the budget may be used as a coordinating tool by management.

6 (*a*) Differentiate between applied research and basic research in the field of retailing. Give illustrations of each type.

(*b*) "Retail research should do more than provide recommendations for solving short- and long-term problems. Just as essential is the obligation to raise provocative questions for consideration by top management." Discuss!

7 What is meant by the "business information revolution"? What factors are responsible for this development and what problems has it created for retailing management?

8 What is meant by the term "the new management"? Precisely how does the "new" management concept differ from the "old" management, *i.e.*, "management" as the word has been used for many years?

9 During recent years considerable emphasis has been placed on the importance of "tough-minded" management in American business, including retailing. Explain in your own words what you consider the term to mean. What are the benefits likely to be derived from, and the risks inherent in, such a management philosophy?

10 Drawing on your library and other available sources of information, prepare a paper of some 2,000 words on the topic "The Social Responsibilities of Business under Today's Conditions with Particular Reference to Retailing Institutions."

Annotated supplementary readings

ANNOTATED SUPPLEMENTARY READINGS

Chapter 1

Applebaum, William. *Super Marketing: The Past, The Present, A Projection.* Chicago: Super Market Institute, 1969. This brief pamphlet, prepared by one of the pioneers of food distribution research, traces the development of the supermarket and mass distribution industries, describes corporate strategies, and predicts renewed urban store development.

Crawford, C. Merle. *The Future Environment for Marketing.* Vol. 17, No. 2. Michigan Business Studies, Ann Arbor: University of Michigan, 1969. Professor Crawford discusses the probable influences of population growth, technological advances, changing consumer expectations, evolving channel relationships, and other environmental forces upon both manufacturer and retailer.

Drew-Bear, Robert. *Mass Merchandising: Revolution and Evolution.* New York: Fairchild Publications, Inc., 1970. Professor Drew-Bear, who has been closely connected with the industry, reviews many aspects of discount-store growth and operations.

Edwards, C. M., Jr.; McCarthy, C. E.; McNair, M. P.; and Wingate, J. W. *A Bibliography for Students of Retailing.* New York: B. Earl Puckett Fund for Retail Education, Inc., 1966. This authoritative bibliography is an excellent guide to pre-1966 books and articles on retailing.

Gross, Walter. "Retailing in the Seventies: A Projection of Current Trends."

Baylor Business Studies, No. 79, February–April 1969, pp. 19–31. The major trends considered here include demographic changes, increased public expenditures and their effect on retailing, the growth of the retail giants, and the development of retail conglomerates.

Lowry, James R., and Davidson, William R. *Leased Departments in Discount Merchandising.* Columbus, Ohio: Bureau of Business Research, The Ohio State University, 1967. This survey covers the major aspects and problems of lessor-lessee relations as well as many other facets of leased department operations.

McGregor, C. H., and Chakonas, Paul C. *Retail Management Problems.* 4th ed. Homewood, Ill.: Richard D. Irwin, Inc., 1970. The 42 new and 16 reprinted cases included in this edition are drawn primarily from the experiences of small and medium-sized firms.

The National Industrial Conference Board. *The Consumer of the '70s.* New York: The Board, 1969. This small pamphlet, sponsored by Time, Inc., predicts that the consumer market will change more in the 1970s than during any preceding decade.

Padberg, Daniel I. *Economics of Food Retailing.* Ithaca, New York: Cornell University, 1968. The massive data collections of the National Commission on Food Marketing provided the basis for this thorough and highly useful volume.

Thompson, Donald N., ed. *Contractual Marketing Systems.* Lexington, Mass.: Heath-Lexington Books, 1971. Most of the papers in this thoughtful collection deal with the problems and implications of franchising, although some also discuss significant aspects of voluntary chain organization and the use of contractual systems in industrial marketing. Professor Thompson's *Franchise Operations and Antitrust,* also published by Heath-Lexington Books, 1971, provides a valuable insight into some of the legal and economic problems of franchising.

U.S. Department of Commerce. *Bureau of the Census Catalog.* Washington, D.C.: U.S. Government Printing Office, quarterly with annual cumulations and monthly supplements. Census publications provide a wealth of information about consumer population changes and competitive developments in retailing. Retailers find the *Census of Population,* the *Census of Business—Retail Trade,* and *Current Population Reports* most useful, but many of the other publications listed and described in this catalog are also helpful in appraising market and competitive conditions.

———. *Statistical Abstract of the United States.* Washington, D.C.: U.S. Government Printing Office, annually. As its title indicates, this volume presents a wide variety of economic, demographic, commercial, and social data. It provides invaluable information for forecasting and for appraising market conditions, and also serves as a helpful guide to other sources of statistical data.

Vaughn, Charles L., ed. *Franchising Today.* Lynbrook, New York: Farnsworth Publishing Co., Inc., 1970. This volume, the fifth in a series summarizing the annual International Management Conferences on Franchising at Boston College, deals with franchisor-franchisee relationships, legal controls on franchising and other aspects of franchise management.

Chapter 2

Some of the readings suggested for Chapter 26 are also relevant to this chapter.

Brion, John M. *Corporate Marketing Planning*. New York: John Wiley & Sons, Inc., 1967. Although this comprehensive guide to the major steps in preparing plans and policies is written from the viewpoint of the industrial marketing manager, the retailing student can easily perceive its applications to the management of a retail store.

Bunn, Vern A. *Buying and Selling a Small Business*. Washington, D.C.: U.S. Government Printing Office, 1969. Anyone who is thinking of buying a small retail (or nonretail) business should follow the procedures and gather the information outlined in this book. The Small Business Administration, which sponsored this volume, also publishes a series of useful booklets called the *Starting and Managing Series* that deal with the specific problems of various types of small businesses. Booklets discussing small retail camera shops, hardware stores, automatic vending businesses, service stations, flower shops, pet shops, music stores, drug stores, jewelry stores, swap and consignment shops, restaurants, credit and collection bureaus, and dry cleaning establishments have been issued and additional ones are in preparation. Publication lists *SBA-115A: Free Management Assistance Publications and SBA-115B: For Sale Booklets,* available from the Small Business Administration, Washington, D.C. 20416 and its field offices describe other SBA publications.

Drucker, Peter F. *The Effective Executive*. New York: Harper & Row, 1966. Professor Drucker draws upon his extensive experience as a management consultant to show how the executive can and must learn to increase his effectiveness through careful analysis of his responsibilities and thorough evaluation of his corporate and personal resources.

———. *The Age of Discontinuity*. New York: Harper & Row, 1969. In this highly significant book, the author discusses the managerial challenges that will result from the revolutionary changes of the future.

Emery, David A. *The Compleat Manager*. New York: McGraw-Hill Book Company, 1970. The writer of this thoughtful book suggests ways to combine an orderly, systematic approach to management with the highly personalistic and individual requirements of leadership.

Levitt, Theodore. *The Marketing Mode*. New York: McGraw-Hill Book Company, 1969. This discussion of the marketing concept's role in corporate growth, prepared by an outstanding authority, contains many suggestions of benefit to retail management.

Richards, Max D., and Nielander, William A., eds. *Readings in Management*. 3d ed. Cincinnati, Ohio: South-Western Publishing Company, 1969. The articles in this excellent collection deal with the basic requirements and tasks of management. In one of these, "The Case of the Oriental Rug," **Lazarus, Ralph,** chairman of the board of Federated Department Stores, demonstrates the importance of understanding human relations as a basic element in retail leadership. **Johnson, Robert H.,** "Retail Policies; Their Selection and Application," is also of particular interest.

Small Business Administration. *Profitable Community Relations for the Small Businessman.* Washington, D.C.: U.S. Government Printing Office, 1961. All retailers, as well as students, can profit from this booklet's advice on how to deal with a firm's many "publics."

Uris, Auren. *Mastery of Management.* Homewood, Ill.: Dow Jones-Irwin, Inc., 1968. The functions, environment and tools of "The 21st Century Executive" are discussed in this provocative book.

Chapter 3

Some of the readings suggested for Chapter 2 are also applicable to this chapter.

Kelley, Pearce C.; Lawyer, Kenneth; and Baumback, Clifford M. *How to Organize and Operate a Small Business.* 4th ed. Englewood Cliffs, N.J.: Prentice-Hall, Inc., 1968. Although this well-known textbook is concerned with the problems of operating all types of small businesses, it contains much helpful advice for the person who is considering a career as the owner of a small retail business.

Kursh, Harry. *The Franchise Boom.* Rev. ed. Englewood Cliffs, N.J.: Prentice-Hall, Inc., 1968. Franchising is growing in significance, and this volume analyzes its pros and cons.

McNamara, Anne, and Shakley, Charlann, eds. *Recruiting and Developing Store Executives.* New York: National Retail Merchants Association, 1967. Placement and guidance officials discuss student reactions to retailing careers and recruitment efforts; and store personnel executives describe a number of successful programs for developing managerial trainees.

National Retail Merchants Association. *Your Opportunities in Retailing.* New York: The National Retail Merchants Association, 1970. This 10-page pamphlet, available on request from the Association, points out the merits of a retailing career and discusses some of the requisites for success.

"New Breeders of Managers," *Chain Store Age.* Supermarket Executives Edition, February 1969, pp. 35–37. The Jewel Company (a 360-store chain) has developed a cooperative program with five Chicago-area junior colleges for training in supermarket management.

Rotch, William. *Management of Small Enterprises: Cases and Readings.* 2d ed. Charlottesville, Va.: University of Virginia, 1967. The readings discuss the managerial and financial requirements of small business and methods for building the firm's reputation and clientele, topics of importance for anyone contemplating opening his own store. The cases illustrate problems that can arise in the operation of a small business.

Steinmetz, Lawrence L.; Kline, John B.; and Stegall, Donald P. *Managing the Small Business.* Homewood, Ill.: Richard D. Irwin, Inc., 1968. The authors of this useful text ". . . feel that small business is here to stay and will continue to represent an important force in the business-economic environment . . ." but presents an opportunity ". . . only to those few men who have adequately thought out and prepared themselves for the immensely satisfying occupation of being a small business manager."

Tingey, Sherman. "Managing Supermarket Managers," *Journal of Retailing,* Vol. 45, No. 1, Spring 1969, pp. 59–69. Approximately 75 percent of the store managers responding to a survey said they would select the same type of work if they could start their careers over again; but many managers also complained about working hours, lack of qualified assistants, problems with store employees and/or poor communications with top management.

"Who'll Run the Stores of the 70's?" *Chain Store Age.* Variety Store Executives Edition, November 1970, pp. 40–43. The major variety chains' policies of hiring more academically trained potential managers and promoting them to store management at an earlier age are described in this article.

Wiggs, Garland D., ed. *Marketing, Business and Office Specialists.* Career Opportunities for Technicians and Specialists series. Chicago: J. G. Ferguson Publishing Company, 1970. Opportunities for retailing specialists are discussed on pp. 214–26. Retailing careers are also considered in the analysis of fashion merchandising, automotive and petroleum, hardware, and home furnishings trades. A detailed list of proprietary business schools, junior colleges and universities offering retailing and other specialized business curriculums is included.

Wilensky, Harriet. *Careers and Opportunities in Retailing.* New York: E. P. Dutton & Co., Inc. 1970. The author, vice president of Filene's in Boston, discusses the variety of positions in retailing and the types of training they require. This volume was sponsored by the National Retail Merchants Association.

Chapter 4

Adde, Leo. *Nine Cities: The Anatomy of Urban Renewal.* Washington, D.C.: Urban Land Institute, 1969. This excellent treatment reviews successes and failures of downtown renewal efforts in Dallas, Denver, Detroit, Midland (Texas), Newark, Peoria, Philadelphia, Pittsburgh and St. Louis.

Applebaum, William. "Guidelines for a Store-Location Strategy Study." *Journal of Marketing,* Vol. 30, No. 4, October 1966, pp. 42–45. In this article, 16 fundamental steps for planning and executing store-location studies are presented.

———. *Guide to Store Location Research with Emphasis on Super Markets.* Reading, Mass.: Addison-Wesley Publications, Inc., 1969. The author furnishes valuable guidelines for research in choosing locations. Also cf. by the same author and publisher *Store Location Strategy Cases* supplying excellent material for discussion.

———. *Shopping Center Strategy.* New York: International Council of Shopping Centers, 1970. This volume reviews the problems involved in developing a regional shopping center—the Del Monte Center in Monterey, California—and the views of authorities related to the decisions made and the results achieved.

Bollens, J. C., and Schmandt, H. J. *The Metropolis.* New York: Harper & Row,

1965. The development and problems of the metropolis discussed by the authors explain much of the current shifting of retail locations.

Chicago Economic Development Corporation. *Retail Location Analysis Manual and Retailing in Low-Income Areas.* Chicago: The Corporation, 1970. The first part of this two-part study furnishes valuable guides for choosing desirable locations for small stores.

Haines, G. H., Jr.; Simon, L. S.; and Alexis, Marcus. "The Dynamics of Commercial Structure in Central City Areas," *Journal of Marketing,* Vol. 35, No. 2 (April 1971), pp. 10–18. Two questions are examined in some depth in this article: (1) Do inner-city neighborhoods have the same retail store mix as other central-city neighborhoods? (2) Is exit and entry of store types the same for all neighborhoods?

Hoyt, Homer. *People, Profits, Places.* New York: National Retail Merchants Association, 1969. Stressing management's responsibility to forecast the course of events influencing sales volume and income over a period of 10–20 years, the author reviews the pertinent elements involved in this 104-page volume. For new concepts affecting land values in shopping center locations cf., by the same author, "Land Values in Shopping Centers," *Urban Land,* July-August, 1969, pp. 3–12.

International Council of Shopping Centers and National Retail Merchants Association. *The Independent Retailer and the Shopping Center.* New York: 1969. This joint publication covers all main aspects of the independent operator's relationships in today's shopping centers.

Kane, B. J. *A Systematic Guide to Supermarket Location Analysis.* New York: Fairchild Publications, 1966. Techniques and sources of information concerning location analysis are offered by the author in this guide.

La Londe, B. J., and Smith, Paul E. *A Selected and Annotated Bibliography on Shopping Center Management.* East Lansing: Bureau of Business and Economic Research, Michigan State University, 1968. As the title indicates, this source contains information on all phases of shopping center operations, including location.

McKeever, J. R. *Factors in Considering a Shopping Center Location.* SMA No. 143. Washington, D.C.: Small Business Administration, May 1970. In this brief treatment, major emphasis is placed on the basic determinants of shopping center locations for small retailers.

Mulvihill, Donald F. *Geography, Marketing and Urban Growth.* New York: Van Nostrand-Reinhold, 1970. Professor Mulvihill's discussion of urban development will be of interest to any one concerned with retail location problems.

Scott, Peter. *Geography and Retailing.* Chicago: Aldine Publishing Company, 1969. Professor Scott of the University of Tasmania "states the major general propositions concerning retailing from a geographical point of view and identifies the key problems" requiring exploration today. Site and shopping center considerations are included.

Urban Land Institute. *Parking Requirements for Shopping Centers.* Washington, D.C., 1965. In view of the still-growing importance of the automobile to the shopper, this extensive study of parking needs is important. Its major conclusion: The typical center should plan on 5.5 spaces per 1,000 square feet of gross leasable area.

Chapter 5

Although valuable material on the topics discussed in this chapter is available in book form, particularly EDP, discussions of current developments will be found mainly in trade papers and magazines. Hence, the prevalence of such sources in the listing that follows.

Alexander, Tom. "Computers Can't Solve Everything." *Fortune,* Vol. LXXX, No. 5, October 1969, pp. 126–129 ff. Pointing out that executives have been oversold on computers, the author emphasizes the fact "that the most important business decisions cannot be reduced to neat mathematical terms."

Architectural Record is an excellent source of information on contemporary developments in store buildings and shopping centers. Cf. the illustrated reviews, for instance, in "Shopping Centers," March 1970, pp. 119–32, and June 1970, p. 82.

Carter, B. L. *Data Processing for the Small Retailer.* New York: Macfadden-Bartell Corporation, 1966. In this concise volume, the small retailer will find assistance in determining if data processing can be useful to him.

Chain Store Age. Executives Edition, published monthly. Cf. especially "Chains Cut Use of Store Front Glass," October 1970, pp. E32–E33; Store Planners Issue, Mid-July 1971; "Construction Trends," March 1970, pp. E19-E25; and *Equipment and Construction Guide,* published annually in January.

Freed, R. N. "Getting the Computer System You Want." *Harvard Business Review.* Vol. 4, No. 6, November–December 1969, pp. 99–108. Stressing the fact that ". . . there has been a serious, inexcusable failure to use normal contracting practices in acquiring the use of computer systems," the author offers valuable suggestions regarding the key matters in negotiations and other pertinent factors.

"Store Improvement." *Hardware Retailer,* April 1970, pp. 41–87. After stating the case for store improvement, trends in construction, store fronts, ceilings and lighting, flooring, fixtures, and decor are outlined in various sections of this report. Leasing and community restoration responsibilities are also discussed.

Super Market Institute. *Facts about New Super Markets Opened in 1971.* Chicago, Ill., 1971. Published annually, this study contains a great deal of information which is of interest in connection with this chapter, including store size, parking facilities, building cost and overall investment, and distinctive features of the stores.

"Super Markets of the 70's." *Progressive Grocer,* July 1969, pp. 58 ff. Anticipated changes in supermarkets in the 1970s, including improvements desired by customers, are discussed in this article. Also cf. "The 70's: Bigger Stores—Electronic Checkouts," *Supermarket News,* January 19, 1970, pp. 12–13, for a forecast of developments by executives of leading firms.

Telchin, C. S., and Helfant, Seymour. *Planning Your Store for Maximum Sales and Profits.* New York: National Retail Merchants Association, 1969. This 151-page volume, with a 24-page appendix on fixture details, provides excellent information on all phases of store construction, including the interior as well as the external features.

Chapter 6

Architectural Record and Chain Store Age. Periodically these excellent publications present valuable material useful to the retailer in planning his store. For example, cf. "How Variety Stores Allot Space," *Chain Store Age,* Executives Edition, October 1969, pp. E46–E51; and "GEM'S One-Isle Mall-Type Store," *ibid.,* January 1970, pp. 26–29. A prototype for the new Gallenkamp shoe stores is shown in "Double-Deck Saves SCOA Backroom," *ibid.,* March 1970, pp. 21–23.

Frank, R. F., and Massy, W. F. "Shelf Position and Space Effects on Sales." *Journal of Marketing Research,* Vol. 7, No. 1, February 1970, pp. 59–66; **Cox, K. K.** "The Effect of Shelf Space upon Sales of Branded Products," *ibid.,* pp. 55–58; and **Kotzan, J. A., and Evanson, R. V.** "Responsiveness of Drug Store Sales to Shelf-Space Allocations," *ibid.,* Vol. 6, No. 4, November 1969, pp. 465–69. As their titles indicate, these articles review the importance of shelf-space allotments to sales in food and drug stores.

Harwell, E. M. *Checkout Management.* New York: Chain Store Publishing Corporation, 1963. This guide to the subject, with its broad coverage of the essential factors determining satisfactory operation, continues to be one of the most authoritative available. Also cf., however, "Checkouts Call for 'Revolution'," *Supermarket News,* January 19, 1970, pp. 12–13.

Kollat, D. T., and Blackwell, R. D. "Recognizing the Limitations of Customer Traffic Pattern Studies." *New York Retailer,* December 1968, pp. 3–7. The authors discuss, among other topics, some of the shortcomings of using customer movement in the store as a guide to store layout.

Mauger, E. M. *Modern Display Techniques.* New York: Fairchild Publications, Inc., 1965. This study, although several years old, is "must" reading for the retailer.

National Retail Hardware Association. *Basic Store Layout.* Indianapolis, Ind.: *The Association Bulletin,* No. 27, n.d. An excellent discussion of the basic principles of layout as applied to a hardware store, this bulletin is a good example of the aid which a retailer can obtain from his trade association. Also cf. "Store Layout Important in Reducing Thievery," *ibid.,* December 1969, pp. 40–42.

Payne, G. K. *Creative Display.* New York: National Retail Merchants Association, 1965. Both window and interior displays are considered in this fairly recent volume by the display director of Woodward and Lothrop, Washington, D.C.

Progressive Grocer. "Customer Traffic Patterns Key to Selling Efficiency." January 1966, pp. 47–59. The plans, illustrations, and diagrams included emphasize the need to lay out the store from the customer point of view. Also cf. "Ways to Make Every Foot of Shelf Space Pay Off," *ibid.,* March 1971, pp. 40–49.

Sommers, M. S. and Kernan, J. B. "A Behavioral Approach to Planning, Layout, and Display." *Journal of Retailing,* Vol. 41, No. 4, Winter 1965–66, pp. 21–26, 62. "This article explains the basis for behaviorally-oriented layout and display, indicates how it can be applied, and considers the obstacles involved."

Wyokoff, William S. "How Merchandise Is Presented Is the Key to Proper Store Layout." *Stores,* Vol. 49, No. 12, December 1967, pp. 30–32. The author advocates grouping merchandise in terms of the customer's interests. Related articles in the same issue are: **Copeland, Peter,** "The Boutique in Store Design"; "Bonwit Teller: Shops That Stop You"; and **Breen, Edward F.,** "Ten Fundamentals for Using 'Shops'."

Chapter 7

Bingham, W. H., and Yunich, D. L. "Retail Reorganization." *Harvard Business Review,* Vol. 43, No. 4, July–August 1965, pp. 129–46. The evolution of R. H. Macy & Co., Inc., from the traditional organization with both buying and selling responsibilities centered in department managers to its present structure in which buying and selling responsibilities rest in different hands, is told by two key Macy executives. A number of leading merchants present various views on the separation of buying and selling duties in: "Most Big Stores Are Perplexed on Question of Buyer Duties." *Women's Wear Daily,* April 8, 1969, Sec. 2, p. 32.

Eisenpreis, Alfred. "The Challenge of Being Top Management." *Retail Overview,* Vol. 1, No. 2, June 1968, pp. 4–15. In this penetrating analysis of retail organization, the vice president of a major ownership group comments: "The most productive aspect of an organization chart is the time spent in preparing it. . . . relationships between individuals are thought out and weighed and the contributions to be made by each unit of the firm are considered."

Helfert, E. A.; May, E. G.; and McNair, M. P. *Controllership in Department Stores.* Boston, Mass.: Harvard University Graduate School of Business Administration, 1965. Recent trends in the controller's responsibilities and organizational status are covered in this analysis. Also cf. **Murphy, W. B.** "Enlarged Role of the Financial Executive," *Financial Executive,* February 1966, p. 32 ff.

Johnston, John Wallis. *The Department Store Buyer.* Studies in Marketing No. 12. Austin, Texas: Bureau of Business Research, University of Texas, 1969. The responses to this detailed survey indicate that buyers are assuming a more managerial role, using more qualified assistants, more staff services, and improved data systems. They intend, however, to continue receiving information through ". . . contact with customers, and sales and supervisory personnel . . ."

National Retail Merchants Association. *The Buyer's Manual.* 4th ed. New York: The Association, 1965. In connection with the present chapter cf. **Bond, R. C.,** "Department Store Organization," chapter 2; **Brown, E. J.,** "The Merchandising Division," chapter 3; **Bluthenthal, David,** "The Buyer as Manager of People," chapter 4; **Burnside, Frank,** "Merchandising by Classification," chapter 17; and **O'Brien, A. J.,** "Working with the Branch Store," chapter 31.

———. *Survey of Organization of Single-Unit Department and Specialty Stores.* New York: The Association, 1959. *Organization in Multi-Unit Department and Specialty Stores,* 1961. The Retail Research Institute of the Association summarizes in these two publications the results of its extensive organizational studies.

———. *The Branch Manager's Manual.* New York: The Association, 1968. Parent-branch store organizational relationships are discussed in Chapter 1 of this comprehensive guide and are also considered in subsequent chapters that analyze the various functional activities performed in the branches.

———. *Merchandising Problems in Opening New Branch Stores.* New York: The Association, 1969. This volume reviews various problems incurred in opening and merchandising new branch stores. A helpful checklist is provided.

"Now Retailing Conglomerates." *Chain Store Age.* Executives Edition, August 1969, pp. 31 ff. Many chain-store firms have acquired or established subsidiaries that handle diverse lines; for example, some supermarket chain-store firms also own chains of drugstores or of restaurants.

Samson, Harland E. *The Nature and Characteristics of Middle Management in Retail Department Stores*. Madison, Wis.: Distributive Education Resource Center, University of Wisconsin, 1969. According to this study, merchandising and operating division middle managers are highly involved in decision making and planning, rather than in policy formulation or personnel selection and training. The emergence of a new group of "ancillary" middle managers (in data processing, logistics, research development, *etc.*) is also noted.

Wigginton, Matt S. "Human Attitudes in Modern Retail Reorganization." *Retail Overview* Vol. 1, No. 2, June 1968, pp. 16–29. A distinguished merchant and manufacturer points out that divisional specialization can hamper communications and cooperation in large retail firms. He argues for the creation of "task forces," or committees composed of members of various divisions, to study problems, to share insights, and to improve communications and understanding among the participants.

Wingate, J. W., and Friedlander, J. S. *The Management of Retail Buying*. Englewood Cliffs, N.J.: Prentice-Hall, Inc., 1963. Part I of this excellent book contains a helpful chapter on "Organization for Buying: Single and Multi-Unit Stores."

Chapter 8 and Chapter 9

Craig, Robert L., and Bittel, Lester R., eds. *Training and Development Handbook*. New York: McGraw-Hill Book Company, 1967. The American Society for Training and Development sponsored this volume, described as "the first comprehensive collection of knowledge from leading practitioners in the field of personnel training and development."

Falberg, Howard. *Personnel Management*. Dobbs Ferry, N.Y.: Oceana Publications, Inc., n.d. Although general in nature, this little handbook, prepared by the executive placement director of one of America's major department stores, can easily be applied to retail personnel problems.

Harrington, Michael. *The Retail Clerks*. New York: John Wiley & Sons, Inc., 1962. Although this history of the R.C.I.A. is now somewhat out-of-date, the author's conclusions concerning the mass merchandising conditions that are conducive to unionization are still valid.

Helfant, Seymour. *Training and Motivating Retail Salespeople*. New York: National Retail Merchants Association, 1969. Designed as a guide for executives in stores not large enough to support professional training staffs, this report includes a list of useful films and training publications.

Jucius, Michael J. *Personnel Management*. 7th ed. Homewood, Ill.: Richard D. Irwin, Inc., 1971. This text "reviews the wide gamut of objectives, policies, functions, and attitudes that must be incorporated in a meaningful, organized approach to people problems in the business world."

McEwen, James L. *Appraising Retail Executive and Employee Performance*. New York: National Retail Merchants Association, 1968. Professor McEwen surveyed the executive and employee appraisal practices of 81 department and specialty stores and suggests ways to improve both the evaluation process and the feedback of ratings to the employees.

Morgan, John S. *Managing the Young Adults.* New York: American Management Association, 1967. Retailers, who employ many people in the 18 to 25 age bracket, will find much of value in this discussion of the special problems and methods involved in working with this group.

National Retail Merchants Association. *Recruiting and Developing Store Executives.* New York: The Association, 1967. Personnel executives associated with Carson Pirie Scott & Co., Wm. Filene's Sons Co., R. H. Macy, Inc., and with academic institutions describe executive development programs and discuss the topics indicated in this booklet's title.

Northrup, Herbert R. *Restrictive Labor Practices in the Supermarket Industry.* Philadelphia: University of Pennsylvania Press, 1967. Dr. Northrup raises crucial questions about labor-management relations in supermarkets and seeks to determine whether various labor practices are working against the best interests of the consumer and efficient marketing operations. The history of the Amalgamated Meatcutters' penetration of the retail grocery trades is presented in **Brody, David.** *The Butcher Workmen: A Study of Unionization.* Cambridge, Mass.: Harvard University Press, 1964.

Paul, Robert J., and Bell Robert W. "Evaluating the Retail Salesman." *Journal of Retailing,* Vol. 44, No. 1, Spring 1968, pp. 17–26. The authors found that salespeople who sold a large volume worked harder, spent more time selling and doing stockwork, and organized their efforts more effectively than low volume people, but their personnel evaluation ratings did not necessarily reflect their higher sales volume.

Rosenthal, Richard. "Maintaining a Positive Non-Union Status." *Retail Overview,* Vol. 3, No. 2, Summer 1970, pp. 19–24. During "a decade that may see more union organizing efforts in the retail arena than in the past decades combined," management should strengthen its communications with employees, even encouraging complaints so as to take remedial action, and should avoid favoritism or indiscriminate layoffs.

U.S. Department of Labor. *Handy Reference Guide to the Fair Labor Standards Act (Federal Wage and Hour Law).* Washington, D.C.: U.S. Government Printing Office, 1970. Retailers should secure a copy of this pamphlet, available from the Government Printing Office, as well as some of the Wage and Hour and Public Contracts Division nontechnical pamphlets, including "Equal Pay under the Fair Labor Standards Act"; "Retail and Service Enterprises and Establishments"; "Executive, Administrative, Professional and Outside Salesmen Exemptions"; and "The Age Discrimination in Employment Act of 1967," all available from Division field offices in the major cities.

Chapter 10

"The Computer and the Buyer." *Stores,* March 1969, pp. 41–42. The current and potential effects of computerization on the buying function are examined in this article.

"Consumerism: What Is It Anyway." *Chain Store Age.* Variety Store-General Merchandise Edition, May 1970, pp. 42ff. The present and future impact of consumer organizations on the merchandising and operating problems of variety and general merchandise chains is discussed in this treatment.

Cox, Reavis; Alderson, Wroe; and Shapiro, S. J. *Theory in Marketing.* Second Series. Homewood, Ill.: Richard D. Irwin, Inc., 1964, Part III, "Consumer Behavior," pp. 233–309. These six chapters, prepared by six different authors, provide an excellent background on the retailer's customers.

Dickinson, Roger. "Game Theory and the Department Store Buyer." *Journal of Retailing,* Vol. 44, No. 4, Winter 1966–67, pp. 14–24. Designed "to improve the performance of buyers in negotiating," Professor Dickinson reviews the "findings and arguments of individuals interested in game theory" applicable to buying.

Gold, Annalee. *How to Sell Fashion.* New York: Fairchild Publications, Inc., 1969. So far as our discussion in this chapter is concerned, the author's explanation of the nature and changing patterns of fashion and their relation to store image are of major interest.

Howard, J. A., and Sheth, J. N. *The Theory of Buying Behavior.* New York: John Wiley & Sons, 1969. In this treatment the authors advance four sets of abstractions determining buyer behavior with emphasis on various environmental factors.

Katona, George. *The Mass Consumption Society.* New York: McGraw-Hill Book Co., 1964. In buying from the customer's point of view, the buyer needs the background offered by this study of consumer psychology in an affluent society.

Kolodny, Rosalie. *Fashion Design for Moderns.* New York: Fairchild Publications, Inc., 1969. The development of designs adapted to changing consumer wants is emphasized in this volume.

National Cash Register Co. *Buying to Sell Profitably.* Dayton, Ohio, n.d. In this brief booklet many aspects of buying from the point of view of the small retailer are outlined.

National Retail Merchants Association. *The Buyer's Manual.* 4th ed. New York: The Association, 1965. This volume, consisting of a number of articles written by individuals of long experience in retailing, covers many aspects of the buying function. An *Assignment Project Workbook for The Buyer's Manual,* prepared by **Krieger, Murray,** is also available.

———. *Status of EDP in Retailing.* New York: The Association, 1970. Presenting the results of the association's 1969–1970 survey of EDP practices among its member stores, this report reflects the growing use of electronic data for buying purposes.

———. *Want Slip Policies and Systems in Department Stores.* New York: The Association, n.d. This publication presents the best discussion of want slips from the point of view of department-store operation. Much of what is said has general applicability to all stores.

75 Years of Men's Wear Fashion: 1890 to 1965. New York: Fairchild Publications, 1965. This collection of photographs, sketches, reprints and informative documents on men's wear is of interest regarding fashion changes.

Walters, C. G., and Paul, G. W. *Consumer Behavior: An Integrated Framework.* Homewood, Ill.: Richard D. Irwin, Inc., 1970. Written mainly from the consumer's viewpoint, this book covers both macro and micro aspects of behavior. Chapters 26 and 27, devoted to product and store image, are probably of chief interest in relation to the present chapter.

Weiss, E. B. "Will Fashion Promotion Sell Women the Midi? Maybe Not." *Advertising Age,* July 27, 1970, pp. 43–44. The question of who determines fashion and the importance of the answer is critically examined by the author.

Wingate, J. W. "Revising the Store Image." *New York Retailer,* May 1966, pp. 7–10. The significance of buying policies and practices to a store's image is suggested by Professor Wingate.

Wingate, J. W., and Friedlander, J. S. *The Management of Retail Buying.* Englewood Cliffs, N.J.: Prentice-Hall, Inc., 1963. Although emphasizing the department store, this book is one of the best available on the retail buying function.

Chapter 11

Some of the suggestions for reading related to Chapter 10 are also applicable to this chapter.

"Computer Use in Food Distribution." *Progressive Grocer,* June 1970, Part II. This interesting article covers all aspects of computer application and demonstrates how this machine helps 1,600 retailers make more money.

McDonald, John. "Sears Makes It Look Easy." *Fortune,* Vol. 69, No. 5, May 1964, pp. 120–27 ff. Various aspects of buying (degree of centralization, use of specifications, buying organization, integration with manufacturers) by this gigantic retailer are treated in this typical *Fortune*-type article.

National Retail Merchants Association. *The Buyer's Manual.* 4th ed. New York: The Association, 1965. Chapters 6, 7, and 40 of this volume are of particular interest in connection with merchandise resources.

"Racking up Profits." *Financial World,* February 4, 1970, pp. 20 ff. Significant financial trends among leading rack jobbers are discussed in this article. Also cf. **Derven, R. P.** "Rack Jobbing 1969." *Merchandising Week,* January 1969, pp. 22–27.

Ringler, Bill. "The Top 50 Food Chains." *Supermarketing,* October 1969, pp. 17–22. The importance of buying in the success of these companies is evident from the figures presented.

Stern, L. W. "Self-Sufficiency: A Fixation in Corporate Supermarket Chains?" *Journal of Retailing,* Vol. 42, No. 1, Spring 1966, pp. 18–25 ff. Despite the advantages of vertical integration, the author concludes "that many large national and regional corporate supermarket chains could find that engaging the services of specialty wholesalers would be more beneficial, at least in the short run, than increasing the size of their organizations."

Wingate, J. W., and Friedlander, J. S. *The Management of Retail Buying.* Englewood Cliffs, N.J.: Prentice-Hall, Inc., 1963. In connection with this chapter, cf. Chapter 3, "Resident Buying and Other Associated Buying Activities"; Chapter 9, "Merchandise Resources"; and Chapter 10, "Techniques of Merchandise Selection."

Chapter 12

Crowther, J. F. "Rationale for Quantity Discounts." *Harvard Business Review,* Vol. 42, No. 2, March–April 1964, pp. 121–27. Among other aspects of quantity discounts, the author suggests a mathematical approach to their construction.

England, W. B. *Modern Procurement Management: Principles and Cases.* 5th ed. Homewood, Ill.: Richard D. Irwin, Inc., 1970. The discussion of price negotiations in Chapter 11, and especially pp. 632–34, concerning escalator clauses, is of particular interest.

Grabner, J. R., Jr. "Legal Limits of Competition." *Harvard Business Review,* Vol. 48, No. 1, November–December 1969, pp. 4–6 ff. In the "Keeping Informed" section of this publication, Professor Grabner "outlines the current regulatory provisions on pricing and dealer policies and other aspects of marketing behavior." His discussion of functional and quantity discounts, as well as delivered prices and "equal terms" discounts, apply directly to the terms-of-sale analysis in this chapter.

Grether, E. T. *Marketing and Public Policy.* Englewood Cliffs, N.J.: Prentice-Hall, Inc., 1966. In this 120-page volume, a distinguished student of marketing examines "the interrelationships between marketing and the marketing system and the public policies and governmental regulations that pertain to them in the United States." He makes many pertinent comments on the Robinson-Patman Act, especially on pp. 58–68.

Howard, M. C. *Legal Aspects of Marketing.* New York: McGraw-Hill Book Co., Inc., 1964. Chapter 3, "Price Discounts," offers a good discussion of the Robinson-Patman Act and its relation to various kinds of discounts and allowances.

Kintner, E. W. *A Robinson-Patman Primer.* New York: Macmillan Company, 1970. The former chairman of the Federal Trade Commission gives an excellent analysis of the Robinson-Patman Act in layman's language. His sampling of FTC guides, especially those relating to advertising allowances and functional discounts, are of special interest.

Lynn, R. A. "Is the Cost Defense Workable?" *Journal of Marketing,* Vol. 29, No. 1, January 1965, pp. 37–42. The author answers "yes," but adds qualifications which limit the positive character of his affirmation.

National Retail Merchants Association. *The Buyer's Manual.* 4th ed. New York: The Association, 1965. Written by leading retailers, chapters 7, 8, 9, 10, 11, and 43 have special applicability to the present chapter.

Scher, Irving. *Manual of Federal Trade Regulations Affecting Retailers.* 2 vols. Rev. ed. New York: The National Retail Merchants Association, 1969. This updated volume, prepared as a practical guide for retailers, covers—among other topics—the impact on retailing of the Federal Trade Commission Act and the Robinson-Patman Act. In connection with this chapter see especially Chapters 3 and 5.

Tarpey, L. X., Sr. "The Woman's Day Case and Cooperative Advertising." *Journal of Marketing,* Vol. 29, No. 3, July 1965, pp. 35–9. After analyzing this particular use of Section 2(*d*) of the Robinson-Patman Act to regulate cooperative advertising, the author concludes that the "Court of Appeals turned its back on the bulk of the marketing facts which, if considered, might have changed the decision."

Werner, R. O. "Marketing and the Supreme Court: 1965–1968." *Journal of Marketing,* Vol. 33, No. 1, January 1969, pp. 16–23. The author presents a well-documented review of the Supreme Court's contributions to the changing legal environment of marketing. Pages 16–19 are particularly relevant to the discussion in this chapter.

Wilcox, Clair. *Public Policies toward Business.* Homewood, Ill.: Richard D. Irwin, Inc., 1966. Certain sections of this volume covering various aspects of price competition are of special interest. See especially pp. 129, 210, and 213.

Wingate, J. W., and Friedlander, J. S. *The Management of Retail Buying.* Englewood Cliffs, N.J.: Prentice-Hall, Inc., 1963. Chapter 11, "Negotiating the Wholesale Price"; Chapter 12, "Vendor Services Available to the Buyer"; and Chapter 13, "The Buyer's Order and Vendor Relations" offer excellent supplementary material for the present chapter.

Chapter 13

Alexander, Alfred, and Moolman, Val. *Stealing.* New York: Benjamin Co., Inc., 1969. Explaining the tricks and methods used by dishonest employees and shoplifters, this concise paperback is worthwhile reading, especially for small retailers and their employees.

Barber, Harold, and Helfant, Seymour. *Retail Merchandising and Management with Electronic Data Processing.* New York: National Retail Merchants Association, 1965. This manual, covering the steps in a storewide system, describes and illustrates coding systems, merchandise classification breakdowns, and required reports. It is "must reading" for retailers interested in EDP.

Berenson, Conrad. "Marketing Information Systems." *Journal of Marketing.* Vol. 30, No. 4, October 1969, pp. 16–23. In this general treatment, the need for, benefits of, and the myths and pitfalls of information systems, among other factors, are discussed.

Brown, R. A. "The Systems Approach to Inventory Management." *Management Review,* March 1969, pp. 27–31. This summary relates specifically to retailing in the areas of automatic reordering and organizational change. Benefits resulting from the systems approach are explained.

Codner, Bernard. "Retail Management Systems—The Present and the Future." *Retail Control,* April–May 1970, pp. 3–11. Professor Codner discusses mainly the minimum conditions for a computerized system and the factors involved in its orientation in a particular firm.

Frankenberg, Paul. *Management Information Systems.* New York: National Retail Merchants Association, 1969. Furnishing a concise treatment of information systems in retailing, the writer stresses the usefulness of the data to management.

Kraus, L. I. *Administering and Controlling the Company Data Processing Function.* Englewood Cliffs, N.J.: Prentice-Hall, Inc., 1969. Although not confined to retailing applications, this volume furnishes valuable information on the planning, organizing, and other management problems involved in EDP operations.

Krieger, Murray. *Merchandising Math for Profit.* New York: Fairchild Publications, Inc., 1968. In this very concise treatment of some 95 pages are found definitions of retailing terms and simple formulas for computations of many merchandising relationships such as stockturn, stock-sales ratios, and stock shortages.

———. *Decision-Making in Retailing and Marketing.* New York: Fairchild Publications, 1969. Using the case study technique, this training book includes 90 cases from *Women's Wear Daily* and other sources covering the main areas of retailing management, including merchandise control.

McConaughy, David. "An Appraisal of Computers in Department Store Inventory Control." *Journal of Retailing,* Vol. 46, No. 1, Spring 1970, pp. 3–19. Based on a survey of 15 departments in 5 major stores, the author evaluates the general effectiveness of computers in controlling inventories.

National Cash Register Company. *REACT (Register Enforced Automated Control Technique) for Total Merchandise Control.* Dayton, Ohio: The Company, n.d. Divided into three parts, this booklet discusses merchandise control in general, NCR's REACT system of control for small and medium-sized stores, and the system's use in larger stores equipped with the company's computer systems.

National Retail Merchants Association. *Operating Guidelines: A Buyer's Aid for Better Inventory Control.* New York: The Association, 1969. As the title indicates, this source presents guidelines for improving control over inventories by the buyer.

———. *NRMA Standard Classification of Merchandise.* 2d ed. New York: The Association, 1969. Updated and enlarged, this revised edition provides four levels of merchandise groupings with definitions and coding for all classes and categories. Also, cf., *Putting Classification Merchandising to Work,* which provides helpful suggestions designed to maximize benefits from use of this classification system.

———. *Readings in Modern Retailing.* New York: The Association, 1969. Two articles in this compilation are of interest in connection with this chapter: (1) **Lebhar, Ruth.** "Inventory Management by Classification," pp. 357–67; and (2) **Burnside, Frank.** "The Application of Taxonomy (the Science of Precise Classification) to Retail Merchandise Data," pp. 333–46.

———. *Retail Control.* Published monthly, September through June, by the Controllers' Congress of the Association, this journal contains numerous pertinent articles in connection with the discussion in this chapter. Typical recent ones are as follows: **Bradley, J. G.; Wodarsky, F. K.; and Gundell, P. F.,** "Are You Willing to Accept a Computer's Discipline?" pp. 3–16, January 1970; and **Karp, B. R.,** "Applications of Computers to Retailing," pp. 13–19, February–March 1970.

Scher, Jay. *Department Store and Specialty Store Merchandising and Operating Results of 1970.* (MOR) New York: National Retail Merchants Association, 1971. In this new two volume edition representing a marked departure from previous annual reports, "every merchandising guideline (needed for) a more profitable operation (is) . . . summarized and presented by classification . . . rather than by company figures as presented formerly." Also cf., by the same author and publisher, *Financial and Operating Results of Department and Specialty Stores in 1970* (FOR) containing a variety of information for stores of various sales volumes. Both publications are issued annually.

Smith, S. B. "Automated Inventory Management for Staples," *Journal of Retailing,* Vol. 47, No. 1, Spring 1971, pp. 55–62. The considerations involved in designing an automated system for staple items in a national chain-store organization and the benefits resulting from its adoption are well presented by Professor Smith.

Weiss, E. B., "The Future of Electronics in Coordinated Inventory Management." *Advertising Age,* May 2, 1966, p. 92. Emphasizing the high cost of distribution, Mr. Weiss foresees electronic mutual assistance between the distributing trades and manufacturers.

Chapter 14

The references for Chapter 13 are also applicable to this chapter and should be consulted for further information. In addition, the following will prove helpful:

Gotlinger, John. "Merchandise Management," *Retail Control,* May, 1966, pp. 20–27. An executive of Peck & Peck, New York City, suggests that "the retail controller . . . should take the lead in developing merchandise management programs in his organization."

Houthakker, H. S., and Taylor, L. D. *Consumer Demand in the United States: Analysis and Projections.* Cambridge, Mass.: Harvard University Press, 1970. An analysis of consumer expenditures for over 80 commodities during the period 1924–1964 are included in this volume. In addition, it also contains projections of the demand for each in 1970 and 1975 plus figures covering total consumption and savings.

Jones, R. L., and Trentin, H. G. *Budgeting: Key to Planning and Control.* New York: American Management Association, 1966. Offering practical guidelines for managers, considerable information useful to retail executives is presented.

Kieta, Ed. "Plan Future Profits." *Hardware Retailer,* June 1970, pp. 54–55. This brief treatment illustrates and explains the Profit Planning Sheet recommended by the National Retail Hardware Association.

Meyer, J. S., and Harling, E. L. *Merchandise Control and Budgeting.* 4th ed. New York: National Retail Merchants Association, 1969. A completely revised edition of *Dollar and Unit Merchandise Planning and Budgeting,* this volume discusses techniques and controls governing what, when, and how much to buy.

National Industrial Conference Board. *Managing the Budget Function.* New York: The Board, 1970. Although not directly applicable to retailing, students and retailers will find the discussion of the budget process and the use of this tool in evaluating performance of interest and value.

Olson, L. G., and Olson, R. H. "A Computerized Merchandise Budget for Use in Retailing." *Journal of Retailing,* Vol. 46, No. 2, Summer 1970, pp. 3–17, 88. Designed to "contribute an improved merchandise control technique, including an operational computer-programmed merchandise budget [and] . . . to refine some . . . existing concepts of traditional merchandise budgeting . . . ," this article should be read with interest by students of retailing.

Stults, F. C. "What Every Manager Should Know about Sales Forecasting." *Management Review,* November 1968, pp. 34–39. Although not directed specifically to retailing, the author's discussion of the kinds of forecasts, the anatomy of a forecast, and forecasting tools constitute valuable reading.

The Values of Total System Reports for Retailers. Dayton, Ohio: National Cash Register Co., n.d. The section on "Merchandise Management Reports," the heart of the NCR Total System, has direct application to this chapter.

Welch, D. T. *Budgetary Control and Cost Reduction for Retail Companies.* London: Macdonald and Evans, 1969. Designed specifically as a practical guide for retailers, this concise treatment (200 pages) covers all aspects of the budgeting process including the use of computers.

Wingate, J. W.; Schaller, E. O.; and Goldenthal, Irving. *Problems in Retail Merchandising.* 5th ed. Englewood Cliffs, N.J.: Prentice-Hall, Inc., 1961. In this rather old but excellent volume, the discussions of "How to Control Markdowns," pp. 92–97; "How to Determine and Control Stock Shortages," pp. 104–12; "How to Plan Sales and Markdowns," pp. 179–94; "How to Plan Stock in Dollars," pp. 195–207; and "How to Plan Purchases and Open-to-Buy," pp. 208–15, are helpful in connection with this chapter.

Chapter 15

Interesting and helpful booklets and descriptions of equipment used in receiving, marking, and distributing merchandise are available from many equipment manufacturers without charge. Among leaders in this field are Dennison Manufacturing Co., Framingham, Massachusetts 01701; Kimball Systems (a Division of Litton Industries), 151 Portland Street, Belleville, New Jersey 07109; Lamson Corporation, 625 Lamson Street, Syracuse, New York 13200; Monarch Marketing Systems, Dayton, Ohio 45401; and Rapids-Standard Co. Inc., Rapistan Building, Grand Rapids, Michigan 49500.

Bowersox, D. H. "Physical Distribution Development, Current Status, and Potential." *Journal of Marketing,* Vol. 33, No. 1, January 1969, pp. 63–70. This excellent treatment covers many aspects of physical distribution of interest to students of retailing.

Braill, Philip. "Merchandise Handling." *Retail Control,* March 1969, pp. 25–40. An executive of Kimball Systems, Inc., reports the results of his study of ". . . the third largest expense factor in . . . retailing." Also cf. **Anderson, James,** "Source Marking and Inventory Control," *ibid.,* April–May 1969, pp. 17–24.

Brown, Earl, and Day, Robert. *Grocery Distribution Center Efficiency Report.* Ithaca, N.Y.: Cornell University, 1970. The authors report the results of a mail survey involving comparisons of operating effectiveness among food chain-owned distribution centers.

Locklin, D. P. *Economics of Transportation.* 6th ed. Homewood, Ill.: Richard D. Irwin, Inc., 1966. With transportation playing an ever-increasing role in the problems associated with incoming merchandise, the retailer needs the overall understanding of this field which is provided by this volume.

National Retail Merchants Association. *The Buyer's Manual.* 4th ed. New York: The Association, 1965. Chapter 38 of this reference guide, written by **Wabler, E. H.,** summarizes information on traffic, receiving and marking. Also cf. *Receiving De-*

partment Operations Manual covering all aspects of the receiving function; *Marking Methods Manual* which describes the best methods of price-ticketing some 2,600 lines of merchandise; and *Manual for Reducing Transportation Costs,* which contains numerous suggestions for minimizing transportation costs as well as a list of 805 shipping points for different kinds of goods.

Taff, C. A. *Management of Traffic and Physical Distribution.* 4th ed. Homewood, Ill.: Richard D. Irwin, Inc., 1968. Although dealing mainly with traffic management from the manufacturer's point of view, the reader can also benefit from this complete coverage of the subject.

Chapter 16

Brown, F. E. "Price Image *versus* Price Reality." *Journal of Marketing Research,* Vol. 6, No. 2, May 1969, pp. 185–91. Professor Brown describes some of the non-price factors that cause customers to evaluate a supermarket as "expensive" or inexpensive.

Dalrymple, Douglas J. "Estimating Price and Markup Elasticities for Advertised Clothing Products." *Journal of Advertising Research,* Vol. 8, No. 4, December 1968, pp. 20–25. Professor Dalrymple found that price was highly influential, that size of advertisement had little influence, and that markup percentage had a moderate influence upon the sales response to a department store's advertisements for 54 women's ready-to-wear items. He suggests: "(1) To maximize sales, emphasize low priced—low margin items . . . (2) To maximize profits, stress low price—high markup merchandise."

Dickinson, Roger. "Markup in Department Store Management." *Journal of Marketing,* Vol. 31, No. 1, January 1967, pp. 32–34. Disagreeing with most writers on the subject, the author holds that the use of a rigid departmental markup percentage can be helpful in negotiating with suppliers, is a desirable control and planning device, and can be an effective decision tool.

Friedman, Lawrence. "Psychological Pricing in the Food Industry," in *Prices: Issues in Theory, Practice and Public Policy,* edited by **Phillips, Almarin** and **Williamson, Oliver E.** Philadelphia: University of Pennsylvania Press, 1967, pp. 187–201. The author outlines a number of "rules" that food retailers seem to follow in setting prices, such as selecting prices that end with the digits "9," "5," "7," or "3."

Harper, Donald V. *Price Policy and Procedures.* New York: Harcourt, Brace and World, Inc., 1966. Chapter 7 of this thorough and well-documented, yet highly readable, survey is devoted to wholesalers and retailers' pricing policies.

National Retail Merchants Association. *The Buyer's Manual.* 4th ed. New York: The Association, 1965. Chapter 13, by **Hirschler, F. S.,** "Price Lines and Price Lining," and Chapter 28, by **Sostrin, Morey,** "Merchandising to a Profit," are helpful in connection with the present chapter.

Scotese, Peter G. "The Retail Level," in *Creative Pricing,* edited by **Marting, Elizabeth.** New York: American Management Association, 1968, pp. 104–11. The author, who is chairman of a major department store, advocates a flexible approach to pricing based upon consideration of each item's supply, demand, cost, and competitive situation. Other relevant articles in this volume include: **Cundiff, Edward W.** "The Discount House," pp. 112–20; and **Oxenfeldt, Alfred R.,** "Introduction: The Role of Price and Pricing Reconsidered," pp. 9–26.

Shapiro, Benson P. "The Psychology of Pricing." *Harvard Business Review,* Vol. 46, No. 4, July–August 1968, pp. 14–25. This article contains a well-footnoted discussion of the various psychological factors that influence customer reactions to prices.

Will, R. Ted. "Causation of Gross Margin Percentage Differences between Intrafirm Discount Stores." *Journal of Retailing,* Vol. 46, No. 1, Spring 1970, pp. 66–71. An investigation of differences between the gross margins obtained by two stores in the same chain showed that the most significant causal factors were differences in freight costs and in competitive pressures.

Wingate, J. W., and Friedlander, J. S. *The Management of Retail Buying.* Englewood Cliffs, N.J.: Prentice-Hall, Inc., 1963. Chapter 14, "Pricing and Selling Merchandise Purchased." Pricing objectives, profit margin controls, pricing individual items, price lines, and repricing are among the subjects included in this valuable chapter.

Chapter 17

The list suggested for the previous chapter is useful, in addition to the following sources:

Fletcher, F. Marian *Market Restraints in the Retail Drug Industry.* Philadelphia: University of Pennsylvania Press, 1967. This study includes discussions of resale price maintenance, pp. 54–67, restrictions on price advertising, pp. 224–41, and other price controls in pharmacy retailing.

Howard, M. C. "Fair Trade Revisited." *California Management Review,* Vol. 9, No. 1, Fall 1967, pp. 17–25. In this excellent article, the author traces the causes of the many legislative and judicial setbacks resale price maintenance suffered during the 1950s and early 1960s.

Journal of Marketing. "Legal Developments in Marketing." Each issue of the *Journal* includes this valuable section on legal developments. A subsection on "Regulation of Price Competition" lists and comments upon legal actions concerning resale price maintenance and sales-below-cost laws.

Kiernan, Gladys M., ed. *Retailers' Manual of Laws and Regulations.* New York: Research Company of America, 1971. This manual, revised at approximately three- to four-year intervals, provides an invaluable compilation of federal, state, and local laws affecting retailing, including state resale price maintenance and unfair practices acts.

Knox, Robert L. "To Preserve Competition or Preserve Competitors." *Arizona Business Bulletin,* Vol. 15, No. 6, June–July 1968, pp. 142 ff; "Competition and the Concept of Sales-below-Cost," *ibid.,* Vol. 16, No. 9, November 1969, pp. 227–32. In these articles, Professor Knox criticizes the anticompetitive effects of resale price maintenance and unfair practices acts.

Lynn, Robert A. *Price Policies and Marketing Management.* Homewood, Ill.:

Richard D. Irwin, Inc., 1967. All aspects of pricing are considered in this book. The discussions of retail markdown practices, pp. 230–34, resale price maintenance, pp. 269–78, and other retail price regulations, pp. 304–8, are especially relevant to the present chapter.

Mulvihill, Donald F., and Paranka, Stephen, eds. *Price Policies and Practices.* New York: John Wiley & Sons, Inc., 1967. The articles in this volume of readings discuss many aspects of pricing and two "Approaches to Achieving Retail Price Stability" by **Stern, Louis W.,** and "Appraisal of State Unfair Trade Practices Acts" by **Paranka, Stephen,** deal specifically with topics considered in the present chapter.

National Retail Merchants Association. *198 Ways to Control Markdowns.* New York: The Association, 1957, fifth printing 1970. Adequately described by its title, this booklet continues to be one of the best available on markdowns.

Scher, Irving. *Manual of Federal Trade Regulations Affecting Retailers.* Rev. ed. New York: National Retail Merchants Association, 1969. Chapter 4, "Retail Price Advertising under the Federal Trade Commission Act," and Chapter 7, "Resale Price Maintenance—Fair Trade," provide authoritative discussions of their respective topics.

Solomon, S. L. "Markdowns," in *The Buyer's Manual.* 4th ed. New York: National Retail Merchants Association, 1965, Chapter 25. In this chapter, the former chairman of the board of a major department store comments on the causes, control, timing, and recording of markdowns.

United Kingdom Monopolies Commission. "Recommended Resale Prices." *The Antitrust Bulletin,* New York, Vol. 14, No. 4, Winter 1969, pp. 1019–52. Although this study of the economic and competitive effects of manufacturers' resale price recommendations was prepared by a British government commission, its comments also apply to the use of preticketing and suggested pricing in American retailing.

Wingate, J. W., and Friedlander, J. S. *The Management of Retail Buying.* Englewood Cliffs, N.J.: Prentice-Hall, Inc., 1963. Chapter 14, of this college text discusses various aspects of leader merchandising and markdown practices.

Chapter 18

Aspley, J. C., and Riso, Ovid, eds. *The Sales Promotion Handbook.* 5th ed. Chicago: The Dartnell Corporation, 1969. Certain sections of this reference volume devoted to store promotions, promoting through chain stores, and mail-order selling are helpful supplements to the material in this chapter.

Barban, A. M., and Sandage, C. H. *Readings in Advertising and Promotion Strategy.* Homewood, Ill.: Richard D. Irwin, Inc., 1968. Students interested in the broad spectrum of advertising will find this compilation of addresses, essays, and lectures helpful in broadening their understanding.

Bogart, Leo. *Strategy in Advertising.* New York: Harcourt, Brace & World, 1967. Valuable as a source on advertising in general, the author's comparison of retail and national advertising objectives in Chapter 2 has particular relevance to our review of retail advertising in this chapter.

Edwards, C. M., Jr., and Brown, R. A. *Retail Advertising and Sales Promotion.*

3d ed. Englewood Cliffs, N.J.: Prentice-Hall, Inc., 1959. Although over a decade old, this volume continues as one of the best single sources on advertising and display from the retailer's point of view.

Engel, J. F.; Wales, H. G.; and Warshaw, M. R. *Promotional Strategy*. Homewood, Ill.: Richard D. Irwin, Inc., 1971. Although general in nature, this volume contains considerable material of interest to the student of retailing. Chapters 13, 14, and 15 relating to advertising media, Chapter 17 on pretesting advertising messages, and the section on "Retailers as Promotional Resources" in Chapter 21 are of special value as a supplement to our discussion of retail advertising.

Haight, William. *Retail Advertising for the 1970's.* Lansing, Mich.: Michigan Retailers Association, 1970. In this practical guidebook, a veteran merchant and advertising man provides helpful advice on the planning of advertising campaigns and the preparation of individual advertisements.

Krieger, Murray. *Decision-Making in Retailing and Marketing.* New York: Fairchild Publications, Inc., 1970. In the chapters concerned with sales promotion and advertising, such topics as what's wrong with retail advertising, how J. C. Penney ties displays to the merchandise, and the use of television are discussed.

Mauger, E. M. *Modern Display Techniques.* New York: Fairchild Publications, Inc., 1965. As the title indicates, this book reviews display techniques helpful to the retailer in promoting sales.

National Retail Merchants Association. *Merchandising Planbook and Sales Promotion Calendar.* New York: The Association, published annually. This comprehensive planning tool is designed to provide assistance to large and small retailers in their budgeting and sales promotion.

"Prospect 70's, Retrospect 60's: TV, Radio to Get More Ad $ in 70's." *Supermarket News,* December 15, 1969, p. 4. This comprehensive report covers all phases of advertising, display, and other forms of sales promotion used by food retailers.

Sandage, C. H., and Fryburger, Vernon. *Advertising Theory and Practice.* 8th ed. Homewood, Ill.: Richard D. Irwin, Inc., 1971. Covering the broad field of advertising, the authors' discussions of the preparation and reproduction of the advertising message, the testing of advertising effectiveness, and the advertising organization are of particular interest to retailers and students. Chapter 30 relates solely to retail advertising.

"Special Display: Key Weapon in the Period Ahead." *Progressive Grocer,* May 1970, Part II, pp. 193–200. In addition to listing 13 ways to prepare more effective displays, 15 common errors in displaymanship which can easily be avoided are given also in this article. Also cf. **Selitzer, Ralph.** "Cross-Merchandising of Non-Foods Boosts Volume at Allied [Super Markets]," *ibid.,* March 1969, pp. 130–35. Non-foods sales were increased 30 percent.

Stidsen, Bent. "Some Thoughts on the Advertising Process." *Journal of Marketing,* Vol. 34, No. 1, January 1970, pp. 47–53. The author emphasizes the fact that ". . . advertising is still a long way from being an effective and efficient information source *from the point of view of the consumer* [and that] an information source that does not serve the consumer's purposes cannot possibly be maximally serving the advertiser's purposes." He suggests criteria for measuring advertising effectiveness and develops a research paradigm for analyzing the advertising process.

Whitney, J. O. "Better Results from Retail Advertising." *Harvard Business Re-*

view, Vol. 40, No. 3, May–June 1970, pp. 111–20. With emphasis on the fact "that retail advertising is plagued by waste," the author discusses this waste in four contexts and then focuses attention on its profit responsibility as a sales function. Internal communications are also analyzed.

Wright, J. S.; Warner, D. S.; and Winter, Willis, Jr. *Advertising.* 3rd ed. New York: McGraw-Hill Book Co., Inc., 1971. This general treatment gives attention to retail advertising in the pertinent areas of application, including a chapter on budgeting and media decisions.

Chapter 19

Allvine, F. C. "The Future of Trading Stamps and Games." *Journal of Marketing,* Vol. 33, No. 1, January 1969, pp. 45–52. After reviewing the conditions which led to the adoption and diffusion of trading stamps and games, as well as the recent decline in their use, Professor Allvine concludes that present trends are likely to continue.

Bell, C. S. "Liberty and Property and No Stamps." *Journal of Business,* Vol. 40, No. 2, April 1967, pp. 194–202. Also cf. **Beem, Eugene,** and **Isaacson, I.,** "Schizophrenia in Trading Stamp Analysis," *ibid.,* Vol. 41, No. 3, July 1968; and **Bell, C. S.,** "Reply" *ibid.,* pp. 345–46. Important questions concerning trading stamps are discussed.

A Blue Print for Telephone Selling and **Selling by Telephone.** New York: American Telephone and Telegraph Co., n.d. These two pamphlets provide suggestions for improving selling efforts by those using the telephone.

Dysart, Edward. *How to Sell by Telephone.* Swarthmore, Pennsylvania: A. C. Croft, Inc., 1969. Covering telephone selling in general, the reader will find much helpful information applicable to retail salesmanship.

Fox, H. W. *The Economics of Trading Stamps.* Washington, D.C.: Public Affairs Press, 1968. Professor Fox reviews the trading stamp process from issue to redemption, provides financial details on leading stamp companies, and discusses the impact of stamps on the retail prices of food and gasoline, among other topics, in this well-documented treatment.

Fulop, Christina. *The Role of Trading Stamps in Retail Competition.* London: Institute of Economic Affairs Limited, 1964. This careful study of the economics of trading stamps adds much to our understanding of how stamps contribute to effective retail competition.

Incentive Marketing. A monthly publication, formerly *Premium Merchandising,* this journal covers current developments in the broad areas suggested by its title.

Margulies, W. P. "Plan Packages to Fit Their Retail Environment." *Advertising Age,* February 2, 1970, pp. 51–53. Emphasizing that properly designed packages contribute greatly to salability, a packaging expert offers several suggestions for attaining this objective. Also cf., by the same author, "Booming Ethnic Food Market Spurs New Packaging Strategies," *ibid.,* April 19, 1971, pp. 59–60.

Modern Packaging. Published monthly, this magazine covers all aspects of packaging, particularly from the manufacturer's point of view. The sections on "Profiles in Packaging" and "Packing Pacemakers" are of special interest.

National Commission on Food Marketing. *Food from Farmer to Consumer.* Washington, D.C.: U.S. Government Printing Office, 1966. This controversial report reviews many aspects of retail food distribution. Of chief interest in connection with this chapter is the "overview and appraisal" chapter and the views of the minority members on pp. 125–89.

"Packaging: Can It Cope with All Its Challenges?" *Supermarketing,* June 1969, pp. 27–37. In addition to reviewing the packaging quantity standards resulting from the "undue proliferation" section of the Fair Packaging and Labeling Act, future packing trends as seen by A. L. Brody of Arthur D. Little, Inc., are discussed.

The Role of Packaging in the American Economy. Cambridge, Mass.: Arthur D. Little, Inc., 1966. Prepared for the American Foundation for Management Research, this study emphasizes the increasing value of packaging to the consumer but points out that the amounts spent on packaging have failed to grow as fast as our economy.

Stone, Bob. "Smart Retailers Jump into Direct Marketing." *Advertising Age,* September 15, 1969, p. 24. A regular contributor to this publication, Mr. Stone discusses why retailers should sell by mail, some main objectives of this form of promotion, and recent practices of such firms as Sears,Roebuck and Co., Kresge's K Mart Stores, W. T. Grant, and Abercrombie & Fitch.

Weiss, E. B. "Today's Sophisticated Consumers Are Killing off Incentive Promotions." *Advertising Age,* December 1, 1970, p. 98. Asserting that "incentive promotions have a strong appeal only to about 15 percent of the market (adults)," this authority indicates why this appeal is shrinking. Also cf. "Are Games Finally Fading?" on the editorial page of the same publication, October 27, 1969, p. 18.

Chapter 20

Ahrend, H. G. "Alphabet of Selling." *Sales Management,* October 15, 1969, pp. 69–70. Excerpted from the author's *Sell Your Way to Success,* an American Business Press guide for salesmen, the 26 points outlined offer valuable suggestions for retail salespeople.

Ashell, Ben. "Let's Make Retailing More Profitable: A Salesperson's Guide to Better Selling." In a series of three articles under this title in the *Department Store Economist,* March 1966, pp. 26–29; April 1966, pp. 26–28; and May 1966, pp. 32–33; the author discusses how to help salespeople improve themselves "at the place where it really counts—the selling floor." These articles still are relevant to the existing situation.

Blake, R. R., and Mouton, J. S. *The Grid for Sales Excellence.* New York: McGraw-Hill Book Co., 1970. In this volume, a behavioral science approach to the fundamentals of selling is used.

Cotham, J. C. "Case for Personal Selling: Some Retailing Myths Exploded." *Business Horizons,* Vol. 6, No. 2, April 1968, pp. 75–81. Professor Cotham examines two major questions in this article: (1) Is personal selling used as a merchandising tool in its twilight years? and (2) How is the current environment influencing retail management?

Gore, Budd. *The Name of the Game Is Sell.* New York: National Retail Merchants Association, 1969. The fundamentals of good retail salesmanship are well-summarized in this volume.

Haas, K. B., and Ernest, John. *Creative Salesmanship: Understanding Essentials.* Beverly Hills, Cal.: Glencoe Press, 1969. Combining a practical approach to salesmanship with aspects of the behavioral sciences directly related to selling, the authors also stress basic selling concepts and techniques.

Paul, R. J., and Bell, R. W. "Evaluating the Retail Salesman." *Journal of Retailing,* Vol. 44, No. 3, Summer 1968, pp. 17–28. Based on their research in a department store, the authors conclude that evaluations of salespeople by the personnel department were invalid because volume producers were not ranked proportionately higher than lower ones in personnel reviews.

Pederson, C. A., and Wright, M. D. *Salesmanship: Principles and Methods* 5th ed. Homewood, Ill.: Richard D. Irwin, Inc., 1971. Although concerned mainly with outside selling, there is much in this general text of value to the retail salesman. The chapters on "Handling Objections," "The Close," and "Building good will" are especially helpful.

Pennington, A. L. "Customer-Salesman Bargaining Behavior in Retail Transactions." *Journal of Marketing Research,* Vol. 5, No. 3, August 1968, pp. 255–62. "This study examines the bargaining behavior of both salesman and customer as it relates to purchase outcomes on retail appliances."

Robinson, O. P.; Blackler, W. R.; and Logan, W. B. *Store Salesmanship.* 6th ed. Englewood Cliffs, N.J.: Prentice-Hall, Inc., 1966. An elementary treatment of retail selling, this volume provides suggestions for improving performance on the sales floor.

Shockey, Ralf. "Selling Is a Science." *Department Store Economist.* In a series of ten brief articles beginning in the April 1965 issue and ending in January 1966, the author treats all aspects of retail salesmanship. The last article, entitled "Department Store Selling Strictly Model T," suggests six important questions for top management to answer.

Steinberg, Jules. *Customers Don't Bite: Selling with Confidence.* New York: Fairchild Publications, Inc., 1970. In this practical approach to retail selling, the author stresses the three traits necessary for maximum effectiveness—imagination, memory, and close listening. The final chapter outlines "100 reasons why sales are lost."

Stute, J. R. "The Buyer as a Salesman." *Journal of Marketing,* Vol. 32, No. 3, July 1968, pp. 14–18. Noting that "a powerful set of forces may exist which compels new buyers of products to act unwittingly as salesmen," the author examines the dynamics involved in this concise article.

Thompson, Joseph W. *Selling: A Behavioral Science Approach.* New York: McGraw-Hill Book Co., Inc., 1966. The author draws upon a wide variety of social science research to develop an effective, problem-solving approach to salesmanship.

Webster, F. E., Jr. "Interpersonal Communication and Salesman Effectiveness." *Journal of Marketing,* Vol. 32, No. 3, July 1968, pp. 7–13. Professor Webster discusses some of the important new insights "behavioral science offers into the determinants of a salesman's effectiveness" in this well-documented article.

Weiss, E. B. "Computers, Corporations, and Committees Hasten Death of Personal Selling." *Advertising Age,* June 1, 1970, pp. 49–50. Directed primarily at "outside" salesmen, this provocative article discusses reasons for the salesman's obsolescence and also related future developments of interest to the student of retailing. Also cf. his "Salesgirl Teaches Buyer as Floor Selling Declines," *ibid.,* May 6, 1968, p. 84.

Zimmer, A. E. *The Strategy of Successful Retail Salesmanship.* New York: McGraw-Hill Book Co., Inc., 1966. In this practical discussion of retail selling the author also includes in Appendix I selling guides for 21 merchandise lines.

Chapter 21

"Are Sunday Hours Really Profitable?" *Chain Store Age.* Executives Edition, April 1970, pp. E19–21, 30. Many of the merchants interviewed in this survey felt that Sunday openings gave them substantial extra business; others said that they stayed open only because of competitive pressure.

Babione, F. A. "Retailer Adjustment to a Rental Economy." *Journal of Retailing,* Vol. 40, No. 3, Fall 1964, pp. 1–5, 48. Although the author believes that "retailers should be able to adapt readily to rental business," he concludes they "have not (yet) ventured far" into this growing area of customer service.

"Food for Thought—Your Restaurant Profits." *Stores,* Vol. 50, No. 3, March 1968, pp. 34–38. In this article four experts on store-operated food services discuss the problems of restaurant operation, the need for strict cost control, and the importance of developing clear-cut goals and operating concepts for the food service department.

Halvorson, Gerald B. "Can You Afford Delivery Service?" *Small Marketers Aids No. 133.* Washington, D.C.: U.S. Small Business Administration, 1968. A worksheet, for outlining the costs of providing delivery service, is a helpful feature of this pamphlet.

Judd, Robert C. "Similarities or Differences in Product and Service Retailing." *Journal of Retailing,* Vol. 43, No. 4, Winter 1968, pp. 1–9. Professor Judd concludes that although product retailing and the retailing of income services are similar in many respects, substantial differences arise in sales promotion, in pricing, and in developing the product or service. Sampling, demonstration, and physical display techniques that are often used in product retailing are inapplicable to many services.

National Retail Merchants Association. *Wrapping Methods Manual.* New York: The Association, n.d. This survey of methods used in more than 60 stores discusses basic wrapping techniques, new materials and mechanical wrapping aids, and ways of handling a variety of difficult-to-wrap items.

"Rentals . . . If the Market Is There, Tap It and Watch Customers Buy, Too." *Hardware Retailer,* June 1969, pp. 54–57. A survey of several hundred hardware stores indicated that rentals can be quite profitable, but that the store must have capable personnel and a wide range of rental products on hand. Typical rental rates for a variety of products are quoted.

Weiss, E. B. "New Retail Services Push Skyward." *Advertising Age,* September 23, 1968, pp. 84–86. A veteran market analyst discusses the increased use of income-producing services in this article.

"Why United Parcel Admits Its Size." *Business Week,* July 18, 1970, pp. 94–100. This article describes the local and long distance delivery services that have made United Parcel Service the country's largest freight trucking company and analyzes its competitive relationship to the parcel post service.

Chapter 22

Anderson, A. H. et al. *An Electronic Cash and Credit System.* New York: American Management Association, 1966. The authors discuss the "tremendous problems and opportunities" which will result from the evolution of computer systems "linking banks, stores, and credit bureaus. . . ."

Beckman, T. N., and Foster, R. S. *Credits and Collections: Management and Theory.* 8th ed. New York: McGraw-Hill Book Co., Inc., 1969. This well-known textbook discusses both commercial and consumer credit.

Board of Governors, Federal Reserve System. *Bank Credit Card and Check Credit Plans.* Washington, D.C.: The Board, 1968. The Board of Governors provides an authoritative study of the growth, operation, and effects of these plans.

———. What You Ought to Know about Federal Regulation Z—Truth in Lending—Consumer Credit Cost Disclosure. Washington, D. C.: The Board, 1969 with amendments. This layman's guide includes a summary of the major provisions of important regulations along with the texts of the basic law, Regulation Z, and numerous official interpretations of the Regulation.

Boggess, W. P. "Screen-Test Your Credit Risks." *Harvard Business Review,* Vol. 47, No. 6, November–December 1967, pp. 113–22. The author explains point scoring to the layman who has had little or no statistical training.

Cole, R. H. *Consumer and Commercial Credit Management.* 3d ed. Homewood, Ill.: Richard D. Irwin, Inc., 1968. This college textbook is written from the credit manager's point of view.

Credit Research Foundation, ed. *Credit Management Handbook.* Rev. ed. Homewood, Ill.: Richard D. Irwin, Inc., 1965. Designed to cover all phases of the subject, this collection of reading contains helpful information for the student of retailing.

National Association of Credit Management. *Credit Manual of Commercial Laws.* New York: The Association, annually. Although much of the emphasis is on legislation affecting commercial and industrial credit, this annual survey is an invaluable source of information about installment credit, bad check, bankruptcy, and credit charge disclosure laws.

National Retail Merchants Association, Credit Management Division. *Credit Management Yearbook.* New York: The Association, published annually. Also cf. *Facts You Should Know about Revolving Credit, Installment Credit and Credit Legislation,* n.d.; and *Credit in the Branch Store,* n.d. These sources of information on various aspects of credit are among the best available.

———. Economic Characteristics of Department Store Credit. New York: The

Association, 1969. The costs of providing credit and the extent to which they exceed credit-charge revenue are analyzed in this detailed study.

———. **Effective Collection Methods and Control.** New York: The Association, n.d. Students and retailers alike will find this manual of interest and help as a "how to" tool in collection matters.

Speake, S. S. *Consumer Credit and Collections Manual.* St. Louis: International Consumer Credit Association, n.d. This practical handbook presents advice on many phases of consumer credit administration.

Chapter 23

General accounting principles applicable to retail stores are covered in all standard textbooks on accounting. The following references are to specialized treatments of particular phases of this subject. Annual reports of retailing firms also provide a valuable source of information on accounting practices.

"Annual Reports Bare Long-Hidden Facts." *Business Week,* April 3, 1971, pp. 65–66. Additional disclosures in annual reports to stockholders by corporations, ordered by the Securities and Exchange Commission, may make 1971 reports ". . . the best read collection in business history."

Copeland, R. M.; Wojdak, J. F.; and Shank, J. F. "Use LIFO to Offset Inflation." *Harvard Business Review,* Vol. 49, No. 3, May–June 1971, pp. 91–100. The authors emphasize the benefits yielded by LIFO inventory valuation in the current period (1971) of rising inflation in this excellent analysis.

Cox, C. R. "LIFO and Retailing." *Retail Control,* October 1969, pp. 49–53. The regional manager of a leading national accounting firm discusses some recent tax rulings concerning LIFO and FIFO in this brief article. Also cf. "LIFO Inventory Price Indexes Continue Upward," *ibid.,* pp. 58–61.

Fairchild Publications, Inc. *Fairchild's Financial Manual of Retail Stores.* New York: published annually. Complete financial information covering more than 200 publicly owned retail organizations in about 10 different types of businesses is given in this annual publication.

Gordon, M. J., and Shillinglaw, Gordon. *Accounting: A Management Approach.* 4th ed. Homewood, Ill.: Richard D. Irwin, Inc., 1969. Chapters 1, 2, 7, and 8, "Accounting and Business Enterprise," "Basic Elements of Accounting Method," "Processing Accounting Data," and "Introduction to Financial Statement Analysis," respectively, are of special interest in connection with this chapter.

Kieta, Ed. "Records for Profitable Retailing." *Hardware Retailer,* June 1970, pp. 41–56. Emphasizing the need for recordkeeping in hardware stores (and among all retailers), this treatment offers suggestions covering several main elements involved in the process. Pages 53–54 deal specifically with the retail inventory method.

McNair, M. P., and Hersum, A. C. *The Retail Inventory Method and LIFO.* New York: McGraw-Hill Book Co., Inc., 1952. Initially undertaken as a revision of McNair's *The Retail Method of Inventory,* the authors have so improved and enlarged on the former treatment that the current volume is really a new book.

McNair, M. P., and May, E. G. "Pricing for Profit: A Revolutionary Approach to Retail Accounting." *Harvard Business Review,* Vol. 35, No. 3, May–June 1957, pp. 105–22. A strong and long-time advocate and student of the "retail method," with the capable assistance of Miss May, emphasizes in this article the need for "a new method of approach, with a new framework, new concepts, and some new terminology" in retail accounting.

National Cash Register Company. *Expenses in Retail Businesses.* Dayton, Ohio: n.d. This compilation of retailing data includes sales, gross margins, net profits, and other factors as well as operating expenses. Covering many types of retail businesses, the information is invaluable for comparative purposes.

———. *The Values of Total Systems Reports for Retailers.* Dayton, Ohio: n.d. Part III, "Basic Financial Statements," and Parts IV and V, Section A, apply directly to the discussion in this chapter. The *Reference Supplement* provides excellent illustrations of the points reviewed.

National Retail Merchants Association. *The Retail Inventory Method in Practical Operation.* New York: The Association, n.d. This small volume contains a concise explanation of the retail inventory method and furnishes helpful illustrative forms and examples.

Wingate, J. W.; Schaller, E. O.; and Goldenthal, Irving. *Problems in Retail Merchandising.* 5th ed. Englewood Cliffs, N.J.: Prentice-Hall, Inc., 1961. This paper-covered volume presents in Part I a clear and simple explanation of the retail operating statement; in Chapters 14–15 and Appendix B the retail inventory method; and in Appendix C, LIFO and FIFO.

Chapter 24

Chain Store Age. *1970 Annual Report of the Chain Drug Industry. Chain Store Age,* 1970. With 30 publicly owned chains continuing to set performance records in 1969, the five-year trends in gross margin and total expense reveal the importance of tight control over expenses.

Fisher, William. "Expense Planning and Control Other than Payroll." *Retail Control,* January, 1970, pp. 35–39. A retail controller offers helpful suggestions concerning budget formation and control in this concise article. Also cf. the related discussion by Sehn, A. A., "Payroll Planning and Control," *ibid.,* pp. 40–50.

National Association of Retail Clothiers and Furnishers. *Annual Survey of Operating Expenses for Men's Wear Stores.* Washington, D.C.: The Association, published annually. These expense figures are classified according to the annual sales of each store.

National Cash Register Company. *Expenses in Retail Businesses.* Rev. ed. Dayton, Ohio: n.d. This small volume stresses the importance of expense control and provides expense data for a variety of retail stores.

National Retail Furniture Association. *Operating Results of Furniture Stores.* Chicago: The Association, annual reports. These reports are of much value to all retailers of home furnishings.

National Retail Merchants Association, Controllers' Congress. *Department Store* *and Specialty Store Merchandising and Operating Results.* New York: The Association, annual reports. Known as MOR, data are now presented in two volumes by classification and classification volume as well as for stores as a whole.

———. *Financial and Operating Results of Department and Specialty Stores.* New York: The Association, annual reports. Known as FOR, these reports are designed to provide "store management a tool to aid in the forecasting and formulation of future operations, plans and policies."

———. *Retail Accounting Manual.* New York: The Association, 1962. The official NRMA accounting manual for retail stores, this volume details the expense accounts in retail stores including expense centers. A recent addition is the grouping of accounts for single-store companies and those operating branches.

———. *Successful Cost Cutting . . . Where and How.* New York: The Association, 1967. This volume contains over 800 practical and proven expense-saving ideas selected from thousands submitted to the Controllers' Congress during the past decade.

Operating Results of Food Chains. Ithaca, N.Y.: New York State College of Agriculture, Cornell University, published annually. This summary of expenses provides valuable information on chains of various sales volumes.

The True Look of the Discount Industry. Published annually by The Discount Merchandiser, this volume contains detailed data on operating and merchandising results as well as significant trends.

Chapter 25

Only a limited amount of information is available on sales transactions systems as such in current literature. Probably the best sources of such data are the manufacturers of the equipment designed to handle these systems effectively. These include, among many others, the American Regitel Corporation, 1011 Commercial Street, San Carlos, California 94070 (Regitel Register); American Totalisator Company, 383 Hillen Road, Towson, Maryland 21204 (Uni-Tote); The Burroughs Corporation, Second Avenue at Burroughs, Detroit, Michigan 48202; Friden Division of the Singer Company, 2350 Washington Avenue, San Leandro, California 94577 (MDTS-Modular Data Transaction System); General Electric Company, 53rd Street and Lexington Avenue, New York, New York 10022 (Tradar); Information Machines Corporation, 8024 John Towers Road, Santee, California, 92071 (Registron); International Business Machines, Armonk, New York 10504; Lamson Corporation, 625 Lamson Street, Syracuse, New York 13200; National Cash Register Company, Main and K Streets, Dayton, Ohio 45400; Olivetti Corporation of America, 1 Park Avenue, New York, New York 10003 (TC 601); and Sweda International, a Division of Litton Industries, Orange, New York 08952 (Dataregister). These firms, most of which feature electronic equipment, serve retailers of all kinds and sizes.

Representative of the kinds of information in this general area of value to the student of retailing are the following:

Barber, Harold, and Helfant, Seymour. *Retail Merchandising and Management with Electronic Data Processing.* New York: National Retail Merchants Association,

1966. Of special interest in connection with this chapter is the authors' discussion of instore equipment needs.

Harwell, E. M. *Checkout Management.* New Work: Chain Store Age Publishing Corporation, 1963. Looking at the checkout in the self-service store as "a huge transmission belt which processes tonnage into consumer transactions," the author covers checker accuracy, scheduling and training of checkout employees, checkout supervision, and equipment for the checkout operation. This treatment should be reviewed in the light of recent developments.

National Cash Register Company. *The NCR Total System for Retailers.* Dayton, Ohio: n.d. The section devoted to sales transactions applies particularly to this chapter. Case histories and procedures manuals are also available for certain kinds of stores.

National Retail Merchants Association, Retail Research Institute. *Proceedings of Annual Electronic Data Processing Conference.* New York: The Association, annual reports. Beginning in 1959, the Institute has published annually the papers delivered at this conference.

Tipper, Harry, Jr. *Controlling Overhead.* New York: American Management Association, 1966. After reviewing problems of managing overhead, the author suggests a positive approach to solving them. The discussion of systems and procedures has particular relevance to the topics in this chapter.

Tomeski, E. A. *The Computer Revolution.* New York: Macmillan Co., 1970. Subtitled "The Executive and the New Information Technology—A Guide to the Better Understanding of Computers and the People who Feed, Use, and Direct Them," this volume may be read with profit by all levels of management.

Chapter 26

Anshen, Melvin. "The Management of Ideas." *Harvard Business Review,* Vol. 47, No. 4, July–August 1969, pp. 99–107. Noting that "current advances in management science stress improved analytical and administrative tools," the author discusses the thesis that "to the traditional skills of managing people, material, machines, and money, they will add a challenging new skill-management of ideas."

Bacon, Jeremy. *Managing the Budget Function.* New York: National Industrial Conference Board, 1970. Stressing the management aspects of budgeting rather than the techniques, Mr. Bacon discusses, in four concise chapters, the nature of budgeting, preparing and approving budgets, controlling operations through budgeting, and the budget executive and the budget organization.

Bower, Marvin. *The Will to Manage: Corporate Success through Programmed Management.* New York: McGraw-Hill Book Co., Inc., 1966. Concentrating on principles, the managing director of McKinsey & Company relates the managing methods employed by successful firms in this interesting book.

Bunge, W. R. *Managerial Budgeting for Profit Improvement.* New York: McGraw-Hill Book Co., Inc., 1968. Noting that "the modern business budget has come to be regarded as one of management's most effective tools," the author covers all major aspects of budgeting. Chapters 1, 2, 7, 9 and 10 are particularly relevant to retailing.

Dunckel, E. B.; Reed, W. K.; and Wilson, I. H. *The Business Environment of the*

70's: A Trend Analysis for Business Planning. New York: McGraw-Hill Book Co., Inc., 1970. This 120-page book presents the findings of a survey covering the major forces and trends now reshaping American society.

Eilenberg, Howard. *Research Techniques for Retailers*. Dobbs Ferry, N.Y.: Oceana Publications, Inc., 1968. The vice president and research director of Frederick Atkins Company, a leading buying organization, describes the "techniques used by successful . . . [retailers] in correctly understanding customer needs and in making the merchandise she has wanted available for sale" in this 92–page volume. Actually, department stores are the focal point of attention.

Feinberg, Samuel. *How Do You Manage?* New York: Fairchild Publications, Inc., 1965. Business leadership and its effectiveness in relation to the main functions of management are discussed by a long observer of the retail scene in this excellent book.

Heckert, J. B., and Willson, J. D. *Business Budgeting and Control*. 3d ed. New York: Ronald Press Co., 1967. This edition of a widely used volume embodies current concepts and practices of budgeting.

Krieger, Murray. *Decision-Making in Retailing and Marketing*. New York: Fairchild Publications, Inc., 1969. Through 90 cases based on experiences taken from various Fairchild publications, Professor Krieger covers all major areas of retail decision making in this stimulating volume.

McDonald, John. "How Social Responsibility Fits the Game of Business." *Fortune*, Vol. 72, No. 6, December 1970, pp. 104–6 ff. This informative article notes that "corporate executives have to find new ways of reconciling their responses to emerging social issues with hard economies." And the head of a national merchandising chain is quoted as follows: "In the fabric of society, unless you make a contribution to enhance human values, your institution is in danger." (p. 106)

National Retail Merchants Association, Retail Research Institute. *Operations Research in Retailing—Case Studies* and *Electronic Data Processing for Retailers*. New York: The Association, n.d. These two publications furnish basic information on various applications of operations research to retailing functions. An updating service is also available to keep retailers abreast of the latest developments in this rapidly growing field.

Odiorne, G. S. *Management by Objectives*. New York: Pitman Publishing Corp., 1965. In one of the first books devoted to the subject, the author sets forth the essential elements of this management philosophy. Also cf. his related volume *Management Decisions by Objectives*. Englewood Cliffs, N.J.: Prentice-Hall, Inc., 1969.

Reilly, P. J. *Old Masters of Retailing*. New York: Fairchild Publications, Inc., 1966. Reviewing the founding and present status of 35 prominent stores in this country, Canada, and England, this treatment provides valuable insights to the managerial problems and tactics of retail executives.

Roland, V. K. *Evaluating and Improving Managerial Performance*. New York: McGraw-Hill Book Co., Inc., 1970. In this valuable volume the author suggests methods and devices designed to strengthen management accomplishments.

Shidle, N. G. *The Art of Successful Communication*. New York: McGraw-Hill Book Co., Inc., 1969. The major emphasis of this volume is on the written aspects of communication.

Super Market Institute. *The Responsibilities of Leadership*. Chicago: The Institute, 1969. This concise treatment includes an analysis of what is expected of the business leader by his community, his company, his family, and others.

Uris, Auren, and Noppel, Marjorie. *The Turned-on Executive.* New York: McGraw-Hill Book Co., Inc., 1970. In this enlightening treatment, two members of the editorial staff of the Research Institute of America discuss the personal qualities of present successful executives and picture the super-manager of the year 2000.

Valentine, R. F. *Performance Objectives for Managers.* New York: American Management Association, 1966. "This handbook sets forth . . . the new dynamic concept of managing by objectives and demonstrates how managerial efficiency can be increased by following logical techniques."

Votaw, Dow, and Sethi, S. P. "Do We Need a New Corporate Response to a Changing Social Environment?" Parts I and II. *California Management Review,* Vol. 12, No. 1, Fall 1969, pp. 3–32. "The authors discuss the traditional corporate responses . . . to changing social environment, the general lack of success of these responses . . . and the effects of these failures on the corporation [and] society." Recommendations for new responses are made.

Walton, C. C. *Ethos and the Executive—Values in Managerial Decision-Making.* Englewood Cliffs, N.J.: Prentice-Hall, Inc., 1969. In this volume the Dean of General Studies, Columbia University, emphasizes the ethical values that are involved in decision making by executives.

Wortman, M. S., and Luthaus, Fred, eds. *Emerging Concepts in Management.* New York: The Macmillan Co., 1969. In this selection of readings, the editors cover several of the newer concepts of current management.

■ ANTHOLOGIES

These helpful volumes contain collections of articles and papers on retailing, reprinted from a variety of business and scholarly sources.

Gist, Ronald, ed. *Management Perspectives in Retailing.* 2d ed. New York: John Wiley & Sons, Inc., 1971.

Krieger, Murray, ed. *Decision-Making in Retailing and Marketing,* New York: Fairchild Publications, Inc., 1969. The items presented here are drawn exclusively from the Fairchild retailing-related newspapers.

Markin, Rom J., Jr. *Retailing: Concepts, Institutions, and Management.* New York: The Macmillan Co., 1971.

McLaughlin, Daniel J., Jr., and Mallowe, C. A. eds. *Food Marketing and Distribution: Selected Readings.* New York: Chain Store Age Books, 1971. Most of the articles in this collection deal with food retailing and the problems of adjusting food distribution to the "new market" and environment of the 1970s.

National Retail Merchants Association. *Readings in Modern Retailing.* New York: The Association, 1969. This collection consists of papers and speeches prepared for various NRMA publications and meetings.

Rachman, David J., ed. *Retail Management Strategy: Selected Readings.* New York: Prentice-Hall, Inc., 1970.

Ryans, John K., Jr.; Donnelly, James H., Jr.; and Ivancevich, John M., eds. *New Dimensions in Retailing.* Belmont, California: Wadsworth Publishing Co., Inc., 1970.

SELECTED RETAILING PERIODICALS

The student of retailing should become familiar with the leading trade papers and periodicals in the field. They provide an excellent source of supplementary readings on all the subjects covered in this text. Some of the leading periodicals are the following:

American Druggist. Hearst Magazines, Inc., 1790 Broadway, New York, New York 10019. Biweekly.

Chain Store Age. Various editions, monthly; *Discount Store News,* biweekly, Lebhar-Friedman Publications, Inc., 2 Park Ave., New York, New York 10016.

Department Store Management. Concept Publishers Corp., 19 West 44th St., New York, New York 10017. Monthly.

Discount Merchandiser. MacFadden-Bartell Corp., 205 East 42nd St., New York, New York 10017. Monthly.

Drug Topics. Topics Publishing Co., Inc., 330 West 34th St., New York, New York 10001. Biweekly.

Hardware Age, bimonthly; *Jewelers' Circular—Keystone,* monthly, Chilton Co., Inc., Chestnut and 56th Sts., Philadelphia, Pennsylvania 19139.

Hardware Retailer. National Retail Hardware Association, 964 N. Pennsylvania St., Indianapolis, Indiana 46204. Monthly.

Journal of Retailing. Institute of Retail Management, New York University, 100 Washington Square, New York, New York 10003. Quarterly.

The Merchandiser/Magazine of Mass Retailing. Merchandiser Publishing Company, 419 Park Avenue South, New York, New York 10016. Monthly.

Merchandising Week, electrical appliances, weekly; *Vend,* semi-monthly, Billboard Publishing Co., 165 West 46th St., New York, New York 10036.

Modern Retailer, discount stores. Larkin Publications, 99 Chauncy St., Boston, Massachusetts 02111. Monthly.

N.A.R.D. Journal. National Association of Retail Druggists, 1 East Wacker Dr. Chicago, Illinois 60601. Semimonthly.

Nargus Bulletin. National Association of Retail Grocers, 360 N. Michigan Ave., Chicago, Illinois 60601. Monthly.

Progressive Grocer. Butterick Company, Inc., 420 Lexington Ave., New York, New York 10017. Monthly.

Retail Overview. Edward Francis Engle & Co., Inc., 103 Park Ave., New York, New York 10017. Quarterly.

Stores. National Retail Merchants Association, 100 W. 31st St., New York, New York 10001. Monthly.

Women's Wear Daily; *Daily News Record,* men's wear; and *Home Furnishings Daily,* daily except Saturdays, Sundays, and holidays; *Footwear News;* and *Supermarket News,* weekly; and *Men's Wear,* semi-monthly, Fairchild Publications, Inc., 7 East 12th St., New York, New York 10003.

Indexes

NAME INDEX

B

C

G

H

S

T

SUBJECT INDEX

F

T